HUMAN RESOURCE MANAGEMENT

Concepts, Practices, and New Paradigms

Second Edition

AF819900

Amitabha Sengupta

Ex-faculty, K J Somaiya Institute of Management Studies and Research, Mumbai

Visiting Faculty

Tata Institute of Social Sciences, Mumbai

Narsee Monjee Institute of Management Studies, Mumbai

K J Somaiya Institute of Management Studies & Research, Mumbai

Cengage

Australia • Brazil • Canada • India • Mexico • Singapore • United Kingdom • United States

Cengage

Human Resource Management, 2e
Concepts, Practices, and New Paradigms

Amitabha Sengupta

For product information and technology assistance, contact us at
asia.infoindia@cengage.com

For permission to use material from this text or product, submit all requests online at
www.cengage.com/permissions

ISBN-13: 978-93-5573-943-8
ISBN-10: 93-5573-943-5

Cengage Learning India Pvt. Ltd.
T-303, 3rd Floor
DAV Complex, Plot 3
Mayur Vihar Phase 1
Delhi-110091

Cengage is a leading provider of customized learning solutions with employees residing in nearly 40 different countries and sales in more than 125 countries around the world. Find your local representative at **www.cengage.com**

Cengage is committed to creating inclusive and diverse products, including perspectives that represent the diversity of people across all backgrounds, identities, opinions, and experiences. If you have any feedback related to this, please contact us at **support.cengage.com**

To learn more about Cengage products, platforms and services, visit at
www.cengage.co.in

Printed by:
Rajiv Book Binding House
D-1518, DSIIDC Industrial Complex,
Narela, New Delhi 110040

Printed in India
Print Number: 04 Print Year: 2024

To

my parents,

my wife Sharmila,

and my son Ateesh

Brief Contents

Detailed Contents

CLUSTER 8: HUMAN RESOURCE BLUE OCEAN

Preface to the Second Edition

Those familiar with the first edition will note that there have been substantial changes in the second edition, increasing the number of chapters of the book from 18 to 21. The additions were thought necessary in view of the emergence of some key trends in the field of human resource management during the internecine period: diversity, equality, and inclusion (DEI or EDI) and challenges of career management in the gig economy and wellness at workplace.

1. (Chapter 20) Diversity, equality, and inclusion and talent strategy

The war for talent has intensified in business world. According to psychologist Dean Keith Simonton, talent is any package of personal characteristics that accelerates the acquisition of expertise, or enhances performance given a certain amount of expertise. Good organizations now prioritize DEI to open a world of new opportunity as a unique talent strategy. They proactively look for ways to integrate DEI across all facets of talent and leadership to create a fair, inclusive, equitable environment that people do not want to leave. When diversity, equity, and inclusion are mainstays of its culture, an organization can accelerate talent outcomes and increase innovation, customer satisfaction, and profitability.

2. (Chapter 7) Career management in the gig economy

According to Niti Aayog's policy brief, 'India's Blooming Gig and Platform Economy', the gig or platform worker, is the 'person who performs work or participates in a work arrangement, and earns from such activities outside of traditional employer-employee relationship'. It is estimated that by 2029-30, India will have 23.5 million workers. Treated as consultants or freelancers, they do not get employment contracts and are made to work long hours to earn a liveable income, wear uniforms, etc., while companies employing them can avoid accountability as it is not a traditional employment relationship.

Research shows that many find themselves caught between two extremes: empowerment and marginalization. Empowerment because they have the freedom to pick their own tasks and choose when, where, and how to complete them. Marginalization because many gig platforms. Managing careers in such an economy poses multiple challenges.

3. (Chapter 21) Wellness at workplace

A *Harvard Business Review* article reports that a comprehensive, strategically designed investment in employees' social, mental, and physical health ensures a hard return on investment. Johnson & Johnson's leaders estimate that wellness programs have cumulatively saved the company US$250 million on health care costs over the past decade.

The COVID-19 pandemic has highlighted the need for employers to prioritize their employees' health and well-being. Employee health and wellness programs are used to improve the health and well-being of employees in a company, usually through preventative care to manage chronic diseases and/or to encourage employees to improve health and avoid behaviors that are unhealthy.

New to This Edition

- The entire book has been revised and updated. The author reviewed every chapter, utilizing extensive feedback from faculty who have used previous editions of the book. The content in some of the chapters has been reorganized and rewritten to present the material more coherently and effectively. Cases have been added and new developments in the specific HR domains have been incorporated.
- In the continued effort to enhance readability, many of the features have been updated. Reflection questions have been included, where appropriate to generate short discussions.
- Another improvement to facilitate faculty experience has been to add a series of short questions at the end of each chapter.

Preface to the First Edition

The field of human resource management (HRM) has been constantly evolving in modern organizations, due to a variety of contextual factors. In a global business environment, a wide spectrum of factors—ranging from recruitment, engagement, compliance, performance management et al—are rooted in the basic domain of HRM. Underlying this strategic focus is the realization that traditional sources of competitive advantage, such as access to capital, sheltered markets, or proprietary technologies, are fading out and the emergent key success factor is the ability to innovate, adapt and learn and leverage the learning globally. These competencies lie in managing human resources.

Intuit Inc. is a business and financial software company that develops and sells financial, accounting, and tax preparation software and related services for small businesses, accountants, and individuals. The company is headquartered in Mountain View, California. More than 95% of its revenues and earnings come from its activities within the United States (Intuit Inc. Annual Report 2016). Intuit has developed TurboTax, a consumer tax preparation application, the small business accounting program QuickBooks, professional tax solutions ProSeries and Lacerte, and multiple payroll products. Intuit India, a fully owned subsidiary of Intuit Inc. USA, based in Bengaluru, started in April 2005. It presently employs around 500 employees.

In 2017, it was featured in the *Economic Times* list of India's best companies (ranked no. 1) to work for, moving up from a previous ranking of 10 in 2016. Some of the employees interviewed were effusive about innovation being a 'buzzword,' the 'energized work climate,' and the 'inclusive and collaborative culture,' among other attributes. Somnath Baishya, the Director and Head HR (India), talks about a particular initiative called 'Intuit Again,' which helps women technologists return to the workforce after they have taken a career break and provide them mentoring during a fresh internship to reach their full potential. This apart, employees are encouraged to innovate on new projects outside their own, as part of unstructured time or about 10% of their working hours. These solutions can be turned into products.[1]

---

[1] *The Economic Times*, 'India's Best Companies to Work for 2017: The Complete List,' *The Economic Times*, July 3, 2017. Available at: https://economictimes.indiatimes.com/news/company/corporate-trends/indias-best-companies-to-work-for-2017-the-completelist/articleshow/59419981.cms (accessed on November 13, 2017).

On the Glassdoor page,[2] an employee, who has been working at the organization for over five years, has written, 'Intuit as a company has evolved in terms of business process, maintenance process and selecting technical stack to support business, which is incredible. Nurturing innovative ideas is one of the keys (sic) for this evolution.'

Examples abound through the corporate landscape. Hyatt Hotels, ranked 16, has collaboration with the Stanford University School of Design, to bring in a design-cantered approach to all areas of business. Following this, empathy interviews are conducted on an ongoing basis to identify an innovation and initiative, or to overcome a challenge. This helps managers build a more personal connection with their colleagues while building a more engaging employment experience.

New kinds of great organizations are ruling the roost in business today. Facebook, Google, JP Morgan, TCS, and ICICI are just a few examples. These high-performing organizations are so nimble and athletic that their product cycles move in months, not years. Their workforce is highly interconnected and digitally literate. Acquiring and retaining talent, innovative organization culture, diversity, flexible employment—all these provide competitive advantage. Conversely, there is no premium for 'disciplined soldierhood' of the traditional organization of the ilk of GMs. Work itself has an uncertain future, and activities in these organizations center around projects and programs, which evolve and change at breathtaking speed. This is the best of times and the worst of times for the HRM function. On the one hand, holding the reins in these new organizations is not the elite torchbearer of scientific management or the time-honored system and process, but rather really the plebian—the customers and the select employees who have talent. It is, of course, the Digital Revolution that has been primarily responsible for the makeover, by enhancing the customers' ability to purchase. It is a strange 'Game of Thrones,' where today's customer and the valued employee hold all the aces—she can compare products, services, and prices, and then decide on what to settle for and how.

Has the time come to write an epitaph for the old, traditional HR function? The answer is yes and no both. In the context of the changed imperatives of business, the durable HR programs—dedicated to policing and enforcing the rules, developing and maintaining formal organization structures, playing power games with trade unions, and crafting rigid compensation structures based on hierarchies and watertight processes—will need to change. The focus has to shift to customer centricity, team culture, empowerment and engagement, continuous learning, coaching, and innovations.

Aims

The book aims to fast-forward the students to the new paradigms of the HRM function while not losing foothold on the enduring, fundamental HR processes of planning, selection, development, and rewards. It attempts to provide a dual perspective of robust frameworks moored in sound theories and the experiential approaches to leverage them. The author has called upon three decades of post-MBA professional experience in a wide variety of public and private sector organizations and of HR consulting and leadership training to present the corporate stories from a practitioner's viewpoint and shared insights in the light of the relevant frameworks.

Organization of the Book

The book is divided into 9 clusters and 18 chapters. Each cluster has a common thread, binding one aspect of HRM. The clusters are Old HR–New HR (chapters 'Human Resource Management—Introduction' and 'Human Resource Business Partner'); Plan and Acquire (chapters 'Human Resource

[2] Glassdoor, July 2017 (Current Employee–Senior Dev Ops Engineer in Bengaluru). Available at: https://www.glassdoor.co.in/Reviews (accessed on February 12, 2018).

Planning' and 'Recruitment and Selection'); Development and Growth (chapters 'Learning, Training, and Development' and 'Competency Management'); Engage and Perform (chapters 'Employee Engagement' and 'Performance Management and Appraisal'); Reward and Compensate (chapters 'Compensation and Benefits' and 'Compensation for Special Groups'); Decent Workplace–Compliance and Dialogues (chapters 'Industrial Relations' and 'Workplace Legislations, Regulations, and Debates on Labor Law Reforms'); Transformation of Work and Work Relationships (chapters 'HR Information System, HR Metrics, and HR Analytics' and 'Employment Relations'); HR Blue Ocean (chapters 'Human Resource Management in Small and Medium Enterprises' and 'Human Resource Management in the Services Sector'); and finally, Innovate and Transform (chapters 'Organization Transformation and the Human Resource Leadership' and 'Human Resource Management Innovations').

Cluster 1, Chapter 1 explains the evolution of HRM, the environmental forces influencing HRM, the 'soft' and 'hard' perspectives, and several unique models of HR value proposition practices in creating competitive edge for the organization. Chapter 2 presents how HR is shifting focus from traditional functional expertise to being immersed in business and thus providing strategic leadership inputs to the organizational leaders through business partnership.

Cluster 2, Chapter 3 describes the HR Planning (HRP) process including the factors that impact it, the barriers, the elements of demand and supply forecasting, the strategic options in formulating and implementing a program by the organizations, and finally the unique challenges that Indian businesses are facing today. Chapter 4 addresses how the critical processes of recruitment and selection have a direct bearing on business strategy. The chapter also addresses questions on what internal and external factors shape the recruitment activities, what are the emergent tools for aiding an efficient and on-time recruitment/selection process, and the future trends in recruitment and selection with the explosion of big data.

Cluster 3, Chapter 5 describes the differences between training, learning, and development, the value and process of building an integrated learning development strategy, the different learning theories, the important elements to watch out for while making a training design, the steps in the training needs assessment, and how to evaluate the effectiveness of training. The chapter also does a crystal-gazing into the future trends such as training partnerships and self-directed training. Chapter 6 takes the readers through the origin of competency studies, the steps in competency modeling, the formulation of competency dictionaries, the linkage with other HR processes, and the various choices in assessment/development centers. The chapter also examines future trends in the context of rapid disruptions occurring in the workplace.

Cluster 4, Chapter 7 examines the way employee engagement differs from happiness or motivation. It explains the current models of employee engagement and explores ways and means of building effective engagement strategies. Chapter 8 tries to answer the dilemma of balancing evaluation of performance with coaching for improvement. It carefully distinguishes the performance management system (PMS) from traditional performance appraisal and describes the process of PMS, the common problems of PMS and how to avoid them, the different kinds of PMS, and the elements of an effective PMS. The chapter ends with a critical examination of the future of PMS and addresses the current trend for doing away with bell curve in favor of continuous review and feedback for performance improvement. Cluster 5, Chapter 9 addresses the subject of compensation in a comprehensive manner. The issues discussed are how to formulate a compensation strategy and set up a system of pay starting from job analysis and conducting salary surveys, what are the components of pay, and what are the different kinds of benefits. It also deals with the shifting focus from financial rewards to a wider field named as total rewards and its attractiveness for talent. In Chapter 10, the compensation for certain special groups such as board-level executives, scientists, and sales personnel have been discussed with reference to their unique needs; the recent controversies around the Chief Executive Officer (CEO) pay have been taken up in some detail.

In Cluster 6, both the chapters deal with the management of collectives and the legal framework that constitutes the boundaries of these relationships. Chapter 11 traces the evolution of industrial relations in the post-Independence era of huge industries and the rise of the trade union power, and the eventual decline in the time of liberalization and the emergence of services sector. It examines the criteria for effective industrial relations and in that mode also examines the models of industrial relations systems. Chapter 12 covers the legal framework, the issues and the agenda for labor law reforms, and the context of it. It also describes the industrial jurisprudence that also exerts significant influence in the workplace, as also the regulations applicable for public sector and government employees.

Cluster 7 deals with the digitization of HR, transformation of work, and work relationships. Chapter 13 deals with the entire landscape of digital HR and the clear portents that HR is in the cusp of a probable metamorphosis of its mental models by prioritizing connectivity, real-time operations, platforms, automation, and mobile-first approach. In Chapter 14, there is a stocktaking of the fundamental changes still occurring in the employment relationships, the challenges faced as a consequence of global competitive pressure, the formidable role played by multinational corporations (MNCs), and the shape of work and the work relationships in the future.

Cluster 8 navigates the hitherto uncharted areas of HR—the so-called HR blue ocean—the HR function in the burgeoning small and medium-sized enterprises (SMEs) and the services sector. Chapter 15 examines how the manufacturing sector essentially varies from the services sector and how the services culture requires the HR function to change its focus and reorganize its activities. It also deals with the trade unionism or the absence of it in services sector, and presents some specific HR challenges within different parts of the services sector such as health care, Information Technology Enabled Services (ITeS) and hospitality industry with the aid of some case studies. Chapter 16 covers the HR challenges in SMEs and the factors influencing the adoption of HR practices and the future of HR in SMEs.

Finally, Cluster 9 presents the complex process of change and disruption in the organizations. Chapter 17 deals with organization transformation and the topics explored at length are the types of change, the factors that enable change, the change barriers and how to overcome them, the change models, and strategies for implementing change effectively. In Chapter 18, on HR innovations (HRMIs), some of the topics covered are determinants of innovations in organizations, the nature of HRMIs, the role of HR in fostering innovations in organizations, current trends in HRMIs in business including the application of design thinking, and the enablers of successful HRMIs.

The Targeted Readers

The book will be relevant for a wide variety of readers—students, professionals, academicians, and researchers. The issues concerning today's business in India will interest students of employment relations in India and abroad. The innumerable case studies in the book are drawn from happenings in the corporate world—both public and private. The innovative practices being reported from all around the corporate terrain make this book entirely topical. The readers will be enlightened about all the out-of-box thinking that are driving new initiatives in HRM, some of which are succeeding and some failing. The readers will also get to know how that the functional boundaries are gradually becoming permeable. For example, the concept of employer branding or creating signature workplaces has drawn from time-honored practices prevailing in the marketing domain; the cost-based approach to manpower studies uses standard costing procedure; the balanced scorecard-based PMS establishes a causal link between a newly developed learning plan and creation of a new market and profitability.

Acknowledgements

A book on human resources management is fraught with enormous challenges now, and one of the keys is being in the know. The great insights, perspectives, and information come from a host of friends, colleagues, and acquaintances.

I would like to thank Ms Monica Khanna, the Director at SIMSR, and Ms Preeti Rawat, the Area Chairperson for HR, for creating the space for me to venture into writing this book with their encouragement and advice. I express my gratitude to the following for their inputs at different stages: Meenakshi Aggarwal Gupta, Associate Professor at IIM, Indore; Shailaja Kurve, Associate Professor SIMSR; Hemangi Bhalerao, Asha Bhatia, and Bhargavi Karamcheti, Assistant Professors at, among many others.

Several friends outside the academic environment helped me with their valuable suggestions from time to time—Arvind Krishnaswami, GM-Strategy at BPCL; K. Padmakar, Executive Director at BPCL, D.N.B. Singh, formerly GM at IOC, currently a Mentor at Welingker Institute, and Meenakshi Narayan, President–HR at Ambuja Cements, among others.

Amitabha Sengupta

CLUSTER 1

OLD HR–NEW HR

Chapter 1

Human Resource Management—An Introduction

Chapter 2

Human Resource Business Partnership

In a recent interview, Charles Handy, the famous management guru *(The Economist)* spoke about preferring the term 'human management,' instead of 'human resource management.' He explained that in his view 'human resources' represents an obsolescent corporate model, given the speed and extent of change in the environment, and belongs to 'the age of elephants.' Elephants lorded over the old economy—'big, powerful, bureaucratic corporations, rich in tangible assets, whose people traded job security for loyalty.' It was suitable in predictable markets, ensuring a long tenure for a good product. Handy explains the shift from dominance to what Tom Peters called 'the nanosecond advantage' before somebody else comes along with a similar or better product.

The implications for the HRM function, according to Handy, are that it will have to learn to manage individuals, rather than 'human resources,' tolerate unconventional attitudes and lifestyles, empower people with freedom to make decisions, and accept the consequences (crisply articulated by the retailer Nordstrom, whose employees carry a message that reads 'do whatever you think is necessary'). Two areas of focus emerge for the new HR, in Handy's view: the war for talent—turning organizations into 'employers of choice—and getting the employees to develop a sense of passion.[1]

Human resource management finds itself at a fork. The emphasis on consistency and administration becomes dated, but the classical processes of acquisition, development, and rewards still remain valid and represent the enduring part of old HRM. The new HRM, which relies on the ability to partner with businesses and to align HR processes with strategic needs of business, enables HR to earn a 'seat at the table.'

Chapter 1 deals with the fundamentals of the HRM. Chapter 2 explores the emergent concepts of new HR in the form of HR business partnership.

---

1 Charles Handy, 'Human Management,' May 21, 2001. Available at: https://www.hrzone.com/lead/strategy (accessed on October 12, 2017).

CHAPTER 1

Human Resource Management—An Introduction

LEARNING OBJECTIVES

After completing this chapter, the student will be able to:

- Learn the importance of human resource management (HRM) functions to an organization
- Understand the environmental factors impacting the HRM
- Describe the different roles in HRM
- Know the possible ways in which human resource (HR) outcomes can be measured
- Acquire clarity about what competencies are appropriate for HR professionals
- Be aware of the successive models of HRM and know how to evaluate them
- Establish linkage between HR strategy and business strategy

Opening Case The Life and Times of Rajeev Sinha

1970-1971

Rajeev Sinha started his career against a backdrop of extremely bleak economic conditions. There was a general recessionary wave in the country, and the industrial environment in West Bengal was particularly dismal. A key reason was the changing political equations. The government had just changed hands from the Congress to the Left Front. The upbeat mood of the Left-oriented trade unions was reflected in a spate of industrial unrest. A new instrument of industrial agitation, named gherao, specially unnerved the employers. The government refused to intervene in law and order violations in the workplace. A number of workplaces were either locked out or facing strikes. After completing a two-year postgraduate diploma in social welfare from the University of Calcutta, he was appointed as a labor welfare officer (LWO) in a jute mill in the suburbs of Howrah.

The Bikaner Jute Mill (BJM) manufactured jute bags (sacking and hessian) and carpet backing, and part of the manufactured goods were exported. The industry was in a downturn for sometime mainly due to fallen demand in the face of competition from now emergent synthetic packing materials manufacturers, as the products were much cheaper, lighter, and far more flexible. There were about 2000 regular workmen and about 5000 temporary workmen engaged in BJM. The temporary workmen were divided into three categories—temporary badli, badli, and permanent badli—based on seniority. Rarely a temporary workman was regularized on company's roll, but when that happened, it was out of the pool of the permanent badlis that workmen were selected. Every day, based on requisitions received from the production departments, the time-office clerk would go to the gate at the beginning of a shift and from a window in the gate call out the names from his list of temporary workmen, based on the seniority list. There would always be a crowd waiting, irrespective of the weather and the time of the day, but only a few lucky ones would actually get engaged for that particular day. Santrupt, as the LWO, was to personally supervise the intake and ensure that the process was fair and that dissatisfaction of the waiting crowd did not turn into a full-scale unrest.

The labor office had the following structure:

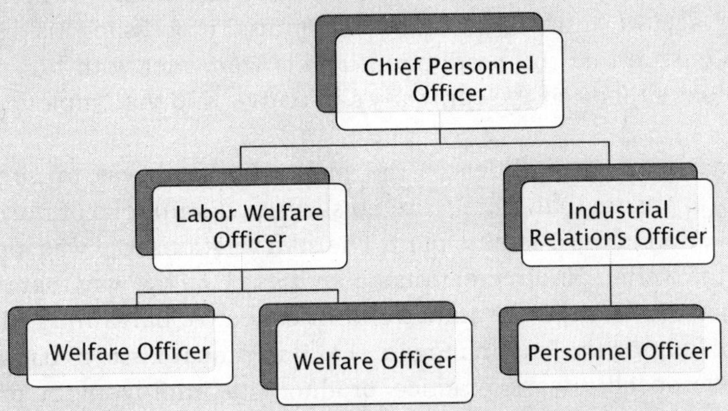

The function of the personnel department was two-fold: the LWO would look after the statutory welfare activities (under the Factories Act), and the industrial relations officer (IRO) would deal with the issues of employee discipline and also with the unions. The industrial relations (IR) work was more complex and more critical for the business impact. Thus, Santrupt looked forward to moving from welfare job to an (IR) job as an essential condition to move up in the functional hierarchy. Santrupt and the other welfare officer would visit the workmen colony to check the hygiene and listen to grievances, visit the ESI hospital to ensure proper medical care of the workmen who were interned there, educate the workmen on the need to fill up nomination forms for their dependents, and prepare absenteeism report and daily engagement statistics for sending to the corporate office. The HR head exclusively dealt with the union leaders (there were three unions), and took decisions on pending disciplinary cases, of which there were many at any given point of time.

1980-1981

Rajeev had, by this time, been 10 years in his profession, having changed jobs and was now on his second job in National Battery Company, a battery-manufacturing and marketing company of 50 years, as the plant HR head. It was a compact new unit of around 350 employees (300 workmen and 50 executives). The company once had a near monopoly market, until Japanese competitors with far cheaper products entered the market and posed serious threats. So the workplace relations, which once had a family environment of industrial harmony promoted by a paternalistic management, started turning adversarial due to constant pressures with regard to increase in productivity and cost cutting and introduction of new technology. It also coincided with the emergence of a Left union that tried to get one up on the existing non-political union by taking militant postures on workmen issues.

National Battery Company had recently set up a new plant with the latest technology in order to produce batteries of sustained quality at a cheaper cost. Rajeev was given the assignment of stabilizing the new plant. It had young work force, around 50% being graduates and the rest being diploma holders in various trades from industrial training institutes (ITIs). Rajeev's key responsibility was managing the IR in such a manner that there was no disruption in planned production due to employee grievances. He was also responsible for selection of employees, administration of the grievance procedure, projection of the requirement of manpower for future and thereby obtain approval from corporate office, employee orientation and training, and administration of welfare budget (e.g., annual picnic) and employee benefits for executives. He also had to manage the annual performance appraisal process for his own staff. The thrust of his role was to ensure that the production targets were met with full participation of the workforce, the unions supported the company's initiative, and the employee cost was kept at a reasonable level.

One of the major responsibilities of the plant HR head was to anchor the collective bargaining process to ensure that there were no surprise disruptions of normal operations and to support the execution of the business plan. The staff relations role was more in the nature of administration of the welfare and recreational activities in such a way that the executives were kept in good humor. He learned the new trend in collective bargaining, that is, productivity bargaining, by first helping the line managers (LMs) to prepare lists of bad practices requiring elimination and the specific work practice/productivity improvement practices that, once agreed by the unions across the negotiation table, would help in improving the productivity of the plant. He also became trained in quality circles (QCs) and anchored the setting up of 10 QCs in the factory, which helped in solving some operational problems such as leakage in the cooker machine.

2005

For the last 10 years, Rajeev had been with Wallace & Magor (W&M), a large liquor manufacturing company with around 65% share in the Indian liquor market. He was the general manager, corporate. There were two plants—one each in Kolkata and Uttaranchal—and 27 branches all over the country. A new plant was coming up in Uttaranchal, in the special economic zone. Santrupt has had a very tough time dealing with strong adversarial unions in their old plants, especially in Kolkata, and advised the management to set up a union-free workplace in the new plant. He also met the labor minister and the labor secretary, and received an assurance that the state government would support the management in a productivity-orientated industry and would ensure that no union is registered for their plant. Some initial efforts by the Kolkata and Kanpur federation of employees were thwarted by a dual strategy of blocking the application for registration at the office of the registrar of trade unions at Nainital, and then by releasing a substantial wage hike for the workmen.

During the last 7–8 years, Rajeev has been concentrating more on the HR work than on industrial or personnel work. He had once gone to attend a personal growth lab (PGL) with

Indian Society for Institutional and Social Development and had met Mr Pulin Garg. He was fascinated by the exciting new development in the domain of the good old personnel relations and IR function known as human resource management (HRM). After having gone through the experience of the PGL in three consecutive years and being accredited as an organization development (OD) practitioner, he felt charged to bring in the transition in HR. He put up an internal proposal and got the top management to agree on creating a new cell in HR called human resource development (HRD). He brought in a new executive with experience in HRD in a good firm and reassigned some personnel executives based on their aptitude.

The initiatives that he took were, introducing a system of performance management, creating a competency model for all key roles in sales and operations, systematizing the recruitment procedure by aligning it to the competency models, and modifying the training and development (T&D) strategy on the basis of training need identification. He also helped introduce a process for strategy formulation based on the techniques of appreciative inquiry. A particularly interesting work was to use a large group facilitation method to facilitate a dealer meeting, which was much appreciated by the dealers' association and the general manager, sales.

2014

Rajeev is now into the role of an adviser in W&M. The company has grown manifolds during the last 20 years and added the division of consumer products and health care. He advises the top management on the people strategy. The company introduced systems, applications, and products (SAP) for several reasons—to streamline business processes, to create an integrated real-time management information system (MIS), for inventory management, and for superior, high-quality customer service. There were many change management issues—the employees needed to be trained before the rollout date, the users needed to be motivated, the surplus staff (around 20% of the total staff) had to be redeployed or given voluntary retirement scheme (VRS).

Rajeev led the experiment of creating non-union workplaces in the new plants and deunionization of some of the existing plants. He pursued a two-pronged strategy—reducing the frequency of dialogues with the union leaders and creating several trust-building initiatives. One specific initiative was known as Umang, an employee-engagement package, which included an annual employee survey, a series of supervisor training, and attractive suggestion schemes to promote the workplace culture.

Rajeev has pruned down the HR department and brought in several youngsters with an engineering background and MBA from Indian Institute of Management (IIM). He plans to have an HR analytics group, which will work on predictive analytics, for example, what factors in recruitment and selection process will factor in performing employees (identifying which campuses predict maximum job fit and longevity in the company), and also bring out the metrics that had the highest impact on the company performance. He has outsourced the functions of manpower staffing (for new projects) and payroll and training (minus the leadership development). He has also made a tie-up with Wharton Business School for the specific functional excellence programs for different functions such as finance, operations, and sales and marketing.

Epilogue

At 65, with about 43 years active career behind him, he looks back with a sense of awe and wonder as to how he went through several hairpin bends in his ever-evolving, chequered professional career to always ride the wave of the current trend in his profession.

Discussion Questions

1. What were the shifts in the evolution of the HRM function?
2. What were the influences driving the shifts?

1.1 INTRODUCTION

Human resource management (HRM) operates on the 'people' dimension of an organization. Its function comprises anchoring the system's processes and practices for acquiring, developing, and motivating people for performance and engaging them for achieving the objectives of the organization. This is valid for all organizations irrespective of their nature—government, business, education, health, recreation, or social action.

The area of HRM has developed from several streams of thinking, which can be put together as an unstructured and free-flowing philosophy regarding managing human resources, but not exactly a specific methodology. It came up in the 20th century, but it also includes previously existing beliefs about people management at work. The constituent ideas have divergent origins and, as a consequence, do not constitute a coherent and uniform body of knowledge. One contentious area of raging polemics has been the issue: How is HRM different from the old field of personnel management? The domain of HRM continues to evolve, with the formulation of new approaches, trends, and fashions of management.

One of the reasons why HRM may appear to be a nebulous and somewhat elusive concept is on account of multiple existing definitions of the term. HRM is a stretchable term, covering a range of applications that have wide variance across industries. Graham describes the purpose of HRM as 'to ensure that the employees of an organization are used in such a way that the employer obtains the greatest possible benefit from their abilities and the employees obtain both material and psychological rewards from their work.'[2] Boxall and Purcell[3] define HRM as '... all those activities associated with the management of the employment relationship in the firm.' Stephen Bach,[4] however, considers the definition as 'a little too broad,' stating that such a broad definition, inter alia, fails to underscore the unique features or values of HRM or map the shifts in the practice of HRM. In Bach's opinion, HRM, as distinct from employee management, is unitarist (where employer–employee interests converge), having organizational effectiveness as the focal point, with emphasis on individual motivation and aspiration as opposed to collective aspirations. Some later definitions of HRM are as follows:

---

[2] H. T. Graham, *Human Resource Management,* 2nd ed. (Plymouth: MacDonald & Evans, 1978).

[3] Peter F. Boxall and John Purcell, *Strategy and Human Resource Management* (New York, NY: Palgrave Macmillan, 2003), 1.

[4] S. Bach, *Managing Human Resources: Personnel Management in Transition* (Oxford: Blackwell, 2005), 3.

- 'A strategic approach to managing employment relations which emphasizes that leveraging people's capabilities is critical to achieving competitive advantage, this being achieved through a distinctive set of integrated employment policies, programs and practices.'[5]
- 'A philosophy of people management based on the belief that the human resource is uniquely important in sustained business success. An organization gains competitive advantage by using its people effectively, drawing on their expertise and ingenuity to meet clearly defined objectives. HRM is aimed at recruiting capable, flexible and committed people, managing and rewarding their performance and developing key competencies.'[6]
- 'A strategic and coherent approach to the management of an organization's most valued assets—the people working there who individually and collectively contribute to the achievement of its objectives.'[7]
- 'A set of interrelated policies with an ideological and philosophical underpinning.'[8]

Despite the divergence in definitions, there seems to be some common ground. HRM comprises people-oriented management practices, where employees are seen as assets, with the objective of creating and maintaining a skillful and committed workforce, which must be used to gain competitive advantage.[9]

1.2 HUMAN RESOURCE MANAGEMENT AND PERSONNEL MANAGEMENT

Grant and Oswick's telephone survey found that 50% of the respondents believed that HRM is very different from personnel management. More recently, Hoque and Noon[10] have used 1998 Workforce Employment Relations Survey data to demonstrate important differences between personnel and HR specialists based on job titles. These titles, they argue, are not synonymous because empirically they represent specialists who operate in distinct ways. Their analysis suggests four key ways in which HR specialists are different from personnel specialists:

1. Level of formal education
2. Involvement in strategic planning process
3. Extent to which authority has been devolved to LMs or supervisors
4. Adoption of strategic high commitment practices associated with HRM

1.3 THE IMPORTANCE OF HUMAN RESOURCE MANAGEMENT

There have always been skeptics about the value of HRM to business. Years ago, in Kolkata there was the legend about an old company called Lily Biscuits, a once popular brand running into hard times. Due to serious industrial unrest, it was locked out for a long time, and then eventually closed. Some years later, with the persistent efforts of the employees, it was reopened with the help of the government and the Board for Industrial and Financial Reconstruction (BIFR), with employee

5 J. Bratton and J. Gold, *Human Resource Management: Theory and Practice,* 4th ed. (Hampshire: Palgrave Macmillan, 2007).

6 Alan Price, *Human Resource Management*, 4th ed. (Hampshire: Cengage Learning, 2011).

7 Michael Armstrong, *A Handbook of Human Resource Management Practice* (London: Kogan Page, 2008).

8 J. Storey, *From Personnel Management to Human Resource Management* (London: Routledge, 1989).

9 Zorlu Senyucel, *Managing the Human Resources in the 21st Century* (Denmark: Ventus Publishing, 2009).

10 Hoque, Kim, and Mike Noon, 'Counting Angels: A Comparison of Personnel and HR Specialists,' *Human Resource Management Journal* 11, no. 3 (2001): 5–22.

shareholding, owned and managed by the employees. The employees decided to do away with the personnel department, saying it was not worth the cost for running the business. In a *Forbes* article,[11] contributor Kyle Smith wrote, 'Everybody has a HR horror story,' which is why, in the words of an author, HR is widely thought of as, 'at best, a necessary evil—and at worst, a dark bureaucratic force that blindly enforces nonsensical rules, resists creativity, and impedes constructive change.'

Has the HR function served its term? Is it to be readied for the corporate guillotine? The answer is an emphatic no. Even the strident critics do not target the function; they target the foibles of the practitioners.

> After close to 20 years of hopeful rhetoric about becoming 'strategic partners' with a 'seat at the table' where the business decisions that matter are made, most HR professionals aren't nearly there. They have no seat, and the table is locked inside a conference room to which they have no key. HR people are, for most practical purposes, neither strategic nor leaders.[12]

'HR, goes the refrain, is too important to be left to HR,' says the contributor in the *Forbes* article. 'HR is the corporate function with the greatest potential—the key driver, in theory, of business performance,' acknowledges the author of the *Fast Company* article. Peter Cappelli in his widely read article 'Why We Love to Hate HR?'[13] has explained it as the 'Personnel Pendulum.'

> How top executives feel about HR pretty reliably reflects what's going on in the U.S. economy. When the economy is down and the labor market is slack, they see HR as a nuisance. But sentiments change when labor tightens up and HR practices become essential to companies.

Dave Ulrich and Wayne Brockbank[14] provide a repartee about the importance of HR in their iconic book *HR Value Proposition* in these words:

> We like HR, we like the HR practices that deal with people, performance, information and work because they create an infrastructure that affects employees, customers, LMs and investors. We like the HR function because it allows functional experts to help sustain organization results We like HR professionals because, for the most part they value people and they work to create both competitive and compassionate organizations.

1.4 MODELS OF HUMAN RESOURCE MANAGEMENT

There are various models of HRM. The famous ones are the Fombrun, Tichy, and Devanna Model; the Harvard Model; the Guest Model; the Warwick Model; and finally, the Ulrich Model. Some of

[11] *Forbes,* 'It's Time for Companies to Fire Their Human Resource Department.' April 4, 2013. Available at: https://www.forbes.com/sites/kylesmith/2013/04/04/its-time-for-companies-to-fire-their-human-resource-departments/ (accessed on September 21, 2017).

[12] K. H. Hammonds, 'Why We Hate HR' (July–August 2005, Fast Company Newsletter). Available at: https://www.fastcompany. com/53319/why-we-hate-hr (accessed on September 21, 2017).

[13] Available at: https://hbr.org/2015/07/why-we-love-to-hate-hr-and-what-hr-can-do-about-it (accessed on September 21, 2017).

[14] Ulrich, Dave, and Wayne Brockbank, *The HR Value Proposition* (Harvard Business School Press, 2005).

the classifications are hard–soft models and normative–prescriptive models. Storey[15] has classified these as conceptual, descriptive, and prescriptive; the four-way classification by Legge is normative, descriptive–functional, descriptive–behavioral, and critical–evaluative. Tyson[16] has a three-way classification: normative, descriptive, and analytical.

The dominant classification of hard and soft forms of HRM has been demonstrated by two schools of HRM known as Michigan and Harvard schools, respectively. ‘Hard’ HRM highlights the resource side, where the management controls the head counts, monitors the numbers, and ensures that the numbers as well as the performances match the requirements of the organization. The focus of ‘soft’ HRM being the ‘human’ facet of HRM aims at eliciting a commitment so that behavior is primarily self-regulated. It lays stress on achieving the strategic objectives by taking people along, leading them through communication and motivation. Soft HRM is connected with the human relations movement and the utilization of individual talents and is in tune with McGregor’s Theory Y on orientation of people.

The soft–hard dichotomy in HRM exists primarily within normative models of HRM, rather than in what Legge[17] terms the descriptive–functional or critical–evaluative traditions. Soft HRM is associated with the human relations movement, the utilization of individual talents, and McGregor’s Theory Y perspective on individuals (developmental ± humanism). This has been equated with the concept of a ‘high commitment work system,’[18] ‘which is aimed at eliciting a commitment so that behavior is primarily self-regulated rather than controlled by sanctions and pressures external to the individual and relations within the organization are based on high levels of trust’ and that communication plays a central role in management.[19]

Hard HRM, on the other hand, stresses ‘the quantitative, calculative, and business strategic aspects of managing the ‘headcount resource’ in as ‘rational’ a way as for any other factor of production’[20] (where HR policies and practices are closely linked to the strategic objectives of the organization, and are coherent among themselves[21,22] with the ultimate aim being increased competitive advantage).[23,24,25,26,27,28]

15 J. Storey. (Ed.), ‘Human Resource Management: Still Marching on or Marching Out?’, In *Human Resource Management: A Critical Text* (London: Routledge).

16 S. Tyson, *Essentials of Human Resource Management* (Abingdon: Routledge, 2015).

17 K. Legge, *Human Resource Management: Rhetorics and Realities* (London: McMillan, 1995).

18 R. E. Walton, ‘From Control to Commitment in the Workplace,’ *Harvard Business Review* (March–April 1985).

19 Storey, John and Sisson, Keith, *Managing Human Resources and Industrial Relations.* Managing Work and Organizations (Milton Keynes, UK and Philadelphia: Open University Press, 1993).

20 J. Storey, *New Developments in the Management of Human Resources* (Oxford: Blackwell, 1992).

21 Baird and Meshoulam, ‘Managing Two Fits of Strategic Human Resource Management Baird, Lloyd; Meshoulam, Ilan Academy of Management,’ *The Academy of Management Review* 13, no. 1 (1988): 116–128.

22 Hendry and Pettigrew, ‘The Practice of Strategic Human Resource Management,’ *Personnel Review* 15, no. 1.

23 G. C. Alpander and C. H. Botter, ‘An Integrated Model of Strategic Human Resource Planning and Utilization,’ *Human Resource Planning* 12, no. 2 (1981): 189–203.

24 M. Devanna, C. Fombrun and N. Tichy. (Eds.), ‘A Framework for Strategic Human Resource Management,’ In *Strategic Human Resource Management* (New York: Wiley, 1984).

25 Cynthia A. Lengnick-Hall and Mark L. Lengnick-Hall, *Interactive Human Resource Management and Strategic Planning* (Washington Papers, 1984).

26 Miles and Snow, ‘Designing Strategic Human Resources Systems,’ *Organizational Dynamics* 13, no. 1 (Summer 1984): 46–52.

27 Storey, John and Sisson, Keith, *Managing Human Resources and Industrial Relations.*

28 Tyson and Fell, *Evaluating the Personnel Function* (London: Century Hutchinson Ltd, 1986).

1.4.1 The Harvard Business Model

The Harvard Business Model is one of the leading models of HRM. In this framework, employees are considered as resources with the only distinctive feature being that, unlike other resources such as money and machine, human resource cannot be managed similarly. In this approach, there is an underlying theme of mutuality: employees are also considered a key stakeholder in an organization, with their own needs and interests, in the same way as other stakeholders such as the shareholders and customers.

The model describes the HR policy areas as (a) HR workflows covering recruitment, selection, placement, promotion, appraisal and assessment, promotion, termination, and so on, (b) reward systems that cover compensation, incentives, and so on, (c) employee influence—delegation of authority, responsibility, and power, and (d) work systems—work design and employee alignment.

The situational factors having a bearing on HR policy choices include workforce characteristics, business strategy, management philosophy, labor market, task technology, and so on.

The HR outcome as a result of the management policy choices are the four Cs in the form of commitment, congruence, competence, and cost effectiveness. It implies that given the right kind of nurturing environment, the employees are likely to contribute to the organization in a qualitative manner.

The aforementioned HR outcomes create well-being in the long term—for both individual and the society, and also ensure effectiveness for the organization.

1.4.2 Michigan Business School—Fombrun, Tichy, and Devanna Model

This model, despite resemblances to the Harvard Model, adopts a hard approach about resources and does not differentiate human resource from other resources. It maintains that people should be acquired cheap, and should subsequently be managed for maximum yield, to be used efficiently and developed to have better values. The Michigan Model, also described as the 'Matching Model' stipulates that HR strategies should aim at matching the business strategies. In this approach, the HR role is a restricted non-strategic role, and the role of environmental factors in shaping HRM is largely played down.

According to Fombrun et al., there are only four common HR processes: selection—matching people to jobs; appraisal of performance; rewards—emphasizing the real importance of pay and other forms of compensation in achieving results; and development of skilled individuals. These processes are interlinked in an HR cycle.

According to the critics of this model, the inherent flaw in the Matching Model is that it appears to presume that in organizations decisions are made following a rational and mechanical path. It is pointed out that, in actual practice, strategy-making is a complicated process—tending to get decided sometimes in a personalized manner, intuitively, even politically, and certainly not always in pure rational method. It has also been described as prescriptive and normative with a clear suggestion that the compatibility to business strategy should decide HR strategy. A revised, and more complex, variation of the Fombrun, Tichy, and Devanna Model was offered by Randall Schuler and colleagues[29] by incorporating some new variables such as technology, organizational structure and size, unionization, and industry sector.

[29] Randall Schuler and Jackson, 'Linking Competitive Strategies with Human Resources Practices,' *The Academy of Management Executives* 1, no. 3 (1987): 207–219.

1.4.3 Guest Model

David Guest's model of HRM flows in six sequential elements building up to a variety of outcomes:

1. HRM strategy
2. HRM practices (hiring, training, appraisal, compensation, relations)
3. HRM outcomes (commitment, quality, flexibility)
4. Behavior outcomes (motivation, cooperation, organizational citizenship)
5. Performance outcomes (positive—high productivity, innovation, quality; negative—low productivity, low turnover, absenteeism)
6. Financial outcomes (profit, return on investments [ROI])

The model differentiates HRM from the erstwhile personnel management, which is claimed to have been moored in strategy. The model has been classified as prescriptive and idealistic in its basic assumptions. It links intangible factors such as flexibility and motivation with profit and ROI in a causal relationship. Guest, nonetheless, admitted to the uncertain relationship between commitment and performance outcomes. The Guest Model is unitary in its belief, and fails to recognize the role of trade unions, emphasizing the employee relationship as the one between the employee and the organization.

1.4.4 The Warwick Model

The model of the Warwick University duo of Hendry and Pettigrew introduced an outer context (socioeconomic, technical, politico-legal, and competitive) and an inner context (culture, structure, politics/ leadership, task technology, and business output). Against these contexts, HRM and business strategy contexts interact to lead to HRM contents (HR flows, work systems, reward systems, and employee relations). The Warwick Model thus emphasized the influence of both external and internal dynamics to shape HRM and, in this way, it is an improvement on the Guest Model.

1.5 EVOLUTION OF HUMAN RESOURCE MANAGEMENT

In the beginning, it was in the avatar of personnel function. It commenced as soon as business started in the USA. As a function, the discipline of personnel management was started around the start of the 20th century as a clerical activity recruiting workers and keeping their records for the emerging industries. Gradually, it metamorphosed into a specialized discipline with wider roles of managing the employees. Some of the milestones of the ongoing march of personnel function are captured in the textbox further.

As can be observed, the function continued to evolve all through the subsequent years in a step-by-step process, absorbing new developments and getting more mature. Some of the significant occurrences, as shown in the textbox further, include the first properly documented strike in America in the year 1796, and continuing to the end of the millennium. It is evident that the contextual factors (government regulations and socioeconomic factors).

A significant watershed in the history of HRM was the setting up of the Society for Human Resource Management (SHRM) in 1948. Having established credibility for the profession, SHRM has directed attention to the changing role of the HR profession by encouraging the development of strategic business partnerships between the HR and the organization, as well as the continued development of professional competencies.

Exhibit Significant Occurrences in the Field of HRM

1796	The first authenticated strike in America
1881	Frederick Taylor starts work in scientific management at the Midvale Steel plant
1924	Point Method of job evaluation developed
1927	Hawthorne studies begun by Mayo, Roethlisberger, and Dickson
1976	HR Certification Institute begins certification
1985	Focus on employee participation in management to improve productivity and competitive position
1991	Focus on global HR practices; greater use of temporary employees
1995	Emphasis on greater diversity in the workforce and on TQM; downsizing or 'rightsizing' of organizations
1990s	Use of Competence Models to guide HR program design

Source: Sherman, Bohlander, and Snell, Managing Human Resources (South-Western college Pub, 1996).

1.5.1 HRM in India

The precursor to the HRM has been identified as Kautilya's *Arthasastra* by some experts, based on its reference to a sound system of management of resources in the 2nd century BC. In modern times, an important event was the emergence of trade unions in the form of All India Trade Union Congress (AITUC) following the World War I. The Factories Act, enacted in 1881 and modified several times in later years, also contained regulations on working hours and employment of children. The institution of LWO, enforced by the amended omnibus Factories Act in 1948 (for factories employing 500 workmen and more), created an important headwind for the progress of the function.

Two factors, however, accelerated the growth of the function, then in the form of labor welfare and personnel: First, India's political independence in 1947 unlocked the awareness for creating decent workplaces, the need for creating platforms to capture employee voice, and a growing government commitment to adhere to the charters of International Labor Organization (ILO). The commencement of Five Year Plans, the building up of huge industries for creating infrastructure along with adoption of industrial policies, formation of tripartite bodies including the employer and employee federations, and the government labor department—all these helped in the evolution of the personnel function that grew beyond the traditional labor welfare. Second, the emergence of two professional bodies in the form of National Institute of Personnel Management (NIPM) and the National Institute of Labor Management (NILM) also helped in the shaping of a new integrated function (with labor welfare, industrial relations, and personnel administration) known as personnel management and in providing a platform of professional networks and sharing of best practices. Later, a body (now merged) came up in the 1980s as NIPM.

The personnel function was also responding to the changing context of the business in the 1970s and the 1980s. Labor welfare activities became largely passé, as many industries had already adopted enlightened policies for employee welfare beyond the statutory requirements and public sector. However, the core work in the function was around dealing with trade unions, fighting litigations, and ushering in experiments in total quality management (TQM) for improved productivity. The predominant skill sets set in the personnel function were collective bargaining, how to downsize in old units, and how to introduce effective productivity incentive schemes in the shop floor.

In the 1980s, the personal computers started being used in the industry, leading to upgradation of technology also in personnel function, in marking attendance, and in running payrolls in-house. The OD interventions in Indian Oil Corporation Ltd (IOCL) and Larsen & Toubro (L&T), among others, were creating the early waves of HR function in India. Mr Udai Pareek, Mr Pulin Garg, and Mr T. V. Rao, with their exposure to the OD intervention technologies in National Training Laboratory were starting to run PGLs and various OD interventions. The erstwhile personal function was receiving a makeover in the form of HRM. For the first time, HR function was being perceived as an asset, requiring to be nurrd, rather than managed and manipulated.

1.6 THE FACTORS INFLUENCING HUMAN RESOURCE MANAGEMENT

1.6.1 Globalization

The term 'globalization' implies unrestricted movement of goods, services, people, and ideas across national frontiers. In a globalized context, organizations fiercely strive for acquiring customers who expect certain standards of performance, quality, and cost. In the closing decades of the last millennium, major shifts in economic thinking fueled an unprecedented surge in international business with globalization of world markets, characterized by the formation of new international business blocs and a thrust in economic liberalization in major developed and emerging economies. Over 75 developing and erstwhile communist economies, having an aggregate of 3-billion plus populations, were poised for assimilating themselves into the global market system. Several other factors such as low labor and manufacturing cost in certain parts of the world, growth in demand for products that are culture-neutral (e.g., cell phones), favorable regulations and tax structures, access to new markets, lower transportation costs, technology advancements (e.g., the Internet), and global accreditations like ISO 9000 propelled this change in the global economy. As a response to these trends, large volumes of capital started flowing in to many such economies in Asia, Latin America, and Central Europe. Significantly, over 30 countries were able to establish stock markets having the potential of attracting international portfolio investments. As a key emerging market in the world, India showcased a capacity for sustained high rates of economic growth, and thus has been marked out as principal actor in the world economy. The effect of all these changes has been the heightened capability of organizations to compete globally.

Many Indian industries reaped the benefit by shifting the gear of competitive strategies. For example, Sundaram Clayton bagged the supplier of the year award from General Motors (GM) for several years with increased volumes every year. Maruti is the chosen supplier of small cars under the Suzuki brand for Europe and, outside of Japan, India is the manufacturing, export, and research hub for Suzuki. Tata Iron and Steel Company (TISCO) is today the lowest cost producer of hot-rolled steel in the world. In general, globalization has caused significant spurt in exports (especially information technology, auto-components, and pharmaceuticals). In the automobile industry, most major automobile manufacturers now procure their components from Indian manufacturers, accounting for a total value of US$1.5 billion in 2003. Hyundai Motors India (HMI) is expected about to become the global small car hub for Honda Motor Company (HMC). In 2003, HMC sourced 25,000 Santros from HMI's plant in India. By 2010, the supply increased more than eight times, to more than half a million.

Ford India, which started outsourcing in 2000, was earning 35% of its sales through outsourcing in three years' time, exporting to Mexico, Brazil, and China, among others. The same trends emerged in retail, textile, and chemicals also. India accounts for 50% of its apparel to Walmart. Gap sources US$500–600 million worth, while Hilfiger sources US$100 million worth from India. Asian Paints has manufacturing units in 22 countries across the globe.[30]

Globalization affects HRM in more ways than one. Like movement of goods and services, successful people practices can also be planted across national boundaries. At the same time, it is also common knowledge that good practices in one part of the globe may not always be replicable in another country, another cultural context. In case of Suzuki and Toyota, the successful Japanese workplace practices have been partly responsible for an opposite, unintended effect in the industrial areas of Haryana and Karnataka in India—the periodical eruption of violent industrial unrest in the automobile units in Haryana and the experiments in no-union workplace of Toyota have largely backfired in Bangalore units. Regarding MNC subsidiaries, Poutsma et al.[31] argued that organizations try to balance the need to standardize best HRM practices across national boundaries with the need to adapt to local practices and customs. Kostova and Roth[32] labeled this phenomenon as 'institutional duality.' The appropriate balance between these two needs will positively affect organizational performance.

Researchers have established linkages between effective international HRM and improved financial and organizational performance. An example supporting this point is that of Maruti Udyog Ltd, a leading company in the Indian automobile industry, which started as a joint venture with Suzuki of Japan. Maruti, which was the undisputed ruler of the automobile market in India (at over 80%) with the quality of its products and services in the regulated environment, started losing its share post deregulation in the wake of entry of new players (Telco, Mahindra & Mahindra [M&M], Daewoo, Toyota, Ford, Mitsubishi, GM, and others). The company responded by launching new models, targeting different market segments, and by an image makeover from a manufacturing company to a marketing company with a service-oriented and customer-centric focus. HRM function also rose from being a mere transactional, unimportant, non-strategic function to a valued function with induction of professional managers. In order to sustain the competitive edge in a competitive environment, HRM initiated systems such as performance appraisals, competency mapping and job rotations, redefining job profiles, simplifying procedures, and so on. The HR outcomes of these measures were in the form of excellent teamwork, admired compensation system, falling employee turnover, improved employee morale, commitment, and increased job satisfaction within the organization.

Globalization also opens up a global labor market for the global organizations. Foxconn, the manufacturer of Apple iPhones, has its large manufacturing units in China and India employing thousands of workers at a relatively low wage rate. Developed countries (the USA, Europe) have been facing backlash against the outsourcing of jobs overseas. Another consequence of globalization is downsizing and restructuring. All big MNCs (Coca-Cola, IBM, GM, and others) have undertaken the process of restructuring at some point of time or the other. The most recent example is Infosys embarking on a job cut of 3000 employees as a result of the loss of Royal Bank of Scotland (RBS) contract. In 1995, M&M Ltd (tractor division), beset with chronic manufacturing bottlenecks, poor

[30] Ashok Som, 'Bracing for MNC Competition Through Innovative HRM Practices: The Way Ahead for Indian Firms,' *Thunderbird International Business Review* 48, no. 2 (March–April 2006): 207–237.

[31] E. Poutsma, E. M. Ligthart and U. Veersma, 'The Diffusion of Calculative and Collaborative HRM Practices in European Firms,' *Industrial Relations a Journal of Economy and Society,* 45, no. 4 (1996): 513–546.

[32] T. Kostova and K. Roth, 'Adoption of an Organizational Practice by Subsidiaries of Multinational Corporations: Institutional and Relational Effects,' *The Academy of Management Journal* 45, no. 1 (2002): 215–233.

productivity, stressed production cycle, and low output, decided to undertake business process re-engineering (or redesign) (BPR) to stay competitive. In a few years' time, the BPR, in tandem with the renovated HR processes such as flattened organizational structure, improved teamwork, outsourcing of non-core processes, and open communication, started achieving spectacular growth at a sustained basis.

Reflection Point

In his recent blog post, Bill Gates made a bold prediction: 'Within the next two or three years, I predict most virtual meetings will move from 2D camera image grids... to the metaverse, a 3D space with digital avatars.'

Many companies are already making leaps to move to the future of work that will be defined by more authentic remote collaboration and potentially the metaverse.

Discussion Question

1. What do you visualize would be the impact of metaverse in the world of work?

Source: Three ways Metaverse could transform the HR. June 2022. https://www.forbes.com

1.6.2 Influence of Technology

The march of technology has brought in phenomenal changes in the arena of business. We have witnessed the exit of the industrial age, and the 1990s have ushered in the digital age or the information age, characterized by extensive use of computers and the Internet. A growing community of business organizations are weighing the options of using technology in preference to employing people with the belief that technology-driven services and products could provide better quality at a cheaper rate. The use of enterprise resource planning (ERP) has changed the way work is organized, creating scores of jobs and skills as redundant. Overall, no business, however traditional, can function without leveraging computer technology. This impact is all-pervasive—covering all aspects of business, including HR, which has regrouped itself and reoriented its various practices in response to the technological advancement.

One area where technology has stimulated significant changes is recruitment and selection. In the pre-Internet era, the recruitment process of a company was heavily tied up in print publications, including newspapers, for advertising vacancies and for attracting applications from prospective job seekers against open positions. Although alternate methods such as networking were in vogue too, the recruitment professionals did not enjoy the freedom to circulate the news of vacancy at multiple locations, thus enabling simultaneous access to vastly larger pool of prospective candidates. The emergence of portals such as Naukri.com, Monster.com, and TimesJobs have made the life of the recruiter far simpler. The availability of large numbers of software has crashed the cycle time of recruitment and, in general, made recruiting more efficient.

The field of training, learning, and development has also been greatly enriched by the availability of various software, which make it possible to offer e-learning options to busy workplaces and to employees to learn in their own time. Information technology also makes it possible to access all relevant information pertaining to programs, trainer profiles, training history, cost of training, training budget spending, and so on. Much of the orientation of new hires can be done virtually covering multiple locations, in a quick time, without the need for traveling. Even the evaluation of the effectiveness of training programs can be done faster and more efficiently through Internet and through computerized testing programs. Similarly, electronic formats and software have brought about a sea change in the way performance management processes are organized, saving time and bringing greater transparency and consistency in the process.

The maintenance of databases has also taken huge leaps by virtue of advanced technology, thus widening the scope and scale of HR processes. In day-to-day functioning, paperwork has become almost extinct. With electronic imaging, files can be stored and retrieved in electronic formats. Various personnel forms and files can be printed on demand, thus eliminating the need for storage space and saving costs.

Currently, businesses are riding on the latest technological waves of big data and cloud computing. The rapid pace and shifts in technology have influenced businesses in diverse ways, from global operations, organizational restructuring to the millennial employees (estimated at 75% of the workforce by 2020) seeking remote and mobile job opportunities. In this environment, HRM function also has to embrace technology at its core, if it wants to play a meaningful role in leading change in businesses and at the same time meet the aspirations of the new employee.

1.6.3 Demographic Changes in the Workforce

All over the world, the composition of the workforce is changing rapidly, and these changes have already had a major impact on the HRM functions. Workforce is getting increasingly diverse, forcing changes in people management approaches in organizations. In some parts of the world (the USA, Japan) workforce is aging, while in India it is predominantly young.

A report titled 'Shaping the Future of HR,' authored by SHRM Foundation and the Economist Intelligence Unit (EIU), informs of several demographic trends, likely to change the profile of the average worker over the next two decades. The major trends include:

1. **Aging workforce in developed world** Due to increased life expectancy, some countries in Europe have increased the pensionable age. As a result, the HRM professionals have to cater to the typical demands of characteristic older workforce requirements, and also to get adept at resolving workplace conflicts between generations.
2. **Generation Y** Ironically, in another part of the world, the challenges are just the reverse—those which come with an increasingly youthful labor force. The Asia-Pacific region, for example, will have 60% of the world's 15–24-year-olds. The millennials have high expectations of their employers, short-term focus on immediate future, need for innovative and exciting work, and a distinct preference for a positive work–life balance. The talent management process will have to be aligned with the new workforce inclinations.
3. **A globalized workforce** People will be mobile and migrating across different parts of the world. This will make the workplace culturally divergent, posing challenges in terms of equality and inclusion (DEI). As a consequence, HR managers would need high cultural intelligence to deal with employees from a multitude of countries, faiths, and ethnic groups.
4. **Rising number of women in workforce** Booz & Company have predicted that in the decade of 2010–2020, some 865 million more women will have entered the economic mainstream, resulting in a surge in female employment particularly in the developing nations. This coincides with the growing share of women in education and rise in equality. The HR processes, practices, policies, and also the physical environment would also have to shift to align to this change.

In conclusion, the EIU and SHRM Foundation report asserts that 'many of the previously trusted techniques for managing culturally uniform, co-located teams, composed largely of male, long-service employees, are now as redundant as the office typewriter.'

1.7 HUMAN RESOURCE MANAGEMENT AND LINE MANAGERS

There is a view that in a highly competitive business environment, it is necessary for LMs to share part of the onus for HRM.[33] It helps by providing the HR specialists adequate time to concentrate on their strategic roles and thus enable the integration of HRM function into the business strategy. In this condition, the LMs take up the primary responsibility for handling the operational tasks connected with HRM activities. The rationale behind this devolution of HRM activities is the belief that the LMs are more tuned in to the local conditions and the specific needs of the people working in close contact with them. They are able to exercise influence on the attitudes and conduct of their team members to navigate them to the direction of an organization's goals, priorities, and strategies. As far as employees are concerned, they are also likely to accept and support their bosses in all their broad directions. It is another matter that very often the LMs are ambivalent in accepting the primacy of this role. The HRM activities in which they can play key roles have been identified as the areas of performance management, training and development (T&D), HRP including recruitment and selection, manpower optimization, employee relations, compensation and rewards systems, career management, and health, safety, and environment (HSE) activities.

Brewster and Larson[34] have attributed the devolution to several factors: emergence of profit center-based approaches, the imperative of a comprehensive approach to managing people, the need for real-time decision-making in a customer-centric environment of the dominant services sector, and so on. It is further determined by the power equation of the line management with the top leadership. An extreme view in this context of devolvement holds that HRM is too important to be left to the specialists; therefore, it has to be shared.[35]

It is necessary to check out the effects of this devolution of HRM role on both the HRM functions and the line management. According to Hoogendoorn and Brewster,[36] devolution creates both threats and opportunities for the HR specialist. The transfer of activities to the line management may create a psychological void in influence among the HR specialists, but it may also open up new HR tasks, which may wield more strategically dominant impact. According to MacNeil,[37] when LMs foster a climate of sharing of learning in work teams, the organization can capture tacit knowledge, as they work in close contact with the employees and have their trust.

---

[33] P. Budhwar, 'Evaluating Levels of Strategic Integration and Devolvement of Human Resource Management in the UK,' *Personnel Review* 29, no. 2 (2000): 141–157.

[34] C. Brewster and H. H. Larsen, 'Responsibility in Human Resource Management: The Role of the Line,' in *Human Resource Management in Northern Europe*, eds. C. Brewster and H. H. Larsen (Oxford: Blackwell, 2000), 195–218.

[35] S. T. Teo, 'Effectiveness of a Corporate HR Department in an Australian Public Sector Entity During Commercialization and Corporatization,' *International Journal of Human Resource Management* 13, no. 1 (2002): 89–105.

[36] Jacob Hoogendoorn and Chris Brewster, 'Human Resource Aspects: Decentralization and Devolution,' *Personnel Review* 21, no. 1 (1992): 4–11.

[37] Christina M. MacNeil, 'Line Managers: Facilitators of Knowledge Sharing in Teams,' Employee Relations 25, no. 3 (2003): 294–307.

Table 1.1 Issues/challenges in LM's role-taking in different HR activities

Areas	LM's role	Issues
Performance management	Jointly set objectives with employee Monitor performance and provide feedback and resources Assess the need of employees' T&D through employees' performance	Ambiguity about role Uncertainty about the depth of their role Limited responsibility and uneven devolution of responsibility Weak involvement
Recruitment and selection	Projects manpower needs for future Participates in selection	Do not bring in the organizational perspectives in selection Decision-making with HR Do not exert great influence on the recruitment and selection process
T&D	Identifies training needs through performance management process Sometimes involved in training design and delivery Evaluates the impact of training on job performance	Uneven involvement Unsure about the efficacy of training on actual performance improvement Perceives training as an HR function. Refusal in role-taking
Managing discipline	Increasing involvement in taking decisions	HR specialist authority and technical expertise outweighs LM influence Perception of limited authority and tendency to refer complex ones to higher authorities
Compensation	Although LMs' role tends to vary, they play an important 'link pin' role between operational and strategic-level activity regardless of the situation facing the organization	Lacks the helicopter view Depends on the HR expertise for basic pay fixation
Career development	Jointly responsible with HR for career development of employees	Lacks basic skills in planning career-development activities Dependent on HR for providing direction

Bredin and Soderlund[38] highlight the value of assigning HR role to LMs in a project-based organization in preference to the traditional hierarchical and bureaucratic role. In this new orientation, which impacts the organizational structure and their role content, the LMs stand at the intersection of the HR function and the firm's operations, and operate as competence coach. This thus represents a shift from managing and supervising functional activities to managing competencies and people.

The problems and issues in the devolution of LM role are innumerable (Table 1.1). A key issue is the perception of HR specialists themselves. Hyman and Cunningham[39] report that while LMs take pride in their key HR capability of 'common sense backed by experience,' it is the HR specialists, who doubt this competency, leading a perceptional gap. Another frequently repeated criticism by HR managers on LM role is of avoidance. There are also perceptions of LMs' capabilities in undertaking these tasks. E. Conway and K. Monks[40] report that the increased bureaucratic layers adversely affect the decision-making by both HR and middle managers. HR managers are emerging as regulators. They retain control of information systems that slow down middle management decision-making.

[38] K. Bredin and J. Soderlund, 'Reconceptualising Line Management in Project-based Organizations: The Case of Competence Coaches at Tetra Pak,' Personnel Review 36, no. 5 (2007): 815–833.

[39] J. Hyman and I. Cunningham, 'Change in Employee Relations—Can Line Managers Deliver?' Management Research News 19, no. 4/5 (1996): 35–37.

[40] E. Conway and K. Monks, 'The Devolution of HRM to Middle Managers in the Irish Health Service,' *Personnel Review* 39, no. 3 (2010): 361–374.

However, one positive effect of devolution is that providing LMs with training and support in HRM has a greater positive impact on perceived effectiveness in organizations that have not devolved compared to those that have.[41]

Reflection Point

A recent trend to hire data scientists and data analysts for HR tech roles is an early sign of the shift of the profile of the HR professional of the future. Innovative learning and development (L&D) interventions such as AI-led learning recommendations, gamification, micro-learning, on-the-job data projects, can help build data-skills from within. HR leaders must learn to be comfortable and adept with data and technology.

Discussion Question

1. How would the future HR competencies evolve? What skills will stay, and what will become obsolete?

According to Brockbank et al.,[42] the following are the important competencies of an HR professional:

1. **Personal credibility** Models the values of the organization, builds a trust-based relationship, and demonstrates a conviction, based on evidence, about how business can win
2. **Change management** Leads change and is able to diagnose problems, build client relations, articulate a vision, and set a leadership agenda
3. **Manage culture** Custodian of the culture, creates culture congruent with the strategy and vision, enrolls employees, and describes behavior specific to the culture
4. **Delivers HR practices** Expert in state-of-the art innovative HR practices
5. **Business knowledge** Understands strategy, market, competitors, finance, IT, and so on

According to CIPD,[43] the HR professional competencies are:

1. Personal drive and effectiveness
2. People management and leadership
3. Professional competence
4. Adding value through people
5. Continued learning
6. Thinking and applied resourcefulness
7. Customer focus
8. Strategic capability
9. Influencing and interpersonal skills

[41] E. L. Perry and C. Kulki, 'The Devolution of HR to the Line: Implications for Perceptions of People Management Effectiveness,' *International Journal Human Resource Management* 19, no. 2 (2008): 262–273.

[42] Wayne Brockbank, Dave Ulrich, and Richard W. Beatty, 'HR Professional Development: Creating the Future Creators at the University of Michigan Business School,' *Human Resource Management* 38, no. 2 (Summer 1999): 111–117.

[43] M. Armstrong, *A Handbook of Human Resource Management Practice* (London: Kogan Page, 2008).

1.8 OTHER KEY STAKEHOLDER ROLES IN HUMAN RESOURCE MANAGEMENT

1.8.1 Top Management

Frederick Taylor had conceptualized the role of top management in ensuring that employees tasks were well defined, measured, and controlled. In that frame of mind, manager perceived their employees as merely as a little more than machines, yielding consistent and reliable output for business. In a study reported in HBR of 20 large companies, it was found that highly effective top-level managers were able to connect with the employees. They can engage the unique knowledge and skills, capabilities of each employee of the organization[44].

It is, therefore, clear that that top management looks at its role as beyond making decisions on behalf of the organizations, to foster people engagement. They often set the bar for the way managers deal with their team and embed such a thrust in the company culture. Therefore, they also take responsibility for championing the change management efforts anchored by HRM.

Role of Employees

Employees need to be aware of being a critical stakeholder in the growth of the organization for their overall growth. They also have a stake in the effectiveness of HRM. Some of the way they can play the role are as under:

- The primary role of the employee is to do the work for which he is contracted.
- It is also the employee's duty to comply with the do's and dont's in the Code of Conduct.
- The employees need to work safely by following safety rules.
- The employees are expected to follow all the Standard Operating Principles.
- Keeping company business information confidential.
- Remain engaged and stay.

In summary, forging a powerful working relationship between the superior, colleagues, and the top management and developing mutual understanding and respect benefits all concerned. This ensures wellness and decent workplace environment.

Case Challenges in Managing Internal Stakeholders

Bhavesh started his career in XYZ company. During his initial orientation, the HR-Head gave him a brief about the company, the HR department, and the HR challenges and opportunities. At the end he asked Bhavesh, given his background as a trained HR professional from TISS, what were the few ideas that he would seek to implement here. The HR-Head added that one of the challenges faced by HR professionals was how to enroll the LMs.

After spending several weeks in the HR department, Bhavesh realized the real importance of what the HR-Head had stated. Many of the activities/plan of HR department found serious obstacles from a few influential LMs. Some of the examples that he noted were:

44 Bartlett, Christopher A., and Sumantra Ghoshal. 'Changing the role of top management: beyond systems to people.' *Harvard business review* 73.3 (1995): 132-142.

1. HR had taken a performance target of training each employee at least for three training days in a year. But often the schedules workshops had very attendees. The workmen, when asked stated that their bosses did not release them for the training.
2. The new online performance management system (PMS) PMS system required the appraisers to hold quarterly reviews and make notes online. But the data from the last two quarters showed that 60% of the LMs defaulted.
3. The HR department had scheduled interviews on an emergency basis for filling up positions across functions. The interview panel consisted of senior managers with an HR representative. But often interviews had to be rescheduled as the Manager/s called off at the last moment stating urgent work.
4. The HR department had launched a recognition program. As part of the same, it instituted a system of 'employee of the month' to an outstanding employee working on the shop floor. But different managers recommended different employees, and when the HR man in charge wanted to build a consensus candidate, the meetings were either not attended, or would prove inconclusive.

Bhavesh discussed the above in an HR departmental meeting. The HR-Head expressed the inability to solve this impasse. Later some of the experienced HR colleagues told him that the impasse is because of ego clash between the HR-Head and the Head-Operations. The HR-Head had brought up the issue of lack of cooperation from the LMs in a monthly Executive Committee meeting, but the CEO suggested that this is an issue between two heads of department, and they should mutually resolve it. The HR colleagues opined that the CEO did not think that the HR department was doing their job and the department was merely a cost center.

Discussion Question

1. If you were to advise Bhavesh on how to overcome the impasse, what would you suggest?
2. How does LMs impact HRM?

1.9 HUMAN RESOURCE MANAGEMENT AND FIRM'S PERFORMANCE

Kaplan and Norton,[45] in their pathbreaking framework of balanced scorecard, had brought out the importance of learning and growth for organizations to do well on a sustained basis. It is obvious that the fulcrum of organizational competitiveness is its human resource and the processes and systems, which ensure optimizing this resource. The linkage between individual employee performance and organizational outcomes has often figured in the literature on HRM for more than two decades.[46] The theme, however, has garnered currency with the rapid pace of globalization, the arrival of the digital age, and the paramountcy of the knowledge worker.

The connection between financial performance of organizations and HRM can also be traced in the strategy framework of Barney, known as the resource-based view.[47] According to the resource-based view, organizations utilize their resources and capabilities to gain a competitive advantage that

[45] Kaplan, Robert S., and David P. Norton. 'Using the Balanced Scorecard as a Strategic Management System.' *Harvard Business Review* (January–February 1996).

[46] M. A. Huselid, 'The Impact of Human Resource Management Practices on Turnover, Productivity, and Corporate Financial Performance,' *Academy of Management Journal* 38 (1995): 635–672.

[47] J. B. Barney, 'Firm Resources and Sustained Competitive Advantage,' *Journal of Management* 17 (1991): 99–120.

translates into better value creation. When resources and skills in an organization help in formulating and executing strategies, then they can be reckoned valuable for that organization.[48] According to Barney, the firm's structure, the skills, judgment, and intelligence of the firm's employees, and HRM systems are sources of competitive advantage. Several researches over a period of time have established correlation between HR practices and organizational financial outcomes. In a study conducted in 1996, Delaney and Huselid[49] reported that HRM practices jointly explain a significant ($p < 0.05$) amount of the variance in perceived organizational performance (R2 = 18.6%) and perceived market performance (R2 = 28.9%). In a later study, Huselid, Jackson, and Schuler[50] also found positive relation between HR practices and organizational outcomes. The study used survey design to evaluate the impact of HR managers' capabilities on HR effectiveness and the impact of effectiveness on corporate financial success. The survey was conducted around the senior executives of around 300 publicly held companies, representing the manufacturing, utilities, financial service, and other miscellaneous service industries.

A more recent study in Haryana, India,[51] investigated the connection between HRM practices and service quality, customer satisfaction, and performance in the hotel industry. It covered 52 hotels in India covering HR managers, 260 employees, and 260 customers. The results established that HR practices have a positive influence on the improvement of service quality as well as on customer satisfaction and hotel performance. The findings indicate that the creation of customer satisfaction/value in the hotel can be achieved through increasing responsiveness to customers' needs and that the creation of customer value that have a positive impact on the firm's profitability.

Closing Case The Empire Strikes Back—The Rise and Fall of a Wave in Gujarat Fluorochemicals Ltd

Epilogue

In the plush chambers of the factory manager, the chief of engineering, Mr Pillai, and manager production, Mr Vakil, had a hearty laugh over their tea. The latter said, 'Poor chaps, they had to learn the hard way.... I kept telling them that HR should not meddle on production and daily operation activities...but then they wanted to impress the top boss.'

Background

Gujarat Fluorochemicals Ltd (GFL) was a large public sector company. Unlike many others of its kind, it had been doing very well, especially on account of its professional management and of course partly because of its monopoly status. It was a multi-locational plant with units spread over Western India, one each located in Maharashtra, Gujarat, and Rajasthan, respectively. The plant in Gujarat was the oldest, and the latest installation was the one in Maharashtra. The plant in Maharashtra prided itself on being the youngest in average age

48 Sundar G. Bharadwaj, P. Rajan Varadarajan, and John Fahy, 'Sustainable Competitive Advantage in Service Industries: A Conceptual Model and Research Propositions,' *Journal of Marketing* 57, no. 4 (October 1993): 83–99.

49 J. T. Delaney and M. A. Huselid, 'The Impact of Human Resource Management Practices on Perceptions of Organizational Performance,' *Academy of Management Journal* 39, no. 44 (1996): 949–969.

50 M. A. Huselid, 'Technical and Strategic Human Resource Management Effectiveness as Determinants of Firm Performance,' *Academy of Management Journal* 40, no. 1 (1997): 171–188.

51 C. Mohinder, 'The Impact of HRM Practices on Service Quality, Customer Satisfaction and Performance in the Indian Hotel Industry,' *International Journal of Human Resources Management* 21, no. 4 (2010): 551–566.

(just 28 yr) and the most professionally qualified plant. The juniormost operators were also diploma engineers or bachelor's of science. The engineers and supervisors were from the best engineering and management colleges in the country. Some of the operators had earlier experience prior to joining GFL, having held positions of supervisors, and were also older than the young engineers (who were direct recruits from colleges), whom they had to report to.

Excerpts from the typical discussions among the operators in their restrooms:

Operator A: These guys are still all wet behind their ears but they lecture us on productivity and discipline.

Operator B: The other day I told this shift in charge that there is steam leakage at pipe no. 213 and he told me to mind my own business and attend to my job instead of meddling in the mechanical chap's work. He said it was none of our business.

Operator A: '...and they give us bhashans on teamwork!'

A typical control room conversation between the supervisors at the same time:

Officer X: Where is B? Oh, why am I asking; he must be fast asleep in the restroom. Every night shift he hits the sack! Totally disinterested in his job!

Officer Y: I agree, these guys are here just for their salary and not to forget their overtime...that's it! No concern for the work for which you are paid. Absolutely lazy characters.

The plant had problems of inconsistent productivity. It was a new plant. Management initially was keen to keep it union-free. However, five years after the commissioning, two unions were formed in rapid succession. Several young MBAs, who had joined the HR department, were unfamiliar about unions, which were dealt with by their older, experienced superiors. They used to go around the shop floor to get a feel of the place, very eager to try out what they had learned in the classroom about empowerment, sometimes joining in conversations during tea breaks at the tea kiosks. They would bring up this 'gap' between their operators and engineers often in every meeting with their senior leaders. It was diagnosed as the root cause of all the communication issues that arose between the supervisors and operators from time to time. Even in interplant meetings, which were coordinated by Mr Vakil, the production manager, such issues were discussed and Mr Raja, the head of HR, who came to this plant on being promoted from an IR role, was requested to do something to improve the 'performance culture' of the unit.

Development

The issue was deliberated in an HR meet, and on the suggestion of the general manager HR, a new entrant to the organization (who had his head office at Gujarat), the local HR department at the Maharashtra unit decided to go ahead with the small group-activity initiative, QCs, which would encourage teamwork among the people and contribute to workers' participation in management. It was the first time that a local unit was going ahead with an HR initiative of its own and there was an opportunity to create some glory of its own. Generally, all HR activities previously were uniformly implemented across all the sites, on the basis of detailed guidelines from the headquarters (HQ). The younger members from the HR team at the Maharashtra complex were very excited about this venture. A young deputy manager was given the responsibility to make a detailed plan and road map, and her team consisted of three young MBAs recruited during the last three-five years. This was going to be a 'high-profile' venture.

Massive training on QC tools was organized for selected facilitators (engineers) from various plants. The names were suggested by the HR teams and generally seconded by the factory manager. Training for workers was also organized. It was decided to undertake this initiative in a few plants of the unit as a pilot case. Accordingly, two plants, one each of urea and ammonia, were chosen for this initiative. Volunteers from the plant operators, who were trained, were invited to form the QCs out of their own interest. The steering committee constituted of the factory manager, engineering head, production manager, and HR head. Everyone had clear-cut roles and responsibilities. An HR coordinator was nominated for each plant separately. A grand launch ceremony was planned on March 27, 1996, where the first five QCs were launched in the ammonia and urea plants.

Over the next six months, the QCs took up various projects and the facilitators helped them whenever required. The HR coordinators attended every QC meeting, kept the minutes, and urged the plant personnel and managers to take an active interest in the activities of the QCs. By the end of the year, there was an annual convention in which the best QC was awarded. The head of overall HR from Gujarat attended this function and awarded the trophy. The next year the company won the Forbes Marshall Award from Quality Circle Forum of India (QCFI) for having done outstanding work in the field of quality movement in India. The QC members interacted closely with the HR department and came into limelight due to their work and presentations in QCs. They also got the opportunity to travel to other cities in the country to attend conventions there. There was a separate identity for a QC member, a special badge, and separate stationary—all in all, they started enjoying a separate status. The good work done by the HR team that worked on QCs was appreciated by overall head of HR. The unions were always invited to attend all QC presentations.

The QC members took up several projects within their own departments that led to savings in energy or small improvements in work processes. However, after a year, it was seen that some facilitators started giving less of time to the QCs, also the concerned plant managers were not conducting regular meetings.

The HR coordinators found that the interest of the plant managers was waning. The unions declared that the QCs should be closed down until some of their demands were met. The HR head and factory manager decided to close the activity. The senior IR oriented HR executives nodded at each other as if saying, 'We told you so.'

Coda

The HR department conducted a brainstorming session within itself as to what went wrong. At the end, when a secret ballot vote was cast within the department (for the sake of anonymity) to find out how many persons of the HR team believed that the activity should continue, most people voted against the idea.

Discussion Questions

1. What went wrong in the quality interventions at GFL?
2. What makes it difficult for HR functions to make a transition from IR to HR?

SUMMARY

Human resource management (HRM) has evolved from several streams of thinking, which can be put together as an unstructured and free-flowing philosophy, regarding management of human resource, but it does not exactly fall in the category of a specific methodology. It emerged in the 20th century but it also includes previously held beliefs about people management at work. The constituent ideas have divergent origins and, as a consequence, do not constitute a coherent and uniform body of knowledge.

Michael Armstrong[52] described it as a strategic and coherent approach to the management of an organization's most valued assets—the people working there who individually and collectively contribute to the achievement of its objectives.

There are various models of HRM. The famous ones are the Fombrun, Tichy, and Devanna Model; the Harvard Model; the Guest Model; the Warwick Model; and finally, the Ulrich Model. Some of the classifications are hard–soft models and normative–prescriptive models. Storey[53] has classified these as conceptual, descriptive, and prescriptive; the four-way classification by Legge is: normative, descriptive–functional, descriptive–behavioral, and critical–evaluative. Tyson has a three-way classification: normative, descriptive, and analytical.

In India, HRM emerged as a new avatar of the erstwhile personnel function in the 1980s owing to the two new developments in the area of people management: the growing use of the personal computers, leading to upgradation of technology also in personnel function; and the OD interventions in IOCL and L&T, helmed by Mr Udai Pareek, Mr Pulin Garg, and Mr T.V. Rao, with their exposure to the OD intervention technologies in National Training Laboratory, were starting to run PGLs and various OD interventions. Some of the examples of such OD interventions are: Role Effectiveness Exercises by Udai Pareek, OCTAPACE culture interventions by T.V. Rao, and Task Analysis for Human Resources by Udai Pareek et al.

The field of HRM has been constantly evolving to keep pace with the changing external environment in which business operates. Some of the most important factors creating impact are globalization, digital revolution, and demographic changes across the world. One major internal factor that also impacts the HRM function is the part played by LMs in sharing part of the onus for HRM.[54] It helps by providing the HR specialists adequate time to concentrate on their strategic roles and thus enable the integration of HRM function into the business strategy.

Doubts have from time to time been expressed as to whether HR function has a future, given the breathtaking speed in which technology is replacing humans at work. Researches have, however, from time to time re-established clear linkages between HR practices and firms performance. The results established that HR practices have a positive influence on the improvement of service quality as well as on customer satisfaction and hotel performance. The findings indicate that creation of customer satisfaction/value in the hotel can be achieved by means of increasing responsiveness to customers' needs and that the creation of customer value does have a positive impact on the firm's profitability. According to Brokebank, Ulrich and other HR scholars, the new HR professionals have to come with competencies such as managing culture, leading change, and creating value.

---

52 Armstrong, *A Handbook of Human Resource Management Practice.*

53 J. Storey. (Ed.), 'Human Resource Management: Still Marching on or Marching Out?', In *Human Resource Management: A Critical Text* (London: Routledge).

54 Budhwar, 'Evaluating Levels of Strategic Integration,' 141–157.

Short-answer Questions

1. Why does HRM appear nebulous and somewhat illusive concept?
2. Define HRM?
3. How has HRM evolved?
4. What are the key differences between HR specialists and personnel specialists?
5. What were the factors that led to the growth of labor welfare and personnel functions?
6. Mention three key factors influencing HRM.
7. Mention some of the challenges in devolution of HRM to LMs.
8. Mention a framework of HR competencie's.
9. Can HR practices lead to improved firm performance?
10. Explain the Harvard Model.
11. Explain the Fombrum, Tichy, and Devanna Models.

Discussion Questions

1. What are the new ways in which HRM can add value to business?
2. What are the essential differences between hard view of HRM and soft view of HRM?

CHAPTER 2

Human Resource Business Partnership

LEARNING OBJECTIVES

After completing this chapter, the student will be able to:

- Discuss the context of HR business partner (HRBP) concept
- Define HRBP
- Discuss the Ulrich Matrix and the multiple roles of the HRBP, and some alternate models for HRBP
- Discuss the challenges for the business partnering
- Discuss the new HR competencies for HRBP
- Differentiate between internal consultant and external consultant
- Discuss the metrics for evaluation of the effectiveness of HRBP

Opening Case Dilemma of an HR Business Partner

Bharat Petroleum Corporation Ltd (BPCL) came into the national mainstream in January 1976, following acquisition of refining and marketing operations of Burmah Shell Company by Government of India. In 1998, BPCL went through an organizational restructuring, in which its business was divided into five strategic units: retail, lubricants, LPG, aviation fuels, and industrial and commercial. As a part of the change, the HR function was reorganized into three segments: HR business partner (HRBP) for the strategic business units (SBUs), HR corporate, and HR shared services (HRSS). Uma Narendran, who was heading the policy-making cell in corporate earlier, became the HRBP for its lubricants business.

The lubricant business was into the deregulated market already, its main competitor being Castrol. Its market was under serious threat. The business, which had to overcome challenges of competition and achieve profitability and market share, relaunched its three lubricants brands—MAK for diesel engine oils, Automol for petrol engine oils, and Glide for two-three wheelers—into an umbrella brand called MAK Lubricants. It also opened a new bazaar channel, and seriously latched onto its customer focus through a marketing strategy of promotion and incentive to dealers.

Uma started with enthusiasm to make her mark in what was seen as a virgin pasture for HR. She wanted to leverage her knowledge of company policy for employees, and also her internal network, especially among the other HR professionals, to consolidate the HR function in lubricants business. She built a team of four members to oversee the business in the four regions. She interfaced with the SBU head and the four regional managers in charge of the business in four regions, created policies for conveyance reimbursements for the sales personnel, created motivational packages for high performers, and acted as the single window between the employees in her SBU and the benefit administration services in the HRSS.

In April, the time came for performance appraisal. Uma, expecting kudos, was in a shock. S. Krishnamurthy, the SBU head, was scathing in his feedback. The summary of it was as follows: Uma was moving in one direction, while the entire business was moving in another direction. She did not know that there were serious problems of imbalance in work distribution among the territory sales representatives, leading to some exits. The regional managers complained that she was not touring enough to understand the problems in the field. She attended the sales review meetings, but did not make any suggestions or contributions. Did she know that getting proper dealers for running bazaar shops was an issue because of high risk in the business? Could not she help in creating a competency profile for the dealers and anchor the selection process? Did she know that sales efforts needed to be incentivized, and the dilemma was to decide on individual or team parameters? Did she know about the unique challenges of lubricants business, where the money came from, and where it went?

Uma was ravaged and clueless. Then she decided to call up her friend Shantanu Sarkar, who was the HRBP in retail SBU. Shantanu had created a success of his role, and her boss often gave the example of what Shantanu was doing.

Shantanu shared what he has been doing. He told her that LMs did not have any respect for HR professionals, unless they (the HR) started talking the same language. For that, he had to learn all aspects of the retail business, be it finance, marketing, or supply chain. He knew their bottom line, which territories were doing well, which were not. So now, while framing the recruitment, training, and employee development strategies, he clearly visualized the work that the various functions do and what kind of employees would suit them. As a result, he could participate in their sales review meetings, and even challenge them on market information, because he had made it a habit to visit some retail outlets regularly and talking to dealers occasionally. The trick he said is 'getting immersed in business.'

Discussion Questions

1. How does the role of an HR generalist vary from that of an HRBP?
2. What are the shifts in competencies?

2.1 INTRODUCTION

Imagine the following scenario in a typical business setup.

It is the month of January. Time for the make or break performance review meeting in a sales and marketing organization. The CEO is fretting and fuming on the reasons that sales have been heading south. After some initial wrangle between the operations and sales (quality and dispatch issues and failure to provide a timely schedule for the launch of a new product), there is an implicit truce: they decide to close ranks and hunt for their favorite target—the HR. So, quality issues are ascribed to slow down by unionized employees and dipping sales to the lack of closure on a proposal for incentives. The CEO now throws up his hands and remarks to his HR head, 'As always, when the business is going in one direction, HR is moving another direction.'

The aforementioned perception is shaped by the way HR professionals defined their roles in the conventional manner. Traditionally, HRM function was organized around four basic management tasks:

1. Entry and exit process for employees
2. Growth and development process
3. Reward and recognition process
4. The overall organization climate

The importance of the above-mentioned activities notwithstanding the tags associated with HR brand has often been uncharitable. HR is often described as a 'policy police' or 'a regulatory watchman.' It is portrayed as a bureaucracy, pushing files on hiring and firing, administering benefits, and implementing compensation decisions made by others. In an empowered environment, it could go one step forward—to add recruitment, training, and development programs—or take steps to improve workplace diversity. But at the heart of all these, HR was described as an ostrich in business—burying its head in the sands of its self-indulgent processes, indifferent to the environment in which the organization is operating and, thus, often woefully disconnected from the work of the organization.

2.1.1 HR Function at the Veritable Fork in the Road

A story is told about an HR professional in a PSU bank, who was once assigned the task of managing the dipping operations in one of its territories. Skeptics interpreted it as a way to sink his career. How he converted adversity to advantage to eventually end up as the bank's chairman and managing director is the corporate folklore of a certain Anil Khandelwal's story of rise and rise at Bank of Baroda.

An article in *Business Standard*[1] reported that Khandelwal's story is merely an anachronism. In actual practice, not many HR professionals get to wear Khandelwal's shoes. Indeed, there are only a handful of CEOs in India who have a background in HR. The level of under-representation of HR professionals in the top jobs is surprising, given the key role they play in the life of an organization. As they say, a company is only as good as its people. HR, then, is on the frontline when it comes to hiring, managing rewards, and retaining employees. Then why is HR seen as less strategic than other support functions? Why is the HR department in most corporations still seen as the last bastion of bureaucracy?

---

1 Sayantani Kar, 'Crisis in HR.' April 15, 2013. Available at: http://www.business-standard.com/article/management/crisis-in-hr-113041400319_1.html (accessed on September 21, 2017).

The isolationism of HR function has, over the years, attracted considerable flak and derision. Sometime back, the Internet went viral with a mocking article titled 'Why We Hate HR?'[2] The author describes a gathering of several hundred HR executives in the faux glam Caesar's Palace at Las Vegas, on what the author snidely refers to as strategic HR leadership (HR being 'neither strategic nor leaders'). In the words of the author, 'The human resources trade long ago proved itself, at best, a necessary evil—and at worst a dark bureaucratic force that blindly enforces non-sensical rules, resists creativity and impedes constructive change.' In another article, by Thomas A. Stewart,[3] HR is compared to the asp in Cleopatra's bosom, poisonous and unproductive, and, therefore, there is a suggestion to 'blow the sucker up.'

A pragmatic perspective is provided by ICICI Bank's Mr Ramkumar as to why HR is often left behind and why getting heard by the C-suite is a tall task for HR. Familiarization with operations will help HR become credible business partners.

> If you speak up only when there is an HR issue, in a room with five other C-suite people, then they will quickly categorize you as just HR. Also, many an HR person gets caught up in bombastic language such as engagement indices, etc. You do all of them but in the boardroom, you have to speak equally in the language of productivity, of turnaround times, of margins.[4]

The central issue with HR through all these jibes and diatribes is about connectedness with business. Ironically, the need to connect HR with the business has become more urgent than ever due to the shifts in business environment. The trends are telltale. Financial markets have been exerting relentless pressure for growth, especially in emerging markets. Customers keep demanding more and better service at lower cost. Cost efficiency, resource conservation, and regulatory compliance have become issues for almost every organization. Turnover among top talent is expected to increase in 2012; globalization is requiring stronger regional HR capabilities; and demographic shifts across the world are dramatically affecting availability of qualified people.

The HR function finds itself at the crossroads. It has a choice to adopt highly automated employee-services operation, evolved from paperwork-driven antiquated processes in a ruthlessly brisk manner—at the best, in impersonal but personalized cafeteria-style services. Alternately, it could head straight to the CEO's office.

Dave Ulrich, the propounder of the concept of HRBP, and an avowed 'HR champion' himself, holds the criticism of HR as 'senseless.' In his influential book *Human Resource Champion*,[5] he recommends a makeover of HR function: from 'doables' to 'deliverables,' from activities to outcomes, guarantees, and results. Ulrich defined four generic HR outcomes (strategy execution, administrative efficiency, employee contribution, and capacity for change) and offered a new HR model based on the same.

---

[2] K. H. Hammonds, 'Why We Hate HR?' (July–August 2005, Fast Company Newsletter). Available at: https://www.fastcompany. com/53319/why-we-hate-hr (accessed on September 21, 2017).

[3] Thomas A. Stewart, 'Taking on the Last Bureaucracy People Need People—But Do They Need Personnel? It's Time for Human Resources Departments to Put Up or Shut Up,' January 15, 1996.

[4] Kar, Sayantani, 'Crisis in HR: If HR Truly Wants to Add Value to Business and Improve its Reputation, it must Transcend its Functional Boundaries'. Available at: http://www.business-standard.com/article/management (accessed on April 15, 2013).

[5] D. Ulrich, *Human Resource Champions: The Next Agenda for Adding Value and Delivering Results* (Boston, MA: Harvard Business School Press, 1997).

2.2 DEFINING HUMAN RESOURCE BUSINESS PARTNERSHIP

2.2.1 Concept and the Framework

The HRBP model indicates a movement by the HR department to participate in strategic planning in respect of the present and future goals of business. It implies a shift in sole focus from traditional HR duties such as benefits and payroll administration and IR. The HR department undergoes a makeover and shows intent to add value to the company through critical processes such as recruitment, training, growth, and placement of new and current employees. According to a 2013 survey by Towers Watson,[6] close to 50% of businesses globally have shown preference for Ulrich's 'three-legged' model of shared services, HR centers of excellence (CoEs), and a team of HRBP. The report goes on to suggest that the Ulrich Model 'is far and away the most prevalent of the available options.' In some organizations, the HRBP role is well defined, while in some others, the HR managers play out the role without the benefit of the title.

The Ulrich Model

Ulrich listed 10 challenges to the business that would necessitate the recasting of HR function:

1. **Globalization** It entails new markets, new products, new mindsets, and new ways of thinking about the business. For example, in case of Motorola, 75% of the profit and 60,000 of its employees are from outside the USA.
2. **Value chain for business competitiveness and HR services** The challenge is to become more customer-responsive through innovation, faster decision-making, leading in price and value, and linking with suppliers and vendors to build a value chain.
3. **Profitability through cost and growth** Profitability is a given and companies have tried to achieve profitability through various means including downsizing, delayering, consolidation, productivity gains, reengineering, and quality focus.
4. **Capability focus** Capabilities have been described as the DNA of organizations, that is, what organizations do better than their competitors.
5. **Change** The challenge is to create organizations that respond faster than their competitors.
6. **Technology** Rapid technological innovations need to be leveraged for business results.
7. **Attracting, retaining, and measuring competence and intellectual capital** Sourcing and retaining key talent becomes a competitive advantage.
8. **Turnaround is not transformation** There is a difference between turnaround and transforma- tion. Turnaround through downsizing and restructuring can make businesses sleeker, but what is needed is transformation that changes the fundamental image of business as seen by customers and employees.

To deal with the above-mentioned challenges, HR and LMs must jointly recast the HR functions, practices, and professionals to build new organizational capabilities. HR professionals must embrace multiple roles to create value and deliver results for business.

Ulrich also presented a matrix of HR roles to build a competitive organization (Figure 2.1). The two axes depict focus and activities for the HR professional. Focus ranges from long-term/strategic to

6 J. Faraghar, 'How to become HR Business Partner,' (October 2013). Available at: https://jobs.personneltoday.com/article/ (December 15, 2017).

short-term/operational. Activities range from managing processes to managing people. Each role has a metaphor, deliverables, and activities. The role of strategic HR, with the metaphor of strategic partner, has strategy execution as deliverables and includes activities of aligning HR strategy with business strategy and organizational diagnosis. The infrastructure role has the metaphor of administrative expert, delivering administrative efficiency, with activities leading to continual reengineering of the work processes. The role of managing employee contribution has the metaphor of employee champion, with the deliverables of increased employee commitment and contribution. The fourth role of management of change and transformation comes with the metaphor of change agent, with the deliverables of capacity to change, and the activities include identifying and framing problems, building trust, and creating action plans.

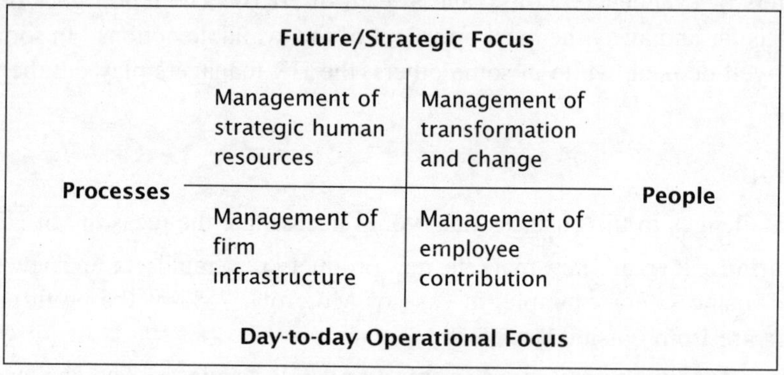

Source: Ulrich, D. *Human Resource Champion* (Boston, MA: Harvard Business School Press, 1998): 24.

Fig. 2.1 HR roles in building a competitive organization

The concept of business partner encompasses all the above-mentioned four roles. It thus becomes an ensemble, with collective synergy being the key to success. The business partnership emerges from the play of the individual roles in this manner: the strategic partner by aligning business strategy with HR priorities; the administrative expert through cost saving by efficient design and delivery of HR systems; the employee champion through securing employee commitment and competence; and finally, the change agent by helping businesses through transformations.

Three-legged Model

Later, certain aspects of the Ulrich Model have come to be presented as a 'three-legged stool' or 'three-box' model for HR. Ulrich also reviewed and further developed his own theories on this issue in his subsequent work.[7] The three-legged model of HR rests on three key elements: HRBPs, shared HR services, and HR CoEs, which may be described in brief as follows:

- **HRBPs (or strategic partners)** Senior or key HR professionals working closely with business leaders or LMs usually embedded in the business unit, influencing and steering strategy and strategy implementation.
- **Centers of excellence** Usually small teams of HR experts with specialist knowledge of leading-edge HR solutions. The role of CoEs is to deliver competitive business advantages through HR innovations (HRMIs) in areas such as reward, learning, engagement, and talent management.

[7] Ulrich, D. (1998). 'A new mandate for human resources'. *Harvard Business Review*, January–February, pp. 124–34.

- **Shared services** A single, often relatively large, unit that handles all the routine 'transactional' services across the business such as recruitment administration, payroll, absence monitoring, and advice on simpler employee relations issues. The remit of shared services is to provide low-cost, effective HR administration. For further information, see our factsheet on HR shared service centers.

2.2.2 HRBP–The Definition

The HR business partnership has been defined in several ways, some of which are being reproduced further.

An HRBP is someone who 'works along with senior managers, providing the link between business and organizational strategies, providing support and challenge to the senior team and developing credible initiatives in a setting of ongoing cost reduction.'[8] CIPD[9] definition says,

The HR business partnering is a process whereby HR professionals work closely with business leaders and/or LMs to achieve shared organizational objectives, in particular designing and implementing HR systems and processes that support strategic business aims. This process may involve the formal designation of 'HR business partners' that is HR professionals who are embedded within the business, sometimes as part of a wider process of restructuring of the HR function.

In actual practice, when an organization adapts an HRBP role, one or more professionals of the HR department become attached to an LM or a business head or a group of managers, with the objective of making him closely acquainted with the working of the business/operations, so that he is able to provide value with appropriate professional, provide effective assistance, improve the working systems, and, above all, get well accepted by the business.

The new role is intended to instigate a paradigm shift in the way HR functions: from doable to deliverables, from operational to strategic, from qualitative to quantitative, from administrative to consultative, from activity-oriented to solution-focused, and from policing to partnering.

2.2.3 Benefits of HRBP

Prima facie, HRBP provides a single window for the internal customer. The intimacy with the customer helps the HR professional to command necessary influence to get desired commitment/buy-in on common HR solutions. By virtue of knowing business inside out, the HRBP is able to champion the interests of the business before the HR department. He can create customized solution addressed to the specific needs/issues of the customer. He can seamlessly forge together cross-functional task forces to iron out complicated organization-wide solutions. He has identified all the critical talents for the organization and can devise talent retention/development programs across functions. Specifically, the advantages of HRBP are as follows:

1. The HR practitioner becomes a more strategic contributor, with increased business focus, greater engagement with LMs, and the ability to move people management issues higher up the business agenda.[10]

---

8 L. Holbeche, *Aligning Human Resources and Business Strategy* (Oxford: Butterworth-Heinemann, 2001).

9 CIPD Factsheet, 'HR Business Partnering,' August 2, 2017. Available at: https://www.cipd.co.uk/knowledge/fundamentals/people/hr/business-partnering-factsheet (accessed on September 21, 2017).

10 Reilly, Tamkin and Broughton, 'The Changing HR Function: Transforming HR,' CIPD Research Paper (2007). Available at: http://www.employment-studies.co.uk/ (accessed on February 12, 2018).

2. Research appears to suggest that HRBPs are able to more easily select and implement HR practices that are most appropriate to developing the business strategy for that unit.
3. This structure allows HR partners to utilize their 'unique' knowledge and skills to support and drive change in people management practices.
4. They can also be well placed to support LMs in considering the people consequences of changes to strategy or policies.[11,12]
5. HRBPs can also work with LMs on HR service delivery, longer-term people resourcing, and talent management planning issues.

Their role in intelligence-gathering and understanding of good people management practices, internally and externally, enables business partners to raise issues that managers may be unaware of.[13]

2.2.4 Implementation of HRBP Model

Although Ulrich's model met with a groundswell of acceptance among business organizations the world over, the role of business partners has been subjected to a wide range of interpretations. Some companies have chosen to appoint hundreds of them; others have appointed just a few. One large organization with 60,000 employees has 350; another, with some 50,000 employees, has just two. A 2004 study of 20 large American companies by PricewaterhouseCoopers' Saratoga Institute found a median ratio of 1 HR business partner for every 1000 employees.[14]

According to a CIPD survey, nearly 40% of survey participants from large organizations in the UK described their HR function structure as the three-legged model (also referred to as the Ulrich Model) including business partners, specialists, and shared services. Among small and medium-sized organizations (less than 250 employees), 'a single HR team with generalists, specialists and administration together' was the most common structure, with just under two-thirds reporting they had adopted this model. There are also interesting sector differences, with public sector organizations much more likely to have adopted the three-legged model than private sector organizations.

Indian organizations have not been far behind in joining the HRBP global bandwagon. The Indian HR domain is abuzz with freshly minted HRBPs, HR generalists, and HR strategic partners, and the practice has evenly spread in hardcore manufacturing sector in the same way as in services sector, IT and information technology-enabled services (ITeS), the MNCs, and the SMEs. Typically, traditional organizations have managed the transformation by easing in the role at junior and middle levels with the traditional functional silos maintained at the top (Tata Steel, L&T).

2.2.5 Challenges for HRBP

Although the idea of reinventing HR and bringing it closer to the business appeals to many professionals, it has not been an easy ride for the HRBP. K. Pritchard, doing a research on the actual transition from an HR generalist to an HR strategic partner role in the HR department of the London operation of an

---

11 CIPAD, 'Employment Relations' (2011a). Available at: www.cipd.co.uk/ hr-resources/survey-reports (accessed on February 12, 2018).

12 Ulrich, Younger and Brockbank, 'Twenty Century HR Organizations,' *Human Resource Management* (November 2008). Available at: http://onlinelibrary.wiley.com (accessed on February 12, 2018).

13 CIPD, 'According to a CIPD Survey, Nearly 40% of Survey Participants Employment Relations' (2011a). Available at: www. cipd.co.uk/ hr-resources/survey-reports (accessed on January 12, 2016).

14 *The Economist*, 'Human Resources Transformation.' May 26, 2009. Available at: http://www.economist.com/node/13724525 (accessed on September 29, 2017).

American investment bank,[15] observed that the HR professionals found it 'difficult to step away from day to day activities, in which they had been involved for many years.' Whereas the business partner role has 'given freedom from previous generalist work and enabled a more strategic focus,' Pritchard[16] has observed that in some cases business partners continued to remain involved in generalist work. Some practitioners, however, feel that this is an 'essential stepping stone' to a more strategic role.[17] Being able to understand how the transactional side of the agenda works and having the ability to continue to resolve HR issues were regarded as essential to building trust with LMs. This was seen by some practitioners involved in the study as a prerequisite to successful partnerships.[18]

Typically, a set of issues cropped up around implementation of a transition plan from traditional to a new HR organization. While redesigning the transactional processes, in the event of the HRBP's role still being part of it, the business partner found it well-nigh impossible to take on a strategic identity, as he was still accountable for routine administrative tasks. The second set of bottlenecks came from the reporting structure of the HR department. Who will command the HRBP—the business or the HR department? In case of reporting to business, the often divergent priorities/interests of both may stir dysfunctional conflicts. Sometimes, the business's adverse mindset, formed in response to the HR generalist's current administrative role, prevented him from accepting the strategic dimensions of the HRBP role.

Another challenge in the process of transition to HRBP is in finding proficient professionals equipped with the relevant competencies and enjoying easy acceptance to LMs. Obtaining people with the right levels of skills and credibility to perform the role of business partner was also cited as an issue with introducing HRBP to organizations.[19]

The HR personnel say that their work, far from becoming less important as they turn administrivia over to others, has become of high strategic importance. We are, they say, the trustees of the asset that matters above all others, proactive custodians of our core competence, holders of the keys to competitive advantage in the new economy. True, true, true—but are these the guys you want to put in charge? Nothing is more dangerous than a group of people trained in the art of monitoring compliance with rules, fluent in a language that does not include a word for 'customer', and who have time on their hands and are looking for something to do.[20]

Third, much of the challenge lies in the perceptions of key stakeholders also. A PWC Annual Global Talent Survey reported that CEOs feel that HR has much to prove and that HR is not ready for the task ahead. On a survey question on how well prepared the major functions in their business were to capitalize on transformational trends, only 34% felt that HR was well prepared and 9% said that it was not prepared at all. The perception also complements the findings in State of Human Capital Report by McKinsey,[21] which stated that people in HR still largely have "a support-function mindset,

15 K. Pritchard, 'Becoming an HR Strategic Partner: Tales of Transition,' *Human Resource Management Journal* 20, no. 2 (2010): 175–188.

16 Ibid., 181.

17 Ibid., 184.

18 Ibid.

19 Reilly, Tamkin and Broughton, 'The Changing HR Function: Transforming HR,' CIPD Research Paper (2007). Available at: http://www.employment-studies.co.uk/ (accessed on February 12, 2018).

20 Stewart, 'Taking on the Last Bureaucracy People Need People.'

21 S. Graber, 'It's not HR's Job to be Strategic,' *Harvard Business Review* (October 2014). Available at: https://hbr.org/2014 (accessed on October 31, 2014).

a low tolerance for risk, and a limited sense of strategic 'authorship'"—all of which has led to "low status among executive peers, no budget for innovation, and a 'zero-defects' mentality."

Furthermore, the demands for new competencies for the HRBP being a 'Strategic Architect,' for example,[22] together with an assumed natural reluctance to move out of the comfort zone of traditional HR work that had earlier been considered valuable,[23] suggests that the introduction of HRBP has not been without its difficulties. Despite this, research has shown that HRBP remains an attractive role for HR practitioners and organizations.[24]

Detractors of the HRBP concept pose a question whether being a strategic partner is the only way to revitalize HR. The comparison is drawn to the role of a sales manager, who has sales goals to achieve, but since, in most cases, he cannot compel customers to buy, he has to invent a value proposition that becomes a win-win situation for both the stakeholders—the potential customer and the business organization. In the same manner, HR needs to draw upon its unique value proposition, which is to look at the organization from the employees' point of view, which becomes a win-win situation for the business organization as well as the employees. It is opined that HR function merely playing the role of a 'strategic business partner' through supposed alignment of employees with the business strategy is adopting a blinkered approach. Failure to engage the employees in a broader sense may help the HRBP achieve business results for some time, but the consequences in the long term are likely to be grievously damaging to the organization.[25]

The skeptics have even suggested reversing the process. In an article in *HBR*,[26] Sean Graber opined that HR 'at least in its current form' should not be a strategic partner. He proceeds to the proposal of Ram Charan about splitting HR into two parts: one to oversee leadership and organization, and the other to handle administration. Graber suggested that instead of grouping all the people-related activities together under HR, businesses should organize them according to types of service provided—and move a couple of them to other functions altogether, much like Deloitte's service delivery model, which divides activities into four categories: site support, transaction processing, center of expertise, and business partner. In this model, Graber feels that the bulk of HR services fall into the first three categories, where a cost-cutting mindset makes a good deal of sense (examples include payroll, benefits, risk and compliance, and labor relations).

2.3 MODELS FOR BUSINESS PARTNERSHIP

1. Business partners as process consultants working alongside the line, with specialist and transactional HR provided centrally or outsourced. Barclays and Prudential Company experimented with this model with success. In this model, the business partners are able to develop strong working relationships with line management. However, for this model to succeed, LMs have to recognize the value of process consultants and allow HR to get into strategic issues.

---

22 Ulrich, Younger and Brockbank, 'Twenty Century HR Organizations. Human Resource Management' (Wiley Online library, 2008). Available at: http://onlinelibrary.wiley.com (accessed on February 12, 2018).

23 Pritchard, 'Becoming an HR Strategic Partner: Tales of Transition.'

24 CIPD HR Survey Report, 'Where We Are and Where We Are Going' (CIPD, 2003). Available at: http://www.cipd.co.uk/subjects/hrpract/hrtrends/hrsurvey (accessed on February 12, 2018).

25 See 'Are You a Strategic Business Partner?' Available at: http://www.greatplacetowork.in/storage/documents/Competencies_ for_HR-_Prasenjit_Bhattacharya.pdf (accessed on September 20, 2017).

26 Available at: https://hbr.org/2014/10/its-not-hrs-job-to-be-strategic (accessed on September 21, 2017).

2. Business partners as process and specialist providers working alongside the line, with transactional HR reporting to them. While it provides HR with a well-rounded role, the problem is that business partners may find it difficult to distance themselves from transactional HR activities. Besides, both expert and process roles might pose challenges in balancing.
3. Business partners as process consultants working along with the line, with specialist and transactional HR provided centrally and a local HR advisor as a focal point for transactional issues. The RBS has adapted a similar approach. In this model, the operational HR and HRBPs are not separated by hierarchy and it also gives the LM the feeling of being supported on operational HR.
4. Business partners working alongside the line on specialist and transactional issues using a process consulting approach. Canon Europe has adapted a similar approach. The advantage is that all HR functions are in close touch with the business. But the role boundaries within HR may appear hazy.

2.4 HUMAN RESOURCE BUSINESS PARTNER ROLE

The role of HRBPs varies widely between organizations. Some activities that HRBPs are likely to be involved with include:

- Organizational and people capability building
- Longer-term resource and talent management planning
- Using business insights to drive change in people management practices
- Advising on the people implications of organization change, making recommendations
- Intelligence gathering of good people management practices, internally and externally, so that they can raise issues of which executives may be unaware

In practice, the activities can vary enormously depending on factors such as organizational size, company culture, and business priorities.

When creating and developing HRBP roles, it is important to consider the knowledge and behaviors required for the position in that particular organization, bearing in mind that creating the title of HRBP will not alone create a strategic contribution from the function. The CIPD's Profession Map sets out the key knowledge, skills, and behaviors required of HR professionals at all stages of their career to maximize their impact on business performance.[27]

2.5 MANAGING CRITICAL RELATIONSHIPS

2.5.1 Line Managers

It is the essence of the concept of business partnering that HRBPs are close colleagues of managers at different levels in a peer, rather than subordinate relationship. They will need to acquire technical and managerial capability and a complete understanding of the part of business area or function being serviced. The HRBP needs to develop the personal skills crucial to making any relationship work, such as the ability to collaborate around a common purpose and effecting HR solutions to the line.

[27] CIPD Factsheet. Available at: http://www.cipd.co.uk/hr-resources/factsheets (accessed on December 5, 2017).

Job Description of an HRBP Executive in an IT Firm in Bengaluru

Position—HRBP Executive

1. Skill: Recruitment, human resource sourcing;
2. Experience: 10–15 years;
3. Responsibilities:
   (a) Provide leadership, direction, and expertise for the full scope of HR functions and General Electric (GE) HR processes within India technology teams including performance management, reward and recognition, succession planning, talent management, salaried and non-salaried employee relations, employee compensation, employee engagement, and recruiting and selection
   (b) Provide HR leadership for the India technology team and strategic HR direction to define roles, organizational vision, and facilitate team performance to become a preferred employer of choice for technologists in India
   (c) Partner with India engineering leaders to plan and execute strategies including those relating to Technology 2025
   (d) Partner with the larger HR leadership team in India and globally to implement strategies and drive HR initiatives that contribute to the development of HR and facilitate the implementation of the business people agenda. Implement HR strategies and drive operational excellence in HR processes across the collocated businesses
   (e) Ensure a dynamic pipeline of talent through rigorous performance management, for example, leadership assessments, coaching and development of employees, and candid and timely performance feedback
   (f) Proactively manage HR systems in order to maintain integrity of employee and organizational data
   (g) Ensure client managers establish a commitment to compliance and quality and communicate the importance of meeting statutory, regulatory, and customer requirements
   (h) Ensure maximum employee engagement while actively managing headcount targets and HR budget
4. Qualifications/Requirements
   (a) Bachelor's/master's degree in business administration or HR/IR, industrial/organizational psychology
   (b) Minimum 10 years of increasing HR generalist and/or HR manager responsibility (i.e., handling employee relations, compensation, recruiting and performance management, organizational effectiveness, and change management) and leadership experience with clear career progression
   (c) Demonstrated ability to make independent decisions, evaluate people, manage conflicting priorities in a fast-paced environment, and effectively interface with high-level global, engineering, and function leaders
   (d) Outstanding communication, coaching, and interpersonal skills with the ability to work effectively with people at all levels of the organization
   (e) Able to energize and inspire others to commit to and take action on business priorities
   (f) Able to support clients in multiple locations and open to global travel
   (g) Strong analytical and problem-solving skills
   (h) Process- and detail-oriented, including strong organizational and prioritization skills

(i) Strong understanding of the application of local labor laws and government requirements
(j) Desired characteristics: Proven team leadership experience and proven ability to drive change in an effective and participative manner
(k) Experience driving business solutions through influence and collaboration in a global matrix organization
(l) Resourceful, innovative, persuasive with strong communication/presentation skills

Source: Glassdoor.

Besides the precondition of a successful partnership are clear roles with delineated boundaries, expectations, and accountabilities, with good communication between the parties concerned.

Sometimes, the HRBPs may have to surmount the past baggage in the form of a manager's biased opinion of HR based on earlier experience. The personal credibility and self-assuredness of an HRBP become crucial in overcoming any residue of inferiority. The transition has been described as one from being an 'order taker' to an initiator, with the expertise that enables them to coach and guide.

Similarly, the LMs also need to embrace a change in mindset from treating people as cost to treating them as capital, and getting ready to act as employee champions.

2.5.2 Centers of Excellence

There are three activities in which CoEs typically engage.[28]

1. **Policy** Formulating suitable practices and processes for the organization
2. **Consultancy** Catering to specific requests from business solution of emergent problems
3. **Services** Specialist know-how or enlarged consultancy work

The setup of CoEs gets liquidated over time, as and when HRBPs and LMs acquire expertise and rely more heavily on automated self-service advice.

The challenges in dealing with CoEs could be around the clarity of role boundaries, the inclination to fall into a silo mentality, the customer ignorance about the thin line between a 'policy' capacity, a client-centered consultancy, and an assistance in execution. The biggest challenge can occur when both business partners and CoEs have mastery over a subject tempting both to 'compete' in guiding the LMs and end up giving disparate counsels.

Senior specialists in a CoE may opt to walk around HRBPs and establish direct communication channel with the business, which would ensure the demise of the experiment. Sometimes CoEs habitually contact external consultants to deal with ambiguous or risk-wrought issues. In such situations, the core factors are accountability for quality, quantity, and cost, and there could be contentious issues on cost allocation.

2.5.3 Support Services

HR restructuring normally takes the shape of HRBP, CoE, and support services.

But for the LMs, HRBP remains the local face of HR, and therefore HRBPs need to take certain responsibilities for the quality of services to avoid poor image of the HR.

1. The idea of centralized service center with common policies and tools and demands of front-line business requirements may often conflict. Only a high quality of communication between

[28] Andrew Lambert, *Effective HR Business Partner* (London: Corporate Research Forum, November 2009).

HRBP and support services can help defuse the issues. Disgruntlement with services may affect perception of quality of the HRBP.

2. LMs' suspicions that their interests are secondary to corporate cost-cutting tend to grow when major parts of their services are outsourced and/or offshored. In such cases, the services function has to work doubly hard to demonstrate its responsiveness to HRBPs and 'end-customers.'

2.5.4 Measurement of HRBP Effectiveness

HR is often criticized for not submitting to measurement of its effectiveness while preaching the same for other functions. Traditionally, the typical HR executive is known to detest specific analytics and is comfortable talking platitudes about morale, turnover, and engagement. The business partner role of HR, however, is unlikely to be credible unless assertions are backed by concrete evidence, ideas by real outcomes, and perceptions by assessments. Dave Ulrich[29] suggests ways in which HR can become a valuable accessory for business decisions: first, by establishing the linkage between specific HR practices and business results; second, by using balanced scorecard to weave HR issues into business measures; and third, by auditing HR practices, professionals, and functions.

2.5.5 Impact of HR on Business Results

Two seminal studies indicate a connection between business outcomes and HR practices. One, a study undertaken by SHRM/CCH Study of 1995,[30] and the other, a comprehensive study of the relationship between HR practices and firm's performance done by Mark Huselid, a professor at Rutgers University, and his colleagues. In the first study, an overall quality of HR index was developed for each firm being studied based on the aggregate ratings of all HR activities adopted by the firm and then related to four financial measures: market/book value (market value of the firm based on stock price divided by the firm's assets, which represents 'value added' by management), productivity (money value of sales divided by number of employees), market value (stock price of three outstanding shares), and sales. All the four financial measures increased dramatically with the quality of HR practices.

The second study drew on research that identified high-performance work practices across a number of firms and worked to show their relationships with financial performance of 968 large (with more than 100 employees) publicly traded firms. They then examined the impact of higher work performance practices on three organizational performance measures: turnover, productivity, and financial results. For turnover, they found that a one-standard-deviation increase (about 25%) in work performance reduced turnover 7.05% on a per-employee basis. For productivity, they found that each standard-deviation increase in work performance practices equaled a 16% increase in productivity (measured by sales per employee). In raw numbers, this meant US$27,044 sales per employee, since the average sales per employee in his sample was US$171,099. For financial performance, a one-standard-deviation increase in work practices yielded US$27,044 in sales, US$18,641 in market value, and a US$3,814 increase in profits.

---

29 D. Ulrich, 'Measuring Human Resources: An Overview of Practices and a Prescription for Results,' *Human Resource Management* 36, no. 3 (1997): 303–320.

30 Ibid.

Balanced Scorecard for HR

Balanced scorecard system recognizes and focuses on stakeholders' interests. The stakeholders include investors, customers, and employees. Among them, employees are found to be hardest to measure. Ulrich reports certain experimentation to develop employee measures on three people dimensions: productivity, people, and process (Table 2.1).

Table 2.1 Developing measures for employees and stakeholders

Employee		
Productivity	**People**	**Process**
Ratio: output/input	Feel, do, know	How do we get things done?
Revenue per employee	Satisfaction	Leadership
Cost per employee	Commitment	Innovation
Unit produced per employee	Competence	Speed/cycle time
	Turnover/reward	Learning
	Grievance	Unity/shared mindset
	Absenteeism	Equity

Source: Ulrich, 'Measuring Human Resources.'

Regarding practices, all key HR practices could be audited on suitable measures. For example, performance management practices could have the following measures:

1. Acceptance of appraisal processes by employees
2. Effectiveness of appraisal process for dealing with poor performers
3. Percentage of employees receiving performance appraisal
4. Percentage of employees whose compensation is performance contingent
5. Percentage of total salary at risk
6. Speed of salary action processing
7. Average merit increase granted by classification
8. Ratio of salary to competitor salary
9. Trends in health care costs to national averages
10. Extent to which measurement systems are seen as credible
11. Labor costs per revenue dollar

Regarding HR professionals, the audit could include the following steps:

1. Develop a model for HR competencies
2. Collect data using the model
3. Summarize data and feedback to HR professionals
4. Create action plans
5. Summarize improvements

Regarding function, the measures could include the following:

1. Ratio of total employees to HR professionals
2. Ratio of money spent on HR to total sales, general, and administrative costs

Huselid and Becker[31] caution against the practice of relying on benchmarked comparisons of cost and other efficiency-based performance outcomes to justify HR contribution to the organization. Such measures fail to capture HR's real contributions to the success of business and can sometimes be counterproductive. Instead, Huselid and Becker make the case that HR professionals should customize their strategic performance measures and focus on their performance in relation to the organization's strategy.

Reflection Point

'... senior HR individuals who counsel managers on talent issues. Despite decades of trying to focus these HRBPs on strategic issues, many of our clients voice a common refrain that a great HRBP is quite hard to find. And while the value of a great HRBP remains unquestioned, the structure of the HRBP role requires reengineering'.

Discussion Question

1. What is the critical conditions necessary for success of an HRBP?

Source: The critical importance of HR Business Partner. Jan. 2018. https://www.mckinsey.com/capabilities/people-and-organizational-performance

2.6 HUMAN RESOURCE BUSINESS PARTNER COMPETENCIES

What abilities the new HR professionals need to have to perform as a business partner? It is important to define the links between performance and skill sets of an HRBP (Table 2.2). Ulrich[32] and his colleagues at the University of Michigan have been credited to create the most influential competency models for HRBP. The versions of competency models have, however, undergone changes over a period of time. The earliest versions brought up three key competencies: 'change management,' 'functional expertise,' and 'knowledge of the businesses.' In the next updated version, two more competencies were added—'culture management' (about changing employee behavior) and 'professional credibility' (modeling the business values of their organization). The next revision of the model indicated five overarching competency categories: strategic contribution, personal credibility, HR delivery, business knowledge, and HR technology.

Table 2.2 How HR architecture drives strategy execution in a retailer

Right HR professionals	Right HR practices and systems	Right costs and investments	Right HR deliverables	Right business outcomes
Objectives				
HR managers possess competencies linked to needs of the business	HR practices and systems are aligned, integrated, and differentiated, as appropriate	Total workforce costs, not HR costs, are appropriate (not just minimized)	Employees deliver performance behaviors that execute strategy	World-class customer buying experience

[31] M. Huselid and B. Becker, 'Measuring HR: Benchmarking Is Not the Answer' (2003). Available at: https://www.shrm.org/ hr-today/news/hr-magazine/pages/1203becker.aspx (accessed on December 5, 2017).

[32] Ulrich, Brockband, Yeung and Lake, 'Human Resources Management Competencies: An Empirical Model,' *Human Resources Management* (December 1995). Available at: http://onlinelibrary.wiley.com/ (accessed on February 12, 2018).

Right metrics				
• Rating on validated competency assessment tools • Knowledge of key business processes • Wrong metrics • HR/full-time equivalent (FTE) total firm employment	• Percentage of employees trained on product knowledge • Percentage of employees completing sales training • Percentage of employees seeing link between training, incentives, and HR deliverables • Wrong metrics • Cost per hire • Recruitment cycle time	• Dollars invested in training and incentives/ percentage increase in customer satisfaction • Dollars invested in training and incentives/dollars in increased sales • Wrong metrics • Training cost/payroll • HR expense/total FTE	• Percentage of front line staff rated 1. Knowledgeable 2. Timely 3. Helpful 4. Courteous • Wrong metrics • HR expense/ operating expense • Gross margin minus labor costs/ total FTE	• Mystery shopper ratings • Customer repurchase percentage • 'Would buy again' ratings • Overall customer satisfaction • Wrong metrics

Source: Brian Becker and Mark Huselid, 'Measuring HR? Benchmarking is Not the Answer,' *HR Magazine*, December 2003.

In a subsequent version by Ulrich,[33] the contents of the competencies have been described as follows:

2.6.1 Credible Activist

It is about practicing what one is preaching. The building block for professional credibility is personal trust that occurs with outcome-based integrity. It requires effective interpersonal skills to strike positive chemistry with critical stakeholders. The HR professional thus acquires influence that contributes to business results. They use data and well-considered views to take strong positions about business issues.

2.6.2 Strategic Positioner

This implies understanding the global business context—the social, political, economic, environmental, technological, and demographic trends that bear on their business—and translate these trends into business implications. The HR professionals develop intense appreciation of the structure of their own business and competitive dynamics. It becomes possible for them to construct customer-focused business strategies and develop annual business plans and goals.

2.6.3 Capability Builder

The HR professional needs to articulate organizational capabilities and thus helps in the process of building and sustaining a strong and successful organization. Capability has been defined as all that the organization excels at and is known for and they survive performance of individual manager or system. Examples of such capabilities are innovation, speed, customer focus, efficiency, and meaningful work.

2.6.4 Change Champion

This points at the crucial competency of developing the organization's ability for transformational change and then converting it into effective tools of change management, including processes, structures, and so on. The ability to change faster than others provides sustainable competitive advantage for the

[33] D. Ulrich, 'What's Next for HR? The Six Competencies HR Needs for Today's Challenges,' *Personnel Today*. Available at: https://www.personneltoday.com/hr (accessed on November 13, 2012).

organization. The competent HR professionals use their grasp of the market and business conditions to make cases for change and effectively deal with the incidence of change aversion by involving the important stakeholders in key decisions, and acquiring their buy-in for implementation. They ensure that the necessary resources (time, people, capital, and information) are made available. Finally, they create process to capture the learning from the change initiatives.

2.6.5 HR Innovator and Integrator

This indicates the ability to innovate and synthesize HR practices around some strategic business issues. The challenge is to adopt a holistic approach so that HR as a whole makes a deeper impact. HR professionals are thus able to ensure that intended business outcomes receive topmost priority, that the organizational capabilities are developed in an effective manner, and there is an alignment of HR practices, processes, structures, and procedures to these capabilities.

2.6.6 Technology Proponent

Traditionally, technology has been used by HR professionals to the limited purpose of improving HR processes (employee benefits, payroll, health care, recordkeeping, and other administrative services). In this mode, technology is used by HR professionals on a wider spectrum. At the organizational level, technological applications are currently used to great effect by competent HR professionals in two ways. First, social networking technology is leveraged to foster connectedness between people—within the firms and outside the firms, especially customers. The second significant use is in the management of information. This includes identifying the information that should receive focus, bundling that information into useable knowledge, leveraging that knowledge into key decisions, and then ensuring that these decisions are clearly communicated and acted upon.

The effectiveness of the competency models for HR business partnerships has certain limitations. In a 2008 survey of the UK's 118 organizations covering HRBP practitioners,[34] it was found that the competency models were considered to be effective in selections, less effective in developing business partners or HR business strategy alignment and business performance, and poor at predicting performance in a business partner role. Besides, four key contextual factors appear to have affected respondent evaluations. Effectiveness varies with the degree of change to the HR function, the consistency in implementing business partnering, the level of reduction in transactional HR, and the extent to which the HR function is centralized or decentralized.

Reflection Point

Good bye HR Business Partner

The core of HR is the HR service center, focused on high-level customer service and using advanced HR tech. And in the end, HR should be a partner of the business, a partner of the workforce, a partner of the clients and a partner of the other stakeholders of the organization.

Discussion Question

1. Do you agree with the view that the concept of HRBP need to be widened to align to the volatility of the business environment now?

Source: https://hrtrendinstitute.com/2020/12/04/goodbye-hr-business-partner

[34] As reported in R. Caldwell 'HR Business Partner Competency Models: Re-contextualising Effectiveness,' *Human Resource Management* Journal 18, no. 3 (2008): 275–294.

2.7 HUMAN RESOURCE BUSINESS PARTNER AS AN INTERNAL CONSULTANT

HRM professionals often get troubled by a recurring self-doubt: Is HRM a legitimate managerial function, and if so, is it held on par with the other functions such as finance or marketing? One of the many ways in which the HRM function has sought to redeem itself and win respectability and legitimacy is by adapting the role of an 'internal consultant.'

A consultant commands a set of diagnostic and behavioral competencies that help him to partner with LMs to generate solutions to performance problems. Much like an external consultant, the internal consultant is also exposed to a range of projects and business activities with a variety of customers. For him, such clientele is constituted of the various departments and teams within the business organization. In the capacity of an internal consultant, HRBPs can leverage their internal consulting skill sets to create a business impact—by catalyzing performance improvements of other departments through a problem solution approach.

As an internal consultant, HRBP also needs to have some other competencies. One such crucial skill could be described as organization awareness: demonstrating deep understanding of formal and informal structures, climate, culture, and the internal politics (without getting personally involved into other people's power games). HR practitioners must also have a capacity for creating their own brands. The internal client needs to be convinced of the relevant expertise of HR and their potential for contributing to the success of a project. The HR professionals need to be credible in the skills of asking effective questions, listening, making impactful presentations, and demonstrating outstanding communication skills—both oral and written. Internal consultants are also expected to be adept in coaching skills.

Broadly, as an internal consultant, an HRBP is required to master three key competencies. First, project management skills. Realistically, HR practitioners are not seen as experts in project management as a discipline. Their contribution is expected more in helping LMs in forging effective teams, identifying competencies, and thorough management development. Second, internal coaching skills. Coaching helps in two ways: first, by impacting the bottom-line success of a business; second, by aiding employee development. In a study on some 86,000 employees in 15 global organizations, the ability of internal coaches to produce results was found to be on par with external coaches. Finally, it is the ability to provide solutions. The credibility of HR as an internal consultant rests largely on resolution of critical business issues, and accurate and relevant counsel to senior management at all times. For example, during a merger and acquisition situation, HR can provide solutions on cultural integration between the two organizations, or on optimization of manpower, or on devising a suitable compensation strategy so that business can stabilize seamlessly (Table 2.3).

Table 2.3 Differences between internal and external consulting

Aspects	Internal consultants	External consultants
Focus of attention	On desired outcomes from the project, maintaining one's job, and long-term relationships with other members	On desired outcomes from the project, on retaining current and all clients, and short-term relationships with members
Client's perception of consultant skills	As another member with known roles, skills, and performance	As a specialist having strong expertise
Source of credibility with client	From consultant's authority, known performance, and quality of relationships	From consultant's reputation and apparent expertise

Contd.

Biases of consultant	Influenced by the culture of the organization, and desires and personalities of other members	Influenced by personal and professional background
Consultant's knowledge base	Already knows much about the organization, in addition to having certain professional knowledge	In addition to certain professional knowledge, has to learn about the organization 'from scratch'
Client's perception of consultant	As a member of the organization who also might be part of the problem	As an outsider, a 'hired gun' who is not part of the problem
Client's acceptance of consultant	Depends on the top leadership's support of the project, consultant's authority, and client's relationship with the consultant	Depends on the top leadership's support of the project and the skills of the consultant to get buy-in from members' influence of consultant
Influence of consultant	Depends on the top leadership's support of the project, consultant's authority and expertise, and client's relationship with the consultant	Depends on the top leadership's support of the project and on the consultant's interpersonal skills the consultant has to learn about power and politics in the organization
Range of influence	Can often readily involve various resources throughout the organization	Operates within the scope and terms of the contract with the client
Options outside the project	Cannot readily opt out of the project	Can leave the project as per any terms of the contract

Sources: Adapted from *Field Guide to Consulting and Organizational Development*; see http://www.authenticitycon-sulting.com

Exercise

You have been assigned an important project in a manufacturing plant. You have to quickly put together a project team by sourcing talents from different functions. You have created job descriptions for each position including the competencies. You have also created a list of employees who are suitable for each position. You require a few from the maintenance department and expect major resistance. The Head, Maintenance Department is a workaholic, but notorious for holding on to his team members, even though he can outsource part of the work and manage with a reduced number. You have received the targeted personnel from the remaining departments.

Task

Create a role-play situation in your group with three roles: HRBP, the maintenance manager, and an observer.

2.8 GAZING INTO THE CRYSTAL BALL—BEYOND HRBP

The 'business partner' model of HR has been around for about 15 years now. The model has had some positive effects, notably considerably improved HR delivery—transactional as well as transformational. There has been greater HR focus on maximizing synergies and providing efficient core services. But this has not led to improving organizational performance to the satisfaction of many CEOs.[35] There appears to be a groundswell of doubts whether the HRBP model, after all, has delivered.

Three problems have been identified by some of the observers. First, the key area of HR deliverables (Ulrich had talked about a shift from doables to deliverables). In contrast to the senior business

[35] Chris Roebuck, 'Bye Bye, HR Business Partner. Hello, HR Entrepreneur,' *HR Magazine*. Available at: http://www.hrmagazine. co.uk/article-details/bye-bye-hr-business-partner-hello-hr-entrepreneur (accessed in September 2011).

leadership's ease with data crunching, HRBPs are still found wanting in developing their own key result areas (KRAs). Second, HRBPs often falter in establishing a true 'valued partnership' with line or business leaders. The perceived failure is perceived in challenging the business strategy, demonstrating that HR understands business, and formulating HR strategies in sync with the business. On occasions, HR has sincerely attempted to support the business better; the efforts have been counter-productive. HRBPs had not grasped the typical misalignment between operational and strategic objectives at middle and lower levels. Clearly, such HR delivery on 'operational' but not 'strategic' agenda would not construe value addition. Third, to compete in a playing field with peers in charge of business and earning their respect, HRBPs need to demonstrate certain key capabilities, mainly BI and functional/behavioral competence.

Responding to the shifting imperatives of business, Dave Ulrich and Dick Beatty designed a brand new HR role that goes beyond the HRBP: HR players.[36] In the new avatar, HR professionals, while retaining their focus on management of talent and intellectual capital, get ready to take on some additional responsibility. This involves helping organizations to 'change quickly, innovate, develop leadership depth, ensure accountability, learn and unlearn, leverage global knowledge, create strategic clarity, establish customer intimacy, etc.,' thus delivering on organizational capabilities and intangibles to generate investor confidence. Ulrich and Beatty propose six ways in which HR players contribute to the organization: coach, architect, builder, facilitator, leader, and conscience.

In yet another review of the HRBP role, Peter Capelli, writing in *Harvard Business Review*,[37] reports on a growing criticism that HR managers focus too much on 'admistrivia and lack of vision and strategic insight.' Although the criticism appears to be cyclical ('When the economy is down and the labor market is slack, they see HR as a nuisance. But sentiments change when labor tightens up and HR practices become essential to companies' immediate success'), Capelli suggests that HR managers can score big wins for their companies by rethinking old programs, making business case for the initiatives that matter and cutting loose pet programs that lack impact.

Experts, however, predict a new dawn for HR through another kind of partnership. In much the same way that chief financial officers (CFOs) became trusted aides to the CEO, the time has come for chief HR officers (CHROs) also to make the same transition. To make this possible, CHRO needs to build and assign talent, but the onus has really been passed on to the CEO to elevate the CHRO and 'bridge any gaps that prevent the CHRO from becoming the strategic partner.'[38]

Case Study Statoil HRBP Initiative

Statoil is one of the largest integrated oil companies with operations in 40 countries, almost 30,000 employees worldwide, and a market capitalization of over US$60 billion. Like many organizations in and outside the energy industry, HR had traditionally been seen as primarily administrative and transactional, responsible for basic services. However, in 2006, and coincident with the merger of the energy assets of Norsk Hydro, HR SVP Jens

[36] Dave Ulrich and Dick Beatty, 'From Partners to Players: Extending the HR Playing Field,' *Human Resource Management* 40, no. 4 (Winter 2001): 293–307.

[37] Available at: https://hbr.org/2015/07/why-we-love-to-hate-hr-and-what-hr-can-do-about-it (accessed on September 21, 2017).

[38] Ram Charan, Dominic Barton, and Dennis Carey, 'People Before Strategy: A New Role for the CHRO' *Harvard Business Review* (July–August 2015): 62–71. Available at: https://hbr.org/2015/07/people-before-strategy-a-new-role-for-the-chro (accessed on February 12, 2018)

Jenssen and his boss, CEO Helge Lund, recognized that the future performance of the company depended increasingly on a more strategic approach to managing and developing the company's human resource.

In 2008, Jenssen and Lund, with the help of Statoil HR-VP Hilde Sannes, embarked on a program of HR transformation including structural change, process improvement in critical capability areas such as leadership development and talent management, and significant investment in HR professional and leader-ship skills. A week-long educational initiative in HR business partnership skills was piloted, working with the RBL Group, combining education in strategic HRM, consulting, and change management with action-learning projects focused on business improvement. This included focus on identifying and addressing areas of measurable opportunity in talent and organization effectiveness, opportunity identification, profit growth, cost reduction, and performance improvement. In short, Jenssen expected his HR team to not 'just' learn and grow as professionals, but also to practically apply what they were learning for the benefit of the company.

With respect to the specifics of developing skill in consulting and change management, the educational process incorporated a number of specific features. Participants were taught a methodology for systematically aligning strategic business goals with HR investments. The methodology is referenced in a number of recent books and papers[39] and focuses on the importance of the following:

1. Clarifying the key external trends impacting the organization
2. Defining the strategic goals of the organization in dealing with these external trends
3. Identifying the critical organizational capabilities required to achieve this strategy
4. Assessing the current effectiveness of these capabilities
5. Investing time and resources in more effectively aligning HR systems and processes to deliver the capabilities
6. Measuring impact and identifying additional or follow-up actions

In addition, the program provided the participating HR professionals with specific tools for evaluating and improving employee engagement, as well as a framework for rigorously managing change. Initially, that framework was the pilot's checklist,[40] but later on Statoil deployed a change management framework of its own development.

Making an Impact

By all accounts, the education these professionals have received, and the application of this education, have proved impactful in a wide variety of areas. For example, a sampling of the projects included:

1. Developing and implementing a more rigorous process for staffing major oil exploration and development projects
2. Increasing employee engagement in the retail business
3. Implementing a more integrated planning process in a support unit
4. Improving the effectiveness of operations teams and teamwork in Canadian operations
5. Increasing rigor-performance assessment and development rigor in the natural gas business

[39] Ulrich, D., Allen, J. and Brockbank, W., *HR Transformation: Building Human Resources from the Outside in* (New York, NY: McGraw-Hill, 2009).

[40] Ibid.

6. Improving the quality of collaboration and communication between HR generalists and functional specialists
7. Development and piloting of a first-line supervisory training program
8. Enhancing safety on deepwater platforms

Over 200 HR leaders and professionals participated in the HR business partner initiative. In some cases, Statoil has been able to identify a specific financial benefit accruing as a result of the action-learning projects begun by workshop participants. In other cases, it has been difficult to specify the economic benefits but it has identified a measured (qualitative) improvement. The success that Statoil HR has achieved through its HRBP initiative has the following common characteristics:

1. As a result of the HRBP educational initiative, Statoil HR professionals have gained the consulting and change management competence needed to effectively identify, plan, and execute improvement projects.
2. The combination of skill development, provided by the workshop, and management support and mentorship provided by HR Head Jens Jenssen and his leadership team, Statoil HR professionals have gained the confidence to take greater initiative as internal consultants and change agents.
3. Over the course of the workshop, the HR leadership and professional community has learned andapplied common tools and methods for consulting and change management. This has increased both the ability and willingness of HR colleagues to collaborate, and reinforced the view of effective HR by line management.
4. HR network building, including the HRBP workshops and other activities, has provided the community support needed to reinforce the importance of application through action learning. While not all participants were successful (this is to be expected), 'good tries' were equally complimented and reinforced. This increased commitment to the overall initiative.
5. Finally, there was effective ongoing communication of the successes and learning achieved by actionlearning efforts. This, in turn, further reinforced success and commitment.

Discussion Questions

1. What were the triggers for HR transformation at Statoil?
2. Critically evaluate the steps taken to implement the program.
3. Recommend what Statoil needed to do differently.

Source: Jon Younger, Aaron Younger, and Nate Thompson, 'Developing the Skills of HR Business Partnership: Consulting and Change Management,' *Strategic HR Review* 10, no. 1 (2004): 6–14.

SUMMARY

Traditional HR function that was perceived as largely reactive, static, and focused on process needs to reinvent itself to proactive, dynamic, and results-focused. This is in response to certain trends in the business environment, namely, globalization, value chain between business competitiveness and HR services, profitability through cost and growth, capability focus, change readiness, rapid technological advances, and the compelling need to attracting, retaining, and measuring competence and intellectual capital.

HR business partnership, which is formulated by Dave Ulrich, is a process whereby HR professionals work closely with business leaders and/or LMs to achieve shared organizational objectives, in particular, designing and implementing HR systems and processes that support strategic business aims.

Although Ulrich's model met with a groundswell of acceptance among business organizations the world over, the role of business partners has been subjected to a wide range of interpretations and models depending on the nature of business, the size of the organization, and the business imperatives.

To succeed in the new role of HRBP, HR professionals require specific competencies. They include change management, functional expertise, and business knowledge. Ulrich has described six competencies: credible activist, capability builder, change champion, HR innovator and integrator, strategic positioned, and technology proponent. HRBP is also seen as an internal consultant, requiring consulting skills.

As the business environment continues to evolve, there is a demand to go beyond HRBP. Dave Ulrich and Dick Beatty have designed a brand new HR role that goes beyond the HRBP: HR players.[41] In the new avatar, HR professionals, while retaining their focus on management of talent and intellectual capital, have to get ready to take on some additional responsibility.

Short-answer Questions

1. Describe four key challenges that according to Dave Ulrich necessitated HRBP.
2. Define HRBP.
3. What are the benefits of HRBP?
4. What are the challenges for HRBP?
5. Mention three models for HRBP.
6. What are the critical relationships for HRBP?
7. Mention some of the metrics for HRBP.
8. How dies HRBP act as an internal consultant?
9. What competencies does HRBP require?
10. Describe four key tasks of HRBP.

Discussion Questions

1. In a large manufacturing organization, the chairman and managing director (C&MD) has mandated that the entire HR function, which was organized functionally, should get reorganized into HRBP, shared services, and CoEs. What would be the challenges for such reorganization? What would be the elements of strategy to successfully effect the transition?
2. What competency sets are required to operate the role of an HRBP in a manufacturing organization, a service organization, and an SME? Are there any differences?

[41] Dave Ulrich and Dick Beatty, 'From Partners to Players.'

CLUSTER 2

PLAN AND ACQUIRE

Chapter 3
Human Resource Planning

Chapter 4
Recruitment and Selection

The planning and acquisition exercise of HR function has acquired a great urgency because of the ongoing war for talent. HRP is the process of identifying an organization's short- and long-term goals and objectives and then selecting the best options for achieving them. A good plan can provide a distinct competitive advantage (in the private sector) or efficiency and excellence (in the public and non-profit sectors) through comprehensive scenario planning. There are complexities presented by the volatile business environment (e.g., consider the IT sector, which at one point of time was on recruitment spree, now having to shed its flab in manpower in a cycle of less than a decade), globalization, and the options of different kinds of employment relations (part-timers, temps, contracted employees, moonlighters, and other). Much of what Charles Handy depicted as the shamrock organizations is coming true.

In selection, the digital immersion of organizations provides positive opportunities. Josh Bersein writes in an article on Forbes.com of how a client improved sales performance by US$4 million in six months simply by implementing a new candidate screening process, based on insights gathered from data the company always had. Xerox also reportedly shrunk the attrition rate at its call centers by over 20% by using big data tools in hiring for its 48,000+ department.[1]

1 PromptCloud, 'Data Analytics for HR: How to Make Effective Recruitment,' December 1, 2014. Available at: https://www.promptcloud.com/blog/data-analytics-for-HR-how-to-make-effective-recruitment (accessed on November 22, 2017).

CHAPTER 3

Human Resource Planning

LEARNING OBJECTIVES

After completing this chapter, the student will be able to:

- Grasp and describe the importance of HRP
- Learn about the factors influencing HRP
- Explain the barriers to HRP
- Understand the process of HRP
- Apply the choices in HR programs in the changing contexts of business through the maturity cycle

Opening Case Options in an HR Program

Nirmal Patel, the HR Manager in Inox Refinery, was in utter confusion. On taking charge as the new HR head, he was instructed by the executive director to pay attention to ensuring that the new refinery modernization project (RMP) plant, due to be commissioned in another three months, does not have staffing issues. Accordingly, he held a series of discussions with the project head and operations head. He was told that the new plant would require 26 technical and non-technical personnel (4 charge hands, 12 process technicians, 6 maintenance technicians, and 4 general workmen).

During discussions, the following facts were reported to him:

- Inox Refinery, with 12 million metric ton capacity, has got 25% more manpower than its closest competitor refinery with same capacity levels.
- A recent manpower survey done by an outside agency revealed that it is carrying excess manpower in unskilled category, while it faces shortage of key technical manpower (instrumentation engineers) due to resignation and retirement in next two–three years' time.
- The new refineries have been able to outsource maintenance and utility activities, which Inox manages with permanent employees.

- Inox is unionized. Manpower complement and employment of dependents is part of collective bargaining agreements.
- Head operations has demanded that technical manpower be placed immediately for three months of mandatory precommissioning training.
- Recruitment cycle for technical personnel requires 45 days' time from advertising to positioning of the selected personnel.

Discussion Question

1. What strategic steps options should Mr Patel look at?

Exhibit The Current Reality of HR Planning

A workforce strategy audit survey by KPMG in 2015 asked HR professionals about their organization's strategic planning activities to respond to the skill gap arising out of older workforce exiting. Some of the findings were as follows:

1. Nearly three-fourths of the respondents recognized the loss of older workers as a problem. But only 5% of the organizations implemented specific policies to resolve the problem.
2. A piecemeal approach was used for strategic workforce planning rather than whole workforce approach, which includes the contingent workforce.
3. When segmenting the workforce in organizations, organizations do not appear to fully understand role characteristics and role differentiation, nor reflect these in HR policies and practices and the way they report HR data.
4. Organizations take a one-size-fits-all approach to developing employment value propositions (EVPs), competency assessment, performance management, and appraisal systems.
5. Organizations tend to be reactive rather than proactive: succession planning is poor, forecasting of recruitment needs is non-existent, career paths are under-developed, there is low focus on workforce risk, and knowledge about future skills requirements is hazy. This may partly be a consequence of under-resourced HR departments.
6. A number of organizations struggle with their HR data and analytics. The current emphasis on adopting HR technology and analytics before having developed a workforce strategy is like 'putting the cart before the horse.'
7. Strategic workforce planning is delivering disappointing results, starting with problematic implementation. This is likely to be a consequence of all of the aforementioned factors and is therefore not surprising. The inevitable consequence is flawed people management, which compromises the organization's ability to achieve its strategic objectives.
8. Executives and senior HR professionals need education in strategic workforce planning, given that managing internal resources are now seen as crucial to sustained effectiveness. Configuring and managing a workforce that is accessible, skilled, motivated, and efficiently deployed, with a strategy that is aligned with the business strategy, will increasingly be a key differentiator of business performance and financial success.

Source: https://home.kpmg.com/content (accessed on August 2, 2017).

3.1 INTRODUCTION

In order to place the right person on the right job at the right time, organizations have been taking recourse to planning their HR in a systematic manner. In the distant past, when business organizations were used to operating in fairly stable and predictable conditions, this planning process was simple and driven by immediate operational compulsions. The last few decades have, however, been witness to certain paradigm shifts in the HRP caused by uncertainty and unprecedented competitiveness in the business environment, changes in demographics, and rapid march of technology. Planning, in general, has moved from being a one-dimensional, short-term exercise to a complex interface between line management and business planners with long-term visions. With a growing strategic role and business partnership status, the HR planners also have assumed increased responsibilities and accepted challenges like never before.

Contemporary HRP occurs within the broad context of organizational and strategic business planning. It involves forecasting the organization's future HR needs and planning for how those needs will be met. It includes establishing objectives and then developing and implementing programs (staffing, appraising, compensating, and training) to ensure that people are available with the appropriate characteristics and skills when and where the organization needs them. It may also involve developing and implementing programs to improve employee performance or to increase employee satisfaction and involvement in order to boost organizational productivity, quality, or innovation.[2] Finally, HRP includes gathering data that can be used to evaluate the effectiveness of ongoing programs and inform planners when revisions in their forecasts and programs are needed.

3.2 THE IMPORTANCE OF HUMAN RESOURCE PLANNING

HR Planning concentrates on assessing the human resources required by an organization through the different stages of the organization's life cycle and through changes in its conditions over time, and then responding to these demands by formulating appropriate strategies in a proactive manner. HRP makes sure that right kinds of people in right numbers are available at the right time and in the right places to help implement business strategies. HRP lends itself the strategic process in business in that it anticipates long-term HR supplies and demands keeping in view the constantly evolving conditions facing the organization, and then formulates suitable programs. It is believed that the organizations that deal with or plan their HR in a strategic manner, tend to perform better than their competitors who lack such strategic thrust in HR plans.[3]

For example, an organization in the growth stage must plan to industrialize and expand. For that, it will require developing jobs and skills relevant to business plans, sales, operations, and productivity. It warrants acquiring external talent based on projected quantified growth plan and eventually drawing up a career plan, which flows naturally from the organic growth of the organization. In contrast, an organization in a mature or changing market, while facing stagnation, can reduce business volume in its primary market leading to manpower optimization strategies. Organizations sans a planned approach with regard to HR will be doomed to take reactive actions by cutting budgets, restructuring, and so

---

[2] Quinn Mills, D. 'Planning with People in Mind,' *Harvard Business Review* (November-December 1983): 97–105.

[3] L. W. Lam and L. P. White, 'Human Resource Orientation and Corporate Performance,' *Human Resource Development Quarterly* 9, no. 4 (1998): 351–364.

on, whereas those ready with a preventive action plan can take such proactive steps as professional reskilling program through training, mentoring, and tutoring.

3.3 MANPOWER PLANNING TO HUMAN RESOURCE PLANNING

Manpower planning, the precursor of HRP, evolved to ensure that there was a systematic approach to make people available to business to execute its plans. It was variously defined 'as a strategy for the acquisition, utilization, improvement, and preservation of an enterprise's human resource'[4] or as 'the process of forecasting manpower requirement and manpower availability, and matching their demand and supply.'[5] John Bramham, an acknowledged expert on manpower planning, spoke about a 'framework for manpower control' approach with an inherent matching, where the control system includes identifying reasons and requirements for deviations, highlighting problems with employee costs and performance and, accordingly, deciding to alter either the supply or the demand.[6]

The conventional approach to manpower planning has, however, been criticized for taking a static and mechanical stance, with the sole purpose of striking a perfect balance between shortage and excess of manpower. This approach is described as a 'tedious mathematical process'[7] as it envisions a utopian world where people issues can be resolved through a logical and rational basis, without considering the unpredictable dynamics of market forces, and the external and internal contexts of organizations. HRP is claimed to have made the planning process more adaptive to the dynamics of business. It presents a 'fundamentally dynamic process that endeavors to monitor and manage the flow of people into, through and out of the organization.'[8] A critical difference between manpower planning and HRP has been brought out by Lundy and Cowling.[9]

> In HRP the manager is concerned with motivating people—a process in which costs, numbers, controls and systems interact and play a part. In manpower planning the manager is concerned with the numerical elements of forecasting supply, demand matching and control, in which people are a part.

To sum up, HRP is the process to determine the way in which the business organization should progress from its existing manpower position to the ideal position. 'It contains quantitative analyses of HR data ranging from head counts and costs to qualitative analyses about culture, learning and knowledge management. The HRP is a dynamic entity that can be changed if turbulence or unpredicted extraneous factors affect the business strategy.'[10]

4 G. Stainer, *Manpower Planning* (London: William Heinemann, 1971).

5 C. J. Verhoeven, *Techniques in Corporate Manpower Planning* (Boston, MA: Kluwer-NIjhoff Publishing, 1982).

6 John Bramham, *Practical Manpower Planning*, 4th ed. (London: Institute of Personnel Management, 1988).

7 S. Rothwell, 'Human Resource Planning,' in *Human Resource Management: A Critical Text*, ed. J. Storey (London: Routledge, 1995): 234–253.

8 R. Zefanne and G. Mayo, 'Planning for Human Resources in the 1990s: Development of an Operational Model,' *International Journal of Manpower* 15, no. 6 (1994): 36–56.

9 O. Lundy and A. Cowling, *Strategic Human Resource Management* (London/NY: Routledge, 1996).

10 Paul Turner, *HR Forecasting and Planning* (London: CIPD, 2007).

Exhibit 780 Accept VRS at Tata Steel as Firm Tries to Lower Employee Costs

Mumbai: Some 780 employees have accepted Tata Steel Ltd's newly introduced VRS, which is part of an attempt by the company to lower employee costs from 12–15% of production cost to less than 10% in the next few years. Tata Steel introduced its *Sunhere Bhavishya ki Yojana* scheme, equivalent to a VRS, in June, as one of its various initiatives to trim employee costs. Margin pressure resulting from lower steel demand and prices has forced not just Tata Steel but also other manufacturers such as Uttam Galva Steels Ltd, Usha Martin Ltd, and Essar Steel India to consider paring employee costs.

Under its scheme, Tata Steel employees can retire while continuing to draw their basic salary and other benefits, depending on their age. Suresh Dutt Tripathi, vice president, HRM, said it was critical to cut down on costs because there is a tremendous pressure on steel prices. The company, unlike its operations in Europe, does not plan lay-offs in India as it is bound by a no-retrenchment agreement with the labor union. But it plans to go slow on hiring blue-collar workers, said Tripathi. 'We need to look at how we maximize productivity with the same set of people that we have,' Tripathi said. Tata Steel employs around 37,000 people, of which around 6,100 are officers while the rest are factory workers.

Tata Steel also has 30 other employee productivity programs where current employees are retrained and redeployed in projects where they may be required more. For instance, under its job-for-job scheme, employees can nominate their ward to take up employment at the time of their separation. The scheme also helps replace higher-salaried employees with less-paid ones, Tripathi added.

Hiring of management trainees from top technical and business schools has also increased, with more than 100 management trainees hired this year alone.

'It is a common practice by large companies to come out with employee-friendly separation schemes when they are trying to operate in a market situation where they have to keep a check on their production cost,' said Sangeeta Lal, senior partner (industrial), Transearch, an executive search firm.

She said, hiring in steel companies has slowed considerably in the last one year as most of the projects are unlikely to take off due to various inherent and external problems.

Some have already cut jobs. Steel wire manufacturer Usha Martin Ltd, in a recent conference call, informed analysts about its job cut plans. 'The company on the call said it has cut about 165 jobs in the first half of this calendar year,' said an analyst with a domestic brokerage firm who did not want to be identified.

Kumar Kandaswam, partner at Deloitte and Haskins Pvt. Ltd, said retrenchment is more likely in areas that are not core to the steel making process. 'Some of the departments are core to the plant operations, those jobs will need to be maintained. However, other departments, such as material handling, that are more temporary in nature, may get impacted due to the stress in the sector,' he said. This could be true for companies such as Uttam Galva Steels, which is both hiring and cutting jobs simultaneously.

'We are in a unique situation, where we are cutting down jobs, but also hiring at the same time. We are restructuring our entire organization, we think certain areas are too burdened and certain areas require additional talent, and hence the combination. Also we are expanding; instead of only hiring fresh, we are also looking to rationalize, so the existing manpower can be adjusted to a large extent,' said Ankit Miglani, director, Uttam Galva, which at present employs 9,500 people.

Certain others such as Essar Steel are yet to decide on their options to rationalize employee costs.

'All cost-reduction opportunities are being aggressively pursued,' a spokesperson for the company said in an email response. The spokesperson added that no decision pertaining to a reduction of the company's employee count has been taken so far. Employee costs amount to around 2% of revenue at Essar Steel.

Discussion Question

1. What factors have affected the HRP in TISCO?

Source: Amritha Pillay and Bidya Sapam, '780 Accept VRS at Tata Steel as Firm Tries to Lower Employee Costs,' Live Mint, May 24, 2016.

3.4 FACTORS AFFECTING HUMAN RESOURCE PLANNING

As the business organizations operate in a volatile and uncertain environment, the planning for HR also becomes a dynamic and continuous process. There are various forces, external and internal, which influence the assessment of the HR needs at any given point of time. For example, the IT sector, at the turn of the century, was on a recruitment drive. But the changes in visa policy by Trump administration completely changed the calculations, rendering large number of employees in IT sector as redundant. The HRP process needs to adapt in order to effectively meet the changing strategies and objectives. Some of the factors are explained further.

3.4.1 External Factors

Economic Factors

The state of the economy has a direct influence on employment situations and the HR needs of an organization. Cyclical downturns have touched off waves of lay-offs and firings as businesses cut back on employment levels to save money on salaries when production demands declined. On the other hand, cyclical economic upturns spur massive call back and hiring as businesses gear up for higher production levels.

If the business organizations wait for the cycle and then react, then certain issues may typically crop up. Workers, retrenched at a downturn, do not want to remain unemployed for long and are likely to look for new jobs or start their own ventures. On the next upturn, as business conditions improve, and businesses require to recruit skilled workforce, they may not be available in the market leading to recruitment of untrained, fresh workforce, who require training and time to get properly productive.

Technological Factors

At Massachusetts Institute of Technology (MIT), a management robot is taught to run a factory and give orders to artificial coworkers, and a BakeBot robot is reading recipes, whipping together butter, sugar, and flour, and putting the cookie mix in the oven. At the University of California at Berkely, a robot can do laundry and then neatly fold t-shirts and jeans.[11] According to Martin Ford, author of *The Rise of Robots: Technology and the Threat of a Jobless Future*, the increasing adoption of robots means that more routine and repetitive jobs such as bricklayers and some office work will be

[11] Cecelia Kang, 'New Robots in the Workplace: Job Creators or Job Terminators?' *Washington Post*, March 6, 2013.

replaced by machines. Ford doubted whether the trend would create massive unemployment, though it would rather increase the disparity between low-skilled workers whose jobs are threatened and top management who are generally safe.[12]

The march of technology means that skill obsolescence will also occur at a faster pace, creating new workforce skills. On the one hand, with the consolidation of the trend of telecommuting, the focus of performance measurement shifts from management by sight to management of product; on the other hand, in the shop floor, the workers are increasingly getting replaced by a growing band of steel-collared workers, especially in automobile majors.

Legal Factors

In India, there are around 250 central and state labor laws governing the workplace. As a consequence, the various statutory requirements, judicial pronouncements, and executive actions also create boundaries for HRP. For example, there are state-sponsored affirmative actions' regulations in the form of presidential directives (on scheduled castes/tribes and disabled groups), which the HR planners have to take into account in public sector units (PSUs). Besides, judicial pronouncements by the hierarchy of courts at the local and apex levels also affect HRP significantly. Laws such as the Employment Exchange Compulsory Notification of Vacancies Act and Contract Labor Regulation and Abolition Act also define boundaries for HRP for industries governed by these laws.

Demographic Factors

While the West, specially the USA, is coping with aging population, the trend is different in Asia where the percentage of youth is swelling in the workforce. Two other trends have significant bearing on HRP: the use of contingent labor and the increasing participation of women in the workforce. Due to competitive pressures to keep the costs under wraps and also to escape the rigors of statutory compliance, employers have been relying increasingly on contingent workers (also known as contract labor). In certain industries, the percentage ratio of contract labor vis-à-vis the permanent workmen is as high as 60:40. Contingent workers pose a critical challenge to organizations. While their attractiveness lies in their being significantly low cost, the differential payment makes them less loyal than their permanent counterparts. Besides, the employers are also less inclined to invest in their skill/knowledge upgradation, thus making them non-productive assets.

Geographic Conditions

HR planning is also impacted by local conditions, the availability of suitable workforce in the neighboring labor market. For example, due to high level of unemployment, in many parts of the country there are local expectations about preference of the 'sons of the soil' in employment. Even for greenfield projects, land procurement deals often include provisions of employment of project-affected persons, known as PAPs.

Globally, since the 1980s, businesses (especially, automobile and telecommunications) have moved from high-cost geographies to low-cost geographies, thereby leading to some spurt in manufacturing activities in places such as Bangladesh and Vietnam. This is also behind the call for 'Make in India' by the Indian Prime Minister Narendra Modi. Telecommuting has, no doubt, fostered this trend, as employers would like to take advantage of skilled manpower at cheaper rates.

---

[12] Jonathan Vanian, 'Robots: Will They Steal Your Jobs?' *Fortune*, November 4, 2015.

Social Factors

Several changes in social processes also have bearings on HRP. The trend for diversity and the rising numbers of women employees have warranted fresh look at reworking the traditional workplaces. The dismantling of the joint family, the spread of nuclear family, and the emergence of the millennial generation have caused erosion in traditional interpersonal skills, requiring change in workplace communication.

3.4.2 Internal Factors

Business Strategy

HR planning has to align itself to the evolving business strategies of the organization and cannot remain stagnant. For example, when Tata Steel found itself carrying 75% excess manpower, it had to revisit the 50-year-old practice of giving employment to dependents of employees and also introduce VRS. Similarly, the HRP has to change when organizations merge or acquire new companies or decide to go global.

Applying the widely accepted typology formulated by Miles and Snow,[13] organizations, according to their business strategy, can be grouped into three broad types—defender, prospector, and analyzer—and their business strategies influence the HR forecasting in significant ways. For example, defender type of organizations (with little product variations, predictable product market, and so on) experience fairly stable and predictable business environments, which make it possible for them to use quantitative forecasting techniques and choose low-cost options on HR; for the prospector organizations, which operate in a volatile, dynamic environment, the choice of qualitative forecasting technique is apt, whereas in analyzer kind of organizations (normally large corporations) where the focus is both stability and innovation, a mixed approach is observed.

3.4.3 Other Factors

The other internal factors affecting HRP include time horizon (short-term or long-term needs), organizational growth cycles (the needs at growth, maturity, and decline vary), and quality of information available (e.g., an organization with advanced HR analytics and ERP will have access to more sophisticated analysis than a small startup).

3.5 BENEFITS OF HUMAN RESOURCE PLANNING

HR planning initiatives are being integrated into business planning and strategic planning processes by high performance organizations, and the number of companies working on workforce planning has increased to over three quarters since 2009, according to a study by the Institute for Corporate Productivity. HRP is being seen as a process that supports the budgeting process and the business plan process, and helps identify shortage of qualified talent to fill critical talent and also skill gap in the workforce. The benefits are as described further.

[13] M. Duane, *Customized Human Resource Planning* (Westport, CT: Quorum Books, 1996).

3.5.1 Talent Acquisition

It is well known that like all other processes, the process of recruitment and selection also has a minimum cycle time. HR departments, normally accountable for filling up vacancies, often struggle to meet the recruitment time schedules, as there are dangers of recruitments done under time pressure. For example, advertising for the open positions, managing the application process, interviewing prospective candidates, and making job offers—all require specific cycles that are difficult to collapse. With a proper HR plan in place, an organization finds sufficient time to prepare in advance for the identified job vacancies, rather than reacting in haste or sudden urgency, and at times in a panic-stricken manner, when a key role holder unexpectedly puts in papers at an inconvenient time for the business. The recruiters are also able to target their job search to find the best candidates.

Thus HRP facilitates talent acquisition by:

- Aligning strategic planning with head count and talent planning
- Surfacing manpower demand and supply issues by costs, reporting relationship, and by location
- Providing dashboard for managers on the impact of their hiring decisions and future talent acquisition priorities
- Minimizing employee costs and throwing lights on bottlenecks for employee productivity
- Creating competitive advantage through planned talent management

3.5.2 Career Development/Succession Planning

HR planning also enables formulating suitable career plans with back up development strategies, to identify the potential leaders and take them through the charted path of grooming and preparing them for future responsibilities. This ensures the building of a leadership pipeline so that the organization does not get adversely affected by the retirement/unexpected attrition of senior leaders and that there is already good bench strength to move up into the vacant slots. Currently, with the war for talent still raging on, career development programs have been found to be an effective tool in employee retention.

3.5.3 Training

With an effective HR plan, an organization can update and draw up suitable learning strategies to develop competencies that would give it the competitive edge over its rivals. It observes the emerging trends and even can anticipate the types of training programs that it needs to offer.

HR planning also helps the training, learning, and development strategies. It covers induction and on boarding plans for new employees, and gets them ready to perform and deliver on skilled positions. The training input also includes acclimatization with the culture of the organization, information about the company products, services, organization structures, projects, and initiatives, as also on personnel policies and practices.

To sum up, in the current environment of rapid and unprecedented change, all organizations, on a planned growth path, whether through expansion, amalgamation and merger, diversification, and adoption of new technology, should have the human resources it needs for execution of its strategy. An HR plan helps offset uncertainty and change in developing a compensation and benefits strategy and provide for infrastructure including office and residential facilities, working conditions, and other support facilities such as canteen, schools, hospitals, transport, and crèche.

3.6 HUMAN RESOURCE PLANNING PROCESS

The HRP planning process is a nine step process (Figure 3.1).

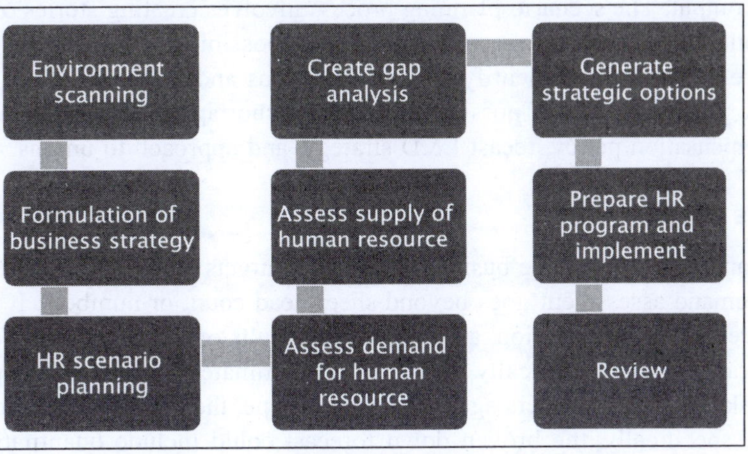

Fig. 3.1 Nine-step HRP process

3.6.1 Environment Scan

The HRP plan process starts with a stock-taking of the business environment, the components of which are economic, technological, political, and social context of business. The economic factors cover the state of the economy, the level of manufacturing activities, and the policies of the government. The technological factors include the digitalization, the degree of automation, and others. The political factors include the impact of the political parties and the balance of power between the executive, the legislature, and the judiciary. The social factors comprise the priorities of the community, the level of social activism, the level of education, and so on.

3.6.2 Business Strategy

According to Michael Porter, an organization has to take a clear strategic position, understand that position, and then make sure that its activities along the value chain (sales, marketing, production, HR, and so on) are aimed at achieving or enhancing that strategy. Assuming that HR has a seat on the table, it should be able to formulate HR strategies arising out of the overall business strategy. For example, if the strategy is about breaking into new markets, the HR strategy should focus around identifying the key competencies required by the people. Similarly, if the strategy is acquisition, then the HR strategy should be to understand how the two cultures are similar or different. Aligning HR strategy with business strategy at the initial stage is important as a wrong organization design, or wrong set of skill sets, or the wild growth of culture could undermine the execution of the business strategy.

3.6.3 HR Scenario Planning

It has been famously said by Patrick Dixon that people should take hold of future or it will take hold of them. Scenario planning is a strategic planning method, originally developed by Pierre Wack, a

French oil executive, working for Royal Dutch Shell's London headquarters in the 1970s, used by organizations to make flexible long-term plans. It is widely used by many a renowned organization (amazon.com and Hewlett Packard, among others) for their strategy-making process. It is essential for HR to be involved at this stage to be able to make contribution with relevant input and also to be able to grasp the output. The scenario planning process involves creating stories of possible scenario, to identify the outcomes, identify success and disaster possibilities, identify the gap between the current and future scenarios, and identify successful actions and measures of success. From the HR perspective, it could be a range of possibilities such as shortage or excess of people, competency gaps, flawed compensation policy, recast L&D strategy, and approach to unions.

3.6.4 Assess the Demand

In HRP, the demand arises out of the business plans with targets of sales, production/throughput, and financials. The demand assessment goes beyond sheer head count or numbers. It widens sufficiently to include the levels of skill, education, and so on. The results of the demand forecast should include for a specific period in future (typically 3–5 years) an estimated number of people required, along with the type of skill and the numbers against each skill type, the places where the people will work, and so on. More specifically, the broken down forecast could include quantitative details such as head count, geography, demographics (age, gender, ethnic groups), functions, and ratios (sales per salesperson, units manufactured per person, and others). It could also include qualitative details such as skills and competencies, knowledge, training needs, different kinds of skills, and so on.

3.7 TOOLS FOR DEMAND FORECASTING

Traditionally, there are two sets of tools for forecasting demand: qualitative and quantitative. The qualitative tools include managerial judgment, Delphi technique, nominal group technique, and unit demand forecasting. The quantitative tools comprise ratio analysis, regression analysis, flow models, and work study methods.

The choice of the forecasters is determined by several factors: the organization environment, the size of the organization, the perceived uncertainty in labor market and economy, and competition. In a stable environment, it is possible to quantify the value of the variable, thus enabling the choice of quantitative methods, and in the same way qualitative method could provide the answers in an unstable environment. Much in the similar way, the perceived certainty (or the lack of it) in the labor market and economy can render the use of sophisticated quantitative techniques redundant (or not feasible). Furthermore, larger the size of the organization, more refined and quantitative tools are called for. Lastly, competition also plays a role in the selection of forecasting tools in so far as organizations in regulated, predictable product markets are observed to use identical forecasting techniques.

To sum it up, organizations need to embrace different tools based on their own unique conditions, and there is no one-size-fits-all that could be prescribed.

3.7.1 Qualitative Forecasting

Qualitative forecasts essentially rely on informed guesswork or assessment by people who are conversant with earlier manpower use or availability.

Managerial Judgments

In this process, managers discuss and agree on a requirement of manpower. There are two common ways of doing it. In the first approach, also known as bottom-up approach, the assessment process starts at the level of the LMs, who send their proposals higher up, and thus through the hierarchy of the organization the proposals finally get looked in and approved by the top management. In the second approach, known as the top-down approach, it is the top management, which initiates the forecast that is examined and concurred by the department heads.

In a variation of the aforementioned, known as the participative or the two-way approach, the two approaches are integrated. The LMs make their own assessment and project a figure based on guidelines provided by the HR function. Concurrently, the top management also makes a forecast. Thereafter, a committee consisting of line and HR functional representatives examines the forecasts of both the aforementioned groups to decide on the certain figure, which is then put up to the top management for final approval.

Theoretically, the integrated approach would appear to be the most inclusive among the different approaches. However, it is the culture of the organization that determines which approach would work best for it.

Delphi Technique

In this top-down method, a group of experts (internal and/or external) are called upon to forecast demand, which are then summarized by the HR functionaries and the collated reports are sent back to the experts. Uniquely, the experts operate individually, and do not sit together, while making their assessments. On the basis of the summarized views of all, the experts give further comments. The cycle of reviews are repeated until all the experts come to a consensus.

The aforementioned technique, while being highly reliable, suffers from the limitation of being expensive, time-consuming, and vulnerable to ego clashes between the experts causing impasse and delayed decisions.

A variation of the aforementioned is known as the nominal group technique, which is a group-based forecasting technique. In this method, a group of four or five participants presents their views regarding workforce requirements. These views are recorded and discussions are only held afterwards as the information is presented. The group takes a decision based on a final ballot.

Unit Demand Forecasting

In this method, the units (a department, a project team, or some other group of employees) furnish certain workforce estimates on the logic that they are fully conversant with what business activity will be undertaken by their units in future. The aggregated estimates for all departments constitute the total forecast for the organization. This is also compared with the demand forecast prepared by the workforce analysts. For example, a unit finds that 5% of its critical workforce will retire in a year's time and that combined with an ambitious capacity expansion, the effect would hamper its functioning. In a proactive response, if the unit recruits the critical employees in a planned manner, the department managers will have time to become aware of the skills, abilities, and desires of their employees, and this could reveal a discrepancy with the organizational forecast. This exercise will perhaps yield a higher quality forecast and a broad organizational forecast may not lack intimate knowledge of employee's performance.

The advantage of this approach is that the results will be quick and fairly accurate as the unit manager knows how many new positions will be needed to achieve output and is therefore the right person to decide. On the contrary, a disadvantage is that it involves organizing large groups and they could work on different assumptions.

Replacement Planning

Manpower estimates are arrived at by using charting techniques, which plot current role holders and critical data about each of them. This often covers a summary evaluation of performance and potential, age, time spent on present role, and the length of service.

Allocation Planning

This method involves judgments about labor supply or demand on the basis of observation of movement of employees across different roles at the same organizational level.

3.7.2 Quantitative

Trend Analysis

Trend analysis examines past employment levels against business variables to predict future manpower levels. This is a quick forecasting technique using past ratios (e.g., between number of operators and output in a manufacturing unit) to predict future ratios while allowing for some changes in the organization or its processes.

Regression Analysis

Regression analysis, in a manner similar to trend analysis, predicts the dependent variable on the basis of understanding of certain independent variables. It is a refined statistical tool to determine the best fit. In a simple linear regression, only one dependent and one independent variables are studied. When the variables are more than one, then it is multiple regression. Most uses of multiple regression emphasize two or more independent variables. With the rapid improvement in computer-processing speed and capacity, it is possible to use any number of independent variables to predict the outcome or dependent variables. In its application to HRP, it implies the use of a mathematical formula to forecast future demands based on a proven relationship between an organization's manpower level (dependent variable) and some measurable factors of output (independent variables) such as revenue, sales, or production level.

In Figure 3.2, throughput is a dependent variable and number of skilled operators is independent variable. There is a regression line in the center, which indicates that at a particular level of throughput, a particular number of skilled operators are required.

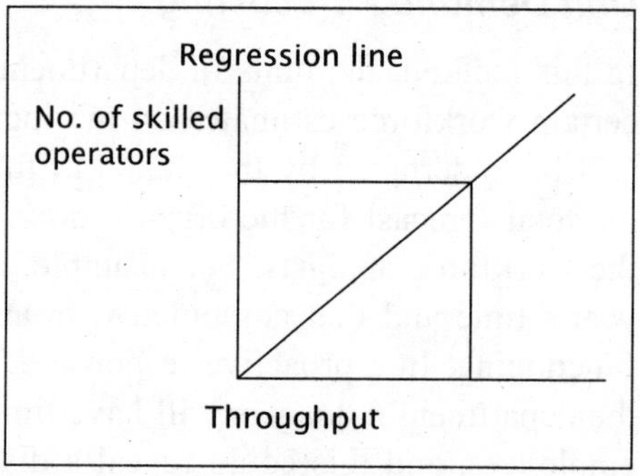

Fig. 3.2 Regression diagram of manpower vis-à-vis productivity

Ratio Analysis

Like trend analysis, ratio analysis uses the ratio between some causal factors (such as production volume) and the number of skilled operators to forecast the requirement (e.g., the number of operators). It assumes that the output per person remains stationary. For example, in case a skilled operator historically produces 1 million units per day and that plans call for increasing the output to 2 million units/day next year, then, if the output–operator ratio remains the same, one new operator would be required for each line (each of whom produces an extra 1 million units).

Work Study Techniques

In situations where the workload can be accurately measured, this technique can be effectively used to predict the estimated total output and the activities for a specific time span in future. When using this technique, the starting point could be the production budget, drawn from the sales plan. Then finally, the number of manpower is calculated based on the number of hours required to yield the planned output. Work study techniques work where it is possible to accurately predict the budgeted figures.

Flow Model

Flow models base the human resource demand forecast on analyzes of different kinds of movement of employees over specific periods in the past. The most basic model is known as the Markov Model (Table 3.1). The steps followed in this model are as follows:

1. Decide on the target time span.
2. Establish employee categories known as 'states'.
3. Count annual movements, called flows, between 'states' for several time periods. These states could include gains (recruitment or transfer), or losses (death), or changes in position levels or employment status.
4. Forecast the probability of movement from one state to another based on past trends.

Table 3.1 A Markov model of HRP (2015–2016) for an imaginary manufacturing industry with multiple plants

2016 / 2015	Superintendents		Function heads		Supervisors		Production/ maintenance technicians		Exit	
Superintendents N = 8	75%	6							25%	2
Function heads N = 40	10%	4	70%	28					20%	8
Supervisors N = 120			5%	6	70%	84	10%	12	15%	18
Production/maintenance technicians *N* = 1200					2%	24	90%	1080	8%	96
Estimated supply		10		34		108		1092		124

Note: N, total strength.

Illustration: In the category of Superintendent, the total strength in 2015 was 8. In 2016, 6 (75%) is expected to stay, 2 (25%) is to exit, and 4 persons are expected to get promoted from Function Head, making the total number of superintendent in 2016 as 10.

Apart from the aforementioned models, there are some recently evolved and less used quantitative models such as Time Series Model where fluctuations in labor levels are projected by isolating trends—seasonal and cyclical, and others; and Economic Model where fluctuations are projected by specified form of the production function.

3.7.3 Assessment of HR Supply

After the organization finds out what is the manpower it requires, the next question is where to get the requisite manpower to fill in the projected demand. The HR supplies have two sources: internal as well as external. Internal sources have to cover the available skill and potential of existing employees, while the larger source of external supplies covers demographics and skill level in the locality.

Internal Supply

Inventory by skill types

This inventory is simply a comprehensive record of the names, critical personal information, attributes, and skills/competencies/capabilities of the current employees. The recorded data fall into three categories: data summarizing the employee's past, data summarizing present, and data focusing on future. The information also covers interests, current performance appraisals, and readiness for promotion. In managerial inventories, in addition to the aforementioned, data about managerial responsibilities/training are also used to indicate internal candidates eligible for promotion or transfer. The skills and management inventories require timely and regular updating, as an obsolete record could result in eligible employees being passed over for filling up vacancies.

Inventory by total numbers

Although it is difficult to accurately predict supply by numbers for such complex jobs such as administration or operations, it is possible to keep an approximate figure in mind for any particular kind of work in future. Currently, organizations on a regular basis keep track of present or possible surplus employees (based on skill obsolescence or closure of units) for future redeployment.

For the organizations key positions, some organizations follow a practice of developing replacement charts that typically contain at least three candidates who could replace the current role holder of a critical position, should it suddenly fall vacant due to sudden contingencies. Such charts typically indicate the age of potential internal candidates (to project retirement dates), the level of current performance, and the potential for growth.

Inventory by location

In the choice of locations for a new business, often an important consideration is known as geographical analysis or the availability of potential workforce suitable for the business. This explains why certain locations become known as IT hub (such as Hyderabad, Pune, and Bangalore) or automobile hub (Gurgaon, Chennai, and others).

Inventory by business unit

Bajaj Auto, originally based in a sprawling factory in Pune, later spread out in multiple locations. While setting up a new unit, one potential source of workforce is the manpower available in existing locations, the advantage being the skill level and the familiarity with the organization culture. Therefore, an inventory by business unit type also becomes an important source of HR supply.

External Supply

While managers can influence internal sources, they cannot hope to fill up all positions with internal candidates. The internal candidates may not have the specific education or the skill required for the position, or the organization might have opened a new product line or business for which it requires specialists. Often, the efficacy of the organization's training, development, and career-planning processes also determines the volume of positions that must be filled externally. To outsource human resource, it is necessary for employers to take stock of the general economic conditions, labor market, demographic factors, and market availability of professionally skilled workforce.

State of the economy

The state of businesses is directly affected by the cyclical fluctuations of economic forces. These include investment climate, inflation rate, GDP growth, and particularly, the unemployment rate. Low unemployment rate means tight supply of skilled manpower and professionals, while an ascending unemployment implies abundance of manpower at relatively cheap rate. It is, however, important to note that unemployment rates vary by occupation and geographic location and can result in an organization's inability to fill certain positions. The state of the economy, whether it is in recession or in boom, also influences the consumer demand and consequently buoyancy of business and the hiring trends.

Demographic factors

Demographic transitions provide a platform for countries to encash their demographic dividend and leapfrog to a higher level of income-employment situation. This prospect arises at a stage of demographic transition when the population pyramid expands in the middle, implying a greater share of working age people in total population and thus a lower dependency ratio. India has an advantage in that 25% of the projected increase in global working population is expected to occur in India, and so it is posed to add over 300 million working age people to its ranks by 2040, making it the largest contributor to global workforce over the next 30 years.[14] Demographic factors also include factors such as education levels, age, gender, and marital status. Some significant trends in the demographic factors in India include higher percentage of women in the workforce and rising diversity in workforce. The labor market data is available from the labor ministry sites, private sources and researches, various associations of industries, and other chambers of commerce.

Professional market conditions

Apart from assessing the general labor market conditions, employers also keep an eye on the availability of potential resources in targeted professions (programmers, instrumentation technicians, financial analysts, and so on) for recruitment. With the boom in several sunrise sectors, industries fought hard to source project engineers, geologists, and investment bankers.

3.7.4 The Gap Analysis

Gap analysis goes beyond mere comparison between the current numerical size of the manpower with the future size as envisioned in the strategic plan. Its larger scope includes training, culture, and succession plan among other areas. Hofer and Schendel[15] define gap analysis as 'a comparison of the organization's objectives, strategy and resources against the opportunities and threats in its environment to determine the extent of change required in the current strategy.'

[14] Seema Raza Bokhari, 'Demographic Dividend-opportunity or Threat? Available at: https://tribune.com.pk/story/275878/demographic-dividend–opportunity-or-threat (accessed on October 17, 2011).

[15] C. W. Hofer and D. Schendel, *Strategy Formulation: Analytical Concepts* (St. Paul: West Publishing Company, 1986).

Based on the forecast of HR demand and supply, an estimate is prepared of the HR needs—both short-term and long-term. Long-range plans typically lack exact numbers and are more likely to be in the nature of general statements of possible HR requirements. Short-term plans, on the contrary, include specific details prepared in the form of a staffing table.

The long-term plan could address the following segments of the gap analysis:

1. Excess or shortage of manpower
2. Disparity between the existing and desired organization culture
3. Discrepancy between the current and preferred organization structure
4. Focus areas for organizational reward-learning, employee relations, and rewards

Reflection Point

A recent trend to hire data scientists and data analysts for HR tech roles is an early sign of the shift of the profile of the HR professional of the future. Innovative L&D interventions such as AI-led learning recommendations, gamification, micro-learning, on-the-job data projects, can help build data-skills from within. HR leaders must learn to be comfortable and adept with data and technology.

Discussion Question

1. How will the digitalization process impact HRP?

3.7.5 Generate Strategic Options

After taking stock of the supply–demand, the next step is to develop HR program and implementation. To effectively leverage the internal supply, organizations need to simultaneously streamline their relevant HR processes, specially performance and careers management. The PMS involves proper job designs, effective goal setting and review process, calibrated measurement system, and proper performance coaching for improvement. Finally, the reward system needs to be aligned to the PMS. Career management would entail formulation of policies. The L&D systems need to complement the development of careers.

At the end of the aforementioned exercise, three possibilities could arise: a state of equilibrium, when the supply and demand are matched; a surplus, when the supply is more than the demand; and shortage, when the supply falls short of demand (Table 3.2).

On the extremely unlikely occurrence of a labor equilibrium, the organization should go ahead with implementation of the existing plans to replace departing employees with suitable promotions or transfers, and where internal candidates are not available, with fresh recruitments.

In a surplus scenario, the common response is to freeze recruitment and to manage the vacancies through work-reorganization and redeployment. Over a period of time, separations gradually reduce the excess manpower. The obvious limitations of this strategy are: It is time consuming and the employers have little choice on who stays and who leaves. A legal method for dealing with surplus is to use lay-off or retrenchment—a temporary or permanent cessation of employment due to business reasons and circumstances beyond the control of the employer. In India, the Industrial Disputes (ID) Act has provided for prior approval for such an action by government labor department for industries employing 1000 or more workmen. A more proactive approach is to offer VRS by incentivizing

Table 3.2 Options for matching supply and demand

<table>
<tr><th colspan="3">Labor shortage</th></tr>
<tr><th>Increase supply externally</th><th>Reduce demand</th><th>Improve retention</th></tr>
<tr><td>• Recruit differently
• Attract people of different age, sex, race, nationality, skill, qualifications, and experience
• Advertise in different places
• Assess and select in different ways
• Improve terms and conditions
• Offer assistance in relocation, transport, childcare
• Internally
• Promote differently
• Train existing staff
• Redeploy existing staff</td><td>• Redesign work
• Redesign job specification
• Use existing staff differently
• Subcontract work
• Relocate work
• Automate</td><td>• Improve terms and conditions
• Improve management style and communication
• Improve promotion and recognition
• Improve training
• Improve inducements, bonus, and the like
• Improve selection, placements, and inductions
• Monitor staff turnover</td></tr>
<tr><th colspan="3">Labor surplus</th></tr>
<tr><th>Increase demand</th><th>Decrease supply</th><th>Discourage retention</th></tr>
<tr><td>• Increase markets for products and services</td><td>• Early retirement
• Assisted career change
• Secondments, sabbaticals, and the like
• Voluntary redundancy
• Compulsory redundancy</td><td>• Short-term contracts
• Flexible working</td></tr>
</table>

Source: Rothwell, 'Human Resource Planning.'

premature separation. VRS, however, needs to be carefully planned to ensure that key role holders do not leave. VRS also means huge outflow of money at the same time. Some employers adopt a form of compulsory retirement policy by pressurizing the targeted workforce to leave. Such a step, however, has a recoiling effect, by causing panic reaction among the employees and creating a negative employer brand. Two other approaches, such as job-sharing and part-time employment, though reduce the working hours and earnings for the employees, are more employee-friendly because they prevent the pain of job loss. The organization also gains in so far it holds on to the skill and wins the confidence of the employees. The employers, however, may find it impractical in an uncertain business environment.

In non-unionized workplaces, especially in the services sector, targeted employees are purged on grounds of non-performance, in smaller number on a regular basis, and in larger number, when facing crisis. Executives negotiate a golden parachute clause in their contract of employment with a guarantee by the employer to pay specific compensation in the case of termination caused by downsizing or restructuring.

Some organizations provide outplacement assistance, whereby an outside agency can help affected employees find employment in other organizations.

The third scenario is about shortage, when demand exceeds supply. There are options for short-term and long-term responses to deal with shortage. A high level of regular overtime hours is an indication of shortage and a popular way of managing it. Subcontracting or outsourcing (temporarily or permanently) and use of temporary employees or *badlis* are two more such short-term responses.

To deal with vacancies, organizations resort to internal employee movements (promotions and transfers), and a deliberate attempt is made to create resultant vacancies at the entry level, because they are easily filled at lower cost and in a timely manner. Transfer means movement from one job to another that is similar in pay, responsibility, or position. Transfers serve multiple purposes: The human resources are effectively optimized through building up skills, perspectives (often through encountering technical and relational challenges) in an employee, and thus the organization gains from the better and properly evolved candidate moving up the corporate ladder. In a promotion, the employee is moved from one job to another job of higher pay, responsibility, and position. Promotion can be merit based or seniority based or a combination of both.

In a wider sense, the HRP process brings to the surface some hidden issues for the organization indirectly triggering employee attrition. It might indicate intervention and course correction on certain related HR processes such as performance management, employee engagement, and compensation and reward practices.

Case Study Dilemmas of HRP in a Business Life Cycle Stage

MIG Batteries Inc has decided to set up a new battery plant B in Kolkata. Their old plant A at the Baranagar area in the northern part of the city is about 50 years old. It was the pride of MIG when it started. Over the years, the workmen have really become skilled and would respond quickly to changes in battery designs and introduction of new products. For a long time, it enjoyed monopoly in the AA- and AAA-size battery market and enjoyed tremendous goodwill due to sustained quality.

Ever since the late 1970s, however, the market dynamics changed with the entry of Japanese products. Consumers suddenly became spoilt for the choice: prices were competitive. Quality was no longer the differentiator, price was. So MIG started losing chunks of its market. There would be inventories of finished products, sometimes the production was stopped for a few days. The workmen, who were the best paid in the neighborhood, started complaining about the fall in earning due to lower production incentive. The union split into two. A new Centre of Indian Trade Unions (CITU)-affiliated union came up by breaking away from the existing apolitical union. The long cherished industrial harmony was broken often with sporadic agitations and incidents of indiscipline.

The new battery plant was planned at a location in South Kolkata. The company planned to adapt the latest technology with imported machines for bobbin, cooking, can extrusion, and finishing departments. Its capacity would be twice that of plant A, with one-fourth of the manpower cost of plant A, and would need only 300 workmen (as against the existing 1,900 at plant A). The challenges were as follows: The productivity had to be sustained at a high level and the core workforce had to be high skilled and quick to adapt to evolving technology (plant A had only 25% high-skilled category). When plant B would operate at full capacity, plant A production could be cut down to one-third of the current level. This would cut down the operating cost for MIG to 40% of the current level after about four–five years.

The dilemmas that the management faced are as follows:

- What would be the desired workmen profile?
- Would the workmen be sourced internally or externally?
- What options does MIG have to deal with the workmen of plant A, once plant B goes full throttle on targeted productivity?
- What HR program should it decide and why?

3.8 ATTRIBUTES OF AN EFFECTIVE HUMAN RESOURCE PLANNING

1. **Structured** A well-formulated and rigorous approach enables HRP to provide value to a business. A proper HR plan creates a clearly visible linkage between the desired workforce capabilities relevant for business success and the actual status of the capabilities existing and the action planning for closing the gap.
2. **Prognostic** The plan must be visionary and should leverage both the available data and emerging trends to visualize the effects of internal and external forces on the organization. Businesses must take a proactive look at country-based, regional, and global trends in workforce demographics, labor availability, and skills gaps.
3. **Strategic** A subset of an organization's strategic plan, workforce planning must be done within the context of market factors that impact the organization and the industry in which it operates. Strategic alignment with the business is imperative.
4. **Flexible** Since the workforce plan reflects the market and organizational realities, it will be subject to continuous change. The fact that workforce planning occurs in a fluctuating environment makes it all the more important that planning does occur.

3.9 BARRIERS TO HUMAN RESOURCE PLANNING

1. **Time frame** Many managers are focused on executing current-year results, but workforce planning has typically addressed a longer time frame and does not show immediate gains that can help meet this year's results.
2. **Integrity** Data integrity concerns when 'getting out of the gate.' Managers are reluctant to review future plans when they feel that they cannot get a proper view of current head count.
3. **Control** Some managers have gut feelings and do not want to reference data without a compelling data story. There is no opportunity to shift this stance until managers experience the actual pain that could have been avoided through workforce planning.
4. **Detail** Organizations have a hard time settling on the appropriate level of granularity of workforce planning, or their job taxonomy. It is generally understood that a workforce plan has to distinguish one type of job from the other, but is it sufficient to look at broad labor categories, narrower job families, individual jobs, or actual skill sets? So many organizations get into self-imposed delays in rolling out their planning program by trying to find the perfect level at which to plan. From a planning perspective, however, if organizations could start by planning out high-level job categories, this is a great start, and may be enough.
5. **Forecasting** Traditional forecasting methods are poor at predicting the actual individuals at risk for turnover and retirement, and, thus, are not sufficiently actionable.

Two recent trends serve to moderate—and sometimes even eliminate—these potential roadblocks. The first is a broad-scale acceptance of data-driven decision-making that is infusing the culture of organizations and making workforce planning inherently more attractive. The second involves recent advances in predictive analytics and modeling technology. These advances provide more compelling, near-term actionable information about granular employee-level supply risk while simultaneously helping with demand-based scenario planning. Coupled together, these trends have a profound ability to move workforce planning from a 'nice-to-have' status to a critical program for high-performance organizations.

3.10 THE CHALLENGES FOR HUMAN RESOURCE PLANNING IN INDIA

A paradoxical feature being noted in India is that of a labor surplus economy, with an unlimited number of workers willing to work at a subsistence wage—where the rising incidence of scarcity or shortages coexist with a situation of potential plenty. The scarcity pertains to skilled labor. It is reported that 15% of Indian trucks are idle owing to a shortage of drivers and India Inc is worried that such scarcity is rampant across the skills spectrum. These trends are predicted to only worsen in the future and can seriously impair the country's rapid growth aspirations. An example is cited of the metals and mining sector, which is booming but plagued by the dearth of qualified metallurgists. An entire new generation of engineers grooves more on IT and management than heavy metal, while it is the steel industry that develops in tandem with the growth of the economy.[16]

But the alarm bell is ringing even in IT, infrastructure, and power, where the demand for skills is not met. A recent survey conducted by the Federation of Indian Chambers of Commerce and Industry (FICCI) and the World Bank conducted on 157 employers across sectors and regions, half of which were large employers, sought answers on: (a) skills employers considered important when hiring new engineering graduates; (b) how satisfied employers are with the skills of engineering graduates; and (c) important skills in which engineers were falling short. In a key finding, around 64% of employers were only somewhat satisfied with the quality of the new hires or worse. They perceive soft skills—core employability and communication skills—to be very important. Gaps were found to be more severe in higher-order thinking skills.[17]

It is feared that skill shortages in construction, for instance, can apply the brakes on the country's rapid growth. This industry is critical to building physical infrastructure since it accounts for more than half the investment required for setting up facilities such as ports, power projects, roads, and bridges. The sector has been growing at a double-digit clip during the last eight years and accounts for 9% of India's GDP. The vast majority of jobs created between 2004–2005 and 2009–2010 was also in construction.

Reflection Point

Lazy Girl Jobs

It means trying to get an easy going job which pays more. It is a response to the hustle culture which is prevailing in many of the business organizations.

Discussion Question

1. What would be the upside and down side of designing roles to suit the preference of the young generation?

3.11 CHALLENGES AND STRATEGIES OF BUILDING A GLOBAL WORKFORCE

Companies have long understood that an important condition of success in global economy is to build a geographically dispersed workforce. Such a workforce comes with top of the shelf functional

[16] N. Chandra Mohan, 'Shortages in a Labour Surplus Economy: Planners Need to Come to Grips with This Paradox in the Labour Market,' *Business Standard*, October 24, 2011.

[17] Andreas Blom and Hiroshi Saeki, 'Employability and Skill Set of Newly Graduated Engineers in India' (working paper, World Bank, April 2011).

knowhow from across the world, cultural diversity, and precious local insight of the high potential markets. Over time such workforce can become a unique mosaic of cross-cultural diversity, a vast repertoire of work experiences and different perspectives on strategic and organizational challenges. These elements create helpful conditions for MNCs to compete effectively in the global business arena.

Globalization of the workforce has, indeed, become an accepted way of life in business and a compulsive need. Businesses recognize that jobs will keep moving from mature rigid markets where talent is scarce, to emerging and flexible markets where talent is more plentiful. This transition makes it imperative that companies pay attention to developing new HR competencies for managing a global supply chain for talent, as a survival strategy, in much the same way the manufacturing companies have learnt the ropes managing a global supply chain for products. All these do not come without back lashes in the form of HRP costs and organizational challenges.

A principal challenge is the mental model of the existing employees. From a young age, they have learned to adore all artefacts of a national identity–the national anthem, the national history, the cultural habits of their country, and a sense of national superiority. All these can pose huge barriers to the building a global workforce causing a hostile work environment and subdued productivity.[18]

Another challenge is the legislations in different countries. The differences in local laws affect areas like recruitment, employee benefits, payroll administration, and termination of employment. According to a survey done for 2019 Global Business Complexity Index, covering 76 different jurisdictions worldwide, in terms of ease of doing business, it was found that 50% of the jurisdiction felt that of countries' labor laws are difficult to understand. Giving some example, the survey also reported that shared parental leave prevailed in 63% of jurisdictions in Americas, but only 33% in APAC. On the other hand, for pension, organizations have to fund in 79% of APAC countries, 63% in the Americas and 50% in EMEA. It is also revealed that payroll legislation is affected by quick changes. Besides 76% of jurisdictions globally require companies to submit employees' payroll data to the government at least once a month. The employers right to terminate an employee varies too: Americas, 52% of jurisdictions allow businesses to terminate employment contracts in less than a day. In APAC this figure is just 8% and in EMEA 6%.[19]

A study report on the basis of interviews with HR managers in eight large companies Karen Roberts and others have reported three challenges and four strategies for building a global workforce. The challenges are deployment, knowledge, and innovation dissemination. The strategies are aspatial careers, awareness building assignments, SWAT teams, and virtual solutions. Managing the global workforce: challenges and strategies.[20]

Closing Case TCS Story

How TCS Manages Its Huge Workforce

Tata Consultancy Services (TCS), the country's largest provider of IT services, has over 300,000 people on its rolls and plans to add another 55,000 in the current financial year. This

[18] The Challenges of managing a global workforce. Walaa Abulmagd. https://www.linkedin.com/pulse

[19] Challenges mount for Global workforce: TMF report. https://www.peoplemattersglobal.com/article/compensation-benefits

[20] Karen Roberts, Ellen Ernst Kossek and Cynthia Ozeki. The Academy of Management Executive (1993-2005). Vol. 12, No. 4, Competitiveness and Global Leadership in the 21st Century (Nov., 1998)

will bring TCS within striking distance of the country's largest employer in the corporate sector, state-owned Coal India which has 357,000 employees. For the HR team of TCS, the challenge is not just the scale but also that these men and women represent 118 nationalities and are located in 50 countries. Employees accounted for 37% of the total cost for TCS in 2013–2014, down from 37.84% a year ago because of the weakening of the rupee. For TCS Executive VP and Head of Global HR Ajoy Mukherjee, the challenge is to strike a balance between the need for a charged-up workforce and profits. IT companies have realized that one way to keep employee costs under control is to hire fresh graduates from campuses in large numbers. They are inexpensive manpower. But getting the wrong people requires substantial investments in training and the cost advantage gets negated.

At TCS, according to Mukherjee, manpower planning is done at least three years in advance. The projections get refined for each year. And the company starts visiting campuses for recruitment one-and-a-half years in advance. Mukerjee's team visits almost 370 colleges every year from September to mid-February. The team creates a pool of students who are assessed through an online test, followed by two rounds of interview. Around 70% of these students join TCS. The bulk of these freshers come from engineering colleges at an entry-level salary, which has remained unchanged for five years now, of ₹3.15 to ₹3.50 lakh.

The bane of the IT sector is high employee turnover. Replacements need to be hired and trained, and there's a cost attached to it. So, most companies want to keep attrition as low as possible. TCS's attrition of 11.43% in 2013–2014 may have risen from 10.57% in 2012–2013 but it is still among the lowest in the industry. At Infosys, attrition was at 18.7% in the March-ended quarter, while at Wipro it was at 15.1%.

But even at this low attrition, TCS has to hire and train at least 30,000 additional hands in a year. One way out of the annual exercise is to give regular increments. TCS gave 10% in 2013–2014 (average of 7% in 2012–2013), which compares favorably with the industry benchmark of 7 to 9% for offshore employees.

The Social Network

Mukherjee says his prime concern is to meet the aspirations of the young employees (those born in the 1980s and early 1990s) who make up 80% of the workforce. To keep in touch with the goals of this generation, Mukherjee has again relied on technology. In 2013, TCS did a survey of India's younger generation, covering 17,500 high school students across 14 cities. The biggest finding was that this generation was a heavy user of smart devices and had a constant need to be online. This led to the creation of Knome, TCS's internal online social network. This is significant as several IT companies do not allow employees to access platforms such as Facebook or Twitter during work hours, but Knome allows employees to connect through posts, discussions, and blogs. This is also a popular platform for the brass to connect with all. CEO N. Chandrasekaran, rather than sending emails to individual employees, has chosen to post his thoughts on this platform, ensuring it reaches out to the largest number. This is also a platform that helps employees reach their voice to the top. For instance, some employees thought that half-sleeve shirts can be a part of formal dressing in India since the country is hot. They created consensus among the employees and now Mukherjee is looking at making such shirts a part of the TCS dress code. In addition, TCS does an annual Pulse Survey which takes every employees feedback on things that matter to them. The feedback is confidential and the HR team works on each of the issues raised during the survey.

More than the sheer number of employees, what worries Mukherjee is how to keep this 300,000-strong workforce relevant in the fast-changing world of technology? TCS does it by shifting employees across departments and organizing training programs. However, because the training programs require its employees to move from one office to another across geographies, they can also be a difficult exercise in compliance, especially to rules pertaining to visas. 'How do we ensure we are compliant? The risk to reputation is very high,' Mukherjee adds.

In spite of the rapid rise in the employee base, TCS's revenue per employee increased from $41,900 in 2011–2012 to $44,600 in 2013–2014.

Discussion Questions

1. Discuss how TCS aligns HRP to business strategy.
2. How is the HRP different from the Tata Steel?

Source: Shivani Shinde Nadhe, 'How TCS Manages Its Huge Workforce,' *Business Standard*, June 5, 2014.

SUMMARY

Contemporary HRP occurs within the broad context of organizational and strategic business planning. It involves forecasting the organization's future HR needs and planning for how those needs will be met. It includes establishing objectives and then developing and implementing programs (staffing, appraising, compensating, and training) to ensure that people are available with the appropriate characteristics and skills when and where the organization needs them. It may also involve developing and implementing programs to improve employee performance or to increase employee satisfaction and involvement in order to boost organizational productivity, quality, or innovation.[21] Finally, HRP includes gathering data that can be used to evaluate the effectiveness of ongoing programs and inform planners when revisions in their forecasts and programs are needed.

The HRP process in an organization is impacted by multiple factors in the internal and external environment of business. The external factors include economic, technological, legal, social, political, geographic, and demographic, and the internal factors include the business strategy, state in the organization growth cycle, time horizon, quality of information, and so on. HRP supports the budgeting process and the business plan process, and helps identify shortage of qualified talent to fill critical talent and also skill gap in the workforce. It also helps the other HR processes such as career development and training.

The HRP process has nine sequential steps: environment scan, business strategy formulation, HR scenario planning, demand assessment, supply forecasting, gap analysis, generating strategic options, prepare HR plan and program, and implement and review. For demand forecasting, there are two sets of tools: qualitative and quantitative. The qualitative tools include managerial judgment, Delphi technique, nominal group technique, and unit demand forecasting. The quantitative tools comprise ratio analysis, regression analysis, flow models, and work study methods. HR supply forecasting uses two sources: internal and external. Internal sources have to cover the available skill and potential of existing employees, while the larger source of external supplies covers demographics and skill level in

[21] D. Quinn Mills 'Planning with People in Mind'. *Harvard Business Review* (November–December 1983): 97–105.

the locality. In gap analysis, based on the forecast of HR demand and supply, an estimate is prepared of the HR needs—both short-term and long-term. Long-range plans typically lack exact numbers and are more likely to be in the nature of general statements of possible HR requirements. Short-term plans, on the contrary, include specific details prepared in the form of a staffing table.

After comparing the demand and supply position, three possibilities could arise: a state of equilibrium, when the supply and demand are matched; a surplus, when the supply is more than the demand; and shortage, when the supply falls short of demand. On the extremely unlikely occurrence of a labor equilibrium, the organization should go ahead with implementation of the existing plans to replace departing employees with suitable promotions or transfers, and where internal candidates are not available, with fresh recruitments. In a surplus scenario, the common response is to freeze recruitment and to manage the vacancies through work reorganization and redeployment. Over a period of time, separations gradually reduce the excess manpower.

In India, there exists a paradoxical feature of surplus coexisting with demand. The scarcity pertains to skilled labor. It is reported that 15% of Indian trucks are idle owing to a shortage of drivers and India Inc is worried that such scarcity is rampant across the skills spectrum. These trends are predicted to only worsen in the future and can seriously impair the country's rapid growth aspirations. An example is cited of the metals and mining sector, which is booming but plagued by the dearth of qualified metallurgists.

Short-answer Questions

1. How does HRP differ from Manpower Planning?
2. What could go wrong if the business organizations wait for the economic cycle and then plan?
3. What according to Martin Ford would be the likely outcome of the increasing use of robotics?
4. Name the laws affecting HRP in India.
5. What are the implications, positive, and negative of the use of contingent labor in India?
6. Who formulated the typology of 'defender, prospector, and analyzer' and what was the context?
7. Explain any two qualitative tools for demand forecasting.
8. Mention the advantage and the disadvantage of Unit demand forecasting.
9. What are the six attributes of HRP?
10. What is Gap analysis?

Discussion Questions

1. Imagine that an HR manager in a small business of manufacturing auto parts is informed about a business strategy of moving into business process outsourcing (BPO) business, and that the manufacturing unit, will cut down its operation by half over the next one year due to fall in demand and competition. What would be the elements in your HRP process?
2. What can be the role of business analytics in HRP process? Conduct a mini research on how IT industry is using analytics to make their HR plan in the context of highly volatile business environment.
3. What are the advantages and limitations of reskilling programs for employees in manufacturing vis-à-vis services sector?
4. There is a retail outlet with 50 sales personnel currently. According to the business strategy of the company, expansion plans will require the following manpower during the next three years:

(a) 2017: 60

(b) 2018: 70

(c) 2019: 80

There are no promotions into the group, and typically two are promoted to the rank of sales supervisor per year. An average of five per year is transferred to other retail outlets of the organization, and two per year transferred in from other retail outlets. Employee turnover averages 50% per year.

(a) What will be the recruitment requirements over the one year?

(b) If the overall number is 70, what difference would it make?

CHAPTER 4

Recruitment and Selection

LEARNING OBJECTIVES

After completing this chapter, the student will be able to:

- Appreciate the value of recruitment and selection in effective HRM
- Identify the critical success factors for effective recruitment and selection
- Understand the pros and cons of internal and external recruitment
- Evaluate selection methods based on criteria of professionalism including reliability, validity, and fairness
- Comprehend the interrelationships between recruitment and selection and other HR processes

Opening Case Use of Selection Instruments

It was April, already a little late for campus selections, the session having already begun since last year for some colleges. For Sambaran Hazra, the new recruitment and talent manager of ABC Chemical & Fertilizer Company, BIIT, Pune, it was the first campus selection process since taking over. BIIT was reputed to be one of the two best colleges for chemical engineering in the country, and many of its alumni were in senior positions in the ABC. It was the policy of the company to visit only the top engineering colleges (on the basis of a MARG annual rating).

In course of the essential research prior to the recruitment, Hazra had found out the trends in executive turnover rates: 0.5–1% in the top tier (10 years and above, senior managers); 10–15% in the middle tier (5–10 years, managers); and 25–30% in the bottom tier (up to 5 years, engineers/executives). There was a system of exit interviews (EIs), held by the HR head. The data was unstructured and qualitative (handwritten notes on the discussion) and used only for discussion with the function heads. The tea-room gossip was that the graduate engineers joined ABC as a launching pad to gain experience of 2 years, prepare for CAT test, and try to gain admission in MBA education in reputed B-schools.

This year the company required to recruit 10–15 fresh engineers from 10 selected campuses. The interview panel had some experienced interviewers, representing different functions. The panel head was S. Varadararajan, a highly regarded chemical engineer from IIT, and the current head, operations.

Based on the preplacement talks, 50 students from the chemical engineering batch were called in for interview. Based on a quick calculation of the available time, it was found that (with 20-minute interview time per candidate) it was possible to interview up to 10 candidates only. So shortlisting of candidates was done initially on the basis of ranks secured (in the last semester exam), and subsequently on the basis of a group discussion (two groups of 15 each, discussion time of 15 minutes).

The interview process (three panelists, including Hazra) was interesting. The interview started with 'tell us something about yourself ' question, probe into the family background of the candidate and any gaps in the education, proceeded with technical questions, and ended with questions such as 'will you be comfortable with a shift job?' Mr Varadarajan had a prepared questionnaire in which he methodically asked questions on basic chemistry, chemical processes, fire and safety regulations, disaster management, and so on. The second panelist presented small scenarios on actual problems witnessed in the company during last 5 years or so and asked questions such as 'what would you do, if...?' Hazra asked questions on values and vision, for example, 'If you caught a subordinate submitting a false claim for transport reimbursement, what action would you take?'

After the interviews, the candidates were administered a well-known psychometric instrument to test parameters such as extroversion–introversion and the like. This was Hazra's choice. He had also suggested inclusion of a psychologist in the panel, which was not approved by the HR head on the ground of cost escalation. So the results of the psychometric test were put down on the interview evaluation score sheet and discussed by the panelists before the final selection was done.

The panel found two candidates suitable. The candidates were given offer letters. The appointment would be subject to medical fitness on the basis of examination by an empaneled physician.

Discussion Questions

1. Critically evaluate the aforementioned selection process by ABC Company.
2. If you had to change some of the processes, what would they be? Give your reasons.

4.1 INTRODUCTION

HR planning exercise ends with a final score card where the outcome could be either scarcity or surplus. In case of scarcity, which indicates the need for additional personnel, also in some situation of surplus (where the organization requires some critical talent), organizations can select one out of the many choices to resolve the issue. The automatic option presenting itself may be a full-scale recruitment and selection process, but sometimes bringing in additional employees is not considered the preferred method for dealing with scarcity. The other choices such as recruitment process outsourcing, contingent employees, fixed-term contracts, temporary employees, and so on may be more suitable for the organization, rather than the conventional single point method. Business organizations habitually handle periodical changes in work volume through overtime or part-time employees of different kinds. The activities of recruitment and selection do entail investment in considerable time and money for an organization and, therefore, decisions to hire new employees are best taken only after having exhausted all other options, when a long-term engagement is considered critical for the organization's business plans. According to Galbreath,[1] estimates on the cost to replace supervisory, technical, and management employees run from 50% to several hundred percentage of employee salaries.

Responsible HRP is expected to take into account the general health and growth prospects of the organization and properly calibrated forecast of future manpower requirements. Recruitment planning commences only after other options have been found to be inappropriate for specific reasons. Two factors have to be borne in mind in this context. First, recruitment is successful only when it is fully integrated with the overall HR plan and does not hang out as an isolated, stand-alone event; and second, recruitment should be viewed as interrelated with all other HR processes such as performance management, L&D, compensation and rewards, and so on. For example, an organization with a negative reputation of poor compensation or repressive workplace practices may find it difficult to attract targeted candidates for recruitment.

Recruitment and selection form part of the nucleus of HRM activities which have a direct bearing on business strategy. This is also an area that witnesses active participation of the line management to ensure its ultimate success. Recruitment has been defined as 'the process of attracting individuals on a timely basis, in sufficient numbers, and with appropriate qualifications, to apply for jobs within an organization.'[2] Recruitment thus aims to create an inventory of such capable applicants. Selection, on the other hand, is the process by which specific instruments or techniques are used by HR specialists and also by the LMs to select from such a body of applicants a candidate or candidates, who have the potential ability to effectively perform the role within the boundaries of management goals and statutory requirements. Selection, therefore, is the combination of processes that results in the choice of one or more persons over others for one or more jobs or roles.

4.2 IMPORTANCE OF RECRUITMENT

Recruitment, if done right, provides a strategic advantage by providing talented people who, through their performance, improve the profitability and enhance the value of the organization. In the opposite way, a wrongly done recruitment burdens the organization with issues of incompetence and non-performance, which sometimes have the negative effect of pulling the organization behind. For example, the recruitment of Vishal Sikka as the CEO of Infosys, eventually led to the company making huge strides in acquiring new business, growth in profits and share value, and all-round growth of employees.

The message 'War for Talent' coined in a *Harvard Business Review*[3] article, reflected a sense of urgency for the businesses to attract and hold on to employees possessing critical talent for the business. In some domains, especially technology, there is an acute shortage of proficient manpower and, therefore, in a typical demand-surpassing supply case, the salaries and benefits of the limited available professionals are skyrocketing. The most rigorous quest in war for talent is for those 'passive

1 R. Galbreath, 'Employee Turnover Hurts Small and Large Organization Profitability' (SHRM white paper, Society for Human Resource Management, Alexandria, VA, 2000).

2 R. W. Mondy, *Human Resource Management* (Upper Saddle River, NJ: Pearson, 2008).

3 Chambers, E., Foulon, M., Handfield-Jones, H., Hankin, S., Michaels III, E. 'The War for Talent'. *The McKinsey Quarterly*, 3 (1998): 44–57.

job seekers' who are happy and comfortable with their current job and unaware that they are the focus of an organized hunt.

Exhibit Jobs in Demand

High-Paying Jobs in India: Here Are Top 25 Skills Most in Demand

LinkedIn came out with a list of 'Hottest Skills of 2015' based on hiring and recruiting activity seen on the networking Website in the past year (January 1 to December 1, 2015). As expected, IT skills dominated the list.

Trends

In 2015, new skill areas—corporate law and governance, military and defense, automotive services, parts and design—featured in the LinkedIn list. They were not listed in 2014. Electronic and electrical engineering jumped 14 places in the 2015 list as compared to 2014 while user interface design rose by 7 spots. Among notable drops, social media marketing slipped 11 spots in 2015 list as compared to that of 2014.

The hottest skills of 2015 (India), according to LinkedIn are:

1. Cloud and distributed computing
2. Statistical analysis and data mining
3. Storage systems and management
4. User interface design
5. Algorithm design
6. Public relations (PR) and communications
7. Network and information security
8. Web architecture and development frameworks
10. Virtualization
11. Electronic and electrical engineering
12. Public policy and international relations
13. Data presentation
14. Corporate law and governance
15. Mobile development
16. Mac, Linux, and Unix systems
17. Social media marketing
18. Economics
19. Game development
20. Shell scripting languages
21. Data engineering and data warehousing
22. Automotive services, parts and design
23. Middleware and integration software
24. Digital and online marketing
25. Military and defense

Source: NDTV Profit, January 27, 2016.

Some other benefits of recruitment could be listed as follows:

1. A proper recruitment process can ensure long-term retention of selected candidates.
2. Success in recruitment also means good ROI or value for the money spent on the recruitment process.
3. In current times of globalization, more than at any earlier times, the trend is to build a culturally diverse workplace, which is also facilitated by a properly orchestrated recruitment process.

To sum up, it is said that recruitment is a kind of business competition and it is intensely competitive. In as much as business organizations compete to develop, manufacture, and market the desired product or services, they must be ahead of the pack in the race to identify, attract, and recruit the most valued people.[4] Recruitment is business and big business. Any management must pay as much attention to it as any other critical activity as, otherwise, even the most articulated and clever business strategy will flounder without the talent to execute it.

Reflection Point

Purple Squirrel refers to candidates who possess both rare skills and who actively seek out new roles, via their motivation and drive, rather than relying on recruiters or third parties to find them a job. In 2012, Google recruiter Michael B. Junge published a book *Purple Squirrel: Stand Out, Land Interviews, and Master the Modern Job Market*. In 2012 Elon Musk tweeted 'Do not search for purple squirrels! Giving them attention only makes them want to be more purple.' which is likely also a reference to this term.

Discussion Question

1. What is the wisdom in recruiting Purple Squirrels or in avoiding them in recruitment?

4.3 RECRUITMENT POLICIES

Recruitment and selection policy is a statement of norms and guidelines describing the manner in which an organization should conduct its recruitment and selection process. The recruitment policy seeks to ensure transparency and absence of any bias in recruitment and selection process; one that results in the appointment of the best candidate, who comes through purely on merit and is compatible with the organizational values, philosophy, and goals.

A model recruitment and selection policy should have the following elements:

- Respect for diversity
- Ethical decision-making
- Merit-based selection
- Equal treatment for all
- Procedural fairness

Adherence to such a policy will not only ensure job applicants are treated fairly, but will also greatly increase your chances of securing the best possible people for your organization.

D. Seligman[5] described four types of company positions on recruitment: (a) passive non-discrimination—with a passive commitment not to discriminate based on community and sex

4 A. S. Wellner, 'Employers Join Forces to Recruit,' *HR Magazine* (January 2001): 86–96.

5 D. Seligman, 'How 'Equal Opportunity' Turned into Employment Quotas,' *Fortune* 87, no. 3 (1973): 160–168.

for hiring, promotion, and pay; (b) purely diversity based—established on commitment to select the best from among an expanded pool of candidates irrespective of sex or community; (c) diversity-based recruitment with preferential hiring with a preferential treatment for women and minority; and finally, (d) hard quotas—with mandate to recruit or promote definite numbers.

In India, reservation of the fourth variety (hard quota) is prevalent in public sector organizations and government offices. In these organizations, recruitment and promotions have to conform to specific numbers (based on percentage of the overall workforce) for Scheduled Castes (SCs), Scheduled Tribes (STs), and Other Backward Castes (OBCs). Such quotas have also been fixed for specially abled persons and ex–service personnel. Some organizations have also adapted internal policies to induct certain percentage of women to their workforce to promote diversity (e.g., XYZ Group of Companies).

Preferential recruitment of locals, euphemistically called 'sons of the soil,' is often a political issue in many parts of the country and organizations informally follow a policy of giving preferential treatment to locals, especially on unskilled jobs. For greenfield projects, there is also a practice of providing employment to the land losers (often known as PAPs) at the rate of one person per family based on requirement.

The ratio of internal and external recruitment is another formal or informal aspect of recruitment policies, as is also specifications about part-time or contingent employees.

4.4 FACTORS INFLUENCING RECRUITMENT

Recruitment is affected by two sets of factors: internal and external. The internal factors include primarily the recruitment policies of the organization, as described earlier. The other internal factors include (a) a well-structured and comprehensive HR plan, which facilitates seamless sourcing of manpower in a systematic and appropriate manner; (b) the size of the firm in as much as the complexities in recruitment planning and process are generally inversely connected with the largeness of the organization; (c) budgetary considerations—requiring pursuit of cost-effective ways of recruiting (e.g., use of social media instead of search firms); (d) stage in the maturity cycle of the business, implying, for example, that an organization in a decline stage would be far less inclined for recruitment than an organization in the growth stage.

The principal external factor affecting recruitment is the labor market condition. A labor market in the classical sense meant a geographical area inside which the dynamics of labor supply and labor demand determine the price of labor. The surplus in supply would explain why unskilled laborers struggle to obtain even the statutorily fixed minimum wage, in the same way that the scarcity in supply makes airline pilots command salaries of their choice. The labor market, however, can no longer be confined to a set geographical area. The employers can now go global and tap the cheapest source of labor. A wider definition of labor market[6] could cover diverse factors such as:

1. Geography
2. Education
3. Industry
4. Licensing and certification requirement
5. Union membership

6 Alison E. Barber, *Recruiting Employees* (Thousand Oaks, CA: SAGE Publications, 1998).

A second external factor in a related way is the unemployment rate in the area. Higher the unemployment rate, larger the number of applicants for a given job. The national skill development program by the government is a step in the direction of managing the issue of unemployment by increasing the employment potential of a person through building marketable skill sets. Another external factor influencing recruitment is the political and legal environment of the organization. There are multiple labor laws governing recruitment in India, including Apprentices Act, Compulsory Notification of Vacancies Act, Contract Labor Abolition and Regulation Act, to name a few. Recruitment is also considerably influenced by issues around reservation for disadvantaged communities.

4.5 THE RECRUITMENT PROCESS

The recruitment process is a sequential chain of activities with three distinct and interconnected stages: pre-recruitment, recruitment, and post-recruitment (Figure 4.1). It is also termed as the resourcing cycle. The core activities commence with the identification of a vacancy and conclude with the selected new employee performing his role to an acceptable standard. Recruitment can also be described as a hydra-headed process. While the candidate is under a scanner by the organization to demonstrate his/her suitability for the given vacancy, the candidate from his side gauging the organization as a suitable future employer. It is, therefore, imperative that the entire recruitment process is helmed in a manner that ensures not only the selection of the most accomplished candidate(s), but also a degree of satisfaction in the rejected candidates of having participated in a fair, transparent, and professionally conducted process. Such an experience will enable him/her to apply again for a job in case of a future vacancy, along with other suitable candidates.

The first step begins with the big picture of the organization: the business strategy. In a scenario where the organization is venturing into new business, the parameters of recruitment may vary from

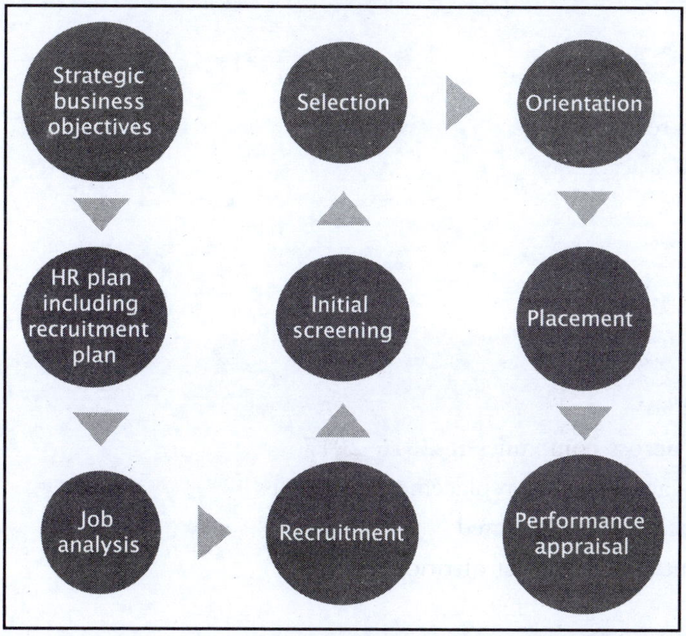

Fig. 4.1 Recruitment process

the traditional business. For example, L&T may pick up their entry-level engineers from campuses, while for L&T InfoTech, they may prefer social media or job fair. The entire recruitment process may remain suspended in air if it does not have a visible linkage with the business strategy.

The second step in the process is the HRP process of scanning the environment, balancing the supply with demand, and arriving at the scenario of either surplus or scarcity. It will end up with HR program that will include the HR plan of identified vacancies with the numbers and skill requirements of the manpower required for a specific period. Increasingly in respect of the identified vacancies, a more strategic and critical approach may be taken. It is possible that in respect of a particular vacancy, which has arisen because an employee has left, managers may plan to manage the work alternatively, on a part-time, job-share, or flexi-time basis. Alternatively, could the job be automated? Organizations, while conducting manpower rationalization drives, manage the scenarios post job cuts through various innovative methods.

To combat the situation arising out of recessionary trends in the global steel market, the two major corporations in India—Tata Steel and SAIL—went on a manpower rationalization drive in the early part of the millennium. The reorganization of work was carried out with such detailed planning that while Tata Steel's head count fell from 48,821 employees in FY'01 to 46,234 employees in FY'02; its per employee sales was 76 tons in FY'02, which was 9.7% higher against its previous year's (FY'01) figure of 70 tons. In value terms, the company recorded a marginal rise of 3.5% from ₹15.9 lakh per

Exhibit Some Findings of a Hiring Attrition and Compensation Trend Survey 2016 Across 410 Organizations

The experience level having most opportunities in 2016–2017

- Freshers 7%
- 1–3 years 35%
- 4–7 years 44%
- 8–15 years 12%
- 15+ years 2%

The top avenues for recruiting

- Consultants 30%
- Job portals 25%
- Referrals 20%
- Campus 10%
- Internals 9%
- Advertisements 4%
- Social media 2%

The hiring scenario across companies in 2016–2017

- 45% both new vacancies and replacement vacancies
- 21% new vacancies will be created
- 19% replacement hiring against attrition only
- 11% no hiring
- 4% lay-offs

Source: Adapted from a research conducted by Genius Consultants.

employee in FY'01 to ₹16.5 lakh in FY'02. Similarly, SAIL, with an employee strength of 1.48 lakh, also saw an increase in its employee productivity. Its staff strength declined to 1.48 lakh from the previous year's count of 1.57 lakh. This resulted in a marginal increase in per employee sales from ₹10.6 lakh in 2001 to ₹10.8 lakh in 2002.

The next step is the stage where the jobs are analyzed in minute detail to cull out the requirements of skill. The choice is for the organization to adopt approaches suiting its needs—whether based on competencies or the classical processes of job analyses resulting in formal job descriptions and job specifications. The exercise should ideally throw up specifications accurately describing the duties and requirements of the job as also the skills, aptitudes, knowledge, experience, qualifications, and personal qualities required to discharge the responsibilities in an appropriate manner. Due attention needs to be paid to enable the recruiter to use precise methods to measure and elicit information concerning such skills/competencies.

The next stage, recruitment—the commencement of the core recruitment process—aims at attracting candidates so as to create a pool of appropriate number of eligible candidates within acceptable cost limits. This stage includes recruitment planning and recruitment strategy development.

Several factors determine the concept of the so-called 'right' person for a particular organization. In the same way, multiple factors work together to make an organization attractive to such target candidates. In drawing up its recruitment plan, the organization aims to align the interests of the two parties by creating incentives for the most desirable candidates to apply, while keeping out the less qualified candidates from the mix. Through the recruitment process, organizations primarily try to attract the highest possible number of candidates and then filter out to select people who have the best potential and fit their specific criteria. Organizations that recruit the more qualified applicants are typically ones that have a larger applicant pool. Questions have, however, been raised whether there can be any magic number of applications for a given vacancy or whether there is any strategic importance for obtaining a high volume of applicants. It is also difficult to generate a benchmarked process for recruiting applicants.

There are various strategies adapted by organizations to lure the desired candidates. One obvious method to attract new employees is compensation and benefits. Organizations follow strategies for paying same, more or less than the competitors. Generally, however, most organizations that compete in the same market space tend to match each other's compensation packages and benefits within a reasonable range. As a consequence, when the differentiation becomes negligible in financial package, what influences the decision process for prospective recruits are numerous other aspects. This includes job satisfaction, quality of work life in the corporate culture, company policies, and the general atmosphere of the work environment. It has been suggested by scholars that because applicants have incomplete information about organizations, they interpret information they receive as signals about the organizations' working conditions. This constitutes the signaling theory, which attempts to explain communication through various signals.

Some of the strategies organizations use to provide such signals include promotional gifts, pre-placement talks, print and digital advertisements, and use of company Websites. These actions constitute employer branding which can be described as the aggregate of an organization's intentional endeavors to communicate to current and potential employees that it is a great place to work. In this context, it needs to be mentioned that an organization must first ascertain certain attributes about its target individuals. According to the Randstad 2008 World of Work study, the Generation Y attaches relatively greater importance to their work life, and therefore many of the old rules of thumb in recruitment

Table 4.1 What millennials look for in employers?

Factors	Rank	Percentage (approx.)
People and culture fit	1	78
Career potential	2	75
Work–life balance	3	74
Compensation	4	62
Challenging environment	5	50
Company mission	6	41
Innovation	7	22
New graduate program	8	21
Market leadership	9	17
Target audience	10	15
Alumni and friends	11	15

Source: Adapted from a study conducted over 15,000 millennials by CollegeFeed. Sanjeev Agrawal, 'How Companies Can Attract the Best College Talent,' *Harvard Business Review*, March 17, 2014. Available at: https:// hbr.org/2014/03/how-companies-can-attract-the-best-college-talent (accessed on December 6, 2017).

strategies are clearly obsolete. Some of these factors have also been suggested in a Harvard Business Review article 'How Companies Can Attract the Best College Talent' (Table 4.1). This explains the increasing use of the social media to connect with the prospective Gen Y candidates. Great influence is exerted by LinkedIn, Twitter, and Glassdoor. It has, however, been observed that candidates are impressed considerably by a good reputation of an organization. An organization's reputation is built through several influencers, one of the most impactful and positive influencers being the occasional award of 'Best Employer.' These awards showcase the positive aspects of working for a particular company and publicize it to potential employees. For example, TCS was recognized in 2016 by the award of 'Global Top Player' by the Top Employers Institute.

> In its assessment of 1072 employers worldwide, the Top Employers Institute rated TCS as an exceptional performer across nine core HR areas including talent strategy, workforce planning, onboarding, L&D, performance management and leadership development, among others. This certification is only awarded to the best employers in the world—organizations that demonstrate the highest standards of employee offerings, the institute said. Others included in the list include CJSC Technip, DHL, Dimension data, Saint Gobain, JT International, Mobinil, Mobistar, Orange and Valeo.[7]

Finally, a potential candidate is also influenced by the contact with the recruiter. In an article[8] written for *Academy of Management Journal* in 1992, Dougherty and Turban reported on the impact of perceived recruiter behavior and attributes on potential candidates, leading to attraction to a particular organization. This highlights the critical importance of choosing the right person to front the organization while dealing with the potential candidates. Some people fit into this role, and excel

[7] *The Times of India Tech*, 'TCS Recognized as Global Top Employer,' February 29, 2016. Available at: https://www.gadgetsnow. com/tech-news/TCS-recognized-as-Global-Top-Employer/articleshow/51195943.cms (accessed on November 24, 2017).

[8] T. W. Dougherty and D. B. Turban, 'Influences of Campus Recruiting on Applicant Attraction to the Firm,' *Academy of Management Journal* 35, no. 4 (1992): 739–765.

in the task of recruiting, while others may need training on how to interest potential candidates to an organization. Dougherty and Turban proceed to comment that a friendly recruiter raises a vision of a warm, friendly work environment to the aspiring employee. The good recruiters go even further to influence the applicants' confidence powerfully to make it through the interview process successfully to merit an offer.

The objective of the next stage—screening—is to make available an adequate number of qualified candidates, based on which a selection can be done in a smooth manner without loss of time over volumes of unsuitable applications. Search firms eminently serve the purpose by providing a small, manageable number of suitable candidates in a relatively cost-effective and professional manner, in comparison to the traditional mode of advertisement campaigns which often require special efforts for eliminating mountainous heaps of ineligible applicants. The choice of method will also be influenced by the availability of candidates, that is, whether there is a likelihood to have a shortage or surplus of candidates?

Exhibit Recruitment Dilemmas for Alectek Shoes

Alectek Shoes is one of the oldest footwear manufacturers and marketers in India with a sizeable market share in the industry. It also exports considerable portions of its premium segment products to overseas markets. This company has a workforce of over 11,000 employees. Being an old company, most of its HR policies are conventional and empirical. Based on its bitter experience in the past, the top management is of firm conviction that candidates with a revolving door approach toward a job are less committed and prone to leave the organization early. The recruitment philosophy and policy of this company clearly reflected this, and thus discriminated against those candidates who changed their jobs frequently in the past. In fact, the HR people were instructed to eliminate the applicants with a poor track record of job stability, irrespective of their levels of skills and abilities. Since its compensation packages are the best in the industry, the company had so far never faced any problem in finding the required number of people to fill the job positions.

Recently, the company developed a huge manufacturing facility in a metropolitan city located in southern India in order to double its production capacity. As part of this expansion plan, it decided to strengthen the manufacturing, sales, and marketing divisions with increased workforce. It conducted a major recruitment drive for filling all the new vacancies in addition to the routine ones. The company ran an extensive advertisement campaign to attract the best candidates for filling the available job positions.

The response to the campaign was good and many prospective candidates applied for the advertised positions. However, the scrutiny of these applications revealed that a significant number of these candidates had poor job stability records, as they seemed to have worked in different companies for short tenures. But for this shortcoming, these candidates were found to be suitable for the offered positions. The company was now in a dilemma. If these candidates were eliminated, the company might not get a sufficient number of candidates with the required skills for filling all the existing vacancies. In contrast, if they were selected, the firm ran the risk of unanticipated and untimely employee desertions and the resultant work disruptions.

Discussion Question

1. What would be your recommendation to the leadership?

Source: Excerpted from Dr Pravin Durai, 'Case Study Resisting for Change in Recruitment Policy with Times,' *Business Manager*, June 3, 2016.

The last stage in core recruitment activity is selection. The shortlist of candidates generated at the end of the recruitment stage is finally funneled on the basis of a choice of instruments into the desired number of candidates who are to be offered employment. Unlike the other stages of recruitment, where the candidate remains in the background, this is the only stage in recruitment processes in which the candidate has a direct and most powerful interface with the organization. It is also potentially the most negative part of the process, where the candidate faces rejection. A critical success factor in selection stage is the choice of instruments of assessment that can accurately predict the job-fit perfect person. Interviews, in various forms, still rule the selection roost in most organizations. Interviewing warrants specific competence building and skilled interviewers are more likely to gauge the suitability of a candidate than inexperienced ones. The techniques of interviews also vary in effectiveness depending on whether it is carefully structured or not.

The post-selection stage starts with the new recruit. The first step in it is orientation/onboarding. Onboarding aims at making the new recruits engaged and productive in a short time through a series of structured activities. Orientation process is intended to familiarize the new hires about the organization's policies and practices, the benefits, and the culture through a process of socialization. Effective, carefully planned orientation and onboarding processes can reduce startup costs and prevent employee turnover by helping new employees to adjust to their job and work environment with a positive attitude and increasing motivation.

Placement is the allotment of individuals to specific jobs after a reasonable period of observation and assessment. It is based on several factors including skill level, work and educational experience, interview results, references, and consultation between the line and the HR function. Following placement, ongoing training programs enable the fresh hires to become comfortable and increasingly proficient in performing their jobs.

The last stage of the recruitment process is the stage of performance appraisal. The performance of the new employee has been monitored over a period of time and feedback given on periodical review of performance. The employee starts getting familiar with a key business process of goal setting, performance tracking, and feedback/reviews for improvement. The end point of the recruitment process cycle is also where the rubber meets the road, and the real test of an effective recruitment policy is in the performance of the new recruits to an acceptable standard.

4.6 EVALUATION OF RECRUITMENT PROCESS

Recruitment process, like all processes, must submit to periodic checks and analytics for efficacy (Table 4.2).

The standard parameters to evaluate recruitment process are quality, speed, and time; it could be applied further to sources and also to the perspectives of the candidates, and the stakeholders (the LMs). Several researches have been reported on each of the aspects. For example, a study of 10 different sources by more than 20,000 applicants for the job of insurance agent revealed that recruitment source only accounted for marginal variation in quality and survival of new recruits and no variance in commissions. It also came out on research that in campus recruitment, students often had negative perception of the recruitment representative's knowledge of the job and the tendency to believe unfavorable information.[9]

---

[9] W. Cascio, *Managing Human Resources: Productivity, Quality of Work Life, Profits* (New Delhi: Tata McGraw-Hill, 2002).

Table 4.2 An illustrative recruitment metrics table

Metric	The question
1. No. of hires per source	Where are the best candidates coming from?
2. Time per stage	How long in each stage?
3. Referral rates	How many hires from employees?
4. Candidate status	How many candidates have reached the hiring stage?
5. Time to hire	How long is it taking to hire?
6. Aging of requisitions	What time since requisition until placement?
7. Present to interview	What ratio between no. of candidates present and no. of candidates
8. Offer acceptance ratio	How many selected candidates accepted the offer?
9. Line manager satisfaction	What is the performance of the new hire?
10. New hire retention	How many new joinees leaving within first two years?
11. Applicant satisfaction	What is the satisfaction with the selection process?
12. Applicant source ROI	Which source is most productive in producing successful

Due to the explosion of the big data analytics, it is possible to leverage technology to monitor the effectiveness of the recruitment process in an organization. The applicant tracking systems (ATS) and candidate relationship management (CRM) systems are known to have nearly 2,500 data points about each prospective candidate, for recruiting managers to analyze. The issue, however, does not seem to be the availability of data, but rather which questions to ask, which data points to select, and how to discern data to predict trends. So, understanding the linkage between business strategy and recruitment is crucial. For example, if the organization needs predictive analytics, then traditional recruitment metrics would be futile, and in case it is the reverse scenario, then the metrics would be too sophisticated to yield any benefit.

Today's organizations have the choice to move beyond recruitment analytics into predictive analytics. It is believed that with predictive analytics organizations can guess which sourcing channel will provide top talent; or match ideal candidates to open positions; or which candidates to hunt, given the data on their job-seeking behavior; or even select the right time to contact potential candidates with a new job offer.

4.7 RECRUITMENT STRATEGY

4.7.1 Internal Recruitment

The recruiting activities against an identified vacancy in most organizations starts with internal search for suitable candidates, the rationale being that should eligible candidates be internally available, and the organization still ignores them and brings in external candidates, such a step will severely undermine the employee morale. Besides, it is also likely to create a negative employer brand and may discourage potential employees from joining the organization fearing career stagnation.

Internal recruitment is normally done in large organizations where employees in a different department may not be aware of job openings in a particular department. Some of the methods that can be used in internal recruitment include career ladders, job postings within the organization, and employee referrals. Internal recruitments are often preferred being cost-effective, faster and easier than external recruitment, great motivators for employees intent on career progress, as they are secure candidates already culture fit and adapted to the organization practices.

Job Posting

Job posting, the procedure to communicate to employees that vacancies exist, is the simplest method used to find qualified applicants from inside the organization. In earlier times the posting would be done in the form of a notice displayed on the internal notice board. The practice is now replaced widely by electronic notices or intranets or emails to all employees. In its model form, job posting should contain clear details about the position, the requisite qualifications, the manner of application, and be accessible to all employees. Job postings can ensure that opportunities are available to all sections of employees without discriminations. The credibility of the process gets undermined when employees believe the organization has already preselected an internal candidate or the LM refuses to sponsor the candidate on grounds of not having suitable replacements.

Employee Referrals

Employee referral is used by organizations to source potential candidates from their existing employees' social networks. Under an employee referral scheme, when a current employee refers a successful candidate to fill a job vacancy, the employer rewards the sponsoring employee with a referral bonus or merchandise. This method of recruiting candidates through employee referral is generally believed to be the most cost effective and efficient method of recruitment and, therefore, employers of all sizes, across all industries, endeavor to maximize the intake through this channel. A Global Employee Referral Index 2013 Survey[10] reported that 92% of the participants preferred employee referrals as one of the top recruiting sources for recruiting.

Employee referral schemes are intended to ensure candidate quality, 'fit,' and retention levels, while at the same time delivering a significant reduction in recruitment expenditure. It engages the employees, reinforces and celebrates them in a tangible way for contributing to the company's success. On the negative side, an overreliance on employee referrals could limit diversity in the workplace.

Exhibit Employee Referrals Schemes in Corporate India

In corporate India, the top 100 companies extensively use employee referral programs with their own referral platforms. Accenture India fills a substantial chunk of its positions through referrals any given year. It offers various incentives to employees—monetary benefit, and even a promotion or other incentivized perks. It differs from each business unit to another and also depends on the candidature. The benefits are even bigger for referring women candidates. The referral programs are considered critical for niche skills and executive positions. At Infosys, employee referrals are one of the key channels for lateral hiring. There is a portal where employees can view requirements, directly submit the profiles of candidates and also can track the status of their referral in real time. Infosys offers monetary rewards defined for different job levels.

At auto major Maruti Suzuki India, the recruitment process is divided into two categories: campus recruitment and lateral recruitment. For lateral recruitments, the job of sourcing is done with the help of internal job postings and employee referrals, besides using the reach of

10 A Global Employee Referral Index 2013 Survey. Available at: https://www.prnewswire.com/news-releases (accessed in February 2014).

the corporate Website and job portals, and the good offices of placement consultants. The first preference for lateral recruitment is given to employee referrals and internal job postings, which together comprise 40% of the lateral recruitments. Likewise, at Ernst & Young, employee referral contributes to 55% of the total hiring, which is a benchmark in this space. Referral hiring lowers the cost of overall hiring by approximately 50–75% across levels.

Several start-ups and job sites are now offering unique platforms to facilitate the referral process. Naukri.com has an interesting referral platform called Hot Vacancies platform, targeted at SMEs and non-IT (those who lack a specific knowledge about how to execute an internal referral) that will cost a company between ₹75,000 and ₹1 lakh annually. The platform enables recruiters to design their own internal referral campaign and upload the email addresses of their employees. Employees can then broadcast this to their social media groups and alumni networks. Once a candidate applies back, the platform is able to tag it to the person who referred it. Among its other offerings, the portal has a shortlisting tool and the Naukri Recruiter, which is free. By using the shortlisting tool, a recruiter can shortlist five resumes from at many as 2000 responses in five minutes flat. The Naukri Recruiter scan saves a company 40–50% of its recruiting cost.

Round One, founded in 2011, has a unique model that incentivizes employees in companies to interact with job seekers. If found suitable, employees can refer suitable candidates for jobs. It works on the premise that, at times, employees are unable to find the right candidate to refer from their own social circle. By providing an alternate network of suitable and qualified candidates, Round One helps employees refer the right candidates and help them increase their efficiency. Round One charges a membership fee from job seekers, but the sum is small—₹50—for lifetime access to request referrals from any employee at any company. When a potential job-seeker is accepted by a potential referrer for an interaction for a particular job, it charges a fee of ₹500, ₹700, or ₹800 depending on the seniority of the candidate. This ensures that only job seekers interested in that job speak with the referrer. Round One has 7 lakh registered users.

Whistletalk, a Bangalore-based start-up, has a social hiring application that enables employees and hiring managers to find the best talent at the earliest. It sells a monthly subscription-based service to the corporates and the charges are calculated on the basis of the number of employees the company has and the job openings at the company.

Source: Adapted from Ankita Rai, 'Referral Hiring can Bring Down Hiring Costs for India Inc,' *Business Standard,* July 22, 2013.

Career Ladders

In business, career ladder describes the advancement from lowest rung up the ladder with growth in pay, skill, responsibility, or authority. This metaphor is spatially oriented and frequently used to denote upward mobility within a stratified promotion model. Since the ladder does not provide for lateral movement, it is assumed to be a singular track with the greatest benefits at the top. Career management programs are offered by reputed organizations by which the employee can follow the path through training and assignments to advance his/ her career in the organization in a self-directed manner. Dual-career ladder programs are prevalent in some industries, such as engineering, scientific, and medical industries, where valued employees, with high technical skills but disinclined for management career path, can progress in technical ladder.

Temporary/Contingent Workers Pool

Currently, organizations manage their seasonal and short-term work through engagement of workers with different names—casual employees, badlis, temporary employees, fixed-term contract workers, or contract/ contingent employees. Jute and textile mills, where demands were often seasonal, even the temporaries had several categories: temporary badlis, badlis, and permanent badlis. There is a time-honored practice in most of the traditional businesses to fill up part or all of their entry-level vacancies from this pool of temporary workmen. An emerging practice in some organizations is to re-engage retired personnel on fixed terms.

4.7.2 External Recruitment

In order to create a wide enough pool of suitable candidates, organizations turn to external labor market, which are known to vary depending upon the size of the organization. Larger the size of the organization and bigger the recruitment purse, more varied is the choice of sources. Some of the key external sources of recruitment are campus recruitment, executive search firms, and Web-based recruitment.

Reflection Point

There is generally a rule in most educational institutions that once a candidate accepts an offer from a company, they are not allowed to attend any further interviews of other companies that visit thereafter.

Discussion Question

1. Does not it appear like a gamble for those who get selected early? Are there ways in which the rule can be tweaked for a fairer system?

Campus Recruitment

Engineering/technical colleges and business schools are happy hunting grounds for recruiters, for entry-level positions. According to an Aon-Hewitt survey over 95 organizations, in the automotive and auto components industry, junior-level hiring is set to accelerate, comprising 56% of open positions. Aon found that while two-thirds of companies in the automotive and auto components industry planned to fill their entry-level positions by recruiting from campuses, with globalization, Indian companies are going for global campuses, and the global MNCs have been regular recruiters at premier Indian engineering colleges such as the IITs and the business schools such as the IIMs. Campus recruitments are expensive, and the attrition at entry levels is high.

> The traditional concept of 'campus' is slowly undergoing a makeover.
>
> SASTRA University, Thanjavur, has inked a deal with the Bangalore-based global support center of Microsoft India to provide students with hands-on experience on technical services. The partnership will enable students of the deemed university to enhance their career potential by making use of tools and facilities offered at the varsity by the Global Technical Support Center of the Indian subsidiary of the US software giant.[11]

It is being increasingly felt that for the campus recruitment process to yield results for the company, it needs to have a well-planned structure, on the basis of a long-term association with specific institutes. Some organizations leverage this relationship through intake of interns. Mobil is known to have pruned down their choice of campuses from erstwhile 200 to about 50, and the recruitment is carried out

11 'Microsoft Opens Tech Lab at Sastra University.' TNN. Available at: https://www.gadgetsnow.com/jobs (accessed on December 20, 2013).

by dedicated teams, composed mostly of alumni. Mobil Foundation sponsors activities in campuses through the year. The campus recruiting is thus given a wider scope in the form of university relations which indicate an ongoing corporate–academic interface for mutual benefit.

Advertisements

For open positions, organizations may place advertisements in the print media (local newspapers, trade journals) or radio/television. Advertising can be a short 'Positions Vacant' ad in the classifieds to an extensive multimedia campaign. Some organizations rely solely on online applications; some follow a mixed bag of online, print, and campus. Traditionally, newspaper advertising was the preferred recruitment method, particularly for entry-level positions, as it generated a vast volume of applicants.

Internet Recruiting

The emergence and growth of online recruiting can be described as the most significant change in recruiting practices for a long time. Job portals such as Monster.com, Naukri.com, and TimesJobs have large databases which help the recruiters access adequate number of profiles within a short time. Currently, companies routinely post job openings on their Websites or on specialized sites such as CareerBuilder and Monster.com. Some companies have moved ahead and consider only online applications, thus completely doing away with the convention of hardcopy applications. There are certain benefits for online recruiting. In the first place, online recruiting is cheaper than advertising. Posting an ad is easy and fast, responses come more quickly and in larger volume, and there is normally a far greater number of applicants. Online processes can also be made to serve multiple purposes to reduce the HR time for creating a list of eligible candidates including applications screening, administration of some selection tests, and the like. The prospective candidates like the online format because they are able to send out as many resumes as they want with a few actions. Of course, while the ease of applying for an online vacancy can result in greater number of applications, HR staff requires to spend more time sorting through applications to screen out ineligible candidates.

Executive Search Firms

In the beginning, until the 1990s, most recruitments for senior levels were done through newspaper ads, or through informal and unstructured channels, or through local recruitment agencies (only a handful of them such as Ferguson and later ABC Consultants). This resulted in a largely unpredictable process, with a contingent model of pricing for the search firm, as opposed to being retained for a search. In the contingency model, the hiring company gets paid only if a candidate recommended by the recruitment firm ultimately joins the organization. The candidates used to target the destination companies or steady state companies with the purpose of settling down. With the coming of the international firms, the processes became more rigorous and formal and there was due diligence in mapping and assessment, and thereby the fees were based on retained exclusive model, whereby the company gets specific requirement exclusively to one provider and the retained executive search firm gave a commitment to find the right person for that position. Gradually around 2006–2007, the executive search position picked up pace.

Currently, most senior-level roles are filled through executive search firms or through references and seldom through advertisement in whatever channel. Starting in the mid-1990s most global executive search firms (Egon Zander, Corn Ferry, and Russel Raynaulds, to name a few) have their footprints in India. Today, the candidate profile has changed. As the market exploded in the early part of the millennium, it provided opportunities to young managers to become CEOs in their mid-30s. Today

Exhibit Current Trends in Recruiting

Employee referrals and direct hiring channels such as LinkedIn, Facebook, Twitter, and company Websites, considered fads at one time, now contribute 70–90% of hires for companies. The once-dominant HR consultants now hire only for critical and niche roles, add up to 20% of the overall pool of hires and resulting in huge cost savings for organizations.

'Due to the slowdown, companies have turned more aggressively towards internal and cost effective channels. It works better as they can wait for a good fit, unlike in a booming market,' says Shiv Agrawal, MD, ABC Consultants. Sectors where these channels are used more often are information technology, IT-enabled services, telecom, BFSI, and start-ups. And the benefits work both ways.

Employees too are motivated to refer others due to cash incentives, rewards in kind, the satisfaction of getting someone a job, and the opportunity to work with like-minded people. The trend has picked up over the past two to three years, post the Lehman Brothers collapse, as companies began looking for cost-effective, efficient avenues for hiring.

If Aircel gets more than 90% of its hires through referrals, LinkedIn, Facebook, direct walk-ins, and unsolicited emails, Cognizant gets 80–85% of recruits, Crisil 75–80%, and EXL 73% through non-consultant channels. Companies like Aircel report saving up to 70% in recruitment costs annually.

Aircel has hired around seven candidates for positions of GM and above in the past three to six months and has reduced its dependence on HR consultants for filling vacant positions to 7% from 30% in 2010. Of the 90 positions that get filled every month, 45 are through referrals.

Aircel offers a cash reward of ₹10,000 per hire. EXL (with 43% coming through referrals) gives a cash reward of ₹4,000–15,000, gold and silver coins, and cars. Cognizant's referral program, called 'Bring Another You,' contributes 40% of the total pool of employees, and offers cash prizes of 5000–50,000, paid vacation, cars, and even double referral money for niche, hard-to-find skills.

At Cognizant, recruitment through referrals has increased by 10–15% in the past three years. Referrals provide higher joining rates, better performance ratings, and higher interview-to-offer conversions as compared to other channels of recruitment, he adds. 'The conversion rate for offers made through our employee referral program is 10–15% more than those made through recruitment firms,' says Rajagopal.

Besides a more focused use of recruiter and management time, candidates, especially at senior levels, stay on longer than those who join through other recruitment modes, he says.

Other direct channels such as company Websites and walkins too have been effective in bringing down the dependence on HR consultants for recruitment. At EXL, they provide 29% of candidates. Rating agency CRISIL gets almost 35% of its hires through postings on its company Website, more than the 30% it gets through referrals. The company has designed an interface and an automated CV screening process.

'Direct channels have their limitations. Employee referral is a limited pool of resource, and while social or professional networks have grown phenomenally, at some level, crowded networks don't work effectively,' says K. Sudarshan, managing partner, EMA Partners International, India.

The market is currently facing a low tide with companies using internal hiring sources to the fullest but when the tide turns, fishing in a small pond (referrals and direct channels) will not work much, says Manish Sabharwal, chairman, TeamLease. 'Most people, especially at the top, are passive job seekers and it needs a lot of ground work to convince them for a switch.'

Source: Shreya Biswas, 'Social Media Critical in India Inc's Recruitments,' ET Bureau, December 21, 2013.

aspiring chief executives (CXOs) no longer live in geographical cache, but are available globally through Internet and mobile networks. They do not look for cradle-to-grave companies, but rather evolutionary companies that guarantee fast growth and zooming compensation.

Other than executive search firms, there are several temping firms or staffing firms (project manpower and seasonal work) and recruitment process outsourcing agencies. Most of these agencies use job descriptions and specifications given by the organization to create an applicant pool, conduct the initial interviews, screen out unqualified candidates, and send the shortlist. This process saves time, but costs more in the form of retention or contingent fees by the agency. Other sources of external recruitment are Employment Exchange (compulsory for certain categories of employees in PSUs) which can produce lists of candidates based on skill, education, age, and other factors on the basis of requisition.

Google uses the following recruitment tools:

- A social media platform that includes an #askagoogler Twitter feed and 2 million videos posted on YouTube
- Google Games, a recruitment event where students team up and solve mind-bending puzzles
- Google Code Jam, a competition where over 14,000 global programmers compete to solve complex coding challenges in a limited amount of time
- Campus recruiting, where students are invited to Tech Talks and open houses
- Google Student Ambassador program, a program that gives students the opportunity to learn about new Google products and services, while also offering feedback from their own university experience

In India, an increasing talent scarcity has plagued the Indian hiring market during the past decade or so with a handful of talented employees calling the shots, and getting the companies to offer excellent compensation packages. IT–ITeS sector has become a highly competitive market, with soaring employee turnover and a widening supply–demand gap.

The prevailing recruitment practices of India Inc. include a variety of sources: job fairs, online talent auctions, talent referral programs, job sites, and walk-in tours of employer campuses. Private sector firms are also poaching into public sector companies and the armed forces. In the war for talent, companies are formulating a combination of strategies to stay ahead of the competition. This includes campus recruitments, internal job postings, employee referrals, availing the services of placement consultants, participating in job fairs, and advertising in newspapers and job portals.

Till about a decade, newspaper advertisements ruled the roost in external recruitment. The need to save cost has triggered an increasing trend to use the Web portals. Online recruiting has been gathering momentum, with the first wave seeing the emergence of Naukri.com. While job portals continue to play a major role in the recruitment process, the second wave (Web 2.0) has been unleashed by social networking Websites such as LinkedIn, Orkut, Facebook, and others. In 2004, the contribution of portals in the recruitment mix was 2%, whereas it is now close to 12% and is being done through job portals. However, the print media still rules the external recruitment market in India with a firm grip on the majority share.

Some of the regular strategies used by MNCs in India:

- Walk-in sessions
- Head hunting

- E-recruiting
- Employee referrals and internal job posting
- Social networking
- Campus recruitment
- Targeting public sector employees, ex-servicemen
- Hiring housewives, senior citizens, fresh school graduates for part-time work
- Partnering with educational and training institutes
- Job fairs

There are as many different methods of recruiting as there are organizations, and there is no one best method for recruiting job applicants. Most organizations use a variety of methods, depending on the nature of the job to be filled, the time needed to properly fill the position, and the size of their recruiting budget. Your organization may already have a valid track record for recruiting and that will determine what methods work best for your situation.

4.8 SELECTION

Case Choice of Criteria for Selection

'What kind of dinosaur would you be?' is a question that Google and other Silicon Valley companies have been known to pose to candidates. Wacky and unexpected, the question is meant to judge the aspirant's ability to think creatively and beyond the obvious.

When Nikhil Tiwari, a final-year student at the National Institute of Industrial Engineering (NITIE) in Powai was shortlisted for a multinational apparel company, he was asked to arrive at the college ground at 7 AM on the day of his interview. The company was conducting an ice-breaker football match between students and the senior management.

'The organization conducted the match to break the ice between managers and candidates. Over kicks and running from post to post, we found out more about what these managers are really like,' says 26-year-old Tiwari.

To hire the best talent for managerial positions, companies are beginning to use increasingly innovative practices, such as asking candidates to dance, record three-minute videos of themselves, and showcase their sports skills. While a written test and an interview were considered sufficient a few years ago, recruiters have begun giving weightage to group discussions, case study analysis, and stress interviews.

'Often, management students have roughly the same technical background, since they have undergone the rigorous admissions process,' says Tiwari. 'A differentiating factor is more likely to emerge if they are surprised.'

'Often, individual HR managers innovate recruitment strategies, depending on the firm's requirements. Students from our college have been invited to a dinner party so that they can be observed, while others have had their interviews taking place in the college garden instead of a closed room,' says Kanwal Kapil, chairperson, placement committee at Management Development Institute (MDI), Gurgaon.

As a candidate, do not be concerned by the confusing questions and tricks. Instead, decipher the recruiter's real purpose. For example, you do not have to know about fossils and reptiles to answer the dinosaur question impressively. 'This is actually a 'describe yourself' question and not a scientific or knowledge-based one,' says Shubham Yadav, final-year student of IIT Bombay, who is placed with Tanaka Holdings, a core-engineering firm in Japan. 'My answer to this would have been—I want to be the dinosaur that would grow into becoming the CEO of this company.'

'In the open-floor corporate life, employees have to constantly alter between roles. This requires improvisation and the ability to think on the go,' says Suman Nair, Managing Director, Atiitya Training and HR Consultants Pvt. Ltd 'Companies are now finding ways to measure that.'

Uncommon Questions

HR interviews are moving beyond the 'Where will you see yourself in five years?' type of questions. According to students, interviews are becoming longer, and more unexpected. Says Neelanjan Bhattacharya, a final-year student of MDI, Gurgaon: 'A student from our college mentioned salsa dancing as one of his interests. His interviewer, the vice-president of the multinational conglomerate, asked him to show them a few salsa moves. He ended up doing a jig with the VP.'

Another student from Narsee Monjee Institute of Management Studies (NMIMS), Vile Parle, Mumbai, was asked to do push-ups and kicks when he said he had a black belt in karate. Such anecdotes define a changing attitude in managers. 'This is the opposite of a stress interview, which involves rapid interrogation-type questioning. Here, students are judged on their confidence, ability to react without stressing, and their honesty,' says Ankit Bawa, final-year student at NMIMS.

Group Games

Teamwork is a major concern at firms today and companies are looking for people who can handle and gauge group dynamics. 'No one wants to hire a person who has an attitude problem against group work,' says Nair of Atiitya Training and HR Consultants. 'They want to pre-empt any problem that could form between colleagues as far as possible, to decrease attrition rates.'

At NITIE this year, a consulting company divided candidates into groups and distributed flash cards. 'Each flashcard had a clue we had to decode together, while the recruiters observed us,' says Tiwari from NITIE.

Moving Toward Multimedia

During summer placements at SP Jain Institute, a consulting firm insisted on video resumes from all its candidates to gauge their confidence. Each student had to record a three-minute video explaining their academic, professional, and cocurricular background.

'To make my digital resume distinct, I began by talking about my passions, which include adventure sports and poetry writing,' says Devavrat Wazalwar, 25, a second-year student at SP Jain. 'I went ahead with describing my previous work experience and the rest of my background.'

'We willingly put in that extra effort of suiting up, writing a 'script', and recording. For the recruiters, the videos made shortlisting easier,' he adds.

Discussion Question

1. Which criteria in your opinion should have greater weightage in selection of a candidate interviews, psychometric instruments, written tests, or job simulation? What are your reasons?

Source: Deeksha Gautam, 'Hiring Managers Are Changing the Game by Making Campus Recruitments Innovative,' *Hindustan Times*, December 17, 2014.

Selection is the process by which an employer uses certain methods to select candidates from a shortlisted group leading to an employment decision. For the candidates, this is the stage in the entire recruitment cycle in which he/she comes in direct, face-to-face contact with the organization.

It is well established that an organization needs to develop effective selection systems which can ensure that it gets the right kind of employees on a sustained basis, who can contribute to the growth of the organization with good performance. Good performance has three essential cornerstones. In the first place, there should be a person–job fit, meaning that there is a perfect match between a person's competencies with the job specifications. Second, there should be a person–group fit, meaning that the employee should fit in with the immediate work group with certain shared beliefs and values, and have attributes, which either complement or support the characteristics of the work group. Finally, there should be a person–organization fit, implying that there is a perfect compatibility between the culture and values of the individual and the organization.

While recruitment is a positive chain of activities producing an optimum number of job-seekers, selection is inherently negative in that it will probably involve rejection of applicants. It would be prudent to argue that selection decisions should be based on a range of selection tools as some have poor predictive job ability.

In Accenture Consulting, for the position of a consultant, the entire recruitment process can take about 6 weeks from application until final offer. The selection process includes application form (with a word limit), the first interview (which includes a behavior-based interview and a case interview), assessment center with multiple individual and group exercises, and finally, a one-on-one interview. In the experience of a candidate, the process has different levels of rigors and time pressure, but the process is relevant to the actual job of a consultant and, therefore, credible.[12] It is but natural that organizational decision-makers will wish to ensure that their selection methods produce results. At the same time, making judgments on an individual's personal attributes and suitability for future employment is wrought with problems and that many conventional selection methods are seriously flawed. Whether the selection process is effective or not depends on three universally accepted criteria: reliability, validity, and utility.

Reliability indicates consistency of measurements. Reliability in the context of workforce selection can refer to the following issues: temporal or 're-test' stability where the effectiveness of a selection

[12] WikiJob, 'My Successful Experience of the Accenture Recruitment Process,' July 2, 2011. Available at: https://www.wikijob.co.uk/ forum/consultancy-consulting-firms/my-successful-experience-accenture-recruitment-process (accessed on September 21, 2017).

tool is assessed by consistency of results obtained over time. An individual could, for example, complete a Myers–Briggs Type Indicator (MBTI) or occupational personality questionnaire (OPQ) test at different times over a period of several years, although in the latter case it would be important to isolate the impact of repeated practice on results. Consistency, in this context, will mean asking a simple question: Does the test assess what it is intended to? For example, if the candidate is administered a psychometric instrument, the test scores would be almost the same even if administered more than once at a time gap of, say, a few months. There is a criticism that elements of IQ tests wrongly emphasizes a person's vocabulary, which could have been shaped by their education and general background, rather than by their innate intelligence.

Validity is described as the extent to which the selection method predicts one or more important criteria. There are two major kinds of validity: content validity and construct validity. Empirical or criterion validity involves the statistical relationships between performance or scores on some predictor or selection tool (interview, written test, and so on) and performance on some criterion measure such as the job effectiveness (sales, supervisory ratings, job turnover, employee theft, and so on). The statistical relationship is usually reported in a correlation coefficient. Higher correlation indicates stronger validity. Content validity assesses the degree to which the content of a section method assesses the requirements of the job. A knowledge-based test for chartered accountants could have content validity for the accountant job.

Another two-pronged classification of validity is face validity and predictive validity. Face validity is about the acceptability of the selection measure, including to the candidate himself or herself. For example, a candidate appearing for a supervisory position in a manufacturing factory will understand a question on the relation between labor laws and the job. He will, however, be skeptical of the questions on use of statistical tools for market segmentation. Predictive validity centers on linkages between results or scores on a selection measure and subsequent outcome—most commonly, job performance at a future point. Here it is important to identify when the comparison will be made, that is, immediately in the case of a simple job requiring little training, or more commonly, at an intermediate point, possibly after a suitable probationary period.

Utility concerns the commercial benefits accrued from the use of a selection method. The basic formula involves estimating the increase in revenue as a function of the use of the selection method after subtracting the cost of the method.

It is often argued by experts that validity and equity should underlie a good selection method in high-performance organizations. These validity measures, however, should be treated with caution because they can be affected by the performance indicators used and the tools applied. They indicate nonetheless both variability between measures and some overall degree of uncertainty when predicting future work performance during the selection process. While it is recommended that validity should be the prime factor in choosing selection tools, it would be naïve not to recognize that other factors such as cost and applicability may be relevant. How practical, therefore, is it to conduct any particular measure? As indicated earlier, an organization aiming for high performance is recommended to adopt valid measures as opposed to merely practical or less costly ones. Again, one should recognize that recruitment and selection is contingent upon other factors such as the work itself. A 'high performance' organization in the fast-food industry may legitimately decide not to adopt some relatively valid but expensive methods when selecting fast-food operatives. It should be noted that the oft derided method of interviewing can in reality be a relatively valid method if conducted skillfully and structured.

4.8.1 Selection Tools

In actual practice, interviews are virtually the centerpiece of the selection process in most organizations. Some organizations still rely almost exclusively on the outcome of interviews to make selection decisions. To have any value, interviews should be conducted or supervised by trained individuals, be structured to follow a previously agreed set of questions mirroring the person specification or job profile, and allow candidates the opportunity to ask questions. The interview is more than a selection device. It is an instrument that can effectively convey to the candidate relevant information about the job and the organization, almost as a realistic job preview contains details about the process, and thereby can reduce the possibility of the candidate spurning the employment offers. Organizations expecting to establish robust and high-performance selection system should, therefore, refrain from overemphasizing the use of interview and instead use a balanced and mixed process by combining interview process with the use of other psychometric tools, as considered suitable.

In order to have a balanced selection process, some of the options available are as follows:

1. **Work samples** Tests in which a sample of the job is performed by the candidate to ascertain his effectiveness in real situation.
2. **Cognitive tests** Generally used for entry-level jobs not requiring technical education. They test the candidate's mental ability to do the job.
3. **Structured interviews** Two kinds of structured interviews are common. Situational/ behavioral interviews use future scenarios with 'what if' questions, based on critical challenges in the job. Criterion-based questions are standard questions related to all aspects of the job prepared beforehand to test the technical knowledge or specific skills of the candidate.
4. **Assessment centers** In a span of 2–3 days of offsite camp, candidates are administered a battery of tests including role plays, group exercises, presentation, in-tray, and psychometric assessments under the watchful eyes of multiple assessors to comprehensively test the managerial and professional competencies of the candidate.
5. **Personality tests** Tests the person–job fit on parameters not available in the resume.
6. **Biodata or CV** Drawn from the biographical details of earlier successful role holders. It aims to predict the right kind of candidates who will succeed in the job.
7. **Unstructured interviews** Unplanned interviews, whose effectiveness will vary based on the experience and the skill of the interviewer.
8. **Reference checks** Feedback sought from the erstwhile superior officers of the candidate, based on information provided by him/her.
9. **Written tests** Tests to ascertain the technical knowledge of the candidate, especially for jobs requiring a threshold of technical knowledge.

All the aforementioned selection tools have varying degree of validity. While work samples, cognitive tests, and assessment centers are considered to have high validity, reference checks and unstructured interviews have low validity and the rest of the tests mentioned earlier range from high to moderate validity.

In situations where the organization has to source candidates from outside for strategic roles where the stakes are high, reputed organizations (Unilever, L'Oreal, and others) have tried out a completely new approach to selection known as competency-based selection. Competency–based selection adapts a two-step approach: initially the unique characteristics that differentiate the superior performers from the average on the specific role are identified through a process known as competency mapping; then, the candidates are tested on the given unique characteristics to determine the gap.

In a recruitment and selection practices survey report by Development Dimensions International (DDI), in August 1999[13] and conducted over 162 organizations, some of the findings related to best practices in selection are as follows:

1. Nearly all organizations use resumes and applications as part of their selection process.
2. Behavior-based interviews are widely used in selection systems.
3. Applicant testing and assessments are not widely used in typical selection systems.
4. Five characteristics differentiate highly effective from moderately effective selection systems:
   (a) Behavior-based interviews
   (b) Training and experience evaluations
   (c) Ability tests
   (d) Biographical data
   (e) Motivational fit inventories.
5. Use of behavior-based interviews are likely to increase substantially.
6. Computerized resume screening will become more popular.
7. Applicant testing and assessment will increase in future.
8. Effective selection systems linked to both higher business and employee outcomes.

To sum up, some of the best practices in recruitment and selections followed by organizations of repute globally are as follows:

1. Building a strong partnership between the recruitment managers and the search consultants
2. Marketing employer reputation or branding
3. Focusing on high ROI sourcing channels. Actively managing the entire candidate experience
4. Searching for knowledge and skills, and interviewing for behavior
5. Reducing administrative effort

4.9 FUTURE TRENDS IN RECRUITMENT

The shrunken volume of print advertisements, the clout of employee referrals as a preferred tool for sourcing, the ever-increasing cost pressure, and the huge canvass of the social media—all these portend ill for the traditional practice of recruitment and selection. The lifeline, however, is provided by the unabated war for talent. Employees with unique skills and competencies are likely be in demand, especially in certain roles, in most business organizations. The practice of recruitment has always been susceptible to dynamics, internal and external to the organization, particularly in respect of technology, globalization, work ethics, and economic factors. The disruptions in recruitment practices are already visible in trends such as employer branding, strategic sourcing, talent pooling, headhunting, candidate engagement, and gauging quality-of-hire and onboarding. The growing application of technology has seen the emergence of intelligent applicant tracking systems, online assessments, job adverts in

[13] Bernthal and Erker, 'Selection Forecast: Recruiting and Hiring Talent' (January 2005). Available at: https://www.ddiworld.com/ ddi/media (accessed on February 13, 2018).

visually appealing infographic formats, YouTube productions, use of mobile-friendly Websites and careers pages, and so on.[14]

As regards the recruiters themselves, the challenges pose great opportunities also. The recruitment agencies will be compelled to forge closer business partner relationships with companies, genuinely know their clients more intimately, and becoming truly a trusted partner. The recruitment function in the organization will learn to use ROI for recruitment planning and to better leverage the options of recruitment process outsourcing.

Closing Case What Ails the Selection Process at Inox?

Inox Corporation is one of India's largest IT services provider with gross revenue of US$5.03 billion in the past financial year. The company is into technology and process solutions at a global level. The company employs more than 85,000 people and is headquartered in Pune, India. The company is involved also in other sectors such as pharmaceuticals, manufacturing, and energy. The company was established in 1974 by Nitin Bhaskar who, along with his nephew and current CEO Sushil Bhaskar, transformed the company into one of the most reputed brands in India. The corporation is currently operating in four continents.

Inox is currently is India's eighth top employer. But the company has a poor track record in HRM, with high attrition and is not even in the top 20 best employers of the country (while some of their competitors are always in the top ten). The company visits all reputed engineering colleges every year in the months of September–October. The selection process is also structured in three rounds:

Round 1: Written Test

1. English Proficiency Paper and Pencil Test: A set of 15–20 questions are asked to test the candidates' proficiency in English language. It includes questions on English grammar related to synonyms, antonyms, similes, prepositions, and so on, and a comprehension passage.
2. Aptitude: Another set of 15–20 questions cover aptitude topics such as time and work, time and distance, puzzles, calendars, ratio proportions, ages, pipes, and such others.
3. Technical: This is quite an important part of the written test and involves 15–20 questions to test the technical knowledge of the applicants in C, C++, Java, Linux, UNIX, DBMS, SQL, programing fundamentals, hardware, software engineering, microprocessors, and so on. The questions are mainly based upon the technical aspects studied as a part of university syllabus.

Round 2: Technical Interview

Many candidates get eliminated at this stage. In this stage, the candidates must have thorough knowledge in the basic technical skills in order to get them cleared from there. Therefore, the candidates are asked to get prepared on their academic subjects before sitting for this round.

[14] Jonathan Rice, 'The Future of Recruitment,' *Human Resources* 17, no. 5 (December 2012/January 2013): 4–6.

Round 3: HR Interview

Considered to be the graveyard of candidates. A panel of HR experts ask questions on the family background, areas of interest, personal vision, preferences in career, and then probing further based on candidate responses. It also includes a panelist asking stress questions. The emotional quotient (EQ) of the candidate is tested in order to check whether he/she is able to withstand the pressures of the job. The other aspects that are tested here involve communication and vocabulary skills of the candidate.

Discussion Question

1. How would you recommend recasting the selection process to improve retention of new recruits by Inox?

SUMMARY

Recruitment and selection of the best-fit candidates is of critical importance for the successful execution of a firm's business strategy. Recruitment has been defined as 'the process of attracting individuals on a timely basis, in sufficient numbers, and with appropriate qualifications, to apply for jobs within an organization.' The central purpose of recruitment is to generate a pool of capable applicants. Selection, on the other hand, is the process by which specific instruments or techniques are used by HR specialists and also by the LMs to select from such a body of applicants a candidate or candidates, who have the potential ability to effectively perform the role within the boundaries of management goals and statutory requirements. A model recruitment and selection policy should have the following elements: respect for diversity, ethical decision-making, merit-based selection, equal treatment for all, and procedural fairness.

Recruitment is affected by two sets of factors: internal and external. The internal factors include primarily the recruitment policies of the organization, as described earlier. The other internal factors include: (a) a well-structured and comprehensive HR plan, which facilitates seamless sourcing of manpower in a systematic and appropriate manner; (b) the size of the firm, in as much as the complexities in recruitment planning and process are generally inversely connected with the largeness of the organization; (c) budgetary considerations—requiring pursuit of cost-effective ways of recruiting (e.g., use of social media instead of search firms); and (d) stage in the maturity cycle of the business, implying, for example, that an organization in a decline stage would be far less inclined for recruitment than an organization in the growth stage.

Currently, the preferred mode of recruitment is through use of social media like LinkedIn and Facebook, use of employee referrals and job fairs, and walk-in interviews for mass recruitments. Manpower staffing firms provide temporary employees for time-bound projects. Senior-level roles are filled through executive search firms or through references, and seldom through advertisement in whatever channel. Starting in the mid-1990s, most global executive search firms such as Egon Zander or Corn Ferry have their footprints in India. Today, the candidate profile has changed. As the market exploded in the early part of the millennium, it provided opportunities to young managers to become CEOs in their mid-thirties. Today, aspiring CXOs no longer live in geographical cache, but are available globally through Internet and mobile networks. They do not look for cradle-to-grave companies, but rather evolutionary companies that guarantee fast growth and zooming compensation.

Selection is the process by which an employer uses certain methods to select candidates from a shortlisted group leading to an employment decision. For the candidates, this is the stage in the entire recruitment cycle in which he/she comes in direct, face-to-face contact with the organization. The effectiveness of selection is judged on the basis of reliability, validity, and utility. Most commonly used selection instruments include written tests, interviews, assessment centers, and personality tests.

Discussion Questions

1. Following the restriction on H-1B visa by the USA, you have been asked to step up efforts to recruit locally in the USA by your CEO. What would you do differently while recruiting in the USA? What would be the critical factors?
2. Opportunity for career progression is one of the greatest motivators of employees, and you are sure that given T&D inputs, your bright employees can be moved up. Your CEO, however, wants you to recruit against some key positions from outside. What would you do?
3. What are the variations you need to make while formulating recruitment strategies for executives and unionized category of employees?
4. For selection, which among the following roles would be suitable for assessment centers?
   (a) India sales manager
   (b) Cashier
   (c) Peon
   (d) Production manager in a pharmaceutical plant

CLUSTER 3

DEVELOP AND GROW

Chapter 5
Training and Development

Chapter 6
Competency Management

Chapter 7
Career Management

According to a Bain report on the future trends in development of human capital, there has been a scarcity of management talent for some time in emerging markets 'as economic growth outstrips home-grown talent growth' and managers in advanced countries preferring entrepreneurship to employment. So, the prescription for companies that plan to expand in India, China, and other fast-emerging markets is to hire and grow—recruit promising managers early and invest in their training and retention, as finding fully capable managers in-market will be hard.[1]

Training and development (T&D), often low on priority and driven solely by the HR function in many companies, can, however, yield enormous value for the organization. Training allows employees to acquire new skills, sharpen existing ones, perform better, increase produc/tivity, and be better leaders. It is considered as a key activity to assist organizations in the HR development. According to Michael Porter, organizations that are highly committed to T&D and integrate such an approach into their culture tend to be more competitive[2] and reach higher levels of productivity and financial performance.[3]

With the emergence of competency studies, organizations have become capable of distinguishing superior from average or below average performance, and to adopt precise T&D plan for employees to bridge the measurable 'gaps' between job competencies or competency proficiency levels, necessary for their jobs, and the competency portfolio processed by the employee. Competency models also enable organizations to align their initiatives to their overall business strategy and thus recruit and select employees who are perfect fit for their organization's performance management, succession planning, and career development. Employers are able to use competencies studies to distinguish superior from average or below average performance.

1 Karen Harris, Austin Kim, and Andrew Schwedel, 'Developing Human Capital,' September 9, 2011. Available at: http://www.bain.com/publications/articles (accessed on August 2, 2017).

2 Michael Porter, *The Competitive Advantage of Nations* (New York, NY: The Free Press, 1990).

3 M. A. Huselid, 'The Impact of Human Resource Management Practices on Turnover, Productivity, and Corporate Financial Performance,' *Academy of Management Journal* (1995).

CHAPTER 5

Training and Development

LEARNING OBJECTIVES

After completing this chapter, the student will be able to:

- Understand the role of T&D in business
- Explain the process for identifying training needs
- Describe how training is designed
- Depict the various modes of training

Opening Case Learning Strategies at Accenture

At Accenture Consulting, learning is holistic and continuous and connected with the growth plan of the employees. At the very basic level, employees (software engineers to managers) are expected to develop capabilities through on-the-job work experience, formalized classroom-based training, self-initiated study, and interaction with specialists. The programs are aimed at enhancing their skills and equipping them with business, technical, and behavioral competencies needed to perform their role effectively.

Since high performance is the promise to Accenture's clients, there is an emphasis on continuous learning as the core of employee development. To enable this learning, Accenture provides an environment that encourages each employee to learn, teach, and share knowledge with his or her colleagues.

Employees undergo T&D activities throughout their time at Accenture. Training is provided to deliver superior solutions, whether in advanced systems development, program management, emerging or established technologies, or professional skills. Accenture's proven experience as the leading provider of innovative technology solutions provides a great environment for honing employee skills.

To support a continuous learning environment and enable the employees to integrate better with their technology professionals across the globe, a global training curriculum is provided. It has three key areas:

- Application delivery training on the Accenture Delivery Suite
- Technology specialty training
- Professional development training

Accenture core seminars are annual events to provide a platform for Accenture's executive leadership to engage with future leaders of the company. As part of L&D, employees also have access to career counseling, 'Leadership Connect,' and town halls for mentoring, coaching, sharing knowledge, and networking.

The My Learning internal Website is available to all Accenture employees. From classrooms to virtual sessions and self-paced computer courses, the employees can enroll in any of the more than 20,000 courses. The Website enables employees to access a wealth of information and create their own curriculum and development plans. The strong e-learning strategy constitutes the very foundation of the learning environment at Accenture and is the starting point in our employees' journey to growth and development.

Community of Practice

Accenture has built strong communities of practice in both industry and technology domains to foster innovation. Specialists in particular technologies or industries share their knowledge and experience with colleagues within the company. This unique knowledge-sharing platform not only helps in honing the skills of individual employees but also creates valuable assets for the company.

Employees (senior software engineers to manager career levels) can continue their education through our continuous learning initiative. Accenture sponsors Master of Business Administration (MBA) programs in various institutes. The educational sponsorship program demonstrates our commitment to the professional and personal development of our employees, giving them the opportunity to pursue part-time Master of Business Administration courses at IIM Bangalore, NMIMS, and XLRI (XLRI).

Accenture also supports certification programs across technologies. To facilitate many of the certification programs, Accenture is associated with premier institutes. For example, through the Accenture Solutions Delivery Academy set up in association with the office of the Professional Education Program of the MIT, Accenture offers international certification to their employees as application developers and/or application designers. Accenture has also teamed with the Indian School of Business, Hyderabad, to pioneer the Accenture Management Development Academy.

Being part of Accenture is as much a learning experience as it is rewarding. Each employee has a growth and development plan that is commensurate with the growth and vision of the company.

Discussion Question

1. What are the insights from the employee development practices of Accenture?

Source: https://www.accenture.com/in-en/careers (accessed on August 2, 2017).

5.1 INTRODUCTION

In year 2016, training is passé; learning is on! Even learning is breaking out of the conventional molds in hitherto unbelievable directions. However, the truth is that it has become urgent and important for each employee in the corporate world to train and learn. According to a recent estimate,[4] the corporate training market is expected to grow rapidly with revenues to reach ₹32 billion by FY'2020. The current market for corporate training is assessed to be highly fragmented with about 700 small- and large-sized companies competing for popular and niche training courses in multiple verticals. The prediction is that the markets will widen the portfolio of niche courses and grow.

In today's volatile, market-driven business environment, if an organization has to deliver according to the customer expectations on a sustained basis, the employees will need the requisite skills to perform the job assigned to them. These skills, which include technical, analytical, and people skills, are developed through proper training conducted by trained and competent professionals. Training helps people to improve their competencies and to perform better on current and also future job assignments. High-quality training also fosters better performance ratings, which leads to employee satisfaction and engagement. A well-trained person rises in his/her own esteem, and derives job satisfaction from his/her work. Sometimes emergence of new technology causes skill obsolescence, requiring the employees to seek training to upgrade their skills, or seek reskilling, or acquire new skills to cope with the new challenges. In a nutshell, training allows employees to acquire new skills, sharpen existing ones, perform better, increase productivity, and be better leaders. Since a company is the sum total of what employees achieve individually, organizations should do everything in their power to ensure that employees perform at their peak.

5.2 TRAINING, LEARNING, AND DEVELOPMENT

5.2.1 Training

'Training is the use of planned instruction activities to promote learning.'[5] It involves the use of formal processes to impart knowledge and help people to acquire the skills necessary for them to perform their jobs satisfactorily. It is considered one of the several responses the organization can undertake to promote learning. Training is useful in building skills relevant to the work, for which there is a pressure of time to master the skill, or which is complex enough to require transfer of learning from experts. It is also useful when the employees require some important information critical for their performance. However, an obvious limitation of training is that those, who impart the training (whether external or internal experts) have designed it in a context, which is removed from the actual workplace of the employee. To obviate such limitations, training is customized to make it as relevant as possible.

5.2.2 Learning

As compared to training, which is event-based, learning is a continuously flowing process to upgrade the skill, knowledge, and ability of an individual. Learning pursues specific goals and is derived from experience.

---

[4] Ken Research, 'India Corporate Training Market Forecasts to 2020—Incremental Allocation of Training Budgets in MSMEs and PPP in Skill Development Initiatives to Propel Growth,' June 2016. Available at: https://www.kenresearch.com/education-and-recruitment/ (accessed on March 6, 2018).

[5] Michael Armstrong, *Human Resource Development*. (London: Kogan Page, 2006): 575.

Learning results in positive changes in behavior and cognition, and the changes are sustained over a long period (Figure 5.1). In the words of Honey and Mumford,[6] 'Learning has happened when people can demonstrate that they know something that they did not know before (insights, realizations as well as facts) and when they can do something they could not do before (skills).'

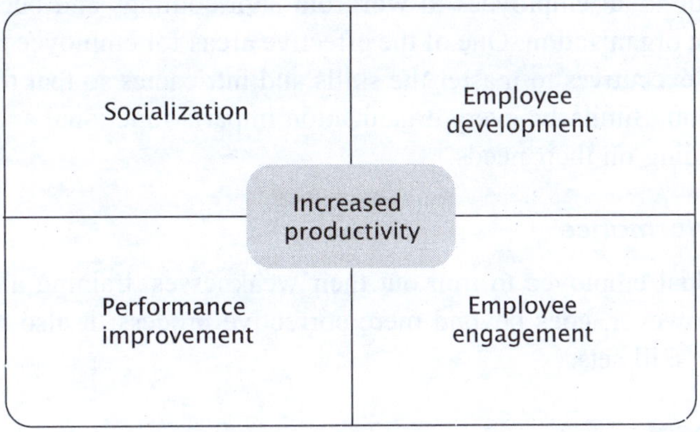

Fig. 5.1 Impact of employee learning

5.2.3 Development

Development is an evolving process that helps people to rise from a current level of knowledge and competencies to a future state in which higher level competencies are required. It has been defined by Harrison[7] as 'learning experiences of any kind, whereby individuals and groups acquire enhanced knowledge, skills, values or behaviors. Its outcomes unfold through time, rather than immediately, and they tend to be long lasting.'

There are four ways normally used to develop employees: formal education, assessment, job experience, and interpersonal relationships. While the focus of training is the improvement of performance in the current job, the focus of development is much wider—to enhance the capability of the employee, even for handling future jobs.

According to Walker,[8] the overall development impact of training, relationship, and workplace experience is 10%, 20%, and 70%, respectively.

Socialization, Employee Orientation, and Onboarding

Socialization indicates the process of gradually embedding in the new recruit the appropriate attitude, conduct, and knowledge for effective participation as an organization member. It represents 'a sense-making process that helps new hires adapt, form work relationships, and find their place in the organization.'[9] For a new recruit, it is done through a training program known as orientation. The purpose of orientation is to prepare the new employees to perform their jobs effectively, learn about the organization, and establish work relationships. According to a new survey by Society of Human Resources, 83% of companies report having a formal orientation program. The current coinage—

6 P. Honey and A. Mumford, *The Manual of Learning Styles* (London: Peter Honey Publications, 1996).

7 R. Harrison, *Employee Development* (London: Institute of Personnel and Development, 1997).

8 Walker, N. 'Creating a Talent Mindset: A Five-step Roadmap,' *Strategic HR Review*, 3 no. 6: 20–23.

9 R. A. Noe, *Employee Training and Development*, 3rd ed. (New York, NY: McGraw-Hill/Irwin, 2005).

onboarding—often used interchangeably with orientation, refers to the orientation process of newly hired managers on a longer term with focus on cultural acclimatization of the new employee.

Employee Development

Training also helps individual employees to work out shortcomings and become proficient in their roles as expected by the organization. One of the effective areas for employee training is sales training that helps rookie sales executives to master the skills and intricacies so that they are able to enhance sales for the organization. Similarly, every organization imparts functional and behavioral training to different groups depending on their needs.

Improvement in Performance

By helping the individual employee to iron out their weaknesses, training also fosters performance improvement. T&D, however, goes beyond mere corrective process; it also reinforces the strengths and acquisition of new skill sets.

Employee Engagement

Investments in T&D also lead to engaged employees. For this, however, the exercise has to be relevant to the employees and one from which they can learn and take back something. No engagement will result if T&D become mere routine, and employees go through the motions mechanically.

Increased Productivity

The total effect of all the aforementioned factors leads to overall productivity of employees and performance improvement for the entire organization. Besides, in a rapidly evolving landscape, productivity is not only dependent on employees, but also on the technology they use. Here also T&D makes a contribution: by getting employees up-to-date with new technology, using existing ones better, and then cancelling the obsolete ones. This goes a long way in enhancing productivity.

5.2.4 Definition and Objectives

'Training,' according to Michael Armstrong, 'is a systematic development of the knowledge, skills and attitudes required by an individual to perform adequately a given task or job.'[10] According to Edwin B. Flippo, 'Training is the act of increasing knowledge and skills of an employee for doing a particular job.'[11] The term 'training' indicates the process involved in improving the aptitudes, skills, and abilities of the employees to perform specific jobs. Training helps in updating old talents and developing new ones. 'Successful candidates placed on the jobs need training to perform their duties effectively.'[12]

5.2.5 The Objectives of T&D

The raison d'être of T&D is to ensure the availability of a skilled and willing workforce to the organization. It endeavors to:

---

[10] M. Armstrong, *A Handbook of Human Resource Management Practice*, 8th ed. (London: Kogan Page, 2001).

[11] E. B. Flippo, *Personnel Management*, 6th ed. (New Delhi: Tata McGraw-Hill Education, 1984).

[12] K. Aswathappa, *Human Resource and Personnel Management* (New Delhi: Tata McGraw-Hill Education, 2000): 189.

1. Prepare the employees to meet the current and emerging demands of the job and the organization
2. Prevent obsolescence
3. Design and impart knowledge/skill inputs for new entrants to enable quick readiness for effective job performance
4. Equip employees for higher-level tasks
5. Upgrade employee skills and knowledge on latest concepts, information, and techniques
6. Build a pipeline of leaders and technical experts
7. Support functional excellence and efficient working of the departments
8. Balance quality with economical output

In a nutshell, one could discern four basic clusters of objectives of T&D: individual, organizational, functional, and social.

1. Individual objectives To help employees achieve their personal goals of growth. This, in turn, creates the drive for individual contribution to the organization.
2. Organizational objectives To assist the organization by focusing on building capability and effectiveness.
3. Functional objectives To help the different functions maintain their contribution at a level suitable to the organization's needs.
4. Social objectives To ensure that the organization is ethically and socially responsible to the needs and challenges of the society.

5.2.6 Investments in Training: Recent Trends

Accenture is a global management consulting, technology services, and outsourcing company, with more than 323,000 people serving clients in more than 200 cities in 120 countries. In 2015, Accenture invested US$841 million on the training and professional development of its employees—covering 15 million training hours, at an average of over 40 hours per employee.

The centerpiece of this investment is an initiative called Accenture Connected Learning (introduced in 2015) that combines a classroom-based training with a digital learning environment and links the company's employees to professional content and world-class internal and external experts. It comprises more than 50 connected classrooms all over the globe, 24,000 online courses, and 900 learning boards (online forums curated by subject matter experts), 5 regional learning centers, and more than 100 professional communities. It has enabled the company to develop highly specialized skills at scale and to respond to quickly changing business requirements faster than ever before. Simultaneously, it helps its diverse categories employees (data scientists, visual designers, information architects, mortgage processors, and others) to enhance their professional capabilities, develop the critical skills needed to stay market-relevant, and enhance their own career opportunities.[13]

Large economies, such as the USA, are known to have always stayed ahead of the disruptive cycles that raged on in business and technology, by sustained focus and large strategic investments in research innovation and human capital. On the human capital front, as per industry reports, US companies on an average would budget 8–10% of their total employee spends on training, with a

[13] Available at: https://www.accenture.com/us-en/careers/your-future-training-counseling (accessed on November 22, 2017).

total annual outlay of over US$100 billion. This is also a market that has been growing at 15% year-on-year since 2012.

India, on the other hand, currently a much smaller economy at about a tenth of the USA, had a relatively smaller spend, estimated at only 1–2% of employee costs and a total outlay of less than US$1 billion. The picture, however, has been rapidly changing. In 2011, Indian organizations on an average spent US$331 per employee on T&D, according to a study on L&D trends in India, by the American Society for Training & Development (ASTD) and Harvard Business Publishing (HBP). The respondents of the survey covered 41 organizations employing 27,394 employees on an average.

The cost figure includes L&D staff salaries, travel costs for L&D staff, administrative costs, non-salary development costs, delivery costs (such as classroom facilities and online learning technology infrastructure), outsourced activities, and tuition reimbursement.

The number of learning hours used per employee on average in 2011 for responding organizations was 49.7, the report revealed. This represents a strong T&D program, putting the organizations in this study on par with ASTD best award-winning organizations, which averaged 49.1 hours used per employee.

In 2011, responding Indian organizations report spending 2.4% of employee payroll on direct learning expenditures. This falls in line with data reported in the ASTD state of the industry report data, which in the past 10 years has reported direct expenditure as a percentage of payroll ranging between 2.2% and 3.2%.

Among the key priorities, building a leadership pipeline topped the agenda for most companies, followed by mid- to senior-level management training and using technology for L&D.[14] Among the different categories of Indian companies, the training spend is particularly high in IT firms. In FY'15, TCS's recruitment and training costs rose by 19% to ₹360.9 crore from a year ago, its annual report showed. That number excludes the cost of the technology TCS builds to train employees and the cost of the time spent in training. TCS also said that, on an average, its employees spent 10.3 days on training during a year. The training cost is expected to rise in FY'16 as TCS continues with its goal of training 100,000 employees of digital technology. Associates at Infosys spent roughly 37 days in training, up from about 21 days a year ago. Middle management spent 2.94 days, senior management spent 1.64 days, while top management 1.83 days. The pattern of investments in training showed another shift. National Association of Software and Services Companies (NASSCOM) had said that five years ago training costs were about 1–2% of the overall costs of an IT company, but it (1–2%) was the percentage of fresher training cost. Currently, the training investment covers mid-career training, design thinking, product management, and many newer things that would be through the employee life cycle and not entry level where the bulk of training costs were earlier concentrated.[15] IT companies are also looking to get more value from the time employees spend in training. HCL is looking at methodologies that crash learning-cycle times by balancing the time for real-time application and content to a size that the employee can absorb.

---

[14] *The Times of India*. 'Companies Spent $331 per Employee on Training, Development in 2011,' September 10, 2013.

[15] J. Mendonca and N. Alawadhi, 'IT Firms like Accenture, TCS Spending Millions to Train Workforce to Meet Increasing Demand for Digital Services,' *The Economic Times*, October 21, 2015.

Reflection Point

Playbook

Organizations are creating Learner Experience Playbooks to generate a holistic, optimized, and engaging learner experience. It comes in the form of an e-book which provides guidance to design and deliver a high quality learning culture for the employees.

Discussion Question

1. What factors make a Learner Experience Playbook more attuned to the new generation of employees in comparison to the traditional methods?

5.2.7 T&D Strategy

There are several issues associated with T&D. What is the cost of training? What are the benefits? Who gets trained? What are the high value trainings? What are the needs for training? What are the ways to capture the effectiveness of training? In order to leverage training efforts, it is necessary to develop an L&D strategy. An L&D strategy is an organizational strategy that articulates the workforce capabilities, skills, or competencies required to ensure a sustainable, successful organization and that sets out the means of developing these capabilities to underpin organizational effectiveness (Figure 5.2). An effective training strategy is vital for the success of your company; it can serve as a means

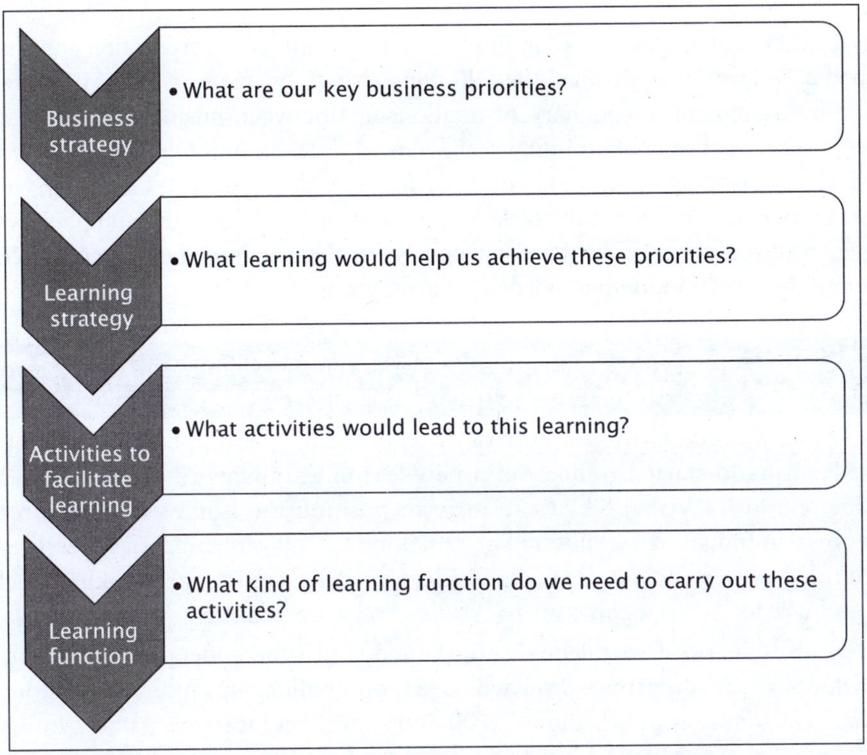

Source: Wendy Hirsh, *Developing and Delivering a Learning Strategy* (London: Corporate Research Forum, 2005).

Fig. 5.2 The flow of learning strategy

to develop your people and can also become an effective recruiting and retention tool. Developing a strategy for training gives your company a competitive advantage and helps propel you into the future. The plan needs to be comprehensive, and every employee needs to understand it so that everyone gets the appropriate training at the right time.

In building a learning strategy, the starting block is the organization's business strategy and mission statement. There are three levels of strategy—at the organizational level, its identity and what it wants to achieve; at the business level, what it is aiming for now; and at the functional level, operational plans to enable the accomplishment of its business strategy. The functional HR strategy has three segments—an umbrella of policies and key programs aligned to the organizational strategy; a series of initiatives that support the business goals; and HR's own functional strategy. The key thrust of HR is to develop human capital by improving capability. Capability is developed through education, training, learning from others, and learning from experience.

The entire cascade of learning strategy can be illustrated with the example of Procter & Gamble (P&G) At P&G, training for skill is no longer viewed as the key L&D process. The years of restructuring saw a deliberate shift from training to learning as part of a strategy to develop learning culture across the company. One major vehicle has been coaching, with almost all the UK and Ireland management sector receiving training in coaching skills. The training started at middle management level, since it is there that the delivery of strategy takes place. Without front line management commitment, flexibility, and competence, strategy cannot deliver. By early 2004, coaching had become adapted as a management technique throughout the whole organization, from top management to the shop floor level.[16]

How does a L&D strategy look like? In the 1990s, the health care corporation Johnson & Johnson (J&J) developed a T&D strategy that had the following structures: the benefits of training strategy, the mission and policy statement, a summary of relationships between business strategy and employee training strategy, steps in systematic training management, roles in training, followed by objectives of T&D strategy. The mission and policy statement of J&J ran like this: 'The Company will ensure that each employee is trained to carry out the tasks required of them. Further the company will encourage each employee to develop his/her skills consistent with the needs of customer driven continuous improvement and their own individual needs and aspirations.'

Exhibit Infosys Gives Makeover to Training Program, Picks 21 'Supercoders' for Futuristic Projects

Infosys, the country's second largest software exporter, has revamped its traditional training program in Mysuru and started rolling out a new learning framework for entry level employees as part of chief executive Vishal Sikka's strategy to position the firm as different from its peers. Amid a slowdown in India's $146 billion IT sector, domestic players are under pressure to innovate as top outsourcing customers such as General Electric and Citigroup are looking to clamp down on budgets and ask for fewer people on backoffice software projects.

Infosys has also identified 21 talented programmers or 'supercoders' across the company—as part of its 'Expert Track' program—who will work on challenging, futuristic customer projects. Infosys, which is currently training about 5,500 entry level engineers on its new Infosys Learning

[16] Rosemary Harrison, *Learning and Development* (London: CIPD, 1997).

Platform (ILP), has introduced several changes to its traditional training program in Mysuru, including increasing the training duration, to make employees adept in areas such as design thinking and artificial intelligence (AI).

Infosys Learning Platform was launched in April, with its first pilot in May. The platform went live in the middle of June. Infosys has included two important changes to the training program—every entry level engineer has to go through a 2-day immersive training session on design thinking. And every employee now is also being trained on a data visualization tool called Tableau.

So far Infosys has trained over 40,000 employees in design thinking, with plans to train several thousands more. 'We increased the amount of training in certain areas and added design thinking and Tableau—we added two weeks to that. It used to finish in 17 weeks earlier, now it finishes in 19 weeks. The fastest person will complete training in 19 weeks and the slowest will probably finish in 24-25 weeks,' said Rangadore.

Training has also been tweaked to train entry level programmers in algorithmic thinking that can help them program in at least three different languages. Infosys is also introducing a new concept called 'Zero Bench,' which will give programmers across the company opportunities to work on different projects.

Source: Anirban Sen, 'Infosys Gives Makeover to Training Programme, Picks 21 'Supercoders' for Futuristic Projects,' *The Economic Times*, August 3, 2015.

5.3 LEARNING THEORIES

5.3.1 Andragogy

Andragogy, a term attributed to Malcolm Knowles, is the process of helping adults to learn by engaging them in specific training activities such as role play, simulations, and so on. According to Knowles, adult learning is based on certain key principles:

The adult learner:

- Prefers, and is capable of, self-directed learning
- Has enough life experiences, which is a good resource for learning
- Has learning needs linked with changing social roles
- Is inclined to apply his knowledge to solve his problems
- Wishes to learn by internal rather than external factors

Based on the aforementioned principles, Knowles formulated a program for the design, implementation, and evaluation of adult learning. Knowles recognized that while designing a program, the learners should be involved building a climate in which they can most effectively learn. The focal points in andragogy were:

- Involvement in the planning and evaluation of their instruction
- Experiential learning activities
- Emphasis on learning, that is, immediately relevant to their job or personal life
- Adaption of a problem-centric rather than content-oriented approach

The most important advantage of andragogy is that it enables the learner to take charge of his own learning and provides a flexible method in different learning contexts. The critics, however, argue that the aforementioned principles are not specific to adult learning contexts only. There are four learning theories related to adult learning. They are action learning, experiential learning, self-directed learning, and project-based learning.

Action Learning

Action learning uses work on a real project or problem as a method to learn. The learning (e.g., how to communicate effectively, how to build trust in each other, and others) occurs from experience through reflection and action. It involves learning from actions that participants, working in small groups (3–4 people), are required to take either to complete their project or to solve issues. In this, the participants are assisted by a learning coach who provides appropriate guidance on how to balance work with learning from that work.

Experiential Learning

The basic premise of experiential learning is that individuals learn best by experience. It can be described simply as 'learning by doing.' Here the learner is involved in a cyclical process of goal setting, planning, making experiments, deciding, and acting, followed by observing, reflecting, and reviewing. The participants learn through reflection on their own experience, rather than through lecture.

Project-based Learning

In this method, the learning occurs through facing difficult and real problems. Learners have to make choices on a problem-solving approach and then to take appropriate action. The participant gathers data information from multiple channels and through a process of synthesis and analysis draws knowledge from it.

Self-directed Learning

Traditionally, the learning takes place under the direction of a teacher and trainer who directs the entire process by virtue of their superior knowledge. In self-directed learning, it is the individual participant who takes the responsibility for their own learning by selecting, assessing, and managing their own specific learning needs. There are three segments in self-directed learning: the goals, the process, and the learner. An adult learner generally has self-determined goals and process. The quality of learning can be improved with skillful facilitation. The critical success factor in self-directed learning is the motivation. The motivating factors are the prospects to acquire new skills, knowledge, and attitudes for improved performance and a general well-being.

5.3.2 Bloom's Taxonomy

Bloom's Taxonomy is a classification of levels of learning ('taxonomy' means classification) formulated by Mr Benjamin Bloom, along with a team of educational psychologists in 1956, based on extensive research in the field. The trigger for the research was to go beyond the conventional rote learning, which emphasizes remembering, to more advanced forms of thinking in education, such as analyzing and evaluating concepts, processes, procedures, and principles. The taxonomy talks about a hierarchy of learning, categorized into three intertwined domains: cognitive, affective, and psychometric.

The Cognitive Domain

Cognitive domain is characterized by a person's intellectual abilities. Cognitive behavior is expressed in intellectual skills such as data comprehension and analysis, organizing ideas, recall or recognition of facts, and so on. Six levels of hierarchy constitute the cognitive domain: knowledge, comprehension, application, analysis, synthesis, and evaluation (from bottom to top, in that order). The hierarchy is indicated in such a manner that those who perform at the higher level are considered possessing superior cognitive skills (e.g., evaluation).

The Affective Domain

The affective domain deals with interests, feelings, values, appreciation, enthusiasm, motivation, and attitudes of the learner. This domain is organized into five levels of hierarchy (from simple to more complex): receiving phenomena, responding to phenomena, valuing, organization, and internalizing values. The affective domain strengthens the emotional competencies of the learner.

The Psychometric Domain

The psychomotor domain covers the use of motor skills to physically manipulate a tool or instrument. Psychomotor objectives normally concentrate on modification in behavior or improvement in skills (e.g., increasing speed of work or precision). Bloom and his associates did not develop the hierarchy for skills in the psychomotor domain on grounds of inadequate experience, but some other educators worked on the psychomotor taxonomies afterwards. Simpson[17] proposed seven levels: perception, set, guided response, mechanism, complex overt response, adaptation, and origination.

Connecting the context of T&D, the above-mentioned framework not only offers a sequential method for organizing the subjects in the curriculum, it also indicates how to categorize levels of learning and keep an expected ceiling for a given program. For example, in the cognitive domain, production operatives may be given training inputs in knowledge, but analysis and higher levels may be kept out of it, while for supervisory training it may cover all the levels including synthesis and evaluation.

Bloom's Taxonomy has attracted some criticism and, in response, undergone modifications over the years. In 2001, Lorin Anderson, a former student, and David Krathwohl, a colleague in Bloom's original academic committee team, formulated a revised version,[18] aimed at being more useful to educators. In the modified taxonomy, three categories were renamed and verbs substituted the nouns to describe the categories ('knowledge' became 'remembering,' and 'comprehension' became 'understanding'). In this modified taxonomy, in one of the many changes, 'creation' switched places with evaluation to become the highest level in the classification system.

5.3.3 Goal Setting Theory

Developed by Locke and Latham,[19] this theory is based on researches on some 400 laboratory and field studies. In summary, specific, hard goals lead to higher levels of task performance than soft and

---

17 Simpson, E. J. The Classification of Educational Objectives in the Psychomotor Domain. (Washington, DC: Gryphon House).

18 Lorin W. Anderson, David R. Krathwohl, and Benjamin Samuel Bloom, *A Taxonomy for Learning, Teaching, and Assessing: A Revision of Bloom's Taxonomy of Educational Objectives* (New York: Longman).

19 E. A. Locke and G. P. Latham, 'New Directions in Goal-Setting Theory,' *Current Directions in Psychological Science* 15, no. 5 (2006): 265–268.

easy goals. So long as a person is committed to the goal, he makes efforts to develop capabilities to attain it.

5.3.4 Social Cognitive Theory

Albert Bandura was the chief proponent of social cognitive theory. This theory describes a psychological model of behavior. The theory underlines that social context provides a strong platform for learning as people can learn by observing others. It is built on several basic assumptions; one such assumption is that a learner can master new behaviors and knowledge by observing a model in a process of vicarious learning, not through direct experience. Another assumption is that learning is an internal process that may or may not lead to a behavior.

5.3.5 Learning Cycles

David Kolb presented his learning styles model in 1984, and then drawing from the cycles, formed his learning style inventory. It is an experiential learning theory, which is anchored in the learner's internal cognitive processes. According to Kolb, with learning people acquire abstract concepts that can be put to use in a variety of situations and new experience generates a drive to develop new concepts.[20]

The learning gets completed only when a person has travelled through the cycle of all the four stages of (a) having a concrete experience followed by (b) observation of and reflection on that experience which leads to (c) the formation of abstract concepts (analysis) and generalizations (conclusions) that are then (d) used to test hypothesis in future situations, resulting in new experiences.

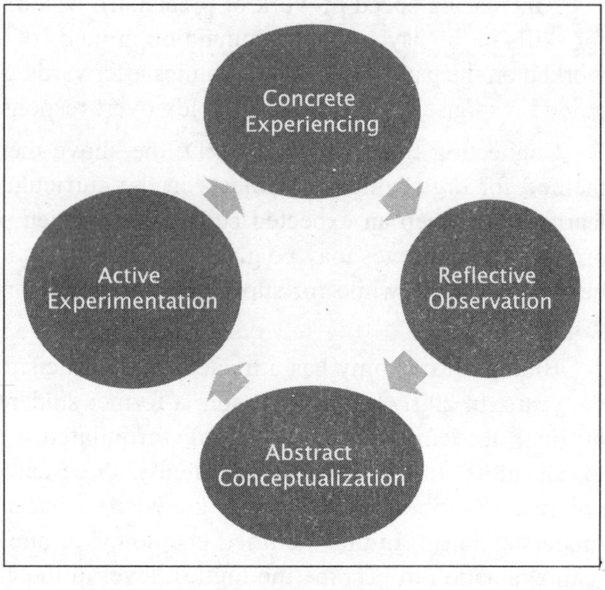

Source: D. A. Kolb, *Experiential Learning: Experience as the Source of Learning and Development*, vol. 1 (Englewood Cliffs, NJ: Prentice-Hall, 1984).

Fig. 5.3 Learning Cycle

In the domain of T&D, there is an opportunity for trainers to design and implement activities in such a way that each learner is able to engage in the manner most suitable for him. It also helps the individual learner to learn more effectively by identifying their least preferred learning styles and deepening these through the use of the experiential learning cycle. The model way of taking the learning cycle concept is by developing the activities and materials to touch upon each stage of the experiential learning cycle and take the learner through the whole experience (Figure 5.3).

20 S. A. McLeod, 'Kolb—Learning Styles,' 2013. Available at: www.simplypsychology.org/learning-kolb.html (accessed on November 13, 2017).

5.3.6 Design of Training

Quite often employee-training activities are undertaken with good intentions, but in a sporadic manner without establishing linkages between the content of training, its delivery, and its outcome, and whether it has served its expected purpose. It is necessary to adopt a systematic approach to training, to make it yield desired outcomes for both the individual and the organization. Taking a systematic approach to training would mean that the end goal is visualized before the training has begun, taking the time to analyze what results the organization needs from its employees, whether employees are accomplishing those results, and what T&D approaches are needed by employees to better accomplish those results. A systematic approach includes evaluating approaches before, during, and after training to ensure employees truly benefited from the training in terms of enhanced results to the organization.

Instructional Systems Design (ISD) is a process for designing training. It takes a formal approach to training where the goals of the training are decided on the basis of multiple assessments of the employees, various training methods are selected and structured to realize the desired outcomes, and evaluation plans are put in place to gauge the quality of the training and degree of achievement of the goals.

A well-known ISD model is known ADDIE. Formulated in 1975 by the Center for Educational Technology at Florida State University, and used first by the US Army and then by the US Armed Forces, it is an acronym for five phases of the training process.

Analyze

Systematically evaluate the gaps in performance and competencies for the organization and individual employees, develop learning/training objectives to bridge the Knowledge, Skill, and Ability (KSA) gap so that at the end of the training, the employee is equipped to perform on the job. The analysis can be elaborate and well documented, or it could be simple and based on informal questions. When the analysis is done well, individual training session achieves its specific goal and training is acknowledged as a value-creating and engaging activity by the employees receiving training inputs. This segment also spells out the duration and timelines and also the target employees for specific training inputs.

Design

The training structure is built in this stage. It covers the learning objectives, the structure and outline, the training content, the method, and so on. Although, the analysis and design may not always happen in a sequential manner, a well-structured process with meticulous design has certain obvious advantages for predicting a desired outcome.

Develop

Details are now added to the structure developed in design stage to create a wholesome learning experience. It includes lesson plan, course materials, and chosen media (presentation, audiovisuals, Webinars, and so on). The entire set of activities needs to be visualized from the learner's perspectives to make the suitable combination (small groups/interactive sessions, ratio of presentation and participation), what the facilitator needs to do—on presenting new information, on strategy for involving the participant. A well-developed design will ensure a well-organized training session creating a satisfied set of adult learners and capable of being repeated by other trainers.

Implement

This segment is conducted by the trainer, who, to be effective need to be familiar with andragogy and a clear strategy to engage the participants. The learners gain knowledge that can be implemented in their work sphere. The training is delivered according to the plan and learning objectives, the activities are conducted on schedule, and at the end, the feedbacks are shared about the program and training techniques. This phase includes administrative activities, such as photocopying, organizing facilities, and taking attendance data.

Evaluate

The evaluation covers the design of the training program, utilization of the resources, and the impact on the learners in terms of overall experience and resultant performance improvement.

5.3.7 Training Needs Assessment

Imagine a familiar scenario in corporate India. In company ABC, the new chief learning officer (CLO) planned a very high profile leadership development program with a famous outbound training company. Based on enthusiastic responses, the CLO secured a budget and conducted the offsite program at Rishikesh, on the banks of the Ganges. There was a virtual scramble for participation and all the powerful LMs influenced their individual bosses to sponsor them for the prestigious program. The program was a success. The participants gave thumbs up to the program in the feedback at the end of the program. Six months later, however, when the training organization came back for some feedback on what has been the impact of the training, the CLO had to struggle securing the feedback. Informally, he was informed by several of the bosses that the above-mentioned training was taken as a part of reward for good performance, and there was hardly any change in behavior as a result of the training.

As much as a journey needs a destination, an effective training also needs a clearly defined end goal based on identified needs. The stakeholders for training could be the individual, the function, or the organization as a whole. In the current competitive environment of shrinking costs, relentless pressure on quality, and truncated budgets, it is imperative that precious resources of the organization are only invested in training after careful planning and based on a strong ROI. Effective training needs analysis (TNA) is critical, given the dynamic nature of today's workplace, where technologies and working practices are continuously changing rapidly, requiring adjustments in relevant skills and competencies.

A training need is a gap between desired level and actual level of employee skills or competencies, which a well-directed training or development program can correct or improve. The deficiency in KSA can be such that prevents the employee from effectively discharging his assigned tasks or adversely affects the performance of the organization. Broadly, the needs can occur at any of the three levels: organization, task, or person. For example, in a situation where there is a rising incidence of quality rejection occurring in a particular manufacturing unit, this might indicate an organizational need for a training intervention. Similarly, if a particular territory is consistently failing to achieve the sales target, the reason could be inadequate sales training of the individual sales personnel there. Training needs assessment (TNA), therefore, intends to solve performance problems, in alignment with the vision and strategy of the organization, through an effective and cost-efficient delivery of training. Thus, the critical success factors for TNA process are: planning, analysis, and coordination across functions setting organizational priorities, avoiding duplication of effort, and aiming at economies of scale.

5.3.8 The TNA Process

Training needs analysis is a three-stage process: organization analysis, task analysis and person analysis (Figure 5.4).

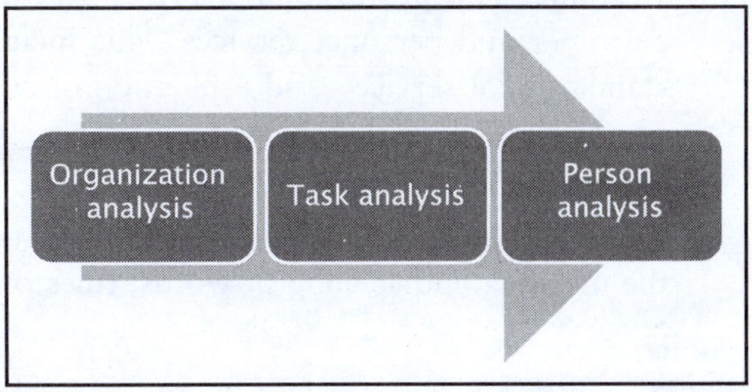

Fig. 5.4 The flow of TNA process

Organization Analysis

Organization analysis scans the external environment (trends, government policies, and others) as also the internal environment (the business strategy of the organization, the resources for training activities, and the pulse of managers, the peers, and the subordinates) to decide which part of the training activities should demand attention and focus. Post Enron, training input on ethics and good governance, whistle blowing, and so on have become part of the environmental requirement. For a public sector organization, knowledge and awareness of the Presidential Directive on Reservation is a requirement for executives, especially those dealing with recruitment, selection, and promotions.

In the second place, the business strategy of the organization also has a linkage with specific training areas. For example, if the company has decided on a strategy of quality improvement, one focus area for training could be the six sigma or TQM. In BPCL, in 2003–2004, it was decided to engage all executives up to a level in strategy formation inputs and, accordingly, a series of appreciative inquiry workshops were conducted to generate such inputs from the participants. In the same way, post merger and acquisitions, companies devise integration programs to align divergent cultures to converge.

Finally, a significant factor in training is the attitude of the managers, peers, and employees toward training. If there is enthusiasm and support for training activities, then it becomes effective, and if there is widespread cynicism, then it is difficult to use learned ideas in workplace.

Currently, with the competitive pressures to cut costs, training budgets also come under severe scrutiny. Therefore, organizations are also driven to look for maximizing returns on training through innovative ways to impart training with reduced costs. One preferred method to optimize returns on training is to take e-learning options and to conduct virtual training and self-directed training. Outsourcing of training activities and tying up with business schools also reduces the cost of training.

Task Analysis

A task is the work activity relevant to a particular job. The task analysis covers a complete listing of all the work activities and the KSAs necessary for performing those activities. It is a four-step process: selection of the job, generation of a primary list of the activities performed on the job, the validation of the list by job incumbents/managers, and finally identification of the KSAs to perform the activities. Task analysis, being a comprehensive, slow, and meticulous procedure, requires commitment of time and resources. Besides, in the current context of rapid changes in procedures and technology in the workplace, it becomes difficult to continuously perform task analysis. There is, therefore, an

Exhibit The KSA of a Cashier

Knowledge

1. **Customer and professional service** Knowledge of principles and processes for providing customer and personal services. This includes customer needs assessment, meeting quality standards for services, and evaluation of customer satisfaction.
2. **Mathematics** Knowledge of arithmetic, algebra, geometry, calculus, statistics, and their applications.
3. **English language** Knowledge of the structure and content of the English language including the meaning and spelling of words, rules of composition, and grammar.

Skills

1. **Active listening** Giving full attention to what other people are saying, taking time to understand the points being made, asking questions as appropriate, and not interrupting at inappropriate times.
2. **Service orientation** Actively looking for ways to help people.
3. **Speaking** Talking to others to convey information effectively.
4. **Mathematics** Using mathematics to solve problems.
5. **Social perspectives** Being aware of others' reactions and understanding why they react as they do.

Abilities

1. **Oral expression** The ability to communicate information and ideas in speaking so others will understand.
2. **Oral comprehension** The ability to listen to and understand information and ideas presented through spoken words and sentences.
3. **Near vision** The ability to see details at close range (within a few feet of the observer).
4. **Speech recognition** The ability to identify and understand the speech of another person.
5. **Speech clarity** The ability to speak clearly so others can understand you.

Source: https://www.onetonline.org (accessed on February 13, 2018).

increasing trend to use competency assessment for determining training needs. Competencies have been described as an underlying characteristic that predicts superior performance. It includes, other than knowledge and skill, self-concept, social role, and motives.

Person Analysis

Person analysis focuses on the individual employee needing training and the kind of training and reasons thereof. It can be occasioned by an issue of non-performance or unsatisfactory performance, or a new role, or the introduction of new technology or work practices. At this stage, it is necessary to have clearly defined performance criteria so that the gap between the current level of performance and the desired level becomes clear.

In order to decide whether specific performance issue needs to be addressed through training, the supervisors need to assess factors such as person characteristics, input, output, consequences, and feedback.[21] Person characteristics include knowledge, skill, ability, motivation, and attitude. Input refers to the resources given to the employee to perform and also instructions regarding performance. Output indicates the performance standards for the job. Consequences mean the rewards for performance. Feedback implies the information conveyed to the employee during performance. The data in respect of all these factors can be obtained through interviews or questionnaires.

The aforementioned factors, along with the learning environment, determine what is known as the employee's readiness for training and, in turn, influences the employee's motivation to learn. For example, a certain residential program for an offsite might have late-night dinner parties thrown in for the high profile training participants every night, leading to the participants being in less than agile state of mind for the subsequent day's training sessions.

Negative performance appraisals are normally neither received nor given in a positive spirit, as it has also negative association with the employee's career prospects. Take the case of a distraught employee, who has been passed over for what he considers a 'deserved promotion' and sent for a training program might lack the motivation to learn. Research, however, has not established any positive difference in motivation to learn when appraisals are only the basis for training, or training is on the basis of self-assessment.[22]

In the final analysis, it is also important to understand the interrelationship between a critical job issue, a critical process issue, and a critical business issue, to be able to really decide when and how to leverage training for maximum impact for the business. For example, a new airport manager, who is not well versed on the guidelines on relaxed norms for last-minute ticket sale from the airport counter, may refuse to lower the rates, originally fixed by the commerce function, thus estranging loyal travel operators to migrate to a competitor airline.

5.3.9 Training Objectives

The training objectives arise out of the assessed training needs. Objectives serve three main purposes: specify the training outcome, describe the sequence of training, and indicate what kind of strategy is to be used.[23] Objective should state what the learner expects to learn, they should be specific, measureable, attainable, realistic, and time-bound.

Exhibit A Sample Training Objective of a Training Program for Negotiation Skills for Junior Executives in a Manufacturing Organization

After attending this program, the participants will:

1. Gain a comprehensive knowledge of the stages in negotiation process and different negotiation approaches
2. Know how to prepare a comprehensive checklist before commencing a negotiation
3. Learn to deal with difficult negotiation situation
4. Acquire skills to negotiate from a position of strength
5. Learn innovative negotiation techniques

---

21 Noe, *Employee Training and Development*, 90–98.

22 I. L. Goldstein and J. K. Ford, *Training in Organizations: Needs Assessment, Development, and Evaluation*, 4th ed. (Belmont, CA: Wadsworth, 2002).

23 R. Buckley and J. Caple, *The Theory and Practice of Training* (London: Kogan Page, 1992).

6. Know how to respond to the changing circumstances of the negotiation itself and the people directly and indirectly involved
7. Master the art of third-party negotiation process
8. Be able to draft a good legal agreement

5.3.10 Training Structure

According to Gane,[24] a training structure should include activities in a logical sequence, theoretical inputs in a balanced manner, the performance outcome, time plan for each module, suitable methodologies, and a concrete plan. There can be three kinds of structure: linear, spiral, and modular. In a linear structure, the themes are arranged in a linear manner. In a spiral structure, the easier interrelated topics are covered first and then the trainee is taken to the next level. In a modular structure, the program is fragmented into small independent units.

Content

While developing the content, due regard has to be given to the attributes of the participants, the training objectives, and the kind of learning intended. A typical training content consists of an introductory stage, a core learning stage, and a summing up and closure stage. The first stage provides opportunity for stimulating interest in the topic and in aligning participant interest with the training objectives. In the middle stage, where concepts are shared, there needs to be proper planning for involving the participants through activities to ensure that there is a commitment to learning the theories and concepts. In the last stage, the training highlights are brought out through a wrap-up session, often by the training role holder, who is in attendance. This stage also is used for review and participant feedbacks.

Table 5.1 Categories of training methods

Categories	Training methods
On the job	Job instruction, job rotation, coaching and mentoring, QCs, deputation, acting
Off the job	Classroom training, assignments, outbound programs, seminars, workshops, and so on
Self-paced training	Internet-based training, self-study
Individual-focused interventions	Counseling, coaching, mentoring
Group-focused interventions	Lectures, seminars, workshops, and so on
Trainer-controlled programs	Lectures, job instructions training
Trainee-controlled programs	Human process laboratories
Training participants together	Classroom
Training participants distributed	Video conferencing, Webinars, and conference calls
Presentation methods	Lectures, audiovisual methods
Hands-on methods	On-the-job training, self-directed learning, apprenticeship, simulations, case studies, business games, role plays, behavior modeling, application planning
Group-building methods	Group-building methods, adventure learning team training, action learning

[24] C. Gane, *Managing the Training Function: Using Instructional Technology and Systems Concepts* (London: Allen & Unwin, 1972).

Table 5.1 lists some training categories and training methods commonly used. Given further is a brief pen sketch of some of the most commonly used training methods:

1. Lecture method is a presentation of a chosen theme to an audience or a class. Cost-effective method of communication of large data in a short time. Lack participant involvement. Highly effective for verbal information, cognitive strategies, and attitudes.
2. Case method is a narration of a true or imagined story where students have to analyze and critique the actions taken and respond to several theoretical and practical questions. Helpful for development of higher skills such as analysis, synthesis, and evaluation. Case study is a standard method in use by the Central Intelligence Agency (CIA), USA.
3. In syndicate group, there are multiple groups or syndicates as against one large group and learning is through facilitated interaction.
4. In programed learning, the subject matter is broken down into small, discrete steps and carefully organized into a logical sequence in which it can be learned rapidly by the students.
5. Business games are classroom exercises requiring the trainees to gather information, analyze them, and take decisions. It involves a competition among individuals or groups against a standard of time or quality. Is commonly used for teaching finance.
6. Role play is simulation in which trainees are required to act out characters assigned to them on the basis of information provided in fact sheets. Used extensively for sales training. Role play, to succeed, requires the trainer to clearly explain the conditions.
7. In-basket activity is a simulation activity where the participant must sort and act on the content of a typical mail box.
8. Behavior modeling presents the participants with a model who demonstrate critical behavior to model and practice. Suitable for teaching skills.
9. Job instruction teaches trainees to systematically acquire routine instructions in key processes from a qualified instructor.
10. In apprenticeship, trainees learn a craft or trade by hands-on experience while working with a skilled worker.
11. Coaching is a process that enables the employee to progress to a desired state.
12. Mentoring refers to a personal developmental relationship in which a more experienced or more knowledgeable person helps a less experienced or less knowledgeable person.

For any training method to be effective, the trainee characteristics also require to be kept in mind while planning. For example, for training a new employee, job instruction by an experienced supervisor is considered appropriate. Similarly, for a computer-programing executive, a computer-based training or Web-based training (WBT) may be effective. In summary, there is no one-size-fits-all method as a recipe for all occasions. Rather it is a blended method that is often most effective.

Reflection Point

Flipped Learning

Flipped learning is an approach that involves reversing the traditional classroom model. In a flipped classroom, students watch lectures or complete readings outside of class, and then come to class to engage in hands-on activities and discussions.

Discussion Question

1. What will be the advantages of flipped learning as compared to the traditional learning methods?

5.3.11 E-learning

According to a recent estimate,[25] the number of Internet users in India currently stands at 462 million (July 2016) and it has overtaken the USA (286 million) as the second largest Internet base in the world. The phenomenal advance in the Internet and mobile connectivity in the recent time provides a serious opportunity for the growth of e-learning in India. A robust Internet ecosystem with a multitude of local and global players is expected to help online learning make important inroads.

The first IT-based teaching tool arrived in India in the 1980s through the introduction of computer-based training, with study material being stored in CD-ROMs. The e-learning market, however, picked momentum with the emergence of the information and communication technology (ICT), and later with Internet and broadband connectivity, which fueled WBT models.[26]

E-learning is defined as 'the delivery and administration of learning opportunities and support via computer, networked and Web-based technology to help individual performances and development' by Pollard and Hillage,[27] who further depict it as 'just in time, just enough, and just for you' learning. In general terms, e-learning describes the sphere of use of technology to deliver learning and training programs through CD-ROM, Internet, intranet, wireless, and mobiles. Introduced in 1995, it went through several avatars such as Internet-based training, WBT, online learning, before it finally took the form of 'e-learning' (the 'e' adopted during the dot-com boom).

There are two varieties of e-learning: synchronous training and asynchronous training. In synchronous learning, which works on fixed time availability, the participants interact live with an instructor through the Web. It thus has a wider reach than the traditional classroom as it can be accessed by larger number of participants located anywhere in the world. The asynchronous, training provides more flexibility as it lets the trainees work on the WBT at one's own pace and there is no real-time interaction with the instructor. A third form, known as blended learning, synthesizes synchronous and asynchronous learning methods. Blended style combines online learning, face-to-face interaction, and other methods for distribution of learning content. Blended learning courses provides learners with the positive features of both face-to-face interaction and technology-based delivery and instructional methods, such as online learning, distance learning, or mobile technologies such as iPods and personal digital assistants (PDAs).[28]

E-learning also takes the form of computer-based training (CBT) which is a programed instruction with a mix of text, graphics, and multimedia stored in a CD. Various companies also develop their own learning management system (LMS) embedding their own strategies and intended training outcome.

E-learning has many advantages. It has wider reach across geographies and trainees have the flexibility to choose what they want to train on, how, and when. It supports the company's business strategy and objectives. The spread of e-learning has been hamstrung due to cost, lack of motivation among employees to learn online, and lack of management buy-in. There is, however, evidence that as the technology further improves and the cost reduces, technology-based training is expected to completely replace the traditional classroom training.

---

[25] *Internet Live Stats.* Available at: www.InternetLiveStats.com (accessed on November 13, 2017).

[26] S. Kaushal, 'E-learning: Moving Toward a Self-servicing Society,' EY. Available at: http://www.ey.com/IN/en/Industries (accessed on November 13, 2017).

[27] E. Pollard and J. Hillage, 'Exploring E-Learning' (Report no. 376, Institute of Employment Studies, Brighton, 2001).

[28] Noe, *Employee Training and Development.*

The prospects for e-learning are widening. By 2015, the global e-learning market is expected to reach US$107 billion by 2015. The global self-paced e-learning market revenues are estimated to reach US$49.9 billion in 2015. The LMS market is expected to worth approximately US$4 billion in 2015 and over US$7 billion in 2018. The mobile learning products and services market is estimated to reach US$8.7 billion in 2015 and US$12.2 billion by 2017. For self-paced e-learning, India is estimated to grow by 55%, better than China at 52%.[29]

5.3.12 Employee Development

The last of the famous 12 Q of Gallop's Employee Engagement Survey runs like this: 'In the last year, have you had opportunities to learn and grow?' Employee development is a key component of an organization's endeavor to foster quality mindset, to meet challenges of global competition, and to adapt to the march of technology in the workplace. There are four approaches to develop employees: formal education, assessment, job experiences, and interpersonal relationships.[30] One or more of these approaches are generally used by majority of the organizations. Formal education is enrolment in offsite or onsite courses, often in tie-up with an academic institution of repute. Assessment, most commonly used to select on the basis of potential, provides data about the employee's competencies. Job experiences are enhanced by rotating the employee through multiple jobs. Interpersonal relationship covers interaction with a seasoned member of the organization and takes the form of mentoring or coaching. Development programs need individualized plans, learner motivation, and support by the superior.

5.3.13 Evaluation of Training

When a training program closes, several questions come to mind: 'Was it worth the money spent on it?' 'What do the participants know that they did not know before?' 'What can they do now, which they were unable to do before?' 'How have their feelings and attitudes improved as a result of the training?' 'What, in a nutshell, is the training outcome?' In order to respond to these questions, it is necessary to have a planned process. Evaluating training is a key to the success of an organization's T&D programs.

There are several issues connected with the evaluation of training:

1. Treating training as an independent event, separated from the overall organizational process
2. Imperfect criteria for measuring the financial benefits of training
3. Lopsided bias on learning without linkage with performance
4. Multiple dimensions of training evaluations leading to confused measures

An L&D survey conducted by CIPD in May 2016 revealed that the majority of employers carry out some evaluation of learning interventions in their organizations. The types of evaluation used by employers who took part in our survey include:

- Happy sheets, that is, post-training questionnaires capturing the degree of satisfaction about program
- Testimonies of individuals and direct observation

---

[29] Available at: https://elearningindustry.com/elearning-statistics-and-facts-for-2015 (accessed on September 21, 2017).

[30] R. J. Campbell, 'HR Development Strategies,' in *Developing Human Resources*, ed. K. N. Wexley (Washington, DC: BNA Books, 1991): 5-1–5-34.

- Return on expected outcomes
- The impact on business key performance indicators
- Return on investment
- Development metrics (such as psychometrics or 360-degree feedbacks)
- Quantitative survey methods to assess behavior change

Source: CIPD Factsheet.

The most famous training evaluation model was authored by Donald J. Kirkpatrick. The model has four levels of evaluation: reaction, learning, behavior, and results.

1. **Reaction** This level is about trainee satisfaction (what the trainees thought/felt about the training). The question being asked is: What did trainees think of this training? What is evaluated at this level is the reaction of individuals to the training or other improvement intervention.
2. **Learning** The focus at this level is learning (the impact on knowledge or capability). The question being asked is: Was there an increase in knowledge or skill level? The degree of improvement in learning here is measured with the aid of course tests.
3. **Behavior** This level assesses the change in behavior (improvement in behavior and capability as reflected in actual practice). The question being asked is: Is new knowledge/skill being used on the job? The measure of the transfer learning to actual behavior change in the workplace.
4. **Results** An outcome measure (the overall impact of training on the organizational environment and business results as a consequence of the performance of the trainee). The question being asked is: What effect did the training have on the organization?

The progression from level one to level four is based on degree of difficulty. The general findings of many surveys indicate that the level one evaluation prevails in most organizations in some form or the other, but the number shrinks as one climbs the levels. In fact, research from the ASTD shows that over 75% of organizations measure only the level of reaction through the use of questionnaires, the 'smile' or 'happy sheets.' The ASTD study also showed that 44% of the US corporations measured how much people learned, while only 21% how much people changed their behavior as a result of training; indeed, a mere 11% measured whether training affected organizational results.[31] It is felt that rather than try to adapt all four levels of evaluations, organizations should concentrate on the level that is most appropriate for them. A common criticism against Kirkpatrick's model is that it cannot be used to determine the cost–benefit ratio of training (i.e., ROI). Among the critics, Jack Phillips went on to improve on Kirkpatrick's four levels to emphasize ROI on the basis of training cost and organizational impact.

5.3.14 ROI Evaluation

The ROI approach to training evaluation uses the cost–benefit method for determining the return-on-investments. The costs can include equipment, facilities, personnel, and materials costs at different stages of training process. The benefits can also be calculated using different approaches. One tested method is to use a controlled group and an untrained group and compare the performance over a period of time on parameters of quality, productivity, and so on. The benefits can also be identified by comparing the original training objectives with the outcome of the program. The ROI is calculated by

31 Robert Craig. (Ed.). Chapter 5. (New York, NY: McGraw-Hill): 575–600.

dividing return or benefits by costs. ROI approach, however, may be suitable only in situations where the outcomes are clearly measurable and the training is long-term as well as strategically focused. Some of the other alternate training evaluation approaches are shown in Table 5.2.

Table 5.2 Examples of some alternate training evaluation approaches

Approach	Components	Focus
Hassett's training investment analysis	1. Needs analysis 2. Information gathering 3. Analysis 4. Dissemination	Profitability
CIPP	1. Context 2. Input 3. Process 4. Product	Systematic evaluation of learning
Kaufman's five-level evaluation	1. Enabling 2. Reaction 3. Acquisition 4. Application 5. Organizational output 6. Societal outcomes	Micro and mega analysis. Considerations of organizational factors
CIRO by Warr	1. Context 2. Input 3. Reaction 4. Output	Achievement of organizational objectives through training
Bushnel's IPO Model	1. Input 2. Process 3. Output 4. Outcome	Tracking the progress of the employees through predetermined key performance indicator (KPI)
Training valuation system model	1. Situation analysis 2. Intervention 3. Impact 4. Value	Systems-based

5.4 THE FUTURE OF TRAINING, LEARNING, AND DEVELOPMENT—CRYSTAL GAZING INTO THE FUTURE WORLD OF LEARNING

5.4.1 Technology-driven Learning

In the shifting landscape of corporate learning, the fulcrum now is the rapidly evolving technology. The easily distracted new corporate executive is looking for instant gratification, and new levers in corporate learning—in the form of immersive games such as 'Gods of War,' 'Sky ream,' and 'Assassin's Creed.' M-Learning or 'learning via mobile devices,' be it smart phones or tablets, are the emergent mainstay for functional training.[32] Collaborative knowledge-sharing, cloud-based systems, Wikis, blogs, online bulletin boards will be the common parlance in the new world of the CLO.

[32] Gautam Bhushan, 'Emergent Trends in Organizational Learning,' *People Matters*, September 1, 2011.

5.4.2 AI in L&D

Artificial intelligence in L&D is a fast developing domain. District possibilities are emerging of AI application in education. It is realized that AI can phenomenally augment learning experience, make instructions more effective, and offer personalized and efficient learning experience.

Despite the fear of job loss in a wake of the emergence of tech infushion, generative AI holds many prospects for more impactful and democratized and easily accessible L&D across geographies. 'In a fast-changing world where work culture has completely revolutionised, the basic problem L&D[33] is information searching, discovering and collecting the information and putting them into a forum,' says Global HR industry analyst Josh Bersin in a conversation with CoRise's Julia Stiglitz and Sourabh Bajaj.

Exhibit Application of AI in L&D

1. **Personalized Learning/Tutoring system** Enable personalized learning by analysing the learner's performance and personalizing the curriculum or content and feedback and guidance.
2. **Content** AI can create educational content, like videos, quizzes/other interactive materials, thus. This can save time and resources for educators and trainers.
3. Testing Design adaptive tests that adjust the difficulty of the questions based on the learner's performance so that a more accurate assessment of the learner's knowledge and skills can be obtained.
4. Chatbots /virtual assistants AI–driven chatbots and virtual assistants can help with continuous resources addressing questions/providing on the material.
5. Predictive analytics AI can predict student performance, identify at-risk students, and provide personalized interventions that can help them improve.

Discussion Questions

1. How is AI going to change the landscape of skills and knowledge in India?
2. What factors would enable the adoption of AI enabled L&D in India?

Source: Seven Roles of Artificial Intelligence in Learning and Development. https://www.hurix.com/role-of-artificial-intelligence

5.4.3 Self-directed Learning

The days of instructor-led classroom training appear to be on the wane. It already seems to be another era, when training was an event. Organizations seem to have come around to the view that behavior modifications cannot and do not occur by virtue of a single training program. There is rather a growing preference of treating training as a continuous process, taken at the learner's choice, at his pace, in bite-sized nuggets. There is a lot of variety in the learning kitty—problem-based learning, experiential learning, and action learning—all of which have evolved to new levels. Add to this the right mix of 'buddy programs' and 'field coaching.'

33 In Focus: L&D in a world of AI and ChatGPT. Jagriti Kumari. Mar 5 2023. https://www.peoplematters.in/article/training

5.4.4 Training to Aid Virtual Work Arrangements

In virtual work arrangements, where employees from multiple organizations work on projects, there will be a growing thrust for training to foster digital collaborations. The specific training inputs in demand will be Web-based delivery on intercultural sensitivity, teamwork, and communication.

5.4.5 Training Partnerships

Corporate training departments will increase partnership with academic institutes of repute to develop content for training, especially on leadership development and strategy. L&T, Bharat Petroleum are some of the companies in private sector as well in public sector who have struck tie-ups with Harvard, Wharton, and INSEAD to develop their leaders. Training will also cover non-employee groups such as suppliers, dealers, and customers to enable deeper knowledge of products, services, and the organization in general. Deloitte's 'Global Human Capital Trends 2015' on the basis of research conducted across 295 US organizations shows that many organizations are increasing their investment in internally developed talent because they realize that they cannot recruit all the talent they need from external sources. The research also reveals that the roles and responsibilities of most L&D practitioners have grown more diverse, and that more time is being spent on sourcing and incorporating a variety of externally produced content into current learning portfolios, ostensibly in the belief that externally produced content can help to better address the changing needs of both businesses and learners. The focus is clearly on long-term goals, to develop baseline proficiencies of existing employees. It is expected to also align workers with the needs of the business, to meet present objectives while ensuring that the talent pipeline is equipped to address future challenges.[34]

Closing Case Training Programs at Toyota Kirloskar Motors (Gurukul)

The training structure at the learning academy of Toyota Kirloskar Motors (TKM, Gurukul) is based on the role and skill requirements with respect to their designations. The structure has two segments: corporate and functional.

The Corporate segment, anchored by the HR, focuses on skill development of all the employees. The programs include Fundamental Skill Training (FST), Element Work Training (EWT) and Standardized Work Training (SWT), in addition to culture-based trainings, such as Toyota Production System, standardized Work and Kaizen, Team Leader Role and Group Leader Role. Other programs include Basic Microsoft Office, Cross Culture Awareness, Planning and Scheduling, Toyota Way Foundation, Power Your Presentation Skills, PDCA and A-3, Toyota Business Practice, Deputy Managers Development Program and Post Promotion for Managers.

The Functional segment, managed by individual sections and departments, is mostly need-based, for instance, Auto-CADD, Macros, Robotics Training, Taxation, and Budget Impact.

The company uses adult pedagogy. Visual manuals are specially developed to make the trainees understand the concepts and their application in an effective manner. Similarly,

[34] 'WhatWorks®market brief,' August 26, 2015, PRNewswire. Available at: https://www.prnewswire.com/news-releases/bersin-by-deloitte-learning-and-development-spending-soars-again-as-organizations-invest-to-close-skill-gaps-300133478.html (accessed on November 13, 2017).

emphasis is on experiential learning, for example, hands-on experience, simulations, activities and competitions.

Toyota Kirloskar Motor's learning model is composed of on-the-job development, self-initiated projects, and classroom training.

Toyota targets 70% development efforts through On-the-job training (OJT). This experience serves as a driving force in developing the next generation. Further, self-initiated projects to cultivate self-motivation and to enhance communication skills (20%) and classroom trainings (10%) supplement the learning inputs for the employees, which cannot be covered by OJT. There is special focus on the development of specialized knowledge, ability and skills for the accomplishment of work operations.

Toyota Kirloskar Motors follows a comprehensive Learning Needs Assessment of employees to decide on developmental needs, and the content is set accordingly. Opportunities are created for each employee to implement their learning in their respective jobs. Continuous monitoring ensures that complete utilization of the learning opportunities is achieved.

Training programs are organized in three stages. The first stage comprises the fundamentals, wherein employees are imparted basic skills and approach to perform the job. Following this, employees move to the next stage—elementary work training, where the focus is on developing a combination of key skills in a single job. In the third stage, which consists of standardized work training, all employees need to work in the same manner repeatedly since manufacturing happens on a conveyor line.

In every step of this training program, employees have to pass through various tests. Then, on-the-job development occurs on the shop floor, offline. After gathering adequate knowledge and skills, the employees are fully equipped to perform their job.

Discussion Question

1. Please make a training evaluation plan for Toyota Kirloskar Motors based on aforementioned information.

Source: HR Katha News Bureau, 'Toyota Transforms Raw Talent into World Class Skill Champions,' New Delhi, October 29, 2015.

SUMMARY

Training allows an employee to acquire necessary skills, produce better results, delight the customer with impeccable and consistent service and product quality, and make the company profitable and competitive. As per the resource-based view, cutting-edge training equips the employees with unique abilities that provide the competitive edge to the business as they cannot be easily replicated. In today's ever-changing market-driven business environment, if an organization has to deliver according to the customer expectations on a sustained basis, the employees will need the requisite skills to perform the job assigned to them. These skills, which include technical, analytical, and people skills, are developed through proper training conducted by trained and competent professionals. Training helps people to improve their competencies and to perform better on current as also future job assignments. High quality training also fosters better performance ratings, which leads to employee satisfaction and engagement.

Effective training systematically incorporates learning principles from the learner's perspective. There are several theories about how a person learns. An influential theory is known as Bloom's

Taxonomy. It is a classification of levels of learning ('taxonomy' means classification) formulated by Mr Benjamin Bloom, along with a team of educational psychologists in 1956, based on extensive research in the field. The trigger for the research was to go beyond the conventional rote learning, which emphasizes remembering, to more advanced forms of thinking. The said Taxonomy talks about a hierarchy of learning, categorized into three intertwined domains: cognitive, affective, and psychometric. Apart from this, other theories of training include andragogy, social learning, action learning, and experiential learning.

Training, to be effective, needs to be based on a training need analysis that includes organization analysis, task analysis, and person analysis. Organization analysis scans the external environment (trends, government policies, and so on) as also the internal environment (the business strategy of the organization, the resources for training activities, and the pulse of managers, the peers, and the subordinates) to decide which part of the training activities should demand attention and focus. A task is the work activity relevant to a particular job. The task analysis covers a complete listing of all the work activities and the KSAs necessary for performing those activities. It is a four-step process: selection of the job, generation of a primary list of the activities performed on the job, the validation of the list by job incumbents/managers, and finally identification of the KSAs to perform the activities. Person analysis focuses on the individual employee's needs for training. The needs are generally caused by non-performance or an employee moving into a new role.

An important aspect of training is its evaluation. Training requires a clear line of sight with the business outcome. An important contribution in evaluation of training literature is the four-stage evaluation by Donald Kirkpatrick. At level one, known as reaction level, the focus is on trainee satisfaction (what the trainees thought/felt about the training). At the second level, known as learning level, the key idea is learning (the impact on knowledge or capability). At the next, that is, behavior level, the effort is to assess the change in behavior (improvement in behavior and capability as reflected in actual practice). Finally, at the last level, that is, results level, there is an outcome measure—the overall impact of training on the organizational environment and business results as a consequence of the performance of the trainee.

In the new millennium, the process of T&D is acquiring new emphasis. The emergent trends include technology-driven learning, self-directed learning, and training partnership, among others. Clearly, the focus is clearly on long-term goals, to develop baseline proficiencies of existing employees. It is expected to also align workers with the needs of the business, to meet present objectives while ensuring that the talent pipeline is equipped to address future challenges.

Short-answer Questions

1. Differentiate between *Learning* and *Development.*
2. Describe the impact of employee training.
3. Mention three objectives of training.
4. Mention three recent trends in training.
5. Define andragoggy and its basic principles.
6. What is psychometric domain?
7. Describe Kolb's Learning Cycle.
8. How is person analysis done?
9. What are the advantages of e-learning to the learner?

10. Explain Kirkpatrick's training evaluation model.
11. Explain self-directed learning and its advantages.

Discussion Questions

1. As a training manager in a continuous chemical process plant, what would you do to improve the participation levels of e-learning and self-learning modules?
2. Your company, a BPO, wants to introduce a PMS based on balanced scorecard and link it with incentive plan. How would you go about making a training strategy for managers and employees?
3. Design a training program for supervisors to ensure that they balance quality with productivity. This is in the context of recent rise in the numbers of customer complaints about product defects.
4. If you have to embed the principles of Bloom's Taxonomy in the aforementioned program, what are the few things that you will do?
5. As a training manager in a new insurance company, you propose a 50% increase in the training budget over last year. What would be your main arguments to convince the CEO?

CHAPTER 6

Competency Management

LEARNING OBJECTIVES

After completing this chapter, the student will be able to:

- Describe the basic terminologies used in competency management process
- Explain the context and evolution of competency studies
- Define a competency dictionary and describe its uses
- Create a competency model in a step-by-step process
- Know the application of competency models
- Describe the importance of assessment centers and how to set up an assessment center

Opening Case Competency Management and Organizational Transformation–The Bharat Petroleum Story

In the year 1997, in a deregulated business environment, BPCL geared up for the competition by refocusing on improving customer service and profitability. It decided to embark on a comprehensive process of organizational redesign and restructuring process with the help of a well-known global strategy consulting firm. In the redesigned organization, the erstwhile business structures, which were based on regions and functional excellence, gave way to an agile system of SBUs. It led to a delayered, flat organizational structure (where eight levels were collapsed to three effective levels), which was to be flexible, entrepreneurial, responsive to external changes and competitive market forces, team-based, and congenial to learning. In this new organization, the key business role was entrusted to the newly created position of territory managers. The territory managers were fully empowered with administrative and financial authority to effectively deal with customer issues.

In the process of implementing change, it soon began to be realized that there was a key challenge in the style and behavior of leaders. The leaders required new competencies, some of the prominent ones being coaching and teamwork and cooperation. The territory managers, who were placed to handle the business in an anchoring role, required the wherewithal for dealing with such a crucial role. They needed to be carefully groomed over a period of time, with appropriate developmental inputs. This brought to the surface the need for developing a model for the required competencies, to assess the gap between the target levels and the levels of the individual role holders, for the purpose of deciding on specific developmental inputs.

In October 2001, after a detailed research into the emerging trends in L&D, the head HRD, learned about the emerging field of competency modeling, and engaged a well-known, premier consulting firm to help implement a competency management process. The purpose was to improve the 'liquidity' of the rookie territory managers by accelerating their learning to eventually obtain enhanced performance. It was realized that the L&D process also needed to be strategic, in sync with the business objectives of the orga- nization, and therefore, it was crucial to identify specific competencies of the territory managers, which were connected with customer services and building profitability.

The first step was to create a steering committee, which consisted of the senior leadership—the heads of SBUs, the directors and HR senior leaders. A competency modeling workshop was conducted where, along with the steering committee members, a broader select group of leaders from the different functions and HR created the competency model for territory managers, based on the inputs of the group as also the recent performance management data in respect of outstanding and average performers among the territory managers. The process followed was as follows:

1. Strategic planning: Identify the role to be studied.
2. Resource planning: Agree on action steps, work plan, accountabilities, and logistics.
3. Train interviewers: Training of selected executives for internal accreditation.
4. Expert panel: Identify outcome measures, key tasks, and preliminary competencies based on expert knowledge.
5. Select sample: Determine who will be interviewed.
6. Conduct behavioral event interview (BEI): Identify competencies and their behavioral indicators.
7. Administer questionnaires: Provide assessment tools to measure competencies, behaviors, outcomes, or other useful information.
8. Transcribe BEI: Transcribe BEI tapes.
9. Code: Analyze each interview for evidence of demonstrated competency in the performance of the job.
10. Data input: Consolidate codes and other data into database through online coder or scan sheets.
11. Data analysis: Run preliminary analysis of competency relationships and differentiation.
12. Concept formation: Identify those characteristics demonstrated more often or better by outstanding performers. Create clean and valid competency model through integration of all data into a useful conceptual framework.
13. Validation: Ensure the model reflects and is fully sensitive to the nuances of the organization culture. Obtain feedback from broader audience to further refine the process. Establish the ability of the competency model to predict performance on the job.

The critical part of the process of competency modeling was the use of BEI to obtain critical competency data that predict superior performance, the identification of competencies that have the most impact on performances in that role, the scales of competency, and so on. The competency model that emerged out of the workshop had 3 clusters and 16 competencies. The model described the threshold level that a territory manager must have and a desired level. While it created a buzz, the questions that were in the wind were: How to leverage the competency approach and how to establish some concrete performance outcomes?

Discussion Questions

1. What are your views about how BPCL went about the competency modeling process? Were there any key steps that were missed out?
2. What should be the way forward? What HR processes need to be linked with the competency models of the territory managers and how to do that?

6.1 INTRODUCTION

Human capital is increasingly being acknowledged as the source of competitive advantage and companies are taking great care to acquire, nurture, and retain the talented employees. Against this backdrop of the scramble for talent, competency-based management has become the new shiny object of HRM for around the last four decades, creating unprecedented surge of interest among the business leaders and academicians alike. A fresh new field in HRM, it provides a clear line of sight between ability and successful performance. Currently, the bulk of Fortune 500 companies, among others, are committed to this approach as the bedrock of their talent management strategy. Competency-based management is helping organizations to identify how their critical performers behave while performing and to create profile of superior performers in important roles.

6.2 THE EVOLUTION OF COMPETENCY MANAGEMENT

The origin of the competency studies can be traced to the endeavors of the renowned educationist Benjamin Bloom and his team in the USA in the mid-1950s with the identification of educational objectives, along with a clear definition of the KSAs to go with them. The group contributed by its painstaking work over a period of time with a concise classification of the educational objectives grouped under the cognitive domain. The competency studies started with Robert White[1] who suggested competency as a human trait. The renowned Harvard psychologist David McClelland is credited with having pioneered the competency movement in organizations across the world. His classic books such as *Talent and Society*, *Achievement Motive*, *The Achieving Society*, *Motivating Economic Achievement,* and *Power the Inner Experience* brought out several new dimensions of the competencies.[2] The competencies uncovered by McClelland relate to the affective domain in Bloom's terminology. The breakthrough in competency movement came with an article published by McClelland in *American Psychologist* titled 'Testing for Competence Rather than Intelligence' in 1973. McClelland clearly turned the focus of the organizations to competence as a new zone for L&D. In that article, David

[1] R. White 'Motivation Reconsidered: The Concept of Competence,' *Psychological Review* 66, no. 5 (1959): 279–333.
[2] T. V. Rao, 'Art and Science of Competency Mapping: An Update,' *NHRD Network Journal* 3 (2010): 46–53.

McClelland described researches that challenged the validity of the time-honored instruments for aptitude and knowledge as predictors of either job performance or success in life. Subsequently, McClelland[3] and R.E. Boyatzis[4] developed the concept further and presented 'competence' as the central piece in planning, organizing, integrating, and improving the entire gamut of HRM systems.

The term 'competency' has got different connotations. In the HRM literature, competency describes outstanding performance of individual employees in specific roles.[5] It differs from competence in a more general sense, meaning a specific skill that an employee has.[6] At the same time, in strategic management studies, competencies implied attributes of an organization as a whole, including core competencies and dynamic capabilities.[7] The terms 'competency' and 'capability' have sometimes been used interchangeably, though capability indicates unique strengths at the collective or organizational level of analysis, which represents the strategy management viewpoint.[8]

6.3 WHAT IS COMPETENCY?

Operationalizing the term 'competency' poses the first major hurdle in competency studies.[9] Initially considerable confusion existed in the difference between the terms 'competence' and 'competency.' The generally accepted position is that 'competence' relates to 'performance of work' and 'competency' describes the behavioral abilities of the manager required to perform the work effectively.[10]

Sparrow[11] conceptualized this in terms of behavioral attributes that can distinguish a superior performer from average. Athey and Orth,[12] on the other hand, stated job-related competency in terms of a set of observable performance dimensions, such as individual knowledge, skills, attitudes, and behaviors; collective team, process, and organizational capabilities that are linked to high performance and competitive advantage. According to Marrelli,[13] competencies are measurable human capabilities

---

3 D. C. McClelland, 'Identifying Competencies with Behavioral-event Interviews,' *Psychological Science* 9, no. 5 (1998): 331–339.

4 Richard E. Boyatzis, *The Competent Manager: A Model of Effective Performance* (New York, NY: John Wiley & Sons, 1982).

5 Boyatzis, *The Competent Manager.*

6 Christopher Rowe, 'Clarifying the Use of Competence and Competency Models in Recruitment, Assessment and Staff Development,' *Industrial and Commercial Training* 27, no. 11 (1995): 12–17.

7 C. K. Prahalad and Garry Hamel, 'The Core Competence of the Corporation,' *Harvard Business Review* 68, no. 3 (1990): 79–91.

8 Klas Soderquist, Alexandros Papalexandris, George Ioannou, and Gregory Prastacos, 'From Task-based to Competency-based: A Typology and Process Supporting a Critical HRM Transition,' *Personnel Review* 39, no. 3 (2010): 325–346.

9 J. S. Schippmann, R. A. Ash, M. Battista, L. Carr, L. D. Eyde, B. Hesketh et al., 'The Practice of Competency Modeling,' *Personnel Psychology* 53 (2000): 703–740. Available at: https://home.ubalt.edu/tmitch/651/competency%20modeling%20 trends.pdf (accessed on February 13, 2018).

10 Pierce, C. 'Tomorrow's Company Director: The Competency-based Approach'. (Conference Paper at RSA Inquiry, National Conference at Leeds, March 17, 1994).

11 P. R. Sparrow, 'Organizational Competencies: Creating a Strategic Behavioural Framework for Selection and Assessment,' in *International Handbook of Selection and Assessment*, eds. N. Anderson and P. Herriot (Chichester: John Wiley, 1997): 343–368.

12 T. R. Athey and M. S. Orth, 'Emerging Competency Methods for the Future Human Resource Management,' *Human Resource Management* 38, no. 3 (1999): 215–226.

13 Anne F. Marrelli, 'An Introduction to Competency Analysis and Modeling,' *Performance Improvement* 37, no. 5 (1998): 8–17.

that are required for effective work performance demands. For Dubois,[14] competencies are those characteristics—knowledge, skills, mindsets, thought patterns, and the like—that, when used either singularly or in various combinations, result in successful performance.

According to Spencer and Spencer,[15] competencies are underlying characteristics of people and 'indicate ways of behaving and thinking, generalizing across situations and enduring for a reasonably long period of time.' Five characteristics constitute competencies: motives (which drive, direct, and select behavior toward certain actions); traits (physical characteristics and consistent responses to situations or information); self-concept (a person's attitudes, values, or self-image); knowledge (information in specific areas); and skill (ability to perform certain physical or mental tasks). The skill and knowledge elements are indicated as visible or surface parts, easily improved, while self-concept, trait, and motive are hidden, deeper part of core personality, and thus harder to develop. For characteristics to become competency, they should also have a criteria reference, the most commonly used criteria being 'superior performance' and 'effective performance.' The authors have also described two categories of competencies being threshold competencies (signifying the minimum, essential abilities in a job) and differentiation competencies (differentiates superior from average performers).

For Boyatzis,[16] competencies are the underlying characteristics of an individual, which are causally (change in one variable causes change in another) related to effective job performance. Competencies also contain intent. It is the intent that describes the competency, not the behavior alone. For example, conducting a feedback session could be with the intent of closing a loop in the PMS, or to create justification for handing over pink slip to a team member, or to use it to coach for development.

Jackson and Schuler[17] defined competencies as 'the skills, knowledge, abilities and other characteristics that someone needs to perform a job effectively.'

For Intagliata and others,[18] most fundamentally, competencies provide organizations with a way to define in behavioral terms what their leaders need to do to produce the results the organization desires and do so in a way that is consistent with and builds its culture. They should provide the 'North Star' by which leaders at all levels navigate in order to create synergy and produce more significant and consistent results.

Hornby and Thomas[19] define competencies as 'the knowledge, skills and qualities of effective managers/ leaders.'

It may be difficult to find a coherent way in this maze of different perspectives. Charles Woodruffe[20] has tried to follow the lead by Richard Boyatzis and described 'competency' as a set of behavior patterns that the incumbent needs to bring to a position in order to perform its tasks and functions with competence. This definition clearly establishes that competencies are about people's behavior. They

---

14 D. D. Dubois, ed., 'Preface,' in *The Competency Casebook: Twelve Studies in Competency-based Performance Improvement* (Amherst, MA: HRD Press, 1998).

15 Lyle M. Spencer, Jr., and Signe M. Spencer, *Competence at Work* (New York, NY: Wiley, 1993).

16 Boyatzis, *The Competent Manager.*

17 S. E. Jackson and R. S. Schuler, *Managing Human Resources Through Strategic Partnerships*, 8th ed. (Mason, OH: Thomson South-Western, 2003).

18 J. Intagliata, D. Ulrich, and N. Smallwood, 'Leveraging Leadership Competencies to Produce Leadership Brand: Creating Distinctiveness by Focusing on Strategy and Results,' *Human Resource Planning* 23, no. 3 (2000): 12–23.

19 D. Hornby and R. Thomas, 'Towards a Better Standard of Management?' *Personnel Management* 21, no. 1 (1989): 52–55.

20 C. Woodruffe, 'What is Meant by a Competency?' *Leadership & Organization Development Journal* 14, no. 1 (1993): 29–36.

are, in fact, a discrete dimension of behavior, which is related to performance in the job. Competencies are 'behavioral repertoires that some people carry out better than others.'[21] So, while undertaking a job analysis, it is the behavioral dimension, which should be the focal point. Thus, an employee's performance is about the way she behaves and, while analyzing superior performance, the behavior aspect must be separated in the job analysis.

6.4 CLASSIFICATION OF COMPETENCIES

Competencies have been classified in several ways by different researchers.

Katz and Kahn[22] categorized competency into the following types: (a) technical or functional (knowledge, attitudes, skills, and such others associated with the technology or functional expertise required to perform the role); (b) managerial (knowledge, attitudes, skills, and such others required to plan, organize, mobilize, and utilize various resources); (c) human (knowledge, attitudes, and skills required to motivate, utilize, and develop human resources); and (d) conceptual (abilities to visualize the invisible, think at abstract levels, and use the thinking to plan future business).

Carrol and McCrackin[23] organized competencies into three main categories: (a) Core competencies:[24] a unique organizational ability in a strategic direction, something a company excels in as compared with its competitors. Core competencies constitute abilities that the employees should have, for example, a core competency in customer service. (b) Leadership/managerial competencies: competencies connected with leadership of teams and the organization. (c) Functional competencies: These are job-specific skills required to perform a particular job role or profession.[25]

Spencer and Spencer have used the term 'competency clusters' to categorize competencies. Clusters have been grouped based on the latent intent. An intent has been defined as 'a level of analysis between social motives and superficial behavior, 'specific to a particular circumstances',' and 'more ephemeral and surface quality than an underlying motive.' The examples of clusters are: achievement and action cluster, helping and human service cluster, impact and influence cluster, and managerial, cognitive, and personal effectiveness clusters.

Shellabear[26] suggests the following classification for a more precise evaluation:

1. **Practical competence** Ability to perform tasks
2. **Foundational competence** Understanding how and why tasks are done
3. **Reflexive competence** Ability to integrate activities along with understanding them so that learning occurs and changes happen in the required moments
4. **Applied competence** Ability to perform a series of tasks along with understanding and necessary response

---

21 Ibid.

22 D. Katz and R. L. Kahn, *The Social Psychology of Organizations* (New York, NY: John Wiley & Sons, 1986).

23 Carrol, A. and McCrackin, J., 'The Competent Use of Competency-based Strategies for Selection and Development'. *Performance Improvement Quarterly*, 11, no. 3 (1998): 45–63.

24 Hammel and Prahalad. Competing for the Future. (Harvard Business School Press, 1994).

25 Ozcelik and Ferman, 'Competency Approach to Human Resource Management Outcomes and Contributions I a Turkish Cultural Context'. *Human Resource Development Review*, 5 no. 1 (2006): 72–91.

26 S. Shellabear, 'Competency Profiling: Definition and Implementation,' 2002. Available at: http://www.consultseven.com/case/ pdf/Competency_Profiling.pdf (accessed on November 14, 2017).

6.5 WHAT IS A COMPETENCY DICTIONARY?

Individual competencies are defined in organization-specific manner, and the divergence of organizational characteristics are reflected in the way the level-specific behaviors for a given origination are described. Take the example of 'teamwork' or 'team management.' At the higher competency levels, one organization has defined it as 'ability to identify, utilize and synergize the contributions of a project team,' and another organization has defined it as 'ability to inspire and carry along the top management team including diversity management.'

A competency dictionary is specific to an organization. It is a record of the competency language used by that organization. It details, in the unique language of the firm, the combinations of competencies (technical, managerial, human and conceptual knowledge, attitudes, and skills). It consists of the general competencies pertaining to all jobs (e.g., communication, focus on results, and so on), the common competencies that are specific to the key jobs in that organization (e.g., initiative, teamwork, and so on), and also the core competencies for the organization (e.g., digital proficiency, customer service, and so on). These competencies are normally developed through research into the available literature, the best practices, and by customization based on the needs of the organization. Each competency is adequately defined, thus providing the user with reasonable clarity regarding the behavior related to a specific competency. The competencies include proficiency levels (3–5) or scales and each level/scale has differentiating behavior descriptors or indicators. The original research group of McBer & Company identified scale dimensions based on intensity or completeness of action, size of impact, and complexity and amount of effort.

Concern for order and quality scale

Level	Behavior description
–1	Lack of order: Lack of concern for order, despite problems caused by disorder.
0	Not applicable: Active order keeping is not necessary, or is done by someone else, or a lack of concern is noticed, but does not cause problems.
1	Keeps an organized workspace: Maintains an orderly workspace with desks, files, tools, and so on in good order.
2	Shows a general concern for order and clarity: Works for clarity. Wants roles expectations, tasks, and data crystal clear and in writing.
3	Checks own work: Double checks accuracy of information or own work.
4	Monitors others' work: Monitors quality of others' work, checks to ensure that procedures are followed. Or keeps detailed records of own or others' activities.
5	Monitors progress of a project against milestones or deadlines: Monitors data, discovers weaknesses or missing data, and seeks out information to keep data in order; general concern for increasing order in existing system.
6	Develops systems: Develops and uses systems to organize and keep track of information.
7	Develops complex systems: Puts new, detailed, complex systems in place to increase order and improve quality of data. Or deduces new needs (not having to do with order) from perceived disorder.

Source: Adapted from Spencer and Spencer, Competence at Work, 30.

It may be mentioned that the levels of proficiency for each competency are additive, meaning that when an employee shows proficiency at a certain level, it would imply that he can operate adequately at the competency levels below. The scales describe the degree of proficiency required by the organization inside a competency field. For example, focus on results are applicable both to the juniormost and the senior leadership levels; what varies between the competency requirements between these two roles is the complexity of the results required. The differentiation based on proficiencies makes it possible for organizations to adopt tangible development plans for individual role holders within the current roles and also across job roles from one level to the succeeding higher levels. In this way, indirectly competency scales help the process of career development, succession management, and HRP in the organization.

The differentiation also helps organizations in another way—in setting targets and levels of proficiency at different stages of their tenure—at the entry level, at the next level when he is fully effective, and finally, at the stretch/mastery stage when the employee has achieved some mastery over his role.

A competency dictionary, when developed internally, is likely to capture the distinctive and unique competencies necessary for the success of the organization and mirror its values, vision, and the characteristic manner of communicating within the organization. This, being an expensive and time-consuming process, sometimes the organizations opt for securing the dictionary from a reliable source. The advantages of a purchased dictionary is that it is likely to be a properly developed and researched, ready to be used, when required, to support employee development plans. The obvious limitation of such a dictionary is that it may not cover all the required competencies, and the competencies may be expressed in a language not suitable for the particular organization.

Very often, organizations go for a hybrid solution. An externally procured competency dictionary is adapted to the specific requirement of the organization by making suitable revisions to reflect the organization's own conventions of communication, sometimes by incorporating an extra behavioral indicator to reflect performance expectations of the organization. This method proves to be an expeditious and cheaper solution, suitable for the unique requirements of the organization.

Reflection Point

A World Economic Forum (WEF) study from 2016 identified 'large mismatches between the actual supply and demand of key-work related skills' leading not only to mismatches between skill demand and supply nowadays, but also between today's skills and future skill requirements. More specifically, there is a growing awareness of the gap between existing and needed digital competencies of the workforce to master the challenges of the digitalised future at work.

Discussion Question

1. Make an Internet research and list out the competencies that will be in demand over the next 5 years.

Source: World Economic Forum 2016.

6.6 COMPETENCY LIFE CYCLE

The competency management process consists of four stages that have an underlying, common purpose of continuous development of competencies for both the individual and the organization. The four stages are: competency mapping, competency diagnosis, competency development, and competency monitoring.[27]

The stages flow in the following manner:

In the first stage, the concept of competency mapping is presented to the organization with a broad outline of all the relevant competencies, which are most critical for it to achieve its business objectives, as contained in business plan, the project needs, and the requirements from key roles. At this stage, the competency levels for each job profile are also worked out in detail. Competency diagnosis is the theme of the second stage, when stock-taking is done of the current status of competencies and equivalent individual proficiency level. This stage also covers a skill gap analysis to inform the gap that exists between the actual and the desired number and level of competencies in accordance to the demands of the job roles. The planning and the scheduling of action plans for development of the number and proficiency level of competencies take place in the third stage of competency development. In the final stage, there is a continuous tracking of the results achieved by the competency development phase.

6.7 COMPETENCY MODELING

Competency model is the assortment or combination of knowledge, skills, abilities, and other characteristics (KSAOs) required for performing effectively on a particular job (Table 6.1). The development of competency models have made the employers turn to information on the job and the skills required to perform it as an aid to managing the employee performance. In that sense, competency models have been metaphorically referred to as the 'Trojan Horse' for job analysis, an indirect way to interest the employers in job analysis.[28] The competency model, by differentiating top performers from average performers, creates a strategic focus on only those characteristics in a job, which explain performance. Another important virtue of competency model is that it connects competencies to the business objectives and strategies.

Table 6.1 Example of a generic competency model of a manager

Weight	Competency
XXXXXX	1. Impact and influence
XXXXXX	2. Achievement orientation
XXXX	3. Teamwork and cooperation
XXXX	4. Analytical thinking
XXXX	5. Initiative
XXX	6. Developing others
XX	7. Self-confidence
XX	8. Directiveness/Assertiveness
XX	9. Information seeking
XX	10. Team leadership
XX	11. Conceptual thinking
	(Organizational awareness and relationship building) Expertise/Specialized knowledge

Source: Spencer and Spencer, Competence at Work, 191.

[27] Fotis Draganidis and Gregoris Mentzas, 'Competency Based Management: A Review of Systems and Approaches,' *Information Management & Computer Security* 14, no. 1 (2006): 51–64.

[28] Michael A. Campion, Alexis A. Fink, Brian J. Ruggeberg, Linda Carr, Geneva M. Phillips, and Ronald B. Odman, 'Doing Competencies Well: Best Practices in Competency Modeling,' *Personnel Psychology* 64, no. 1 (Spring 2011): 225–262.

There are several other ways in which competency models differ from the traditional process of job analysis. Unlike job analysis, which relies on interaction with the jobholders in a bottom-up way, competency modeling moves in a reverse way, the process starts with collective information from the leadership levels. Another important difference is that while job analysis is related to existing jobs, competency models can cover emerging future roles in emerging business also.

HRM Competency Model

An early model of HRM professionals (School of Business Administration, University of Michigan) consisted of business qualifications, change management, and HR activities.

A second model developed by McBer company includes three fields: objective management and practical management; interpersonal management and people management; and analytical reasoning.

A third model developed by Larson lists five groups of competencies: objective management and practical management; functional and organizational management; influence management; business knowledge; and technical skills of HRM.

Source: M. Beheshtifar and M.N. Moghadom, 'Studying the Competency Related Models in Succession Planning,' *European Journal of Economics, Finance and Administrative Services,* no. 34 (2011).

6.7.1 Steps in Competency Modeling

Scan the Environment

There are multiple factors, internal and external; having a bearing on the competencies of employees in an organization. They include the culture and values, the stage in the organizational life cycle, the market, the preferences of the customer, the presence of unions, and so on. The competency models need to be in harmony with the specific contexts of an organization. It also needs to align itself to the vision, goals, and the strategies of business to provide a sense of direction to the developmental needs of the employees. A model competency framework can create a clear line of sight and perfect alignment between the mission–vision, strategy, the core competency for the organization, the job family competency models, the technical/ managerial competencies required of the employees, the critical behavioral indicators, and finally the measureable performance and metrics for the employees.[29]

Secure Commitment of the Top Leadership

Support of the top management is desirable for several reasons: the budgetary approval for a process that could be time-consuming as well as expensive, for insight into the right direction for the business, the competency language appropriate and meaningful for the organization, and so on. Such engagement of senior leaders, leading different functional areas, also ensures valuable inputs in preparation of the models at different levels of the hierarchy.[30]

Specify the Standards of Performance

Since the construction of the competency model for a job solely rests on superior performance, it is imperative to select the right criteria for evaluating the performance. The source of the information

[29] Campion et al., 'Doing Competencies Well.'

[30] Ibid.

could be concrete outcome measures or the feedbacks from relevant groups like superior, peers, or stakeholders. The concrete measures or the hard data normally include sales volume or sales growth of market share in a marketing organization, or the number of policies sold in an insurance company. A combination of lead and lag measures could be useful to provide a balanced set of criteria for superior performance. For example, for an insurance company, the balanced performance criteria could be a combination of outcome measures, such as return on equity, combined mix, loss ratio, expense ratio, and performance measures, such as agency performance, policy holder satisfaction index, price monitors, underwriting quality survey, claims frequency, claims severity, and so on. Similarly, for an airline industry, while the lag parameters such as yield, optimized traffic mix, third-party revenues are important, the lead parameters such as safety audits and safety trends are also equally important.

The performance measure may not always be easily available and, therefore, it may be necessary to develop the criteria in certain situations. For example, in case of a refinery, despite having standard measures like throughput and profitability, the safety record may require to be built through measures like number of near miss accidents. Besides, in the absence of hard measures, the alternate criteria could be the performance ratings by superiors, or even better would be a 360-degree feedback of superiors, peers, and subordinates.

Determine the Composition of Comparison Groups

In competency modeling process, the two groups taken for comparison based on performance effectiveness normally are the outstanding performers group and the average performers group. The inclusion of a third group of poor performers can add complexity and enrich the process by making it possible to create a threshold level for related competencies, especially for selection and for career progressions. Many organizations are reluctant to experiment with the third group for fear of backlash against the process from the staff members so identified, or even from the supervisors who decline to categorize their subordinates as poor performers.

The recommended sample size for the criteria sample is 20 with 12 outstanding and 8 average,[31] the logic being that the size suits the statistical tools for testing hypotheses competencies.

Obtain Information

A principal tool for collecting competency data, established by David McClelland and his team at McBer & Company in the pioneering study, is known as BEI. It is a combination of Flanagan's critical incident method and the thematic apperception test, the former providing data about the cognitive style and the latter about facets of the job. This method offers competencies data that is beyond the reach of traditional task analysis, provides algorithms for differentiating competency levels, and generates data suitable for assessment. On the contrary, it is an expensive and time-consuming method, requiring specific expertise in BEI protocols, and excludes non-critical incidents from job analysis.

Competency modeling process has often been criticized for lack of rigor—'a hodgepodge of job and worker-oriented KSAOs' and 'ill-defined concepts with no clear meaning.'[32] A rigorous way of collecting competency data is through job analysis route, by listing details of each task and function by employees or observers. Importantly, job analysis can complement and validate the data provided by BEI.

31 Spencer and Spencer, *Competence at Work.*

32 P. R. Sackett and R. M. Laczo, 'Job and Work Analysis,' *in Industrial and Organizational Psychology*, vol. 12 of *Handbook of Psychology*, eds. W. C. Borman et al. (Hoboken, NJ: Wiley, 2003), 21–37.

The other methods of obtaining information include expert panels (through formation of focus groups), surveys (which, inter alia, explore the skill differentials between the superior and average performer), and direct observation. A novel method for data collection is through use of SMEs to build scenarios. It helps with current jobs and also future-oriented roles. Microsoft created Project Oxygen to use extensive analytics to create a competency profile for managers.

Data Analysis, Organization, and Presentation

All the information, thus compiled through various channels, are now analyzed to create the model of competencies for a job. Multiple analysts browse through the piles of data to eventually form hypothesis on the distinctive characteristics of the superior performer. The analysts also search for competencies typical of the organizations. Through repeated rounds of refinement the competencies descriptions achieve what is known as 'inter-rater reliability.' The process ends with a behavior codebook where each competency is described with citations from the BEI and the criteria for scoring.

Spencer and Spencer[33] suggested the following steps:

1. Conduct of thematic analysis to discover competencies from the data collected so far by
   - (i) Coding BEI transcripts for recognizable competencies from the dictionary
   - (ii) Conceptualizing new competency themes
     - (a) Form the analysts teams
     - (b) Individual analysis of BEI
     - (c) Team definition of competencies
     - (d) Preliminary testing of the competency coding system
     - (e) Reconciliation
     - (f) Statistical analysis of the BEI sample
     - (g) Coding the remainder BEI sample
     - (h) Final statistical analysis
     - (i) Final competency codebook for the job

6.7.2 Application of Competency Models in HRM

Selection

The application of the competency model starts with the selection process itself. Competency model can serve useful purpose in any of the following situations, when

1. There is abnormal employee turnover rate as compared to the trends in the industry, and it is hurting the business
2. There is consistent poor employee performance and low productivity, especially in a new business
3. New employees take too long to learn the skills required to perform adequately on their roles
4. There is urgent need to fill in managerial vacancies by identifying which of the new recruits would have the potential to make it
5. It becomes necessary to decide on the learning strategy for the new hires

33 Spencer and Spencer, *Competence at Work.*

6. There is a need to move people outside the organization following a merger–acquisition scenario

A competency-based selection system presumes a competency model for the target jobs with competency levels and behavioral descriptors. The choice of assessment tools for the selection will depend on the cost, the administrative convenience, and candidate acceptability. The selectors need to get trained in the interview protocols, especially in BEI techniques. Preferably, the selection process could be pilot run for validation. Later, based on experience, some database for job–person fit could be constructed for different jobs in the organization.

The assessment methods include assessment centers, BEIs, work sample tests, ability tests, and so on. BEI is a structured interview process developed by David McClelland and his colleagues at McBer & Company. It combined Flanagan's critical incidence method with thematic apperception test. If conducted properly, BEI can be used as a psychometric assessment instrument to assess individual competencies.[34] The tests could include operant tests (which require the taker to act) or respondent tests (where the taker plays a passive role).

6.8 ASSESSMENT CENTERS

Assessment centers originated around the time of World War II. The driver for the centers was the felt need for identifying competent candidates for dealing with the arduous and somewhat uncommon assignments required by the Office of Strategic Services (OSS) of the US government. Their initial negative experiences of a significant number of their selected candidates subsequently proving wrong fit for the job, prompted the OSS to decide on overhauling their entire traditional selection process with the help of external experts, to eventually formulate a new design of selection process that would more consistently predict the best fits for their crucial but unusual assignments. What came out of this experiment was the first assessment center in the USA in the year 1943, designed by and implemented with the advice of a team of psychologists hired by OSS.

In the center, the participants were instructed to perform on an assortment of simulated on-the-job situations. On the conclusion of the workshop and as an outcome of it, the OSS was able to successfully select candidates who proved to be better fit and more effective than earlier sets of candidates. The key element which was largely seen as having contributed to the success of the experimental method was the behavioral component of the design. The performance of the assessees during the various simulated, customized assignments, modeled on real-life job situations connected with the assignments, provided clear indications to OSS on which of the candidates were more likely to succeed than others. After the story of the OSS experiment became well circulated in the corporate world, there was a growing curiosity and interest about the potential of the assessment center technique as an effective predictor of a reliable selection process. The next to follow the footsteps of OSS was American Telephone & Telegraph (AT&T) to whom, however, the credit goes for being the first business organization to conduct research, and then to actually operationalize the assessment method in HR practices.

In a well-known study on longitudinal management research, begun in 1956, AT&T set out to identify the attributes which could predict an executive's potential ability to move up the management ladder. A customized assessment center served as the pivotal piece of measurement instrument for the research. Groups of managers were identified for assessment based on certain criteria, then assessed

[34] Spencer and Spencer, *Competence at Work.*

in a three-day assessment center, and later, the same group was reassessed after eight years. In 1958, AT&T used assessment centers for identifying employees from hourly rated categories for promoting to the level of supervisors. Gradually, many other large organizations (Sears, IBM, and GE, among others) followed suit in the use of assessment centers for selection, promotion, and employee T&D. By 1977, around 30,000 employees underwent assessment in the assessment centers covering at least 1000 organizations. It is now well established, based on many researches, that assessment centers are a valid and reliable instrument in employee selection.

6.8.1 The Center

An assessment center can have 4:1 to 1:1 assessee–assessor ratio. The assessors are drawn sometimes from inside the organization, sometimes from outside. While the external assessors can be psychologists, academics, and/or management professionals, the internal assessors are chosen from senior leadership levels. The internal candidates undergo training of varying duration in the protocols, especially in BEI techniques. All management consulting firms rely to a large extent on freelance assessors, some of whom may have been taken through the rigors of a standardized assessor accreditation process. The assessees are normally the junior-level managers.

The duration of the centers varies from 1 day to 10 days, from morning until night, with a social assessment event thrown together (typically, a dinner with premarked sitting arrangements).

The assessors write reports during and after the assessment process, event-wise and competency-wise in standard templates. The process closes with the most delicate phase of the center: the feedback process. This is handled with skill and much preparation to avoid any negative baggage or spillover effect. The best feedbacks build agreement on the assessments and leave the candidate with a definite map for his own development of competencies.

6.8.2 Exercises

In-basket

Describes the imaginary day in the life of a manager and the typical activities. Participants are presented with a bundle of memos, report notes of telephone calls received by others, letters, and the like. The candidates have to prioritize and plan actions on problems such as requests for leave, interpersonal conflicts, invitation for major and minor events, management meetings, and letters from the unions, and so on. The participant responses are classified into competencies such as problem-solving, decision-making, analytical thinking, conceptual thinking, and quality orientation. Sometimes the actual processing of the in-basket exercises is followed up with a questionnaire or a structured interview process with one or two assigned assessors, and the candidate is questioned on his logic for opting for a particular response in relation to an item and the rationale behind his priorities.

Leaderless Group Discussions

In a leaderless group discussion (LGD), a topic is presented to the group for discussion and for coming to a conclusion at the end of a specific time period. Problems could be how to use and allocate a tight budget, whom to retrench in a difficult situation, whom to select for a particularly crucial assignment, and so on. During the course of the meeting, the behavior of each participant is observed and his/her comments are coded to make assessment on how they interact and what leadership and communications skills each person displays.[35] The competencies observed in LGDs are interpersonal understanding, communication, impact and influence, team leadership, and teamwork and cooperation, among others.

Role Plays

A standard role-play theme is the irate customer (J. C. Penny's famous exercise of irate customer phone calls), dealing with an unhappy subordinate over a performance feedback session, breaking a bad news, and striving to prepare a contract negotiation with a supplier. The exercise is meant to test the participant's emotional self-control, information seeking, impact and influence, and so on.

Presentation of Vision and Strategies

The participants are given a limited time to prepare a presentation to be given to the top leadership group on the vision of the work group or the organization. The tools provided to the participants are flip charts, markers, transparencies, or laptops without Internet connection. After the oral presentation, the candidates are questioned on each item to look out for discrepancies in logic or data and to test the emotional involvement in the theme.

6.8.3 The Uses of Assessment Centers

A good number of assessment centers are used for selection and promotion. However, assessment centers can also yield good data on certain other domains of HR function such as career development, organization development, and succession planning. The combination of exercises in the assessment centers and the focus of the exercises vary depending on the intended use of the center outcomes for the specific HR processes. While the tools used reflect diversity, a common feature in all of them is the essential use of job simulation exercises. The participants are expected to demonstrate job dimensions of performance and typical employee characteristics in exercises that imitate critical incidents in the target jobs.

In selection and development contexts, the assessment center exercises replicate the basic tasks of the target jobs, so that the participants can demonstrate the important skills and dimensions, also the degree to which the employee characteristics can be applied effectively.[36] In the cases of career development/planning and organization development, the exercises would be less job specific, more broad based, and ranging across several rungs in the organizational hierarchy and competencies, which are common to all those levels. There is a shift in focus from precision in the assessor scores to quality of the assessor findings, because the end use is to generate data suitable for performance feedbacks and suggestions for development.

When the aim of the assessment center includes obtaining OD data, the target information will need to be culled from a summary of the aggregate information acquired across all participants by dimension. In case of succession planning, the source of the key data is the compared competency profile of the candidate to the competency model of the future role profile. This database proves vital in deciding on growing talent (if the competency can be developed) or importing talent (if the competency gap is unbridgeable). In order to avoid the expense on account of multiple assessment centers for different purposes, it is common to use the products of the selection/promotion assessment

---

[35] Schultz, D. P. and Schultz, S. E. *Psychology and Work Today: An Introduction to Industrial and Organizational Psychology*. 8th ed. (New York: McMillan, 1994).

[36] Dennis A. Joiner, 'Assessment Centers: What's New?' *Public Personnel Management* 31, no. 2 (Summer 2002): 179–185. Available at: https://doi.org/10.1177/009102600203100204 (accessed on June 1, 2002).

centers for the purposes of drawing information on career development, succession planning, and organization development.

Reflection Point

Shifts in Assessment Methods

Based on working with a wide and varied client base, here are the top five trends we've identified that are changing how assessment is delivered:

1. Movement away from traditional assessment delivery methods.
2. The end of the road for pen and paper.
3. Much more engaging and effective assessment.
4. Increasing levels of automation.
5. Assessments are much more candidate centric.

Discussion Question

1. Consider the role of a Junior Financial Analyst in a Fintech company. Discuss the pros and cons of automating the assessment process.

6.8.4 Criticism of Assessment Centers

Before commencing with the assessment centers, the organization should be clear about what purpose they are going to use the data for. The candidates, who are rated high, may get positive reputation inside the organization, but if no premium is attached to high performance, then it might eventually deflate the morale of such employees. The same is true of the reverse. In case of those candidates who have a low score, the damage done to their reputation is considerable, and if the organization does not clarify the implication of the scores, then it may be the 'kiss of death'[37] leading to serious disengagement. In the third place, assessment centers may also lead to the 'proliferation of the organizational man.'[38] An IBM study indicated that the supervisors may nominate those higher on conformity and lower on independence. Nevertheless, this problem is not inherent in the assessment center, but in the process of nomination.

Assessment centers have been described as more evolutionary than revolutionary. The tests that it bundles together were all there before. The key insight from assessment centers has been to know how to combine all these tests most effectively in a given situation.

6.9 PERFORMANCE MANAGEMENT

A purely outcome-based PMS suffers from several limitations:

1. Employees may not have control over the results.
2. Some employees have to be pushed down forcibly in rating due to the bell curve system.
3. Intangible process goals in some functions (HR, finance) may have to be compared with intangible outcome goals (sales, operations).

[37] Ann Howard describes the later situation in 'An Assessment of Assessment Centres,' *Academy of Management Journal* 17, no. 1 (March 1974): 115–134.

[38] Ibid.

4. Employees may not have been consulted over the targets.
5. Skepticism among sections of employees regarding the relevance of appraisal process.
6. It does not always cover the strategic direction of the organization.

A competency-based PMS aims to address all of the aforementioned issues. It endeavors to shift the focus from pure outcome orientation to competencies that an employee needs to acquire, to be able to perform effectively on not only the current job, but also on any future role that he may be found suitable for.[39] In a competency-based performance system, the employee receives a clear signal as to what capabilities the organization values and would want him to master. Thus while traditional PMS relies on the 'what' of the performance, uses qualitative measures, and adopts a short-term approach, a competency-based PMS relies on the 'how' of PMS, uses quantitative measures, and adopts a long-term approach. In a nutshell, the primary orientation in the former is rewards, whereas it is development in the latter.

In order to overcome the limitations of either approach, organizations often prefer a hybrid system known as a mixed model where the PMS incorporates a larger segment of KRAs as results (between 80% and 90%) and a smaller segment on competencies (between 10% and 20%). The aim is to provide a balanced opportunity to the employees to obtain results and they become more skilled and versatile.

The situations in which competency-based performance can be appropriate are:

1. When the business environment is dominated by external factors beyond the control of individuals. For example, the government decision to cancel the allotment of coal blocks created crisis for the aluminium industries for procurement of fuel.
2. When performance depends on teamwork. For example, execution of an IT project based on roles.
3. When the quality of the process is more critical than the result. For example, in a hospital and healthcare services, it is important how the quality processes are complied with in patient care.
4. When an organization adopts a blue ocean strategy to grow business in an unfamiliar field. For example, when a petroleum marketing and refining company ventures into oil exploration, it needs to give emphasis to quick learning rather than immediate results.

The building blocks for a competency-based PMS are as follows:

6.9.1 Describe Critical Competencies

In this step, the organization first explores and then specifies the core and cultural competencies that are critical success factors for the business and that each employee must possess along with the levels and the behavior descriptors. A marketing organization may specify customer/service orientation that each employee must exhibit at different intensity or scope; a research organization may select comfort with numbers and analytical ability as the core competencies.

6.9.2 Design the PMS Based on a Combination of Outcome Orientation and Competency Orientation

This step should also include setting targets and performance standards for competencies. The typical competency targets for customer service could include:

[39] David Martone, 'A Guide to Developing a Competency-based Performance Management System,' *Employment Relations Today* 30, no. 3 (2003): 23–32.

- Determine customer needs and expectations
- Address requests promptly and effectively
- Contact customers to follow up on services, solutions, or products to ensure that their needs have been correctly met
- Make extra efforts to understand customer needs

6.9.3 Coach for Performance Improvement

The coaching should cover both the employee and the manager. It should be based on a competency improvement plan owned by the employee with a targeted behavior-improvement road map. A critical condition for the success of the initiative would be the quality of training input to the manager regarding the process of coaching.

Competency-based T&D

Is competency learnable? Douglas McClelland responded in the affirmative, even for hard to train, deeper levels of the competency iceberg-like motive, for example, achievement motive.[40] This includes difficult to change traits such as self-confidence, which can be improved.[41]

The competency-based learning basket has many ingredients: training programs, individual development plans, computer-based online programs, developmental feedbacks, to name a few. An effective method of learning competencies uses four theories of learning and change.[42] One of the methods use the principles of andragogy through David Kolb's Learning Cycle (abstract conceptualization, active experimentation, concrete experience, and reflective observation. In the second place, McClelland formulated his famed theory of motive acquisition in a step-by-step process. Thirdly, the social learning theory emphasized the value of learning through behavior modeling. Lastly, the self-directed learning process of actual and desired goal and action steps.

A competency-based training program could involve the following structures:[43]

1. Formulate a competency model indicating the desired level of key competencies.
2. Identify specific competencies that can be developed with minimum effort and costs.
3. Choose an appropriate method, some of the options being development center, computer-based, or self-development.
4. Develop assessment centers and training curricula.
5. Conduct training programs for learners/trainers (where appropriate).
6. Evaluate training effectiveness.

Competence-based Compensation

Under the competence-based pay system, employees are paid not on the basis of their job but their competencies to do the jobs. Under this scheme, the more they learn, the more they earn.

Competency-based pay may be appropriate when (a) the organization is losing talent and unable to acquire the targeted talent; (b) certain employees with strategic skills are worth more than others; or (c) there is a felt need to motivate employees with incentives to acquire or upgrade key skills.

---

40 D. C. McClelland and D. G. Winter, *Motivating Economic Achievement* (New York, NY: Free Press, 1979).

41 Martin Seligman, *Learned Optimism* (New York, NY: Knopf, 1991).

42 Spencer and Spencer, *Competence at Work.*

43 Ibid.

While performance-based pay systems supplement base salary determined by organizational role with organizational output, with actual performance, results and economic benefits are brought into the firm. Competency-based pay systems pay for individual input characteristics for the ability to add economic value to the company at some future point in time.[44]

Case A Virtual Competency Assessment Model

In the United Kingdom, the adoption of a simulation based virtual assessment system by UK Fire and Rescue Service had led to a significant reduction of operational incident by approximately 40% in a decade.

The competency model named as 'Introspect model' lays down the process of assessment and simulation based training for the Fire Service personnel, and has been used, in conjunction with the use of XVR simulation software, in development sessions and during competence assessment over the last 6 years. The model focuses on the understanding of decision rationale, striving towards a state of unconscious competence within the crisis decision maker at the incident, to effectively compensate for the skill fade or inexperience, due to diminished incident exposure.

The need for the adaption of the competency model arose when a fire fighter in the Oxfordshire Fire and Rescue Service (OFRS), while attending a cross-border incident received life changing injuries. As a response, a process was introduced to within OFRS to assess and monitor the competence of all incident commanders within the service. This assessment process is now referred to as the 'Introspect Model', and has effectively readdressed this incident evaluation imbalance, over the last 5 years.

The key to 'Introspect Model's' success, is the unique method of self-reflection, which plays a key role in enabling employees to become metacognitive in their crisis management decision making skills. In crisis at a period of ill-defined goals and unique situations, the individual needed to recognize that typical 'pattern matching' techniques, used in their normal day-to-day decisions or application of standard policy or procedure, may not work. Instead, now the people made confident, robust decisions, being flexible at the same time to learn.

The key mantra in the Introspect model for all the decision makers was 'The right person, making the right decisions at the right time, for the right reasons'. The 'right person' is identified through a series of selection process covering aptitude, knowledge, and practical ability for the role. The 'right' decisions, 'right' time and the 'right' reasons, being much harder to define and measure, was done through a process of simulation.

A software (XVR) produced by a Dutch company (E-Semble), helped with the simulation used in assessments and development sessions. Assessment facilitators used the scope of simulation to create scenarios that are characteristic of their geographical or topographical area. It is also possible to recreate specific incidents for particular training issues or debriefs and to develop an array of incident types.

Discussion Question

1. What do you think are the positive and negatives of virtual competency assessment?

Source: Inspection Model: Competency Assessment in a virtual world. *Lamb K.* et al.; 2015.

44 Ibid.

6.9.4 Challenges for Competency Models

1. While competency models have curved a niche in the domain of HR practices by unifying multiple languages into a common language, at the workplace they cannot provide a recipe for every selection situation.[45] According to Ashworth and Saxton,[46] using competencies as an outcome can overlook 'the mental and personal processes that are utilized in developing and exhibiting skills and utilizing knowledge.'
2. It is also argued by some that sometimes individual employees succeed in their roles by making use of some unique competencies, which are difficult to articulate or categorize. The moot point is that such competencies have played a part in enhancing the competitiveness of the organization. It is quite probable that such 'idiosyncratic competencies' may be ignored where the sole emphasis for selection of an employee rests on the candidate fit to the model. Similar is the implication where the organization, again caught in the rigidity of the model, does not visualize the potential for use of developmental resources to where a gap exists.[47] In both situations, the organization stands to lose out on vital talent.
3. The use of competency models for appraising certain areas of performance and for developmental inputs in the performance feedbacks has also been criticized by some authors.[48] Besides, the process of defining or assessing competencies is still not an exact science. Sometimes, competencies cannot be precisely captured in behavioral terms, but rather there are behaviors related to these competencies. These competencies, thus, defy objective measurements and it is likely that they will be based on erratic notions of behaviors that reflect maturity, flexibility, cooperation, autonomy, and independence, among others. For these competencies, it is important to develop measures that confirm to certain standards of quality and professionalism.
4. Where the organization chooses to weave in competency models into the whole fabric of their HR practices (including performance management, L&D, talent acquisition, and compensation), the competency frameworks must be known to all managers and employees. It can also enhance the acceptance and general awareness of the competency model, if employees are involved in the process of development of the model.[49]

   The employee participation in the competency model-building process can also help in creating ownership and in melting the resistance to change. With the strategy of involvement of the entire organization in formulating the competency models and describing the meaning of individual competencies for that particular organization, there will be awakening of an organizational awareness of what causes the success of the organization. To fill up the white spaces in competency buildup, necessary learning strategies can be developed and offered.
5. The factor of employee communication, obtaining and securing trust as well as speaking to the hearts of employees poses one of the make or break challenges for competency modeling

---

45 T. Cockerill, J. Hunt, and H. Schroder, 'Managerial Competencies: Fact or Fiction?' *Business Strategy Review* 6, no. 3 (1995): 1–12.

46 P. D. Ashworth and J. Saxton, 'On Competence,' *Journal of Further and Higher Education* 14, no. 2 (1990): 3–25.

47 A. A. Lado, and M. C. Wilson, 'Human Resources Systems and Sustained Competitive Advantage: A Competency-based Perspective,' *The Academy of Management Review* 19, no. 4 (1994): 699–727.

48 Boyatzis, *The Competent Manager*.

49 A. D. Lucia and R. Lepsinger, *The Art and Science of Competency Models: Pinpointing Critical Success Factors in Organizations* (New York, NY: Pfeiffer, 1999).

initiative for an organization. In any competency implementation process, there are likely to be some managers who will be far from being receptive to the emergent competency models. The reasons could be their loss of trust in leadership, depressed levels of general motivation, and general mood of pessimism.

To brighten up the general mood of pessimism and to work around it, the employees have to see how new competencies can mold the growth of the organization. At the same time, they should be provided adequate resources in tools and time to develop the new competencies.

> If employees trust their management's strategy is the right one, they (regardless of level) will align themselves. Therefore, leaders need to take sufficient time to communicate and build trust. In many organizations where the focus hardly goes beyond the next quarterly report, this is a tall order. Those companies that understand the value of truly engaging their employees also emotionally will differentiate themselves from the pack in the long run.[50]

6. There are times when organizations adapt their competency models for future and make them in an aspirational manner. Long-serving employees, who may have been part of a conservative workplace that valued steadiness and risk aversion, had grown up with the organization with certain expectation of the future, the value the management team espouses, and the behaviors that are expected of the employees. If, at some point, there is a change of market dynamics, the takeover of a new management, or a merger, there may be change occurring, including adoption of new competency models and recruitment of new profile of employees to confirm to that framework.

   In such a scenario, to many of the old employees the entire exercise may appear strange, unreal, and unsettling, while to some others the same models may actually appear inspiring and exciting.

   In the aforementioned situation, there might be some buildup of tensions and there is bound to be some frictions. Although the truth is that future-oriented competency models fundamentally change the EVP, but the organization has to tread with caution. To be used successfully in an organization or other professional networks, competencies must be inclusive or integrated throughout all of the HR practices.[51]

7. The credibility of the HR function and its level of maturity also sometimes hold the key for the effectiveness of the competency management initiatives in an organization. In some cases, if the HR function finds the going hard, and fails to shape up in response to the demands of a competency approach, it may actually create roadblocks to the march of change. In such a situation, an external consultant is sometimes inducted to help implement the process by bringing in insights of the best practices.

   What may help is for the HR function to be brought on the same page at the beginning, to get aligned with the strategic direction. When HR's is a voice at the table that is not shy of pointing out the risks, and feels part of the end decision, it will be well positioned to help guide the human capital in the right direction.[52]

---

50 J. C. Hayton and G. M. McEvoy, 'Competencies in Practice: An Interview with Hanneke C. Frese,' *Human Resource Management* 45, no. 3 (Fall 2006): 495–500.

51 R. M. Fulmer and J. A. Conger, 'Identifying Talent,' *Executive Excellence* 21, no. 4 (2004): 11.

52 Hayton and McEvoy, 'Competencies in Practice.'

8. Finally, although competency models make available valuable information for employees, it requires a systematic implementation strategy to make use of the information effectively.[53] In the absence of a strategic implementation plan and a support structure, competency modeling ends up having a short shelf life, like many other HR initiatives having similarly flawed implementation approach. Competency model involves a transformational effort, affecting the way information is used to commence new HRD initiatives such as job design, career management, and so on. Overall, the drivers of the process should manage the new data with due discretion and confidentiality.

Case Competency Development Initiative at Zen Air

Zenith Airlines (India) Ltd. is the aviation sector of the Raman Group. It was founded in 2005 with the brand name Zen Air. Maintaining its forte in the domestic sector, it was created with an aim to offer affordable flight options across the country. Zen Air flights have been recording an average load of 86% and the highest load factors in the airline industry since 2007.

The top sectors for Zen Air are New Delhi to Mumbai, Mumbai to New Delhi, Srinagar to New Delhi, and Mumbai to New Delhi, where it operates 54, 54, 35, and 35 weekly flights, respectively. They also have occasional flights from Mumbai to Nagpur, Port Blair to Kolkata, and Kolkata to Patna.

In 2014–2015, Zen Air embarked on a comprehensive competency development process in order to ensure acquisition, retention, and competency upgradation of its managerial cadre. The new VP Sales and Marketing, who recently came over from the highly successful Zettihad, sought to introduce all the good practices in his earlier organization. In the first stage, Zen Air wished to cover the sales and marketing team. Currently, there is no competency model in place that has competencies, definitions, and proficiency levels for the sales and marketing team. There were some adverse customer feedbacks that were recurring on the Air Travelers.com site. Two such comments are cited here:

> Goa–Mumbai flight on Zen Air. The experience was simply horrible. The flight was delayed by more than 2 hours. On landing at Mumbai airport, we had to wait for more than 1 hour for our baggage as there was no Zen-Air staff for the same. I will never ever book any flight from Zen Air in future.
>
> I had the worst experience with Zen Air. I had a flight from Patna to Pune via Delhi. Due to poor visibility in Delhi they landed the flight in Lucknow, and kept us for 5 hours on plane without food. Staff were very rude, finally after 5 hours we were flown to Delhi. My Delhi to Pune flight was cancelled and they had no arrangement for it, neither were they giving us accommodation nor arranging any other flight.

The top leadership of Zen Air felt that there was a need to:

- Create a competency model with levels and behavior indicators
- Design a bouquet of assessment instruments to evaluate managers against this competency model
- Conduct the assessment centers and provide detailed feedback to the individuals and organization

[53] Richard J. Mirabile, 'Everything You Wanted to Know About Competency Modeling,' *Training and Development* 51, no. 8 (August 1997): 73–77.

- Create individual development plans for the individuals with a clear alignment with the organizational strategic focus
- Design development guides for learner-directed development actions

Based on the population details, the following numbers are available. However, 31 people have been identified by the organization. Details of the balance two people still need to be sent.

1. City managers: 15
2. Area sales managers: 2
3. Managers: 5
4. Senior managers: 2
5. Regional general managers: 3
6. General managers: 3

The group comprised of two levels: (a) junior-middle level and the (b) middle-senior level. The competencies were identified accordingly.

The following steps were taken:

Step 1: A Competency model was created based on

- Visionary interviews with the senior management of the organization to understand the objectives and goals of the organization
- Secondary research was conducted on the existing competency models of similar high-performing organizations through
- Competency definitions and proficiency levels were described based on the discussions and back-ground research
- Finally, the draft competency model was validated through discussions with HR department

Step 2: Assessment center was planned with following steps:

- Design of assessment matrix (Table 6.2)
- Assessment exercises for measuring individual competencies were identified
- Evaluation sheets were designed
- Planning and conducting of the logistics of assessment centers
- Preparation of a feedback report and individual development plans
- Feedback to individuals and validating the individual development plans
- Submission of reports to the organization

Table 6.2 Assessment—exercise matrix

Competency/ exercise	In-basket	Presentation	Subordinate role play	Customer role play	Leaderless group exercise	BEI	Final scores
1. Deliver results	✓				✓		
2. Focus on customer	✓			✓			
3. Business awareness	✓	✓					
4. Leads by example	✓		✓		✓		
5. Communication	✓	✓	✓		✓		
6. Networking	✓				✓		
7. Decision-making	✓		✓	✓	✓		
8. Global mindset		✓			✓		
Assessor	TSG	NG	SD	NN	MRC	CS	

Step 3: Assessment centers were conducted in three batches of 10–12 participants each. Six assessors with two data analysts. At the end of the center, each candidate was given feedback on the results, the agreement was obtained, and an individual development plan was created covering one or two of lagging competencies.

Future of Work and the Implications for Competencies for Future Work

We live in a highly disruptive environment in which the future of organizations and even of work itself is in doubt. There are two headwinds of disruptions—globalization and virtualization of workplace. Globalization occurred in two waves: industrial and knowledge. Industrial globalization (in the 1980s to 1990s) changed manufacturing (the Toyota model) and retail (the Walmart model). Knowledge globalization is expected to disrupt knowledge industries, which today include financial services, life sciences, media, entertainment, communications, and information technology, and dominates the list of Fortune 100. Virtualization, which accelerated post the recession and is spread across technology, people, and business model, is eliminating the physical environments.[54] The forces of disruptions are also altering the equilibrium in man–machine interrelationship at traditional workplaces. Armies of newer smart machines are substituting human effort in offices, factories, and homes. This poses a challenge of redesigning the work and processes, as a condition for adapting. It will require crafting new levels of man–machine collaborated work. To be successful in the changed work context, people will need to show foresight in plotting a course in the quickly shifting terrain of organizational models and competency requirements. The organization men will be required to continually reevaluate their competencies, and marshal resources to quickly build them. Future organizational workers in the future will have to be adaptable and committed to continuous learning. Businesses also likewise have to align strategies for workforce planning and development to future competency sets. This will imply that the conventional processes for mapping of critical competencies and selection of talents will not hold.[55]

Beset with unprecedented challenges and opportunities, the future workforce, whether in traditional or more entrepreneurial work environments, will need to collaborate with others from different disciplines and cultures to solve problems and to create positive outcomes.[56] It may require a mixed new assortment of old and emergent competencies, for example, sense-making, adaptive thinking, computational thinking, design mind-set, ability to interact respectfully, and respect for cultural otherness. There is, however, no doubt that much of it will be attributes of a global mind-set.

SUMMARY

The trend for competency studies in businesses was started by renowned Harvard psychologist David McClelland, who is credited with having pioneered the competency movement in organizations across the world. His classic books *Talent and Society*, *Achievement Motive*, *The Achieving Society*, *Motivating Economic Achievement*, and *Power the Inner Experience* brought out several new dimensions of the

---

[54] Malcolm Frank, *The Future of* Work, December 2010. Available at: https://www.cognizant.com/worldwide_olt/FutureofWork-A-New-Approach.pdf (accessed on November 13, 2017).

[55] Institute for the Future, 'Future Work Skills 2020.' Available at: http://www.iftf.org/futureworkskills/ (accessed on November 13, 2017).

[56] OECD, 'Global Competency for an Inclusive World' Available at: https://www.oecd.org/education/Global-competency-for-an-inclusive-world.pdf (accessed on November 13, 2017).

competencies. The breakthrough came with the article published in *American Psychologist.*[57] In it, the author clearly turned the focus of the organizations to competence as a new zone for development and learning. In that article, McClelland described researches that challenged the validity of the time-honored instruments for aptitude and knowledge as predictors of either job performance or success in life.

Some confusion existed initially in the difference between the terms 'competence' and 'competency.' The generally accepted position is that 'competence' relates to 'performance of work' and 'competency' describes the behavioral abilities of the manager required to perform the work effectively. According to Spencer and Spencer, competencies are underlying characteristics of people and 'indicate ways of behaving and thinking, generalizing across situations and enduring for a reasonably long period of time.' Five characteristics constitute competencies: motives (which drive, direct, and select behavior toward certain actions); traits (physical characteristics and consistent responses to situations or information); self-concept (a person's attitudes, values, or self-image); knowledge (information in specific areas); and skill (ability to perform certain physical or mental tasks). Competencies have been classified into different categories. Katz and Kahn[58] have demonstrated four groups: technical, human, managerial, and conceptual.

The competency management process consists of four stages which have an underlying, common purpose of continuous development of competencies for both the individual and the organization. The four stages are competency mapping, competency diagnosis, competency development, and competency monitoring.

Competency approach has usefulness for various HR processes: recruitment and selection, T&D, performance management, and compensation management. The competency linkage ensures accuracy and impact of the processes in a more scientific manner than the traditional approaches.

Competency management is not without attendant challenges just like any other process. There are problems of over expectations. Sometimes it does not describe the unique abilities of individuals. Besides, it cannot be considered as an exact science.

Finally, looking into the crystal ball on the future of work, virtualization of workplace and globalization are going to require a new set of competencies, evolved perhaps on the basis of a new method of competency mapping. Some new competencies are likely to emerge, for example, global mindedness or value for human dignity, virtual collaboration, and others.

Short-answer Questions

1. How did the breakthrough in competency movement come?
2. What is the difference between competence and competencies?
3. Competencies have been defined as 'underlying characteristics of people'. Elaborate.
4. Explain Competency Clusters.
5. What is the use of a Competency Dictionary?
6. What are Competency Clusters?
7. What are the steps in Competency Modeling?
8. How can the limitations of either traditional PMS or competency-based PMS be avoided?
9. What is In-Basket exercise?
10. How is the purpose and structure of Behavioural Event Interviews?

---

[57] D. C. McClelland, 'Testing for Competence Rather than Intelligence.' *American Psychologist*, 28, no. 1 (1973): 1–14.

[58] Katz and Kahn, *The Social Psychology of Organizations.*

Discussion Questions

1. What are the different ways in which competency-based management creates value for business?
2. Discuss the situations in which assessment centers will be the appropriate instrument for selection. What could be some of the unforeseen problems?
3. Is competency-based approach suitable for SMEs?
4. Brainstorm and create a competency dictionary for a start-up, a management consultancy, and a municipality.
5. What would be some of the methods for using analytics for competency studies?

CHAPTER 7

Career Management

LEARNING OBJECTIVES

After completing this chapter, the student will be able to:

- Understand the context of Career Management
- Know why Career Management is necessary
- Examine the roles of various stakeholders.
- Understand the challenges of Career Management
- Examine the instruments of Career Development
- Know the stages of Career Development
- Analyse the theories/models of Career Management

Opening Case The Choice of a Career

Sharmistha Jalan graduated with Commerce from Goenka College, Kolkata. While pursuing Masters, she wanted to earn some money, and got herself a paid internship with a Search organization dealing with the Financial Services vertical. During the Covid time, she also enrolled for a CA course. She cleared the Foundation and one group of the Intermediate, and got an Articleship in an Audit firm in Kolkata. She juggled the internship and the Articleship by working long hours. But the dual occupation proved too exhausting for her and she gave up the internship after six months.

She could not clear her Intermediate second group in the first attempt. In the meanwhile, her father, who was working with a multinational FMCG firm as a Regional Sales Manager got transferred to Bangalore, and she also relocated with her family. The relocation created a disruption, and she found it hard to concentrate on her studies and decided to do it afterward. Meanwhile, she decided to try out an MBA course and joined a coaching academy for CAT.

In the first attempt, her CAT score qualified her for 2nd tier Management Institute, but she was interested only in IIMs. Therefore she decided to wait and have a crack at CAT to improve her score. Meanwhile, she decided to join a Civil Engineering Design start-up, run by a friend of hers, where she did accounting, admin, and recruitment work. Eventually, she fell in love with the partner's friend and decided to get married.

Post-marriage she decided to try her hand in a completely different area, and started her own a start-up – a takeaway restaurant specializing in Lebanese food and Turkish desserts. She ran it for a year and found it hard to break due to tough competition, and small margin, forcing her to close it down.

The twists and turns in her career left her a little drained so she decided to take a break to mull things over by taking a long break and planned a holiday in Thailand. There she got fascinated by scuba diving and did an instructor course in it. She loved the sport and also wanted to earn some money so, she decided to stay in Thailand for three months.

When she came back and talked things over with her husband and in-laws, she found herself clearly at crossroads career-wise. Would she go back to CA and complete it, take a crack at MBA, or resume her restaurant by changing the product mix, or do something new? How would she decide?

Discussion Question

1. What should Sharmistha do?

7.1 INTRODUCTION

The concept of career management has, from time to time, drawn different metaphors, ladders, pathways, pyramids, timelines or tournaments, which also surface several issues of career management. Each symbol describes a process. A tournament evokes the image of competing for a promotion. A timetable indicates racing to touch the finishing line for an aspired role. One of the most potent images for career management is a ladder or pyramid depicting an ascent.

Not so long ago, the new employee would cross the portals of a decent workplace armed with two contracts – a printed one (the Appointment letter) and one in the mind (the psychological contract) with the intention of working hard, earning well, and, if possible, staying in the same place by moving up the ladder of hierarchy. The new digital age has replaced that picture with a refreshed psychological contract according to which the refrain is continuous learning and learning agility, learning faster than the competitor, and adapting multiple careers rather than one.

Deloitte in their *Global Human Trend Report* 2018 defined the career as 'a series of developmental experiences' providing opportunities for mastering 'new skills, perspectives, and judgment'.[1] The report visualized modern careers as moving in an 'upward arc', instead of a 'stairway', where progressions/promotions occur periodically. In the context of collapsing hierarchies and team-based functioning, designing new career models based on relevant skills came up as important to 47% of respondents.

A Forbes article 'What kind of jobs do Generation Z looking for' highlighted the trend of the youth Millennia' and Generation Z to seek work based on passion and alignment with their values and goals. The choice, according to the author, ranged from the tech industry to unusual career paths like music,

[1] *From careers to experiences: new pathways.* https://www2.deloitte.com/us/en/insights.

sports, and fashion. However, most are ignorant about the choice of jobs available in their preferred areas. An example has been cited about sports enthusiasts being unaware of how being proficient in maths or data science, make them fit into roles of business intelligence (BI) for a sports team. Rob Kingyens, Founder and CEO at Yellow Brick.co talked about collaborating with industry leaders to make more deliberate linkages between academic studies and 'passion industries,' to enable students to pursue meaningful careers that go beyond attractive salaries.[2]

The outlook for a career has become widely varied according to the successive generational cohorts. Gen X looked for stability in seeking jobs; Gen Y swung from one job to another; Gen Z rejected both approaches. According to experts, they are not lured by the chintzy tactics of the employers in the form of free food or gymnasiums, but clearly valued opportunities for professional development. A recent survey predicted that millennials are unlikely to stay in their job for more than 2 years, because of a lack of support in pursuit of their careers by the employers. They represent a clear break from their preceding generation in embracing face-to-face interactions and networking.

Exhibit Career Development at ITC

ITC has a systematic process for career development. Career counseling is a regular practice that involves a 'dialog' with employees to plan their progress within ITC. Faculty from reputed business schools, like Harvard and INSEAD, are also invited to conduct workshops on strategy and product development.

Alongside, employees are rotated across various business segments, for exposure to new roles and responsibilities. The CEO also has undergone the process several times during his 30-odd years with ITC. Here people never find themselves stagnating.

In Glassdoor, one can find many employees expressing views appreciating the job security, ample opportunities to learn, good interaction within the company, making a lot of connections, fast-paced, many verticals, great exposure for freshers, scope for upskilling, great mentorship, etc. There have been some views about the slow pace of progression and work-life imbalance.

Discussion Question

1. The business environment has been described as Volatility, Uncertainity, Complexity, and Ambiguity (VUCA). What are the upside and downside of a systematic career development process in an organization like ITC?

Source: https://www.businesstoday.in/magazine/features/story/people-first-71629-2017-02-18

7.2 WHAT IS CAREER?

In the early days of management, there was no concept of careers. The workers were hired to do specific assignments, and any arrangements later were made on ad hoc basis. Later, as William Whyte said in his famous 'The Organization Man' that employees need longevity of their employment and upward movement in the corporate ladder can only be achieved through dedication, commitment, and loyalty. The Oxford Dictionary defines the career as 'an occupation undertaken for a significant period by a person's life and with opportunities for progress. A career in simple words is advancement or progress at work. But, Hall defines the career as 'individually perceived sequence of attitudes and

[2] https://www.forbes.com/sites/quora/2020/01/17

behaviors associated with work-related activities and experiences over the span of an employee's life.'[3] Glenview. It represents a duality, Janus-like, where career is at the same time a chain of actual events, as also a perception or drive by the individual employee.

7.2.1 Career and Job

A job is an implicit trade, between the individual and the organization, where the individual works in accordance to some specifications and within certain boundaries, in exchange of pay. A career, in contrast, indicates a long-term endeavor, which a person builds over time with regular effort. A job is restricted within the walls of a role, but a career is a mosaic of roles, aspirations, experiences, and a map for achieving a goal.

Exhibit Why a Career is not the Same as a Job?

Job	Career
1. It is short-term exchange of work for rewards.	1. It is long-term assurance of financial security based on systematic acquisition of skills and new learnings.
2. Changes in environmental factors (strategy, technology, and market dynamics) can eliminate a job.	2. A career can make one optimistic that hard work and acquisition of new skills will reward one in the future in enhancing value to the employer and increased pay and benefits.
3. Satisfaction derived from doing a job will depend on the inherent nature of the work in it, requiring job enrichment or job enlargement from time to time.	3. A career can cushion a fall caused by loss of a job, assuring that the more capability one acquires, more enduring the cushion.
	4. A career involves a goal directed pursuit, generating excitement in dealing with challenges, motivation in doing so and the joy of continuous learning over time.

Discussion Question

1. 'In Gig economy employees should focus on the job, rather than the career'. Do you agree with this view?

Source: Based on The Difference between a career and a job and why it is important. http://cwa.ac.uk

In the conventional understanding, a career is expected to proceed in the following sequence:

1. Entry
2. Progress
3. Mid-career
4. Later-career
5. Exit

[3] Hall DT Careers in organizations.

Currently, another view of career has emerged. According to this view, careers, instead of moving sequentially, move in unpredictable, subjective, and discontinuous manner. Its elements are employability, network, boundaryless, and present orientation.[4]

7.2.2 Career Plan

'Career path is an intentional effort by an individual to discover his/her 'skills, interests, values, opportunities, constraints, choices, and consequences.'[5] It also describes the process of developing a pathway and setting visions regarding career. It includes choice of occupation, choice of roles, choice of the organization, and choice of self-development.

7.2.3 Career Development

It is a system that balances human resource needs of an organization with employee career desires in systematic and planned manner. For example, an IT company may need a programing officer, and an individual having the requisite programing skills and competencies may want to join the company with a desire to become the Project Team at a future point. A development system is a way to match the current and future personnel requirements of the organization. According to Stanford Professor Pfeffer, formal mechanism of career development yields a strategic advantage. 'Career systems that emphasize promotions from within not only promote advantages in terms of managing the employment relationships, but also make it more likely that strategies for achieving competitive advantage through people will be understood and pursued.'[6] Pfeffer believes that for deriving such a competitive edge, the manpower plan needs to be in sync with the career development plans.

7.2.4 Career Management

Career management[7] is about opportunities for employees to advance and develop in careers while making sure that the organization has the pipeline of strategic talent it values. The components of career management are the scope for continuous learning, opportunities to build competencies, and career/succession planning.

Aims:

Two-folds—To guide the employees to take a path to realize their innate potential, and to make available regular learning opportunities to enhance capabilities.

Dynamics–The movement of employees to go up or to widen their roles by deepening skills. Armstrong describes it as expanding, establishing, and maturing.

Process–It involves development processes and programs, succession/ career plans, performance/ potential assessments, talent audits, and demand-supply forecasts.

Policies–It will include the critical decisions to grow or buy talent and also to deal with plateaued managers who work effectively but are content with where they reached.

---

4 Nick Wilson. Human Resources Management. Sage. 2012. P.343

5 Hall DT & Ors. Career Development in Organizations. Jossey-Bass.

6 Pfeiffer. Competitive advantage through people. HBR.

7 Human Resource Management. M. Armstrong. PP-400-401

7.2.5 Career Path

Encompasses varied forms of career progression such as traditional vertical career ladder, dual career ladder, horizontal career lattices, career progression outside the organization, and encore careers.

7.2.6 Career Ladder

Career ladders or career lattices are carefully designed and structured stairways which the employees expect to climb as they spend time in organizations honing their skills and acquiring new capabilities. According to the Cambridge dictionary, career ladder is a series of jobs from the lower paid with less responsibility to the highest paid with the most responsibility within a company or particular profession.[8]

According to SHRM career ladder is about progression of jobs in an organization specific occupational field ranked from highest to the lowest based on level of responsibility and pay.[9]

7.2.7 Career Portfolios

It comes from the Italian word 'portare' to carry and 'folio' a sheet of paper. A career portfolio is a new way to think about, talk about, and craft one's professional future in order to navigate the ever-changing world of work with purpose, clarity, and flexibility. It is different from a career path in the sense that a path tends to be a single pursuit in a linear manner, a career portfolio is a never-ending source of discovery and fulfilment. It represents one's vast and diverse professional journey, including various twists and turns whether made by choice or circumstances.

At the beginning of one's career, one may not have everything figured out. The ability to navigate ambiguity and not knowing are some of the valuable skills. Curating one's career portfolio is more than professional development. It is about how one designs one's life.

A typical portfolio looks like a network with many add those to my drawing. different nodes. As one adds new skills, roles, or experiences, I add those to my drawing. A couple of times in a year I refresh my drawing to make sure it still aligns with my broader professional and life journey.[10]

Exhibit Organizations of Choice

According to LinkedIn's 2022 Top Companies list for India employees voluntarily and anonymously share what their job and company are like when it comes to career opportunities. The sixth annual edition reveals the 25 best workplaces where professionals in India can grow their careers.

1. Tata Consultancy Services (TCS)	2. Accenture
3. Cognizant	4. Infosys
5. Capgemini	6. Wipro
7. IBM	8. HCL Technologies
9. Larsen and Toubro	10. Deloitte

8 http:// dictionary.cambridge.org

9 Developing Employee Career Paths and Ladders. www.shrm.org

10 Ascend why should you build a career portfolio (not a career path) HBR.org

7.2.8 Career Salience

Salience is derived from the Latin word 'salire', to exit, as through a gate. An alternate meaning could be 'standing out from the rest' or 'prominent', as was given by Psychologist Donald Super to present his famous theory on career development and also its uses in career counseling.

The uniqueness of the idea of career salience is that it needs to be visualized in the context of other life roles and not as separate from them. It describes the prominence for an individual of his or her career in relation to other life aspects like family or leisure. A person may have more salience for other roles. For example, getting married or bringing up children or taking care of old parents or other close family members may become more urgent for a person, driving concern for career to the back burner. Thus, career salience for any person does not remain static, but, depending on the life stages or the circumstances, its value may shift relative to the salience of other life roles and obligations at a given time. There are three components of career salience according to Super: commitment, participation, and knowledge.[11]

Subsequently, Nevill and Super formulated Developmental Assessment Model which is a method of career counseling. Career counselors use this model to plan a preliminary interview with the client, explaining the life-role planning process and the interrelationships of multiple life roles a person plays at different points in time. The Life-Career Rainbow described earlier is a useful tool in this initial stage. The developmental assessment model of career counseling includes collecting a large array of information about the client prior to engaging in career decision making. Super, along with Nevil also developed the Salience Inventory, which was found useful in individual counseling, group counseling, and career development sessions and career counseling. The Salience Inventory is used to measure the current commitment and participation in five life roles: student, worker, citizen, home and family, and leisure.[12]

Career salience is dependent upon many factors such as sociological, financial, educational, or economical. The socio-psychological features (beliefs, motives, personality et al.) for different people vary differently, impacting their career salience. It has been established through multiple studies that women rarely represented in CEO/CXO positions both in government and in private sectors largely due to self-imposed barriers. 'Such barriers can broadly be considered as the often dramatic 'push and pull' between family-personal issues and the time of life during which promotions to higher ranks typically take place'.[13]

7.2.9 Work Life Balance and Career Salience

The balance between work life has been an area of great priority by employees in VUCA world, where the millennial generation is known as the Standby generation, kept for work on a 24/7 basis. There is an ever increased demands on time, energy, and work commitment. Katie 2011 studied how work-life programs enhance employee retention and proposed that in addition to time-based conflict, social identity should be considered concurrently.[14] He found that as time spent in the work role and the identity that an individual derives from the work role became incongruent, the conflict increased. Furthermore, individuals who have strong identities with either role, or significant identities in both the work and non-work roles, experience more role conflict.

[11] Super, D. E. 1980. *'A Life-span, Life-space Approach to Career Development.'* Journal of Vocational Behaviour 16: 282-298.

[12] Super, D. E. and Nevill, D. 1986. The Salience Inventory. Palo Alto, CA: Consulting Psychologists Press.

[13] Brizendine, L. 2008. One reason women don't make it to the C-suite. Harvard Business Review 86 (6): 36.

[14] Work-life programs enhances employee retention

7.2.10 Career Resilience

The American Psychological Association (APA) defines resilience 'as the process of successfully adapting to adversity, trauma, threats, and sources of stress' and the 'ability to bounce back from challenging circumstances', it is also reflected in a person's capacity to grow and evolve to overcome obstacles. The APA also recognizes this trait as something that can be learned by anyone since it involves a combination of thoughts, behavior, and actions that can be developed over time.

Robert H. Waterman and others have defined career-resilience as 'being dedicated to the idea of continuous learning' and 'standing ready to reinvent themselves to keep pace with change' taking 'responsibility for their own career management' and, being 'committed to the company's success'. In brief, the employee needs to know two things: one, how the market is playing out and what future competencies it will value; and other, his/her own competencies, strengths and limitations and a development plan for future employability.[15]

Career resilience represents a shift from expecting the company to provide long-term job security and manage the employee's career to encourage them to grow and become far more capable to manage their career themselves, and more employable whether inside the organization or outside. In other words, it describes a transition from career dependence to career resilience. The action seems to be appropriate, in a time when downsizing and lay-offs have rendered the earlier covenant of life-time employment an anachronism.

Exhibit Careers After a Break for Women

1. **Phoenix at Marico** Phoenix is a career transition program that offer opportunities to professionals who have taken a one year minimum career break and are keen to return to the corporate world. The company said about this program in a release. The program respects individuality and welcomes candidates that may have taken a break to prioritize their health, fulfil their aspirations or explore their passions.

   The key components of the hiring process include project-based hiring, wherein the candidates will be hired as consultants for a duration of six months, nine months and twelve months, and their absorption will be based on their performance and role availability. In lateral hiring, based on experience, the candidates will be hired directly in lateral roles.
2. **Career Reboot by Accenture** A program for women, having been on a career-break for over two years, and want to re-join the workforce as an intern or a full-time employee. The program promises to support holistic development and offers a blend of curated trainings, experiential learning boards and world-class online resources with skill-based mentorship.

   The program is powered by Accenture's Vaahini Network – a network of 120,000 women professionals. The platform was created to help women reach their professional goals through trainings, mentorship and a network that its members can leverage to help them succeed in their careers.
3. **Tata SCIP** Tata Second Careers Inspiring Possibilities (SCIP) is a platform for women transitioning into a career after a break. With an on boarding methodology, that makes the process faster and more efficient, it offers multiple career options, providing women the choice to select either part-time or full-time employment.

[15] Harvard Business Review, 'Towards a career resilient workforce' https://hbr.org/1994/07.

Discussion Questions

1. What are the challenges faced by women returning to workplace?
2. What are the gains for an organization in providing opportunies to women to re-join the workplace?

Sources:

1. Marico launches Gender neutral second career program https://hr.economictimes.indiatimes.
2. *Career Reboot program at Accenture* https://www.accenture.com/in-en/careers/local/career-reboot-program
3. *Tata Scip* https://www.tata.com/careers/tata-scip-second-careers-inspiring-possibilities-women-jobs

7.2.11 Second Career

A second career is a change in career sought by one after being on the same role for a reasonably long period of time. It may also include taking a job after retirement or about women who want to resume work after a break on personal grounds. In the first situation, the driver could be passionate or have interest in a particular domain, or may have been laid off or terminated on other grounds. In the second situation, the individual may still find himself/ herself employable or may have financial/ security reasons to earn.[16]

Reflection Point

Guy Standing has used the term Precariat (a neologism for Proletariat and Precarious) to describe a 'dangerous class' of people emerging in the gig economy, who spend considerable amount of their daily time in unpaid activities include continually having to search for work (including preparing for and attending job interviews).

Discussion Question

1. What challenges are to be faced by HR professionals to manage careers for the Precariat?

7.3 CHALLENGES OF CAREER MANAGEMENT

Helen Tupper and Sara Ellis, writing in Harvard Business Review suggests that four assumptions pose a challenge for career management

1. There will be a time for doing career management (the when)
2. Somebody will help manage my career (the who)
3. Not knowing what skill needs to have priority (the what)
4. Career can only be developed in a congenial workplace (the where).

In current VUCA business environment, some of the challenges[17] could be:

(a) Multi-generational workforce and the difference in aspiration and worldview leading to communication bottlenecks. Specifically, the issues are technology adaption, goals, and how to navigate their careers.

(b) Issues arising out of advancement to a higher role, especially how to deal with erstwhile peers as leader.

(c) Acquiring proficiency in conducting a career growth conversation.

---

[16] https://www.indeed.com/career-advice/finding-a-job/second-careers#:~:text=What%20is%20a%20second%20career,retiring%20from%20their%20professional%20life.

[17] How to overcome career development challenges in the workplace. https://www.insala.com/blog.

More serious challenges arise when the business goes downward due to changes in the business environment. The challenges arise because of the need of reorganization and the uncertainty and anxiety unleashed by it. It arises at times of downsizing—especially, the fairness in the criteria in downsizing, the manner in which it is communicated, the spread of the downsizing across the ranks, etc.

7.4 THE IMPORTANCE OF CAREER DEVELOPMENT

During the phase of the Great Resignation people started leaving in hordes. It turned focus on one major issue which the businesses were suspecting, but not admitting–about the withering commitment and loyalty of people to the organization. People were quitting, because they saw no career pathways in their organization, and they were searching to see it in elsewhere.

Career development was intended to boost employee motivation and improve performance. Focus on career development enables talent acquisition. The need for an organization to embrace formal career paths and career ladders can arise when-

There is a scarcity of right talent to man specific roles for the organization at the right time.

- The company feels the need to engage its employees.
- When employees raise the voice for the need of increasing workplace flexibility.
- There is a lack of diversity at the senior leadership roles.
- There are rising numbers of Gen Y and Gen Z.
- The organization is flat, limiting the scope for advancement.

Exhibit The Value of Career Pathways

A LinkedIn's 2018 Workplace Learning Report, reported that 94% of employees declared their intention to stay at a job longer if provided pathways for career development.

The workplace is changing. Companies that want to retain employees and better their bottom line will need to pivot. Talent is valuable, and the relationship between companies and employees needs to shift to a win–win. Creating a vigorous career development program within an organization is a great way to roll with changing times and retain talent.

July 2021 poll conducted by Monster found that:

- 86% of workers feel that their career has stalled during the pandemic.
- 79% feel pressure to push their careers further as the pandemic ends.
- 29% of workers named lack of growth opportunities as their reason to quit.
- 80% of workers do not think their current employer offers growth opportunities.
- 49% of workers expect their employer to play a part in career development

Source: Five Reasons Offering Career Development to Employees Benefits Companies https://www.forbes.com

7.5 CAREER MANAGEMENT PROCESS

The step-by-step process of career management in an organization[18] are as follows:

1. **Career management strategy** Make or break, fast-track for talents, career based on long-term stay/loyalty or on short-term commitment or employability

[18] K. Aswathappa – Human Resources Management—Texts and Cases. Pp 304-305.

2. **Assessment** Talent audit, Identifying gaps or strength finder approach
3. **Career planning** Creating career pathways, performance-potential data, succession plan
4. **Career development** Career counseling, coaching/mentoring
5. **Evaluation** Review of effectiveness of the career management process; possibilities of varying perceptions of employee organization

Exhibit List shows Indian Start-ups that have Laid-off Employees since 2022

As many as 26,000 employees have been laid off by Indian start-ups since 2022, according to a list compiled by Money control. Among these, nearly 6000 employees were let go within the first quarter of 2023 itself. Companies that laid off the highest number of employees included BYJU'S, WhiteHat Jr, Blinkit, Ola, Vedantu, and Lido Learning, as per the Money control list.

Discussion Questions

1. In the given business conditions of uncertainty and volatility, what choices do the employers have to do for career development of the employees?
2. What would be your recommendations?

Source: Short by Hiral Goyal/12:40 pm on 29 Apr 2023, Saturday

7.6 ROLES IN CAREER MANAGEMENT

Organizations play a key role in the career management of the employees. To assess the inter-relationship between the role of organization and career management of employees, a study was conducted in the education sector of Pakistan with a sample of 100 people. Regression, correlation and beta value was determined. Positive relation was found in both the variables.

In developing career, however, it always takes two to tango. According to Lips–Wiersma and Hall, there are five ways the roles are taken mutually. first, development of capacity and employability in the individual: the employee wants to enhance skill, and the organization provides the resources through T&D; second, by strategic and structural integration: the employee seeks secured employment, the organization makes career tracks and communicates it; third, by cultural integration: by creating a culture that enables the employee to feel resourceful enough to take charge of career; fourth, diversity management: balancing work–life through flexible work timings; fifth: communication: obtaining information of employees keen on career development.[19]

The mutual role taking between organization and the employee can be segregated through the following table:

Table 7.1 Mutual responsibility

Employee	Organization
1. Choice of occupation	1. Recruitment and selection
2. Choice of organization	2. Stuffing
3. Choice of work assignment	3. PMS
4. Individual development plan	4. T&D

[19] Lips-Wiersma, M., & Hall, D. T. (2007. Organizational career development is not dead: A case study on managing the new career during organizational change. Journal of Organizational Behavior, 28, 771-792.

The actions that employee and the organizations should take are summarized as under:

Table 7.2 Key actions

Employee	Organization
1. Increase employability and portable competencies. 2. Take independent control of own career. 3. Acquire ability to self-assess. Drive protean/ boundary less career. 4. Create visions about career. 5. Maintain a technical expertise/strength. 6. Build a personal brand based on past success. 7. Improve project skills 8. Network 9. Seek feedback 10. Commit to continuous learning	1. Provide tools and opportunities to support employees career plans. 2. Create a culture of automatic learning. 3. Provide help in assessment and guidance 4. Encourage coaching/mentoring by managers. 5. Provide family support facilities to help employees strike a balance between work and personal lives. 6. Embed career development in all HR systems 7. Reskill employees before downsizing

In the current context of ups and down of business, and massive lay-offs and downsizing, the role of the organization in supporting the career aspirations of individual employees is changing, and the role is getting redefined. Lips–Wiersma and Hall have offered a ten-point reckoner for the changed role:[20]

1. Recognise that the employee owns the career
2. Support the employee's own career development efforts
3. Play a broker's role and link employees with assignments and other people
4. Provide employees with career information and opportunities for career assessment
5. Communicate career development and management expectations to employees
6. Focus on employee's work planning rather than career planning
7. Promote employee's learning through work tasks and relationships
8. Engage employee in decisions regarding career development and management
9. Define employee's success by ability to switch tasks/jobs, not by mastery of one
10. Develop a mind-set of continuous learning in employee and organization.

Exhibit The Role of a Career Counselor

'My career counselor, Patrice Mueller, helps me achieve my professional aspirations. With his advice and support, I carry out my plans and goals. I'm lucky that he's been my coach since I joined the firm as an analyst. At key moments and crossroads in my career, I benefited from his insights and perspectives.

Patrice and I meet at least once every quarter to discuss my work priorities, which evolve as I grow and step into new roles. We found that we shared an interest in transforming the world of business, a pursuit we both find very exciting! Hence, we include time for bouncing ideas off each other on technology, industry and the future of work in our conversations.'

Excerpts from a Blog.

Hong Yi Lim. Building up greatness: How learning and career counseling fuelled my growth journey at Accenture

Discussion Question

1. What makes it difficult for organizations to use resources for developing their employees' careers?

Source: https://www.accenture.com

[20] Lips-Wiersma & Hall. Ibid

7.7 INSTRUMENTS FOR CAREER MANAGEMENT

Since, career management is recognized to be the responsibility of the employee and supported by the organization, there are a number of tools/ activities which can be used by both the individual and also the organization:

7.7.1 Individual

1. **Self-Assessment Tools** They may include Big Five Locator, OPQ, Strong Interest Inventory, Holland Code Self-Assessment, MAPP Test, MBTI tests.
2. **Career Planning Workshops** These workshops which demand commitment of limited time from participants aim to help individuals take more personal responsibility for their career paths, grow more intentional in their career conduct to enable them to identify, implement, and, then achieve career goals.
3. **Career Workbook/Playbook** It contains guidelines, questions, tips and perspectives for pursuing career. James Citrin's Career Playbook is quite resourceful. According to him each career goes through three phases–aspiration phase, promise phase and momentum phase. Each individual has to pursue a career by balancing three points of the career triangle–job satisfaction, compassion and lifestyle. The other resources that are used in this context are–O*net and 'What color is your parachute'.

Exhibit What Color is Your Parachute?

It is a Career Playbook by Richard Bolles written for the benefit of job-seekers. Published in 1970, it has remained an influential career guide book since. For example, the author advocates networking to because one needs to identify who is the person with the authority to hire, and desist from the futile practice of despatching resumes in random manner.

An important part of the book is an exercise called the Flower Exercise which involves looking at oneself from seven different viewpoints: compatibility with people, workplace conditions, skills, purpose, knowledge, money, and location. In the exercise, each angle is visually represented by a flower petal. At the end of the exercise, one comes up with a one-page flower diagram of your flower that contains a visual summary of one's personality in the context of one's career.

Discussion Question

1. Do Internet research on adoption of career playbooks and their impact on employees decision to stay.

Source: What colour is your parachute: Flower Exercise. https://www.shortform.com

7.7.2 Organization

1. Individual career counseling Generally organized by HR. Price Waterhouse Company (PWC) covers all employees on Counseling/Coaching assistance. Marico uses career counseling based on Schein's career anchor after individual assessment.
2. Job posting
3. Skill inventories

4. Career ladders and career paths
5. Assessment centers
6. Development centers
7. Mentoring
8. Succession planning

For special groups, organizations have specific programs:

1. Fast-track
2. Outplacement
3. Stationary employees
4. On boarding/socialization of new employees
5. Retiring employees
6. Women employees

Exhibit Career Growth and Talent Progression Path at Infosys

At Infosys, the career pathway has three overarching philosophies covering nine guiding principles:

1. Future Readiness: It has three guiding principles
   (a) Master a digital skill reskill program in digital technologies. The online learning platform, 'Lex', curates learning paths and certifications.
   (b) Bag a skill tag tagged employees earn incentives and get higher visibility and preference for internal movements.
   (c) Dive deeper to specialize opportunity to specialize as power programmers to get opportunities to learn and work in niche technologies and move up.
2. Agile Careers: Provides opportunities to move people who have learnt new skills to the right roles.
   (a) Chart your experience move to a new project once you complete 18 months in a project after joining us as a fresher.
   (b) Join the internal marketplace Internal job postings offer you the avenue to apply for lateral or vertical movements.
   (c) Make the shift Power programmers to get opportunities to learn and work in niche technologies.
3. Always on learning: Continuous learning through a robust digital ecosystem
   (a) Transform your learning with AI Zoiee, the virtual learning assistant, acts as a personal quiz master and suggest relevant learning content.
   (b) Learn anywhere, anytime Upskilling and reskilling at convenience.
   (c) Skill up, step up Developing proficiency through experience, expertise and increase in knowledge.

Discussion Question

1. Critically evaluate the effectiveness of the above system at Infosys.

7.8 CAREER DEVELOPMENT STAGES

'Choose a job you love, and you will never have to work a day in your life' *(Confucius)*

Eli Ginzberg, an economist, working on a grant from Columbia University, researched on how upper middle class young people make career choices and published his work[21] The key points in his theory are: selection of occupation is a process, which is irrevocable and each choice has a component of compromise.

Ginzberg indicated three stages of career development: (1) the Fantasy stage, in which children engage in playing, simulating occupations like cops, car race driver, but also begin to be aware of occupations; (2) the Tentative stage, which again has four stages-'Interest,' where children learn likes and dislikes; 'Capacity,' where the child learns how much his/her abilities align with his/her interests; 'Values' when she/he learns how work may satisfy his/her values and finally 'Transition' when the individual becomes responsible (for his/her own actions), independent and exercises her choices. (3) 'Realistic 'when adolescents gradually take stock of interests, abilities, and values. It has three stages: 'Exploration': when she/he chooses her career path but also remains open to other opportunities; 'Crystallization': when she/he becomes more engrossed in a particular career, committing to one direction more than she/he ever has and finally 'Specification': in which she/he commits to or develops a preference for a specific area of her occupation.

However, it must me born in mind that this concept has a number of practical limitations as it concerns solely the period before starting professional life and is highly one-dimensional as it concerns youth studying at universities.[22]

Donald Super, who formulated the career development theory, conceptualized career development as a lifelong process, rather than a once-in-a-lifetime decision. According to him an individual goes through five successive developmental stages, each marked with its own career concerns: (1) Growth (9 to 14): When the child grows its capacities, attitudes and interests; (2) Exploration (14 to 24): When the young adult engages in self-reflection and pursuit of education, tackling challenges of 'crystallization, specification, and implementation' of career preferences as developmental tasks. (3) Establishment (24 to 44): The young adult starts his first job, and establishes himself at work\place, and starts climbing the career ladder. (4) Maintenance: the aging worker tries to maintain his or her current position, and updated his skill. (5) Disengagement (over 65): Slow withdrawal from active, career preparatory to retire, retirement planning and retirement living.[23]

A subsequent view advanced by Thompson et al. suggested four stages of career development: (1) The work is supervised. Tasks are simple, routine and the employee has no status or influence; (2) The employee gets independent and more responsible tasks. He gains confidence, capability, power, and credibility; (3) Employee's becomes more skilled, starts to work in multiple areas and contribute. Starts coaching others; (4) Employee gets into leadership roles, representing organization internally and externally and grows considerable power and influence. This model presents an assumption that

---

21 *'Toward a Theory of Occupational Choice' Hitchcock W.L. and Kemp Maybry M., eds. Readings in guidance.* MSS Educational Pub. Co. pages 74–78.

22 The Career Theories of Eli Ginzberg. Johnny Kilhefner. https://woman.thenest.com/career-theories-eli-ginzberg-15464.html

23 Super, D.E. (1951). Vocational adjustment: Implementing a self-concept. Occupations, 30, 88-92.

new entrants prefer. They embrace challenging assignments that would provide scope to acquire new skills, whereas employees at Stage 2 may seek varied work experiences as more critical for them. In the same way, other organizational career management strategies, such as training, mentoring, and appraisal, need to be selectively applied depending on the particular stage of the employee.[24]

7.9 TWO INFLUENTIAL CONCEPTS

7.9.1 Career anchors–Edgar Schein

Schein offered the concept of anchors as internally driven directions aligned to self-perceived abilities, motivators and values. He identified eight anchors: (1) Technical and Functional - looks to apply own skills and deepen it further; (2) General management - seeks to rise high enough in the organization, to be able to integrate the efforts of others across functions and be responsible/accountable for results; (3) Autonomy and independence - seek flexibility to define one's work in own way; (4) Security and Stability - concerned about financial/employment security and willing to do whatever it takes to for the employer to assure job tenure; (5) Entrepreneurial creativity - wants create own organization/ enterprise, built on own abilities and willingness to take risks and to overcome obstacles; (6) Service and dedication to a cause - likes work that achieves something of value, such as making the world a better place to live, solving environmental problems, improving harmony among people, etc.; (7) Pure challenge - enjoys work to solve difficult problems, to win out over tough opponents, or to overcome difficult barriers; (8) Life style - clear about balancing and integrating personal needs, family needs with the demands of career, in sum, to make all the major sectors of life work together towards an integrated whole. Schein made two important points: an individual has only one career anchor; career anchors are shaped by early career experience.

7.9.2 RIASEC–John Holland

Holland composed his vocational choice theory by proposing six distinct worker personalities—Realistic, Investigative, Artistic, Social, Enterprising, and Conventional. This is known as RIASEC. Each of the personality types is comfortable in a particular work environment. While some elements of each type may appear true of individuals. The general thesis of the theory is that salient types (work personalities) will rise in each individual. People look for the environment that support them in manifesting their skills and abilities, express their attitudes and values, and assume suitable circumstances and roles.

Holland's work has been recognized in contributing immensely to the domains of career development and counseling. Holland's theme of interests as demonstration of personality aids career counselors. Student's specialists also gain critical self-understanding. Studying the personalities and work environments fit is a basic aspect of using this concept for student development.

Helping students to explore and learn about different careers that may be of interest to them is congruent with the goals of higher education institutions and student development theories. In the opinion of the *Committee on Scientific Awards*, Holland's 'research shows that personalities seek out and flourish in career environments they fit, and that jobs and career environments are classifiable by the personalities that flourish in them'.

---

24 Career development, planning and management from the organizational perspective. Peter creed and Michelle Hood.2009 ttps://www.researchgate.net/publication/44180091)

Exhibit The RIASEC Model

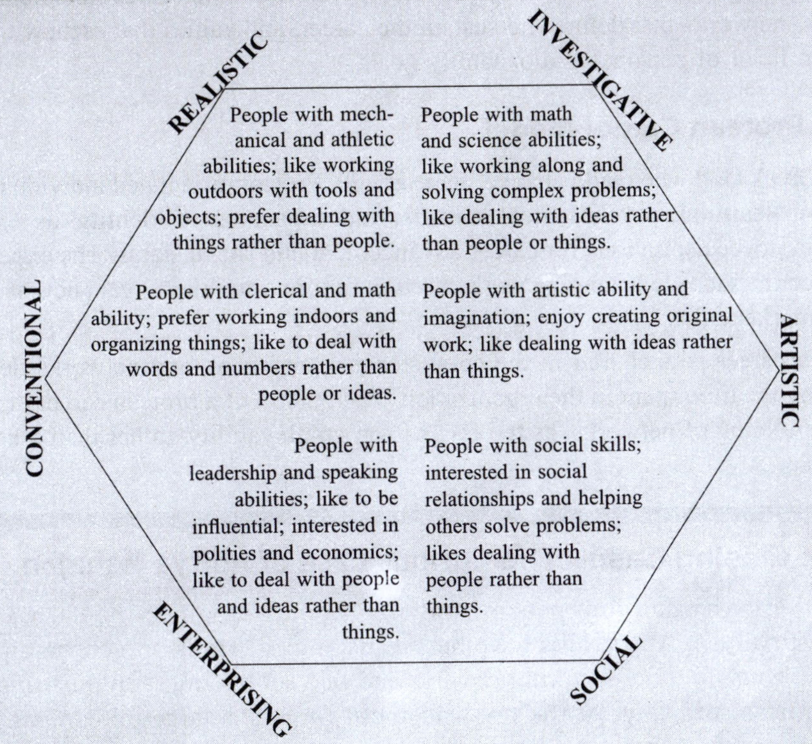

Source: https://www.thecareerproject.org/blog/how-are-you-intelligent-an-introduction-to-the-holland-codes-riasec/(accessed July 2023)

In a nutshell, Holland believed that the selection of a vocation is an expression of personality. Two things, however, need to be highlighted in this connection. John Holland emphasized that all six personality types have equal value. According to him our myriad interests, values, competencies, and choices pull us toward specialized vocational roles, all of which make for a sustainable society in equal manner. Secondly, people rarely confirm to a specific perfect type. Rather, more often than not a person will demonstrate the attributes of one type most vividly, while showing few traits of some other types also. In Holland's descriptions, thus people and work environments fall in three categories: primary, secondary, and tertiary.[25]

7.10 MODELS OF CAREER MANAGEMENT

7.10.1 The Boundaryless Career Model

Boundaries are perceived to be inherent in the idea of career. Boundaryless careers, which sound like an oxymoron, was formulated to indicate the capabilities necessary from employees confronted with new organizational realities. De Fillipi and Arthur define it as 'sequence[s] of job opportunities

[25] Holland's Theory of Career Development. Stoltz, Kevin. https://connect.springerpub.com/content.

that go beyond the boundaries of single employment settings'[26] It is characterized by career paths unbound by single organization's several employers, 'portable competencies suitable for project-based activities, social networks that define and sustain the career, and values that eschew traditional career advancement in favor of personal and/or family goals'.[27]

7.10.2 The Protean Career Model

Proteus was a Greek God who could change shape at will. Protean-orientated individuals are perceived to be driven by 'learning, psychological success, and expansion of identity' as contrasted to the conventional employee aspirations for career advancement and social status. The expectations around the protean career includes 'exchanging work in return for opportunities to gain new skills, networking and enhanced marketability.[28]

The protean career is anchored in the competencies, endeavor, and networks developed by the individual during the time spent in the organization. The pursuit of a protean career demand relentless upskilling and building of networks, as the focus is on employability, rather than job security within an organization.

Closing Case The Curious Case of Aditya Mahajan

Aditya Mahajan is a bright young person, studying Chemical Engineering at UICT in Mumbai. He is in the final year. His results have been outstanding. He is one of the top five in the class. He had consulted the Alumni network, and had set his mind on pursuing a career at a large Chemical Company. At the pre-placement rounds, a large oil company came and they liked his profile. What drew him about the company was that it was large, profitable, growing at the rate of 20% per year continuously since last five years, much higher than the industry curve. He liked compliments from ex-employees for its inclusive culture, and growth prospects. The HR manager promised that the workplace is an engineers' delight, and a good engineer can have a fast-track advancement. Even the current CEO is a Chemical Engineer.

Aditya cracked the selection process of written exam, GD, panel interview and a Psychometric Test, and joined as an Operations Officer on probation for one year. He worked very hard, and discovered that he had excellent skills and problem-solving ability. His boss took a liking to him. Aditya found out that the majority of his peers from engineering colleges spent time cracking the CAT/GMAT and then joining an MBA course of choice. But Aditya reasoned that being on the job would help him in deepening his expertise in chemical engineering, a subject he had passion for. Besides, the company had introduced the system of fast-track promotions about two years back, as a response to high attritions among the younger employees, and acting on the feedback of the EIs. The fast-track promotions were done in case an employee had received a performance appraisal rating of outstanding for three consecutive years.

[26] DeFillippi, Robert J., and Michael B. Arthur. *'The boundaryless career: A competency-based perspective.'* Journal of organizational behavior 15.4 (1994): 307-324.

[27] Lichtenstein & Mendenhall, 2002. Non-linearity and response ability: Emergent order in 21st century careers. Human Relations, 55, 5-31.

[28] (Altman & Post, 1996 Beyond the 'social contract': An analysis of executives' views at 25 large companies. In D. T. Hall (Ed.), The career is dead-long live the career: A relational approach to careers. San Francisco, CA: Jossey-Bass.)

His probation was shortened and two years later, he received his first promotion as Senior Operations Officer, incharge of a shift. His next two promotions also occurred on fast-track. He enjoyed the confidence of his boss, who gave him visible work and projects, talked highly of him in senior leaders' circles and fought for his promotions in the Promotion Committees. The only point of regret that he had was when his boss declined to send him for trainings: first, to an Executive MBA course at an IIM, and, second, a TQM program. The boss told him that those programs are a waste of time, and he will ensure that his career continues to advance on a fast-track.

His boss, in the meanwhile, was going up the ladder too, and became the Head, Operations at the Refinery. Suddenly, there were some developments deeply impacting Aditya's career. An incident of fire occurred leading to some unfortunate fatalities, and damage to some costly machines. An inquiry headed by a Senior Process Expert from another refinery found serious laxity in observation of standard operating principles and company's safety policy in the name of need for higher throughput. In the reshuffle of personnel which was ordered by the Director, the Head–Operations got replaced by another senior engineer from another refinery, and was posted on an advisory role in the headquarters without much power or authority.

From that point, the tailwinds in the career of Aditya Mahajan turned into headwinds. In the twists and turns of organizational politics, the new Head of Operations hounded out the close confidantes of the ex-head of operations. Aditya was also marked out. His performance rating went south, coming down from outstanding to very good or good. He was removed from fast-track as a consequence. Eventually, he was transferred out to the materials function at another refinery, on the plea of job rotation. Aditya, a manager, knocking at the band of the senior leadership found the change hard to accept, as it was a white-collar work dealing with technologies. He found that he had to master it before he could command respect from his team. His performance declined, and he applied for jobs overseas, and eventually, he resigned and went to a refinery at Bahrain.

Discussion Questions

1. Evaluate the approach of the organization in managing the career of Aditya.
2. From the point of view of a Protean career-oriented employee, what could Aditya have done differently?

SUMMARY

The concept of career management has, from time to time, drawn different metaphors, ladders, pathways, pyramids, timelines or tournaments, which also surface several issues of career management. Each symbol describes a process. A tournament evokes the image of competing for a promotion. A timetable indicates racing to touch the finishing line for an aspired role. And one of the most potent images for career management is a ladder or pyramid depicting an ascent.

Career management is about opportunities for employees to advance in careers while making sure that the organization has the pipeline of strategic talent it values. The components of career management are the scope for continuous learning and opportunities to build competencies, career/ succession planning.

Career management uses different terms: for example, career salience is derived from the Latin word salire, to exit, as through a gate. An alternate meaning could be 'standing out from the rest' or 'prominent'. It was preferred by Psychologist Donald Super to present his famous theory on career development and also its uses in career counseling. Career resilience—Robert H Waterman and others have defined career-resilience as 'being dedicated to the idea of continuous learning', 'standing ready to reinvent themselves to keep pace with change' 'taking responsibility for their own career management', and being 'committed to the company's success'.

Both the organization and the individual employee are responsible for careers. The individual through taking charge of own career and using all resources; and organization by creating career pathway. In the current context two approaches have emerged—Protean career and Boundary less career.

Career choices are facilitated by two theories—Edgar Schein's Career Anchors, and Holland's Vocational Choice theory or RIASEC.

Short-answer Questions

1. What is the key point on career preferences in Deloitte's Global Human Trend Report 2018?
2. Explain the Flower Exercise.
3. What are the four assumptions described by Tupper and Ellis (in HBR) that challenge career management process?
4. Define RIASEC.
5. Explain career anchors.
6. Describe the boundary less career model.
7. What, according to Ginzberg, are the three stages of career development?
8. Describe some of the instruments used as self-assessment for career development.

Discussion Questions

1. What are the benefits of career management?
2. In the gig economy, when companies are employing alternate workforce and precariat, what career development strategies would benefit both the individual and the company?
3. Explain the different stages in career management.
4. How can Holland's Vocational Choice theory be leveraged for creating right fit between individual and the job?
5. Explain the term employability. What strategies should the organization adapt to enhance employability of employees?

CLUSTER 4

ENGAGE AND RATE

Chapter 8
Employee Engagement

Chapter 9
Performance Management

In 1972, Studs Terkel, a Chicago-based writer and radio journalist, published what has been described as a documentary masterpiece, 'Working: People Talk About What They Do and How They Feel About What They Do,' a collection of narratives, based on 133 interviews across America. The stories reiterate the wisdom obtained in thousand workplaces that work, when it is satisfying, when it is about purpose, that success is based in what we do, not how much money comes from it. In a telling statement, one interviewee, a pharmacist, says, 'I never cared about being rich. I like to feel needed.'

Employee engagement 'is a measurable degree of an employee's positive or negative emotional attachment to their job, colleagues and organization that profoundly influences their willingness to learn and perform' at work (Scarlett Surveys[1]). In a study of 15 steel mills, 17 apparel manufacturers, and 10 electronic instrument and imaging equipment producers, Eileen Appelbaum and her colleagues sought to compare traditional production systems with flexible high-performance production systems involving teams, training, and incentive pay systems. In all three industries, the plants utilizing high-involvement practices showed superior performance. In addition, workers in the high-involvement plants showed more positive attitudes, including trust, organizational commitment, and intrinsic enjoyment of the work.[2]

Organizations gain competitive advantage through cutting-edge performance. Performance of organizations is the sum total of the performance of individual employees. Effectively high performance occurs when an employee is working on something that he is passionate about. There are controversies around the dampening effect of appraisal system and the bell curve or the forced ranking method. Therefore, organizations should remove the bottlenecks, and try to create an environment that fosters learning and creates a platform to demonstrate their abilities so that their work can be acknowledged and appreciated.

---

1 Scarlett Surveys. 'Your Employee Engagement Value Chain and Improvement System'. Available at: www.scarlettsurveys.com (accessed on August 2, 2017).

2 I. S. Priya and J. Vijayadurai, 'Employee Engagement in Organizations,' *European Journal of Business and Management*, 6 no. 34 (2014): 5–10.

CHAPTER 8

Employee Engagement

LEARNING OBJECTIVES

After completing this chapter, the student will be able to:

- Define employee engagement
- Explain the impact of employee engagement on business performance
- Describe the evolution of the concept of employee engagement
- Explain the barriers to employee engagement
- understand the various models of employee engagement
- Explain the various techniques for measurement of employee engagement

Opening Case 'I Have to be there to Start the Cooker Machine'

Sujit Sarkar is the production operative in the battery plant ABC. He joined the company three years back after graduating with a diploma in the trade of operations from Industrial Training Institute, Tollygunge, Kolkata. He was inducted along with 30 other trainees from different backgrounds such as quality control, technicians, electricians, and so on, and was involved in the pre-commissioning activity of the new plant. The company deployed experienced supervisors from other plants to train up the new employees well in advance. The commissioning of the plant was smooth and the production stabilized quickly because the operatives and the supervisors were already familiar with each other.

Sujit worked hard on his job, and established a reputation as the best operative in the plant. He not only ensured that the machine yielded the desired level of production consistently but also worked on the machine for small repair work, instead of asking the maintenance crew to take charge. If he anticipated issues like raw material shortage, or the illness of a colleague, he would go out of his brief to alert the supervisors so that timely corrective action could be taken.

When the union was formed in the plant for the first time before a wage settlement, Sujit consulted his immediate supervisor, with whom Sujit had a close bond from the days of his training. The supervisor advised him to join the union, as he would otherwise stick out like a thumb, and would become an object of ridicule and pressure from the union activists. Besides, it would also alienate him from the other workers and affect his effectiveness. Over the years, Sujit had won several interplant and intraplant performance awards based on his outstanding performance. He also was an enthusiastic participant in the suggestion scheme when it was first launched. Several of his suggestions led to efficiency improvement of the machines.

The plant legend has it that once during the monsoon season, there was an occasion of heavy flooding in the city. The entire transport system went out of gear. In the morning, the employees could not report for duty, and one supervisor, who lived in the vicinity, was advised by the plant manager to go over to the plant to take care of emergency maintenance. The supervisor, to his surprise found Sujit inside the plant, with his trousers rolled up. The supervisor was surprised because he knew that Sujit lived in a place about 10 km away. Sujit explained that he was worried with overnight rain and felt that since he was the one to start the machine, he should somehow reach the plant ('I have to be there to start the Cooker machine'). Since transports were off the road, he, therefore, had started early and trudged for three hours through the waterlogged streets to reach before the start of the shift at 6 AM.

Discussion Question

1. What factors could have led to the level of commitment demonstrated by Sujit Sarkar toward his job and toward the organization?

8.1 INTRODUCTION

Aconsensus seems to have emerged among employers that engaged employees is a key requisite for organizational success. A high degree of employee engagement drives business outcomes through retention of talent and customer, and improved organizational performance and stakeholder value creation. In the frenzied scramble for scarce talent in the marketplace, the talent seems to be having the last laugh. The balance is loaded in favor of the talented employee, who enjoys enhanced bargaining power. Scouting for candidates with high skills is a competitive activity in a job market, which is highly transparent. Recent research undertaken by Bersin by Deloitte indicates that the factor of 'retention and engagement' ranks number two in the opinions of many business leaders, next only to the challenge of building global leadership.

> In short, in many cases, the balance of power has shifted from employer to employee, pushing business leaders to learn how to build an organization that engages employees as sensitive, passionate, creative contributors. The shift taking place is moving from improving employee engagement to a focus on building an irresistible organization.[3]

[3] 'CFO Insights: Unlocking the Secrets of Employee Engagement.' Available at: https://www2.deloitte.com/us/en/pages/finance/articles/cfo-insights-employee-engagement.html (accessed on November 14, 2017).

Who is an engaged employee? What does he do differently, which other employees do not? A DDI *report*[4] quotes Woody Allen: 'Eighty percent of success is showing up.' And asks a rhetorical question whether mere showing up for work every day implies success in the workplace. The answer is a loud 'no.' It is attendance in body and mind that holds the key. The bad news is that researches across divergent countries and workplaces indicate that employees who are passionate about their jobs and the organizations in which they work constitute a minority. DDI's aforementioned research puts the number of highly engaged employees at only 19%. This finding resonates with another extensive research done by Corporate Executive Board across 50,000 employees around the world, and the figure of highly engaged employees (described as 'true believer') at only 11%. A third report, by Towers Perrin[5] finds a marginally higher level at 17% of the 35,000 employees surveyed.

Is an engaged employee the same as a happy employee? An engaged employee is not the same as a happy employee, if his happiness does not get translated into actions at the workplace. While the practices of lavish company cafeteria, state-of-the-art gym or dinner coupons for the newlyweds may provide great topics for sharing on the Facebook or Glassdoor, happy is not the synonym for engaged. In the same way, satisfaction and engagement are also two different terms. The customary 'employee satisfaction' surveys can tell lies about deep-rooted, hidden issues, apart from being too shallow, for a meaningful trigger for action. A satisfied employee may always be on time for work, but if he insists on catching the company bus punctually at 5 PM, irrespective of urgent work pressures, then he is not an engaged employee. An engaged employee, on the contrary, has an emotional connect with the organization and is always ready to put in discretionary effort as a matter of habit. In this way, an engaged telephone operator, may get up from her perch during the lunch hour, make an unannounced customer comfortable with a seat at the reception and organize tea from the neighborhood coffee shop, until the customer relations manager returns from his lunch at the cafeteria. Similarly, an engaged operations officer in a manufacturing unit may provide relief to the overworked assembler and sit with other assemblers and put jackets on pairs of AA batteries until the operator returns from his smoking break.

8.2 IMPACT OF EMPLOYEE ENGAGEMENT ON ORGANIZATIONAL PERFORMANCE

Does employee engagement impact business performance? Various research findings have established linkages between employee engagement and business outcomes: employee retention, productivity, profitability, customer loyalty, and safety. The findings suggest a positive correlation between employee engagement and revenue growth. Employee engagement is found to be higher in double-digit growth companies; it is also positively related to customer satisfaction.[6] Engaged employees facilitate organizational performance by championing the organization to coworkers, potential employees, and

---

4 R. S. Wellins, P. Bernthal, and M. Phelps, 'Employee Engagement: The Key to Realizing Competitive Advantage,' 2005. Available at: http://www.ddiworld.com/ddi/media/monographs/employeeengagement_mg_ddi.pdf?ext=.pdf (accessed on November 14, 2017).

5 Towers Perrin, 'Working Today: Understanding What Drives Employee Engagement' (The 2003 Towers Perrin Talent Report, Research Report, Towers Perrin, Stamford, CT, 2003).

6 Ibid.

customers; by staying on despite opportunities; and making serious endeavors to contribute to the success of the business.

Studies have found correlation between employee engagement and strategy execution and improved results. Various studies conducted by Gallup, Hay Group, and Towers Watson have indicated that employee engagement has a quantifiable impact on business performance. A Gallop survey in 2006 over 23,910 business units found, among other things, that units with high engagement scores averaged 12% higher customer advocacy, 18% higher productivity, and 12% higher profitability; units with low engagement scores averaged 31% to 51% more employee turnover, 51% more inventory shrinkage, and 62% more accidents.

Another study by Towers Watson of 50 companies found a 19% increase in operating income and nearly 28% growth in EPS for organizations with high engagement scores. A Hay Group study similarly found organizations with high engagement scores having a revenue growth 2.5 times higher than companies with low engagement.[7]

Furthermore, there have been multiple studies that found an interrelationship between employee engagement and turnover intent.[8] A study of 22 companies over 5 business sectors by International Survey Research identified and determined some key drivers for turnover intent: recognition and rewards, individual development, career advancement, empowerment, management leadership, respect for employees, retaining talented employees, supervisory issues, culture fit, and job security. Several of the factors constitute employee-engagement factors, mentioned by Buckingham and Coffman[9] (i.e., recognition, development, opportunity, encouragement, care, best friend, progress). Besides, in another study[10] 66% of highly engaged employees indicated no plans to leave compared to 36% of moderately engaged individuals and 12% of disengaged employees. Furthermore, a lower percentage of highly engaged employees (2%) reported search for another job than moderately engaged (8%) and disengaged employees (23%).

Disengaged employees, on the other hand, are likely to waste their effort on work below their capability, lack full commitment and may leave without waiting for things to change in their organization, and have far more misgivings about their organization in terms of performance measures such as customer satisfaction.[11]

8.3 WHAT IS EMPLOYEE ENGAGEMENT?

There are many definitions of employee engagement.

[7] Diane Berry, Lily Mok, and Thomas Otter, 'CFO Advisory: Employee Engagement Impacts Financial Outcomes and Business Risk,' Gartner Executive Programs (Stamford, CT: Gartner, Inc., March 13, 2013).

[8] Mary Lynn Berry and Michael L. Morris, *The Impact of Employee Engagement Factors and Job Satisfaction on Turnover Intent* (Knoxville, TN: The University of Tennessee, 2008).

[9] Buckingham, M. and Coffman, C. 'First, Break all the Rules: What the World's Greatest Managers Do Differently (New York: Simon & Schuster, 1999).

[10] Perrin, 'Working Today.'

[11] White, B. 'Employee Engagement Report 2006' (Princeton, NJ: Blessing White, Inc., 2006). Available at: www. blessingwhite. com (accessed on November 15, 2008).

Corporations

Caterpillar

Engagement is the extent of employees' commitment, work effort, and desire to stay in an organization.

Dell Inc.

Engagement: To compete today, companies need to win over the MINDS (rational commitment) and the HEARTS (emotional commitment) of employees in ways that lead to extraordinary effort.

Intuit, Inc.

Engagement describes how an employee thinks and feels about, and acts toward his or her job, the work experience, and the company.

Consultants and Researchers

Corporate Leadership Council

Engagement: The extent to which employees commit to something or someone in their organization, how hard they work, and how long they stay as a result of that commitment.

Development Dimensions International

Engagement is the extent to which people enjoy and believe in what they do, and feel valued for doing it.

The Gallup Organization

Employee engagement is the involvement with and enthusiasm for work.

Hewitt Associates

Engagement is the state of emotional and intellectual commitment to an organization or group, producing behavior that will help fulfill an organization's promises to customers, and, in so doing, improve business results.

Engaged Employees

- Stay—They have an intense desire to be a part of the organization and they stay with that organization;
- Say—They advocate for the organization by referring potential employees and customers, are positive with coworkers, and are constructive in their criticism;
- Strive—They exert extra effort and engage in behaviors that contribute to business success.

Institute for Employment Studies

A positive attitude held by the employee toward the organization and its values. An engaged employee is aware of business context, and works with colleagues to improve performance within the job for the benefit of the organization. The organization must work to develop and nurture engagement, which requires a two-way relationship between employer and employee.

Kenexa

Engagement is the extent to which employees are motivated to contribute to organizational success, and are willing to apply discretionary effort (extra time, brainpower, and effort) to accomplishing tasks that are important to the achievement of organizational goals.

Towers Perrin

Engagement is the extent to which employees put discretionary effort into their work, beyond the required minimum to get the job done, in the form of extra time, brainpower, or energy.

Source: Robert J. Vance, *Employee Engagement and Commitment: A Guide to Understanding, Measuring and Increasing Engagement in Your Organization* (Alexandria, VA: SHRM Foundation). Available at: https:// www.shrm.org/ hr-today/trends-and-forecasting (accessed on February 13, 2018).

The many definitions of employee engagement lack uniformity, causing ambiguity. The lack of a universally shared definition poses problems of measurement, management, and benchmarking. Kahn[12] suggests that employee engagement occurs when employees 'engage in occasional innovative and cooperative behavior beyond the requirements of the role but in the service of organizational objectives.' Employee engagement, according to Kahn, is the 'harnessing of organization members' selves to their work roles; in engagement, people employ and express themselves physically, cognitively, and emotionally during role performances.' Kahn further laid down triple psychological conditions for engagement: meaningfulness (positive sense of ROI of self in role performance), safety (ability to show one's self without fear or negative consequence to self-image, status, or career), and availability (sense of possessing the physical, emotional, and psychological resources necessary).

Several writers have equated employee engagement as emotional and intellectual commitment to the organization and passion for work. Harter, Schmidt, and Hayes define employee engagement as 'the individual's involvement and satisfaction with as well as enthusiasm for work.'[13] Robinson, Perryman, and Hayday[14] define employee engagement as

> A positive attitude held by the employee towards the organization and its value. An engaged employee is aware of business context, and works with colleagues to improve performance within the job for the benefit of the organization. The organization must work to develop and nurture engagement, which requires a two-way relationship between employer and employee.

The DDI[15] uses the definition, 'The extent to which people value, enjoy and believe in what they do.' DDI also states that its measure is similar to employee satisfaction and loyalty.

The term `employee engagement' has been defined in so many diverse ways, to imply so many different things, that it can be truly overwhelming for someone trying to make sense of it. Some common strands, however, can still be made out in this clutter. These indicate employees' immersion with their work and 'pride in their employer, the extent to which people enjoy and believe in what they do for work and the perception that their employer values what they bring to the table.'[16] The degree of engagement determines the intensity of discretionary effort and the thrust for great performance. It

12 W. A. Kahn, 'Psychological Conditions of Personal Engagement and Disengagement at Work,' *Academy of Management Journal* 33, no. 4 (1990): 692–724.

13 J. K. Harter, F. L. Schmidt, and T. L. Hayes, 'Business-Unit-Level Relationship Between Employee Satisfaction, Employee Engagement, and Business Outcomes: A Meta-Analysis,' *Journal of Applied Psychology* 87, no. 2 (2002): 268–279.

14 D. Robinson, S. Perryman, and S. Hayday, 'The Drivers of Employee Engagement' (Report No. 408 Institute for Employment Studies, Brighton, 2004).

15 DDI (2005, 1).

16 R. J. Vance, *Employee Engagement and Commitment: A Guide to Understanding, Measuring, and Increasing Engagement in Your Organization* (Alexandria, VA: SHRM Foundation, 2006).

also predicts 'stickiness' (a term coined by IES) in deciding against quitting the organization. In the estimate of software giant Intuit, for example, there is 1.3 times more probability of highly engaged employees to be high performers than less engaged employees and five times less likely to voluntarily quit the organization.

8.4 EVOLUTION OF EMPLOYEE ENGAGEMENT

The precise beginning of the coinage 'employee engagement' is difficult to plot at a specific time, but undoubtedly the term gained currency by virtue of the trend setting practices of Gallup Organization towards the end of the last millennium. Gallup's initial surveys covering some 100,000 employees on strong workplaces were first reported in the book *First, Break All the Rules* by Buckingham and Coffman.[17] The use of 12 questions to capture employee perceptions of their workplaces led to powerful revelations about what drove employee engagement, the crucial role played in it by the managers, and in this way the legend of Q12 was born.

Gradually, the trend caught on and became staple for big consulting firms looking for new thrust areas. The sudden surge of interest in making the workplace the focus perhaps was symptomatic of the waves of changes happening in the world of business at the start of the new millennium. In the first decade itself, the number of publications on the theme of employee engagement crossed 1500. William Kahn's first writings came out in 1990 in the *Academy of Management Journal*, and the positive psychology movement, spearheaded by Martin Seligman, coupled with the growing importance of human capital, added wind to its sail.[18]

8.5 CHALLENGES FOR EMPLOYEE ENGAGEMENT

When the new employees cross the corporate threshold and start their work life with stars in their eyes and spring in their steps, and sometime lose the shine as they grow with the organization, the reasons are not blowing in the wind always. It has been observed that engagement can work like a double-edged sword. The wide-eyed enthusiasm of a new recruit may turn somersault into despair with a careless and flawed action by the management. A recent survey by consultants Bain & Company, covering 200,000 employees across 40 companies in 60 countries, reported some disturbing statistics: decline of engagement scores with age and tenure, low engagement levels in the frontlines of business, and lack of engagement in customer fronting roles like sales and service.

8.5.1 Strategic Alignment

If the engagement programs are conceived and initiated as stand-alone HR initiatives, unconnected with the big picture, and with the sole objective of keeping up with the Joneses, achieving sustainable engagement levels may be a difficult proposition. The shift that one needs to make is 'to redefine engagement beyond an annual HR measure to a continuous, holistic part of an entire business strategy.'[19]

For the admired organizations, this constitutes a critical shift in paradigm. During the past three decades, employee engagement has emerged as a strategic area for any organization, intrinsic to its

[17] Buckingham, M. and Coffman, C. *First, Break All the Rules* (1999).

[18] W. B. Schaufeli, 'What is Engagement?' in *Employee Engagement in Theory and Practice*, eds. C. Truss, K. Alfes, R. Delbridge, A. Shantz, and E. Soane (London: Routledge, 2013).

[19] John Bersin, 'It's Time to Rethink the 'Employee Engagement' Issue,' *Forbes*, April 10, 2014. Available at: https://www.forbes.com/sites/joshbersin/2014/04/10/its-time-to-rethink-the-employee-engagement-issue/#c8c2c06cf363 (accessed on November 23, 2017).

success in the marketplace. A business plan sans a differentiating employee-engagement program is doomed to fail like a jigsaw puzzle for which a main piece has gone missing. In the Deloitte *Global Human Capital Trends* research, 78% of business leaders rate retention and engagement urgent or important. Employee-engagement measures are aligned with customer satisfaction measures. So, an employee-engagement strategy that is integrated with the organization's business strategy is considered to be a lever for business success.

8.5.2 Sustained Approach

Shifting employee-engagement scores from disengaged to highly engaged cannot be expected to be accomplished with one annual survey. An engaged workplace with focus on high performance demands a multi-layered, holistic approach. The employees need to soak in the organization's values, the leadership and the managers need to demonstrate these values, and the selection process needs to bring in employees with culture fit. Simultaneously, systems and process also need to align based on continuous efforts. A model workplace thus takes shape only with time by virtue of a holistic and sustained approach. So, while embarking on an annual survey is an important step in measuring engagement, it should be kept in mind that it is only a tool to provide inputs for action and transformational change. In the constantly evolving business environment, the input data also needs to be updated in a relentless manner.

Already, the talk is on to move beyond annual surveys for more real-time surveys to keep track with the employees and enable timely interventions. There are suggestions for pulse surveys to measure the heartbeat of an organization, suitable to detect emergent engagement issues, and also to know if the initiatives on engagement are yielding benefits or need to be modified.

8.5.3 Customization, Rather Than a Single Panacea

Research findings have established that different groups of employees respond to different engagement drivers and therefore a one-size-fits-all approach is not likely to work. In a survey conducted by Institute for Employment Studies (IES) for National Health Services, UK, it was found that while feeling valued and involved was the key driver for employee engagement in most job groups, except for the pharmacists, where, quite inexplicably, job satisfaction turned up as the key factor.

The need to watch out for divergent drivers and to adapt becomes even more imperative with the surge of the millennials in the workplaces and the glut of technology at work. A traditional engagement survey, based on standard drivers and models, while serving as benchmarks, cannot provide all answers. John Bersin[20] while dismissing the much-repeated old axiom about people leaving managers cites research (TINYpulse research[21]) findings that peers have much greater impact on commitment than managers.

8.5.4 Service Tenure

Several research findings have established that engagement levels dip as service tenure increases.[22] The organization loses out on the valuable resourcefulness of a rich segment of employees in case

---

20 Bersin, 'It's Time to Rethink.'

21 McPherson, J. With Development Opportunities, Having A Good Manager Matters. Available at: https://blog.cultureamp.com/its-about-development-opportunities (accessed on February 13, 2018).

22 Robinson et al. 'The Drivers of Employee Engagement.'

the engagement levels are low. The low engagement levels could be the effect of a myriad factors such as career frustration, boredom arising out of routine work, cynicism, and so on. A strategy to uplift the engagement levels of this group, despite the rigors involved, could be deeply rewarding for the organization.

8.5.5 Balance of Accountability and Freedom

Finally, the challenge is to strike a delicate balance—in creating a workplace that is attractive, the one that creates a sense of belonging in the employee as also a strong sense of accountability. A modern day's flat organization demands each employee to own her part in the whole system. There is no margin for transferring the responsibility upwards. The key to success in the reverse pyramid structure is the spirit sense of autonomy and valuing each employee as a key contributor.

Closing Case Umang: The Ambuja Cements Story

Ambuja Cements Ltd, a part of Lafarge Holcim, is a premier cement company in India. It was established in 1983 as Gujarat Ambuja Cements Ltd by Narotam Sekhsaria in partnership with Suresh Neotia. In 2006, it was taken over by Holcim. Currently, it has a capacity of around 30 million tons, with 5 integrated plants and 8 grinding units in different parts of the country. The group has 115,000 employees and has presence in 90 countries.

A few years after the takeover by Holcim, the leadership group (Exco—the Executive Committee) of Ambuja Cements decided to invite Gallup to conduct an employee-engagement survey. The purpose was to feel the pulse of the employees, whose numbers were swelling along with the growth of the company's business. A competition was held among the employees to create a title for the survey and the name chosen for the initiative was Umang (happiness). A logo was created with multiple colors to depict diversity. A group of 20 LMs was selected to act as 'champs.' They were given training by HR and the consultants to further train the LMs to interpret the survey results (or the scorecards) of the 12 questions and to draw action plans. Each champ had up to 10 LMs to coach.

As the Gallup's employee engagement model has a focus on the role of the LMs, the surveys provided useful feedbacks to the LMs. It also revealed gaps in the perceptions of the LMs and the employees. For example, one particular LM used to take his team for dinner, as a token of recognition of good work. He was unaware that the team members would have been happier with a more explicit gesture like being praised in front of the whole team. Thus, the feedbacks helped the LMs to improve the engagement scores. The first survey, conducted in 2010, placed the company in the 30th percentile among all organizations globally. The successive surveys done improved the organization's position to 54th and then to the 76th percentile.

HR, while anchoring the initiative, kept on the sidelines, providing necessary support, but leaving it to the line to take the ownership and drive it. Every year HR organized a champ's event to share best practices and to award the best performer in eliciting highest responses to the survey.

In 2015, Ambuja Cements switched over to the Hewitt model of Say–Stay–Strive. The surveys were done not on the LMs, but on the unit as a whole. The engagement initiative, however, provided a direction to LMs to continuously improve the engagement levels of the employees.

Discussion Questions

1. What are the triggers for building an engaged workplace?
2. Evaluate the approach taken by Ambuja Cements for building an engaged workplace?

8.6 HOW TO BUILD AN ENGAGING WORKPLACE?

The employee-engagement consulting market is currently estimated to be over a US$1.5 billion in size. Over 50% of the consultants claim internal tools and programs to find solutions to engagement and retention issues. Bersin of Deloitte has identified more than 30 different vendors serving this market, and they provide widely ranging types of tools and solutions. The solution is driven by the definition that one follows, and is, therefore, varied and inconsistent. For example, Glassdoor.com tries to provide data on how happy the employees are with a particular organization; a manufacturing organization may interpret employee engagement through the lens of IR. There is little uniformity in the findings and the opinions vary over a range of choices that the employer can have while trying to create engagement.

There have been some important studies on what creates an engaged work/place. Towers Perrin-ISR has identified 10 key drivers through employee surveys, the top driver being the degree to which the employees were convinced of the genuine interest of the senior management in their well-being. In the same study, in response to a question whether they think their senior management actually exhibit this attitude and behavior, 39% of the respondent employees indicated negatively, and 32% were neutral. The employees' belief that they had improved their skills and capabilities over the previous year constituted the second driver. Here the employee responses were far more encouraging with only 15% responding negatively, 23% being neutral, and thus the remaining 62% believing that they had indeed built their skills and capabilities.

A significant study, requisitioned by the Secretary of State for Business in the autumn of 2008 to 'take an in-depth look at employee engagement and to report on its potential benefits for companies, organizations and individual employees,' was conducted by David Macleod and Nita Clarke. The review came up with four factors that drive employee engagement:

- Leadership that articulates the directions of the organization
- The managers, who motivate, empower and support their employees
- Employee voice, including participation in decision-making
- Organizational integrity that includes its values

Leadership is recognized as the prime mover of employee engagement. The Towers Watson 2012 Global Workforce Study covering 32,000 employees across 30 countries indicates that among employees, who are highly engaged ('sustainably engaged' is the term used) 74% were convinced of the sincere interest of senior leaders in their well-being, while only 44% of traditionally engaged employees and 18% of disengaged employees felt similarly.

For leadership, to act as the enabler of engagement, the key is to begin thinking of themselves as chief energy officers. Energy is contagious, for better and for worse, and disproportionately so for leaders—by virtue of their influence. 'The manager is at the heart of what we might think of as a personal employee ecosystem,' the Towers Watson study concludes, 'shaping individual experience... day in and day out.' Visible leadership that walks around the workplaces lifting the morale of the employees and bringing them on board on what the organization is trying to do in difficult times. It authors a powerful narrative on the journey that the organization is taking, the purpose of the organization, its vision, and the role individual employee is expected to play to achieve the vision. To engage in the workplace, the employee needs to enroll into the strategy and mission of the organization. But the Institute for Corporate (I4CP) recently released a study, done in partnership with HR.com, on the ability of employees to recall or recite their organization's mission statement.[23] The findings look like this:

- 84% of organizations surveyed have a mission statement.
- Of these organizations with a mission statement, 62% reported that less than half of their employees would be able to recall their mission statement if asked.
- 20% of the organizations with a mission statement indicated that only 10% of their employees would be able to recall their mission statement if asked.

Exhibit How Leaders Engage–The Ten Cs of Engagement

Connect

In *First, Break All the Rules*, Marcus Buckingham and Curt Coffman argue that managers trump companies. Employee engagement is a direct reflection of how employees feel about their relationship with the boss. Employees look at whether organizations and their leader walk the talk when they proclaim that, 'Our employees are our most valuable asset.'

Career

Leaders should provide challenging and meaningful work with opportunities for career advancement. Most people want to do new things in their job. Do leaders hold people accountable for progress? Are jobs enriched in duties and responsibilities? Good leaders challenge employees; but not giving people the knowledge and tools to be successful is unethical and demotivating; it is also likely to lead to stress, frustration, and, ultimately, lack of engagement.

Clarity

Leaders must communicate a clear vision. People want to understand the vision that senior leadership has for the organization, and the goals that leaders or departmental heads have for the division, unit, or team. Success in life and organizations is, to a great extent, determined by how clear individuals are about their goals and what they really want to achieve. In sum, employees need to understand what the organization's goals are, why they are important, and how the goals can best be attained. Clarity about what the organization stands for, what it wants to achieve, and how people can contribute to the organization's success is not always evident.

[23] Young, C. 'Talent Management Guide for Executives'. Available at: http://cdn2.hubspot.net/hub/115950 (accessed on October 26, 2016).

Convey

Leaders clarify their expectations about employees and provide feedback on their functioning in the organization. Good leaders establish processes and procedures that help people master important tasks and facilitate goal achievement. Good leaders work daily to improve the skills of their people and create small wins that help the team, unit, or organization perform at its best.

Congratulate

Surveys show that, over and over, employees feel that they receive immediate feedback when their performance is poor, or below expectations. These same employees also report that praise and recognition for strong performance is much less common. Exceptional leaders give recognition, and they do so a lot; they coach and convey.

Contribute

People want to know that their input matters and that they are contributing to the organization's success in a meaningful way. In the Sears Roebuck and Co. turnaround plan in 1992, the implementation of total performance indicators, which gauged how well Sears was doing with its employees, customers, and investors, led to three startling conclusions. First, an employee's understanding of the connection between her work—as operationalized by specific job-relevant behaviors—and the strategic objectives of the company had a positive impact on job performance. Second, an employee's attitude towards the job and the company had the greatest impact on loyalty and customer service than all the other employee factors combined. Third, improvements in employee attitude led to improvements in job-relevant behavior; this, in turn, increased customer satisfaction and an improvement in revenue growth. In sum, good leaders help people see and feel how they are contributing to the organization's success and future.

Control

Employees value control over the flow and pace of their jobs and leaders can create opportunities for employees to exercise this control. Do leaders consult with their employees with regard to their needs? Are leaders flexible and attuned to the needs of the employees as well as the organization? Do leaders involve employees in decision-making, particularly when employees will be directly affected by the decision? Do employees have a say in setting goals or milestones that are deemed important? Are employees able to voice their ideas, and does leadership show that contributions are valued? A feeling of 'being in on things,' and of being given opportunities to participate in decision-making often reduces stress; it also creates trust and a culture where people want to take ownership of problems and their solutions.

Collaborate

Studies show that when employees work in teams and have the trust and cooperation of their team members, they outperform individuals and teams that lack good relationships. Great leaders are team builders; they create an environment that fosters trust and collaboration. A continuous challenge for leaders is to rally individuals to collaborate on organizational, departmental, and group goals, while excluding individuals pursuing their self-interest.

Credibility

Leaders should strive to maintain a company's reputation and demonstrate high ethical standards. People want to be proud of their jobs, their performance, and their organization.

Confidence

Good leaders help create confidence in a company by being exemplars of high ethical and performance standards.

Source: Excerpted from Dan Crim and Gerard Seijts, 'What Engages Employees the Most OR, the Ten Cs of Employee Engagement,' The Workplace (March–April 2006).

Engaging manager is the next key driver, according to the study findings. The manager makes significant difference to the levels of engagement of the employees, both in a negative and positive sense, since an employee spends most of his workplace time dealing with his manager. While an engaged manager can role model commitment and engagement, he may find it impossible to hold necessary candid discussions with the employee faced with difficult times for the organization unless the employee sees him practicing the espoused values. A manager also influences the discretionary effort of the employee, according to a research finding by Corporate Leadership Council (CLC). It is the manager who makes discretionary work possible by explaining how to do one's job, the importance of it, and how to complete one's work. The report identified three conditions for being engaging managers: clarify expectations from individual employees, taking care to create stretch goals, appreciate good work, and provide feedback and developmental inputs; treat employees with fairness and respect, and be concerned with their well-being; and finally, ensure efficient work design.

According to Frederickson's 'broaden and build model,' positive emotions broaden people's 'momentary thought action repertoires' and develop their long-term personal capabilities. Do positive emotions have a direct bearing on work performances? Frederickson lists four of them that can be linked most highly to business outcomes—joy, interest, contentment, and love. Joy, interest, and love come closest to describing employees' emotions in high-performing business units. Individuals experience theses emotions through various events in their daily lives. If in the workplaces such events occur frequently, then the effect of these positive emotional experiences would be a deep bonding with each other, their work, and their organizations. The managers, by paying attention and responding to each unique employee they manage, can facilitate occurrences of such daily experiences, which may lead to higher frequency of these emotions among their employees.[24]

The role of the manager is the hidden structure underlying the Gallup Q12 questions, which includes 'I know what is expected of me at work,' 'in the last seven days I received recognition and praise for doing good work,' and 'at work my opinion seems to count.' 'Knowing what is expected of me' seems to be enhanced when it is accompanied by some positive stretch. The importance of coaching is corroborated by a Watson Wyatt survey that indicates that engaged employees have frequent work-related discussions with their immediate manager and a high percentage (43%) of highly engaged employees receive feedback at least once a week. A Towers Perrin study in 2008 indicated

[24] B. L. Frederickson, 'What Good Are Positive Emotions?' *Review of General Psychology* 2, no. 3 (September 1998): 300–319.

a correlation between recognition of employee performance by manager and a significant growth in engagement levels (33–52%).

The crucial importance of managers in driving employee engagement is also amply supported by researches. According to one research done on workers and employers in the UK in 2005,[25] around 40% of manual workers (skilled and unskilled) vouch not having experienced a positive management style in their present role. This falls in place when it is also indicated that 18% of the middle managers surveyed confirmed lack of pride in working for their current organization and 21% expressed their resolve not to recommend their organization to their friends as a place to work. The majority of employers recognize the importance of management appreciation (61%), integrity (58%), and respect (50%), and believe they are providing this positive style.

Aon Hewitt Report[26] 'Managers: Your Strongest (or Weakest) Link in Driving Employee Engagement?' highlights the influence the managers can have over employee engagement in the workplace. It is found that the more engaged the managers are, the more time and effort they tend to spend on engaging their own teams. It is indicated in the aforementioned findings that managers who reviewed their survey results and identified actions had an engagement score of 63%, as compared with an average score of 52% for managers who only reviewed their results but did not take action. Further, 47% of managers indicated that they spend between two and five days per year on activities related to the annual engagement survey. Organizations need to change the focus from engagement as a once-a-year set of tasks and activities to something addressed as business-as-usual.

Exhibit Engagement–A C Suite Perspective

Universally, employees are a worried lot. All of these are alarming trends and need to be taken seriously. Solutions must be found and implemented at the firm level. Within the firm, it must be focused upon at the departmental level and at the level of the individual relationship. Employees feel engaged or disengaged at the transactional level within departments.

A firm-level approach: Managers must consider a four-pronged approach.

First, the subject of employee engagement needs to be driven down the company by the CEO. I think there is a general lack of awareness of the problem down the line. It is also mixed up with the general economic downturn. Poor employee engagement, it must be clearly understood, is a precursor to some other problem that is brewing. That is why there needs to be top-level engagement. If enough employees feel disengaged, the consequences will certainly be disruptive. Operating managers have to act. It cannot be left to the HR department.

Source: Excerpted from R. Gopalakrishnan, 'Employee Engagement: A Leadership Priority,' *The Economic Times*, December 7, 2009.

The next engagement driver is employee voice. Employees experience a sense of belonging in an organization when they are listened to, and they believe that their actions can have an impact. Employees become more engaged when employees are able to express their views to the senior levels

25 Penna, *Meaning at Work: Research Report* (2007). Available at: http://www. e-penna.com/newsopinion/research.aspx (accessed on November 10, 2008).

26 Aon Hewitt, 'Managers: Your Strongest (or Weakest) Link in Driving Employee Engagement?' (AonHewitt European Manager Survey, 2011) Available at: http://www.aon.com/attachments/human-capital-consulting (accessed on March 6, 2018).

of management, when they feel updated about the happenings in their organization, and when they believe in the commitment of their manager to the organization.[27] The employees' voice also includes collective voice, which is important in an organization, despite the rapid decline in union density all over the industrialized world and the burgeoning number of non-unionized workplaces. The bad news is the role of collective representation in improving workplace effectiveness is yet to be developed and the joint participative forces in the workplaces have to show an appetite for rising beyond small issues related to welfare to focus on strategic issues like performance and productivity. 'Optimal results are achieved where there is a mix of direct employee involvement and indirect participation through a trade union or works council.'[28]

Integrity is the fourth enabler of employee engagement in an organization. When there is congruence between the professed values in an organization and the values in practice, an environment of trust emerges. Any gap between the two, leads to distrust—more the gap, larger the level of distrust. An example of the variance or distance between espoused values and values in practice could be an organization that emphasizes safety, but tolerates its employees to bypass important safety provisions in the standard operating practices (SOPs) for meeting a business target of production.

Work itself, when meaningfully designed, becomes a powerful driver of employee engagement by creating a sense of community and making employees content about contributing to the organization. Research by Roffey Park in 2003 covering employees working in different organizations in UK found that 70% of employees seek more 'meaning at work.' What then is good work? It is, according to a Penna report (entitled 'A Good Day's Work') that work which 'is individually satisfying, organizationally productive and socially, with all the three levels aligned together.'

Penna Research group conducted an online survey in 2005 covering 1765 British workers in the summer of 2005. The questions aimed to identify what created meaning at work for working class and employers' respondents in the UK on creating meaning at workplace. A model presented in the compiled Penna Report in 2007 (titled 'Hierarchy of Engagement') describes the evolution of engagement drivers in a hierarchy, similar to Maslow's need hierarchy. The steps, from bottom to the top include pay and benefits, L&D, the possibility for promotion, the leadership style to the higher levels of complexity—an alignment of value-meaning, which is demonstrated by a real 'sense of connection, a common purpose and a shared sense of meaning at work.' As an employee goes up the ladder and 'meaning' is created, his engagement or 'stickiness' loyalty increases. The research findings corroborate this: 42% of the respondents indicated rising level of loyalty to their employers if work became meaningful, and 55% spoke about improvement in their motivation levels.

While work can create meaning, a balance in engagement is achieved by a time away from work. The percentage of respondents who confirmed a positive experience at work by being able to leave work on time and strike a work–life balance was 44. The Penna Research (2007) also found that 54% of those working on clerical and administrative work valued leaving work on time. Manual workers are nearly half as likely to have access to any form of flexible working arrangement than anyone else. Little wonder that so many (40%) take the opportunity to leave work on time when it is available.

---

27 Independent research by Kingston Business School and Ipsos Mori for the CIPD in 2006.

28 Macleod and Clarke. 'Engaging for Success'. (BIS, 2009): 109. Available at: http://engageforsuccess.org/engaging-for-success (accessed on January 15, 2018).

8.7 MEASUREMENT OF EMPLOYEE ENGAGEMENT

Is it necessary to measure employee engagement? There are influential arguments against measurements. The old business adage that says, 'If you cannot measure it, you cannot manage it,' was famously rubbished by Edward Deming. The critics say that measurement serves no purpose, as it requires 'stopping the action, getting outside of it and holding it up against a yardstick, exactly the opposite of the activity that would create products or ship them, make customers happy or move our business forward in any way.'[29] For employee engagement, the measurement poses additional difficulties as it refers to one's emotional commitment to their organization and the organization's goals. How does one measure a salesperson's voluntary immersion in hard work through the week in grueling marketplace, or a technician's obsession with the new machine to make it fully productive, or both their decision to stay on with their respective organizations?

However, despite difficulties of creating meaningful rubric, or of placing a numerical value on a variety of actions, attitudes, and process that constitute employee engagement, employers have been making serious efforts to assess their employees' engagement levels for two reasons: to understand the impact of employee-engagement initiatives on business results, and to assess the levels to take corrective actions. The two principal methods for going about the measurements of employee engagement are EIs and employee surveys.

8.7.1 Employee Engagement and the Neuroscience of Trust

Leaders know that low employee engagement is a sign of lost value. It is clearly something the employers seek to correct. So what is done to improve engagement is a series of random actions. It is much like the story of Nasiruddin Molla watching a frustrated drunk person looking for the lost key for his house on certain areas because they were the only areas lit up by street lamps. So, organizations they scatter benefits in the name of rewards which do not motivate employees, or they hire a consultant and adapt a model without realizing when they transplant of a model suits the ecology of their work environment.

It is known by now on the basis of research that what is required is an employee driven culture, which can enthuse employees about their work and workplace. Neuro scientist Paul J Zak has a solution based on his detailed research for many years. He believes that building a culture of trust can make all the difference. He gets support from unusual quarters. In a survey of CEOs, PWC reported that 55% of the CEOs felt that lack of trust is a menace to the organization. It is also found that high trust organizations consistent outperform low trust organization by a big margin. What is also interesting is that employees in the former organizations have 74% less stress than employees in the later organizations.

Experiments conducted by Prof. Zak[30] and his team also establish that having 'a sense of higher purpose' stimulates oxytocin production, as does trust. 'Trust and purpose then mutually reinforce each other, providing a mechanism for extended oxytocin release, which produces happiness'.

So, the case for the ideal solution for low engagement has been suggested. Enjoyment at doing the work is caused by 'doing purpose-driven work with a trusted team'. Based on a rigorously obtained

---

29 Liz Ryan, 'If You Can't Measure It, You Can't Manage It: Not True,' *Forbes*, February 10, 2014. Available at: https://www.forbes.com/sites/lizryan/2014/02/10/if-you-cant-measure-it-you-cant-manage-it-is-bs/#303cdc9d7b8b (accessed on November 22, 2017).

30 The Neuro science of Trust. Paul J. Zak. HBR. Jan-Feb. 2017

widely valid data set, the 'correlation between (1) trust reinforced by purpose and (2) joy is very high. It means that joy can be considered a 'sufficient statistic' that reveals how effectively your company's culture engages employees. So it all boils down to the basic question: how much do you enjoy your work?

Exhibit Current Situation at NTC Plant, Trichy

The plant has 108 unionized employees (all men), which excludes the managerial staff, contract workers, and the casual labor. The plant has two unions constantly at competition with each other. There are only four female employees in the managerial staff.

The union elections were scheduled on 16 May 2012 but due to some disputes, the elections had to be stalled and further dates on the union elections is yet to be decided. Stringent measures against forming groups on the campus, holding any meetings, holding placards, etc., have been taken.

NTC, Trichy follows Lean Manufacturing Process (LMP) and is Level 2 certified of LMP and trying for Level 3 certification. Its other counterparts, NTC Bhadrachalam, Kovai, and Tribeni are still at level 1.

Every machine has its owners name and details under the title 'My Machine'. Short-term goals like zero defects, doing it right the first time, etc., and warnings like 'Do Not Enter without Safety Gear' are hung at several locations on the shop floor.

About the blue-collared employees, the workforce is

- Quite young, mostly in the age group of 30-35 years.
- Immature due to their young age (according to our guide at NTC)
- Well educated, minimum qualification being polytechnic graduates
- Very focused on developing their technical expertise

Recent incident on the shop floor:

- The plant failed to get one of the certifications from a British organization as during the time of audit, a part of the campus was housing a couple a pigeons which had also dirtied the place. To make sure that this episode does not repeat, huge mannequins of eagles have been hung at several locations.
- One of the employees had taken a picture at the canteen to report the quality of the food being served, but it also created a lot of tension as clicking photos on campus was prohibited.
- One of the operators was severely injured where the thumb and the index finger were crushed due to his negligence.
- The union elections scheduled on 16 May 2012 was postponed to another date due to some conflict (which the management has not yet disclosed).

Some points observed at the plant:

- Power distance (untold but understood) between the managerial staff and the workforce is quite high. This we could figure out by some informal discussions with the staff and their attitude towards the blue collared employees and also the seating arrangement followed at the canteen.
- The employees are not frisked at any point.
- Check for alcohol is also not done.

- There is no doctor available on the plant but only first-aiders, who happen to be the employees themselves. Details of the first-aiders are displayed at different locations in the plant, above every first-aid kit. In case of any accident, the first aiders tend to the injured first and then if necessary the injured is transferred to a hospital (recognized by NTC, which is nearly 5-6 kms away) in the emergency vehicle or any other vehicle.
- Various options are available for increasing the technical knowledge of the employees like provision for higher studies, technical library, etc.
- The workshops conducted for improving the behavior and attitude of the Blue collared employees is negligible. This is primarily because it is a continuous manufacturing process. Involving all the employees of the same team is highly impossible as the machines cannot be stopped.
- No incentives are provided for superior performance. Everybody is given the same hike or reward according to their level irrespective of their contribution. This is mainly because the union is against recognizing individual performers.

Discussion Questions

1. What should be done to increase the level of employee engagement at NTC Trichy?

8.7.2 Exit Interviews

The traditional method for gauging the level of employee engagement is the instrument of EIs. An EI is a formal interaction with an exiting employee with the aim of learning the reasons why the employee wants to depart from the organization and to and use the data for taking some corrective actions. In practice, however, EI programs often fail to yield useful information. In the first place, the data quality, which hinges on the candor of the exiting employee, becomes doubtful when such employees choose to be guarded for multiple reasons, such as time constraints, lack of motivation, or simple reluctance to openly express any negative feelings about their line bosses. Lack of consensus on best practices also undermines the effectiveness of EIs. There are wide variance in the objectives and the conduct of EI programs. A survey[31] conducted in 2012 and 2013, covering 188 executives and 32 senior leaders, representing 210 organizations in 33 industries in more than 35 countries reported the following practices:

1. Three-quarters of the companies conducted some type of an EI for at least some departing employees.
2. 70.9% had their HR departments handle the process.
3. 19% had the departing employees' direct supervisors do it.
4. 8.9% delegated the job to the direct supervisor's manager.
5. 1% turned the job over to external consultants.
6. About 8.2% of organizations used more than one interviewer.
7. Only 4.4% used questionnaires.
8. 1.9% used a questionnaire accompanied by a face-to-face or a telephone interview.
9. 2.5% used questionnaires as the sole form of EI.

[31] Everett Spain and Boris Groysberg, 'Making Exit Interviews Count,' *Harvard Business Review* (April 2016). Available at: https:// cb.hbsp.harvard.edu/cbmp/product/R1604G-PDF-ENG (accessed on January 15, 2018).

Exhibit Stay Interviews

Stay interviews are a relatively underused retention tool, but things are looking up. More and more companies are now warming up to it. They (stay interviews) are a continuous process of enquiry that enables the management to find out how engaged valuable employees are. It is a proactive step and is not to be confused with trying to retain an employee who has decided to leave. A stay interview may help a company find out the factors that have made an employee stay in the organization for the duration he/she has and reinforce those factors.

Aditya Narayan Mishra, CEO, CIEL HR Services, says,

> Around 2000–2006, when there was a boom in ITeS sector, retaining talent was harder. With many opportunities beckoning them, employees in the sector changed jobs frequently. This forced companies to assess level of employee engagement across their workforce. Based on this assessment, employees were marker in amber and red (those likely to leave). Yet, most companies were not sure of the action that needed to be taken to ensure all the reds changed to amber. Over a period of time, some companies evolved action plans to improve employee engagement and retention. Stay interviews were part of these action plans.

Source: Excerpted from K. Sarumathi, 'It's Time to Show Exit Interviews the Door,' The Hindu, June 9, 2016.

8.7.3 Employee Survey

Perhaps the most consistent measure finding wide acceptance in organizations is the use of a survey. Each survey is, however, different from each other and known by different names—engagement survey, attitude survey, work climate improvement survey, and so on. The surveys could indicate which engagement initiatives are on target, which need to be jettisoned off, which need to be tweaked for making even greater impact.

The survey questionnaires have also graduated from the conventional general assertions of climate or well-being into more pointed, more sharpened enquiries on focused areas such as superior subordinate relationship, work organization, and even connecting with specific business objectives. Some examples of the survey questionnaires are given further:

Gallup's Q12

Among the engagement measures, Gallup's Q12 is well known. It is a 12-question survey that tries to assess the levels of employee engagement by exploring various aspects of the employee's perceptions of his working conditions. The questions are:

1. Do you know what is expected of you at work?
2. Do you have the materials and equipment you need to do your work right?
3. At work, do you have the opportunity to do what you do best every day?
4. In the last seven days, have you received recognition or praise for doing good work?
5. Does your supervisor, or someone at work, seems to care about you as a person?
6. Is there someone at work who encourages your development?
7. At work, do your opinions seem to count?
8. Does the mission/purpose of your company make you feel your job is important?
9. Are your associates (fellow employees) committed to doing quality work?
10. Do you have a best friend at work?

11. In the last six months, has someone at work talked to you about your progress?
12. In the last year, have you had opportunities at work to learn and grow?

8.7.4 The Engagement Index

The JRA employee engagement index has been successfully run on thousands of New Zealand employees since its first use in 2000. This basic instrument has six items to assess the rational–emotional–behavioral dimensions of employee engagement.

The six questionnaire items are:

1. I look for ways to do my job more effectively.
2. Overall, I am satisfied with my job.
3. I take an active interest in what happens in this organization.
4. I feel inspired to go the extra mile to help this organization succeed.
5. I feel a sense of commitment to this organization.
6. Overall, I would recommend this organization as a great place to work.

The CLC uses the following four questions:

1. I am proud to work at COMPANY.
2. Overall my satisfaction with COMPANY is high.
3. I would recommend COMPANY as a great place to work.
4. If offered a similar position and compensation at another company I would stay at COMPANY.

Dell

1. Even if I were offered a comparable position with similar pay and benefits at another company, I would stay at Dell.
2. Considering everything, Dell is the right place for me.

Development Dimensions International

DDI's tool, known as E3, measures three facets of engagement (individual value, focused work, and interpersonal support) and includes a standard measure for employee satisfaction, which is the outcome of engagement.

1. My job provides me with chances to grow and develop.
2. I find personal meaning and fulfilment in my work.
3. I get sufficient feedback about how well I am doing.

Institute for Employment Studies

The survey by IES also provides 12 attitude statements depicting engagement, but they vary from those of Gallup. IES also has a subset of 5 questions, in the event 12 questions cannot be used. A sample of a few such questions are:

1. A positive attitude toward, and pride in, the organization.
2. A willingness to behave altruistically and be a good team player.
3. An understanding of the bigger picture and a willingness to go beyond the requirements of the individual self.

8.7.5 Linkage Research

Certain common themes running across in such engagement measures have been found to be:

1. Pride in employer
2. Satisfaction with employer
3. Job satisfaction
4. Opportunity to perform well at challenging work
5. Recognition and positive feedback for one's contributions
6. Personal support from one's supervisor
7. Effort above and beyond the minimum
8. Understanding the link between one's job and the organization's mission
9. Prospects for future growth with one's employer
10. Intention to stay with one's employer

The aforementioned elements constitute employee engagement as per linkage research, which links survey outcomes to financial outcomes. Linkage research was developed by psychologist Benjamin Schneider and colleagues in 1980 to demonstrate a correlation between employee perceptions of service to customers and customers' evaluations of service quality. Employee engagement survey items are those having the strongest correlations with business results.

8.8 STRATEGIES TO IMPROVE EMPLOYEE ENGAGEMENT

The reason why employee engagement has caught the imaginations of the leadership in corporate organizations is that they see it contributing to the business outcomes either directly or indirectly, and there certainly is a line in sight. What strategies maximize such engagement, and what are the most powerful ways to structure employee-engagement initiatives to yield positive business outcomes? The key strategy to link employee engagement to business outcomes is to identify those HR processes that promote engagement and then enrich them in a planned manner. These practices cover the design of the job, the recruitment and selection processes, performance management, T&D, and others.

8.8.1 Design of Work

As mentioned earlier, while sharing the Penna research findings, work itself is a powerful driver of employee engagement. This brings up the importance of design of work. In the job characteristics model, formulated in 1971, Hackman and Lawler[32] suggested five core job characteristics that create meaningfulness of work: skill variety, task identity, task significance, autonomy, and performance feedback. With the evolution of flatter and nimble organizations and the emergence of team-based work, a new dimension being extensively researched on is social characteristics of work that seem to powerfully impact the level of employee engagement, specifically their commitment and retention.

8.8.2 Recruitment

Employers look for the ideal employee, who will stay and walk the extra mile to help achieve the organization's vision and values. This makes recruitment as a crucial HR process. Employer branding is

[32] J. R. Hackman and E. E. Lawler, 'Employee Reactions to Job Characteristics,' *Journal of Applied Psychology* 55, no. 3 (1971): 259–286.

a commonly used way to attract the potential employee by showcasing the characteristics relevant to aid engagement, such as great work environment, community of professionals having similar background, and so on. Instituting an internal promotions policy and using employee referrals for recruitment are some ways employers can create cues for loyalty and commitment through recruitment practices.

8.8.3 Selection

When a new employee is placed on a regular job without being made to wait in the transit places in the organizations, he is impressed and positively motivated. Therefore, creating a right fit through focused selection process is a method for developing employee engagement. Besides, the use of behavior-based interviewing, aligned to job competencies, or situations-based interviewing, with inputs drawn from actual situations on the role, the candidate gets the whiff of the real job and this enhances his alignment to the work itself.

8.8.4 Training and Development

The onboarding process or the orientation program for a new employee provides a platform for the employer to start the engagement process by providing inputs about the organization's mission, vision, and values, and familiarizing the employee with the organization structures, the location, the products and services, and the people among other items. All these activities can create the initial positive experience of the employee that provides the bedrock of emotional and intellectual alignment of the employee to the organization.

The subsequent T&D inputs through different assignments, classroom, and through digital platforms help enhancing the capabilities of the employee to perform the work and make him increasingly confident, satisfied, and aligned to the job, the workplace, and the organization. T&D process also improves the employability of an employee.

8.8.5 Compensation

To drive engagement through compensation, employers need to embed certain elements in the compensation system: internal and external equity, incentive for high performance, competency based pay, and a cafeteria approach to adapt to the individual requirements of talented employees.

Younger employees may have a preference for financial package, while older employees may opt for a total package with retirement benefits. Compensation also provides strong signals about the intent of the employer to construct a performance-based culture or a loyalty, seniority-based culture, through the way the rewards are planned and administered. It is also essential to develop a total rewards strategy by carefully including financial as well as non-financial component in the reward basket.

8.8.6 Performance Management

The engagement process can be implanted in the starting block of the performance management process: the target/goal setting. If the performance goals are set with involvement of the employee, it shall go a long way in fostering commitment. The easily achievable targets dampen enthusiasm of the performing employee, who likes challenging goals with sufficient stretch in them. Due care, however, needs to be taken to strike a balance: goals should not be too stiff to discourage endeavor; at the same time, it should not be so soft that it would not propel performance improvement efforts.

An SHRM sponsored study in 2011[33] by Dr Elaine Fernandez and others reported the following key findings:

1. Performance management process, when broadly driven by a wide range of outcomes such as T&D, pay, career plans, and so on, has the most impact on employee engagement.
2. The target setting stage in the performance management process cycle is connected with employees having positive feelings about their job and the organization as a whole. The frequency of performance evaluation also had linkage with increased employee state engagement.

8.9 ROLE OF HUMAN RESOURCE IN EMPLOYEE ENGAGEMENT

Whose role is it to anchor employee engagement in the organizations? There are clear evidences emerging from numerous researches that support the view that it is the role of the leaders to spearhead employee engagement in an organization. It is also similarly acknowledged that it is for the LMs to lead it in the workplace. But a big chunk of work belongs to the HR professionals to play. David McLeod and Nita Clarke quote Jackie Orme, the Chief Executive of CIPD, to emphasize that employee engagement 'gets put on the table' in companies. 'HR can't manufacture engagement, but we have a key role in helping companies develop the kind of organizational culture where engagement can thrive, and ensuring that managers have the skills to make engagement a reality.'[34] According to CIPD's recent discussion paper 'An HR Director's Guide to Employee Engagement,'[35] the HR role is two-folds: emphasize the importance of engagement and to make available the diverse tools and techniques to facilitate line management effectiveness at engagement.

For HR, however, to play the role of the facilitator, it will need to first develop its own business literacy levels—to know the business strategy and to focus on the specific HR policies and practices that have a positive bearing on engagement. The aforementioned report by David MacLeod and Nita Clarke also refer to the opinions expressed by many of those surveyed to the 'strategic opportunity' that employee engagement provided to the HR function to reincarnate itself as a key profession, placed at the heart of business and organizational success, rather than being looked at as 'a cost center' or administrative function.

Closing Case Employee-engagement Survey at Infinity Motors

Infinity Motors Company (IMC) is a joint venture company between Hokkan Motor Company and JVT group in India with an investment of about ₹1,500 crore. The company operates in the passenger car segment. It has two large manufacturing plants in Chennai and Karnataka, with an installed capacity of 25,000 cars annually, and a plan to increase it to 40,000 over the next 5 years. The company has created a niche for itself in the market

[33] Elaine Farndale, Veronica Hope Hailey, Clare Kelliher, and Marc van Veldhoven, 'A Study of the Link Between Performance Management and Employee Engagement in Western Multinational Corporations Operating Across India and China' (Report, SHRM Foundation, Alexandria, VA, 2011).

[34] David MacLeod and Nita Clarke, *Engaging for Success: Enhancing Performance Through Employee Engagement, a Report to Government* (Department for Business, Innovation and Skills, corp creator, 2011). Available at: http://dera.ioe.ac.uk/1810/ (accessed on November 14, 2017).

[35] CIPD, 'An HR Director's Guide to Employee Engagement,' Discussion paper (London: CIPD, June 2009).

segment, commanding a 25% share in the market and has a reputation for reliability, fuel efficiency, and low cost.

The company has had some mixed experiences as far as the employee relations are concerned. The Japanese model of operations based on Toyota culture, and the thrust on high productivity with low compensation levels created employee unrest from time to time. In 2013, its unit at Karnataka went to three months of agitation and even a 7-day lockout. In 2016, the executive council of IMC decided to have an employee engagement survey, conducted with the help of a reputed consultant company with the purpose of initiating some actions to improve the employee perceptions and also its brand image.

About 1,080 employees of IMC were covered in the survey with 430 in the executive cader and 650 in the non-executive unionized cader that constituted about 80% of the total employee strength. The responses were about 88% among executives and about 45% in non-executive caders. The questionnaire included three parts: questions on the engagement factors (pride in the organization, alignment to organizational vision, camaraderie, growth and recognition), further exploration on each engagement factors, and demographic factors. The responses were on a five-point scale with 1 indicating strongly agree and 5 indicating strongly disagree.

Based on the survey, the key findings were as follows:

1. Overall engagement score at IMC was 56%.
2. The ratio of actively engaged to actively disengaged employee was 7:1.
3. The engagement scores for different factors were as follows:
   (a) 69% in peers relations and camaraderie.
   (b) 35% in alignment to organizational vision.
   (c) 55% on pride in the organization.
   (d) 21% on growth and recognition.
4. 27% said that their managers recognize their contribution.
5. 13% said that the organization has an effective process to identify their need for development.
6. 27% of the employees said that their opinions and suggestions were given due importance.

Discussion Question

1. What would you consider for further areas for exploration to decide on corrective actions for IMC?

SUMMARY

An engaged employee is not a happy or a satisfied employee; he/she has been described as the one who has an emotional connect with the organization and is always ready to put in discretionary effort as a matter of habit. It is well recognized now that a high degree of employee engagement drives business outcomes through retention of talent. In the ongoing war in a market driven by scarcity and high value, talent seems to be holding all the aces. Recent research undertaken by Bersin by Deloitte indicates that the factor of 'retention and engagement' ranks number two in the opinions of many business leaders, next only to the challenge of building global leadership.

Several researches have established that employee engagement and improved productivity are clearly correlated. Various studies, conducted by Gallup, Hay Group, and Towers Watson, have indicated that employee engagement has a quantifiable impact on business performance. A Gallup survey in 2006 over 23,910 business units found, among other things, that units with high engagement scores averaged 12% higher customer advocacy, 18% higher productivity, and 12% higher profitability; units with low engagement scores averaged 31–51% more employee turnover, 51% more inventory shrinkage, and 62% more accidents.

Many business organizations have succeeded in building engagement. Some of the building blocks are: leadership that articulates the directions of the organization; the managers, who motivate, empower, and support their employees; adoption of process to capture employee voice, including participation in decision-making; and taking steps to develop organizational integrity that includes its values. The employee-engagement initiatives can be linked to business outcomes, and a key strategy to that would be to identify those HR processes that promote engagement and then enrich them in a planned manner. These practices cover the design of the job, the recruitment and selection processes, performance management, T&D, and so on.

Can employee engagement be measured? However, despite difficulties of creating a meaningful rubric, or of placing a numerical value on a variety of actions, attitudes, and processes that constitute employee engagement, employers have been making serious efforts to assess their employees' engagement levels for two reasons: to understand the impact of employee-engagement initiatives on business results and to assess the calculated levels to take corrective actions. The two principal methods for going about the measurements of employee engagement are EIs and employee surveys.

Short-answer Questions

1. What does DDI's survey report on employee engagement reveal about the number of employees engaged?
2. How has the term employee engagement evolved?
3. Mention two positive outcomes of employee engagement.
4. What can go wrong if the employee engagement programs are not aligned to business strategy?
5. What, if at all, is the correlation between the length of service and service tenure?
6. Describe the basic steps in building an engaged workforce.
7. What is the role of LMs in employee engagement?
8. Explain the ten Cs of engagement.
9. How can employee engagement be measured?
10. Explain Engagement Index.

Discussion Questions

1. Who is an engaged employee? Is it necessary for business to have 100% employee engagement?
2. What is Gallup's Q12? How does it differ from Aon Hewitt model of employee engagement?
3. What steps should be taken to build employee engagement in a unionized workplace? What could be the potential areas of discord?
4. It is said that an employee does not leave his job, he leaves his boss. What implication has this statement for the role of manager in creating employee engagement?
5. What HR processes need to be focused on to create a line of sight between employee engagement and business outcomes?

CHAPTER 9

Performance Management

LEARNING OBJECTIVES

After completing this chapter, the student will be able to:

- Discuss the objectives of performance management
- Understand the difference between performance management and performance appraisal
- Identify some of the common problems with the performance appraisal process
- Describe the performance appraisal process
- Identify the features of an effective PMS
- Identify the instruments for performance management
- Discuss the future of performance management

Opening Case The Inner Game of Performance Evaluations

At the end of the daily management committee meeting, Tarneja, the works manager and my boss, took me aside and said softly, 'Can you see me in my cabin in ten minutes? I want to complete your performance review work. I have been putting it away for one reason or another.'

It was Friday, June 21. I knew that Tarneja would leave after lunch, as he had to catch an evening flight to Newark, USA. He will be away for the next fortnight to attend a leadership development program at Berkeley. Various thoughts crossed my mind. Did he keep this review deliberately for the last minute? Why did he not give me sufficient time to get mentally prepared? What is going to happen at the review meeting? Would I get a proper performance bonus?

He was having coffee, when I entered his spacious chamber. We sat at the small, oval meeting table, overhung by a Hussein print of Mother Theresa. He opened the inner door, and told Henrietta, his secretary, not to let anybody in. Without beating around the bush, he opened his briefcase, pulled out a report and pushed it across me. Tarneja wears a nervous grin when he is uncomfortable. 'I have to do this. This is what Haran and I have written together.' Haran, Nadan's predecessor, was transferred in October last year to another division, in mid-March.

With a premonition of what was coming, my spirits sank. The report truly was disappointing.

Throughout the last appraisal period, as the plant HR head, I had to bear the brunt of an aborted lockout that occurred in 2013. But now things were different. Productivity was near normal. There was no lost time due to industrial actions. A Gallup poll showed several areas of good engagement levels. Hostile employee groups were coming a round to support the new six sigma projects. A suggestion scheme was being launched. Tarneja was fully aware of my efforts. The report, however, contained very little of the efforts. There were some far-fetched comments like 'Needs to manage time better, and prioritize issues,' 'Needs to demonstrate more awareness of business issues' without a single concrete example. I asked Tarneja, what did all these phrases mean? 'I was never told about any during the appraisal period.' He smiled and said vaguely 'Well, perceptions also need to be managed.' When I asked, 'Whose perceptions?' he avoided answering directly. Instead, he asked 'How did you get along with Haran?' The needle of responsibility for the report was diplomatically being maneuvered to point at Haran.

In the meantime, a telephone call came through and he got talking by walking to another corner of the room. I waited, and eventually lost my lines. Already the lunch hour was coming to an end. When Tarneja finished his call, he shook hands with me, and said, 'Don't worry, keep your spirits up, I am there to take care this year.'

In the executive cafeteria, P. K. Bose, the operations manager, came to sit next to me. PK was a seasoned warhorse, my agony uncle, and an astute interpreter of reality in Signal Ltd. He had overheard Tarneja's conversations with me in the meeting room and observed my hangdog looks now. With a knowing wink, he asked, 'What did he tell? That he will take care of you this year?' I opened my heart to him about the pitifully truncated appraisal interview, deliberately structured by Tarneja. Later, gradually, through sips of the tepid sweet corn soup, PK unraveled the mysterious patterns in the inner game of managerial performance evaluations in Signal Ltd. 'Our plant is under fire from the head office since the last, failed lockout. For the bell curve, the plant manager needs a scapegoat to save his backside. Last year, it was the engineering manager. This year, you have been chosen as the sacrificial lamb at the altar.'

I was aghast. Where is 'performance' in this cesspool of corporate gamesmanship?

Discussion Question

1. How would you evaluate the performance appraisal practices at Signal?

9.1 INTRODUCTION

Performance management has always stirred passionate polemics. 'Is There Any Organizational Practice More Broken Than Performance Management?' screamed a *Forbes* article in 2013.[1] The answer is predictably negative. The article reported universal concurrence on several areas:

1 Sylvia Vorhauser-Smith, 'Three Reasons Performance Management Will Change in 2013,' *Forbes*, December 16, 2012. Available at: https://www.forbes.com/sites/sylviavorhausersmith/2012/12/16/the-new-face-of-performance-management-trading-annual-reviews-for-agile-management/#10ff057537ae (accessed on November 14, 2017).

1. It is loathed by everyone—employees and managers in equal proportions.
2. Nobody seems to be adept at it, as it is an elusive skill despite substantial training efforts.
3. It fails the test of what is known as 'construct validity'; it is unable to deliver what it is designed for.

Traditional PMS has been thus described as an 'organization wallpaper' appearing in the background, but seldom expected to make an impact. Ironically, the low level of popularity notwithstanding, performance management, for individual employee as well as for the organization, as a concept, has remained an enduring feature of business organizations.

To collect information about the current status of effectiveness and outcomes performance management, WorldatWork and Sibson Consulting gathered feedback from a sample of WorldatWork members through participation in a confidential online survey. In May and June 2010, 750 individuals, primarily senior-level HR professionals, responded. More than half of the respondents (58%) gave their organization's PMS a grade of 'C' or below. Only 43% view their organization's PMS as effective (with an overall grade of 'A' or 'B'), with very few selecting an 'A' grade (extremely effective).

Why then have business organizations persisted with the performance management process? In today's competitive world, the quality of human resource being considered the key differentiating factor between successful and average organizations, performance management process is expected to help to assess the relative worth of individuals and seeks to maximize their contribution to the organizational goals. This actual process is sometimes formal and, in many cases, informal, both having varying degrees of impact, depending largely on the strength of the organization's philosophy and the conviction of the leadership.

9.2 OBJECTIVES OF PERFORMANCE MANAGEMENT

Performance management aims at energizing people, boosting productivity, and shaping a community of people into a committed workforce. It benefits both the individual employee and the organization.

9.2.1 Objectives for the Employee

1. Personal development
2. Work satisfaction
3. Engagement in the organization

9.2.2 Objectives for the Organization

1. Provide information about employees and their development
2. Measure the efficiency with which human resource is being used and improved
3. Provide linkages to compensation and rewards to employees
4. Maintain organizational control

In short, performance management should balance the personal goals of the employees and the organizational goals. Employees can grow only when the organization succeeds in the marketplace. The dual purpose of performance management promotes harmony and enhances the value of human capital in organization.

9.3 PERFORMANCE MANAGEMENT AND PERFORMANCE APPRAISAL

Performance management is the continuous process of identifying, measuring, managing, and developing the performance of individuals and groups in an organization. At the basic level, it is about finding out the current level of employee performance so that appropriate steps can be taken to eventually upgrade the performance level. Performance management is a systematic assessment of employee performance (including transmission of that evaluation to the employee) that is used for performance improvement over time.

Performance appraisal, on the other hand, is the ongoing process of reviews of employee performance over time, and is one component of the entire performance management process. It is a formal system, which requires a manager to carry out this activity in a continuous manner (Table 9.1).

Table 9.1 Performance appraisal and PMS–A comparison

Performance appraisal	Performance management
Focus is on performance appraisal and generation of ratings.	Focus is on performance management.
Emphasis is on relative evaluation of individuals.	Emphasis is on performance improvements of individual officer and his departmental or team performance.
Annual exercise, though normally periodic, evaluations are a continuous process with quarterly or periodic performance made.	Continuous process with quarterly or periodic performance made review discussions.
Emphasis is on ratings and evaluation.	Emphasis is on performance planning, analysis, review, development and improvements.
Rewards and recognition of good performance are an important component.	Performance rewarding may or may not be an integral part.
	Defining and setting performance standards is an integral part.
Designed and monitored by the personnel/ administration department.	Designed by the personnel/HR department, but could be monitored by the respective departments themselves.
Ownership is mostly with the administration/ personnel.	Ownership is with LMs; personnel/administration facilitates its implementation.
Key performance areas (KPAs) and key result areas (KRAs) are used for bringing in objectivity.	KPAs or KRAs are used as planning mechanisms.
Developmental needs are identified at the end of the year on the basis of the appraisal of competency gaps.	Developmental needs are identified in the beginning of the year on the basis of the competency requirements for the coming year.
There are review mechanisms to ensure objectivity in ratings.	There are review mechanisms essentially to bring performance improvements.
It is a system with deadlines, meetings, input, and a format and output.	It is a system with deadlines, meetings, input, output, and a format.
Format-driven with emphasis on the format as an aid linked to promotions, rewards, T&D interventions, placements, and so on.	Process-driven with emphasis on the format as an aid linked to performance improvements and through them to other career decisions as and when necessary.

Source: T. V. Rao, 'Lessons from Experience: A New Look at Performance Management Systems,' *Vikalpa* 33, no. 3 (September 2008): 1–15.

Performance appraisal has frequently been criticized as a negative activity, wasteful, causing fissures in the employee–supervisor relationship, and one that is hard to master. Managers dread to give them while employees hate to receive them. So unpopular are appraisals that Jim Heskett, writing for the Harvard Business School says, employee performance reviews rank alongside 'undergoing root canal dentistry work on the list of least favorite things to do both for employees and managers.' A survey done by SHRM concluded that more than 90% performance appraisal systems are a failure.[2]

In her article 'Is It Time to Give Up on Performance Appraisals?'[3] Gabriella Jozwiak notes, in UK 'management consultancy Hay Group found half of public sector workers and one-third of business leaders describe appraisals as a box-ticking exercise.' In a US poll from San Francisco consulting firm, Achievers, it was revealed that 98% of staff found annual performance appraisals unnecessary.

Despite that, performance appraisals have survived because they are designed to furnish extremely relevant information to both individual employee as well as the organization about performance and progress. Performance appraisal is considered necessary for the effective management and evaluation of staff. Appraisals are expected to help develop individuals, improve organizational performance, and feed into business planning. Annual performance appraisals also can enable management and monitoring of standards, agreeing expectations and objectives, and delegation of responsibilities and tasks. Staff performance appraisals too establish individual training needs and enable organizational TNA and planning.

9.4 COMMON PROBLEMS WITH PERFORMANCE APPRAISALS

The issues with performance appraisals cover a wide range. The harshest critics challenge the raison d'être or the rationale for having a performance appraisal system. At the other end of the continuum, there are flaws that can be repaired.

Case Giving it to Alexa

I was on the road for some errand. Suddenly I heard a shout 'No, No, no, no, no.' Looking back I saw a young couple about ten meters behind me, and the young man talking excitedly on his mobile. I stopped, curious.

'You called Roshan and told him you will do 450, as you did 425 last year. You asked Javed how much he wanted to do, and he said 400, and you said Ok. You did not listen to me and gave me 500, just because I did 470 last year. It is a new, and very tough area. I can only do what others are doing 400-450. You are not being fair. Hello, hello.'

The conversation ended abruptly, pulling the curtains down on an absurd mini drama around a performance goal setting meeting. Watched by several by-standards, the young man looked at his mobile in bewilderment, despair, and helpless rage writ large on his face, their day ruined. In a physical workspace, he could have walked to the boss' chamber and talked it out.

I thought of the enormous labor HR professionals put in on first creating the process of performance management and then chiseling it over the years. Was Dr. Denning right in describing performance appraisal as one of the seven deadly sins? 'The idea of a merit rating is alluring. The sound of the words captivates the imagination: pay for what you get;

2 Michael Moran, 'Making the Appraisal Process More Constructive,' March 20, 2013. Available at: http://www.hrmagazine. co. uk/article-details/making-the-appraisal-process-more-constructive (accessed on November 14, 2017).

3 Gabriella Jozwiak, 'Is It Time to Give Up on performance Appraisals?' October 22, 2012. Available at: http://www. hrmagazine. co.uk/article-details/is-it-time-to-give-up-on-performance-appraisals (accessed on November 23, 2017).

get what you pay for; motivate people to do their best, for their own good. The effect is exactly the opposite of what the words promise'.

Time bosses off load the process of performance appraisal and give it to Alexa?

Discussion Question

1. Is it the end of the road for performance management? Why? Why Not?

9.5 PERFORMANCE APPRAISAL AND TOTAL QUALITY MANAGEMENT

In the first category, fall the oft quoted views of Edward Deming, the quality guru. In his book *Out of the Crisis*,[4] Deming expressed a view that performance appraisals foster short-term performance, stifle long-term planning, generate fear, destroy teamwork, and breed rivalry and politics.

Indeed, Deming lists 'evaluation of performance, merit rating and annual review' as the third of his 'Seven Deadly Diseases.' To Deming, performance of anybody follows from the interplay of combination of several forces—the individual performer, the others he works with, the job, the material that he works on, his tools, his management, his supervision, and his environmental conditions (noise, confusion, and poor food in the company's cafeteria). These forces create 'unbelievably large differences between people' and, as a matter of fact, 94% of performance outcomes are attributable to the system, not to people. People are, therefore, left' bitter, crushed, bruised, battered, desolate, despondent, dejected, feeling inferior, some even depressed, unfit for work for weeks after receipt of rating, unable to comprehend why they are inferior.[5]'

On being asked about what to replace performance appraisal with, Deming would indicate organizational investment in leadership, use of statistical data, boss–subordinate supportive interactions of sufficient durations, and accommodation of solitary individuals.

The proponents of TQM, taking cues from Deming, argue that performance appraisal militate against the basic values and principles of TQM. Essential conditions of TQM include customer-centricity, systems thinking, an appreciation of variation, motivation and learning, and teamwork. These conditions of TQM are undermined by performance appraisal. For example, performance undermines teamwork because solo performers are actually individual contributors to a group effort, irrespective of whether that group is a formally constituted one. By implication, when an individual's contribution is evaluated, the presumption is that the specific value creation by an individual member can be extracted from the net outcome, by separating those contributions for which others deserve credit or discredit.

In short, TQM is targeted at enhancing customer value by enabling the employee to understand, control, and improve processes. Performance appraisal relies on regulating the behavior of the employee to the satisfaction of the superior officer. The approaches are, therefore, mutually exclusive, in which either of performance appraisal or TQM can operate successfully.[6]

The second set of problems with the system of performance appraisals is that it is often a flawed process. The common flaws are discussed further.

---

4 Edward Deming, *Out of the Crisis*, (MIT, 1982): 102.

5 Edward Deming, *Out of the Crisis*.

6 Peter Scholtes, 'Total Quality or Performance Appraisal: Choose One.' Available at: http://pscholtes.com/articles/total-quality-or-performance-appraisal-choose-one.htm (accessed on November 14, 2017).

Inaccurate

Researches done by David Schoorman showed that supervisors, who were party to a recruitment or promotion decision and had concurred with the choice, would positively bias subsequent performance appraisal ratings for that employee. Conversely, supervisors who, having participated in the original decision, differed with the decision would demonstrate a negative bias in subsequent performance appraisal ratings. The phenomenon of rater bias in performance reviews is also observed in favor of gender and race preferences. 'Like me' is an important element of interpersonal attraction and thus subordinates 'unlike me' tend to get discriminated against.

Researches done by Longenecker, Sims, and Gioia have highlighted the political, almost Machiavellian, underpinnings of the system of performance appraisal, which run contrary to its stated objective of a rational, objective, and accurate process. Managers, while evaluating the performance kept in mind the impact of it on their future relationship. Thus, what follows is deliberate manipulation of the process in the latent belief that accuracy in appraisal is neither attainable nor desirable. Thus, the managers in the researched organization confirmed having used appraisals to get their subordinates better raises in difficult years, to pull up indifferent performers, and remove people who were not falling in line. In brief, performance appraisal served as an instrument to get the job done.[7]

Infrequent

The infrequent nature of performance reviews also impedes meaningful feedback. The performance reviews that commonly occur at the year-end, appear more of a ritual and less of an event to look forward to. Add the fact that the actual performance and the feedbacks are often removed in time, creating a disconnect, which makes learning difficult. Peter Cappelli, Head of Wharton Center for HR comments, 'If you wait a year to tell employees how they are doing, they are almost always surprised and unhappy if the results are not positive.' Cappelli further notes, 'Humans are hard-wired to focus on the negative.' 'So 'balanced' feedback always leaves us concentrating on the bad parts' of the reviews.[8]

Managers also get influenced by what is known as the 'recency factor,' whereby they consider more recent events and ignore/forget things that took place in the relatively more distant past.

Comparison with Peers

Being ranked against the peers also creates a mental block for constructive performance reviews. Peer comparison stokes competitiveness, and thereby a natural reluctance to help or collaborate. This undermines the spirit of interdependence that sustains a healthy work environment. Researches in educational settings have shown that best performances emerge from benchmarking against the past performance of one's own, not of the peers. This has often been the experiences of organizations, which have struggled with the bell curve or the forced ranking systems.[9]

---

7 C. O. Longenecker, H. P. Sims, and D. A. Gioia, 'Behind the Mask: The Politics of Employee Appraisal,' *Academy of Management Executive* 1, no. 3 (1987): 183–193.

8 Peter Cappelli, 'Should Performance Reviews Be Fired?' Wharton Center for Human Resources, April 27, 2011. Available at: http://knowledge.wharton.upenn.edu/article/should-performance-reviews-be-fired/ (accessed on September 25, 2017).

9 Jeffrey Pfeffer, 'The Trouble with Performance Reviews,' *Bloomberg Businessweek*, June 30, 2009.

Unsuitable for the Millennials

With the coming of the digital age, large numbers of workplaces have undergone significant transition from command-and-control, hierarchy-driven functioning to teamwork and matrix-style, networked management. 'They're designed as though they're Russia in the '60s,' says management adviser Marcus Buckingham. The traditional review, which comes entirely from the people who manage you but likely know less about your skills than those who work with you day to day, is 'totally out of date.'

That is especially the case for workers of a younger generation, the generation of 'millennials' (those born between the late 1970s and early 1990s) who are accustomed to constant and instant feedback—from parents, text messaging, friends, or social media sites—in nearly every other aspect of their lives. They want the same from their employers. 'They put something on Instagram, and in 15 to 20 seconds they're expecting to know if it's any good or not,' Buckingham says. 'So it's crazy for them to come into a workplace that's like, 'We don't care about you, and twice a year we're going to tell you what the company wants'.' As Daniel Pink, a workplace expert and author, noted in a recent article in *The Telegraph* titled 'Think Tank: Fix the Workplace, Not the Workers,' millennials have 'lived [their] whole lives on a landscape lush with feedback.' Yet when they enter the workforce, they find themselves 'in a veritable feedback desert.... It's hard to get better at something if you receive feedback on your performance just once a year.'

Even though both performance appraisal and PMSs aim at improving employee performance, most of the modern-day business organizations have shifted to PMSs. Performance management seeks to monitor and improve the performance real-time to ensure performance reaches the desired levels. It adapts a continuous and ongoing, proactive mechanism to ensure that the employee achieves the set targets on a real-time basis, without reviews or corrective actions, at some point in the future. It thus constitutes a line activity and remains embedded in an employee's day-to-day work.

9.6 PERFORMANCE MANAGEMENT PROCESS

TISCO, an iconic, over 100-year-old company of India involved in manufacture and marketing of steel products is acknowledged for successfully implementing an effective PMS. The company initiated an organization restructuring program with the objective of transforming a 100-year-old, archaic structure into a high-performing organization capable of accelerated learning and growth. In the HR front, the management focused on providing exciting career opportunities and building a team of high-performing professionals for which they hired Mckinsey and Co. The consultants first started with building a lean and a flat SBU with enriched jobs, increased accountabilities, and autonomy. A performance ethic program was also introduced for promoting young and dynamic professionals and this was a replacement of seniority-based promotions. A new PMS helped in aligning the individual employee's KRAs with the business strategies and identifying outstanding performers in the organization by defining clear career paths and accountabilities. The compensation and rewards were coupled with the PMS. The new measures in the direction of performance management energized the employees and boosted their performance. The job satisfaction also improved due to the introduction of a fair and transparent reward system.

Performance management is an interactive process by which the superiors and the subordinates in an organizational setup work in unison to plan, monitor, and review an employee's performance against a set of specific/general objectives for the growth and success of the organization. More than just an end-of-the-year performance appraisal, performance management constitutes a continuous process of setting objectives, tracking progress, and imparting constant, real-time guidance and feedback to the employee to facilitate the attainment of organizational and personal goals by the employees. The circular process consists of six interconnected stages of (a) contextual preparation, (b) planning, (c) execution, (d) assessment, (e) review, and (f) renewal of performance.

Armstrong and Baron[10] define performance management as

> [a]process which contributes to the effective management of individuals and teams in order to achieve high levels of organizational performance. As such, it establishes shared understanding about what is to be achieved and an approach to leading and developing people which will ensure that it is achieved.

The authors further elaborate that performance management is

> [a] strategy which relates to every activity of the organization set in the context of its HR policies, culture, style and communications systems. The nature of the strategy depends on the organizational context and can vary from organization to organization.

The aforementioned definition brings out two key elements of performance management: strategic (covers broad issues and long-term goals) and integrated (links various aspects of the business, people management, individuals, and teams).

9.6.1 Step One–Contextual Information (also described as pre-requisites)

The performance management process, in order to take off successfully in an organization, requires two key pre-requisites. In the first place, it pre-supposes that the organization would have clarified its organizational vision, mission, and strategy planning. Strategy and goals should be clearly defined and understood by all levels so that the efforts are directed toward the realization of the organizational ambitions. It is necessary because organizational goals provide the bedrock on which a successful performance management process can be constructed. On establishing the organizational goals, employee goals can logically be made to cascade from there. This is all the more relevant in the light of one of the important expected outcomes of the performance management process, which is to enhance employees' contributions to the organization's objective.

A mastery over the requirements of the jobs, and more specifically, clear definition of the roles for performing a given job within the organizational framework is the second pre-requisite. An important instrument for acquisition of comprehensive job knowledge is job analysis. Job analysis is suitable not only for new jobs, but also for existing jobs, especially those in respect of which some time has passed since the last exercise. It is useful to start the performance management process with a correct job description. As an abundant caution, new, comprehensive analyses can be carried on all key jobs before commencement of the performance management process. The contextual information also requires that the linkages of a role with other roles are also indicated. Once the strategic planning goals are set and the job analysis information is updated, the performance management process can take off.

[10] Armstrong and Baron. *Managing performance: Performance Management in Action*, 2004, pp. 3–5. London: CIPD.

The pre-requisite stage also covers one more important element: the commitment and support of the senior leadership and top management. The support is manifested through various steps, which include:

- Challenging work for star performers
- Healthy investment in L&D projects
- Appropriate structure for dealing with poor performance
- Reward and recognition aligned to PMS

9.6.2 Step Two–Planning

Employees cannot be expected to deliver outstanding performance, if they are fuzzy about how the organization describes and measures outstanding performance. Thus, at the next step, the organization establishes the criteria and expectations for employee performance. It is a formal structured process for identifying and communicating the organizational and individual goals. The planning stage has two components: performance outcomes and individual development plans. The plans are arrived at through a collaborative interaction between the boss and the subordinate. An effective planning process includes high-quality communication not only building commitment of the subordinate to achieve the organizational objectives, but also integrating his personal career goals through competence building. In a nutshell, the goals of the performance planning are:

1. To build agreement on the employee's job responsibilities
2. To clear doubts about targets and objectives that need to be achieved
3. To bring into focus the competencies relevant for the job
4. To develop a career development plan for the employee

Performance plan has the following elements:

- Key accountabilities
- Specific objectives
- Performance standards

Key accountabilities are broad areas of a job for which the employee is responsible for producing results. Objectives are statements of outcomes. A model way to develop outcomes is by using the acronym SMART. It stands for specific, measurable, attainable, realistic, and timely.

1. **Specific** Includes who, what, when, where, why, and/or how in developing the goal.
2. **Measurable** Contains numeric or descriptive measurement.
3. **Achievable** Indicates the necessary resources required to set a realistic goal.
4. **Relevant** In sync with the vision, mission, values, and strategy of the organization.
5. **Time-bound** Indicates the timeline.

Example (for an operations executive) Reduce rejection rates to increase annual battery production by 10% while confirming to the quality specifications and within approved budget. This objective is specific and measureable (the employee knows the expected deliverable: 10% increase in production). It directs the employee on what to pay attention to—rejection rates. It describes for him the timeline: one year. The budget and specifications indicate measureable dimensions. The objective, therefore, is specific, measurable, attainable, realistic, and timely.

Performance standards or performance criteria are management-approved expression of performance threshold(s), requirement(s), or expectation(s) that have to be met to be evaluated at a particular level of performance. They provide yardsticks to assess how well the employee has achieved the objectives. The performance standards/criteria used in organizations are as diverse as traits, behaviors, competencies, goal achievement, and potential to improve.

Traits

A trait is a characteristic that an individual possesses. Traits include things such as appearance, attitude, initiative, work ethic, leadership ability, a sense of ethics, loyalty, adaptability, and judgment. A common criticism against traits approach is that it can lead to subjective evaluations. The appraisal can be tainted by how much the manager likes the employee. There is also a possibility of substandard performance being ignored because employee traits are compatible with what the manager values. One way organizations get around this bias is by involving multiple raters, including other managers and even peers, in a consensus.

On the other hand, if the traits are selected on the basis of relevance to the job, then it can create some value in appraisal and be appropriate. Traits such as timeliness, judgment, and attitude are used to good effect when the job connection is established.

Behaviors

Behavior-based approaches are used mainly in conditions when an employee's task results are difficult to assess. This approach covers what the employee does and should do differently, in other words, specific action by employees on the job and use of techniques such as critical incidents and behaviorally anchored rating scales (BARS). This approach may be relevant, for example, in a BPO; the team leader may be assessed based on his leadership style, teamwork, and cooperation. If the employees are assessed purely by their behavior, the focus is on measuring what they do against what they get done. If certain behaviors are identified as leading to business results, then reinforcing such behaviors through rewards and recognition may lead to the desired behaviors being repeated.

In the negative side, in a behavior-based approach, there is sometimes a tendency to eliminate less tangible but important criteria such as rapport with customers, positive contributions to meetings, and optimism.

Competencies

Competencies have been defined by Boyatzis as 'an underlying characteristic of a person in that it may be a motive, trait, skill, aspect of one's self-image or social role or body of knowledge which he or she uses.' Competencies indicate the interrelationship between perceived performances, anticipated future, and expected performance. Competencies may be technical, behavioral, or managerial. Competencies such as ethical orientation are preferred by many organizations for their executives. Other competencies such as analytical thinking, result focus, and initiative are related to jobs.

Organizations have tried to integrate competencies into the performance management process in either of the two ways: first, by identifying the competencies relevant to the performance objectives; second, by incorporating the employee's job competencies into the performance management process. In the first case, the manager and the employee identify the competencies for each objective (typically, 1 to 3), and the same are evaluated along with the employee's performance at the end of the performance cycle. This method, while correctly ensuring the development of goal-related competencies, clearly misses out on other competencies within the competency model of the role, but not directly connected with goal performance.

In the second case, the performance plan includes the complete set of competencies from the competency profile for the employee's role/job. The balance of gains and losses get reversed as compared to the first case. In both cases, however, the feedback on competencies provides learning opportunities for the employee.

Goal Achievement

This approach lays emphasis on outcomes and considers ends as more important than means. Outcomes can have the following dimensions:

- **Quality** Furnishes information on how well a task is performed or to what standard it is completed. It covers accuracy, appearance of work, usefulness, and effectiveness. The measure may be expressed as an error rate or a percentage of errors allowable per specific unit.
- **Quantity** Indicates the volume, how much or how many of the results have been achieved. It is expressed through numbers or percentages.
- **Timeliness** Within what time, how fast the result is achieved.
- **Manner** The way or style of task is performance.
- **Method** The policies, procedures, and technical considerations that are applied to complete the task.
- **Cost** The effective use of resources including human, organizational, and physical resources to complete a task.

Potential Appraisal

Traditional performance criteria have often been past-oriented, which from a performance management perspective provides no scope for action, as past cannot be undone. The process can, however, yield results if the spotlight is reversed to future instead on behaviors and outcomes necessary to grow the employee, who in turn, can catalyze goal achievement for the business. This brings up the need to assess the employee's potential so that meaningful career planning and development process can be embedded in the performance management process.

The above approaches are not independent of each other. In actual practice, appraisal systems are cross breeds of different systems. Along with the outcome ('what' of performance), the competencies ('how' of performance) have also been considered important. While performing the task, the manner in which it is accomplished has not been ignored.

The planning process also covers the formulation of individual developmental goals. In this segment, areas of improvement, if any, are identified for correction during the period. This apart, discussions are held on overall improvement of selected competencies to enable the employee to pursue a career plan and build future capabilities. Developing employees is a value adding activity not only for the individual employee, but also for the manager as well as the larger organization in the long run.

9.6.3 Step Three—Performance Execution

Execution is famously acknowledged to be 'the missing link between aspirations and results.' Plans need to be translated into reality through management of performance by the employee, performance monitoring and feedback and coaching by the superior officer. This is the critical zone of learning and performance improvement. Elaborate and impeccable strategic objectives notwithstanding, failure to pay attention to this phase may abort performance improvement plans and lead to employee disengagement.

Performance execution is the joint responsibility for both the employee and the manager.

Employee Responsibility

Committing to goal achievement

For attainment of goals, the key driver is the employee himself, not the manager. Goals are not tasks, but are the results of efforts. The focus shifts from mere performance of tasks and work routines to work outcomes. The employee needs to feel motivated enough to put in the desired level of endeavor, and to invest the time and energy to obtain the results. The manager's task is to set challenging goals, to energize the employee, and to make the working conditions congenial enough, so that the employee finds it worthwhile to go the extra mile to achieve the results.

Seek performance feedback

The onus is on the employee to solicit feedback and work on the data to enhance his performance. It is for him to take the initiative in reviewing performance plans with manager, describe planned actions, and ask for help/guidance, if necessary.

Effective and periodical communication with manager

The employee should actively plan/schedule review sessions at regular intervals to discuss performance issues and the progress of any ongoing project.

Collection and sharing of information on performance

On completion of projects and achievement of targets/goals, the individual employee should advise the manager of the current status of the objectives that were set at the beginning of the period.

Active participation in performance reviews

The employee is expected to cooperate in making the review process meaningful, by being prepared and open.

Manager Responsibility

Creating suitable work environment to motivate the employee

Managers can motivate the employee by allocating work/projects that are challenging enough, thereby providing opportunities for achievement. Appropriate delegation and empowerment also go a long way in stimulating high performance. Employees also feel stimulated when they are provided with developmental experiences in the form of training inputs through workshops.

Timely documentation of performance

Recording of performance information in real time, formally or informally, generates confidence in the minds of the employee about the fairness of the process. It also helps to provide useful feedback on specific behavior or actions.

Upgradation of initial goals

Managers need to be flexible to adjust the performance plans, if warranted by changes in environmental conditions.

Feedback and coaching

Feedbacks are meant to be presentations of information. A properly furnished feedback is non-evaluative, neither positive nor negative. Its sole purpose is to help an employee become aware of the effect of his behaviors on others, so that he can modify some of his behavior. Managers should develop skills in providing feedbacks on performance and behavior in a descriptive, specific, and timely manner.

Feedback alone, however, rarely impacts performance in a positive manner. On the contrary, it can have a negative impact unless the manager backs it up with developmental inputs in the form of coaching.

9.6.4 Stage Four–Performance Assessment

In this phase, the manager should review any documentation that he may have of the employee's performance during the assessment period. As mentioned earlier, keeping an ongoing file of records of the employee's work throughout the year becomes useful so that the manager has the data readily available to complete the performance assessment. Using multiple sources (peers, customers, and subordinates) improves the ownership of the employee and also opens up wider area of information.

As for the employee, he facilitates the process with a self-assessment using performance data documented desirably in real time and with supporting documents, if necessary.

Rater Problems

A study undertaken by Michael Mount, Steven Scullen, and Maynard Goff and published in the *Journal of Applied Psychology* in 2000 revealed that 62% of the variance in the ratings could be ascribed to individual raters' peculiarities of perception. Actual performance accounted for only 21% of the variance. The researchers thus concluded:[11] 'Although it is implicitly assumed that the ratings measure the performance of the ratee, most of what is being measured by the ratings is the unique rating tendencies of the rater. Thus, ratings reveal more about the rater than they do about the ratee.'

Some of the common rater problems are:

(a) **Problems with standards of evaluation** Perceptual divergence in the use of words (e.g., good, adequate, satisfactory) among multiple evaluators.

(b) **Halo effect** Assigning values on the basis of an overall impression of the ratee, created by a positive first impression.

(c) **Leniency or harshness** Seeing everything good, or everything bad in a ratee.

(d) **Central tendency error** Avoiding use of high or low ratings, rather rate all employees on an average basis.

---

11 Manuel London, ed., *How People Evaluate Others in Organizations* (Mahwah, NJ: Lawrence Erlbaum, 2001).

(e) **'Recency of events' error** Rating an employee more on the basis of recent past behavior (e.g., last 5 weeks) rather than overall performance.

(f) **Contracts effects** Raters let another employee's performance influence the ratings.

(g) **Personal bias (stereotyping, 'similar to me')** Rating an employee on the basis of sex, race, and favoritism.

In order to eliminate the aforementioned rater problems, organizations have tried out dual methods of providing rater training and improving the performance appraisal instrument. Typical rater training focuses on eliminating rating errors and improving the quality of supervisor observation and recording competencies. Behavior-based rating scales sought to make the ratings objective, but when it did not show consistent superiority over other rating templates, the improvement efforts were concentrated on the rating process itself. Efforts are being made to help the raters accurately observe, recall, and report behavior at the time of evaluation (Table 9.2).

Table 9.2 Comparative efficacy of different rater systems

Rater	Advantages	Disadvantages	Remedies
1. The immediate supervisor	The supervisor is the most natural choice as he is the one most likely to know what the employee should be doing.	1. The supervisor may not be in regular contact. In modern organizations with virtual teams, Internet-linked offices, telecommuting, and complexity of tasks, the supervisor may not be familiar either with the employee in person or his tasks. 2. Personal bias might hinder objective evaluation.	Use multiple evaluators, including the supervisor to improve the objectivity quotient.
2. Peers	1. Often know the job of the employee more closely than the supervisor and are more directly affected by the employee's actions. 2. In a team environment, peers can accurately assess the interpersonal competencies of the employee.	Possibilities of a different kind of bias. Ego conflicts and personal biases can color perceptions of individual employees in respect of their peers.	1. Can be suitably moderated by the manager based on observed patterns. 2. Possibilities for personality conflicts/ bias notwithstanding, peer evaluations can provide clear insight into the inner functioning of a team, especially when the supervisor has infrequent interaction with the team.
3. Subordinates	Can provide valuable insight into the managerial practices of people in control other employees in the organization.	1. Evaluations may get tinted by wanting to punish the supervisor for unwanted tasks or for disciplining them for lapse in work. 2. Evaluations can be inaccurate for lack of familiarity of the supervisor's actual responsibilities.	1. Outliers can be identified and biased ratings can be moderated. 2. Keeping the evaluations anonymous.

Contd.

Rater	Advantages	Disadvantages	Remedies
5. Customers	Is relevant when the employee regularly interacts with internal or external customers.	Can get subjective, inaccurate, or biased.	The known bias can be adjusted. Negative and positive comments can be compared.
6. 360 degrees	Originally designed by DuPont, but currently considered a useful talent assessment tool, especially in teams systems.	Requires huge investments in time and money.	Best used for 360-degree individual development, rather than for administrative evaluative decisions.

9.6.5 Stage Five–Performance Management Process

At the review meeting, the employee and the manager discuss the 'what' and the 'how' of results achieved against performance plans. It also includes the performance rating and progress on development plan.

The performance review conversation is intended to be a conversation. For holding effective conversations, the records and the forms serve as aides to support the conversation. In course of the conversation, the manager and the employee should discuss:

- Commitments, if any, from the last review meeting
- Specific achievements since the last conversation
- Difficulties hampering performance, the reasons and the ways and means of overcoming them, including use of skills in past achievements
- The implications of changing behaviors
- Action plan for future

As regards the conduct of the meeting, the appraisal should be conveyed in simple language sans jargons and preambles. While communicating unsatisfactory appraisals, it helps if the manager talks clearly and in a straightforward manner. If the manager hedges and haws and 'dances around the issue at hand,' the employee detects his discomfiture accurately, almost 'like a shark sensing blood in the water.' If the employee senses that the manager is not confident in his appraisal, the whole evaluation loses credibility and the employee may even be encouraged to try to improve the ratings. On the other hand, by papering over the employees' shortcomings or inflating their ratings, in deference to their feelings, managers actually deprive the employee of a chance to improve and expose the organization to long-term liability.

The moment of truth for the manager in the review meeting comes not only in breaking bad news, but also in communicating good news sometimes. The manager's occasional hesitation in openly conveying good news is attributed sometimes to an apprehension that in the event he is called upon to take tough measures in future involving the same employee (e.g., giving pink slip for redundancy), he may lose the flexibility to do so if he places on record his appreciation of the employee's success now.

Finally, one important way to make the performance review meeting count is to leave the employee with the resolve and motivation to keep up the good work and to improve in the areas where there is a scope for growth. To make that possible, the manager should provide encouragement even when the appraisal does not meet the employee's expectations by first, reminding the employee that he is still valued and second, by committing to support him in his development.

9.6.6 Stage Six–Renewal

In the last phase, the manager uses insights and learning from the last cycle to more effectively plan performance in the next cycle. The manager and employee review and make appropriate adjustment of goals in tune with the organization's mission, vision, values, and strategy. This could lead to setting new objectives, standards, and new accountabilities; development of new competencies for the upcoming performance period; and fostering the ongoing and continuous nature of the performance management cycle.

9.6.7 The Critical Success Factors for PMS

A pulse survey on performance management in March 2014 by Towers Watson reported that while 96% of the respondents believe that performance management is important for their organization, only 64% reported having either an effective or very effective approach or less than one-third believed that it has caused a marked improvement in employee performance.

Strong Commitment from the Top Management

An effective PMS requires visible commitment from the top management. The commitment is demonstrated through creation of powerful, shared vision and values and by using PMS to cascade the same through the organization. The top leaders inspire and help build credibility for the process by role modeling, communicating, supporting the system, and rewarding compliance. Management support would imply that senior leadership follow all the parameters of the system themselves and develop similar expectations from their direct subordinates by incorporating performance management as a key input in their evaluations.

In the initial stages, if the organization lacks a performance management culture, the executives need to be educated in the importance of PMS. The best practice is to pilot the new system with the senior leadership team to achieve credibility in the minds of the employees.

Alignment with Strategy

Some recent surveys have revealed that

- Only 29% of companies create individual goals aligned to the organization.[12]
- A full 52% of midlevel managers and 74% of lower-level employees perceive the linkage between individual goals and corporate goals as very weak.[13]
- Up to 50% of employee time is spent working toward non-strategic objectives.[14]

In effective PMS, the process links individual goals to strategic company objectives, while recognizing that goals will be dynamic, flexible objects that must mirror the ever evolving business needs. It is, thus, not only about setting SMART goals, but about setting the right goals—the ones that

[12] Bersin & Associates, 'High Impact Talent Management Research,' 2006; Bersin & Associates, 'High Impact Performance Management Research,' 2007.

[13] WorldatWork and Sibson Consulting, 'The State of Performance Management' (A Survey Brief, July 2007. Available at: https://www.worldatwork.org/waw/adimLink?id=20261 (accessed on November 14, 2017).

[14] FranklinCovey, Execution Quotient Survey. Available at: http://franklincoveysouthasia.com/pdf/client

align the organizational strategy with its employees. As a consequence of this strategic alignment, the employees develop a clear line of sight with the organization's goals, and understand how their actions impact the organizational performance in a negative or a positive way. With a wider understanding of the big, hairy, audacious goals, the employees can clearly envision how their actions drive the business closer to achieving its performance goals.

Alignment with Other HR Systems

The same set of competencies, which form the basis for performance management, should be consistently used for recruitment and selection, placement and reward, T&D and recognition. This alignment clearly conveys what employee behaviors are valued by the organization.

Acceptance by All Levels of Employees

Two key players in the success of a performance management process are the individual employee as also the manager. The employee needs to feel inspired by the goals and take accountability for achieving them. The manager needs to believe in the process and not take it as merely a box-checking paperwork. In order to gain wide acceptance, the PMS should have several attributes. It should be easily comprehensible, time-efficient to use, contain relevant and meaningful metrics, evaluate only those tasks that the employee has control on, use reviewers who are familiar with the performances of the employees, and use the performance data for decisions related to promotion, increments, training, and so on.

Lastly, a model PMS is developed in a participative and inclusive manner by soliciting necessary inputs/feedbacks from employees and encouraging the employees to freely voice their concerns on the process, and incorporating the same in the designs. Frequent and comprehensive two-way communication with all concerned regarding the design and implementation of PMS goes a long way in ensuring the buy-in.

Adequate Organizational Training

Organizations need to develop certain specific skill sets for making the PMS work. The manager requires to learn how to set goals and how to coach and counsel for performance improvement. The employee needs to develop thorough understanding of the system. There are several formats for such training that includes structured classroom training, manualized instructions, WBT, and use of a hotline to address questions by both the employee and the manager.

Automation

Owing to the overwhelming stress on paperwork and administrative process in the traditional appraisal system, a large number of organizations prefer to automate their PMS process. The advantages are multiple: reduction in time spent and administrative workload for both employees and managers; improved compliance by facilitating monitoring of various milestones of the PMS process by HR; enhanced analytics through widespread accessibility of variety of data and integration with other systems and packages.

Automated PMSs, however, do not provide a magic potion to cure all of the ills in traditional performance appraisal systems. At the very best, it provides a tool, which, if used rigorously by both managers and the employees, can make the process more efficient. The decision to automate, however, should require a balanced evaluation of time, resource, and development and maintenance costs.

Reflection Point

Human resource (cost) accounting method is a new and simple method of performance evaluation which analyses an employee's performance through the monetary benefits he/she yields to the company. It is done on basis of a comparison of the retention cost of the employee the monetary benefits (contributions) an organization has ascertained from the particular employee.

Discussion Question

1. Discuss in a group the challenges in implementing such a system and the ways to overcome them.

9.7 TYPES OF PERFORMANCE RATING SYSTEMS

The performance rating systems can be classified into two broad groups: relative and absolute. The absolute group includes narrative method or essays, BARS, critical incidents, graphic rating scales, management by objectives (MBO); the relative group includes rank ordering, paired comparisons, and forced ranking. It is believed that the appraisal rating system, absolute versus relative, affects an employee's perception of the appraisal's fairness.[15] Although an experiment with undergraduate students on a videotaped performance of a lecturer indicates no specific advantage for absolute ratings, studies by Roch and others suggest that absolute appraisal formats are perceived to be fairer than relative formats. Organizations have, however, adapted systems from both the groups with equal comfort and effectiveness.

9.7.1 Rank Ordering

There are two methods: simple and alternation. In simple rank ordering, the rater orders all rates, from lowest to highest. In alternation methods, also referred to as multi-person comparison methods, each employee's performance is matched with that of his/her peers, eventually producing a rank order from top to bottom. In some cases, comparing employees can be based on any number of criteria conjured up by the managers themselves. In fact, it can be as basic as asking managers to rank their employees from the best to the worst, and then the second best rate and the second worst rate and proceed in that manner until the list is exhausted. In other cases, the ranking process and strategy can be more focused, structured, and sophisticated.

It is a method of evaluation in which each employee is compared with each other employee. Scores derived from paired comparison are often compared with the standard deviation and mean of all scores to arrive at standard scores for future comparisons.

In this method, the number of pairs of rates to be compared may be calculated from the formula $n(n-1)/2$, n denoting the number of employees. Hence, if a firm has just 10 employees, all 10 individuals will be compared in this process, (10(9))/2, requiring 45 comparisons. The rater's task is simply to choose the better of each pair and each individual's rank is determined by counting the number of times he or she was rated superior.

---

15 S. G. Roch, A. Sternberg, and P. Capuro, 'Absolute Versus Relative Performance Rating Formats: Implications for Fairness and Organizational Justice,' *International Journal of Selection and Assessment* 15, no. 3 (2007): 302–316.

9.7.2 Forced Ranking

In this method, the organization provides clear and strict guidelines for raters on how the expected distribution of ratings should appear. It is also known as vitality curve, rank and yank, and forced distribution. Jack Welch is credited with introduction of this method in GE (in a distribution of 20:70:10, indicating A, B, and C players) as a 'way of creating a true meritocracy.' The 'top 20%' of the employees being the most productive, the productivity of the middle 70% (the 'vital 70') being adequate, and the bottom 10% constitute the group of non-producers, requiring elimination from the organization. Supporters of the system link Welch's rank-and-yank system with a 28-fold increase in earnings (and a 5-fold increase in revenue) at GE between 1981 and 2001. The forced ranking system is based on the much debated assumption that ratees confirm to a pattern of normal distribution. The rationale for introducing this method is that it effectively controls certain common rater biases such as leniency, severity, and central tendency.

According to a 2013 survey by WorldatWork, the method is used by about 12% of US corporations. According to Corporate Executive Board (CEB), it is used by 29% of companies. According to Dick Grote, a consultant who specializes on the topic, 60% of the Fortune 500 companies used some form of ranking in 2012.

There are long lists of organizations that have used this system (GE, Motorola, IBM, GSK, and Yahoo, among others) and those who have moved out of it (Microsoft, Adobe, and Ford, among others).

One of the criticisms of forced ranking system is that the system may introduce a great deal of error, if a group of ratees does not conform to the usual distribution and may, as a group, be either superior or substandard. In short, rather than eliminating error, forced distribution may introduce another kind of error. Some critics, while acknowledging that the procedure may in fact improve the overall quality of a company's workforce, argue that the price paid may be steep, leading to unintended negative effects on employee morale, teamwork, and collaboration, thus affecting shareholder perceptions. Researchers examining the possible consequences of introduction of a forced ranking have reported that in every case the compelling benefits were evenly balanced by potential problems.

The debate on the efficacy and evil effects of the forced ranking system has continued to rage. A moderated view[16] recommends the use of forced ranking system for only a few years and later, once the obvious and immediate benefits have been achieved, replacing the same with other talent management initiatives. Scullen and his fellow researchers[17] have reported the difficulties in continually improving workforce, and the enormous challenges involved recruiting candidates who are superior to the current employees who would be eventually fired. The researchers have observed, on the basis of mathematical simulation, that the greatest benefits came in the first 3.5–4.5 years after initiating a forced ranking system.

9.7.3 The Narrative or the Essay Method

In this method, considered one of the simplest among absolute ratings, a rater is required to write a description of the ratee's performance, his strengths, weaknesses, and areas of improvement. The narrative structure provides the rater with the opportunity to make their evaluative assessment form

[16] Dick Grote, 'Forced Ranking: Making Performance Management Work,' *Harvard Business School Working Knowledge*, November 14, 2005. Available at: http://hbswk.hbs.edu/item.jhtml?id=5091&t=organizations (accessed on November 14, 2017).

[17] Steven E. Scullen, Paul K. Burgey, and Lynda Aiman-Smith, 'Forced Distribution Rating Systems and the Improvement of Workforce Potential: A Baseline Simulation,' *Personnel Psychology* 58, no. 1 (2005): 3.

that can go beyond a mere ticking of a box. Very often, it does not have a standard template, but there can be a form to write the narrative. The underlying belief is that a rater who is conversant with the rate and his work can produce a narration that can be as powerful and acceptable as a formal appraisal system. Narratives can be used alone, or combined with another method or form.

The positives of a properly executed narrative rating include scope for detailed feedback. The difficulties with this form: it is without quantitative information and comparisons between individual employees, groups, or teams become virtually impossible.

9.7.4 Critical Incidents Method

It was Flanagan who held that the critical requirements of a job are those behaviors that make a difference between effective and ineffective performance. The critical incident method is a set of procedures used for collecting direct observations of employee behavior that have critical significance and meet methodically defined criteria. Critical incidents refer to reports prepared by knowledgeable observers of specific employee behaviors that focus on either particularly outstanding behaviors or particularly questionable behaviors. Supervisors document critical incidents as they occur usually in a file folder (kept for each employee, either a hard copy or an electronic one). Critical incidents relate to important employee actions, not trivial ones, which positively or adversely impact performance. Examples could include successfully meeting a stiff deadline or effectively handling an irate customer to protect the business relationship with the organization, or anything that the employee has successfully done. Similarly, derailing behavior such as regularly fighting with coworkers, or neglect in complying to quality specifications in work can be recorded and placed in the employee record.

The critical incidents method of performance appraisal is based on the raters spending time during the year observing and collecting behavioral data on their employees, especially on critical incidents.

The advantages of the critical incident method are that they provide rich source of data, represent the employee's perspectives adequately, and can capture rare incidents that may not be captured in any other formal method. The supervisors can concentrate on actual behavior on job, rather than exercising one's mind about abstract traits, and use them to provide meaningful feedback to the ratees. The disadvantages are excessive reliance on memory, requirement of accurate and truthful reporting of them, a bias for recent events, and difficulty experienced by employees in telling a complete story in necessary details. The supervisors may resend the workload arising out of meticulous process of documentation, and give it low priority, as a consequence of which the feedback may be delayed.

9.7.5 Graphic Rating Scales

A graphic rating scale, defined as 'any rating scale consisting of points on a continuum,' is a generic label given to a broad category of rating formats.[18] The ratees get evaluated on a continuum with anchor points that demarcate levels of effectiveness. For each ratee, the level of effectiveness is indicated at specific points on the continuum. The scale typically features a Likert scale. The number of points on the rating scale can vary from 1–3, 1–5, or 1–9 with the maximum end point of 5–9 being considered suitable to yield the highest quality of ratings on the basis of research (Table 9.3).[19]

---

[18] W. F. Cascio. 'Costing Human Resources: The Financial Impact of Behaviour in Organizations' (Boston, MA: PWS-Kent, 1991): 15.

[19] R. H. Finn. 'Effects of Some Variations in Rating Scale Characteristics on the Means and Reliabilities of Ratings'. Educational and Psychological Measurement, 32, no. 1 (1972): 255–265.

Graphic rating scales are one of the most used rating systems. One reason for this preference is its adaptability to a diverse variety of formats, and is considered user-friendly. These scales are also easy to construct, have quick process, and have face validity.[20] They can be differentiated based on the type and amount of information presented in the anchors. The common formats include fuzzy adjectives (e.g., 'Marginal,' 'Average,' or 'Outstanding;' or 'Poor,' 'Average,' or 'Excellent') as anchors.

One of the common criticisms against graphic rating scale is that it can hardly be used without the rater taking 'the judgment call.' As each rating has a small label such as 'Poor,' 'Excellent,' and so on, the rater tends to call upon their judgment to do the rating. Besides, the scales often do not elaborate in adequate detail what is meant by either rating someone with a '1' or a '3,' which leaves enough space for ambiguity.

Table 9.3 Factors in a graphic rating scale

How would you rate this employee in respect to the quality of work he turns out, the neatness, and the accuracy evident in the job he does?
☐ Careless worker. Tends to repeat some types of errors.
☐ Work is sometimes unsatisfactory because of errors or untidiness.
☐ Usually turns out acceptable work. Not many errors.
☐ Checks and observes his work. Can be relied upon.
☐ Work is of highest quality. Errors extremely rare, if any. Little wasted effort.
Comments: ______________________________
____
____

9.7.6 Behaviorally Anchored Rating Scales

Typically, BARS comprises 5–10 vertical scales, depending on the nature of the job under review. Each scale describes a key performance dimension of the job. Each dimension is typically depicted by five or more critical incidents corresponding to 'highly effective' to 'highly ineffective' visible job behaviors on the job dimension.[21] The critical incidents are allocated scale values indicating the estimated degree of effectiveness. The most highly effective behavior receives the highest value on the scale. The performance dimensions and the critical incidents are derived from job analysis. The critical incidents, which are developed around observable job-related behaviors, reflect calibrated levels of desired performance (Table 9.4).

Table 9.4 Sample BARS for sales performance by sales trainee

Excellent	7	Can expect the trainee to make valuable suggestions for increased sales and to have positive relations with customers all over the country.
Good	6	Can expect to initiate creative ideas for improvement of sales.
Above average	5	Can expect to keep in touch with the customers throughout the year.
Average	4	Can manage, with difficulty, to deliver the goods in time.
Below average	3	Can expect to unload the trucks when asked by the supervisor.
Poor	2	Can expect to inform only some of the customers.
Extremely poor	1	Can expect to take extended tea/lunch breaks and loiter without purpose.

[20] Cardy, R.L. and G.H. Dobbins, *Performance Appraisal: Alternative Perspectives* (Cincinnati: South-Western, 1994).

[21] Scott A. Snell, Shad Morris and George W. Bohlander, *Managing Human Resources*, 7th ed. (Cengage Learning, 2016).

Development of BARS evaluations requires a thorough awareness of key tasks for each job, along with a clear grasp of the entire repertoire of behaviors demonstrated by individual employees in performing the tasks. BARS system is considered to have an edge over other appraisal methods by virtue of its attributes and the detailed process used in building the instrument. The process covers the complete performance zone of a job and major job dimensions with the aid of job analysis.[22] The use of critical incidents is considered to enhance its 'face validity.' The process and the structure of BARS can help in identifying an individual employee's specific behavioral competency levels, which can be used for performance improvement, selection, promotion, and for validating selection criteria, justifying disciplinary actions, and developing training programs.[23] Besides, the involvement of employees in the development process renders it as a fair and accurate instrument.

The limitations of BARS method include interrater reliability and rater errors (due to multiple developmental processes and formats) and high cost associated with the employee time and effort required to develop and use the instrument.

9.7.7 Managing by Objectives

The phrase 'management by objectives' (MBO) was first spelt out by Peter Drucker in 1954 in his book *The Practice of Management,* where he talked about several priorities for the manager of the future. MBO implies a management approach by which employees participate in a vertically cascading process of setting objectives, covering production, costs, sales and profits, together with their superiors. Some goals are collective in nature, for the organization or for the department, while the others are individual. Managers have the responsibility to define the enterprise mission and set the time period of goal achievement. The goals set in the participative manner become the basis of subsequent periodical evaluation and rewards (Figure 9.1).

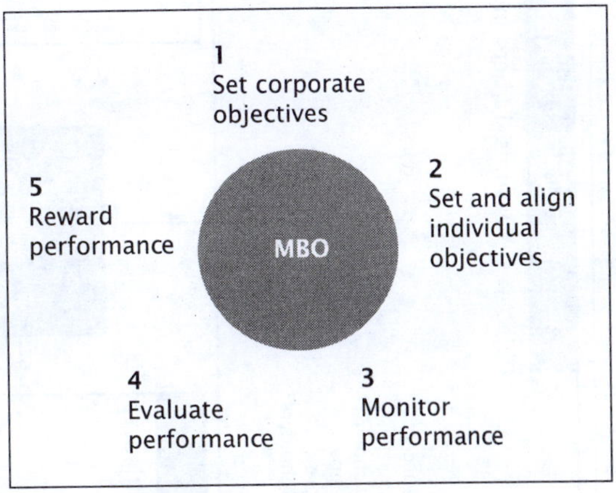

Fig. 9.1 MBO process

Management by objectives was incorporated as an integral part of 'The HP Way,' the much widely applauded management style of Hewlett-Packard. Inside the HP organization, managers at all levels were required to set objectives and assimilate them with those of their colleagues and of the entire company. Plans were prepared indicating what employees must do if they were to reach those objectives. The plans were then shared with others in the company. The MBO approach, hugely popular in the 1960s and 1970s, has run its course and is largely an ignored system. There was one criticism that it encouraged organizations to constantly revise their plans, just to stay on course to their latest objective. Many firms came to prefer the vague overall objectives of a mission statement to the firm, rigid ones demanded by MBO.

22 R. Jacobs, D. Kafry, and S. Zedeck, 'Expectations of Behaviorally Anchored Rating Scales,' *Personnel Psychology* 33, no. 3 (1980): 595–640.

23 Ibid.

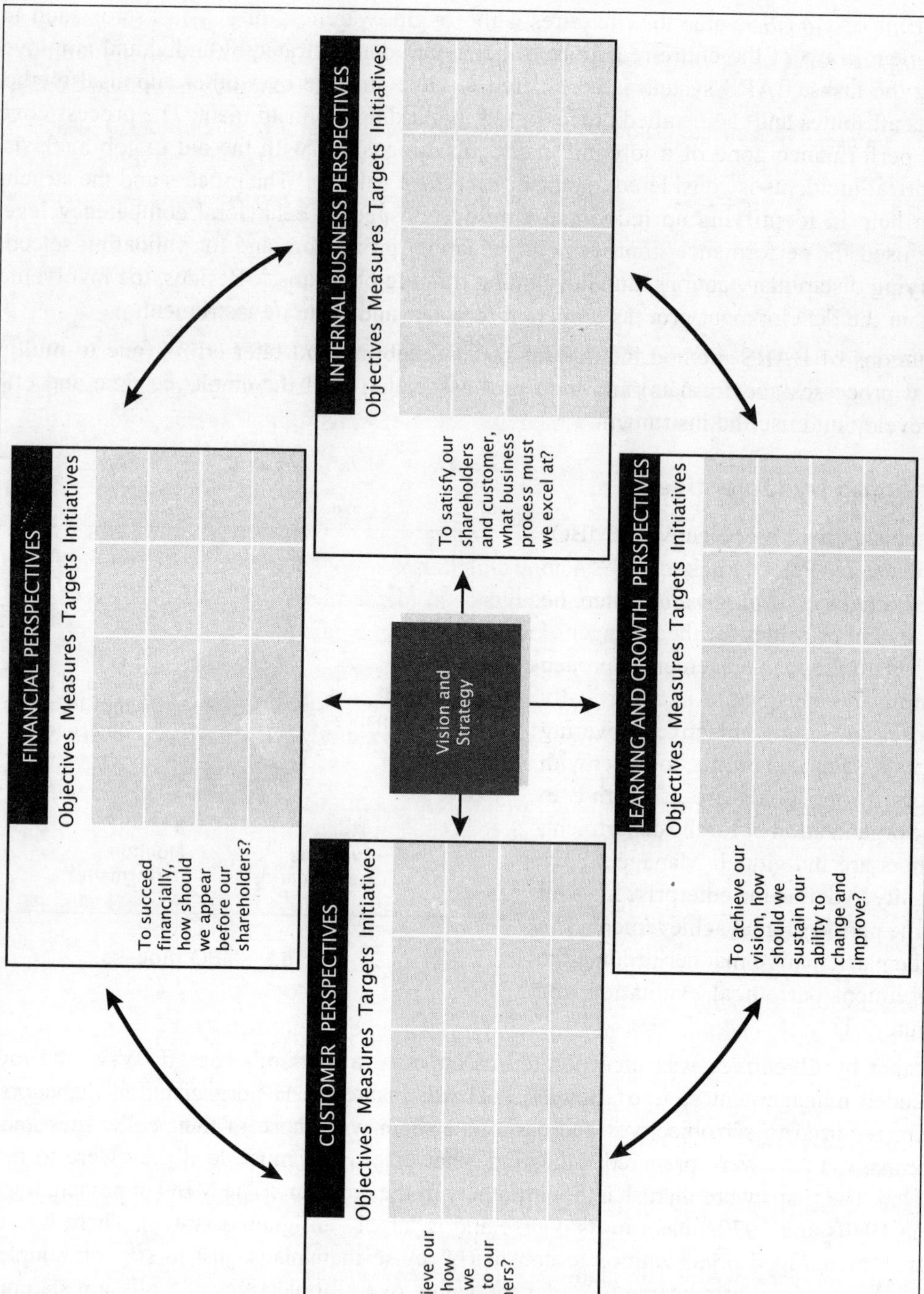

Source: Kaplan and Norton (1996). *Balanced Scorecard*, Boston, MA: Harvard Business Review Press, 1996.

Fig. 9.2 Balanced Scorecard

9.7.8 Balanced Scorecard

Balanced scorecard is a strategy performance management tool that can be used by managers to keep track of the execution of activities by the staff within their control and to monitor the consequences arising from these actions. It was popularized by Robert Kaplan and David P. Norton in a 1992 article in *Harvard Business Review*. The key features of a balanced scorecard include a focus on the strategic agenda of the organization and the selection of a combination of financial and non-financial metrics items to monitor. It talks about four domains of performance (Figure 9.2):

- **Financial** Measures that answer the question 'How do we look to shareholders?' Examples: cash flow, sales growth, operating income, return on equity.
- **Customer** Measures that answer the question 'How do customers see us?' Examples: percentage of sales from new products, on-time delivery, share of important customers' purchases, ranking by important customers.
- **Internal business processes** Measures that answer the question 'What must we excel at?' *Examples:* cycle time, unit cost, yield, new product introductions.
- **Learning and growth** Measures that answer the question 'How can we continue to improve, create value, and innovate?' Examples: time to develop new generation of products, life cycle to product maturity, time to market versus competition.

Reflection Point

In 2002 Colorcon, a US pharmaceutical company, abolished the system of performance appraisal. Over time technology companies like such as Adobe, Juniper Systems, Dell, Microsoft, and IBM followed the example. Now many other like Accenture, PwC, Gap, and even General Electric, joined the bandwagon.

Discussion Question

1. Is it time to abolish performance appraisal? What will be gained and what will be lost?

9.8 FUTURE OF PERFORMANCE MANAGEMENT

At a time when globalization and digital age have compelled organizations to continuously refresh their business models, the virtual freeze frame of the performance management process (for at least last 30 years) makes a case for a serious makeover.

A story narrating the adventures at Deloitte to initiate bold changes in their performance management process[24] elicited a glad quip by a single commentator:

> Welcome to the real world. PMSs have never worked and never will work. Performance management is a day to day, hour by hour body contact activity. While systematic, centrally organized and data rational paper–based programs deskill managers and alienate employees. Great to see.

If the architecture of PMS is demolished by a sudden quake, and a new one is erected in its place, how would it appear? The writers list several attributes. It should be 'something nimbler, real-time,

[24] Marcus Buckingham and Ashley Goodall, 'Reinventing Performance Management,' *Harvard Business Review* (April 2015). Available at: https://hbr.org/2015/04/reinventing-performancemanagement?referral=03758&cm_vc=rr_item_page.top_right (accessed on August 2, 2017).

and more individualized—something squarely focused on fueling performance in the future rather than assessing it in the past.' It will have no cascading objectives, no once-a-year reviews, and no 360-degree-feedback tools.

Deloitte envisions three features of the PMS of the future. One, performance should be recognized. Two, managers should be able to 'see performance clearly,' using a balanced evaluation system. Lastly, managers should be able to 'fuel' performance. The futuristic PMS is built on competent raters with clarity and simplicity, timeliness, and transparency.

Towers Watson in a white paper[25] created a scenario based on a mythical company called FutureCo, outlined the contors of the future performance management architecture: forcing forced ranking out; using a performance-point system to help determine rewards such as salary increases, bonuses, and other forms of recognition; ushering in a culture change through ongoing communication about the new performance management approach, leadership involvement, the collaborative nature of the feedback, and managers' understanding of the importance of the process. Finally, FutureCo created the conditions for great performance by embracing real-time, streaming feedback and other social media tools to help connect, enable, and empower talent development. It had the courage to go beyond conventional thinking and incorporate social media and breakthrough creativity into the workplace to create a fundamentally better company.

The jury seems to be finally out on the bell curve. Iconic organizations are falling over one another like dominoes to see the back of this system of forced ranking.

> In September, management consultancy firm Accenture will join the growing list of companies such as Google, Microsoft, Adobe, and KPMG which have discarded the bell-curve or similar mechanisms for conducting annual performance appraisals of their employees. The move at Accenture is aimed at ongoing real-time feedback and spells good news for its 3.36 lakh global employees, nearly 30% of whom are based in India.[26]

So what do we see, gazing at the crystal ball? The annual 'performance management' process has yielded place to a new 'performance achievement' system. The focus is on real-time, forward-looking conversations about setting priorities, growing strengths, and creating rewarding career opportunities for employees. With a holistic view of performance management, the future process will foster achievements and talents of each employee with the help of leaders, who will spend more time coaching and talking with employees.

Closing Case Green Mart–Challenges for Growth

Green Mart is the retail chain of the large Signal Group of companies. Set up about 15 years back, it has quickly become the second largest retailer in India. The stores sell good quality and competitively priced vegetables, fruits, staples, fresh juice, groceries, bars, and dairy products. A Green Mart store covers approximately 2500–4000 sq ft and caters to an area of about 3–5 km. Green Mart serves over 1.5 million customers every week, and its loyalty program, Green Mart Card has the patronage of more than 5 million customers. It has

[25] 'What's the Future of Performance Management? Exploring One Potential Model for the Future, via Performance Management in Real Time.' Available at: https://www.towerswatson.com/en/Insights/IC-Types (accessed on March 6, 2018).

[26] *The Times of India*, 'Accenture Too Drops Bell-curve Appraisals,' July 27, 2015.

presence in around 500 cities and 4500 towns in the country. These retail outlets are a mix of company-owned and franchisees. Important Indian cities would have larger versions of the retail store than the tier II cities of India.

In India, convenience stores are considered to be only 75% as efficient as stores in the US in terms of display, accessibility of products and services. The vision of Green Mart stores is to provide international class shopping environment with latest technology, a seamless supply chain management coupled with value-added services and ultimate customer satisfaction.

Green Mart has an outlet in Nerul, Navi Mumbai. The outlet has been performing indifferently, at a rate of around 15% of same store sales growth, whereas the average same store sales growth for the company has been 20%. Its biggest competitor in the neighborhood is a DMart store that has a sales growth of 30%. The shop has been dogged with customer complaints and employee turnover. Some of the complaints (as listed on www.customindia.com) are as follows:

Customer complaints samples:

1. 'Green Mart counter assistants cheat you in many ways. Today I bought 4 Quaker Oats small packets each ₹10. The counter assistant asked me to get two more packets as there was an offer of Buy two gets one free. When I came back with those 2 Packets, she had already billed me for four packets (₹40) and given discount of ₹10. She again billed me for two packets (₹20) and gave a discount of ₹10 only. When I asked for a further ₹10 discount which I was eligible, as I had been billed for ₹60 and given a discount of ₹20 only, she called some other colleagues, abused me saying that my contention was wrong and refused the discount. Although the amount involved was only ₹10, the integrity and behavior of the green mart staff is highly questionable.'
2. 'I observed on several occasions that the staff of Green Mart store, at Nerul allows local traders to lift the entire lot of the items which are for sale with some scheme. On 16-08-14 he sold the entire Nirlep brand non-stick Frying Pans to a local trader. When I made enquiries, he informed me that all has been sold.'
3. 'Today i.e. 14/08/2014 I visited Green Mart Nerul outlet. I purchased 4 deodorants Park Avenue, but could not understand the way the bill was written. When I ask to the counter person she said 'Read the bill and you will know'. I did not like the way she spoke in a dismissive manner. I paid with my SBI Credit card. When I got sms in my mobile, the amount deducted is shown as ₹553.50, while the actual amount was ₹550.50. I tried to call several times, but number is not picking up. Can I register complaint to Consumer forum?'
4. 'I purchased some item from Green Mart store at Nerul. The product was charged at a price more than what was mentioned at the cutout pasted near product. When I checked my bill after payment, I asked them to take back the product and return me money, but they told me to come back the next day that they cannot take the product on same day.'
5. 'This is the complaint about the Green Mart outlet, Nerul. I am a regular customer of that store. Being a big retail store chain of the country, I find that there is no updating of stock of different products which are readily available in the market. Many a time I have asked the Supervisor for a product, who informed that it has stocked out. Laster on a closer

search, I could find some of them, kept in a haphazard manner. I have complained to the Store manager about this issue but he only says 'the staff are new' and does not take any other action from his side.'

The Nerul Store was opened about three years back. It has touched sales of about 40 lakh per day, but the DMart store across the street has a sale of 75 lakh per day. It has the following employee structure:

1. Store manager
2. Assistant store manager
3. Supervisor
4. Commercial associate
5. Customer service associate

There are 15 permanent employees and 10 temporary workmen. Turnover rate is 45%, which is higher than industry rate at 35%. The continuous influx of untrained staff affects the quality of service and the housekeeping.

K. K. Menon joined as a stores manager about a month back. He is responsible for the overall P&L of the store and to ensure a high level of customer service. His other responsibilities include:

1. Day-to-day sales tracking and store operations management.
2. Ensure proper presentation and display of products as per plannogram.
3. Promotional offer management and execution.
4. Ensure that the visual merchandising in the store is as per guidelines.
5. Ensure that store operations are carried out to comply with both company policy and all relevant legal requirements.
6. Ensure that cleanliness and hygiene are up to the mark and as per set standards of the organization.
7. Exercise effective control over the cash office operations and general administration.
8. Shrinkage management.
9. Team management and employee training.

Akhil Dhawan the area manager and K. K. Menon's boss, is visiting Nerul store today. He has indicated that he will discuss the performance objective for 2015–2016 for K. K. Menon.

Discussion Questions

1. Make a list of possible objectives that should improve the functioning of the store.
2. What format would you recommend—results-oriented, behavior-oriented, or competency-oriented? Give reasons.

SUMMARY

The practice of performance management is considered as vital to the long-term success of any business. The performance of an organization is the summation of the performance of all individual employees and teams within the organization, and therefore, it is essential that the employees carry out their jobs well, if the organization has to compete effectively in today's business condition. An ideal PMS enables business success by aligning personal objectives with business strategy; motivates employees to give their best; and creates a clear line of sight between performance and compensation.

Performance management is defined as a continuous process of identifying, measuring, managing, and developing the performance of individuals and groups in an organization. At the basic level, it is about finding out the current level of employee performance so that appropriate steps can be taken to eventually upgrade the performance level. It is a systematic assessment of employee performance aiming at performance improvement over time. Performance appraisal, on the other hand, is the ongoing process of reviews of employee performance over time, and is one component of the entire performance management process. It is a formal system, which requires a manager to carry out this activity in a continuous manner.

The critics of PMS challenge the raison d'être or the rationale for having a performance appraisal system. In his book *Out of the Crisis*, Deming expressed a view that performance appraisals foster short-term performance, stifle long-term planning, generate fear, destroy teamwork, and breed rivalry and politics. In actual practice, it is found to be infrequent, suffers from serious rater bias, and is generally held to be unsuitable for millennials in its application of bell curve.

Performance management follows a circular process of six interconnected stages of (a) contextual preparation, (b) planning, (c) execution, (d) assessment, (e) review, and (f) renewal of performance. Each stage has logic and the process is holistic. There are multiple rating systems, which can be classified into two broad groups: relative and absolute. The absolute group includes narrative method or essays, BARS, critical incidents, graphic rating scales, MBO; the relative group includes rank ordering, paired comparisons, and forced ranking. The instruments offer a wide range—from simple to highly sophisticated.

One of the most widely used forms of PMS is balanced scorecard. It is a strategy performance management tool that can be used by managers to keep track of the execution of activities by the staff within their control and to monitor the consequences arising from these actions. It was popularized by Robert Kaplan and David P. Norton in a 1992 article in *Harvard Business Review*. The key features of a balanced scorecard includes a focus on the strategic agenda of the organization and the selection of a combination of financial and non-financial metrics items to monitor.

Finally, PMS, like all HR processes, has witnessed disruptions. The most debated component of PMS seems to be the use of forced ranking or bell curve. Organizations are in a haste to join the bandwagon for discontinuing the bell curve system. The annual 'performance management' process has yielded place to a new 'performance achievement' system. The focus is on real-time, forward-looking conversations about setting priorities, growing strengths, and creating rewarding career opportunities for employees. With a holistic view of performance management, the future process will foster achievements and talents of each employee with the help of leaders, who will spend more time coaching and talking with the employees.

Short-answer Questions

1. In a survey conducted in 2011, performance management was found to be not effective by more than 50% of the senior HR managers? What could be some of the problems?
2. Edward Deming describes that employees are left 'bitter, crushed, bruised, battered, desolate, despondent, dejected, feeling inferior, some even depressed, unfit for work for weeks after receipt of rating, unable to comprehend why they are inferior'. Give two suggestions to improve the PMS.
3. What is your view on bell curve? Is it a necessary evil or is it to be dispensed with?
4. What, according to Armstrong and Baron, are two key elements in an effective performance management?
5. What are the common rater bias?

6. Explain SMART with one example.
7. Differentiate critical incidents method and BARS.
8. What is the supervisor role in performance review?
9. Why is it necessary to align PMS to company's vision, values, and business plan?
10. Explain the key domains of Balanced Scorecard.

Discussion Questions

1. Make a complete PMS for the administrative staff of your college. What measures will be suitable for the cashier or an administrative officer, for example?
2. How will the objectives and measures be different for a faculty member?
3. It is said that PMS is not suitable for unionized category of employees. Do you agree? List out some of the constraints.
4. What would be the important steps in introducing an online PMS for a small organization used to an informal appraisal system?

CLUSTER 5

REWARD AND COMPENSATE

Chapter 10
Compensation and Benefits

Chapter 11
Compensation for Special Groups

In the war for talent, reward and compensation strategy of an organization can make a crucial difference. 'organizations that pay for performance are more likely to attract those interested in performing,' said Jay Schuster, a partner at consultancy Schuster-Zingheim and Associates, Inc., speaking at the 2013 WorldatWork Total Rewards Conference.[1] The rewards package is 'a powerful communications tool that defines the kinds of people who will want to join the organization,' he explained. 'You can't change the corporate culture without changing rewards.'

HRM professionals are called upon to rewire their compensation approaches— from focusing on competitive practice and 'best' practice, 'buying solutions that import the value systems of someone else' to customizing compensation 'to reward the people who produce the most value for our organizations.'

There are different special groups for whom the compensation rules do not apply. Among them, the CEO compensation has attracted much polemics in recent times. An effective reward and executive compensation strategy must be able to (a) attract executives with the skills, experiences, and behavioral profile necessary to succeed in the position; (b) to help retain these individuals, so they do not leave for alternative employment; and (c) motivate them to perform in a manner consistent with the strategy and risk profile of the organization and discourage self-interested behavior.

The CEO compensation has three elements: expected pay, earned (realizable) pay, and the realized pay. The ultimate value of executive compensation will be determined by the CEO's ability to realize performance targets, based on changes in stock price and operating performance.[2]

---

1 Stephen Miller, 'Tie Pay to Value, Not to Market Data,' May 2, 2013. Available at: https://www.shrm.org/resourcesandtools/hr-topics/compensation/pages/pay-to-value.aspx (accessed on November 14, 2017).

2 David F. Larcker and Brian Tayan, 'CEO Compensation' (2015). Available at: https://www.gsb.stanford.edu/faculty-research/ publications/ceo-compensation (accessed on November 14, 2017).

CHAPTER 10

Compensation and Benefits

LEARNING OBJECTIVES

After completing this chapter, the student will be able to:

- understand the difference between different concepts of compensation—compensation, rewards, total compensation, and total rewards
- Identify the different elements of compensation
- List the various factors that influence compensation
- Explain the steps for setting up pay
- Discuss the different theories of compensation
- Explain the concepts of employee benefits

Opening Case 'The Impact of a Compensation Strategy'

Three months ago, Mr Atwal, 31, announced a new compensation policy, fixing the minimum salary at ₹30 lakh per annum (LPA) at his e-business firm, Clip Cart, and taking a cut in his own multi-crore pay package to be able to do it. He was not thinking about the current political clamor over low salaries or the growing disparity between salaries of CEO and that of the ordinary employees, he said. He was just thinking of the 120 people who worked for him and, let us be honest, a bit of free publicity. The idea struck him when a friend shared her worries about paying both her rent and student's loan on a 15 LPA salary. He realized, a lot of his own employees earned that or perhaps less.

Yet almost overnight, a decision by one small businessman in the southern corner of the country became a swashbuckling blow against income inequality.

The move drew attention from around the world—including from some outspoken skeptics and conservatives such as Sikha Sawant, who smelled a communist agenda—but most were enthusiastic. Talk show hosts lined up to interview Mr Atwal. Job seekers by the thousands sent in résumés. He was called a 'thought leader.' IIM Ahmedabad business professors flew out to conduct a case study. Third graders wrote him thank you notes. Single women wanted to marry him.

What few outsiders realized, however, was how much turmoil all the hoopla was causing at the company itself. To begin with, Clip Cart was simply unprepared for the onslaught of emails, Facebook posts, and phone calls. The attention was thrilling, but it was also exhausting and distracting. And with so many eyes focused on the firm, some hoping to witness failure, the pressure has been intense.

More troubling, a few customers, dismayed by what they viewed as a political statement, withdrew their business. Others, anticipating a fee increase—despite repeated assurances to the contrary—also left. While dozens of new clients, inspired by Mr Atwal's announcement, were signing up, those accounts will not start paying off for at least another year. To handle the flood, he had already had to hire a dozen additional employees—now at a significantly higher cost—and was struggling to figure out whether more are needed without knowing for certain how long the bonanza would last.

Two of Mr Atwal's most valued employees quitted, spurred in part by their view that it was unfair to double the pay of some new hires while the longest serving staff members got small or no raises. Some friends and associates in Bangalore's close-knit entrepreneurial network were also piqued that Mr Atwal's action made them look stingy in front of their own employees.

Then potentially the worst blow of all: Less than two weeks after the announcement, Mr Atwal's older brother and Clip Cart's cofounder, Jagdish Srinath, citing longstanding differences, filed a lawsuit in Karnataka High Court that potentially threatened the company's very existence. With legal bills quickly mounting and most of his own paycheck and last year's profits plowed into the salary increases, Sudarshan Atwal said, 'We don't have a margin of error to pay those legal fees.'

Mr Atwal said, 'I have offered to give up everything I have personally and everything I'll have for years to come.' A court date has been set for May.

For now, at least, Mr Atwal has undoubtedly made an immediate difference in the lives of many of his employees. Sangram Nijjar, 30, who supervises an equipment team, was able to afford to move into the city and replace the worn tires on his car. Ms Kalpana, who was briefly homeless as a child, can now visit her family in Coonoor; Mike Gonsalves, 22, who handles operations out of his rented Indiranagar flat, said he and his wife finally felt financially secure enough to start a family.

There have been other ripples. Mario Kutty, who runs Mario's Pizza & Pasta, switched to Clip Cart's policy after seeing Mr Atwal on the news. When he learned his monthly savings would be around ₹50,000, Mr Nijjar decided, 'I was not going to keep the difference for myself.' He used the savings to raise the salaries of his eight employees.

Mario's Pizza aside, Mr Atwal's plan is not easily replicable, said Naren Dastoor, a Cochin venture capitalist and an early champion of fair wages for employees. Still, he noted, 'These individual acts can create a new kind of perception of what's possible and what's righteous.' After all, he said, two years ago, no one would ever have guessed higher threshold salaries would be catching fire in cities around the country. 'Who can tell what that last thing is that catalyzes big change?'

In that sense, Mr Atwal's foray into the public debate on salaries is not unlike his newfound passion of rock climbing. Sweating atop the curves of a Chamunda Hill is not easy. Lean too far heavy on the rope or relax your grip and you are gone. For the moment, he is balancing on the rope, enjoying the climb, and doing his best to keep from falling off.

Discussion Question

1. If you were in Mr Atwal's position, would you raise the minimum salary to 30 LPA? If not, what would you do?

Source: The fictional case is modeled on Patricia Cohen, 'A Company Copes with Backlash Against the Raise that Roared,' The New York Times, July 31, 2015.

10.1 INTRODUCTION

A normal business spends between 15% and 30% of its gross income on paying its employees. The rate would, of course, vary depending on the nature of business—whether the spending is more on raw materials or on people. In the retail or manufacturing business, the endeavor is to keep the cost way below 30%. In a service industry, however, like a private bank, the cost of compensation may even touch 50%. The variance notwithstanding, there is little doubt that compensation makes one of the higher expense items for a business and, for that reason, is forever in the radar of the top leadership and the boards. The other interested stakeholder, analyzing the compensation program for an organization with similar vigor and interest, is the employees. Compensation is the most important determinant of the organization's ability for acquiring and managing critical talent.

The pay system, in this manner, couples business strategy and its execution. A thoughtfully architected compensation plan can boost the effectiveness of the organization many times in enabling the performance of talented and engaged employees.

1. On July 18, 2012, following two months of agitation by unionized workers, violence broke out at the MSIL-Manesar facility. One of the burning issues behind a long agitation in the month was the 'rich–poor divide' reflected in the disparity of compensation between contract labor (₹7000 per month) and permanent workers (₹17,000–18,000 per month).
2. In March 2015, Infosys announced its lowest average wage increase in five years, causing widespread dampening of sentiment among employees and portending anemic pay raises for workers in India's US$146-billion IT industry. It was felt that

> [t]he average wage increase of 6.5% could set the tone for the rest of the industry, but it may not be such a bad thing after all from the perspective of investors keeping a wary eye on margins. Shares of Infosys rose by 2.6% on the National Stock Exchange, outperforming the benchmark Nifty index.[3]

Compensation forms a key theme for all those who work for a living. Issues related to wages and bonus trigger, on a conservative estimate, about one-third of all industrial conflicts in India. According to the statistics of labor department, during the year 2011, disputes due to 'Wages and Allowances' and 'Bonus' accounted for 37.32% (5,395,098 man-days) of the total time loss.[4]

'Even Parliamentarians Fight over Their Salary and Benefits'—screamed a headline.[5] The report revealed the recommendations of a parliamentary committee headed by BJP MP Yogi Adityanath: a

3 *The Economic Times*, 'Infy Sets a New Low in Pay Hikes,' *The Economic Times*, March 28, 2015.

4 http://labourbureaunew.gov.in/UserContent/Statistics_ID_Layoffs_2011.pdf (accessed on November 14, 2017).

5 Zee Media Bureau, 'Even Parliamentarians Fight over Their Salary and Benefits,' July 2, 2015. Available at: http://zeenews.india. com/news/india/parliamentary-panel (accessed on December 11, 2015).

100% hike in the salary, increase in pension amount from ₹20,000 to ₹50,000, revised daily allowance of ₹2000 during Parliament sittings, 20–25 free air travels in a year, additional free AC first-class ticket for companions, including personal secretaries, health benefits for self, children, and grandchildren. The news item also revealed details of heavy subsidy (up to 67% on some items) received by the Lok Sabha Secretariat to run the Parliament canteen.

10.2 DEFINITIONS

1. Compensation
2. Rewards
3. Total pay/compensation

'Compensation' has been traditionally considered as a key factor in driving, motivating, and rewarding employees. Frederick Taylor, the pioneer of concepts of scientific management believed that economic gain was the primary thing that motivated everyone. Traditional view of management held that work is inherently unpleasant for people and therefore money that they earn is more important to employees than the nature of job they are performing. Putting it differently, employees could be expected to perform any kind of work, if they were compensated adequately.

According to Milkovich and others,[6] compensation has multiple connotations viewed from multiple perspectives. From the perspective of the society, compensation and benefit are measures of justice. Thus, a comparison in the earnings between a permanent employee and a contract labor or between men and women highlights what many consider as inequities in pay decisions. From the perspective of a stakeholder, compensation in the form of stocks create a sense of ownership, fueling improved performance leading to increase in shareholder wealth. Managers look at compensation in terms of affordability from the viewpoint of competitiveness—should it be over 50% of the total cost (in case of financial and professional services) or 9–12% (in case of supermarkets)? A second perspective for the managers is to view compensation as instruments of motivation to influence employee behaviors for better performance of the organization. Finally, to employees, compensation embodies an exchange with the employer and themselves, or a privilege as an employee, or as a prize performance. Integrating all the multiple perspectives, compensation has been defined as 'all forms of financial returns and tangible services and benefits employees receive as part of an employment relationship.'[7]

'Reward' implies all the tangible benefits and provisions an employee obtains as part of 'employment relationship.'[8] Bratton and Gold[9] define rewards as all the cash, noncash, and psychological payments provided by an organization in return for their contribution. Buch[10] found in his study, the concept of six sigma that indicates the four categories of rewards: intrinsic, extrinsic, social, and organizational

[6] George Milkovich, Jerry Newman, and C. S. Venkataratnam, *Compensation* (New Delhi: Tata McGraw-Hill Education, 2009).

[7] Ibid.

[8] Ibid.

[9] John Bratton and Jeffrey Gold, *Human Resource Management: Theory and Practice* (Basingstoke: Palgrave Macmillan, 2003).

[10] Kim Buch and Ann Tolentino, 'Employee Perceptions of the Rewards Associated with Six Sigma,' *Journal of Organizational Change Management* 19, no. 3 (2006): 356–364.

remuneration. Intrinsic rewards refer to internal feelings of satisfaction, involvement, growth, autonomy, and self-competence an individual experiences during his career.[11] Extrinsic rewards are based upon organizational participation and performance and further categorized into direct and indirect form. Larson[12] considered the direct reward as a small token of appreciation while indirect reward refers to the financial security and better future prospects. Social rewards that are related to Alderfer's social relatedness and affiliation are associated with team-based projects that reinforce the employees to interact with peers in order to obtain the shared goal outcomes.[13] Organizational rewards refer to the probability of increased profits and productivity: extensive training that streamlined the main business processes and good communications between the employees and the management.

Zingheim and Schuster[14] comment that the conception of 'total rewards' can be categorized into four components: convincing future, encouraging workplace, individual growth, and total pay. Silverman and Reilly[15] explained the total pay as the combination of basic salary, performance-based salary, benefits, and acknowledgement or feedback.

10.3 TOTAL COMPENSATION

John Tropman of University of Michigan Business School[16] classifies pay in three ways: Old Pay, New Pay, and New New Pay. Old Pay is the frozen system based on 'tenure, entitlement, and internal equity.' The New Pay is linked 'to the success of the employee and the firm.' The New New Pay suggests a new system of ten variables that form the *total compensation* or the *cafeteria compensation*.

It is evident, therefore, that although the value of compensation has never been in doubt, the scope of it has progressively got widened to include new terminologies such as total compensation and Total Rewards. According to experts, this deepening of the import of compensation has occurred due to certain issues with compensation:

- Obsolescence—With significant shifts in workplaces such as changes in workforce profiles and expectations, flatter organization structures, the existing systems of narrow pay ranges, rewarding traditional values, overreliance on cash incentives are some of the symbols of an outmoded system.
- Changes in psychological contract—The old contract of 'if you work hard, the firm will take care of you' has been replaced by 'if we outperform the market, we shall share the rewards.'
- Lack of alignment with business strategies.
- Gap between espoused theories and theories in action.
- Double standards displayed by senior leadership.

11 R. S. Allen, M. B. Takeda, C. S. White, and M. M. Helms, 'Rewards and Organizational Performance in Japan and the United States: A Comparison,' *Compensation & Benefits Review* 36, no. 1 (2004): 7–14.

12 A. Larson, *Demystifying Six Sigma* (New York, NY: AMACOM).

13 Ibid.

14 Patricia K. Zingheim and Jay R. Schuster, 'Total Rewards for New and Old Economy Companies,' *Compensation & Benefits Review* 32, no. 6 (2000): 20–23.

15 M. Silverman and P. Reilly, *How Flexible Is Total Reward?* (Brighton: IES Research Network, 2003).

16 John E. Tropman, *The Compensation Solution: How to Develop an Employee-driven Rewards System* (San Francisco, CA: Jossey-Bass, 2001).

The concept of the 'new new pay' is expressed in terms of an equation with ten variables. The equation is based on Tropman's research at the University of Michigan Business School with MBA students (on what they wanted from their workplace) and numerous interactions with corporate executives and HR professionals.

$$TC = (BP + AP + IP) + (WP + PP) + (OA + OG) + (PI + QL) + X$$

TC = total compensation BP = base pay, or salary

AP = augmented pay, that is, any one-time payment, even if received at regular intervals (such as overtime)

IP = indirect pay (benefits)

WP = works-pay, that is, employer-subsidized equipment, uniforms, and so on

PP = perks-pay, that is, special benefits—anything from accessories to employee discounts on company products

OA = opportunity for advancement and increased responsibility

OG = opportunity for growth, both through on-the-job training and through offsite training and degree attainment

PI = psychic income, the emotional enhancements provided by the job itself and the setting (the people)

QL = quality of life, that is, opportunity to express other important aspects of life (location close to home, flextime, onsite child care, ski to work, or whatever)

X = any unique element that an employee wants that the workplace can facilitate ('Can I bring my dog to work?')

The aforementioned 'expanded view of compensation' is meant to be a practical instrument to attract, motivate, and retain employees. This represents an approach, targeted at customer needs, applied so long only for external customers, now to the internal customers, that is, the employees to good effect. This wider view could define the compensation systems of the future. Tropman projects a compensation strategy with a three-fold goal with respect to the workforce: to encourage retention of the best (the top 20%), to balance inflow and outflow of the middle mass (the middle 60%), and to facilitate departure of the rest (bottom 20%).

10.4 TOTAL REWARDS SYSTEM

The concept of total rewards seeks to emphasize the entire canvas of the work experience to hold value to employees, going beyond the limited spheres of pay and employee benefits. It integrates the financial and non-financial elements of rewards into a unified whole. Adam Smith is believed to be the originator of the concept with his notion of 'total net advantage,' which included, besides pay, agreeableness or disagreeableness of work, difficulty and expense of learning it, job security, responsibility, and possibility of success or failure (Figure 10.1).

Several of HR organizations and compensation consultants have fallen over one another to advance their own models of total rewards strategy as part of the process for creating a vibrant employer brand. One such prominent model, known as the WorldatWork Total Rewards Model, depicts the strategic elements of the employer–employee exchange, and indicates how external influences and an

Pay	Benefits
• Base salary • Variable pay • Recognition • Shares	• Health care • Retirement • Savings • Time off • Perks
L&D	**Work environment**
• Career development • Performance management • Succession planning • Training	• Organizational climate • Leadership • Performance support • Work and life balance

Source: http://www.csae.com/Portals/0/CSAE%202014/Anderson%20Handout%201.pdf

Fig. 10.1 Total rewards model

increasingly global business environment affect 'attraction, motivation, retention and engagement[17]' of employees.

The WorldatWork Model represent six elements of total rewards that collectively define an organization's strategy to attract, motivate, retain, and engage employees are (Figure 10.2):

1. **Compensation** Pay provided by an employer to the employees for services rendered (i.e., for their time, effort, and skill). This includes both fixed and variable pay tied to performance levels.
2. **Benefits** Programs an employer uses to supplement the cash compensation employees receive. These health, income protection, savings, and retirement programs provide security for employees and their families.
3. **Work–life effectiveness** A specific set of organizational practices, policies, and programs, plus a philosophy that actively supports efforts to help employees achieve success at both work and home.
4. **Recognition** Either formal or informal programs that acknowledge or give special attention to employee actions, efforts, behavior, or performance and support business strategy by reinforcing behaviors (e.g., extraordinary accomplishments) that contribute to organizational success.
5. **Performance management** The alignment of efforts—of organization, team, and individual—toward the achievement of business goals and organizational success. Performance management includes establishing expectations, skill demonstration, assessment, feedback, and continuous improvement.
6. **Talent development and career opportunities** Provides the opportunity and tools for employees to advance their skills and competencies in both their short- and long-term careers.

Several other variations of total reward strategy have also been formulated. Towers Watson's total rewards framework, shown further, helps illustrate this expansive view of a compelling work experience.

---
[17] Available at: https://www.worldatwork.org/aboutus (accessed on August 2, 2017).

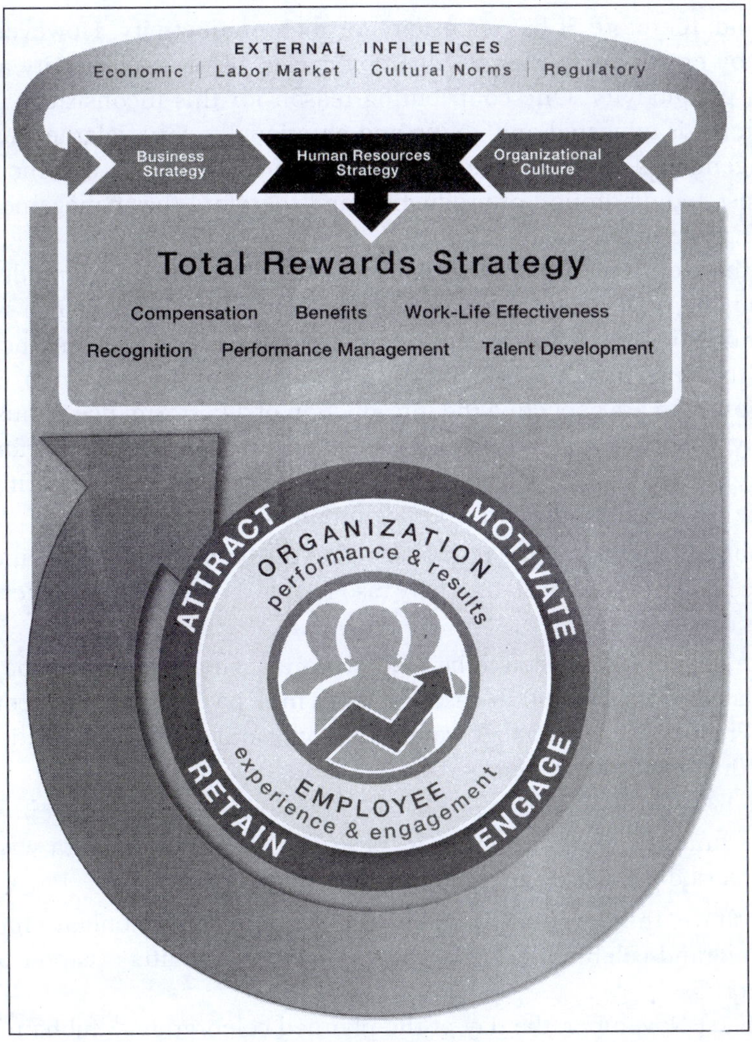

Source: The WorldatWork Handbook of Compensation, Benefits & Total Rewards, p.6. Hoboken, New Jersey: *John Wiley & Sons.*

Fig. 10.2 WorldatWork – Total Rewards Model

The upper two quadrants—pay and benefits—represent transactional or tangible rewards. These are financial in nature and are essential to recruit and retain staff but can easily be copied by competitors. By contrast, the relational or intangible non-financial rewards represented in the lower quadrants cannot be easily imitated and can, therefore, create both human capital and human process advantage.

Case Is Performance Bonus the Panacea for Sustained Performance?

Shubham is the HR Executive of a plant which produces batteries of different sizes. Out of the three plants of the company in Kolkata and Mumbai, this plant was the most recent and most technology driven. The plant had considerable capital investment in automatic machineries and, therefore, it has a capacity for high productivity. However, the plant has been plagued by erratic performance, whereby cycles of low productivity are followed by cycles of high productivity. One contributing reason for this inconsistent performance is that the workforce is educated and young and emotionally very volatile. Sometimes, even a small management action like the issue of caution letters to a chronic latecomer has triggered protest and disruption of production and therefore the management has to tread on thin ice to handle them.

All through the month of October the plant witnessed a stage of high productivity, which, everyone is hoping, will augur a positive turnaround for the plant. The workforce is in high spirits, and they seem to be fired by a spirit of competition with another plant as they want to show that they are the best. In informal chats with the workmen, Shubham got a sensing that workmen are expecting the introduction of a Performance Bonus scheme. Very enthusiastically Shubham made a paper suggesting introduction of a Performance linked Bonus scheme, in consultation with his colleagues in Industrial Engineering Cell, but the proposal was rejected by the Corporate Office on the following grounds:

(a) A production Incentive scheme may also add to the compensation bill and increase cost beyond the budget. Such escalation may also lead to a chain of consequent escalation in other units of the company.

(b) Much more deliberations need to be made before such a scheme can be introduced. If not formulated properly, and in case it fails, it may have unintended consequences in the form of reduced income and lower productivity and employee dissatisfaction arising out of less than expected income.

(c) There may be legal issues. The plant has an existing Wage Agreement with the trade union. The union is committed not to raise any demand for extra wage component during the period the wage agreement is in force.

In view of the above, the Corporate office recommended a non-monetary incentive, which could include a grand celebration in the form of a feast and gifts of sweet packets for the family members.

But today, on 1st November, the day of the planned celebration, Shubham had a difficult situation to handle. With good intention, the management had decided to celebrate the rise in productivity during last month with a sumptuous lunch in the canteen today. But the workers union came to him in the morning saying that they would go on hunger strike as they are opposed to the lunch which has been decided by the management without consulting the workmen, who are hurt about the condescending approach by the management. Shubham was surprised at the way the good gesture of the management has misfired. But the arrangements in the canteen cannot be reversed. However, the major challenge is to watch the impact on the trend of rising productivity.

Discussion Questions

1. Evaluate the stand taken by the Corporate Office.
2. What are the benefits of a Performance Bonus Scheme? Does it motivate in the long run?

10.5 FORMS OF PAY

10.5.1 Basic Pay

Basic pay is the base holding up the compensation package. This is similar to the base of the pyramid, with various other wage components fixed as a percentage of it. For example, house rent allowance (HRA) and additional pay as a certain percentage (say 15% or 30%) of the basic.

10.5.2 Variable Pay

Variable pay is the variable component of the compensation, which is fixed as a percentage of the basic pay. Variable pay is linked with the performance of the company, group, and the individual. It is, therefore, also known as performance-linked pay.

There could be three elements of variable pay:

1. The company performance-linked pay, being the percentage of the basic that is connected with the overall performance of the company. For example, in case of exceptional performance of the company in a particular period, the employee might get a higher pay (say, 100% or 150% of the base pay) than when/if it does relatively poorly (say, at 50% or 75%).
2. The group performance-linked pay tied to the performance of the group or the division in which the employee works.
3. The individual performance-linked pay, being the payout based on the performance of the employee and determined by the performance rating during the appraisal period.

10.5.3 Fringe Benefits

The benefits include a variety of items such as provident fund, gratuity, medical care, canteen facilities, uniforms, club facilities, paid time off, and individual or group accident insurance. Some benefits arise out of law while others are voluntarily offered in keeping with the employer's brand or according to the special needs of the working population.

10.5.4 Perquisites

Benefits associated with executive cadres including air travel, use of company car and driver, club membership, furnished accommodation, and stock options.

10.5.5 Allowances

An important allowance in India is known as dearness allowance (DA). DA was introduced to compensate the employees from erosion in income due to the rise in prices. It is linked to a consumer price index and compensates the employees for the rise in inflation through neutralization of increase in the index. Some organizations pay DA on fixed basis, while others use a variable system linked to consumer price index (CPI). DA is a contentious issue especially among the government employees and the PSUs in respect of the amount and the periodicity of payment.

Other allowances include city compensatory allowance, transport allowance (TA), hazard allowance, and educational allowance for children.

10.6 THEORIES OF COMPENSATION

There are several conceptual frameworks or theories of employee remuneration, which need to be examined to enable a better understanding of the entire spectrum of compensation and benefits.

10.6.1 Reinforcement and Expectancy Theories

Reinforcement theory takes off from Thorndike's Law of Effect and proposes that a response followed by a reward has a good likelihood of recurrence in the future. In terms of compensation management, the implication is that superior employee effort rewarded by money will make future high performance more probable. Conversely, superior effort, not rewarded is unlikely to be repeated in the future. The theory highlights the value of an employee actually experiencing the reward.

The expectancy theory,[18] in a similar manner, underlines the causal chain between rewards and behaviors (instrumentality perceptions), the difference with the reinforcement theory being that it highlights expected (rather than experienced) rewards (i.e., incentives). Two other factors combine to create motivation: expectancy, the perceived link between effort and performance, and valence, the expected value of outcomes (e.g., rewards).

By and large, different compensation systems have the maximum impact on the element of instrumentality: the assumed link between behaviors and pay, which is also referred to as the employees' 'line of sight.' Valence of pay outcomes are expected to be unaffected under different pay systems. Expectancy perceptions, however, are influenced more by job design and training than compensation.

10.6.2 Equity Theory

Equity (or fairness) is a key premise in theory and practice of pay, having impact on multiple spheres, some of the important ones being:

- Equal pay, equal work concept
- Differentiated compensation driven by market pressures/competitiveness
- The fairness of individual pay rates for people on the same job
- Individual employee views of their value relative to their pay

Definition

Equity is commonly defined as 'anything of value earned through providing or investing something of value.' Fairness occurs when the return on equity is equivalent to the investment made. As it relates to compensation, fairness is achieved when pay equates to the value of the work performed. Inequity, on the other hand, occurs when 'the value of the work performed does not match the value of the compensation received'.[19]

10.6.3 Theoretical Constructs Instead of Equity Theory

Researches suggest that absence of equity directly impacts employee conduct and output. J. Stacy Adams in his book *Equity Theory: Toward a General Theory of Social Interaction*[20] opined that an

[18] V. H. Vroom. *Work and Motivation* (New York, NY: Wiley, 1964).

[19] K. Romanoff, K. Boehm, and E. Benson, 'Pay Equity: Internal and External Considerations,' *Compensation & Benefits Review* 18, no. 3 (1986): 17–25.

[20] J. Stacy Adams, *Equity Theory Toward a General Theory of Social* Interaction (New York, NY: Academic Press, 1976).

employee regularly tracks his or her inputs and outputs on work. He perceives equity when the inputs and outputs are in equal ratio, as compared to his peers. In the event of the ratio being unequal, the employee may get annoyed for not being paid adequately or feel guilty for being paid excessively. According to Adam, when an employee perceives inequity in his or her rewards, he seeks to restore equity.

It is important, therefore, for the employees to perceive that they are being treated equitably by the organizations they work for. The maxim 'a fair day pay for a fair day's work' captures the sense of equity the employees should feel. Perceptions of inequity can lead to reduced productivity, absenteeism, or staff attrition.

Cowherd and Levine[21] used sample of 102 business units in 41 corporations to examine whether the size of the pay, differential between lower-level employees and top management, had any impact on product quality. They took the premise that discretionary work, or citizenship behaviors, such as freely offering to help others, following the spirit rather than letter of rules, and correcting errors that would ordinarily escape notice would be less likely when pay differentials between hourly and top managerial employees were large. Their results supported this hypothesis.

External Equity

External equity denotes employee perception of fairness while comparing with the wages prevailing in external labor markets. Practically, however, the labor market lacks uniformity in indicating wage rates for a particular job. Markets are shaped by laws of supply and demand, which vary considerably among markets, leading to differences in wages across labor markets.

Some of the factors accounting for wage variance among markets are: geographic location, industry sector, impact of unions, the size of the organization, competition, brand of the company, and level of education and experience of the workforce. So while defining the market the employers need to take care and avoid defining the market either too narrowly or too broadly, as in the first case, it might end up paying wages more than necessary, and in case of the latter, underpaying the employees.

Internal Equity

Internal equity exists when the employees perceive that the wages are commensurate with the relative internal value of each job. Job evaluation process provides a systematic basis for establishing the relative worth of the various jobs in the organization, by identifying the compensable factors (education, physical demands, working conditions, and so on) and then determining the price for each. However, whether a firm uses a systematic approach to job evaluation or a simplified one, the approaches are still subjective, since they depend on managerial judgment commitment for the choice of methods and their implementation.

Individual Equity

When individuals who on similar jobs are compensated on the basis of variations in individual performance, in so-called pay for performance, individual equity occurs. It implies a situation when excellent performance is rewarded with additional compensation in comparison to what is deemed as

[21] D. M. Cowherd and D. I. Levine, 'Product Quality and Pay Equity Between Lower-level Employees and Top Management: An Investigation of Distributive Justice Theory,' *Administrative Science Quarterly* 37 (1992): 302–320.

average performance. This constitutes a key area of complex compensation decisions: How to create the pay differentials based on performance differentials for employees working on the same job?

Personal Equity

Personal equity involves no direct comparison between employees. It exists when the compensation that an employee receives matches an employee's own image of his/her worth. Individual employees create their own standards based on his/her previous experiences and his/her knowledge of the market value of similar jobs. These internal parameters can govern the employee's pay satisfaction or dissatisfaction.

Procedural Equity

It refers to the perceived fairness of the processes and procedures used to make decisions regarding the allocation of pay.

10.6.4 Agency Theory

The agency theory focuses on the divergent interests and goals of the organization's stakeholders and the way that employee remuneration can be used to align these interests and goals. Employers and employees are the two stakeholders of a business unit, the former assuming the role of principals and the latter the role of agents. The remuneration payable to employees is the agency cost. It is natural that the employees expect high agency costs while the employers seek to minimize it. The agency theory says that the principle must choose a contracting scheme that helps align the interest of the agents with the principal's own interests. These contracts can be classified as either behavior-oriented (e.g., merit pay) or outcome-oriented (e.g., stock option schemes, profit sharing, and commission).

At the first sight, outcome-oriented contracts seem to be the obvious solution. As profits go up, rewards also increase. Remuneration falls when profits go down.

Agency theory—drawn from the domains of economics, finance, and law literatures—argues of differences in interests and goals of the organization's stakeholders, and how employee compensation can be an instrument in aligning them. In the modern corporation, the owner and the manager are different entities, unlike in the initial days. The agency costs (i.e., costs that arise from the interests of the principals/ owners and their agents/managers not converging) are created because the major stakeholders are not involved in day-to-day operations. Thus, agency cost accrues when the management spends money on perquisites (corporate jets) or 'empire building' (acquisitions merely enhance the manager's prestige or pay) rather than concentrating on shareholder wealth maximization. Agency cost is also involved in differences in risk-taking abilities between shareholders and managers. Research shows that the risk aversion by managers is reflected in preferences for base salary to bonuses or incentives, which are uncertain. Agency costs also result from divergent decision-making windows, for example, causing the managers to want to maximize short-run performance, sometimes at the cost of long-term success.

Agency theory stipulates that the principal must go for a contracting scheme that will help integrate the interests of the agent with the principal's own interests, thereby reducing agency costs. Such contracts can be classified as either behavior-oriented (e.g., merit pay) or outcome-oriented (e.g., stock options, profit sharing, commissions). There is no one-size-fits-all formula for the choice of the contract. The outcome-oriented contracts work in certain conditions: If profits are high, compensation goes up. If profits go down, compensation goes down. A limitation of this approach is that such

Exhibit Factors Influencing Compensation

Q. What would be the key focus areas for rewards professionals in 2014?

A. With the new government, there is a sense of optimism in the country today. The system and things on the ground have not changed but there is a belief that they will. The increase in commitment is a precursor to the change happening. Thus, very soon, expectations around compensation and rewards will rise and those challenges will trickle in. There is a 'reason to pay,' 'willingness to pay' but the most important part in any compensation decision is the 'ability to pay.' Hence, while 2015 looks like a positive year, the businesses that are not performing well, their 'ability to pay' will not be altered significantly. Hence, your ability to manage that will be a challenge that each C&B person should be geared for. We, at Hinduja, are trying to raise expectations related to performance and create an incremental variable pay plan where an additional bonus payout happens when there is additional revenue. So, while the pay remains within the budget, it creates an incentive and sense of optimism in the firm.

Source: 'Performance and Pay,' Total Rewards Quarterly 4, no. 3. Available at: http://www.aon.com/india/total-rewards-quaterly/volume4-issue-3/default.jsp (accessed on November 14, 2017): 3, Excerpts from a conver-sation with Sudhanshu Tripathi, Group President, Human Resources, Hinduja Group.

contracts increase the amount of risk borne by the agent who may require higher pay. Behavior-based contracts, on the other hand, do not transfer risk to the agent, and thus do not require a compensating wage differential. However, the principal must be able to monitor with little cost what the agent has done.

A combination of 'external' and 'internal' factors can influence, directly or indirectly, the rates at which employees are paid (Figure 10.3).

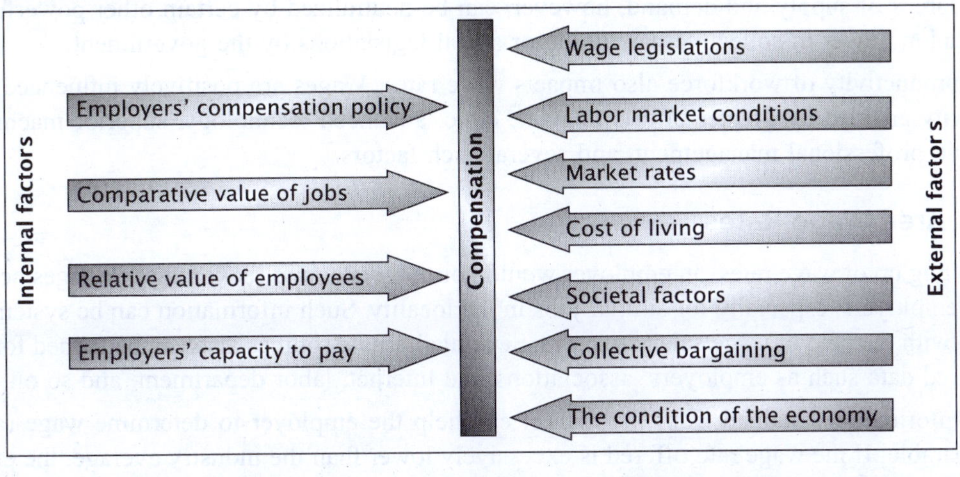

Fig. 10.3 Factors influencing compensation compensation

10.7 EXTERNAL FACTORS

The major external factors that influence wage rates include labor market conditions, area wage rates, cost of living, legal requirements, and collective bargaining if the employer is unionized.

10.7.1 The Condition of the Economy

The general economic condition of the country in which the organization is located plays an important role in influencing the pattern of compensation for employees. In a sluggish economic condition or in times of recession, an employer looks at reducing the manpower cost and takes such unusual steps as pay cuts. Contrarily, in a buoyant economy in times of high growth trajectory, the employers are more likely to open their purse strings and give the employees pay hikes and bonus.

In a research on the short- and long-term career effects of graduating in a recession by National Bureau of Economic Research, Canada, it was observed that graduating in a recession leads to large initial earnings losses. These losses, which amount to about 9% of annual earnings in the initial stage, eventually recede, but slowly, halving within 5 years but not disappearing until about 10 years after graduation. Second, initial random shocks affect the entire career. Graduating in a recession leads workers to start at smaller and lower paying firms, and they catch up by switching jobs more frequently than those who graduate in better times.

10.7.2 Labor Market Conditions

The forces of supply and demand for qualified labor shape the labor market within an area. The balance in the supply and demand substantially tilts the wage rates either negatively or positively for acquiring or retaining the right profile of employees. In India, a paradoxical situation created by abundance of unskilled labor combined with scarcity of workforce with specialized skill sets leads to abnormally low wages contrasted by high-wage islands in organized and unorganized sectors. For instance, premium skills such as consulting and accountancy are paid more as are the technology professionals who might be experts in their chosen field. The combination of expertise and the relative scarcity of such experts determine how much the employer is willing to pay.

The forces of supply and demand, however, can be neutralized by certain other powerful forces such as union power in collective bargaining or social legislations by the government.

The productivity of workforce also impacts wage rates. Wages are positively influenced by high productivity enabled by greater efforts or work ethic, advanced technology, superior machines and equipment, professional management, and several such factors.

10.7.3 Area Wage Rates

While setting up of wage rates, an employer would normally take into reckoning the wages being paid by other employers, especially for similar jobs in the locality. Such information can be systematically collected with the help of wage/salary surveys. Several alternate sources also can be tapped for getting the required data such as employers' associations, the Internet, labor department, and so on.

The information obtained from the market can help the employer to determine wage rates that are comparable. If the wage rate offered is excessively lower than the industry average, the employer runs the risk of not getting employees of required skill sets or may lose skilled existing employees. If the wage rates become higher than the industry average, it will lead to a bloated wage bill, thus creating avoidable financial burden for the employer.

10.7.4 Cost of Living

As a consequence of inflationary pressures, the real wages of employees tend to continuously diminish. This requires a mechanism to upwardly adjust the compensation to offset the adverse effects of price rise at a periodical interval so that the employees can maintain their purchasing power for essential commodities. This is done normally through DA, which is linked with the CPI. The CPI is a measure of the average change in prices of certain listed commodities of everyday consumption over time in a fixed 'market basket' of goods and services. In some industries, not covered by dearness allowances, this is done through what is known as 'escalator clauses' in various labor agreements. In ways similar to DAs, these provisions enable quarterly cost-of-living adjustments (COLA) in wages based on changes in the CPI.

The index is based on prices of food, clothing, shelter, and fuels; transportation fares; charges for medical services; and prices of other goods and services that people buy for day-to-day living. The Bureau of Labor Statistics collects price information on a monthly basis and calculates the CPI for the nation as a whole.

10.7.5 Collective Bargaining

A principal reason why workers join unions is the hope that unions will help raise wages through collective bargaining. It is being increasingly recognized that institutional factors such as trade unions and the process of collective bargaining play a significant role in determining the levels of wages and standard of working conditions. How much unions raise wages and for whom, and the consequences of unionization for workers, firms, and the economy have been studied by economists and other researchers for over a century (e.g., the work of Alfred Marshall). A recent research presents evidence from the 1990s that unions raise the wages of unionized workers by roughly 20% and raise total compensation by about 28%.[22] In a study to analyze the impact of trade union on wages covering blue-collar male workers employed in manufacturing industries in Chennai district of Tamil Nadu, it was observed that union sector workers earned estimated 19% more wages than comparable workers in non-union sector.[23]

Historically, the bigger beneficiaries of such collective bargaining tend to be the 'low-skilled' workers rather than the 'high-skilled' workers. As a consequence, unions act as instruments for reducing wage inequities. According to some researchers in a 'universal finding' of the extensive literature on unions, wages, and worker skills, unions improve wages more for low- and middle-wage workers.[24] It can be argued that, logically, unions standardize wages by decreasing differentials across and within job positions, so that low-skilled workers receive a larger premium relative to their alternative non-union wage.

The agreements negotiated by unions set up compensation trends within the labor market. Consequently, in areas marked by strong organized workforce, wage levels climb higher in comparison with unorganized areas. The impact of unionization on wages, in a chain effect, goes beyond the workers covered by collective bargaining to influence non-union wages and labor practices. For example, in industries and occupations, where sizeable chunk of workplaces are unionized, non-union employers are also expected to follow suit and match the standards set in unionized workplaces, especially regarding compensation and benefit practices, thus clearly going beyond what they would

22 Lawrence Mishel and Matthew Walters, 'How Unions Help All Workers' (Briefing paper, Economic Policy Institute, Washington, DC, August 26, 2003).

23 K. Shanmugam and Subramaniam Madheswaran, 'Wage Differentials Between Union and Non-union Workers: An Econometric Analysis. Econometric Society,' paper presented at the Far Eastern Meeting of the Econometric Society, Yonsei University, 2004, 4–6.

24 B. T. Hirsch and E. J. Schumacher, 'Unions, Wages, and Skills,' *The Journal of Human Resources* 33 no. 1 (Winter 1998): 201–219.

have provided had there been no union presence. This pressure is often described as the 'union threat effect,' implying the extent to which non-union workers get paid more because their employers are trying to prevent unionization. The impact of collective bargaining therefore extends beyond that segment of the labor force that is unionized.

10.7.6 Societal Factors

The prevailing dominant social philosophy also has a bearing on the fixation of the compensation structure. The concept of welfare state had influenced the fixation of wages especially in public sector undertakings post-Independence. One of the drivers of the decision to nationalize sectors such as coal and banking was the perceived poor working conditions in those sectors and the soaring expectations for improvement in the aftermath of nationalization. The social norm is also reflected in the judicial decisions on ID related to wages.[25]

10.7.7 Legal Provisions

In India, a Tripartite Committee on Fair Wages was set up in 1949 to determine the principles on which fair wages should be fixed. Its recommendations, besides providing the guidelines for wage fixation, laid down the key concepts of the 'living wage,' 'minimum wage,' and 'fair wage' as follows:

- **Minimum wage** The wage that provides for the bare sustenance of life and preservation of the efficiency of the work.
- **Living wage** The wage that provides a standard of living to the workers.
- **Fair wage** The wage that is above the minimum wage but below the living wage.

Although the committee suggested that workers should get 'reasonable and fair wages, which are sufficient to meet the needs of the worker and his family,' its recommendations did not lead to a uniform and comprehensive wage policy for all sectors of the economy. As per practice, wages in the organized sector are determined through negotiations and settlements between employer and employees.

Over the years, several labor laws have been enacted on various aspects of wages and benefits of employees, the notable ones being the Payment of Wages Act 1936, the Minimum Wages Act 1948, the Payment of Bonus Act 1965, and the Equal Remuneration Act 1976. The Payment of Wages Act aims to protect the covered employees against irregularities in payment of wages and unauthorized deductions by the employers. The Minimum Wages Act requires the employer to pay the specified minimum wages prescribed by the government to workers engaged in scheduled industries. The Payment of Bonus Act provides for payment of minimum bonus to employees in certain covered establishments. The Equal Remuneration Act prescribes equal pay for equal work to workers irrespective of gender.

The government has also constituted from time to time wage boards, tribunals, and committees to recommend wages payable to workers working in specific industries.

As regards managerial remuneration, the Companies Act 1956 (Sections 198 and 309) deals with the provisions relating to managerial remuneration of all Directors and also its manager. It applies to all public companies and any private company that is a subsidiary of a public company. Section 198(1) lays down that 11% of net profits of the company will be the overall ceiling on the total remuneration of the company. As per section 309(3), a whole-time director or managing director may be paid either

[25] Standard Vacuum Refining Co. of India vs Its Workmen and Another, 1961.

by way of monthly payment or at a specified percentage of profits or partly by one way and partly by the other to the extent of 5% of net profit for one such director and 10% for all of such directors.

10.8 INTERNAL FACTORS

The internal factors that influence wage rates are the employer's compensation policy, the worth of a job, an employee's relative worth in meeting job requirements, and an employer's ability to pay.

10.8.1 Employer's Compensation Policy

Kevin Hallock in his book *Pay: Why People Earn What They Earn and What You Can Do Now to Make More*[26] reports about meticulousness and high formalization of compensation administrations in some organizations.

> They include clear compensation grids, matching to external data, use of surveys and so forth. Even for jobs that are not common in a company's particular market, there are ways to slot them in and figure out what the market might pay someone [who has skills important to the organization].

At the same time, Hallock adds, some employees feel decisions about compensation are arbitrary, because organizations do not always communicate well about pay. Some companies, on the other hand, both for-profit and non-profit, make it a point to give employees a printout every year that clearly explains their benefits and what it costs the company to provide them.

The diversity in the approach to compensation and rewards among different organizations is caused by variance in compensation strategies, policies, and practices. Compensation policy of an organization can cover the following areas:

1. How internal compensation levels should compare with market rates?
2. How external competitiveness is balanced with internal equity?
3. How much information will be communicated about compensation policies and levels?
4. How would pay rates be fixed on appointment or promotion?
5. How employees will be assimilated into revised grade and pay structures?
6. How employees whose pays exceed the maximum for their grade should be protected from a reduction in salary?

10.8.2 Valuation of a Job

Organizations determine the value of a job in two ways. First, those without a systematic compensation policy rely on the subjective assessment of senior employees conversant with the jobs. There is a likelihood of the pay system being either modeled on the market rates, or in a union-backed workplace by the process of collective bargaining.

Second, organizations with a systematic compensation plan follow a process of a methodical evaluation of the compensable factors in the jobs known as job evaluation to help in determining the relative value of each job. This process is useful even when the wage rates are subject to collective bargaining process, as it provides some reference point on which the negotiations can be loosely based to ensure some control over the eventual wage structure.

---

26 Hallock, Kevin F. 'Pay: Why People Earn What They Earn and What You Can Do Now to Make More' (New York: Cambridge University Press, 2012): 226.

10.8.3 Employee's Relative Worth

There are several employee-related factors influencing the decision to compensate him/her, the more common among them being work experience, technical/professional education, seniority, performance, and potential. In industrial and office jobs, differences in employee performance can be recognized and rewarded through promotion and with various incentive systems. Superior performance can be rewarded by granting merit raises on the basis of steps within a rate range established for a job class.

Performance of an employee in an organization is evaluated through a formal or informal system of appraisal. In the 'pay for performance' work culture, it is essential to have an effective performance appraisal system that accurately captures the difference in outputs between those employees who deserve the raises and those who do not. There needs to be a clear line of sight between performance and the eventual reward received. Over time, merit systems, however, have tended to rapidly deteriorate into a comfortable equilibrium of automatic pay hikes irrespective of performance. As a result, employees tend to be rewarded more for merely being present than for being productive on the job.

10.8.4 Employer's Ability to Pay

In the private sector, an organization's ability to pay hinges on a few factors that include the productivity of its employees, the profitability of business, and financial resources available to employers. The general economic conditions and competition faced by employers can also significantly affect an organization's capacity to compensate its employees. Competition and recessions can force prices down and reduce the income from which compensation payments are derived. In such situations, employers have little choice but to reduce wages and/or lay off employees, or, even worse, to go out of business.

In the public sector, the Department of Public Enterprises issues guidelines for revision of pay for various categories of employees from time to time. Typically, the guidelines mandate a percentage of increase up to a ceiling (say 30%), within which the PSEs are required to structure their pay revisions.

Exhibit Starting Salaries in India Among Lowest in Asia-Pacific Study

New Delhi: Entry-level salaries in India are amongst the lowest in the Asia-Pacific region, a study by professional services firm Towers Watson says.

The average monthly starting pay in India is around US$400 (₹24,000), less than one-fifth of the equivalent paid in South Korea and Singapore, said the study by Towers Watson's Data Services.

Graduate Indian employees sit towards the bottom of the Asia-Pacific countries in terms of starting salary, it said, adding that it augurs well for the 'Make in India' campaign as this would give the MNCs a competitive advantage over other Asia-Pacific countries.

'Although dependent on prevailing exchange rates, the findings clearly highlight India's position as a competitive and attractive workforce and talent market,' said Sambhav Rakyan, Data Services Practice Leader, Asia-Pacific, at Towers Watson.

Out of the top 11 Asia-Pacific economies, the average monthly Indian starting salary was ranked ninth. 'The disparity in salaries also illustrates how a large knowledge pool and a significant cost arbitrage makes India a front runner in providing outsourced services. After achieving great success in IT/BPO, India can now become a natural choice for other sectors, like manufacturing,' he added.

Further up the ladder, wages for experienced professionals at middle management levels in India are slightly more competitive, but still below their Asia-Pacific peers.

Notwithstanding the recent push in its manufacturing sector and popularity of the IT sector, an engineering manager in India earns an average salary of US$56,530—almost half of his Chinese counterpart (US$112,070) and one-third of his Singaporean counterpart (US$151,168), the report said.

'Despite a common labor market in the region, it is striking to see how divergent guaranteed cash levels remain amongst top economies,' Rakyan added.

Discussion Question

1. What could be the reason that India Inc. pays the lowest start-up salary in Asia-Pacific?

Source: The Times of India, 'Starting Salaries in India Amongst Lowest in Asia-Pacific: Study,' September 8, 2015.

10.9 ESTABLISHING PAY RATES

An effective compensation system embeds the principles of equity in the various stages of its design. The test of a model compensation system is in being perceived by employees as fair and equitable, comparable to prevalent rates in the market, correctly based, motivating, and easily comprehensible. There are several steps to designing a pay structure:

1. Collect and summarize work content information for each job through job analysis.
2. Establish relative worth of different jobs through job evaluation.
3. Gather compensation data from other employers for comparable jobs through salary survey.
4. Formulate the compensation policy in respect of external competitiveness.
5. Integrate the internal structure (Step 2) with the external market pay rates and create a compensation structure.

10.9.1 Job Analysis

Job analysis is the process of studying jobs in an organization through collection and analyses of the content and the human requirements, as also the context in which work is done. The outcome of this process is a job description (JD) that includes the title, the summary of responsibilities, a list of the key tasks and responsibilities, and a description of the job context. It also includes the KSAs necessary to perform the job.

10.9.2 Job Evaluation

Job evaluation is the process of assessing the comparative worth of different jobs in an organization, eventually leading to formulation of a hierarchy of jobs and a salary structure aligned to it. The underlying principle for job evaluation is that jobs that call for greater responsibilities, higher qualification, and more complexities should have a higher compensation tag than jobs that require less of these.

The essential process of job evaluation is to compare one job with another in order to establish the relative merit to eventually price them. The comparison can be done instinctively on the basis of experience and judgment, or it can be done methodically on the basis of some identified standard job attributes or characteristics. In compensation lexicon, these factors are known as compensable factors. An employer can either develop compensable factors relevant for his business or use more formalized job evaluation techniques. For example, consulting firm Hay Group makes use of three compensable factors: know-how, problem-solving, and accountability. The choice of compensable factors for managerial positions, however, leans on the strategic direction that the organization wants to take. For example, Walmart has 'impact on cost containment' as a compensable factor, while for P&G and 3M 'multi-national responsibilities' is a chosen one.

The primary step in implementing a job evaluation program is to ascertain the need for it. Some of the triggers are high degree of employee attrition, frequent workplace conflicts such as work stoppage, or other evidence of employee unrest arising out of differential pay rates. Once decided, the next step is to bring employees onboard for spontaneous cooperation. One of the reasons why job evaluation sometimes flounders is the employee's apprehension that the process shall result in reduction in pay. Selection of a job evaluation committee is the third step. The committee members should be knowledgeable about different jobs and have employee representatives to instill confidence in the process. While implementing the program, the committee has mainly three functions to perform: identify some key jobs to benchmark (usually 10–15 jobs), so that other jobs can be evaluated in comparison; to identify the compensable factors; and finally, to evaluate the worth of each job.

10.9.3 Qualitative Methods

There are several methods for job evaluation: ranking, job classification, point method, and factor comparison.

Ranking

Job ranking in a Nursing home (imaginary)

Ranking order	Annual pay scale (₹)
1. Superintendent	30 Lakh
2. Head nurse	12 Lakh
3. Accountant	12 Lakh
4. Nurse	10 Lakh
5. Assistant nurse	8 Lakh
6. Helper	2 Lakh
7. Peon	2 Lakh

In the simplest of job evaluation methods, each job is ranked in relation to all other jobs, usually based on general attributes such as job complexity.

Job ranking method uses the following steps:

1. Job analysis and creating JDs for the all jobs. It is not necessary to formulate multiple compensable factors since this method compares jobs in their totality.
2. Jobs are grouped in similar clusters (such as technical workers in one group and unskilled workers in another group).
3. One compensable factor 'general complexity' is selected for ranking.

4. Jobs are ranked. One way to do it is that each rater gives a ranking from lowest to the highest on a set of index cards that contains the JD for each job. A different method is to select highest and lowest from the card, then on to the next highest and lowest and so on.
5. Ratings are integrated. For multiple ratings, a simple method is to average them.

Ranking method has the advantage of being simple, easy to understand, and easily implementable within a short time method. Conversely, the method suffers from the disadvantages of relying too heavily on guesswork and approximation, not providing any scientific criterion for quantifying the value of one job in relation to another and is probably suitable for small organizations only.

Job Classification Method

It is a simple method of classifying all jobs into several groups. These groups are either termed as 'classes' when they include similar jobs or 'grades' if they are dissimilar, but paid the same rates. The classification is done on various bases. One method is to create a grade description like a JD and then put into grades based on how closely these jobs correspond to the grade descriptions. The grade definitions refer to such factors as key tasks carried out, skill, competence, experience, initiative, and responsibility. A second way is to develop the classification on the basis of compensable factors for each grade and then see how each job fits into the grade on the basis of the compensable factors.

Generally, classification systems work between four and eight grades. It has been empirically found that classification systems exceeding eight grades pose difficulties in creating clear boundaries between successive grades; likewise, less than four grades present difficulties in framing a clear definition distinguishing one grade from another.

Job classification system is easy and cheap to develop, implement, and maintain. Second, jobs can be quickly slotted into the structure. In the third place, the grouping of jobs into classifications makes pay determination problems easy to administer. The most important advantage of the classification method is that eventually it does exactly what the employer is comfortable doing: clustering jobs, rather than go through the painstaking process of pricing individual jobs separately. On the contrary, this system cannot cope with complex jobs that do not fit neatly into one grade. Second, the grade definitions tend to be so generalized that they may not be of much help in evaluating borderline cases, especially at senior levels.

10.9.4 The Quantitative Methods

Point Method

The point method, devised by Lott,[27] was the first quantitative method of job evaluation. Under this system, a number of job factors are identified and defined. For example, Motorola has identified five factors: knowledge, communications, complexity, impact, and span of control. Each factor has multiple levels or degrees. Each factor is assigned a value (in the form of points) to indicate its relative significance in the job. The job evaluation committee allocates scores based on degree to which each job factor (such as knowledge) is present in the specific job and add together to produce a total score.

The point method involves the following steps:

1. Decide the jobs or groups of jobs to be evaluated
2. Conduct a job analysis

[27] Lott. *Wage Scales and Job Evaluation* (New York, NY: Ronald Press).

3. Identify and define the job factors
4. Define degree for each factor
5. Determine comparative values of factors
6. Assign values to factors and degrees
7. Develop a factor plan and manual
8. Rate the jobs

Advantages

1. By compelling the evaluators to adapt a number of factors, this system prevents over implication or use of non-analytical methods.
2. The defined parameters help in certain degree of accuracy, consistency, and objectivity in evaluation.
3. It provides a logic that helps in structuring the graded pay scales.
4. It is useful in comparing with external jobs for market pricing.
5. The data makes for smooth computerization.

Disadvantages

1. It is a complex system and requires time and cost to develop, install, and maintain.
2. It is not immune to subjectivity, as judgment is required in selection of factors, defining the degrees/levels, and assigning values.
3. The attributes of a job may defy easy quantification.

Factor Comparison Method

Eugene Benge is credited with developing the factor comparison system, which was subsequently refined by Benge, Burk, and Hay.[28] Similar to the ranking method, the factor comparison method ranks each job several times, once for each compensable factor. Benge had suggested five factors as universally present in all jobs:

1. Mental requirements
2. Skill requirements
3. Physical requirements
4. Responsibilities
5. Working conditions

A factor comparison exercise is usually carried out in the following steps:

1. Select the benchmark jobs
2. Agree factors
3. Analyze benchmark jobs
4. Rank benchmark jobs by factors
5. Determine the relative importance of factors in each job
6. Allocate money value to factors
7. Evaluate other jobs

---

28 Benge, Burke and Hay, *Job Evaluation Manual* (New York, NY: Harper, 1941).

Advantages

1. By following a detailed step-by-step set of instruction, it allows a more methodical comparison of jobs than the qualitative methods.
2. It is fairly accurate, flexible, and objective; it avoids arbitrary selection at any stage.
3. There is logic in comparing the jobs on compensable factors.
4. It limits to a few factors and thereby reduces the probability of overlapping.
5. It lends itself to an automatic determination of wage rates.

Disadvantages

1. It is relatively complex and difficult to explain to employees.
2. It is expensive to install, difficult to operate for those who are not conversant with job-evaluation techniques.
3. The contents and the value of the key jobs may alter over time, and therefore, the linkage of wage to the present jobs may lead to future errors.
4. The method of evaluating jobs and fixing their wages simultaneously may lead to errors.
5. The use of the aforementioned five factors for all organizations may not always be appropriate.
6. The need to use experts particularly in selecting weightages may make the process expensive.

10.9.5 Compensation Policy

The compensation policy or stance of an organization is usually expressed explicitly or implicitly as where it wants its rates to be positioned relatively to the marketplace. Does the organization want to lead, lag, or meet the market in compensation?

The compensation policy could cover the following matters:

1. How will internal compensation levels compete with market rates?
2. How will internal equity and external competitiveness be balanced?
3. How much information is to be shared on compensation?
4. How will pay be fixed on appointment or on progression?
5. How will employees be fitted into revised grades?
6. How will employees' pay be covered to avoid stagnation at maximum of the grade?

The compensation policy or strategy has an impact on employee attraction and retention. Decisions on compensation policy are influenced by the organization's own assessment of the expected impact of its pay on attracting and retaining talent. There can be divergent pay policies across different job families and job levels, if the top management has a conviction that there should be horses for courses, that different strategies are required in different areas of the organization.

10.9.6 Market Survey

Salary survey is the process of analyzing compensation data gathered from other employers in a survey of the relevant labor market. An organization's relevant labor market could be local, regional, or national depending on the job. A common method of defining the labor market is to describe the area from which employers obtain certain types of workers. For example, the labor market for electrician for a factory would be local, whereas the labor market for sales engineer would be national.

Gathering external pay data (e.g., base pay, bonuses, stock options, and benefits) is essential to keep the organization's compensation externally competitive within its industry. Employee attraction and retention can be improved by maintaining externally aligned pay structures.

The essential objective of a salary survey is to enable an organization achieve external equity, that is, to pay its employees equally in relation to similar employees working in other establishments. Employers use these surveys to price benchmark jobs, to adjust pay level in relation to the rates by the competitors, to analyze pay related issues, and to assess the employee costs of competitor companies. Although surveys are primarily conducted to gather competitive wage data, they can also collect information on employee benefits or organizational pay practices (e.g., overtime rates or shift differentials).

Surveys can be done in formal or informal manner. Some organizations prefer to conduct their own salary surveys. In the United States, an important source of salary data lies in comprehensive surveys conducted by governmental agencies such as Bureau of Labor Statistics. MNCs can purchase international surveys through large consulting firms such as Hay, Aon Hewitt, Towers Perrin, and others. The overseas compensation survey offered by TPF&C reports on the payment practices in 20 countries. The third-party surveys, while offering certain benefits to their users, suffer from certain limitations such as incompatibility with the user's context and the user's inability to specify the required data. To overcome these problems, organizations may collect their own compensation data.

Following steps are used in conducting wage and salary surveys:

1. Select the jobs to be used in the survey.
2. Identify the target organizations to include in the survey based on who they actually compete with for sourcing employees.
3. Identify the key jobs for survey, since it is not feasible to survey all the jobs in an organization.
4. Decide on what information to gather on wages, benefit types, and pay policies.
5. Send the survey questionnaire.
6. Tabulate the survey data.

10.9.7 Pay-structure Creation

Once the job evaluation committee has concluded the determination of relative worth of each job, the process of creating a pay structure begins. In constructing a pay structure, the internal structure (Step 2 as stated earlier) is superimposed on the external market pay rates (Step 4 as stated earlier) in a simple regression to develop a market pay line. Depending on whether the organization wants to lead, lag, or meet the market, the market pay line can be adjusted up or down. Pay structure also includes pay grades and pay ranges.

The Wage Curve

A wage curve is typically depicted in the form of a scatter gram with a series of dots that present the current wage rates. A freehand curve is then drawn through the bunch of dots in such a manner that almost an equal number of dots appear above and under the curve. The curve indicates the relationship between the comparative value of jobs and their established wage rates. It may variously reflect the present pay rates for jobs inside an organization, the revised rates consequent on the job evaluation, or the market rates for similar jobs based on what other organizations are paying.

Pay Grades

It is administratively convenient to group jobs into pay grades and to apply the wage rate/range within the same grade. A pay grade consists of jobs of approximately equal difficulty or importance. In job classification system, jobs are grouped into grades as part of the process. In point- and factor-comparison systems, pay grades need to be established at selected intervals that represent either the point or the evaluated monetary value of these jobs.

Grade Structures

A grade structure consists of a sequence of grades, bands, or levels into which groups of jobs that are broadly comparable in size are placed. The number of grades in a wage structure depends on a variety of factors including the incline of the wage curve, the number and distribution of the jobs within the structure, and the compensation policies and career progression policies of the organization. The number utilized should be sufficient to permit difficulty levels to be distinguished, but not so great as to make the distinction between two adjoining grades insignificant.

The main types of graded structure are narrow graded structure, broad graded structure, broad banded structure, career family structure, job family structure, and pay spines.

Rate Ranges

Rather than having a single rate, it is normal practice to provide a range of rates for each pay grade. The pay ranges usually have a minimum, midpoint, and a maximum. This allows for pay progression related to performance, contribution, or competence. Rate ranges have a series of steps that ensures that employees receive increments up to the maximum of the range based on merit, seniority, or competence. Grade structures normally provide for overlaps with preceding/succeeding pay grades. Overlaps allow an employee with experience to earn equal to or more than a less experienced person placed in the succeeding grade.

10.10 EMPLOYEE BENEFITS

10.10.1 Coverage and Objectives

Employee benefits (also covering fringe benefits, perquisites, or perks) constitute the indirect financial and non-financial remuneration, which employees are eligible to receive in addition to their normal wages or salaries by virtue of being employed. The benefits can be classified as statutory and discretionary (Table 10.1) Benefits include housing accommodation, accident insurance, retirement benefits, crèche, scholarships, educational assistance, various kinds of leave, leave fare assistance, social security, profit sharing, and such specialized benefits.

The objective of employee benefits is to address the economic security concerns of the employees, and while doing so, to improve employee retention in the organization. As such, it is one component of reward management. The packaging of employee benefits has been a strategic instrument of employee value proposition in the raging war for talent in the corporate arenas of India.

Table 10.1 Employee benefits—statutory and discretionary

Statutorily required	Discretionary
1. Provident Fund (EPF Act and Scheme 1952)	1. Group insurance schemes
2. Pension (EPF Act 1952)	2. Housing accommodation
3. Gratuity (Payment of Gratuity Act 1972)	3. Allowances
4. Employee compensation for temporary/permanent disablement (Employee Compensation Act 1923, ESI Act 1948)	4. Festival/casual leave
5. Maternity leave (Maternity Benefits Act 1961)	5. Company car
6. Annual leave with wages (Factories Act 1948)	6. Education assistance

10.10.2 Components of Benefits

Employee benefits have two major components: allowances and perquisites. Allowances include DA, compensatory allowances (city compensatory, hill allowance, duty allowances, hardship allowance, shift allowance, and hazard allowance), conveyance allowance, HRA, deputation allowance, and education allowance. Perquisites include leave travel concession, advances, soft furnishing reimbursements, club membership, and expense account.

Another way of categorizing employee benefits is pay for time not worked, insurance benefits, and retirement benefits and services. Pay for time not worked includes annual leave with wages, sick leave, casual leave, festival leave, maternity/paternity leave, and VRS. Insurance benefits include employee compensation, domiciliary and hospitalization benefits, accident insurance, and disability benefits. Retirement benefits cover pension and superannuation systems, gratuity, and such others. Services include personal services such as employee assistance programs, crèche/day care centers, and time off.

Reflection Point

Trends in Compensation and Benefits in 2023

1. Employee turnover remains high among all industries
2. Pay for performance matters
3. Pay transparency remains a challenge
4. Compensation training and communication is the key

Discussion Question

1. Which area, in your opinion, should receive the maximum attention by organizations in India and why?

Source: Compensation Management Trends for 2023. Eric Dirks. January 2023. https://hrsoft.com/compensation-management-trends-2023/

10.10.3 Current Practice in India

The employee benefits provided by IBM India cover seven areas: insurance, health and wellness, financial and retirement, family and parenting, vacation and time off, perks and benefits, professional support, and diversity program.[29] At HCL Infosystems, an initiative named 'Employees First' provides

[29] www.Glassdoor.co.in

for a five-fold path to individual enlightenment and ensures that people are given support, knowledge, recognition, empowerment, and transformation. At Wipro, a counseling initiative called 'Mitr' helps employees to cope with crises faced in their personal and professional lives. Most of the campuses at Intel Corporation have onsite facilities that provide recreational opportunities such as basketball, volleyball, fitness centers, exercise classes, and other activities. At Bharti Airtel, employees can opt for leave of six months for personal reasons and up to one year to pursue higher education. At Canon Corporation, the frontline sales and service employees are provided with the facility of virtual working wherein they do not need to come to office for reporting or attendance and can directly report in the field. Standard Chartered Bank has a day-care center called 'Colors of Joy' that was started specially to facilitate women employees. The bank also has 'Happy Fridays' where a fun activity between 4:00–6:00 pm is planned on any one Friday in a month. At Kotak Mahindra 'Family Day' is scheduled to encourage bonding of office colleagues with immediate family. MakeMyTrip company organizes fun activities such as theme day, rock band, and sports activities to engage its young workforce.

All the aforementioned, however, come at a cost. According to the findings of India Benefit Trend Survey by Towers Watson,[30] employers are grappling with two current issues, which are making them rethink employee benefit strategy: first, the rising inflation and increasing cost of employee benefits; second, low employee awareness and appreciation—one in three Indian employers is spending more than 20% of total payroll on benefits, yet a sizable 43% believe their employees do not sufficiently value the benefits provided by the companies.

10.10.4 Factors Influencing the Choice of Benefit Package: Design Principles and Issues

In designing an effective employee benefit plan, some of the underlying principles are: statutory requirements, employer branding strategies, concern for security, tax angles, and utilization of leisure time. Another classification could be based on employer–employee factors (Figure 10.4). The aforementioned examples of employee benefits indicate three main approaches: innovation, flexibility, and harmonization. For example, Siemens India, in a demonstration of innovative practice, used outplacement (training surplus staff in marketable skills) instead of

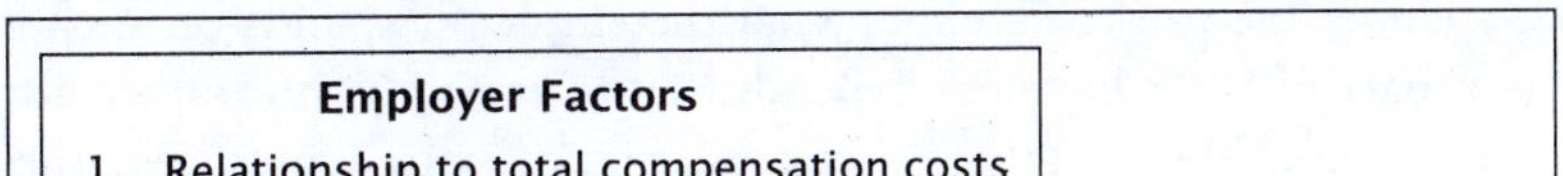

Source: Milkovich and Ratnam, 'Compensation.'

Fig. 10.4 Employer—Employee factors influencing benefits

[30] *Business Standard*, 'Companies in India to Review Employee Benefits Strategy,' *Business Standard*, March 3, 2014.

Exhibit Paying Taxes on Gifts from Employers

A friend of mine was ecstatic about the free air tickets to Goa that he had received from his employer, and why would not he be? It is usual for us to think of gifts as having no tax consequences for the receiver. Unfortunately, as I told my friend, this is not always the case. Most of us are not aware of this, but gifts above a certain monetary value are taxable in the hands of the employee/receiver.

What is considered a gift?

Gifts are given voluntarily without any legal or moral obligations and generally represent payments without any consideration. Items given as awards for good performance or as incentives cannot be considered gifts.

Under the Income Tax rules relating to the valuation of perquisites, the value of any gift, voucher, or token received by the employee or by their family members on ceremonial or other occasions (or in any other way) is considered at the market price of the gifted item.

Previously, the burden of paying taxes on a gifted item was the responsibility of the employer and he was liable to pay a Fringe Benefit Tax (FBT) on the value of the gift given to the employee. With the abolition of FBT from 1 April 2009, the tax liability has now shifted to the employee. The good news here is that if the value of a gift, voucher or token (as the case may be) is below ₹5000 (in aggregate, for all gifts received during the year), the perquisite value shall be taken as nil. If the value exceeds ₹5000, the entire gift amount shall be taxable in the employees' hands. For instance, if the value of the gift given by the employer to an employee during the tax year 2011–12 is ₹9000, the entire sum would be subject to tax on the employee for that financial year.

Under the present regime, what the employer spends on such gift items is fully tax deductible as a part of their business expenditure, fortunately, no longer attracting FBT. If as an employer you are considering giving a taxable gift to your employees, then it is advisable to coordinate this with the payroll department so that the taxable amount can be included in the employees' salaries during a payroll period, and appropriate tax is withheld.

Source: Subramanya HP, 'Paying Taxes on Gifts from Employers,' The Indian Express, June 18, 2012.

simple golden handshake to deal with redundant staff. Similarly, use of 'cafeteria' approach to benefits package displays the organization's flexibility in responding to employees' varied needs. The practices of single lunchrooms for white-/blue-collar employees are an example of harmonization.

Due care, however, needs to be taken on the following aspects:

- The targeted beneficiary
- The extent of choice to be given to employees
- The funding of the programs
- The legal defensibility
- The eligibility gates, if at all (coverage of probationers or trainees)
- The coverage of dependents
- The differentiation between full-time/part-time employees

Fringe Benefit Tax

The concept of tax on fringe benefit was introduced in India in 2006. Currently, the rate is applicable at 30% of the value of fringe benefits. It includes:

(i) Any privilege, service, facility, or amenity provided by an employer directly or indirectly including reimbursements.

(ii) Any free or concessional ticket provided by the employer for private journeys of his employees or their family members.

(iii) Any contribution by the employer to an approved superannuation fund for employees.

(iv) Any specified security or sweat equity shares allotted/transferred, directly or indirectly by the employers free of cost or at concessional rate to his employees.

(v) Expenses incurred by the employer or payments made for purposes, namely, entertainment, provision of hospitality, conference, sales promotion including publicity, employee's welfare conveyance, tours and travel, use of hotel, boarding and lodging, and such others.

Some of the benefits not covered are:

1. Expenditure incurred on the distribution of free/concessional samples and payments to any person of repute for promoting the sale of goods or services of the business of the employer.
2. Free or subsidized transport or any such allowances provided by the employer to his employees for journeys from residence to the place of work.

Exhibit The Impact of Code of Wages 2019

In the new Labor Codes, enacted by the government in 2019, the term 'wage' has been made uniform in all the four codes. In the new definition, it includes all monetary payments and any benefits provided in kind except for the specified exclusions. It leaves out wage components like conveyance allowance, house rent allowance (HRA), amounts paid to defray special expenses (e.g., telephone reimbursements, etc.), and contribution to pension and Provident Fund (PF).

According to the code, the excluded wage elements must be capped at 50% of the total remuneration. This means that for the purpose of social security contributions such as PF, gratuity (accrual and payout), etc., at least 50% of the 'total remuneration' shall be considered. This 'total remuneration' includes wages (as defined in the paragraph above) plus specified exclusions (e.g., HRA, conveyance).

However, a part of HRA and bonus are non-taxable as per the existing rules. The non-taxable part will reduce significantly under the new code and will range between 20 and 25%. Due to increased basic salary, the taxable part of HRA will also rise, and hence tax on HRA will also rise.

Discussion Questions

1. Do a short research to list the action the employers need to take due to the above changes.

Source: The Code on Wages 2019: understanding the key changes. Dec 2019. https://economictimes.indiatimes.com/small-biz/legal/the-code-on-wages-2019-understanding-the-key-changes-to-wages.

10.10.5 Reward and Recognition (R&R)

Rewards and recognition (R&R) program of a company aims at motivating the employee for their good performance. Includes social and monetary recognition, while rewards provide monetary recognition only. The R&R programs yield many benefits in the form of: increased employee engagement, building of a performance culture, good employee retention, better teamwork and a sense of belonging among the employees. Results from a 2022 Gallup and Work human study found that when employee recognition hits the mark, 73% of employees are less likely to feel burned out and 56% less likely to look for new job opportunities. (https://www.peoplekeep.com/blog/what-are-employee).

Some examples of R&R are:

Rewards	Recognition
1. Financial-bonus, gift cards, stock options	1. Kudos
2. Non-financial time off, flexitime	2. Certificate of appreciation
3. Experiences- nomination for seminar	3. Leader board
4. Company events- group cooking, sports	4. Lunch with the CEO
5. Personalized gifts	5. Company retreats
	6. Recognition wall
	7. Social media features
	8. Shout out

In designing an employee R&R program, due care should be taken to ensure that employees are recognized frequently, recognition is linked to specific actions, and feedbacks are sought and acted upon.

Reflection Point

Do reward and recognition programs really matter? According to Daniel Pink, the author of Drive external rewards not only narrow our focus, it causes functional fixedness, which in turn stifles creativity. Instead, humans are most strongly motivated by three innate psychological needs – competence, autonomy, and relatedness.

Discussion Question

1. What are the different ways in which companies can embed the above insight in their Reward and recognition program?

Flexible Benefit Programs

Flexible benefits schemes or 'cafeteria benefits'/'flex plans' provide the employees choices to personalize their pay and benefits package in line with their personal needs. Usually, in such plans/ schemes, employees retain their existing salary, while varying the mix of various benefits they receive or adjust their salary up or down by taking fewer or more benefits, respectively. Each employee is allotted a budget to spend on his/ her benefits of choice subject to a maximum cost for each benefit and mandatory inclusion of certain essential items such as social security and employee compensation. The flexibility also includes mid-course change of plans if personal circumstances change.

Some of the advantages of flexible benefits plans are: freedom of choice to suit personal needs, increased involvement leading to better understanding of benefits, and cost containment for benefits.

The negative consequences include employee vulnerability to bad choices and additional cost of administration.

Steps in implementing a flexible benefit program:

1. Setting up a menu of benefits options
2. Working out the cash value for each option
3. Estimate the likely take-up of specific benefit

4. Present the choice of benefits to employees
5. Fix dates for next review

Flextime, job sharing, and telecommuting are some of the other examples of flexible benefit programs.

Closing Case The Chalk Circle of Fifty Grand

Sudhir Prakash, the Chief Finance Manager, India Petroleum Co, had just come back from his meeting with the Corporate Finance. It was 5:30 pm. The office was deserted, with most of the staff having departed for home. Sudhir was surprised to find Shantanu Poddar, the young chartered accountant, waiting outside his room.

'All well? Anything urgent, Shantanu?' he asked. Shantanu had joined his department about three months back, after his initial training at the corporate learning center. He was a bright, performing employee, very keen on learning, and a well-accepted team player.

Shantanu smiled and said, 'Everything fine. I wanted to see you on something personal.' As he followed Prakash into the room, Shantanu opened the envelope that he was holding and gave him a sheet of paper. Prakash took a look. It was his resignation letter. Shantanu looked embarrassed and explained, 'I am sorry, having to resign. I enjoyed working here. I also respect you for your guidance. I wanted to tell you personally before submitting it.' Prakash did not melt with his praise. He was disappointed and a little clueless. He believed that this was a good organization for CAs. They progressed on fast tracks, rotated well on a variety of work profiles, worked with professionals and the current chairman also started his career here as a finance officer.

Shantanu proved a hard nut to crack why he was resigning. It is not 'better career prospects,' he clarified. It was a personal decision to be near his mother at Bangalore, who was getting old. He did not reveal where he was joining. Prakash immediately knew that the story about his mother was a cover-up. He was very well aware that Shantanu's widowed mother, though aged, was very actively engaged with NGO work at Bangalore and, therefore, did not seek him to be around, at least for now. Shantanu, there-fore, had some other undisclosed reason for leaving. After some patient prodding, Shantanu revealed the real reason.

Shantanu was recruited along with two other rank holders from the batch of 2014 of chartered accountants. At the time of interview, the total package projected was 7 lakhs, translating to 50k+ per month. With his first month's salary Shantanu realized that the actual salary came to around 45k, not more. He asked the HR about it and was told that 7 lakhs was the COC (cost to the company, which included contribution for PF, gratuity, and medical expenses among other items). It was another matter that some of the expenses included in the COC were hypothetical, and not real, and this point was not clarified by the recruitment team amply at the time of the offer. 'You see, sir, in my batch, 50k is the figure that all CA rank holders have asked for and got, and 45k is certainly below par, unfair and unacceptable. Since these are fixed in this organization, and cannot be renegotiated, I have no choice but to quit.' He said it with finality. All my efforts to explain that at Indian Petro the hidden benefits (the club, the subsidies in canteen, travel, and so on) make it much more than 50k, floundered against the imaginary wall of 50k, and I had to shake his hands at the end, and wish him all the best for future.

Discussion Question

1. What does the case reveal about the importance of perceived fairness in compensation structuringin an organization?

SUMMARY

'Compensation' has been traditionally considered as a key factor in driving, motivating, and rewarding employees. Frederick Taylor, the pioneer of concepts of scientific management believed that economic gain was the primary thing that motivated everyone. Traditional view of management held that work is inherently unpleasant for people and, therefore, money that they earn is more important to employees than the nature of job they are performing. Putting it differently, employees could be expected to perform any kind of work, if they were compensated adequately.

Under pressure in the war for talent, the conventional concept of compensation has been widened to include various financial, non-financial, and psychological elements relevant for talent management. Total compensation includes base pay, augmented pay (such as overtime), indirect pay (benefits), works-pay (such as subsidized equipment and uniforms), perks-pay, that is, special benefits (accessories to employee discounts on company products), opportunity for advancement and increased responsibility, opportunity for growth, both through on-the-job training and through offsite training and degree attainment, psychic income, the emotional enhancements provided by the job itself and the setting, quality of life, that is, opportunity to express other important aspects of life (location close to home, flextime, onsite child care, ski to work, or whatever), and any unique element that an employee wants that the workplace can facilitate.

A combination of external and internal factors can influence, directly or indirectly, the rates at which employees are paid. The major external factors that influence wage rates include labor market conditions, area wage rates, cost of living, legal requirements, and collective bargaining if the employer is unionized. The internal factors include valuation of the job, the employee's perceived worth, the compensation philosophy, and the employer's capacity to pay. An effective compensation system embeds the principles of equity in the various stages of its design. The test of a model compensation system is in being perceived by employees as fair and equitable, comparable to current rates in the market, correctly based, motivating, and easily comprehensible.

There are several steps to designing a pay structure. It includes job analysis, job evaluation, market survey, creation of pay structure, and grades and pay ranges.

Employee benefits (also covering fringe benefits, perquisites, or perks) constitute the indirect financial and non-financial remuneration, which employees are eligible to receive in addition to their normal wages or salaries, by virtue of being employed. Benefits include housing accommodation, accident insurance, retirement benefits, crèche, scholarships, educational assistance, various kinds of leave, leave fare assistance, social security, profit sharing, and such specialized benefits. An important current trend in employee benefit is flexible benefits schemes or 'cafeteria benefits'/'flex plans,' which provide the employees choices to personalize their pay and benefits package in line with their personal needs. Usually, in such plans/schemes, employees retain their existing salary, while varying the mix of various benefits they receive or adjust their salary up or down by taking fewer or more benefits, respectively.

Short-answer Questions

1. Describe two issues with the traditional compensation concept that led to the emergence of total rewards.
2. Mention two non-financial elements of the concept of total rewards.
3. Mention two components of variable pay.
4. Define equity.
5. How does labor market condition impact compensation?
6. Explain job analysis and its importance.
7. Mention two advantages of point method.
8. What is rate range?
9. Narrate the steps in setting up flexible benefit system.
10. What are the employee factors influencing benefits?

Discussion Questions

1. It is generally believed that formal job evaluation systems are rarely adapted in a traditional organization in India. What is your view? What could be the reason(s) of avoidance of the job-evaluation procedures?
2. What are the various ways the total reward components could be monetized to arrive at a total cost to the company?
3. What different strategy should be adopted to design incentive systems for the executives and the unionized categories of employees?
4. What are the different ways a BPO could balance individual incentive for superior performance with team incentives? What are the costs of a lopsided incentive scheme?

CHAPTER 11

Compensation for Special Groups

LEARNING OBJECTIVES

After completing this chapter, the student will be able to:

- Differentiate the compensation needs of different special groups
- Present the challenges in executive compensation
- Offer some perspectives to the issues of executive compensation
- Analyze the different architectures for building compensation strategies for sales personnel
- Explain the future trends in CEO compensation

Opening Case A Story of Unequals

Two long-lost friends met at the airport suddenly. They hugged each other, backslapped a lot, went down the memory lane over cups of Cappuccino, and eventually exchanged notes about the tracks covered by them since they lost contact.

Robin and Kushal did their graduation in commerce together. Robin secured a rank in the chartered accountant's exams. Kushal cleared in the third attempt. Both served their articleship in a small firm at Dalhousie Square, Kolkata. Kushal then cracked the probationary officer exam for a well-known bank. After that, they lost touch.

About a month after their chance encounter, a wedding card arrived at Kushal's flat at Nepean Sea Road. A stunningly beautiful and obviously expensive wedding card accompanied by a gift packet bearing the logo of a well-known boutique shop with expensive gifts and a box of sweets. It was a marriage invitation for Robin's daughter to be held at some luxury resort in the Himalayas, off Kufri, Shimla.

Kushal was thrilled with the prospect of meeting his old friend again and the possibility of meeting some more of the common acquaintances and friends at the same venue. Suneira, Kushal's wife, took in the content of the card and coldly announced that she would not like to attend the ceremony. Taken aback, when Kushal pressed for her rationale, she mentioned that they are 'upper class,' 'rich,' 'rolling in money,' and she knows their types. Their women, she continued, would all be showing off their diamonds and emeralds, and Gucci and Versace's, arriving and exiting in their latest BMWs, and talking about holidaying in Sicily. Kushal was aghast. He tried to reason with his wife. Both of us are CEOs of our companies, he said. 'I run a humongous public sector bank as the C&MD, and Robin is the CEO of a private sector petroleum company, and in fact my bank has five times more employees and ten times the PBT [profit before tax] of Robin's company.' But Suneira was adamant. She would not like to appear in an assembly of glitterati, dressed like a 'maid servant' and even talking like one. 'We are middle class. We do not belong to the set,' she said. She gave him the final punch line: 'You may be friends and both may be CEOs. But you are PSU and he is private sector. We are divided by the pay packets that both of you bring home.'

Suddenly, the truth flashed across his mind. Yes. He drew a salary of 3 lakhs a month, and Robin took home a neat ₹3 crore and hefty hidden benefits, with a provision of a golden parachute should he leave the organization. The world indeed is unequal.

11.1 INTRODUCTION

In the world of work, the rules of compensation are fairly linear. It starts with work content for a job being assessed; then the relative worth of each job is ascertained and priced. Formal processes such as job evaluations and compensation surveys are used to establish internal and external equity. At the end, the differences in performances account for differences in payouts. Different rules, however, are applied in case of special individuals or groups in all organizations, especially in hunting for talent at CXO levels. Infosys, for example, paid Vishal Sikka an astronomical compensation package, in a total departure from what its established norms set by the promoters. Reliance Industries follows a highly flexible compensation approach for those for hiring into the senior leadership group, in contrast to clearly structured broad bands and reward structures for rest of the levels. An experienced salesman of insurance policies in Bharti Axel, for example, can command a package of three times of those working in other areas in the organization with similar qualification, span of experience, and age. A perfumer can command a fancy salary in an FMCG specializing in personal care products.

There are of course some methods in the apparent chaos. Each organization has some special groups or individuals who are treated differently from the standard compensation programs on account of their unique nature of work and competencies, which are sometimes of strategic importance to the organization. When an oil downstream company, seeking to diversify into upstream business (oil exploration), requires experienced geologists for helping it to prepare bids for an oil block in Venezuela, the compensation package has to be custom-made to attract the target individuals. There are distinct competitive advantages in acquiring and retaining people of such competencies. Similarly, there are special groups in organizations warranting tailor-made compensation structure. For such groups, there seems to be some 'built-in conflict, conflict that arises because different factions place incompatible demands on members of the group.'[1] Milkovich et al. list the special groups as comprising the following: the supervisors, the top management, the board of directors, the sales representatives, the professionals, and the contingent employees (Table 11.1).

[1] George T. Milkovich, Jerry M. Newman and C. S. Venkata Ratnam, Compensation (New Delhi: Tata McGraw-Hill, 2009).

Table 11.1 Compensation strategy variance in different special groups

Special group	Compensation strategy
Shop-floor supervisor	• Between 5% and 30% differential in the base pay with the top earning workmen supervised by them.
	• Variable pay on target achievement.
Top executives	• Link pay to performance standards. Stock options.
	• Expense accounts and benefits.
	• Perks—luxury office, dining room, special parking, club membership, reimbursement of expenses on transportation.
	• Personal perks—low cost loans, counseling, free home repairs, expenses for vacation homes.
	• Monitoring of benefits
	o Tally sheets—tally up the value of base salary, incentives, benefits and perks, even the current value of stock options.
	o Government regulations.
Scientists and engineers in hi-tech industries	• Create dual career ladder system: (technical and managerial) to deal with technical obsolescence and career plateauing.
	• Link with market price. Follow maturity curve (which reflect the relationship between the scientist/engineer compensation and years of experience in the market).
	• Relatively higher base pay and small percentage of variable pay.
Sales personnel	• Large component of pay being incentive based, in some cases even 40% because of unsupervised nature of their work.

Source: Michael Armstrong, *Armstrong's Handbook of Reward Management* Practice (London: Kogan Page, 2010).

11.2 THE SUPERVISORS

This group of employees acts as the buffer between the leadership and the ranks and absorbs pressures from both. It needs to balance the pulls of implementing the organization's business plans with the pushes for keeping the employees happy, motivated, and productive. This group typically is the nowhere group—belonging neither to the unionized, non-exempt cadre, nor to the managerial or exempt cadre. The compensation plan for such a group needs to be alluring enough for a unionized employee to seek promotion. In the conventional approach, however, the job valuation scores for this role may not fully reflect the rigors of supervision, leading to a lower score than some of the technical worker roles. Sometimes there are instances where the new supervisor draws less salary than his erstwhile in the worker role. In a PSU bank, for example, it is not unusual for a clerical employee to refuse promotions to the supervisory cadre because the total rewards package is not attractive enough.

There are several ways organizations get around the challenges of formulating effective compensation strategy for this special group: by creating a separate grade and scale (a practice used by Indian Oil Corporation Ltd (IOCL), a large PSU behemoth, and several old traditional private sector units such as Tata Steel, L&T, and others). Metaphorically, this grade is sometimes referred as the '0' Grade (as in IOCL). The two other ways to compensate the supervisors is by paying incentive or by paying for the excess hours at twice the rate.

11.3 THE TOP EXECUTIVES

'Infosys CEO Vishal Sikka has taken home ₹49 crore (US$7.45 million) salary in 2015–2016, according to the company's annual report. This includes basic salary variable pay of US$4.33 million and RSUs (restricted stock units) granted to him that is valued at US$2 million.'[2] It has become quite common for important business magazines to publish gist of compensation survey reports by influential compensation consultant firms about the state of executive compensation and the CEO pay. The information is received with renewed debates, the core issue being 'Do they really deserve so much?'

For Vishal Sikka, the positives are: reducing the attrition rate, winning more business from the existing clients, restoring the morale of the employees, and winning the customer confidence.

11.3.1 Disparity Ratio

A critical part of the debate is also the widening chasm between the CEO's pay and the median remuneration of employees (MRE). As per the annual report of Infosys, the ratio between Sikka's salary and MRE stands at a grand 935. It is also reported that the company's MRE excluding that of whole-time directors (WTDs) in 2016 stood at ₹520,946, higher by 6.4% from 2015 level of ₹489,468. Including WTDs, the MRE stands at ₹5 and ₹20,964 in 2016.The aggregate remuneration of employees (excluding WTDs) grew by 14.4% for the company and for WTDs and other KMPs the rise was 11.5% over the previous fiscal. For Vishal Sikka, the salary growth over 2015 was a staggering 752%.

11.4 THE GROWTH IN EXECUTIVE COMPENSATION

The spurt in the executive pay packages has generally been attributed to the following factors:

1. **Agency theory** The belief that the owners can only claim loyalty from the paid managers by providing adequate financial incentives, so that they are motivated enough to perform in order to augment the wealth of the owners.
2. **Tournament theory** The belief that the compensation package of the executive is a trophy that needs to be won by competing in performance. According to this view, like in sports, 'what matters for winning is not the absolute level of performance, but how well one does in relation to the other competitors.'[3]
3. **Star culture** The emergence of the CEO as the celebrity.[4]
4. The sharing of the CEO compensation due to regulatory requirements goads the CEOs to compare salaries and demand equity.
5. The greater pressure and accountability of the CEO for organizational performance.
6. The talent scarcity and the 'war for talent.'
7. The approach and mindset of remuneration committees. It has become an accepted convention to constitute committees to set policy frameworks for executive compensation. It is claimed

[2] Firstpost, 'Infosys CEO Vishal Sikka Rakes in ₹49 cr Salary in FY16: Here's Why It Is Justified,' May 21, 2016. Available at: http://www.firstpost.com/business/infosys-vishal-sikka-ceo-salary-mre-wtds-attrition-2790678.html (accessed on December 7, 2017).

[3] Martin J. Conyon and Dennis Leech, 'Top Pay, Company Performance and Corporate Governance,' *Oxford Bulletin of Economics and Statistics* 56, no. 3 (1994): 229–247.

[4] Armstrong, *Armstrong's Handbook of Reward Management Practice.*

that the consultants who were appointed to advise the committees were engaged in 'ratcheting up of top pay' and driving the reward levels to the top quartile of the comparison group.[5]

11.4.1 The Variance in CEO Compensation

Mr Sridhar Ganesan, Rewards Practice Leader, Hay Group, attributes the variance in CEO pay to what he terms as four potential context clusters—'the Carers, the Contractors, the Cultivators, and the Fundamentalists.'[6] The Carers have been defined as organizations that operate in an environment of social capitalism, the Contractors endeavor to squeeze business value from contracts and closing them, in case it does not work; the Cultivators are adept at constructing a compelling story and enrolling investors and employees with their risk-taking ability, and the last one, the Fundamentalists thrive on an ambience of continuous innovation without 'compromising on the company's identity and cultural strengths.'

Mr Ganesan refers to the Tata Group as a 'carer'—'where the organization uses social and environmental consciousness to create a powerful employee and customer brand,' the CEO compensation package mirroring the organization's values. In contrast, the current CEOs of online portals such as Flipkart and Jabong mark the 'cultivator' approach, 'reflecting dynamism and highly leveraged payout norms.'

11.4.2 The Executive Compensation Package

The constituents of executive pay are basic pay, bonuses (both long-term and short-term), share option schemes, performance share schemes, and so on. The benefit package includes pension scheme requiring a faster accrual rate than the normal pensions. The basic pay of the executives is fixed on the market trends, the negotiation process, and the views of the remuneration committee. The basic pay is crucial because both bonuses and share options are connected with the base pay (either as percentage or multiples of). Bonuses are a percentage of the base pay (up to around 70%), usually linked to the profits and subject to a ceiling. The flip side of bonuses is that it occasionally drives efforts to manipulate the profits for hiking share price and encourages short-term performance growths, in preference to the long-term investment of efforts. Bonuses can be short-term or long-term and sometimes are deferred over more than a year.

Share options, which provide the executives the facility of purchasing a block of shares at a fixed price, are based on the assumption that the executive will be motivated to boost the performance in order to cash in the consequent hike in share prices. The critics, however, indicate that the enormous wealth the executives collect by offloading the shares at a suitable time is vastly disproportionate to the effort of the executives. The intended objective of bonding the executives' interests with those of the shareholders, therefore, remains a myth, according to the detractors of share options. According to Hay Group Compensation Report 2012–2013 for top executives, (covering 158 organizations across auto, chemicals, basic resources, oil and gas, FMCG, retail, construction and materials, telecommunication, utilities, industrial goods, and transportation sectors), there is a bias for leveraged pay or pay for performance for executive pay—for the top team, including the CEO. The report pegs performance incentives at around 30 to 44% of the overall compensation mix, for the CEO and the top team.

---

5 S. J. Perkins and C. Hendry, 'Ordering Top Pay: Interpreting the Signals,' *Journal of Management Studies* 42, no. 7 (2005): 1443–1468.

6 R. Srinivasan, 'Buck Stops at the Top,' *Business Line*, Chennai, December 20, 2012.

Exhibit FMCG, IT, ITeS Take Lead in CEO Compensation

Compensation levels for CEOs show a wide variance, especially in large companies, according to the fifth edition of the Aon Hewitt Executive Compensation Study 2014–2015. According to the survey, total compensa tion for CEOs in companies in the ₹5000 crore to ₹10,000 crore revenue range has a median of ₹5 crore and goes up to ₹9.2 crore. For companies in the ₹10,000–30,000 crore revenue range, CEO compensation is at ₹6.1 crore at median levels and goes as high as ₹9.6 crore.

The survey covered 319 participants across industry clusters. FMCG and IT/ITeS take a lead in CEO compensation as compared to other industries. While the FMCG sector has traditionally been at the higher end, CEO compensation in IT/ITeS also reflects the pay philosophy adopted by Indian companies listed in countries such as the USA. These companies have become relatively aggressive on long-term incentives (LTIs) (share-based compensation) as compared to other Indian organizations.

'Three important factors that will impact executive pay in India are: increased regulatory requirements and disclosures, growing shareholder activism and opportunity to create wealth. All these will force executive compensation to move towards high long-term pay linking the executives' rewards with shareholder returns and long-term health of an organization,' says Anubhav Gupta, Solution Lead, Executive Compensation, Aon Hewitt India.

Source: Sreeradha Basu, 'FMCG, IT, ITeS Take Lead in CEO Compensation: Survey,' *Economic Times*, March 11, 2015.

11.5 DETERMINANTS OF EXECUTIVE COMPENSATION

All organizations are interested in acquiring and keeping their important employees, but the task poses some serious difficulties, given the intense competitiveness in the talent market. The high performers are spoilt for choices. The design of compensation packages have, therefore, assumed strategic importance for luring targeted talent to accept a job in the organization. Compensations, thus, largely dictate the attitude, engagement, and performance of the employee in the organization.

There are several factors that are believed to influence the compensation levels of the CEOs.

11.5.1 Personal Attributes

Factors such as age, experience, tenure, and skills of an employee, which constitute human capital, are considered to be key factors in determining CEO compensation. It is argued that investments in acquiring job relevant skills should get the managers an edge in claiming higher differential rewards. According to Hambrick and Snow,[7] functional expertise/background and prior experience had a positive relationship with the compensation.

11.5.2 Firm Size

The size of the firm is another factor that has been found to be a determinant of executive compensation. In what is described as the sales maximization hypothesis, it is reasoned in big organizations that executives endeavor to maximize sales, in preference for profit or shareholders' income. In an ideal competitive condition in the managerial job market, the CEO is logically expected to earn a marginal

[7] D. C. Hambrick and C. C. Snow, 'Strategic Reward Systems,' in *Organization Design and Human Resource Management*, ed. C. C. Snow (Greenwich, CT: JAI Press, 1989), 333–367.

revenue product. The marginal revenue product is the incremental profit that the CEO earns for the company by virtue of better skills and competencies. In a small firm, the volume of sales will be comparatively lower than in a large firm, and therefore, no matter how capable the CEO is, the total profit is unlikely to show a substantial leap. In comparison, a large firm provides a platform where a marginal rise in sales volume can lead to a big leap in profits on account of magnitude of numbers of units sold. As a result CEOs in larger organizations command better compensation as the firms have a higher capacity to pay their CEOs. According to Agarwal,[8] the complexity of structures of big firms also warrants superior compensation package to the CEOs.

11.5.3 Managerial Discretions

Performance-based pay (bonuses, stock options) would be effective if managerial discretion is high since high managerial discretion means many options available for decision-making (few constraints), behavior and decisions are difficult to pre-determine, impact of their decisions is unobservable or ambiguous, and firm's performance is volatile.[9] Complex/diverse business strategy and uncertain (dynamic) environment and firm diversification are some of the conditions in which the managerial discretion becomes necessary for deciding on CEO compensation. Some researchers indicated that in banking industry high managerial discretion (wholesale customer, foreign, international business, and so on) leads to the choice of performance-based compensation.[10]

11.5.4 Power of the CEO

Some researchers have concluded that the CEO can wield decisive power in influencing his compensation levels irrespective of the economic factors such as firm-specific factors, job, and so on.[11] There are various findings suggesting that the influence of CEO is derived from factors such as tenure, expertise and prestige, and equity ownership. It has been observed that although the CEO has primary duty to safeguard the interest of shareholders, there is a tendency to prefer compliant directors. A trend has also been reported that directors, who are CEOs in other firms, agree with proposal for high compensation level of CEO. The constitution of the board offers an opportunity to leverage professional and demographic heterogeneity in the board for better compensation decision (à la resource dependence theory). In actual practice, however, there is often the phenomenon of professional homogeneity, whereby directors come from the same demographic category having similar belief. Such homogeneity cramps the objective processing of data, because of the natural reluctance to since look for other alternatives. The prevalence of the phenomenon of 'group think' and a tendency for consensus limits critical thinking, and can prove to be a dysfunctional mode of group decision-making by resulting in poor data processing and poor decisions. Professional and demographic homogeneity inhibits the information flow and compensation fixed by them is not optimal for the firm. Similar group of people do not challenge each other's decisions.[12]

---

8 N. C. Agarwal, 'Determinants of Executive Compensation,' *Industrial Relations* 20, no. 1 (1981): 36–46.

9 Jatinder Kumar Jha and Sunil Maheshwari, 'Determinants of Executive Salary in a Competitive Market,' *The Indian Journal of Industrial Relations* 50, no. 4 (April 2015): 575–587.

10 M. L. Magnan and S. Stonge, 'Bank Performance and Executive Compensation: A Managerial Discretion Perspective,' *Strategic Management Journal* 18, no. 7 (1997): 573–581.

11 I. E. Brick, O. Palmon, and J. K. Wald, 'CEO Compensation, Director Compensation, and Firm Performance: Evidence of Cronyism V,' *Journal of Corporate Finance* 12, no. 3 (2006): 403–423.

12 M. E. Turner and A. R. Pratkanis, 'Twenty-five Years of Groupthink Theory and Research: Lessons from the Evaluation of a Theory,' *Organizational Behavior and Human Decision Processes* 73, no. 2–3 (1998): 105–115.

11.5.5 Diversification of Firm Business

Exploring the nexus between CEO compensation and firm diversification over a period of 5 years (1985– 1990), two researchers found that the CEO of a firm with two lines of business averaged 13% more in salary and bonus than the CEO of a similar sized but undiversified firm, ceteris paribus. Two explanations were explored for this disparity: the match of higher ability CEOs with firms that are more difficult to manage, and the association of diversification with CEO entrenchment. The data are more consistent with ability matching: the premium is invariant to CEO tenure, and incumbents who diversify their firms earn less than newly hired CEOs at already diversified firms.[13]

It has also been reported by Deckop[14] that higher international diversification, accounting earnings, investment opportunities, and firm size positively influence the CEO compensation. With diversification, monitoring of executives becomes a costly affair, hence agency cost increases. With the diversification of business, complexity in managing the business increases.[15] With increase in the size of firm, responsibility of CEOs increases and requires greater ability and knowledge to manage the complex firms, so they are paid higher compensation for their efforts.[16,17] Sales volume[18] and total sales are two ways to measure firm size. International diversification, firm size, and accounting earnings are positively related to CEO compensation. Large-sized firm has more international investment opportunities and this international diversification leads to firm profits and CEOs are being paid higher. Staying on top of what is new in executive pay is a challenge even for the most dedicated experts. It is particularly daunting for those broad-based HR practitioners who do not focus on executive pay regularly. But the need for a broader understanding of the key terms and concepts surrounding executive compensation has never been more acute, as compensation committees look to develop stronger connections between HR programs for the top team and for the overall employee population.

11.6 ISSUES IN EXECUTIVE COMPENSATION

11.6.1 Governance

Executive pay decisions entail maintaining a delicate balance of the divergent interests of multiple stakeholders, some of whom are visible and some not so visible—the shareholders, board members, executives, and the public. These decisions are subjected to unparalleled scrutiny, sometimes rocking even the board. The complexities in such decisions arise from the fact that executive pay has dimensions beyond just pay; they also include aspects of succession planning and leadership pipeline. Often the compensation committees are assigned the responsibility for preparing roadmaps for leadership succession. This explains the growing immersion of the boards in the process of talent management agenda of the organizations. The HR function in the organization is expected to anticipate enquiries

---

13 N. Rose and A. Shepard, 'Firm Diversification and CEO Compensation,' *Rand Journal of Economics* 28, no. 3 (Autumn 1997): 489–514.

14 J. R. Deckop, 'Determinants of Chief Executive Officer Compensation,' *Industrial and Labor Relations Review* 41, no. 2 (1998): 215–226.

15 Duru and Reeb. 'Geographic and Industrial Corporate Diversification: The Level and Structure of Executive Compensation,' *Journal of Accounting, Auditing & Finance,* 17 no. 1 (Winter 2002).

16 J. Gaver, K. Gaver and J. R. Austin, 'Additional Evidence on Bonus Plans and Income Management'. *Journal of Accounting and Economics*, 19, no. 1 (1995):3–28.

17 Rosen, 'Authority, Control and the Distribution of Earnings'. *Bell Journal of Economics*, 13 (1982): 311–323.

18 Newman, H. A., and Bannister, J. W., 'Cross-sectional Difference in Corporate Compensation Structure'. *Journal of Managerial Issues*, 10 (1998): 223–239.

from the board about its leadership development strategy and thus proactively keep data in readiness about the critical leadership development programs and the succession plans to senior leadership positions.

11.6.2 Shareholders–Say on Pay

'Say on pay,' a term used in corporate law, indicates the right of shareholders to vote on the pay of executives in the company. It is in the same space as the agency theory that presumes that executives will tend to overpay themselves because, directly or indirectly, they can determine their own pay as a matter of general management power. The board, and the directors being part of it, has a fiduciary responsibility to safeguard the interests of the company. There is a growing trend of executive compensation decision being based on recommendation of a compensation committee, constituted with board members. 'Say on pay' reforms are claimed to cement the bond between the board of directors and shareholders, making sure of performance of the fiduciary duty by the board members. Critics, however, question the wisdom in 'say on pay' initiatives on the ground that it diminishes the authority of the board of directors.

The United Kingdom spearheaded the trend in regulatory stipulation that shareholders be allowed a say on executive pay in the form of a 'non-binding,' or advisory vote. In the UK, Section 439 of the Companies Act 2006 mandates a vote on director pay at the yearly accounts meeting. Directors

Exhibit Incidents at Large UK Companies in Which Shareholders Have 'Revolted' Against the Size of Pay Awards Given to Board Members, Since the 'Say on Pay' Legislation was Introduced

- Vodafone shareholders voted 10% against and 30% in abstention from £13m in shares for CEO Sir Chris Gent. (July 2001)
- Royal and Sun Alliance shareholders voted 28% against a £250,000 retention bonus for CFO Julian Hance and £1.44m severance pay for CEO Bob Mendelsohn. The share price had just dropped. (May 2003)
- GlaxoSmithKline shareholders voted 50.72% (advisory) against a £22m bonus salary and stock severance package for CEO Jean-Pierre Garnier. Chairman Sir Christopher Hogg said it was just the difference in culture to the USA that was holding Britain back and they should accept it. The TUC had been lobbying pension funds. (May 2003)
- ITV shareholders were 40% against a £15m (£1.8m cash, rest shares) payoff to Chairman Michael Green. It was justified on the basis that he would have taken legal action were it not paid, because he was removed prior to the Carlton–Granada merger.
- Berkley Managing Director and founder of the property company had 47% of shareholders vote against his £1.2m (out of a total £4.7m package) under a an LTI scheme that he had not actually belonged to. (August 2003)
- Unilever former chairman Niall Fitzgerald got £1.2m after profits fell. (April 2005)
- Tesco shareholders voted 15% against an £11.5m bonus on Sir Terry Leahy's salary as CEO. It was linked to the success of the firm's Fresh & Easy chain in the USA. The Association of British Insurers and PIRC were against. (June 2007)

Source: Neelam Verjee and Steve Hawkes, 'Shareholder Revolt over Planned £11.5m Payout for Tesco Chief,' *The Times*, June 30, 2007.

are expected to have disclosed their remuneration package in a 'Remuneration Report' (Section 420). Failure to do this leads to fines. Pay increases for top executives in the United States have also slowed in response to shareholder pressure, although they still gained by 14% in 2011. 'High pay for success is perfectly acceptable, it is high pay for failure that needs to be addressed,' said Mark Boleat, Policy Chairman at the City of London Corporation, which promotes the capital's financial sector.[19]

11.6.3 Objectivity of the Compensation Consultant

In the matter of selecting consultants for working on compensation proposals, the companies are under pressure to use extreme caution and discretion. In light of stepped-up oversight under financial regulatory reform, boards and compensation committees no longer can afford to retain executive pay consultants that earn significant streams of revenue doing other work for the company, giving the appearance of a conflict of interest.[20]

The current reality is that consulting relationships could be firmly entrenched in an organization, but use of the services by the tried and tested consulting firms for providing executive compensation pay services to the board may become a harder option.

11.6.4 Aligning LTI Awards to Performance

There is a growing preference of companies to link the LTI awards of the executives to performance-vested share plans. Unlike stock options or restricted stock plans, these programs typically vest in accordance with three-year company-wide performance and might not vest at all. The communication of this kind of performance equity programs poses certain challenges to HR professionals, who might find it far more difficult to explain than the programs on stock option. Due care is therefore required to set up an appropriate communications infrastructure capable of handling the added complexity of these programs and to explore ways and means to create a line of sight between employee behavior and long-term plan payouts.

11.6.5 Peer Groups

In formulating the executive compensation packages, boards show a preference to compare the pay of the executives at other enterprises in similar industries and of similar size and complexity called as peer groups. A peer group indicates a list of organizations that is used by the compensation committee to benchmark on the basis of information collected on the executive pay practices and policies. In what is described as 'competitive benchmarking,' pay levels are typically set at either the 50th, 75th, or 90th percentile. The logic of this exercise is that it provides an effective gauge of 'market wages' that are necessary for talent retention. According to a report by *Wall Street Journal* 's Maxwell Murphy,[21] 96% of Standard & Poor (S&P) 500 companies in USA disclosed in their 2015 proxy statements that they used a peer group to gauge executive pay. Generally, peer groups used for benchmarking are arranged to reflect the target company in some way. Peers usually include close competitors, companies of a

---

[19] Paul Klein, 'Can Say on Pay Increase Social Responsibility?' *Forbes*, July 3, 2012.

[20] David Wise, Shawn Hamilton, and Irv Becker, '10 Executive Comp Issues for Aligning Pay Issues,' July 28, 2010. Available at: https://www.shrm.org/resourcesandtools/hr-topics/compensation/pages/alignpay.aspx (accessed on November 15, 2017).

[21] Mercedes Erickson, 'Peer Benchmarking and Trends in Executive Compensation,' Audit Analytics, November 19, 2015. Available at: http://www.auditanalytics.com/blog/peer-benchmarking-and-trends-in-executive-compensation/ (accessed on November 20, 2017).

similar size and stature, and regional companies. But for whatever reason, the names of a handful of companies seem to pop up over and over again. 3M, Honeywell, and Eaton are cited as a peer by a surprising number of companies. Their popularity, according to research firm Equilar, is largely attributed to their 'breadth of operations or easily comparable company size.'

3M is known to use the following factors to select its compensation peer group:

- The companies regularly tracked by the same market (investment peers).
- The companies having identical commercial and compensation models, market capitalization (based on an eight-quarter rolling average), and annual revenues.

Interestingly, the aforementioned data indicates that the yardsticks used for peer selection goes beyond pure financial metrics such as market capitalization or revenue, but also covers 'investment peers' and companies with a similar business and pay model.

The opponents to the aforementioned practice alleged that this conception of the peer group or a pay market was created purely by 'happenstance and based upon flawed assumptions. In applying the practices uniformly across companies, there is a serious possibility of design flaws adversely influencing the level of executive pay. 'It has been observed in both the academic and professional communities that the practice of targeting the pay of executives to median or higher levels of the competitive benchmark will naturally create an upward bias and movement in total compensation amounts.'[22] The critics claim that regardless of the fact of this escalation being dramatic or merely incremental, this practice of uniform application of implementing compensation practices of a comparison group has resulted in a wide chasm between the compensation levels of the CEOs and what is fair and appropriate to the companies they run.

Another significant aspect related to the executive pay is the compensation structure of the CEO, which has a domino effect on the incentive structure across the hierarchy of employees. Fattened pay packet comes with a cost far bigger than what goes to the pocket of the CEO. There is thus a case made for reducing the focus on peer comparison and benchmarking. The essence of this argument is: (a) Theories of optimal market-based contracting are misguided in that they are predicated upon the chimerical notion of vigorous and competitive markets for transferable executive talent; (b) that even boards comprising only the most faithful fiduciaries of shareholder interests will fail to reach an agreeable resolution to the compensation conundrum because of the unfounded reliance on the structurally malignant and unnecessary process of peer benchmarking; and (c) that the solution lies in avoiding the mechanistic and arbitrary application of peer group data in arriving at executive compensation levels. There is an advocacy for independent and shareholder-conscious compensation committees and internally created standards of pay based on the individual nature of the organization concerned, its particular competitive environment, and its internal dynamics.[23]

11.6.6 Relative Performance

Considering that precise assessment of the worth of the executive contribution and the formulation of suitable compensation contracts is a controversial issue and also the potential high cost of directly supervising executives, there is a practice of finding the value of the executives indirectly, through

22 Charles M. Elson and Craig K. Ferrere, 'Executive Superstars, Peer Groups and Overcompensation: Cause, Effect and Solution' (Paper, Alfred Lerner College of Business and Economics, University of Delaware, Newark, DE). Available at: http://tcbblogs.org/ public_html/wp-content/uploads/Elson_Ferrere_Paper.pdf (accessed on November 15, 2017).

23 Ibid.

relative performance evaluation (RPE). Relative performance refers to team-based goal-setting on performance-based incentives that are targeted toward outperforming peers rather than on absolute goals. In an uncertain business environment, many companies that cannot predict their absolute results are forced to turn to benchmarking their performance against other companies. The performance data captures a company's output level and return level; it is therefore considered to be reliable under modern accounting and auditing systems. RPE theory assumes that companies inevitably face industry-level or macro-level external risk (common risk), and an optimal compensation contract that eliminates these common risks will be more efficient.

It can, however, be argued that company performance is not necessarily the result of the executives' efforts, the company being an open system, influenced by a myriad external factors unconnected with the endeavors of the executives. Besides, RPE theory does not produce consistent empirical results. For example, Antle and Smith[24] have found no support in favor of this theory; Janakiraman and others[25] find only weak support.

11.6.7 Clawbacks

A clawback or clawback provision is a special clause in employment contracts, by which money already paid must be paid back under certain conditions. It refers to recoupment of previously earned incentive pay in the event of new information about performance. The provision enables the employer or trustee to put a lid on bonuses, compensation, or other remuneration in case of ruinous shifts in the fortune of the business, or an economic crisis like the one witnessed in the first decade of the millennium.

To illustrate the system, in case an executive's bonuses are, in the clawback provision, linked specifically to the performance of the financial product(s) the executive may have conceived and/or sold in expectation of a certain level of return, if the expected return is realized, the executive keeps his bonus. In case of default in meeting the expected return, even if much later than the launch of the product, the bonus is liable to be revoked or reclaimed by the company.[26] It has, however, been found on the basis of research that managers who have inked clawback provisions in their employment contract frequently attempt to balance the risk of loss by negotiating higher base salary that is immune from clawback.[27]

It has been reported that Fortune 100 companies increasingly adapted the clawback provision from less than 3% to more than 80% during the five years between 2005 and 2010.[28] In the USA, the increasing trend for the provision has been attributed to the Sarbanes–Oxley Act of 2002, making it mandatory for US Securities and Exchange Commission (SEC) to pursue the repayment of incentive compensation from senior executives that are involved in a fraud. In the UK, according to a report

---

[24] Rick Antle and Abbie Smith, 'An Empirical Investigation of the Relative Performance Evaluation of Corporate Executives,' *Journal of Accounting Research* 24, no. 1 (Spring 1986): 1–39.

[25] S. Janakiraman, R. Lambert, and D. Larcker, 'An Empirical Evaluation of the Relative Performance Evaluation Hypothesis,' *Journal of Accounting Research*, 30, no. 1 (Spring 1992): 53–69.

[26] John Cassidy, 'What Good Is Wall Street? Much of What Investment Bankers Do Is Socially Worthless,' *The New Yorker*, November 29, 2010.

[27] Ed deHaan, Frank D. Hodge, and Terry J. Shevlin, 'Does Voluntary Adoption of a Clawback Provision Improve Financial Reporting Quality?' (Contemporary Accounting Research, April 2, 2012). Available at: https://papers.ssrn.com/sol3/papers. cfm?abstract_id=2049442 (accessed on November 15, 2017).

[28] 'Focus on Clawbacks,' *C-Suite Insight*, 2011. Available at: http://www.equilar.com/pdf/c-suite/CSuiteInsight (accessed on August 2, 2017).

from the *Financial Times*, more firms are putting in place provisions to claw back compensation from top executives whose performance falls below the expected standard.[29]

In India, while the quantum of executive compensation has progressed substantially, the emphasis on governance is reported to be lax. In a report, titled 'Navigating the Path to Maturity' by PwC India Executive Director (Consulting) Padmaja Alaganandan, it has been revealed that, among other items, the pay proportions of companies who are using 'claw back' condition is only up to 25%, and the use of performance-linked conditions, such as employee stock option, has also been found to be at less than the desired level.

On the flip side, in implementing the clawback provisions, the challenges include creating infrastructure to recover payments already made. Besides, since the focus is on employee behavior, clawbacks should also have be developed keeping in mind the particular internal and external environment of the organization and also linked with the key leadership and talent programs.

11.6.8 The Role of the Government

While there have been endless, unresolved debates whether government should rein in runaway executive compensation, questions have been raised whether government should also cap the salaries of movie stars, sportspersons, singers? At the same time, the government role in protecting the interests of the shareholders and the economy from a reckless incentive system cannot be denied. Government must create non-interfering regulations that will encourage responsible corporates to voluntarily provide greater share to the shareholders in executive compensation. The clawback system to recall bonuses resulting from incorrect reporting or outright fraud needs to be strengthened. It can also legislate on tax benefits for firms that voluntarily set reasonable executive compensation limits.[30]

11.7 THE FUTURE OF EXECUTIVE PAY IN INDIA

Executive compensation in India has gone through many changes in recent times. Organizations have largely embraced the system of compensation committees. Some of the factors influencing the compensation decision are the growing bias for pay for performance, the drift in the opinions of the shareholders, and the disparity ratio between the top executive and the lowest wage earner in an organization. There is also the pull for talent where the demand far outweighs the supply—all these function in the backdrop of growing executive expectations regarding compensation packages that present a prospect for wealth creation. Striking a balance among all these features will be necessary.

11.7.1 Pay for Performance Linkage

With the swelling of the pay package, compensation committees have a responsibility to establish linkage to performance stronger than before. Globally, the shareholder advisory bodies are demonstrating a growing trend to monitor the performance compensation alignment. Questions have been asked in the recent past on compensation being greater than performance in comparison to peer firms, hefty bonus payouts, and ad-hoc stock-based grants that have not been justified to shareholders.

The mandatory requirement under Companies Act to disclose performance in terms of change in price–earnings ratio and market capitalization may influence a new trend of designing pay programs

29 Kate Burgess, 'More Companies to Claw Back Executive Pay,' *Financial Times*, August 29, 2011.

30 Prabhudev Konana, 'The Executive Compensation Debate,' *The Hindu*, December 17, 2016.

based on these lag metrics. The report highlights the value of keeping an accent on not only outcomes, but also processes and the need to incentivize for strategy execution. It is hoped that effective incentive programs for top executives, including the CEOs, will emphasize both lag and lead measures. The idea is to see that value creation, in the form of increased market cap, occurs in a sustainable manner aided by strong fundamental performance of the company. This is particularly crucial in the context of the large quantum of variable pay (between 50% and 70% of total compensation) in large-cap firms. In a desired scenario, if the compensation structure is constructed in the proper manner, then it should tell the story of how the company has performed in long run.

11.7.2 Risk Mitigation

While the issue of risk mitigation (specially post the 2008–2009 crash) warranted by the rise in short- and LTIs has been addressed through deferrals and clawback provisions, the report recommends two simple measures for India Inc.: (a) formulating ownership guidelines, that will make it mandatory for executives to part own the company's equity within a specified timeframe, the rationale being that the executive team has skin in the game as globally the ownership requirements range from three to five times of a CEO's fixed pay; (b) creating holding guidelines, also called lock-in. This measure makes it mandatory that a certain percentage of the shares, acquired by exercise of options or through vesting of restricted or performance shares, has to be held for a specific time period during which they cannot be sold.

11.7.3 Long-term Incentives (LTIs)

The trend for LTIs will continue, with the reduction in emphasis on fixed pay, as the preference of both the executives (for better wealth creation opportunities) as also the shareholders (for better alignment with their interests). The choice of different kinds of LTI instruments, however, should be governed by the objective for which it is visualized. The report cited the case of some Western countries such as the USA, where the average number of LTI instruments used can be 2.4 compared to 1.4 in India. Stock options and performance shares are effective instruments, when the shareholder value creation is the primary driver of the executive compensation plan. On the other hand, restricted stock unit (RSU) is an effective tool for retention.

Exhibit As Companies Get Performance-driven, India Inc. CEOs Could Soon Lose Comfort of Fixed Pay

NEW DELHI: India Inc.'s big bosses are losing a compensation comfort they enjoyed vis-à-vis chief executives in other major economies—more than half of Indian CEOs' pay will soon be variable, linked to performance. This is a big change. Just five years ago, less than a third of Indian CEOs' pay was variable.

Data from a CEO compensation survey of 380 companies in India show that more than half of the CEO pay is tied to performance. This means that just about 50% or less of the CEO salary is fixed, and the remaining is performance linked and distributed in annual bonus and LTIs.

And the fixed pay component of CEOs is likely to shrink further.

If global compensation structures are any indication, CEO compensation in India will get increasingly geared towards results in the coming years. The executive compensation survey 2015–2016, shared exclusively with ET, was conducted by Aon Hewitt across eight industries. One of the leading factors for high percentage of pay for performance is pressure from shareholders, which has prompted companies to tie a greater percentage of their CEO compensation to outcomes and results.

'CEO compensation is outcome driven. Shareholders need to see there is connection between compensation and outcome. As CEO compensation increases so does percentage of performance-linked pay,' said Anandorup Ghose, partner, Aon Hewitt.

Fortune 250 companies have almost 70% allocation to LTIs, according to compensation experts. Globally, pay for performance can account up to 85% of CEO salary.

Listed companies have higher proportion of variable pay and LTIs compared with non-listed counterparts, reveals the survey. Close to 60% of CEO salary in listed companies is at risk.

'Listed organizations are more aggressive in pay for performance, and these would also pay a chunk of CEO salary in ESOPs (employee stock option plans). The upside for listed companies is that markets are funding the CEO compensation,' Ghose adds.

Compensation experts point out that the promoters who were earlier very conservative in sharing gains or ownership with professional CEOs are enabling LTI and wealth creation to attract and retain best talent—senior executives from MNCs.

Professionals are too welcoming this change, as they consider it fair that companies structure compensation in a way where they have potential to earn more if they contribute to the growth of the company.

Sense of ownership 'Companies are looking for professionals who come with a sense of ownership. The best way to demonstrate that is if a professional is willing to have a major part of his/her compensation come through LTIs,' says Pallavi Kathuria, who leads Asia-Pacific technology practice for leadership advisory firm Egon Zehnder.

Across sectors, the 'pay at risk' is highest in the financial services, followed by services sector, according to the survey.

However, the quantum of variable pay is determined less by nature of the industry and more by the impact on the business in a particular industry of variables that are either in the control of the executive or doors that are beyond his/her control.

In sectors such as infrastructure, large capital goods and mining industries—where the intervention of the government policies and regulation is quite high—the total proportion of variable pay is on the lower side between 20% and 30%, another compensation expert said.

So what does the future hold? 'We may see a little bit of stabilisation in the structure from here on in India. However, as the companies grow in size and if Western markets are any example to go by, we believe that greater amount will be allocated to LTIs in future,' says Anubhav Gupta, Solution Head (executive compensation), Aon Hewitt.

In terms of salary increment at CEO and CXO levels, the survey shows a marginal drop in fixed pay increase to 9.5% in 2015–16 from 9.7% last year.

According to the survey, stock options continue to be most dominant LTI being used by companies.

Executive compensation survey 2015–16 conducted by Aon Hewitt saw participation from 380 companies across eight industries. It was conducted between July 2015 and November 2015.

Source: Saumya Bhattacharya, 'As Companies Get Performance-driven, India Inc. CEOs Could Soon Lose Comfort of Fixed Pay,' *The Economic Times*, April 26, 2016.

To sum up, the key to manage executive compensation is to adopt programs that aim to balance competitive edge, the executives' value creation for shareholders, and creation of sustainable, long-term value for the firm.

11.8 COMPENSATION FOR SALES PERSONNEL

Sales and customer service personnel of an organization have a direct impact on the business outcomes of an organization and their compensation plan needs to align their activities with the company's objectives.

The pay of a salesperson consists of multiple elements of compensation components adopted by the company. The principal among the elements is of course salary, which is typically adjusted annually, but the one that is detached from any sales or profitability measures; the other elements being those in response to some aggregate measures of market pay norms and salesperson achievement. So, the pay decisions for sales personnel rest on not only how much should be paid in aggregate but also how that amount should be apportioned over salary and the various incentives. The optimal balance between the twin elements of certainty and at-risk compensation, mediated by the salesperson's degree of risk aversion, thus holds the key to an effective compensation design for sales personnel. The compensation metric of the sales personnel aims to ascertain the right combination of salary, bonus, and commission that will boost the performance of the sales force to the maximum level.

The compensation architecture of the sales personnel has to be based on four important factors: level of pay, mix between salary and incentive, measures of performance, and performance–payout relationships. The level of pay or compensation is the amount that a company plans to pay a salesperson over the course of a year. This can be viewed as a range because its total will vary with bonuses or commissions.[31] There are four approaches to rewarding the sales personnel: salary only, basic salary plus commission, basic salary plus bonus, and commission only. Table 11.2 gives a bird's eye view of the different aspects of the schemes.

Table 11.2 Compensation architecture of sales personnel

Approach	When suitable
Salary only	When customer service is more important than sales maximization. When the staff are new or are in an unproductive territory. Not suitable when sales staff need to push for high sales growth and therefore require the motivation for more money.
Salary plus commission	When the underlying need is to strike a balance between attracting many people who want a reasonable base pay and motivating people to get more sales. May, however, foster a trend to go for volumes and for easy-to-sell products and not for products with higher margins.
Salary plus bonus	When the approach requires flexibility and the sales force is required on various aspects of their sales rather than simply augment sales.
Commission only	When the priority is sales only and not non-selling work, or customer relationships. Encourages high pressure selling by providing direct financial rewards.
Additional non-cash rewards	When the premise is that methods other than money need to be tried out and enhanced. Poses a difficulty in administering.

Source: Based on Michael Armstrong, 'Summary of Payment and Incentive Arrangements for Sales Staff,' in *Armstrong's Handbook of Reward Management Practice*, ed. Michael Armstrong (London: Kogan Page, 2010), 350–351.

---

31 Paul W. Farris, Neil T. Bendle, Phillip E. Pfeifer, and David J. Reibstein, *Marketing Metrics: The Definitive Guide to Measuring Marketing Performance* (Upper Saddle River, NJ: Pearson FT Press, 2010).

Over the years, researches based on field experiments have continued to generate fresh wisdom on how to motivate the sales personnel. One field of research was influenced by the agency theory that underlines the basic challenge in compensation arising out of conflicting interests between a principal and an agent hired by the principal. According to this theory, the dichotomy lies in the fact that while the company seeks maximum performance, the salaried employee tends to relax, if he is not closely monitored and observed. The system of payment by commission is a way of integrating the company's interests with the material interests of the salesperson. The commission-based compensation, which is the traditional method, has three perceived advantages: ease of measuring the short-term results of the sales personnel; managerial control over the movements/activities of the sales personnel without need for physical supervision; and alignment to the greater risk-taking propensity of sales personnel than normal office workers.[32]

Based on research carried in Dartnell Corporation, Coughlan and Narasimhan[33] report that the presence of a career path for salespeople is associated with less leverage in the pay plan. This is hypothesized to hold because it offers the promise of a job promotion. Thus, future payoff for today's effort (career progression) substitutes for current payoff for today's effort (incentive pay). Thus, when individual sales personnel are optimistic about career progression in an organization, incentive pay ceases to be a key effort motivator on the margin in the optimal sales compensation plan. Another finding of the same research reveals that the longer horizons tend to be set for incentive pay (e.g., commissions paid out every quarter rather than every month), the longer is the sales performance horizon (as measured by the time a salesperson has to make quota). This also establishes the norm for aligning incentives to sales performance timing.

Another study by Harvard Professor Rajiv Lal and others[34] established the linkage between the level of uncertainty in an industry's sales cycle and compensation system for sales personnel. The study reported that the more uncertain a firm's sales cycle, the more a salesperson's pay should be based on a fixed salary; the less uncertain the cycle, the more pay should depend on commission. An example was drawn from Boeing company, where the actual sales in the form of an order placement for a new Boeing 787 by a client happens only after years of sales effort by the salespeople, and in such an environment the sales personnel were sure to get demotivated if their compensation was largely commission based. On the contrary, commission-based pay is entirely apt in an industry in which sales happen fast and regularly, and there is less uncertainty and more direct correlation of sales with effort.

In the late 1980s, economists Bengt Holmstrom and Paul Milgrom recommended a formula of 'straightline commissions' that provides for commissions at the same rate irrespective of the differential sales as the optimal way to pay sales personnel. The authors' case is that if the sales compensation formula is made excessively complex, the sales personnel find 'ways to game it.' In practice, however, most companies decide to build complex incentive plans for their sales, in acknowledgement of uniqueness of individual salesperson, with different motivations and needs. The flip side of an individualized sales compensation plan is that it would be difficult and costly to administer, and may be susceptible to the 'water cooler effect' whereby information regarding

32 Doug J. Chung, 'How to Really Motivate Salespeople,' *Harvard Business Review* (April 2015). Available at: https://hbr.org/2015/04/how-to-really-motivate-salespeople (accessed on November 15, 2017).

33 A. T. Coughlan and C. Narasimhan, 'An Empirical Analysis of Salesforce Compensation Plans,' *Journal of Business* 65, no. 1 (1992): 93–121.

34 Rajiv Lal, John D. C. Little, and J. Miguel Villas-Boas, 'A Theory of Forward Buying, Merchandising and Trade Deals,' *Marketing Science* 15, no. 1 (1991): 21–37.

compensation are shared eventually raising issues of fairness. It is also recognized that sheer luck also influences sales. Sometimes crucial external circumstances favor them or disable them despite efforts. Keeping in mind such complexities, many companies choose to keep their sales compensation plans complex in the hope of appealing to different types of salespeople and limiting the impact of luck by utilizing caps or compensating people for inputs or effort (such as number of calls made) instead of simply compensating for closing sales.[35]

11.8.1 Issues in Sales Personnel Compensation

- An important issue in compensation for sales personnel is around the relative pay and structural differences of sales professionals at different levels of the sales organization: field salespeople, sales managers, and key account managers. A study covering comparative compensation patterns of field salespeople versus sales managers in five European countries by Rouzies et al.[36] show that sales managers receive take-home pay from 25 to 50% higher than field salespeople; field salespeople's take-home pay increases at a decreasing rate with job challenge, while sales managers' take-home pay increases at an increasing rate with job challenge (consistent with the multiplier effect of a good sales manager on his or her many subordinates); and more aggressive taxation systems lead to more highly leveraged pay for both field salespeople and sales managers.
- The second set of issues is about the choice of right parameters for developing the sales compensation architecture and also information about what metrics are being preferred by organizations currently. One of the grey areas in sales compensation research is the lack of consensus on a base rate beyond which bonus should be applicable. There is also absence of definitive answer on whether individual or group performance should be incentivized and what program should be preferred under what conditions. It is necessary to evolve common standards, despite the divergence in industries, size of the sales force, and so on to connect sales personnel commission pay on conditions such as profit, margin, gains in market share, or sales volumes.
- The time horizon for sales force compensation is also an unresolved issue. The choice is between a monthly, quarterly, or annual bonus. Should one use a quarterly bonus in addition to an annual bonus? In the education literature, researchers have argued that frequent testing leads to better performance outcomes.[37] Is the same learning valid for performance improvement of sales personnel? Like in the education literature, where frequent exams keep students prepared for the comprehensive final exam, frequent quota-bonus plans may serve as a mechanism to keep the sales force motivated to perform in the short-run well enough to be in striking distance of the overall annual performance quota. In the study of Chung and others,[38] quarterly bonuses serve as a continuous evaluation scheme to keep sales agents within striking targets of their annual quotas. In the absence of quarterly bonuses, a failure in the early periods to accomplish targets caused agents to fall behind more often than in the presence of quarterly bonuses. Thus, the quarterly bonus serves as a valuable sub-goal that helps the sales force stay on track in achieving their overall goal. A key finding is that annual bonuses are not as effective for the sales force without quarterly

[35] Chung, 'How to Really Motivate Salespeople.'

[36] Rouzies, Dominique, Anne T. Coughlan, Erin Anderson, and Dawn Iacobucci. 'Determinants of Pay Levels and Structures in Sales Organizations'. *Journal of Marketing*, 73, no. 6 (2009): 92–104.

[37] Robert L. Bangert-Drowns, James A. Kulik, and Chen-Lin C. Kulik, 'Effects of Frequent Classroom Testing,' *Journal of Educational Research* 85, no. 2 (November–December 1991): 89–99.

[38] Doug J. Chung, Thomas Steenburgh, and K. Sudhir, 'Do Bonuses Enhance Sales Productivity? A Dynamic Structural Analysis of Bonus-Based Compensation Plans,' *Marketing Science* (March–April 2014).

bonuses for the low productivity segments. For the most productive segments, quarterly quotas do not seem to matter much. In summary, we find that bonuses have an overall positive impact on all segments of salespeople. Overachievement commissions serve to increase performance among the highest performers, while quarterly bonuses are most helpful to increase performance among the weaker performers. The opinions of Misra and Nair[39] demonstrate some disagreement: 'There exists no straightforward algorithm that would implement an exhaustive search over the multi-dimensional compensation space and uncover the optimal second best compensation policy,' including the right horizon over which to pay salespeople. Their study suggested that shortening the quota horizon from three months to one month improved profitability. Some researchers have found a positive correlation between the sales performance horizon and the incentive pay horizon.

Coughlan and Joseph[40] have mentioned the following issues:

1. How does the combination of training and compensation impact sales force turnover, and what is the best ensemble of compensation structure, training levels, and turnover? It has been pointed out in Murthy and Mantrala's[41] research that it is important for the organization to decide on the relative allocation of marketing and sales funds across training and compensation. Training initiatives can catalyze the creation of higher productivity salespersons who can bring in more revenue, though they also cost more in terms of compensation. If, in addition, the firm's training program is so excellent as to spur competitors to 'pick off ' already-trained salespeople, the firm's turnover costs may swamp the benefits of better-trained salespeople. Additional theoretical and empirical research on this question thus is warranted.
2. What is the overall optimal compensation plan, and why should the firm prefer one type of extra incentive component to another? We indicate in this review a few examples of comparative analyses of one compensation investment versus another, but more such comparisons across multiple alternative incentive plans could uncover general rules for preferring one to another incentive type.
3. More generally, how do compensation decisions interact with other important decisions, such as sales force structure, territory design, sales force selection, marketing–sales coordination, and so forth? For example, territory design can moderate salesperson productivity and, thereby, the incentive effects of compensation.

11.9 COMPENSATION FOR SCIENTISTS AND ENGINEERS IN HIGH-TECH INDUSTRY

Michelle Pfeiffer once claimed that she acted for free, but charged only for 'the annoyance of being a public personality.' The scientists, working in industry, may likewise be driven by the work itself, charging only for the drudgeries of form-filling, meetings, bureaucracy, and so on, which characterize life in business organizations. A Glassdoor survey in July 2017 in Bangalore among 915 respondents

[39] Sanjog Misra and Harikesh Nair, 'Quota Dynamics and the Intertemporal Allocation of Sales–Force Effort' (Working paper, Stanford University, Stanford, CA, 2010).

[40] Anne T. Coughlan and Kissan Joseph, 'Sales Force Compensation: Research Insights and Research Potential' (2011). Available at: http://www.kellogg.northwestern.edu/faculty/coughlan/htm/personalpage_files/Papers/LILIEN%2026%20Anne%20T.%20 Coughlan%20and%20Kissan%20Joseph.pdf (accessed on November 15, 2017).

[41] Murthy and Mantrala's, 'Allocating a Promotion Budget between Advertising and Sales Contest Prizes: An Integrated Marketing Communications Perspective'. *Marketing Letters*, 16, no. 1 (2005): 19–35.

put the average salary of a scientist at ₹8.25 lakh per annum, with minimum of ₹3.75 lakh and maximum of ₹20.3 lakh. The organizations covered ranged from IBM to ISRO and included junior scientists to scientists.

For industries, having a heavy technology element, value addition is done through scientific and technical research. Talent management is a serious challenge for this much sought after, nomadic group of employees. A compensation approach suiting such a special group needs to rely on the total rewards approach. Firms that have aligned their rewards plan to offer differentiation based on the unique needs and preferences of such employees have won the war of talent. Using the total rewards approach to compensation, a survey done by Towers Perrin on over 500 North American and European executives in a variety of industries revealed that 100% included pay elements, 96% included benefits, 83% included L&D, and 75% included work environment rewards. A second research (covering Microsoft, IBM, 3M, Marriot, and others) identifies an overall preference for pay and benefits and, in comparison, lower priority for L&D and work environment. Conversely, research on the rewards preferences of technical workers shows a strong preference for work environment rewards. The logical inference could be that total rewards may be an appropriate rewards management framework for technical workers.[42]

11.10 COMPENSATION FOR CONTINGENT WORKERS

Contingent workers are those who are engaged through staffing or manpower leasing firms for fixed time periods. The definition covers a wide variety of non-permanent employees—part-time temporary workers, contractors, consultants, contract employees, leased employees, and direct recruits. Most contingent workers are considered 'temporary,' and therefore the terms 'contingent' and 'temporary' are often used synonymously. Companies follow divergent practices in employment of contingent workers—some recruit only a few at a time, while some may man their entire workforce on a semipermanent basis. Due to the irregular expansion of the economy, employers are wary about adding to permanent roll. As a consequence, contingent employment has been witnessing rapid growth. Contingent workers continue to insulate businesses from demand fluctuations and companies are embracing this fact across industries and geographies. Used strategically, contingent workforce planning could be the solution to cost optimization, workforce utilization, right fit of candidates, and various other HR problems that ail organizations. This approach also leads to precise focus on the kind of skills required to execute the job. The trend for hiring increasing number of contingent workers is a significant shift in the makeup of a company's internal workforce. The contingent workforce is now estimated to comprise up to 30% of procurement expenditure for some companies, and represents a larger share of the workforce than company employees, for others.

In the findings of a recent survey titled *Human Capital Trends 2016* of 7000 executives, a global management consultancy firm reported that 42% of executives surveyed plan to increase, or significantly increase the use of contingent workers over the next three to five years. Conversely, only 16% of executives expect to decrease the size of their contingent workforce. According to the survey, 62% of Canadian executives surveyed rated the trend towards a more flexible workforce

[42] Steven Rumpel and John W. Medcof, 'Total Rewards: Good Fit for Tech Workers,' *Research Technology Management* 49, no. 5 (2006): 27–35.

as 'important' or 'very important.' The survey considered a variety of types of contingent workers, including contractors, freelancers, and part-time employees.[43]

In Indian Inc., contingent workers belong to two different strata: At the top end, it consists of professional/technically skilled workers, who often receive payment or commission for the completed work and unlike a full-time worker do not receive a fixed amount as salary. Consequently, a company's focus is not on how the work is done, rather the focus is on the outcome. This is in the background of the rise of the Generation Y, who are expected to make up a big part of the contingent pool in the next 15 years, their primary motivation being they want to be their own bosses. Contingent or contract staffing gives a pool of candidates who have worked in multiple projects have the required expertise in the field of work, and are ready to come, see, and conquer. The time invested in orientation and training is reduced significantly due to the expertise and experience of most of the contractors. A contractor will cause only a minimal amount of disruption to the existing operation when they are hired and even lesser when their contract ends, thus reducing administrative and HR friction. Contingent workers also bring with them the option of flexible work schedules and the option of working onsite. There are many instances when contingent workers have outperformed the company's permanent staff because they feel the need to prove themselves on the job, in order to land either an extended contract or a full-time position. They often boost innovation in an organization as they bring in fresh ideas and knowledge, which could be leveraged by using them as change agents for organizational initiatives.

The lower stratum of contingent workers in India consists largely of what is known as 'contract workers' and is covered under the Contract Labor Regulation and Abolition Act 1970 and Migrant Labor Act. India's rigid labor laws are considered to be a huge deterrent for industry, and employers have hit upon a panacea in the form of contract workers. The contract labor, largely unskilled, come cheap, and are easy to procure, replace and terminate (when the work gets over). They are paid at the minimum wage rates specified by the government, which vary between states and consist of basic wage rates and some allowances. According to newly available data, contract employees account for 34% of the total workforce (contract plus regular) of India's top companies. The numbers have been collected from a sample of 82 companies that employ 2.12 million regular employees and 1.08 million contractual employees. The sample had a 64% share of market capitalization and 46% of revenue among all listed companies.[44]

A persistent issue for contract labor in India is the wages paid to them by many employers in comparison to the wages paid to the permanent employees in situations when the work done by both are similar. In a recent verdict that brings relief to lakhs of contractual employees working in government departments and agencies, the Supreme Court (SC) ruled that temporary workers are entitled to wages at par with permanent employees. A bench headed by Justice J. S. Khehar based its judgment on the principle of 'equal pay for equal work.' The rule, it said, constitutes a clear and unambiguous right vested in every employee—whether engaged on regular or temporary basis. The principle has been under-scored in various judgments rendered by the SC and is law of the land, the bench said.

---

43 Liebenthal, M. 'The Rise of the Contingent Worker'. Available at: https://www.hcmworks.com (accessed on August 17, 2016).

44 Ravi Ananthanarayanan, 'Contract Workers Make Up 46% of Workforce of India's Largest Industrial Companies,' *Live Mint*, June 12, 2017.

Anyone, who is compelled to work at a lesser wage, does not do so voluntarily. He does so, to provide food and shelter to his family, at the cost of his self-respect and dignity, at the cost of his self-worth, and at the cost of his integrity. For he knows, that his dependents would suffer immensely, if he does not accept the lesser wage.[45]

In conclusion, the same logic that makes them attractive to organizations can also make them unattractive to the contingent workers. The pay is typically limited to basic wage and allowances, without the perquisites that come with permanent employment. Even though the contract labor have a social security net, because of the problems of law enforcements many employers are lax in covering them under statutory health insurance, sick leave, and overtime pay. In addition, job insecurity and the looming danger of contract termination as well as the absence of unemployment benefits in India render them nomads, continuously on the run for jobs—a condition of life that is unattractive and stressful. To maintain the balance, an organization needs to keep an eye where it will find the exact fit and number of temporary workers, when it needs them, to ensure they are not left hanging when the chips are down. Putting a process in place to manage intelligence, hiring, training, and managing of contingent labor will definitely allow your organization to meet constantly changing business demands in the best possible manner.

11.11 NEW DIRECTIONS IN DEVELOPING COMPENSATION FOR SPECIAL GROUPS

Different special groups need different approaches to compensation. For the CEOs, the thrust for the future seems to be increasing accountability for sustained performance bounded by the 'say for pay' of the shareholders. For sales personnel, it is the fine tuning of the incentive to create clear line of sight between performance and outcome. For the contingent workers, especially in India the direction is for fair wages and equal pay for equal work. But interesting challenges exist for the scientists and engineers in high-tech industries.

The experience of Microsoft is interesting. In the late 1990s, Microsoft was in search for ways to make its compensation package attractive. Between 1992 and 1999, employees who had stock options, got a windfall in terms of a 27-fold increase in the stock price. With plateauing of the stock price and the emergence of newer technology startups with deep pockets, the pay became unattractive. Microsoft successfully rejigged its pay package on total rewards by incorporating insights from internal research on the value employees placed on various financial and non-financial rewards. RBC Financial Group, in developing its total rewards framework, sought information from over 16,000 employees, approximately 25% of its workforce. Employee participation and feedback was also a key component in Marriott's development of its total rewards strategy. The valuable lesson learnt is that involving employees in determining the touch points of an effective compensation could set a future trend.[46]

SUMMARY

Each organization has some special groups or individuals who are treated differently from the standard compensation programs on account of their unique nature of work and competencies, which are

[45] Bhadra Sinha, 'Contractual Staff Must Get at Par Wages: Supreme Court,' *Hindustan Times*, October 27, 2016. Available at: http://www.hindustantimes.com/india-news/contractual-staff-must-get-at-par-wages-supreme-court/story-xLVvtjK2rOQZjGYY7JVrBK.html (accessed on November 15, 2017).

[46] Rumpel and Medcof, 'Total Rewards: Good Fit for Tech Workers.'

sometimes of strategic importance to the organization. There are distinct competitive advantages in acquiring and retaining people of such competencies. Similarly, there are special groups in organizations warranting tailor-made compensation structure. For such groups, there seems to be some 'built-in conflict, conflict that arises because different factions place incompatible demands on members of the group.'[47] Milkovich and other others list the special groups as comprising the following: the supervisors, the top management, the board of directors, the sales representatives, the professionals, and the contingent employees.

1. **Supervisors in shop floor** The compensation plan for such a group needs to be alluring enough for a unionized employee to seek promotion. The job evaluation scores for this role may not fully reflect the rigors of supervision, leading to a lower score than some of the technical worker roles. Sometimes there are instances where the new supervisor draws less salary than his erstwhile in the worker role. The pay approach needs to be flexible and sensitive to those caught in the middle rigors of this group.
2. **Sales personnel** Sales and customer services personnel of an organization have a direct impact on the business outcomes of an organization and their compensation plan needs to align their activities with the company's objectives. The pay of a salesperson consists of multiple elements of compensation components adopted by the company: some are fixed like basic pay, while some are risk pay in the form of incentives. The optimal balance between the twin elements of certainty and at-risk compensation, mediated by the salesperson's degree of risk aversion, thus holds the key to an effective compensation design for sales personnel. The compensation metric of the sales personnel aims to ascertain the right combination of salary, bonus, and commission that will boost the performance of the sales force to the maximum level.
3. **Contingent workers** Contingent (temporary) workers continue to insulate businesses from demand fluctuations and companies are embracing this fact across industries and geographies. Used strategically, contingent workforce planning could be the solution to cost optimization, workforce utilization, right fit of candidates, and various other HR problems that ail organizations. In India, they include contract labor who are paid at the minimum wage rates specified by the government. According to newly available data, contract employees account for 34% of the total workforce (contract plus regular) of India's top companies. The numbers have been collected from a sample of 82 companies that employ 2.12 million regular employees and 1.08 million contractual employees.
4. **Scientists and technical employees in hi-tech industries** A Glassdoor survey in July 2017 in Bangalore, conducted among 915 respondents in Bengaluru, put the average salary of a scientist at ₹8.25 lakh per annum, with minimum of ₹3.75 lakh and maximum of ₹20.3 lakh. The organizations covered ranged from IBM to ISRO and included junior scientists to scientists. For industries having a heavy technology element, value addition is done through scientific and technical research. Talent management is a serious challenge for this much sought after, nomadic group of employees. A compensation approach suiting such a special group needs to rely on the total rewards approach. Firms that have aligned their rewards plan to offer differentiation based on the unique needs and preferences of such employees have won the war of talent.

[47] Milkovich et al., *Compensation*.

5. **CEO and top leadership** Compensation levels for CEOs show a wide variance, especially in large companies, according to the fifth edition of the Aon Hewitt Executive Compensation Study 2014–15. According to the survey, total compensation for CEOs in companies in the ₹5000 crore to ₹10,000 crore revenue range has a median of ₹5 crore and goes up to ₹9.2 crore. For companies in the ₹10,000–30,000 crore revenue range, CEO compensation is at ₹6.1 crore at median levels and goes as high as ₹9.6 crore. There are various factors determining the CEO salary: personal attributes, firm size, managerial discretion, power of the CEO, and so on. The major issues regarding executive compensation include governance, shareholders' say on pay, legislation, disparity ratio, and several others.

Short-answer Questions

1. Mention some key challenges for compensation for supervisors.
2. What is disparity ratio?
3. To what factors would you attribute the spurt of CEO compensation?
4. How do personal attributes influence executive compensation?
5. How does diversification of firm business impact CEO salary?
6. Describe 'Say on Pay'.
7. Define 'Clawback'.
8. Narrate at least four key issues in Sales compensation.
9. How are contingent workers differentiated in pay in India?
10. What is the focus of total rewards approach for compensating scientists and engineers in High Tech Industries?

Discussion Questions

1. What is your view on the disparity ratio being a basis for determining executive compensation? What should be the bideal disparity ratio?
2. What is the right mix of a fixed–variable pay package for the CEO?
3. How do you incentivize the efforts of sales personnel in varied sectors such as insurance and petroleum products such as LPG, where the effort has to balance between volume and other parameters such as transparency (insurance) and safety (LPG)?
4. Conduct an online research on the issue of 'equal work, equal pay' for contract workers in India.

CLUSTER 6

DECENT WORKPLACE—COMPLIANCE AND DIALOG

Chapter 12
Industrial Relations

Chapter 13
Workplace Laws and Regulations

International Labor Organization's concept of decent work involves work that is productive and yields a fair wage, security in the workplace and social protection for families, opportunities for growth and social integration, freedom of expression, organizing and participation in workplace decisions, and equal opportunities irrespective of gender.[1] Modern, global workplaces are already moving beyond reactive, risk aversion–driven compliance of law/regulations to developing a culture, where internal values are as important as compliance driven by external requirements. In India, the shackles of legal compliance that employers complained had restricted flexibility and ease of business are getting removed gradually, keeping in mind the need of the workers for a minimum level of security and social protection.

Social dialog, a condition of decent workplace, describes the process of negotiation by social partners (trade unions and employer organizations), sometimes with government intervention, to influence the arrangement and development of work-related issues, labor market policies, social protection, taxation, or other economic policies.[2] Industrial relations (IR) aim at generating solutions between the conflicting objectives and values, between the profit motive and social gain, between discipline and freedom, between authority and industrial democracy, between bargaining and cooperation, and between conflicting interests of the individual, the group, and the community.[3] In India, IR is marked by decline of trade unionism, the gradual slackening of state control, the employer militancy, and sector–specific explosion of industrial unrest.

---

1 Available at: http://www.ilo.org/global/topics (accessed on November 15, 2017).

2 Alexandre Afonso, *Social Consultation in Times of Austerity* (Amsterdam: Amsterdam University Press, 2013).

3 Richard A. Lester, 'Labor Policy in a Changing World,' *Industrial Relations: A Journal of Economy and Society* 2, no. 1 (October

CHAPTER 12

Industrial Relations

LEARNING OBJECTIVES

After completing this chapter, the student will be able to:

- Learn the concept of industrial relations (IR) and the roles played by the actors
- Distinguish between the different approaches to IR
- Understand the conflict resolution process
- Know the value of collective bargaining
- Appreciate the importance of an employee grievance handling mechanism
- Describe the various levels in which the employees can participate in decision-making

Opening Case IR at Everest

Background

Everest is one of India's fastest growing building solutions company. Currently, it is one of the most respected and renowned business entities in India, and has dominated the market ever since. It has continuously introduced innovative and modern building products with a promise of strength, speed, and safety. Everest offers a complete range of world-class building solutions—roofing, ceiling, wall, flooring, cladding, door, and pre-engineered steel buildings—for the industrial, commercial, and residential sectors.

Historically, Everest has provided rural shelters, by making corrugated roofing sheets available to farmers at a competitive price. The company is poised to capitalize on the opportunities in rural India, where various housing and infrastructure initiatives are envisaged by the government.

The company started in India in 1934 with a first manufacturing unit at Kymore in Madhya Pradesh. Presently, the company has three other plants in Kolkata, at Podanur in Tamil Nadu, and at Nashik in Maharashtra. ACC acquired 50% in the company from copromoter Etex for ₹16.3 crore in December 2001, taking its shareholding to 76.01%. It has a modern R&D center at Nasik. The company has a wide and well-organized sales and distribution network all over the country. With a turnover of around ₹200 crore (₹2 billion), the company is going through a phase of consolidating its recently launched new generation products and maintaining the leadership status in fiber cement Industry.

Everest Industries facility at Lakhmapur, Nasik, was the first to manufacture non-asbestos roofing sheet and fiber cement board in India. This plant has advanced manufacturing facility for manufacturing AC corrugated roofing sheets, fiber cement boards, compressed boards, and solid wall panels.

Conflict

Workers at Lakhmapur production facility in Nasik went on strike from November 8, 2011. As a result of the strike, the building solutions company has seen a 50% dip in its profits in the past two quarters at the Nasik plant. 'The factories are still running as our executives are running operations in Nasik. However, we would have seen additional profits had there been additional manpower,' said Manish Sanghi, Managing Director, Everest Industries. He added, about 135 permanent employees were on strike on issues related to wages and reinstatement of three sacked workers.

This area had faced some unrest in the mid-1990s, but has been peaceful since then. But now fresh trouble has erupted at a company, Everest Industries, which manufactures cement roof material and pipes. The flashpoint being striking workers demanding higher wages and the management calling in contract laborers to keep its operations going. The deputy labor commissioner of Nashik has held 42 meetings to resolve the dispute between union leaders and the Everest Industries management, but failed to find a solution.

The collector of Nasik could not break the impasse either and things just got worse, jeopardizing peace and industrial activity in this buzzing region. The worrying factor is that friction exists between local workers who are permanent employees and laborers who have been brought in from other parts of the country to work on a contract basis.

Escalation of Violence

Last week, a member of one union stabbed three managers of Everest Industries as they were coming out of the factory. All three have been admitted to hospital and one of them, an HR officer, is believed to be critical. Some of the union leaders have been arrested, which led to 140 factories in the region staying shut for two days. While they have resumed work now, the tension is quite palpable.

'We condemn the violence. Confrontation leading to physical assault can only aggravate the situation. CII has been working toward bringing more investment in this region and incidents like these send a wrong signal to the industry,' CII Nashik region's vice-president N. Balakrishnan told ET. Satpur and Ambad are Maharashtra Industrial Development Corporation (MIDC) zones near Nashik and have hundreds of factories. The police have already arrested two office-bearers of the Left-affiliated CITU and six more people in connection with the violence.

The Trade Union's View

Centre of Indian Trade Unions, however, has a different stand on the issue. K. L. Bajaj, vice president of the trade union, said they would launch an all-India agitation if the issue was not resolved. Bajaj said,

> The management has shown an unsympathetic attitude towards the whole issue. We had held a two-day strike in Nashik, where thousands of workers from other industries also participated. A deputation will then meet the Maharashtra home minister. If our demands are not met, we will intensify the strike.

Centre of Indian Trade Unions is demanding the dismissed workers be reinstated and the employees be given a reasonable wage hike. Further, CITU officials are of the view that there is a conspiracy to arrest the two office-bearers, who have had no involvement in the violence.

Industrial bodies in Nashik have also come together to resolve the situation. The Nashik Industries and Manufacturing Association (NIMA) has come forward to maintain peace and has had several talks with the management. NIMA representatives had also met the district collector to find a way out of the situation. This is not the first time Nashik is witnessing such a major agitation. In 2009, the M&M plant at Nashik had witnessed a 10-day strike over the suspension of a union leader.

In 2011 too, workers at the M&M plant had gone on a one-day strike in support of union leaders, who were on a hunger strike, demanding 'equal pay to equal work.'

Meanwhile, officials of CITU have met both the state labor ministry and the chief minister to resolve the situation as soon as possible. 'No concrete results have been reached. The negotiations are still on between the two sides,' said a CITU official. The official added that the workers' demands included flexible working hours and wage hike apart from revoking the dismissal of certain workers.

The union official further said that while permanent workers are paid around ₹12,000 per month, contract workers at the plant who are more than 300 people are paid only upto ₹1500 per month. He added that the government would very soon find a solution to the labor issues and has requested the workers to remain peaceful in their agitation.

Things had taken a violent turn three weeks ago at the plant when three management officials of the company were stabbed by some workers. The management officials are currently recuperating from the injuries.

Centre of Indian Trade Unions officials have also met key ministers in the center to discuss the strike issue and the freeing of two CITU leaders, D.L. Karad and R.S. Pande, who had earlier been arrested for the violence and later released on bail.

Meanwhile, sources from the union said that there had been attempts by the company to freeze the DA of the workers. However, a senior company official dismissed it as a routine development.

Widening Industry-Worker Gap

The fresh bout of violence, in which three officials of an industrial unit were injured, has vitiated the atmosphere and shattered the overall industrial peace here, creating serious labor–industry rift.

The incident has come at a time when Nashik is poised for growth. With Mumbai and Pune having reached saturation levels, many industries are now eyeing the district to set up their base. There are around 4,500 micro, small, medium, and large industries across the district, with some 200 CITU-affiliated unions. There have been two incidents of violence here in the past six months involving management and laborers. The executive director

(ED) of Sanjyot Metal Industries was attacked by his own workers in February. Six months later, three officials of Everest Industries were attacked by company workers last Friday. Both companies have CITU-affiliated unions.

While industrial associations have decided to cancel CITU's registration, CITU leaders have threatened to sue the industrial bodies.

The Management View

Y. Srinivasan Rao, ED, Everest Industries Ltd, strongly condemned the attack. Rao said,

> The workers are being misguided. We had several rounds of positive talks with the union office-bearers. The workers should have not taken the law in their hands. We already have expansion plans at our exist- ing Nashik plant and to generate future employment possibilities. But this will only be possible if there is a positive and healthy work environment.

Former NIMA president D.G. Joshi said,

> There are other ways to get justice. They (the workers) must settle their issues through negotiations. They should not have broken the law. Such attacks are tarnishing the image of Nashik. The city's growth has already been affected due to union problems and the situation will worsen if this continues.

Former NIMA president Dhananjay Bele said,

> We strongly condemn the attack on the senior company officials. It has been decided that the industries across the district having unions affiliated to CITU would not negotiate with the CITU. The further course of action by the industry is to be decided following the joint meeting with the Guardian Minister Chhagan Bhujbal, Police Commissioner Kulwant Kumar Sarangal, and Dy Labor Commissioner Ratnadeep Henre on Wednesday.

AIMA president Suresh Mali said,

> It is an attack on patron and it is really a matter of grave concern for the industry. All the disputes can be sorted out in peaceful manner. The police commissioner has already set up a peace committee of office-bearers of industry bodies and unions. They also had option to settle their issues through peace committee, but whatever happened was really unfortunate.

Tushar Andhrutkar of Nashik Industrial Co-operative Estate (NICE) said, 'The company workers were already on strike for the last few months. This unfortunate incident could have been avoided if the police department would have taken precautionary measures during the meeting at the Office of the Dy Labor Commissioner.'

The Fall Out–100-Crore Everest Capex Held Up

Nashik: Everest Industries has put on hold a ₹100-crore expansion plan at its existing manufacturing unit near Dindori here due to labor unrest. The decision follows the assault on three of its officials. Y. Srinivasa Rao of Everest Industries said, 'We could not invest at our Nashik plant in the past two years due to union problems. We moved a ₹70-core project to Orissa. We have also put on hold expansion plan worth ₹100-crore for Nashik. We are waiting for IR to improve here.' Rao further said,

> Nashik was an ideal place for industrial growth. From a strategic standpoint, Everest had good infrastructure here. There is lot of room for expansion and Nashik is on our list of priorities, but labor conditions have to be a little more conducive.

Discussion Questions

1. Formulation of a possible roadmap for resolution of the current impasse at Everest. What role should each of the actors play to bring about industrial harmony? (10 minutes)
2. One role play out of the following situations (10 minutes):
   (a) Conciliation proceeding
   (b) Individual grievance handling
   (In the role play, a group member should be identified to play the role of the management while the faculty will announce the role player for the worker.)

In Charles Chaplin's famous film *Modern Times*, the protagonist, Charlie, is a factory worker, literally shown as a minor cog in the grinding wheels of industry. His job is to mechanically tighten bolts on a moving belt. He becomes literally trapped in the machine and, in one of the classic episodes of dark humor, he is battered and buffeted by an automatic feeding machine, tried by his bosses to save time and money. The big boss is forever watching, even when he is in the washroom or smoking a cigarette. At the end, the monotony of the work drives him berserk. Taken to the hospital, he soon recovers and is discharged, cautioned to avoid excitement. Cured after his breakdown, he is arrested when he picks up a red flag that has fallen off the back of a lorry and runs down the street to return it, exactly the same time as a left-wing demonstration comes round the corner.

The film bears uncanny similarities to some of the stories of workplace rigidities in some of the industries wrecked by labor unrest, especially in the cost-driven automobile industries. It brings up some important issues. Are there checks and balances to ensure that the workplaces do not lapse back to the primitive conditions of the post-Industrial Revolution times? Are there laws to prevent the excess? Are there norms and processes for decent workplaces?

12.1 DECENT WORKPLACE—INTERNATIONAL LABOR ORGANIZATION

International Labor Organization, set up in 1919, is a specialized agency of the United Nations (UN) with the aim of improving labor conditions and living standards throughout the world.

The functions of the ILO include the development and promotion of standards for national legislation to protect and improve working conditions and standards of living. The ILO also provides technical assistance in social policy and administration and in workforce training; fosters cooperative organizations and rural industries; compiles labor statistics and conducts research on the social problems of international competition, unemployment and under-employment, labor and IR, and technological change (including automation); and helps to protect the rights of international migrants and organized labor.[4]

In the context of the widespread feeling shared by many people that globalization has thrown up several challenges in the form of economic and job crisis, ILO has come up with its own 'Decent Work' for all agenda based on the following four 'strategic conditions' where

[4] Karen Mingst, 'International Labor Organization (ILO),' Encyclopedia Britannia. Available at: https://www.britannica.com/ topic/International-Labor-Organization (accessed on November 15, 2017).

1. People are gainfully employed (and there exist adequate income and employment opportunities).
2. Social protection system (labor protection and social security) is fully developed and accessible to all.
3. Social dialog and tripartism are promoted and encouraged.
4. Rights at work, as specified in ILO Declaration on Fundamental Principles and Rights at Work and Core ILO Conventions, are practiced, promoted, and respected.

'Decent Work,' a term first used by ILO in 1999, has also been adopted by UN as one of the measurements of Millennium Development Goals (MDGs). Since 2005, Decent Work has been included as a target on the first MDG and ILO does all the reporting with regard to the achievement of this target.[5]

12.1.1 Social Dialog

The concept of social dialog covers all types of negotiation, consultation, or exchange of information between or among representatives of governments, employers, and workers on issues of common interest relating to economic and social policy. The underlying principle of social dialog is that 'management by agreement is preferable to management by Diktat. Negotiation is more democratic than unilateral imposition. Hence collective bargaining and social dialog are the most appropriate means of regulating employment relations, a principle which has been widely reasserted in the current crisis.'[6]

12.2 INDUSTRIAL RELATIONS

According to *Encyclopedia Britannica*, IR denotes

> The relations of the state with employers, workers, and other organizations. The subject, therefore, includes individual relations and joint consultation between employers and workers at their places of work, collective relations between employers and trade unions; and the part played by the State in regulating these relations.

Dale Yoder[7] considers IR to be 'a designation of a whole field of relationship that exists because of the necessary collaboration of men and women in the employment processes of Industry.' According to Armstrong, IR is 'concerned with the systems and procedures used by unions and employers to determine the reward for effort and other conditions of employment, to protect the interests of the employed and their employers and to regulate the ways in which employers treat their employees.'[8]

Some authors have provided views different from these. Bain and Clegg[9] defined IR as 'the study of rules governing employment and the way in which the rules are changed, interpreted and

5 International Labor Organization (ILO). 'Decent Work'. Available at: http://www.ilo.org/global/topics/decent-work/lang-en/index.htm (accessed on February 14, 2018).

6 Richard Hyman, 'Social Dialogue and Industrial Relations During the Economic Crisis: Innovative Practices or Business as Usual?' (Working paper no. 11, ILO, Geneva, March 2010).

7 Dale Yoder, *Personnel Management and Industrial Relations* (New York, NY: Prentice Hall, 1942).

8 Armstrong, *Human Resource Management*.

9 G. S. Bain and H. A. Clegg, 'A Strategy for Industrial Relations Research in Great Britain,' *British Journal of Industrial Relations* 12, no. 1 (March 1974): 91–113.

administered.' According to Flanders,[10] 'IR deal with certain regulated or institutionalized relationships in an industrial unit.' In Richard Hyman's[11] opinion, they are 'the study of control processes on employment relationship.' Teed and Metcalfe observed that

> Industrial relations are the composite result of the attitudes and approaches of employers and employees towards each other with regard to planning, supervision, direction and coordination of the activities of an organization with a minimum of human efforts and frictions with an animating spirit of cooperation and with proper regard for the genuine well-being of all members of the organization.[12]

The term 'industrial relations' was in vogue in the pre-HRM times. It covers the interrelationships between employer, represented by management, and workmen, represented by unions, involving the processes of collective bargaining at the organization and industry level. A more recent and wider definition is provided by Singh and Kumar:[13]

> Industrial relations is a discipline concerned with studying the relationship between employers and employees at organization's level, industry branch or national level. It also refers to two-way interaction that state could have in influencing relations. These relationships are shaped by social, economic, political and technical factors that exist at a certain time. The study includes players and their objectives, structures and their functions, conflicts and their origins, solutions over conflict, environmental contexts and their impact, processes and their results.

Integrating the various perspectives on the term, IR we find that IR describes a formal collective relations between employers and employees, dictated by needs and aspirations of both parties, influenced by economic, political and social, technological, and market contexts, and governed by the State. It includes aspects of cooperation and conflicts, and relies on collective bargaining as a rule-making process.

12.3 THE OBJECTIVES OF INDUSTRIAL RELATIONS

The basic objective of IR is to bring about harmonious relations between employers and employees. The larger objectives, however, encompass improvement in productivity; securing the rights and interests of both labor and management based on cooperation; minimize conflict and adopt effective conflict resolution processes; avoid stoppages, go-slows, gheraos, strikes, lockouts; and promote industrial democracy. The State, which plays a watchdog role, also seeks to mend imbalances in social and economic order in the wake of technological and economic advancements, sometimes by controlling and directing the parties to adjust their disparate interests. All India Organization of Employers (AIOE), an allied body of FICCI, has spelt out the following criteria for outstanding IR:

1. Number of strikes and lockouts and their intensity—mandays/manhours lost and production loss—during last five years

[10] Allan D. Flanders, *Industrial Relations: What Is Wrong with the System? An Essay on Its Theory and Future* (London: Faber and Faber, 1965).

[11] Richard Hyman, *Industrial Relations: A Marxist Introduction* (London: Macmillan, 1975).

[12] Ordway Tead and Henry C. Metcalf, *Personnel Administration: Its Principles and Practice* (New York, NY: McGraw-Hill Book Co., 1970).

[13] P. N. Singh and Neeraj Kumar, *Employee Relations Management* (New Delhi: Pearson Education, 2011).

2. Productivity improvement initiatives and result achieved
3. Welfare measures and corporate social responsibility (CSR) activities launched by the company
4. Training/retraining and skill development initiatives taken by the company for employees' development
5. Number of ID pending
6. Information about grievance machinery set up by the management at various levels for redressal of genuine grievances of workers
7. Whether works committees have been set up—if so, details about their composition, functioning, and settlement of issues referred to it
8. Voluntary welfare measures initiated by the company
9. Whether the company has initiated steps toward involving workers in various decision-making processes
10. Formal as well as informal forums and number of committees
11. The system of communication adopted with employees and its relevance in the IR
12. Employee retention rate during the last five years

12.4 APPROACHES TO INDUSTRIAL RELATIONS SYSTEM

An IR system may be defined as comprising the totality of power interactions of participants in a workplace, when these interactions involve IR issues. Based on different elements and characteristics of IR, several authors have tried to formulate their own unique approaches to IR, which are given further.

12.4.1 Systems Approach

Professor T. J. Dunlop of Harvard University in his pathbreaking book *Industrial Relations Systems*[14] presents IR system as 'comprised of certain actors, certain contexts, an ideology' and 'a body of rules created to govern the actors at the workplace and work community.' Professor Dunlop thus introduces three sets of independent variables: the 'actors,' the 'contexts,' and the 'ideology' of the system. The actors consist of hierarchy of managers and their representatives in supervision; a hierarchy of workers and the trade unions; and the government (their specialized agencies). The context is the environment that includes the technological characteristics of the workplace and work community, the market or budgetary limits that restrict the actors, and the locus and distribution of power in the larger society. The ideology is a systematized body of beliefs and feelings held by the actors. The rules consist of procedures for establishing rules, the substantive rules, and procedures for deciding their application to particular situations.

12.4.2 Oxford Approach

It is a study of institutions of job regulations, which could be internal (wage systems, consultation processes) or external (trade unions). It emphasizes the substantive and procedural rules. It is also expressed through an equation: $r = f(b)$ or $r = f(c)$ (where r is rules governing IR, b is collective bargaining, and c is conflict resolved through collective bargaining). It is criticized for being a blinkered approach, and totally disregards the impact of contextual factors such as market on IR.

[14] T. J. Dunlop, *Industrial Relations Systems* (New York, NY: Holt-Dryden Book, 1958).

12.4.3 Sociology Approach

Authored by G. Margerison, an industrial sociologist, this approach centers around conflict and its causes, rather than its resolution. Conflicts can be either caused by intraplant factors (such as job content, work task, and technology) and fall into three buckets—distributive, structural, and human relations—or they can also be caused by external factors.

12.4.4 Marxist Approach

The Marxist approach highlights the power relationship between capital and labor, marked by their power struggle to consolidate and strengthen their own positions with an aim to exerting greater influence on each other. The capitalist's ownership of the enterprise places him in an advantageous position to pay the minimum price possible for maximizing his profit. The lower the price paid by the owner of the means of production for the labor he employs, the greater is his profit.

12.4.5 Pluralist Approach

In this approach, organization is seen as a coalition of strong and divergent subgroups (including management and trade unions), each having its own legitimate loyalties and respective set of objectives and leaders. The effectiveness of management role would demand more of persuasion and coordination than of control, and thus conflicts would need to be resolved through collective bargaining with trade unions who are legitimate representatives of employees.

The focus is on the resolution of conflict rather than its generation, or, in the words of the pluralist, on 'the institutions of job regulation.' Kerr is one of the important exponents of pluralism. According to him, the social environment is an important factor in industrial conflicts. The isolated masses of workers are more strike-prone as compared to dispersed groups. When industrial jobs become more pleasant and employees get more integrated into the wider society, strikes will become less frequent.

12.4.6 Unitarist Approach

The unitarist view looks at organization as an integrated and harmonious whole and one happy family. In this approach, the management and the employees have a shared goal, and it is but natural that they would cooperate with each other for organizational advancement. Unitarists adopt a paternalistic posture, expect loyalty from employees, and believe conflicts as aberrations more the results of managerial inefficiency than system-driven. Trade unions are irrelevant and avoidable since the employee loyalty cannot be split between organizations and trade unions as they are considered mutually exclusive.

12.4.7 Gandhian Approach

The Gandhian concept of trusteeship is a departure from the other approaches in its humanitarian undertone. In Gandhiji's view, employers, despite being the legal owners of the property, should regard themselves as trustees, or co-owners, in the same way that the workers also should behave as trustees with a responsibility to safeguard them. At a deeper level, the bedrock of the trusteeship concept is the belief that properties and human accomplishments are gifts of nature and, therefore, belong to the larger society and not to individuals. It works at establishing economic equality and the material well-being of the workers in a capitalist society through non-violent means. Gandhiji believed that industrial harmony could fuel the growth of the industry itself, and at the same time improve the conditions of work. He endorsed the workers' right for collective bargaining, and even the right to strike by following a democratic internal process.

12.4.8 The Strategic Choice Model

Kochan, Katz, and McKersie[15] presented a three-tiered approach to IR: strategic decision-making at the top level; collective bargaining or personnel policy-making at the functional level; and workplace supervision (involving supervisors, workmen, and trade unions). The traditional activities of IR occur in the middle level through the processes of collective bargaining and personnel policy formulation. While the key strategic choices are made at the top tier, all the basic decisions (where to invest in, where to set up factories, and so on) affect the lower levels of the system.

The model suggests that IR processes and outcomes are determined by the continuously evolving interaction of environmental pressures and organizational responses. The shifting market forces influenced changes in IR approach even in organizations acclaimed for their harmonious IR (e.g., in Tata Steel from employment of dependents in the 1950s to the VRS in the 1990s). Another important change has been the shifting of power within management, for example, the shift from the old IR approach to the new HRM approach explained the change from the focus on industrial peace and harmony to productivity and commitment to organizational objectives.

Exhibit Labor Unrest Plagues Indian Auto Industry News

Continuing labor unrest in various parts of India has begun to tarnish the image of the booming Indian auto and auto parts industry. After reports of repeated labor problems at Hyundai Motor plant at Chennai in Tamil Nadu, labor unrest has now hit the facility of Volvo Buses India Pvt Ltd, the Indian subsidiary of Swedish bus maker Volvo Bus Corporation.

This is the first strike in Volvo's bus plant in India. Volvo Buses India Pvt. Ltd is a joint venture between Volvo Bus Corporation of Sweden and Azad Group of Bangalore. Volvo holds a 70% stake in the joint venture. The factory started operations in January 2008.

More than 600 workers have launched an indefinite strike at Volvo's plant at Hoskote set up two years ago.

Their demands are similar to those at other auto manufacturing units where labor strife has been reported—confirmation of temporary or reinstatement of sacked employees, in addition to wage hikes.

At Volvo's plant in Karnataka, workers began a go-slow movement three months ago, with a wage hike being among the other demands. The go-slow has led to a loss of close to ₹50 crore to the company until now, following loss of production of over 60 buses.

Major auto companies at the receiving end of labor unrest in India in the recent past include Hyundai Motor India, Ford Motor India, Bosch India, and Ricoh India in Gurgaon, among others.

In June this year, Hyundai Motor India's operations in Chennai were hit by union action following a protest by 150 workers demanding the reinstatement of employees sacked last December that led to a production halt.

---

[15] Kochan, Katz and McKersie. *The Transformation of American Industrial Relations*, (New York, NY: Basic Books, 1986).

The industrial action was the fourth one in two years and led to losses of around ₹65 crore. Hyundai Motor's Chennai facility employs more than 10,000 people.

Hyundai Motor is also the second largest carmaker in India by sales and produces cars such as the i10 and i20 hatchbacks as well as the Verna and Accent sedans.

A protest last year by about 1800 workers at the Gurgaon, Haryana-based auto parts maker Rico Auto Industries Ltd affected production at local and global automobile makers. In both cases, the protesting workers were seeking better wages.

The stir forced Rico customers such as General Motors Co. and Ford Motor Co to either temporarily cut vehicle production or shut factories.

Auto makers had faced a similar predicament caused by the lockout at the plant of German auto components major Bosch in Bangalore. The Bangalore-based company declared a lockout at its Naganathapura plant on the outskirts of the city after employees went on a tool-down strike demanding a wage revision.[16]

The workers justified the strike saying that they had been negotiating a long-term wage settlement with the company since January 1, 2009, after the previous settlement ended on December 31, 2008.

Bosch's facility, located near the electronics city on Hosur Road, about 30 km from the city, employs well over 1000 people and manufactures spark plugs, alternators, and generator starters for the Indian automotive industry and for exports to the Germany-based Bosch GmbH's global operations. Similar problems were reported at Pricol Ltd where the labor issue resulted in the murder of a company official by agitating workers. Similarly, the management of Volvo says, the suspension of workers at its plant was due to 'an act of misconduct, which is grave in nature,' when certain employees used physical force against their managers, including the unit head, an expatriate.

They kept the managers hostage for eight hours without food and water in the night, the company said. The management maintained that for the sake of the organization principles and for all employees and their working environment, such an incident is not negotiable. Clearly, the labor unrest at the affected companies is leading to financial losses that has pushed some, such as Korean auto major Hyundai Motor, to voice the possibility of withdrawing from India.

In most cases, the workers' demands were uncannily similar.

The Volvo Buses Workers' Union says, the management has not been responding to their demands. They say, several temporary workers have been awaiting probation, and probationary workers have been waiting to be made permanent for the past two years and the company has not acted on the union's demands.

Thousands of workers were part of a strike in an important North Indian industrial hub Tuesday, under-scoring touchy labor relations in Asia's third largest economy.

At Ricoh Auto, the strike was sparked off by the death of a protesting worker, which the police attribute to a clash between groups of striking and non-striking employees.

The trade unions claimed that workers in Gurgaon were being denied the right to form a union.

[16] Domain-b.com, 'After Naganathapura, Bosch May Declare Lock-out at Bangalore Plant,' March 11, 2010. Available at: http://www.domain-b.com/companies/companies_r/Robert_Bosch/20100311_bangalore_plant_oneView.html (accessed on October 30, 2017).

The auto industry in and around Gurgaon, Haryana has provided employment to more than 200,000 people, according to the district Website.

A number of automobile firms have their plants in Gurgaon, while IT companies such as Hughes Software, Tata Consultancy Service, Alcatel, HCL, Siemens, GE Capital, and Silicon Graphics also have their units located in Gurgaon.

Commentators say, companies in India have to face tough labor issues because of archaic laws and company policies on hiring and retrenchment.

At a time when states in India are competing to offer incentives to auto companies to set up their bases in their respective locations, such labor issues are sending wrong signals to potential investors, particularly worrisome since rival emerging markets such as China, Brazil, and Russia are also in the race for such investments.

Discussion Questions

1. Analyze the aforementioned case using any of the IR approaches.
2. What was the influence of contextual factors in shaping the IR?

Source: Mohini Bhatnagar. Available at: http://www.domain-b.com/industry/Automobiles (accessed on August 4, 2010).

12.5 THE ACTORS IN INDUSTRIAL RELATIONS

12.5.1 Trade Unions

Trade unions came up to fight for the rights of the industrial workers who sensed loss of control over time and labor while being engaged in the production process in the wake of Industrial Revolution. The erstwhile tillers of the land and the tradesmen got converted into industrial workers, exposed to the exploitation by owners, evident through long working hours, poor pay, unsafe and unhygienic working conditions, and whimsical termination of employment. The precursors of trade unions were the trade guilds of merchants, artisans, and traders, which were created primarily as a bulwark against price competition.

Trade unions originated in Britain. In the beginning, it consisted of workers belonging to the same trade, limited to a region, and generally funded by membership dues. Gradually, trade unions spread their wings, even forming international alliances. National Union of Cotton was the first national trade union, coming up in 1829. In 1834, several unions joined under the Great Trade Union, causing great concern among manufacturers. The panic-stricken employers lobbied hard with the government, who enacted a bundle of restrictive laws known as the Combination Acts prohibiting combination of workers. Eventually, the Combination Acts were repealed in 1824, enabling a boom of workers' associations that had gone underground. Around the same time in France, workers began to gain more rights, such as a reduction in the working shift from 18 or 16 hours to 10 hours a day. In the year 1871, trade unions were legalized in Britain, ushering in the era of unionism worldwide.

The evolution of the trade unions continued in the post-World War II era, with focus on improvement of working conditions for all workers. As a result of certain combinations of strategic actions such as strikes, collective bargaining, and mobilization of public opinion to pressurize the legislatures, conditions in the workplace showed considerable improvement. In Australia, New Zealand, the UK, and partly in Canada, new political parties came up backed by trade unions, giving further boost to workplace reform.

Since the 1960s, the percentage of union membership (density) has, however, shown southward dip. The global growth of the labor movement has reversed since then, however, in response to market imperatives and the attrition of labor-friendly legislation. Culturally, the contemporary emphasis on individual rights systematically undermines collective rights. This is particularly difficult for labor organizations. Nevertheless, trade unions may be reviving through grassroots associations worldwide, which continue to organize for collective bargaining in favor of the most vulnerable members of society.

12.5.2 Employers' Associations

Employers' organizations (EOs) are 'entities that promote the collective interests of business, across sectors, irrespective of enterprise size.'[17] Depending on the diversity in range and content of such 'collective interests' across countries, the structure, membership basis, and functions of employee associations also vary considerably from one another. The primary role of the employers' associations is to influence the government, on behalf of the business community, for appropriate changes in policy and regulatory processes, which will foster an economic environment congenial for enterprise creation and development. This is notwithstanding the fact that individual enterprises may have their own specific objective to join the employer association (e.g., obtaining data in respect of market or regulatory frameworks of the opportunities to network) or a specific service (e.g., representation at an industrial tribunal). It is through the function of being an advocate that the employers' association strengthens its public profile, increases membership, and builds its reputation and brand necessary to promote the other revenue-generating services that the organization offers.

Well-functioning business organizations are the link between enterprises and government, between the micro and the macro level, and crucial for establishing a business environment that benefits all sectors and society. Furthermore, there is a direct link between strong business associations and good economic performance, both from a micro- and a macroeconomic perspective.[18]

Employers' Organizations in India

Employers' organizations in India have a three-tier structure, namely, local associations, regional industrial associations, and all-India federations. The local associations function largely through the chambers of commerce, spreading across all industries in a particular area. They have relatively limited coverage of the labor field. The regional bodies fall into the general pattern of organization of employers in India. They are established in the local or regional level and also at the national level, and normally have linkage with the apex central industrial organizations. The national-level associations also include individual employers.

The objective of the industry-wise development of associations is to help solve common problems facing each industry and trade.

---

17 'The Role of Employers' Organizations in Growth and Sustainable Enterprise Promotion' (Working paper, ILO, Geneva, 2010).

18 ILO. White Paper on 'The Role of Employers', *Organizations in Growth and Sustainable Enterprise Promotion* (2010).

The formation of wage boards on an industry-wide basis, industrial committees at the central and state levels, and development of collective bargaining at the industry level in certain regions have facilitated the consolidation and growth of the various employer associations.

Multiplicity of such industrial association in a particular industry could throw up challenges and has sometimes prevented the evolution of an integrated approach to collective bargaining on an industry-wide basis. At the national level, there are federations, namely, AIOE, EFI, and AIMO, which have been given representation on different tripartite labor consultative bodies.

Some of the EOs in India are:

1. **AIOE** The All India Organization of Employers. Established in 1953. Its membership covers manufacturing, banking, insurance, and commercial establishments. It is a national-level association and has no subsidiaries at local or regional level.
2. **EFI** The Employers' Federation of India. Established in 1933. EFI was registered as a trade union in 1963 under the Indian Trade Unions Act of 1926.
3. **IOE** International Organization of Employers. Represents the employers on matters of social and labor fields at the international level. Established in 1920 with headquarters in Geneva.
4. **SCOPE** The Standing Conference of Public Enterprises. Covers the public sector organizations.
5. **CIE** The Council of Indian Employers. Established in 1973.

A survey of members of EOs in India[19] cited a survey data covering EOs in India indicating that 70% of the respondents believe that EOs:

- Are active in disseminating information to members and making representations whenever an issue or problem arises; henceforth need to be proactive
- Are not going as well as they should be doing in their advisory role and in providing a guidance on issues relating to collective bargaining, and so on
- Should pay more attention to:
  - studying problems of concern to employers
  - improving their interaction with members, unions, and government
  - concentrating on training workers and members
  - strengthening advisory services
  - taking up projects for social and family welfare
- Need not participate, as before, directly in enterprise-level negotiations or settlement of ID at firm level

The employers' associations have also helped in providing standards on specific IR for improvement in the overall IR climate in their member organizations. Notable among them is the whitepaper on 'Industrial Relations and Contract Labor in India' by AIOE. Some recommendations for the member countries included the following extra legal steps to create equity in the administration of contract labor:

1. An establishment employing contract labors through contractors in both peripheral and non-core activities would pay 4.81% of the workers' basic pay as gratuity in the social security account of the worker.

---

[19] Venkata Ratnam, *The Employers' Dilemma* (Bombay: Employers' Federation of India and SOLAR Foundation, 1989).

2. Skills level be considered during wage fixation. The minimum wages including the perks and benefits of the contract labor be fixed as per the criteria laid down by the government demarcating unskilled, semiskilled, and skilled labor.
3. The workers who are engaged as contract workers, that is, employed through a contractor, are to paid 20% above the fixed minimum wages at entry level.

12.5.3 Government

IR have continued to be rooted in national institutions despite the winds of globalization and global business environment. All national governments have formulated legislations and policies that deeply impact how the other two actors in IR—employers and employees—deal with each other, and in this way lay down the ground rules. The answer to the question as to why the State intervenes in employment relations is to be sought in the broader economic and social goals for the nation as a whole. The goals include making the economy prosperous, while creating full employment opportunities. Along with the stated economic and social objectives, the state, depending on the party in power, pursues the political ideology about the desirable nature of society.

Hyman[20] in a review of the common polemics regarding the role of government in shaping IR described six possible roles (Table 12.1).

Table 12.1 Role of government in shaping IR

Role	Task
1. An employer in its own right	1. Set the standards of responsible employment practice
2. A regulator of incomes and prices	2. Control prices and wages, either through direct intervention or in its management of the economy
3. An economic manager	3. Formulate macroeconomic policies of the State, which affect labor market demand, employment, and manpower utilization
4. A protector of standards	4. It establishes and monitors minimum standards through its agencies
5. A rule-maker and legislator	5. Enacting legislation to create auxiliary, restrictive, and regulatory rules that affect the other parties in employment relations
6. A promoter of social citizenship guidelines	6. The extension of political citizenship rights to the workplace through legislation and policy

Source: Hyman, R., 'The State in Industrial Relations', *The SAGE Handbook of Industrial Relations,* P. Blyton, N. Bacon, J. Fiorito and E. Heery (eds) (London: SAGE Publications, 2009).

12.6 INDIAN CONTEXT

In India, the intervention strategy of the State in IR is embedded in India's colonial history under the British. During World War II, the British government, eager to ensure the uninterrupted flow of industrial production, enacted the Defense of India Rules, forbidding strikes and lockouts. The battling parties were encouraged to settle their issues through the media of conciliation and adjudication. In the immediate post-Independence era, when planned economic development became the most important vision for the new nation, industrial strife had to be avoided at any cost. It came to be believed that with a democratically elected government social justice could be achieved in a peaceful, harmonious

[20] Hyman, R., 'The State in Industrial Relations,' in *The SAGE Handbook of Industrial Relations*, eds. P. Blyton, N. Bacon, J. Fiorito, and E. Heery (London: SAGE Publications, 2009).

manner. 'The ironic consequence of this line of reasoning was to continue the emergency measures adopted by the British to fight the war as being in the best interests of a newly independent India.'[21]

The inheritance of this triadic system had a continuous run for 50 years since then, with the result that the state assumed the key role as an umpire in cases of conflicts between the two principal actors and to restore harmony in IR. The state is authorized to seize control of ID, require labor and management to give notice of a strike or a lockout, mediate to resolve their issues, have the final say on whether to bury the dispute as having no merit, or take it forward for court proceedings and judicial decision; if conciliation fails, institute courts that will adjudicate disputes, provide interim solutions pending final disposal by courts, ban strikes and lockouts, and even compel labor to get back to work and management to run the enterprise.

Three principal labor legislations have impacted the shaping of IR in India. These laws are: Trade Union Act 1926, Industrial Employment and Standing Orders Act 1946, and ID Act 1947. The provisions of the Trade Union Act include the registration of trade unions, their rights, their liabilities and responsibilities, and also categorize their funds and manner of their utilization. It also confers on the trade unions the legal and corporate status and protection against civil or criminal prosecution, to enable them to discharge legitimate activities for the benefit of the working class. The Act is applicable not only to the union of workers but also to the association of employers. The law is silent on recognition of bargaining agents. It makes it simple to form a trade union (minimum seven workers required to form a trade union), thus contributing to multiplicity of trade unions, a bane in IR in India. The Industrial Employment and Standing Orders Act 1946 aims to provide a uniformity of working conditions, irrespective of whether there is a union or not. It requires all industrial establishments with 100 or more workers (50 or less in case of Maharashtra) to have a standing order.

The objective of the ID Act 1947 is to secure industrial peace and harmony by providing for appropriate machinery and procedure for the investigation and settlement of ID by negotiations. This Act lays down procedure for resolving conflicts, for going on strikes and declaring lockouts, creates conditions for termination of employment including lay-off and retrenchment, and also closure and transfer of undertakings. One of the most controversial provisions of the Act is about requiring the employer to present a 21 days' notice of change before carrying out certain changes in the workplace.

Case Issues in Trade Union Recognition

While confrontation has new teeth with technology and a more educated workforce, a discourse is only possible if unions get recognition from their managements for all labor-related discussions. There are umpteen cases, including Maruti's Manesar plant union, that are awaiting recognition. In its turn, Maruti says that it recognizes only one union at its Gurgaon plant (not Manesar), the Maruti Udyog Kamgar Union, which, says Managing Executive Officer (Admin), S.Y. Siddiqui, 'has been at the forefront of new initiatives like flexible manufacturing, kaizen and regular training of workers.'

Last year, when workers of multinational giant Foxconn demanded that their union be recognized by the management for all labor-related discussions, the subsequent strike led

[21] E. A. Ramaswamy, *Industrial Relations* (New Delhi: Oxford University Press, 2000).

to 400 arrests. Almost simultaneously, workers of the MRF United Workers Union were arrested by the police in Tamil Nadu for raising a similar demand. A few years ago, a workers' agitation in the plant of Graziano Italiano in Greater Noida over the refusal to recognize a workers' union ended with the company's managing director being killed. Currently, workers at Tata Motors' Rudrapur plant that produces the Nano have formed a union and are awaiting recognition. 'There are about 6000 workers in the factory of which 750 permanent employees are union members,' claims Dinesh Bhatt, president of the union, which is demanding wage revision and more downtime, among other things. Bhatt, though, is hopeful of his union getting recognized by August.

Wages are always a sore point but Nestlé India workers seem to have sorted out their problems uniquely—by approaching international bodies. In 2009, unions representing more than 1200 workers at Nestlé India's factories in Moga, Ponda, and Bicholim signed agreements on wages and benefits for the first time marking a major achievement in their yearlong struggle for the right to wage bargaining. In November 2008, the unions, which are members of the International Union of Food-affiliated Federation of All India Nestlé Employees, called for an end to the system of unilaterally imposed annual wage increments and demanded the right to negotiate wages.

Nestlé India management stood its ground and instead obtained court injunctions permanently banning union actions within 50–200 meters of four factories (Moga, Samalkha, Ponda, and Bicholim). In its defense, a Nestlé India spokesperson states that 'the court injunctions were not against the workers' right to assembly...(but) to ensure smooth entry and exit of people and materials and to ensure proper functioning of the factory operations.' There were demonstrations and a formal complaint filed against Nestlé for violations of the *OECD Guidelines on Multinational Enterprises*. With a barrage of pressure at local, national, and international levels, Nestlé India management finally entered into wage negotiations for the first time in September 2009.

Internationally, trade unions have delinked from politics. In the UK and the USA, they are powerful in negotiations with individual employers, but have no significant political clout. Ditto in Japan. Even in Germany, France, and Italy, the role of trade unions has become more focused on negotiations with employers rather than on politics.

Trade unions in India have come a long way since 1918 when the first organized trade union, the Madras Labor Union, came into being under Bahman Pestonji Wadia, a theosophist who found the Madras textile mill workers' conditions oppressive, to say the least. Though B.P. Wadia got disillusioned with the Theosophical Society in Madras and left a year later for Los Angeles, one of his descendants would return more than six decades later to lord over Mumbai's mills and set up one of the greatest clashes between labor and capital in post-Independence India—Nusli Wadia, the enfant terrible of India Incorporated, and one of the nemesis of the late Dutta Samant. But that, again, is another story.

Discussion Question

1. Do you think that government should have a role in resolving conflicts or in the process of recognizing a trade union? State the reasons.

Source: Adapted from Moinak Mitra, 'India Inc.'s New Age Unions Are Pushing for Reformation—and How,' *The Economic Times*, July 29, 2011.

12.7 INDUSTRIAL RELATIONS AND HUMAN RESOURCE MANAGEMENT

There are some fundamental dissimilarities between the old discipline of IR and the emergent discipline of HRM. The key differentiator between IR and HRM is that while the former is essentially a tripartite process involving three principal actors, the latter is a bipartite process, eliminating the role of the State. The activities of IR have often been targeted at collective outcomes at national and/or sector/industry levels, which are then brought down to each enterprise. HRM is solely meant for the enterprise and its endeavors to integrate the interests of managers, individual workers, and groups of workers around corporate objectives, for the ultimate aim at securing competitive advantage for the business.

12.7.1 HRM and the Decline of Trade Unions

According to a large number of researches, trade unionism has been on the wane since at least three decades. In the USA, from a high of 20 million members in 1979 the trade union membership declined to 14.5 million in 2013 and from 12 million to 6.5 million in Britain. According to the OECD, European countries, including Germany and France, have also seen huge drops in membership. Union decline has been particularly evident in Britain over the past 25 years. In the late 1970s, over 13 million people—or around 58% of workers—were trade union members, and wages for over 70% of workers were set by collective bargaining. Since reaching its peak in 1979, unionization (however measured) has fallen year after year, so that by 2004 less than 30% of workers were members of a trade union.[22]

The picture is similar in Asia also. In Japan and Singapore, the slide in trade union density started in the late 1970s. In Philippines, it decreased under martial law, increased later, and decreased again in the 1990s; in Korea, it increased after democratization in 1987, only to slump in the decade of the 1990s. In India, information obtained from diverse sources indicates the onset of a decline around the same time. Bhattacherjee[23] mentioned drop in the number of unions submitting annual 'returns' to the central government. Even in the last bastion of trade unions, in the state of West Bengal, a sharp fall has been reported.[24] Das[25] cites the data that during the period 1982–1990 prior to liberalization, 4,380 new unions with a total membership of 629,151 were registered, but in the subsequent nine years post-liberalization, the number shrank to 2,686 with 240,624 new members. In Taiwan and China, union density rose in the 1980s, but fell in the 1990s. In China, trade union membership increased around 100% between 1979 and 1995, but declined by about 15% in 1998, a 15% drop.[26]

A key change, however, coinciding with the decline of trade unions has been the consolidation of HR practices and new forms of work organization. Phrases such as 'high-involvement,' 'high-commitment,' and 'high-performance management' are emblematic of the emergent HRM. The increased adoption of HR practices has been presented, particularly in the prescriptive management literature, as providing the basis for a new win-win relationship between workers and managers. It is often advocated that the HR practices provide opportunities to the management the hope of improved

[22] *The Economist*, 'Why Trade Unions Are Declining,' *The Economist*, September 29, 2015.

[23] Debashish Bhatttacharjee, 'Organized Labor and Economic Liberalization India: Past, Present, and Future' (International Institute for Labor Studies discussion paper, ILO, Geneva, 2001).

[24] S. Das, 'A Note on Trade Union Density in India,' (Working paper, Department of Collective Bargaining, Cornell University, Ithaca, NY, 2000).

[25] Ibid.

[26] Sarosh Kuruvilla, Subesh Das, Hyunji Kwon, and Soonwon Kwon, 'Trade Union Growth and Decline in Asia' (Cornell University ILR School, Ithaca, NY, 2002).

productivity while enhancing the engagement and satisfaction level of the employee, job security, and possibly better compensation.

As Legge[27] points out,

> Employer/Union power is manifested in three ways: who wins industrial actions; who succeeds in controlling the agenda of IR; who succeeds in moulding employees' definition of their interest and ideological stance. On all three counts, since the end of 1970s, unions have lost ground.

According to Bratton,[28] innovative HRM practices pose a threat to trade unions in four ways: the individualization of employment contract, the demise of union representation, the intensification of work, and undermining of union solidarity through organizational commitment. Mcgraw and Harley [29] have found that MNCs are moving toward more sophisticated HR practices, but there is no evidence to pursue anticollective approach to the management of IR.

Has unionism been replaced by adoption of HRM practices? A series of surveys in Britain between 1980 and 1998[30] finds no evidence to support the hypothesis of HRM/union substitution. This finding emerges from several empirical strategies. First, the study team compared changes over time in the incidence of HR practices across union and non-union sectors, and found little difference between sectors. Second, the surveyors asked whether newer workplaces (because these have been shown to be more likely to be non-union) have experienced differentially faster HRM incidence. Again, the data threw up no such pattern and no evidence of statistically significant union/non-union differences. Third, an analysis of longitudinal changes also failed to yield any evidence of faster union decline in workplaces or industries with faster adoption of HR practices. Overall, one can only conclude that HRM substitution does not seem to be a very important factor in explaining trade union decline in Britain.

In a study to assess the impact of HR practices on the union–management relationship covering 640 respondents from seven manufacturing organizations of Odisha (both sectors), India, the major finding was that the HR practices are not adverse to the union–management relationship. Performance feedback, promotion, and reward systems helped both union and management in maintaining a cordial relationship. However, the training system is perceived negatively by the unions as a mechanism for building direct relationship with the workers. Unions have to leave the path of confrontation and cooperate with the management for their sustenance as well as for organizational growth and development.[31]

---

27 Karen Legge, *Human Resource Management: Rhetoric and Realities* (New York, NY: Palgrave Macmillan, 1995).

28 J. Bratton, 'Human Resource Management and Industrial Relations,' in *Human Resource Management: Theory and Practice*, eds. J. Bratton and J. Gold (London: Macmillan, 1999): 306–357.

29 McGraw, P. and Harley, B., 'Global or Local? Industrial Relations and Human Resource Management Practices in Australian and Overseas Owned Workplaces', *Journal of Industrial Relations*, 45, no. 1 (2003): 1–26.

30 Stephen Machin and Stephen Wood, 'Human Resource Management as a Substitute for Trade Unions in British Workplaces,' *ILR Review* 58, no. 2 (January 2005): 201–218.

31 Manoranjan Dhal, 'HR Practices and Union Management Relationship,' *The Indian Journal of Industrial Relations* 50, no. 4 (April 2015): 652–666.

12.7.2 HRM with Union Consent

A question will come up at this stage: Can HRM be introduced with union consent? In unionized workplaces, it is difficult for HR initiatives to make impact with union involvement. Ramaswamy[32] reported about convergence of union-centered IR and individual-centered HRM in the USA, specifically on quality of working life (QWL) and employee engagement. Further, Japanese practices in their large enterprises have reflected a successful blend of collectivist IR and HRM, made possible to some extent by their enterprise union system, which has facilitated union involvement in HRM initiatives through mechanisms such as their joint consultation system.[33]

A three-track system has been suggested to classify the different kinds of union–HRM interface existing in different organizations.[34] Track 1 captures the traditional combative relations over common workplace issues; Track 2 describes participation of the individual employees in such workplace decision-making activities; in Track 3, there is a direct union involvement in a number of issues. According to Blackstone, the Track 3 model compels the union to adopt joint responsibility for quality and partnership, and thereby its adversarial role gets seriously undermined.

In the final assessment, the tightly drawn frontiers between HRM and IR needs to melt, and IR thinking would need to change to become strategic. Two-way communication, training, and motivation of individual employees are irreversible processes. But the bottleneck appears to be in workplace flexibility (functional, working time, types of contracts, workforce size), job design, and pay systems, where traditional IR and HRM are bound to lock horns. For example, a strategic HR initiative such as introduction of performance pay system may undermine wage fixation through collective bargaining. The process of collective bargaining may be rendered a retrograde process and require restructuring. The lingering role for IR could be in brokering peace in collective industrial conflicts and in finding ways and means to avoid conflicts.

In India, there are some heartwarming stories about transformational efforts of inspired management to enroll the trade unions in the new realities and to curve out a role for them. At an ITC factory in Nepal (Surya Nepal P Ltd), all managers and employees assembled in one room after preparations for two days. They did a group exercise—'WorldCafe.' The preparatory two days were spent with a group of managers and then with other employees preparing for the third day. On the third day, all engaged in developing a common answer to a single question: What kind of work culture should we develop in that factory? And how? At ITC's Ranjangaon factory, the plant management started all practices with the intention of keeping a close interaction with employees. But a union was formed. ITC then decided that if a union was formed they must do everything to foster good relations with the union. So, a series of workshops were organized. This approach has resulted in essentially a healthy relationship. If you go to this factory, you will see two boards or standees like you see those at the petrol pumps. One tells you that you are at the gate of ITC factory. The other was also built by ITC in an identical way—it tells you that ITC Kamgar Sanghatana leads employees. The signboard tells the visitors of the inclusive approach of ITC without saying so.

---

32 E. A. Ramaswamy, *Managing Human Resources: A Contemporary Text* (New Delhi: Oxford University Press, 2000).

33 S. R. de Silva, *The Theory of the Conflict Between Industrial Relations and Human Resource Management* (ILO ACT/EMP Publications, 1998).

34 Barry Bluestone and Irving Bluestone, *Negotiating the Future: A Labor Perspective on American Business* (New York, NY: Basic Books, 1994).

Closing Case Industrial Unrest at Tata Nano Plant

At the Sanand works of Tata Motors, Gujarat, the production of its all-new hatchback Tiago got seriouslydisrupted when on February 23, in the night shift, 422 employees out of the total 2,200 working at the plant, went on a strike, demanding reinstatement of 28 colleagues suspended on disciplinary grounds.

The Sanand plant came into the limelight in November 2008, when in response to an offer from then Gujarat Chief Minister Narendra Modi, the company shifted the trouble-ridden factory to manufacture Nano from Singur in West Bengal. However, the difficulties for the company did not disappear fully, as new problems surfaced. Commencing its operations in 2010, the Sanand plant of Tata has experienced several bottlenecks in the production of Nano.

Against the installed capacity of 250,000 cars per annum, it is reported to have produced roughly 42,560 Nano cars in the two years between January 2014 and December 2015, after the demand for what was once dubbed the cheapest car in the world fell dramatically.

Trouble was simmering for quite some time. The production at the plant has dropped considerably since its launch in July 2009. The plant is operating at 10% of the total capacity of 2.5 lakh units per annum with only one shift.

Around 2,200 workers are employed at the plant, which was shifted from West Bengal following protests over land acquisition to Gujarat that is known for its trouble-free labor. There is no union at the plant.

Labor Commissioner's View

Assistant Labor Commissioner (Ahmedabad) M. S. Patel, who is mediating between the workers and the management, said,

> Two months back, Tata Motors' management suspended two workers on disciplinary grounds. While one had allegedly abused his supervisor, the other was suspended for having walked into another department. The workers went on flash strike but we had immediately intervened and resolved the issue. A compromise was reached that the management will conduct an inquiry into the matter within one month and submit a report.

Patel also said, 'It was decided that out of the two suspended, one would be taken back while the other will face action as per the report,' adding that since the inquiry report did not come in two months, the workers went on strike on Monday night.

Management Version

According to the company's management, the striking workers behaved in a disorderly manner and scratched and damaged around 50 cars. So the management was forced to suspend another 26 workers. They wanted all 28 suspended workers to be reinstated. The management is firm in its stand that the reinstatement can only happen after an inquiry.

'There have been continued agitations for monetary increases as well as protests over disciplinary actions against those provoking the workmen, resulting in serious threat to company personnel as well as losses due to tampering,' said a Tata spokesperson. Cops were deployed at the plant on Tuesday to prevent violence as workers were likely to continue the strike on Wednesday too even as their talks with the management were on. According to the management of Tata Motors, the key problem for the plant was that, located on the outskirts of Ahmedabad city, it did not have an organized trade union. 'Though all of them are salaried and permanent employees of the plant, there is no single leader. They have a panel of seven people with whom we are now trying to have a dialog,' he said.

'While the management team is continuing to make efforts to talk to the workmen on strike and convince them to restore normalcy, plant operations are simultaneously continuing,' the management said.

Discussion Questions

1. What would be a good strategy to resolve the impasse in the aforementioned case?
2. What are the implications of the view that the key problem was that Tata Motors plant 'did nothave an organized trade union'?
3. What are the strategies of effective conflict resolution in a non-unionized workplace? What couldhave been done to prevent the conflict?

Source: Prepared on the basis of reports TNN at http://timesofindia.indiatimes.com (accessed on February 24, 2016) and *The Financial Express* at http://www.financialexpress.com IANs. 24/2.

SUMMARY

According to *Encyclopedia Britannica*[35], IR denotes

The relations of the state with employers, workers, and other organizations. The subject, therefore, includes individual relations and joint consultation between employers and workers at their places of work, collective relations between employers and trade unions; and the part played by the State in regulating these relations.

Dale Yoder[36] considers IR to be 'a designation of a whole field of relationship that exists because of the necessary collaboration of men and women in the employment processes of Industry.'

The basic objective of IR is to bring about harmonious relations between employers and employees. The larger objectives, however, encompass improvement in productivity; securing the rights and interests of both labor and management based on cooperation; minimize conflict and adopt effective conflict-resolution processes; avoid stoppages, go-slows, gheraos, strikes, lockouts; and promote industrial democracy. The State, which plays a watchdog role, also seeks to mend imbalances in social and economic order in the wake of technological and economic advancements, sometimes by controlling and directing the parties to adjust their disparate interests.

An IR system may be defined as comprising the totality of power interactions of participants in a workplace, when these interactions involve IR issues. Based on different elements and characteristics of IR, several authors have tried to formulate their own unique approaches to IR, and these include systems approach, Oxford approach, unitary and pluralist, Marxist, and Gandhian approaches.

In India, IR is characterized by state intervention through legislations, preference for litigations by both parties, namely, employers and trade unions. The intervention strategy of the State in IR,

35 *Encyclopaedia Britannica*, Vol. 12, p. 297 (London).

36 Yoder, *Personnel Management and Industrial Relations*.

which is embedded in India's colonial history under the British, is being eroded with clamor for labor law reforms and flexibility in the workplace post-liberalization of the Indian economy and the rapid globalization. The new millennium has witnessed the shrinking power of the trade unions, and the new workplaces are marked by union-avoidance strategies of the employers. Side by side, there has been rise in industrial unrest, especially in the auto sector, with two new issues pertaining to contract labor and recognition of emergent trade unions.

Finally, on the subject of whether HRM can co-exist with IR, the last word has not yet been spoken. In unionized workplaces, it is difficult for HR initiatives to make impact with union involvement. Ramaswamy[37] reported about convergence of union-centered IR and individual-centered HRM in the USA, specifically on QWL and employee engagement. Further, Japanese practices in their large enterprises have reflected a successful blend of collectivist IR and HRM, made possible, to some extent, by their enterprise union system that has facilitated union involvement in HRM initiatives through mechanisms such as their joint consultation system.

Short-answer Questions

1. What is social dialog?
2. Define industrial relations.
3. What are the objectives of IR?
4. Describe Strategic Choice Model.
5. How does Unitary approach to IR differ from Pluralistic approach?
6. What are some of the employer's organizations in India?
7. Mention some key features of HRM with union consent.
8. Narrate some key issues in Union recognition.
9. What is the role of government in IR?
10. Describe Oxford approach to IR.

Discussion Questions

1. Conventional wisdom is that IR is based on power equations between the employer and the trade unions, and HRM focuses on tapping the potential of the individual. Is it possible to create a new workplace where the two approaches can be integrated?
2. How does IR fit in ILO's concept of decent workplace?
3. Comment on the State's intervention strategy in IR. What role should the government be playing in the emerging workplace?
4. What is your view about whether IT industries should be unionized? What could be the positives and what could be the negatives?

[37] E. A. Ramaswamy, *Managing Human Resources*.

CHAPTER 13

Workplace Laws and Regulations

LEARNING OBJECTIVES

After completing this chapter, the student will be able to:

- Discuss the history and evolution of labor law in India
- Apply the knowledge to solve compliance issues in workplace
- Form an opinion on the relevance of some legal provisions in current context of business
- Present the basic features of the major labor laws in India

Opening Case Change in Service Conditions

ABC is an FMCG company with a factory at Sewri and employs 3,000 employees. The Sewri factory produces, among other things, vegetable oil and soaps. From the outset of 1988, the plan witnessed protracted industrial unrest marked by continuous go-slow for about 17 months. The management responded by declaring lockout (which according to company estimates, resulted in production loss of ₹100 crore). After the imposition of lockout, several meetings were called by the labor department of the Government of Maharashtra. Ultimately, on June 19, 1989, it was agreed by the union and the management that the lockout would be lifted on certain conditions.

According to the management, the union initially agreed to the conditions as discussed in this tripartite meeting, and the terms were chalked out and the notice was put up on June 22, 1989, together with the copy of the draft agreement under Section 2(p) of the ID Act 1947 to be entered into with the individual workman/the union, as a pre-condition for lifting the lockout. The union, however, later backed out and did not sign the agreement. The individual workmen, however, signed the agreement.

On June 22, 1989, the employer lifted the lockout and permitted all the employees to report back for their normal duties. On resumption of their duties, the workmen found that the employer has closed down several departments or parts of the departments. In the hard soaps department, where hard soaps under the brand name of 'Moonlight' and 'Lifebelt' were being manufactured, three lines of hard soaps and three lines of toilet soaps machines were stopped as were two lines of toilet soaps department also. Further, several machines were dismantled that included three Rose wrapping machines, three Jones stamper machines, Mazzeni machines 2 and 3, conveyer belt, and T. S. M. machine. The employer had also closed down the printing department employing about 18 workmen. The EPCC (machine building department), talcum department, and sulphanation plant were also closed.

The union alleged in the complaint that the workmen working in certain departments were getting incentive wages. Now such workmen have been deployed to the departments and the places where there was no incentive payment. As a result of closure of departments, about 500 workmen employed at the factory were rendered surplus. Certain lines of products were discontinued. Certain other lines of products that could be run viably were introduced. This provided employment to about 250 workmen. The union complained that the closure of departments, rationalization, and reduction in wages and allowances are subject matters of Schedule IV of the ID Act 1947. The employer did not give any notice of change under Section 9A of the ID Act 1947 and, therefore, the act of the employer in closing down the said departments or part of it was contrary to the provisions of law and illegal.

The union further alleged that the workmen in skilled grades have been directed to perform semiskilled jobs and workmen requiring definite mental, physical, and intellectual ability are required to do jobs inconsistent with the mental, physical, and intellectual requirements as set out in the settlements.

According to the management, such redeployment will not lead to any retrenchment of the workmen, that no workman has been retrenched so far, nor will they be retrenched in future. According to the employer, it was only in the interest of business exigencies and on the demand for the products, and with a view to modernize and make the unit run viably, that it had become necessary to remove certain machinery, and as such dismantling and removal of such machinery did not constitute any unfair labor practice. The employer averred that the operations that became irrelevant in the present context, keeping in view volume/technological changes, environment and commercial necessity, have been discontinued in order to run the unit viably.

The management also averred that the workmen had no vested right to receive incentive wages as such, and, therefore, the union cannot complain if the workmen were not earning their incentive wages. According to the management, they have not done anything that required any notice to be given under Section 9A of the ID Act 1947. They denied that the workmen have been asked to perform duties that were not consistent with their grades or classification. The employer submitted that the individual workmen had entered into the settlement and they agreed for redeployment as also for introducing new machinery and new method of working. The employer, thus, prayed that the complaint be dismissed.

The Judgment

The relevant provision was Section 9A of the ID Act requiring the management to give a notice of change for 21 days before changing any conditions provided under Fourth Schedule. The management contended that in order to run the factory at Sewri as a viable unit, the redeployment became necessary and that was agreed to by the individual workmen in the agreement. The redeployment was to meet the business exigencies regarding the existing and new products as also the introduction of new products/processes/technologies and improved system of work.

The Court's View

The employer introduced certain new lines in the soaps department and rescheduling of the production was in the interest of business exigencies and depending on the demand for the products and with a view to modernize and make the unit run viably it had become necessary to remove certain machinery. As a result of redeployment about 500 workmen employed at the Sewri factory were rendered surplus. Certain lines of products were discontinued. Certain other lines of products that could be run viably were introduced. This provided employment to about 250 workmen. The workmen agreed to the introduction of new products/processes/mechanization and improvement in quality, reduction in manufacturing costs, improvement in productivity, and new system of working, and in order to do this, certain machineries were removed and fresh machines were installed and layout of the factory was modernized. This entire exercise of discontinuing some lines and introducing some new lines could be classified as rationalization.

For an act of rationalization to be covered under Item 10 of the Fourth Schedule, it is sufficient if such an act is likely to lead to the retrenchment of workmen and not its actual happening. The evidence on record is a clear pointer to that effect.

In light of the preceding discussion, there is no doubt that the action of the employer resulted in change of service conditions of the workmen covered by Items 1, 10, and 11 of the Fourth Schedule of ID Act. The fact that the surplus employees upon redeployment were not paid incentive clearly shows that the wages of the workmen were affected and, thus, there was change in the conditions of service under Item 1 of the Fourth Schedule.

Discussion Questions

1. There is a view, especially among employers, that labor laws in India hinder flexibility in running business. In the light of the above case, do you agree with the above view? Give reasons.
2. Based on a reading of the ID Act, what provisions in your opinion, should be altered?
3. What should be done to strike a balance between protecting employees' and employers' interests?

Source: Adapted from a court case reported in www.Indiankanoon.com

13.1 INTRODUCTION

Ever since the time of the Industrial Revolution, the evolving world of work has thrown up new and complex economic and social challenges for the worker. In India, as the story goes, children below age of seven were working at factories, before the first Factories Act of 1881 prohibited such practice. Legislations governing the conditions of work are intended to help the workers cope with them. Such legislations attempt to do it in three ways. First, they provide a legal system that helps productive individual and collective employment relationships, thereby building a productive economy. Second, they design a structure for worker–employer interface on work-related issues. Third, they act as a catalyst for industrial harmony based on some basic principles and rights at work. It has, however, been found that for laws to play these roles effectively, the labor laws need to be aligned to the demands of the labor market and the interests of the main actors. Such an alignment can happen in a seamless manner if those concerned are allowed to participate at the formulation stage of the legislation through processes of social dialogs. 'The involvement of stakeholders in this way is of great importance in developing a broad basis of support for labor legislation and in facilitating its application within and beyond the formal structured sectors of the economy.'[1]

Labor legislations in India cover the rules pertaining to the contractual aspect of the employer–employee relations. Introduced during the British rule of India, the Indian Contract Act 1872 draws heavily from the British law of contracts and stands on the premise that the parties to the contract enjoy the freedom to develop their own terms of contracts. The employer–employee or the master–servant relationship is based upon voluntarism, indicating the parties can evolve their specific terms formulated by themselves within the bounds of the law of contract.

The underlying presumption in the law of contract that the parties have equal freedom to enter into a contract is a flawed one, as all employment relationships are essentially unequal. In this lopsided relationship, the employer is decidedly the stronger of the two—in economic might as well as in bargaining strength, in contrast to the employee, who depends on his job to survive or perish. Employees try to restore the equilibrium in their favor by being organized, by joining trade union and through collective bargaining. Another process of restoring this balance is through mobilizing political power and seeking intervention of the State. The State responded by creating an umbrella of legislative protection and privileges regarding safety, health and welfare, regulation of hours of work, leave and holidays, and social security. And, depending upon their organizational strength, employees have also sought regulatory legislation for protection and enhancement of their material well-being and security of their employment.

The major labor laws in India were enacted around 1947–1948, at the time of political independence. Prior to that, there were a few laws, such as Factories Act, Payment of Wages Act, and Trade Unions Act, which sought to protect the workers' essential conditions of work and rights at workplace. In India thus, the State stepped in the space meant for the play of the contract between the employer and the employee, by arranging for extensive legal protection of labor, thereby nullifying the principle of freedom of contract. Labor laws thus emerged as key social and economic legislation in India, targeted at safeguarding the interests of the downtrodden.

The rationale for the State acting as the guardian angel of workers' rights lies in the concept of the 'welfare state,'

> whose responsibility it is to assure to its citizens not only physical liberty to pursue their avocations according to their liking, and political liberty to choose their own government at reasonable intervals, but also assure social well-being and economic and material opportunities to make the foregoing liberties meaningful and effective.[2]

The concept of welfare state is enshrined in the Indian Constitution through the Directive Principles of State Policy that assure

---

1 ILO. 'Labor Legislations Guidelines'. Chapter 1, *Labor legislation in the contemporary world.* Available at: www.ilo.org/legacy/english/dialogue/ifpdial/llg/noframes/ch1.htm (accessed on December 14, 2016).

2 Anand Prakash, 'Labor Law.' (1987): 392. Available at: http://14.139.60.114:8080/jspui/bitstream/123456789/738/16/Labor%20Law.pdf (accessed on November 15, 2017).

just and humane conditions of work and maternity relief; public assistance in cases of unemployment, old age, sickness and disablement and in other cases of undeserved want; protection of the health and strength of workers, and avoiding circumstances which force citizens to enter avocations unsuited to their age or strength.[3]

Apart from the Directive Principles, the state role in workers' rights is also indicated in Article 19 which recognizes the right to form associations and unions as a Fundamental Right. It must, however, be mentioned that one very powerful body of labor is the body of judgments by courts, mainly in the arena of adjudication of ID.

13.2 HISTORY AND EVOLUTION

At the heart of the labor legislations was the intent to provide to the workers better conditions, the right to organize, and to the employers the powers to limit disruptive worker actions and to hold down the cost of labor. The level of labor legislations at any time, therefore, is the outcome of this pull between divergent interests in society.

International Labor Organization was set up, as a wing of the League of Nations, to deal with labor issues. Protection of workers' interests constituted a major part of the post-World War redevelopment work. As part of the Reconstruction Commission, the Whitley Commission in the UK pushed for the setting up of 'industrial councils' in all parts of the world. An international labor rights body was recommended by a conference consisting of representatives from Great Britain, France, Belgium, and Italy. Two visions emerged of the post-War world: one by International Federation of Trade Unions, which in a meeting in Berne demanded an end to wage labor and the establishment of socialism and also an enactment and enforcement of labor legislation by League of Nations to safeguard workers and trade unions. The UK also mooted the idea of labor laws by an international parliament that each member of the League would be required to implement. The representative of USA opposed this and instead suggested that such an international body should only make recommendations and that the League of Nations could be entrusted to enforce them. The US proposal, which was accepted, included the stand that labor should not be treated as a commodity, that all workers had the right to a wage sufficient to live on.

The other proposals that were adapted were: 8-hour work day or the 40-hour work week; one or more days for weekly rest; equality of laws for foreign workers; and regular and frequent inspection of factory conditions. In October 1919, after the signing of Versailles Treaty, the International Labor Conference adopted six international labor Conventions, pertaining to hours of work in industry, unemployment, maternity protection, night-work for women, minimum age, and night work for young persons in industry. The ILO became a part of the UNO after the League of Nations was wound up in 1946.

13.3 LABOR LAWS IN INDIA

The history of labor legislation in India spans over 125 years, starting with the Apprentices Act 1850. The law sought to enable children brought up in orphanages to get employment when they come of age.

With the establishment and growth of small manufacturing units, factories, and industries in India from the middle of the 19th century, labor started moving from villages to industrial areas in search of

[3] Ibid.

employment. Due to the absence of any state control over employers, there was rampant exploitation of the workers with complete disregard for their needs. Thus, low wages, long working hours, and poor working conditions were the order of the day. This condition eventually triggered off a series of labor legislations, starting with the Factories Act 1881.

The Factories Act constituted the first set of real legislations to regulate workplaces. The Factory Acts were a series of UK labor law Acts passed by the Parliament of the United Kingdom to regulate the conditions of industrial employment. Initially, the provisions were on hours of work and welfare of young children employed in cotton mills, and by 1833, a professional factory inspectorate was set up. The Indian Factory Act was enacted much later in 1881. It was enacted on the basis of recommendation of the first Factories Commission, which was appointed to ameliorate the appalling condition of workers, especially women and children, in factories. It has been speculated that the law was brought under pressure from the textile magnates of Lancashire and Manchester, and the real purpose was to make Indian labor costlier and to neutralize the competitive advantage enjoyed by Indian textile goods over British textiles. The Act prohibited employment of children below age 7 and employment in two separate factories on the same day. It introduced 9-hour work per day, four holidays in the month, and rest intervals. This Act was successively amended in later years (1891, 1911, 1923, 1926, and 1931), eventually growing into the larger law enacted in 1948.

The Factories Acts were followed by other laws including the Workmen's Compensation Act 1923, Mines Act 1923, Trade Unions Act 1926, Trade Disputes Act 1929, Payment of Wages Act 1936, Employment of Children Act 1938, Maternity Benefit Act, and the Bombay ID Act 1938. The last Act introduced a permanent setup for industrial conflict resolution in the form of an industrial court. This Act was later replaced by a still more comprehensive legislation known as the Bombay Industrial Relations Act 1946.

In independent India, bulk of the current labor laws were enacted in 1947–1948, with only a few exceptions. The labor laws post-Independence have been shaped by various influences: the philosophies and opinions of the important nationalist leaders who led the freedom struggle, the deliberations in the constituent assembly, the constitutional provisions such as Fundamental Rights and Directive Principles of State Policy, and the ILO standards and other important international standards and norms. Another set of influencers were the tripartite labor-related bodies like the National Commissions on Labor. In some cases, even important landmark court judgments have left their mark on a future legislation. For example, the principles laid down for prohibition of contract labor in Contract Labor Regulation and Abolition Act 1970 were enunciated in an earlier case (*Standard Vacuum vs Their Workmen*, 1960).

In terms of the enactment and enforcement, the labor laws in India can be classified into four categories: enacted by Parliament and enforced by the Union government (ESI Act, EPF Act, etc.); enacted by the Parliament and enforced by both the Union and state governments (Contract Labor Regulations and Abolitions Act, ID Act); enacted by the Parliament and enforced by the state governments (Factories Act, Trade Union Act); and enacted by state legislature and enforced by state governments (Shops and Establishment Act).

13.3.1 Indian Constitution and Labor Laws

The Constitution of India is the fountainhead of all legislations. There are three ways in which the Constitution impacts the labor legislations. First, the Seventh Schedule vests the legislatures with legislative powers. Most of the areas pertaining to labor are part of concurrent list, indicating that both the Parliament and the state legislatures can enact laws in these areas. In actual practice, most labor laws have been enacted by the Parliament and are uniform across the various states. Some of the Acts have been modified by the state legislatures to suit their conditions.

The second way in which the Indian Constitution impacts the labor laws in the country is through the enlistment of certain basic rights of citizens known as Fundamental Rights in Part III. They are so called because these rights are essential for each citizen to live life like human beings with dignity, and cannot be denied even by the State. The relevance of these rights lies in the fact that neither the Parliament nor the legislature can enact laws contrary to any of them. Several provisions of Part III are connected with labor matters (Table 13.1).

Table 13.1 Fundamental rights and labor laws

Article	Provision	Brief contents
12	Definition	It defines the state. Whether a corporation can be considered a state has been decided from case to case basis, depending on the ownership pattern of the corporation.
13	Laws inconsistent with or in derogation of the Fundamental Rights	Laws contrary to the fundamental rights shall be void.
14	Equality before law	The rulings specifically indict sexual harassment of women in workplace.
15	Prohibition of discrimination on grounds of religion, race, caste, sex, or place of birth	It allows for special provision for women and children.
16	Equality of opportunity in matters of public employment	It allows pursuit of reservation policy for SC/ST and OBCs.
19	Protection of certain rights regarding freedom of speech and the like (this includes freedom to form associations and unions)	It includes the right to close a business. But the right to carry on a trade or business is subject to the legal boundaries.
20	Protection in respect of conviction for offences	No person shall be punishable for any offence except for violation of the law in force at the time of commission of the act.
21	Protection of life and personal liberty	Scope widened through court rulings. Includes right to livelihood also and has been invoked to contest dismissal by the employer.
21A	Education for children	Ensures right to education up to 14 years of age.
22	Protection against arrest and detention in certain cases	No person to be detained in custody without being told the grounds of arrests and be denied consultation with a legal practitioner.
23	Prohibition of traffic in human beings and forced labor	It prohibits bonded labor; includes the responsibility of the State to ensure that workers live with human dignity, free from exploitation of any kind.
24	Prohibition of employment of children in factories	Prohibits employment of children below the age of 14 in factories, mines, and other such places.
32	Remedies for enforcement of rights conferred by this part	It contains the right to move the Supreme Court or any other court so authorized to enforce Fundamental Rights. It describes writs (orders or directions) that are of five types: habeas corpus, mandamus, prohibition, certiorari, and quo warranto.

13.3.2 The Current State of Labor Laws in India

Labor laws in India can be loosely categorized into four groups: laws on working conditions, laws on trade unions and ID, laws on terms and conditions of employment, and laws on social security.

Laws on Working Conditions

This cluster includes Factories Act 1948, Plantation Labor Act 1951, Mines Act 1952, Motor Transport Workers Act 1961, and Indian Dock Laborers Act 1934. Apart from these, the Shops and Establishments Acts of the various states also provides for the working conditions of employees in shops and commercial establishments. The main areas covered by these laws are hours of work, weekly holidays, prohibition on employment of women and young persons in certain conditions, safety, and health and welfare. The accompanying rules made by the state legislatures specify certain standards, which are then monitored by the inspection machinery and penal measures. The standards are generally the minimum requirements allowing room for collective bargaining or industrial adjudication to further improve these standards.

Laws on Social Security

According to ILO,

> Social security is the security that society furnishes through appropriate organization against certain risks to which its members are exposed. These risks are essentially contingencies of life which the individual of small means cannot effectively provide by his own ability, or foresight alone or even in private combination with his fellows.

Prior to Independence, there were only two social security legislations enacted by the British government— Fatal Accident Act 1885 and Workmen's Compensation Act 1923. These two Acts were intended to protect the workers against accidents, but the provisions of these Acts were inadequate and expensive. Besides, the process for claiming compensation under these Acts was rather complicated. post-Independence there were major legislations to fill in the gaps in the social security laws and the laws included Employees' State Insurance Act 1948, Employees' Provident Fund Act 1952, Maternity Benefit Act 1961, and Payment of Gratuity Act 1972.

The Workmen's Compensation Act recognizes the need of the employee for suitable compensation in cases of injury caused by accident 'arising out of, and in the course of, their employment.' The employer, however, is not liable to pay compensation in case of injury resulting in disablement up to three days. The compensation is payable in case of death, total disablement—temporary or permanent and temporary disablement due to the injury caused by an accident. The expressions used in the Act 'in course of ' and 'arising out of ' has led to judicial interpretations from time to time and has been subject to tests of time, place, and casual relationship. The time criterion seeks to establish whether the accident occurred while the workman was working on activities directly arising out of or incidental to his employment. The place test is used to decide whether the accident occurred in a place within or under the control of the employer, or at which he normally carries on his trade or business. The casual relationship seeks to get the answer to the question whether there is clear connection between the employment and the injury.

The ESI Act of 1948 has a much wider coverage compared to that extended by the Workmen's Compensation Act 1923. The Act extends to all factories other than seasonal factories. The benefits include periodical payments to employees in case of sickness, maternity benefit, for disablement as a result of an employment injury, payment to dependents in case of death of the employee from an employment injury, medical treatment for the employee and the family, and funeral benefits towards expenditure on the funeral of the deceased employee. Benefits are also available in case an employee contracts an occupational disease. Besides, the Act also extends protection to an employee who cannot be dismissed or discharged or otherwise punished during the time the employee is in receipt of sickness or maternity benefit.

The Employees' Provident Fund and Miscellaneous Provisions Act 1952 is a major social security legislation in India. Currently, the Act and the Schemes framed under the Act provide three types of benefits—contributory provident fund, pension to the employees/family members, and an insurance cover to the members of the provident fund. Each employee of a covered establishment becomes a member on the first day, contributing between 10–12% of the basic salary (plus dearness allowances, if any) into the EPF account. The entire 12% of employee's contribution goes into the EPF account along with 3.67% (out of 12%) from the employer, while the balance 8.33% from the employer's side is diverted to the employee's Employee's Pension Scheme (EPS).

Changes in Social Security Laws in the Wake of Internationalization of Workplace

The special provisions in the provident fund law for 'International Workers' were first introduced in October 2008. The definition of international workers was divided into two parts—one applicable for Indian employees going overseas and another for foreign nationals coming to India. Though there has been no change in the definition of international worker under the law since then, there have been frequent changes in the interpretation by the Employees' Provident Fund Organization (EPFO) on the definition as applicable to Indian employees going overseas.

In the first set of FAQs issued by the EPFO in 2009, it was clarified that an Indian employee working abroad in a country with which India has entered into a social security agreement is an international worker. Then, on August 30, 2011, a circular was issued by the EPFO, which clarified that an Indian national is to be treated as an international worker with effect from the date of commencement of the certificate of coverage issued by the EPFO. For the benefit of readers, a certificate of coverage issued to an Indian employee going overseas is a confirmation of continued coverage from the EPFO, which entitles such an employee for exemption from the overseas social security.

The aforementioned circular seems to suggest that only those employees who obtain certificate of coverage from the EPFO will be classified as international workers. International workers are subject to a higher allocation of contributions towards the Pension Scheme and restrictions on withdrawal from the Provident Fund Scheme, until retirement after attaining 58 years of age. Consequently, most Indian employees who went on overseas assignment avoided obtaining certificate of coverage from the EPFO to stay out of the international workers categorization.

Now on May 25, 2012, the EPFO has issued a fresh set of FAQs and a circular, which reflect a major change in their view and completely overturns the earlier position. As per the latest clarification, the category of international workers comprises only those Indian employees who are employed by an Indian employer and have contributed to the social security of host country, which has a social security agreement with India, and are eligible for social security benefits in the host country under that social security agreement.

Source: Gupta, P. 'Provident Fund for Employees Going Overseas'. *The Indian Express.* Available at: archive. indianexpress.com/news/provident-fund-for-employees-g (accessed on June 19, 2012).

The Maternity Benefit Act 1961 protects the employment of a woman during the time of her maternity and entitles her to fully paid leave of absence for 26 weeks for the first two children and for 12 weeks for subsequent children. The leave of up to 12 weeks is also extended in case of adoption and surrogacy. It is estimated that there are around 1.8 million women at the workplace in the organized sector.

The Payment of Gratuity Act 1972 provides for payment of a lump sum to employees for the total period of service rendered in the establishment with minimum continuous service for at least five years. The benefit is payable on cessation of employment (either by resignation, death, retirement or termination, and so on) on the basis of last drawn salary. It is a defined benefit plan. The Act covers factories, mines, oilfields, plantations, ports, railway companies, shops, or other establishments. The current limit, which is pegged at ₹10 lakhs, is likely to rise to 20 lakhs.

Laws on Terms and Conditions of Employment

In India, the relation between employers and employees was loosely governed by the Indian Contract Act 1872, which implied that, especially in unorganized sector, the worker would be at a disadvantage given the supply surplus labor market. With the emergence of the modern system of industrial jurisprudence and political independence, the State took over the responsibility to often tilt the balance in favor of the employee.

The Contract Labor (Regulation and Abolition) Act 1970

The CLRA Act has a dual objective of abolishing contract labor in certain kinds of work and of providing for certain basic welfare amenities such as drinking water and first-aid facilities and, in certain cases, restrooms and canteens by making the employers (immediate and the principal) responsible for them. Provisions have also been made to guard against delays in the matter of wage payment.

The Industrial Employment (Standing Orders) Act 1946

The IESO Act constitutes intent by the legislature to intervene in the contractual relations between the employer and the employee. The Act requires the employers in industrial establishments employing 100 workmen or more to define conditions of employment by adopting a certified standing order and to communicate the same to the employees. The certified standing order acquires the force of law in the sense that there cannot be any individual contract of employment that violates the standing orders.

In respect of the right to hire and fire, the provisions of the standing orders, in tandem with the ID Act, provide a certain protection to the individual employees against arbitrary termination of services (whether as a way of disciplinary action or otherwise) in the opinion of the courts or the appropriate governments.

Caselets Legal Requirements in Workplaces

1. Nilesh is a bus conductor with BEST. He could not report for duty one day due to emergency at home. He could not inform his supervisor also. As a result, the bus scheduling got disrupted causing a chain reaction and inconvenience to passengers. The next day Nilesh's supervisor refused to allow him to resume his work. Instead, after asking him to wait for a couple of hours, the supervisor handed him a signed order dismissing Nilesh from service (the order was signed by the supervisor).
2. Prabha has recently joined a factory manufacturing pharmaceutical products as a chemical engineer. From next week, she has been asked to report for duty in the night shift from 10 PM to 6 AM.
3. Balwant is a Grade 1 welder in an automobile manufacturing factory at Manesar. His duty hours are from 8 AM to 12 noon and then again from 5 PM to 9 PM. He therefore works for eight hours per day.
4. The linesmen of an electricity distribution company in Mumbai have gone on a flash strike. They have not given any notice. The management has put up a notice to the effect that appropriate disciplinary action will be taken against the strikers and there will be deductions of wages for the day.
5. Sakharam is a peon in an auto-component plant in Thane. One day due to some altercation, he slapped his supervisor. The supervisor has issued a show-cause notice to Sakharam.
6. Mr Paranjpe is the branch manager of a PSU bank at Vikhroli. The normal office timing for the staff is from 10 AM to 5 PM with a 30-minute lunch break. The bank stops all public dealings after 2 PM. However, with the increased competition in the banking sector, all the new banks have staggered working hours from 9 AM to 9 PM. Mr Paranjpe wants to change the timings in his bank also as otherwise he will lose all his business.
7. United Technology company has engaged sales representatives on fixed-term contracts for two years. At the end of the tenure, some are given fresh term engagement, others are terminated.
8. The workers at a major engineering firm in Mulund are very agitated regarding delays in the payment of their wages. Though they get their salaries every month, the payment sometimes gets delayed beyond 10–15 days. The workers are not sure when they will receive their salaries.
9. V. Subramanyam, chargeman, Grade III at a steel factory at Jamshedpur, while supervising pouring of hot metal into ladles, suffered serious burn injuries when the molten metal accidentally spilled over the floor. One such metal fragment pierced one of his eyes causing complete damage to vision in the eye. Subramanyam was given alternative employment by the same employer without any loss in salary, but he has not been given any other compensation.
10. ABC Aluminium Manufacturing Co in Renukoot, UP, employs labors on contract for unloading of their raw materials from the railway wagons. These workers, who have been

working at the plant for the last nine years, have demanded permanent employment with ABC.

Discussion Question

1. Please indicate against each case whether there is any violation of laws governing workplaces in India.

13.3.3 Challenges for Labor Laws in the Context of Globalization

On a stock-taking of the impact of labor legislations globally since its early days post-1919, it is possible to see how the legislations served the needs of the times that saw their enactment, and also to count some clear benefits. In the first place, across the industrialized workplaces in the democratic territories of the globe, there has been an acceptance of the right of the worker to form association. Second, it has also gained acceptance for working out a convergence between international trade and labor law, so that workers enjoy certain basic freedom and quality of life and work. Significant progress has been observed in several other areas, for example, acceptance of the fundamental rights of the worker, diversity, and freedom of thought and expression. In many places, work conditions have continued to remain suboptimal, and the worker is in a weak and helpless state. The domain of labor legislation has been rocked by the winds of globalized marketplace, particularly due to the digital revolution, the delocalization of production throughout the world, and the increasing competition between high-wage and low-wage countries. The challenge is how to render labor law more effective, so that the balance does not tilt in favor of capital and the weak and the vulnerable in the workforce can get protected.

Arturo Bronstein[4] has identified five major challenges for labor legislations globally:

1. Flexible employment arrangement To meet the fluctuating business cycles, permanent employment is giving in to unusual employment arrangements, which include part-time work, fixed-term contract, long probation period, and work on call.
2. Coverage of unorganized sector workmen Labor law covers only the formal sector, although throughout the world, informal economy is increasing. In India, about 93% of the total workforce works in unorganized sector.
3. Outsourcing or contractization of the non-core processes The principal employers are passing on the responsibility of compliance to the subsidiaries or contractors.
4. The dilution of the control of national laws In MNC environment, the national laws are not applicable to international workplaces.
5. The shift in ideology The 'welfare state' concept is giving way to market determination, where the labor turns from being human to bring resources.

13.3.4 Labor Law Reforms in India

There is a raging polemics on the validity of labor regulations in the context of a changed business environment brought about by globalization and liberalization of the Indian economy. The theoretical

4 Arturo Bronstein, *International and Comparative Labor Law: Current Challenges* (Geneva: ILO and Palgrave Macmillan, 2009).

arguments take mainly two divergent stands, namely, the distortionist and the institutionalist views.[5] According to the distortionist view, labor regulations interfere with the normal flow and automatic adjustment of the labor market, thus reducing the rate of job creation and foster unemployment. Regulations are also likely to undermine the pace of the entire economy, causing dip in growth and productivity and aggravating poverty. The failure to carry out the necessary reforms in labor law is cited as the key reason for the relative lack of growth (manufacturing accounting for a stationary 17% of GDP) in Indian manufacturing sector, as compared to some of its Asian neighbors such as Malaysia, Indonesia, and even Bangladesh, not to speak of China or South Korea, who have dealt with these challenges and managed to develop a prosperous manufacturing sector.

It is also claimed that, paradoxically, labor market protectionism through various statutory regulations, intended to protect the weak labor, does exactly the opposite—eventually acting against their larger interest.[6] On the other hand, the dynamics of market forces in a free market economy makes it possible to swiftly reallocate the labor elsewhere. 'The process, therefore, is more likely to benefit labor by paying at least its marginal productivity without making them jobless.'[7]

The school of thought that believed in economic progress through dilution of labor regulations, acquired currency in the 1980s boosted by what is known as 'the Washington consensus.' According to this approach, State interference causes distortions and inefficiencies in the operation of markets, and that markets, if unfettered by regulations, can move naturally or spontaneously to a state of equilibrium. Various researches[8] have concluded that worker-protective labor laws are negatively correlated to labor demand in a number of countries, including India. These findings were corroborated by a subsequent oft-cited research on labor laws across the world by Botero et al.[9]

The most cited work in this context with special reference to India is a study carried out by Besley and Burgess,[10] who used state-level data on aggregate registered manufacturing output, investment, employment, and productivity, and concluded that all these variables diminished with pro-employee (restrictive or rigid) labor regulations. The corresponding aggregates for informal manufacturing established the reverse correlation with such labor regulations, showing that the informal sector picks up the growth on the bounce from labor market rigidities in the formal sector. Champions of labor flexibilities cite this study to support claims that one of the important reasons why the formal economy in India is restricted in size is lack of flexibility in labor laws in India.

The general aspects of the labor laws that are normally cited for creating rigidity and for indirectly stifling employment growth and productivity are: multiplicity of labor laws, variance between the legal requirements from state to state (e.g., Certified Standing Orders are required under the Industrial Employment and Standing Orders Act (1961) by establishments having 100 or more employees in West

[5] Praveen Jha and Sakti Golder, 'Labor Market Regulation and Economic Performance: A Critical Review of Arguments and Some Plausible Lessons for India' (Economic and Labor Markets Paper 1, International Labor Office, Geneva, 2008).

[6] Timothy Besley and Robin Burgess, 'Can Labor Regulation Hinder Economic Performance? Evidence from India,' *The Quarterly Journal of Economics* 119, no. 1 (February 2004): 91–134.

[7] Anup Kumar Bhandari and Arun Sudarsan, 'Institutionalist Versus Distortionist Views of Labor Market Reforms: An Investigation into the Post-liberalized Manufacturing Sector in India,' *Journal of Economics, Finance and Administrative Science* 21, no. 41 (2016): 63–72.

[8] Fallon, P. and Lucas, R. 'The Impact of Changes in Job Security Legislation in India and Zimbabwe', *World Bank Economic Review*, 5 (1993): 395–413.

[9] Botero J., Djankov S., La Porta R., Lopez-de-Silanes F. and Shleifer A. 'The Regulation of Labor'. *Quarterly Journal of Economics*, 119 (2004): 1340–1382.

[10] Besley, T. and Burgess, R. 'Can Labor Regulation Hinder Economic Performance? Evidence from India'. *Quarterly Journal of Economics*, 199 (2004): 91–134.

Bengal, but 50 in Maharashtra), restrictions on the employers to lay off, retrench employees, or close business, and so on. There have been various suggestions by different tripartite bodies to classify the labor laws into fewer clusters (e.g., the working group under Twelfth Five Year Plan recommended the creation of four baskets: laws governing employment; laws governing wages; laws governing welfare; and laws governing social security). The key labor laws in the eye of the storm are: ID Act (1947), Contract Labor (Regulation and Abolition) Act (1970), Trade Union Act (1926), Apprentices Act (1961), and Factories Act (1948).

At the other end of the spectrum, there is an opposite viewpoint about labor regulatory frameworks being given too much of focus as a condition of economic progress. The institutionalist view holds that, in fact, there is a growing empirical literature that suggests otherwise.[11] In their opinion, the labor regulations and trade unions might combine to protect not only the downtrodden of the society, but prove beneficial for the economy as a whole as well. For instance, labor regulations might end up boosting productivity. Arun Maira in an article in the *Indian Journal of Industrial Relations*[12] asks, 'Do we want a sustainably strong manufacturing sector, or do we merely want to change our labor laws?' He suggests that the focus should be on the 'goals of a competitive manufacturing sector and more jobs' and that the government should 'not get distracted by a rather shallow presumption that easier firing of workers will lead to growth of competitive manufacturing enterprises.' Bhattacharya[13] has presented an antithesis to the study of Beasley and Burgess, saying that there are two approaches to understand the impact of amendments of the ID Act (1947) on manufacturing performance: the first approach based on contradictory results and the second approach based on a 'flawed' index of regulation. Bhattacharya, nonetheless, makes a case for labor law reforms through rationalizing them, avoiding correcting inconsistencies, and smoothening the compliance process. He also wonders whether reforming Chapter VB, whose coverage is limited only to the organized manufacturing sector constituting 6% of the total workforce (the balance 94% being in the unorganized sector), would make any difference to the national employment situation in spite of labor flexibility creating employment in this small portion of the sector.

The trade unions have opposed the labor law reforms and have shown their disapproval through a one-day strike in September 2014. The ILO has criticized some of the recent labor reforms proposed by the government, as these would take away a chunk of workers from the protection of basic laws. The ILO is also helping the trade unions to prepare a position paper on the recent labor law reforms, IR, and industry development. The ILO has invited various central trade unions' leaders to its Delhi office on Thursday to present the final inputs of the position papers, incorporating their views. This would be followed by a national-level trade union conference on June 29–30, 2017 in Delhi where these position papers would be discussed in detail. The conference would be organized by the Bureau of Workers' Activities of the ILO, along with the Centre for Informal Sector and Labor Studies of the Jawaharlal Nehru University, New Delhi.

From an objective evaluation of all the theses and antitheses of labor law reforms, it appears clear that there is no single panacea to the challenges of jobless growth, and that labor law reforms perhaps have a marginal, if at all, impact on employment generation. To cite Gunnar Myrdal (Asian Drama),[14]

---

11 Andrew J. Oswald, 'The Missing Piece of the Unemployment Puzzle' (Inaugural Lecture, Department of Economics, University of Warwick, Coventry, November 1997).

12 Arun Maira, 'Rethinking Labor Law Reforms,' *Indian Journal of Industrial Relations* 50, no. 1 (July 2014): 34–32.

13 Bhattacharjea, A. 'The Effects of Employment Protection Legislation on Indian Manufacturing'. *Economic and Political Weekly*, 44 (2009): 55–62.

14 'The Curse of a Soft State'. *Live Mint.* Available at: http://www.livemint.com/Opinion (accessed on December 26, 2012).

one of the problems in a 'soft state' (India being in that category) is the overwhelming dependence on enactment of laws to deliver solutions and the yawning gap such systems throw up between law and its implementation. To put the focus back to the entire debate on labor law, the solution could lie elsewhere.

Moving ahead, few things could be done differently. First, let the government revisit the past. Several times, the Government of India had set up committees, many of which had thrown up ideas that are worthwhile. For example, the Second National Commission on Labor (NCL) 2002, appointed to look into the broad framework of labor laws including the ID Act and suggest changes, had suggested a fine balance between business need and workers' interest. It had suggested that prior permission may not be necessary in respect of lay-off and retrenchment, but it would serve the workers' interests better than currently if the retrenchment compensation is revised from the present 30 to 45 days. For closure of the enterprise too, the compensation, which is 30, should be raised to 60 days' salary depending upon whether it is a sick and ongoing industry. Second, there needs to be serious rethinking on dilution of the inspection system (which needs to balance with self-certification to conform to ILO standards of decent workplaces). It calls for serious restructuring, induction of technically skilled personnel, and empowerment of the inspectors and design processes to prevent corruption. Third, government needs to pay attention and initiate action to extend the coverage of minimum threshold of protection laws to unorganized sector (constituting around 93% of the manufacturing sector). Finally, the government needs to initiate a broad-based dialog to create a shared vision of economic progress by engaging all the stakeholders, including employers and employee groups in the same manner, as carried out recently by Germany and followed by France.

Exhibit Inspection of Labor Laws

In 2015, following an instruction from the commerce ministry, several state governments introduced the system of self-certification, generally applicable to factories, shops, and commercial establishments, covering several labor laws. In the relaxed process, there will be a single inspection in a cycle of three years, and targeting of a firm will be avoided through randomized selection, thus penal inspections will give way to guidance inspections. Employers also can submit consolidated annual returns in lieu of multiple returns. The relaxations aim at projecting a reform-oriented image to investors and improve the index of ease of doing business initiated by the Center. There are two reasons for being cautious about going easy on inspections:

1. Does it benefit the employer? Compliance assurance in the form of an affidavit, covering multiple labor laws, is fraught with risks for the employer, as non-compliance even in a minor matter could result in removal from the scheme or forfeiture of security deposit. Considering that labor laws are huge and complex and contain some difficult-to-implement provisions, the old labor inspection system seems safer on hindsight. Therefore, the assumptions that employers will be naturally lawcompliant need to be questioned, because stories of violation of the labor laws, especially Minimum Wages Act and Contract Labor Act, and the frequent incidences of fatal accidents are plenty.

   Besides, the trend in labor inspections shows that, instead of being excessive, there has been a steep decline in inspections and prosecutions. In the absence of adequate inspectorate staff and with resources at their disposal being extremely limited, very few inspections take place. Since there is no database on the universe of firms to be covered under each labor law, a fewer number of firms are visited more frequently, which creates the image of excessive inspections.

2. Measures such as self-certification system, complaint-driven inspections, randomized inspections, prior authorized inspection systems, and the poor inspection record in India are constitutive of violation of various provisions of the ILO Convention No 81, which India has ratified. The violations make India vulnerable to being questioned by ILO's supervisory institution, the Committee of Experts on Application of Conventions and Recommendations (CEACR), which acts on complaints raised to it by trade unions/employers. The matters handled by CEACR move to the International Labor Conference's Standing Committee on Application of Standards (CAS).

As an evidence of ILO's concern, inspection reforms have figured in the committee's deliberations held in June 2015. Acting on the complaints from trade unions in India, the committee has requested information from the government on the self-certification system, such as frequency and thoroughness of inspections, results of labor inspections, verification of information supplied by the employers under the self-certification system, and so on.

Source: K. R. Shyam Sundar, 'The Much-vilified Labor Inspector Raj,' August 9, 2015. Available at: http://www.thehindubusinessline.com/opinion/the-muchvilified-labor-inspector-raj/article7519064.ece (accessed on November 1, 2017.)

13.4 WORKPLACE REGULATIONS APPLICABLE TO GOVERNMENT/ PUBLIC SECTOR

13.4.1 Reservation Policy

Reservation in Indian law is a form of affirmative action whereby a percentage of seats are reserved in the PSUs, Union and state civil services, Union and state government departments, and in all public and private educational institutions, except in the religious/linguistic minority educational institutions, for the socially and educationally backward communities and the SC/STs, who are inadequately represented in these services and institutions. The reservation policy is also extended for the SCs and STs for representation in the Parliament of India.[15]

The relevant provisions in the Indian Constitution are as under:

- Under Article 15(4) and 16(4), the state and Central governments are authorized to reserve seats in public services for the members of the SC and the ST.
- Article 16(4A) provides for reservation in promotion to any class or classes of posts in the services under the State in favor of SCs and STs.
- According to Article 16(4B), the State can fill the unfilled vacancies of a year that are reserved for SCs/STs in the succeeding year, thereby nullifying the ceiling of 50% reservation on total number of vacancies of that year.
- Under Article 330 and 332, specific representations can be done through reservation of seats for the SCs and the STs in the Parliament and in the state legislative assemblies, as well as in government and public sector jobs, in both the federal and state governments.

[15] Available at: http://visionias.in/home/resources (accessed on June 1, 2017).

Fundamental Rules and Supplementary Rules (FRSR)[16]

Fundamental Rules (FRs) are a set of general rules by which all government servants are covered. The different provisions of these rules are supplemented by further elaboration through Supplementary Rules (SRs). These rules had been brought into force with effect from January 1, 1922. These rules are in respect of the following:

1. General conditions of service
2. Pay, additions to pay, and combination of appointments
3. Deputation out of India
4. Dismissal, removal, and suspension
5. Retirement
6. Leave
7. Joining time
8. Foreign service
9. Traveling allowances
10. Central Civil Services (Leave) Rules, 1972
11. Dearness allowances
12. House rent allowance and city compensatory allowance

13.5 INDUSTRIAL AND SERVICE JURISPRUDENCE

Jurisprudence is the 'formal science of positive law'[17] and as the 'scientific synthesis of the essential principles of law.'[18] According to Patten,

> Jurisprudence is a particular method of study and not of the law of one country but of the general notion of the law itself which is not primarily interested in cataloguing uniformities, nor in discovering rules which all nations accept, but to study the nature of law, the nature of legal institutions and their relationship with the society.[19]

Industrial/Service jurisprudence covers almost all the aspects of service conditions of labor in industry and in service. Specific areas dealt with jurisprudence are rules on employment, recruitment, leave, lien, discipline—need and ways and means to, disciplinary or departmental proceeding, departmental or domestic enquiry—in different employments such as government, PSU, and industrial, punishment, natural justice, judicial review, courts' interpretations.

1. The Supreme Court has played a powerful role to protect the interest of employees by holding that a rule providing that service of a permanent employee could be terminated by giving 'three months' notice in writing on either side' was arbitrary and discriminatory, and therefore violative of Article 14. In Delhi Transport Corporation vs DTC Mazdoor Congress,[20] the Court, by a majority of four-to-one, affirmed the decision in the case of Central Inland Water Transport Corporation Ltd. The Court held that the regulations that empowered the authority

---

[16] Available at: www.istm.gov.in/home (accessed on November 15, 2017).

[17] Sir Thomas E. Holland, *The Elements of Jurisprudence* (Saint Paul, MN: The Lawbook Exchange, 1896).

[18] Sir Carleton Kemp Allen, *Law in the Making* (Oxford: Clarendon Press, 1964).

[19] Simon N. Patten, *The New Jurisprudence. University of Pennsylvania Review*, 1 (1913): 2. Available at: http://scholarship.law.upenn. edu/penn_law_review/vol62/iss1 (accessed on February 14, 2018).

[20] S. C. Srivastava, 'Industrial Jurisprudence.' Available at: https://academy.gktoday.in/article/sexual-harassment-at-workplace (accessed on January 17, 2018).

to terminate the services of permanent employees by issuing notice to that effect, or by making payment in lieu of notice—without assigning any reason and without providing any opportunity to the employees to be heard before passing the impugned order—were arbitrary, uncanalized, unrestricted, and violative of the principles of natural justice as also Article 14.

2. While deciding 'contract *for* service,' employer–employee relationship, the Supreme Court affirmed the norms laid down by the House of Lords in Union Public Service Commission vs Girish Jayanti Lal Vaghela (2006) as follows:
   (a) the master's power of selection of his servant;
   (b) the master's responsibility of payment of wages or other remuneration;
   (c) the master's right of suspension or dismissal; and
   (d) the master's right to control the method of doing the work.
3. Disciplinary action–Principles of natural justice Basically there are two principles of natural justice:
   (i) no one shall be a judge in his own cause (*nemo judex in causa sua* or *nemo debet esse judex propria causa*); and
   (ii) no one shall be condemned unheard (*audi alteram partem* or hear the other side).

   The principles of natural justice are an integral part of the guarantee of equality assured by Article 14. Therefore, any law made or action taken by an employer must be fair, just, and reasonable.[21]
4. Disciplinary action–Power of interference by courts

   In the case of Indian Iron and Steel Company vs Their Workmen,[22] the Supreme Court ruled that when a dispute arises, the industrial tribunal has the power to see whether the termination of services of a workman is justified and to give appropriate relief. The tribunal cannot, however, act as a court of appeal and substitute its own judgment for that of the management. It will interfere: (a) when there is want of good faith; (b) when there is victimization or unfair labor practice; (c) when the management has been guilty of a basic error or violation of a principle of natural justice; and (d) when on the material the finding is completely baseless or perverse.
5. Definition of industry

   In Bangalore Water Supply Board vs Their Workmen case, the Supreme Court laid down the following tests for determining the scope of 'industry': (a) Where (i) systematic activity, (ii) organized by cooperation between employer and employee (the direct and substantial element is commercial), (iii) for the production and/or distribution of goods and services calculated to satisfy human wants and wishes. Absence of profit motive of gainful objective is irrelevant, be the venture in the public, joint, private, or other sector.
6. Right to strike

   In All India Bank Employees Association vs National Industrial Tribunal case,[23] the court while determining the scope of Article 19(1)(c) of the Constitution declined to include right

21 D. K. Yadav vs JMA Industries Ltd [May 7, 1993] 3 SCC 259.

22 See http://14.139.60.114:8080/jspui/bitstream/123456789/713/17/Industrial%20Jurisprudence.pdf (accessed on December 8, 2017).

23 Ibid.

to strike when it observed: [E]ven a very liberal interpretation of Sub.cl.(c) of Clause (1) of Article 19 cannot lead to the conclusion that the trade unions have a guaranteed right to an effective collective bargaining or otherwise strike, either as part of collective bargaining or otherwise.

7. Sexual harassment in workplace

A three-judge bench of the Supreme Court in *Vishaka vs State of Rajasthan*[24] made a significant contribution in evolving a code against sexual harassment. The court ruled that it shall now be the duty of the employer or other responsible persons in workplaces or other institutions, whether in the public or the private sector, to take all steps required to: (a) prevent the commission of acts of sexual harassment; (b) deter the commission of the acts of sexual harassment; and (c) provide the procedure for: (i) the resolution of acts, (ii) the settlement, or (iii) the prosecution of acts of sexual harassment.

Closing Case Issues in Compliance of Labor Laws in SMEs

The textile and garment sector has been witnessing rapid growth post-Independence, and is one of the top earners of foreign exchange. It employs 350 million people (and is the 2nd largest employer), generates one-fifth of the total export earnings, and contributes 4% to the GDP, thereby making it the largest industrial sector of the country. This textile economy is worth US$37 bn and its share of the global market is about 5.90%. The product comes out of complex structures that cover home-based units to large manufacturing factories. The apparel industry, a subset of the textile industry, employs around 1 million workers of widely diverse nature including women, Hindu backward castes, Muslim workers from Bihar, and so on.

The industry employs highly ingenuous methods for achieving competitiveness and profitability. One of the methods is subcontracting—the use of several layers of contractors and subcontractors. It helps them to dodge the labor laws, because the identity of the employer remains shrouded in mystery. The typical worker is employed on casual basis and, therefore, vulnerable to being paid low wages and terminated without any compensation. The employers in this manner enjoy high degree of flexibility by unrestricted power for hire and fire.

Arif Khan, aged 13, hails from a village near Sitamarhi, a border town of Bihar. His family of parents, grandparents, and eight siblings, lived off a small piece of farm land. The income from the crops were so meagre that for several months the family would live on a state of near starvation. Three years ago a distant uncle brought him and his younger brother to Delhi for work. Currently, he works in a small garment unit near Ghaziabad on the outskirts of Delhi as an embroiderer. He gets paid on the basis of the embroidery work that he completes. On the days when he cannot come due to sickness, he does not get paid. He normally works from 8 AM till about 9 PM, with breaks in between for eating the daily meal of crushed lentil with green chilies. The current job of Arif Khan is his third in three years, although the owner has remained the same. The first unit, employing around 49 workers, was closed after about a year, and the entire operations shifted to a second unit in the same area, which again operated for about 10 months before all being shifted to the third unit. It

[24] Ibid.

has created some difficulties for Arif because the chawl, where Arif lives with his brother and uncle, is a little distant from the current location.

Arif does not know the name of the company he works for, because the signboard gets repainted once in a few months and a new name is written. He earns around ₹2,500 a month. There is no deduction for provident fund or ESI from his salary, and no welfare facility in the unit. He fetches his own drinking water and for attending to nature's call he has to go to an open ground outside the workplace.

Discussion Question

1. What do you think are the workplace laws applicable to the workplace of Arif Khan?

SUMMARY

Workplace laws help in three ways. First, they provide a legal system that helps productive individual and collective employment relationships, thereby building a productive economy. Second, they design a structure for worker–employer interface on work-related issues. Third, they act as a catalyst for industrial harmony based on some basic principles and rights at work. It has, however, been found that for laws to play these roles effectively, the labor laws need to be aligned to the demands of the labor market and the interests of the main actors. Such an alignment can happen in a seamless manner if those concerned are allowed to participate at the formulation stage of the legislation through processes of social dialogues.

Most of the major labor legislations in India came around 1947–1948, at the time of political independence. Prior to that there were a few laws, such as Factories Act, Payment of Wages Act, and Trade Unions Act, which sought to protect the workers' essential conditions of work and rights at workplace. In India thus, the State stepped in the space meant for the play of the contract between the employer and the employee, by arranging for extensive legal protection of labor, thereby nullifying the principle of freedom of contract. Labor laws thus aimed to right the legacies of colonial repression and denials of fair working conditions, and emerged as key social and economic legislation in India, targeted at safeguarding the interests of the downtrodden.

The major labor laws, largely based on ILO conventions, which India had ratified, were: Factories Acts 1948, Workmen's (now changed to Employee's) Compensation Act 1923, Mines Act 1923, Trade Unions Act 1926, Trade Disputes Act 1929, Payment of Wages Act 1936, Employment of Children Act 1938, Maternity Benefit Act 1961, and the Bombay ID Act 1938. The last Act introduced a permanent setup for industrial conflict resolution in the form of an industrial court. This Act was later replaced by a still more comprehensive legislation known as the Bombay Industrial Relations Act 1946. Currently, India has around 200 labor laws enacted by states and 50 labor laws enacted by the Center. In terms of the enactment and enforcement, the labor laws in India can be classified into four categories: enacted by Parliament and enforced by the Union government (ESI Act, EPF Act, etc.); enacted by the Parliament and enforced by both the Union and state governments (Contract Labor Regulations and Abolitions Act, ID Act); enacted by the Parliament and enforced by the state governments (Factories Act, Trade Union Act); enacted by state legislature and enforced by state governments (Shops and Establishment Act).

The government is seized with an agenda for reforming some of the labor laws, mainly to improve the investment climate in the country. The criticism against the labor laws hinges on their antiquity, excessiveness, ambiguity, and rigidity. There is a prevailing belief that certain structural adjustments are essential to fuel economic growth, and labor regulatory framework is one of the key areas demanding such structural adjustments. The demand for changing labor laws is especially those provisions that deny the employers the right to 'hire and fire,' carry out necessary adjustments in the workplace, and employ temporary workmen. The failure to carry out the necessary reforms in labor law is cited as the key reason for lack of growth (17% Of GDP) in Indian manufacturing sector, as compared to some of its Asian neighbors such as Malaysia, Indonesia, and even Bangladesh, apart from China or South Korea, have dealt with these challenges to develop a prosperous manufacturing sector. The attempts to push through the labor reforms have met with resistance from most national unions. There is need to tread cautiously, to balance reforms with creation of decent workplace, in line with norms set by ILO. Besides, there is also need to cover large multitude of unorganized workers, who constitute around 94% of the workforce in India.

The general aspects of the labor laws that are normally cited for creating rigidity and for indirectly stifling employment growth and productivity are: multiplicity of labor laws, variance between the legal requirements from state to state (e.g., Certified Standing Orders are required under the Industrial Employment and Standing Orders Act by establishments having 100 or more employees in West Bengal, but 50 in Maharashtra), restrictions on the employers to lay off, retrench employees, close business, and such others. There have been various suggestions by different tripartite bodies to classify the labor laws into fewer clusters (e.g., the working group under 12th Five-Year Plan recommended the creation of four baskets: laws governing employment; laws governing wages; laws governing welfare; and laws governing social security). The key labor laws in the eye of the storm are: ID Act (1947), Contract Labor (Regulation and Abolition) Act (1970), Trade Union Act (1926), Apprentices Act, and Factories Act (1948).

Short-answer Questions

1. What were the reasons for enactment of the first labor law in India?
2. What are some links of fundamental rights and labor laws in India?
3. Describe the law on working condition.
4. Describe the importance of EPF and Misc Provisions Act, 1952.
5. Narrate the purpose and key contents of Industrial Employment Standing Orders Act.
6. What are the challenges mentioned by Arturo Bernstein for labor laws globally?
7. What are the key issues of labor inspection in India?
8. Describe the key features of the Reservation Policy.
9. What is FRSR?
10. What is industrial jurisprudence?

Discussion Questions

1. A provision of the Factories Act debars women from being employed in a factory between 7 PM and 6 AM. Is this a discriminatory practice? How do you suggest should it be modified?
2. In the USA, employers are free to hire and fire. In India, as in many other countries, terminating permanent employees is made difficult, especially those covered by ID Act, without prior permission

of the government and without paying compensation. What are your views on this matter? Find out the rules governing termination of an employee in various countries.

3. In India, there is a demand of the trade unions for providing equal wages for equal work. Some of the recent cases of industrial unrest, especially in the auto sector, were the unequal treatment of permanent and non-permanent workers, engaged on the same work. What are your views on it? Do some research on the practices prevailing in different countries on the principle of equal pay for equal work.

CLUSTER 7

TRANSFORMATION OF WORK AND WORK RELATIONSHIPS

Chapter 14
Human Resource Information and Analytics

Chapter 15
Employment Relations

The traditional workplaces, with a physical space and regular working hours, have been fast giving way to an entirely new working environment—the digital workplace. By assimilation of the technologies that employees use (email, instant messaging, social media tools to HR applications, and virtual meeting tools), the digital workplace dismantles communication barricades and creates opportunities for enhancing employee experience by nurturing efficiency, innovation, and growth. There is a simultaneous process of excitement in opportunities and discomfort in work disruptions, posing new challenges for HRM.

While businesses are acknowledging the value of embedding big data and analytics in business processes, choice is between two approaches: a craft approach versus the industrial approach. A craft approach is an ad hoc effort in support of decision-making, while the industrial approach integrates analytics into decision-based work processes. Industrial analytics can potentially be automated or assisted, but a firm must decide how extensively these analytically enabled decisions should be automated. The key is to find the right mix of fully automated decisions, automated decisions with human review, and human decisions informed by analytics.[1] The analytics–driven approach to HRM is likely to cover the entire fabric of employee life cycle—from recruitment to performance management, employee development, and succession planning, by use of a language that both HR and its key stakeholders including the CEOs can comprehend. The digitalization of workplace and a host of environmental factors, including globalization, have deeply impacted the traditional employment relationship and brought in some fundamental changes. A new framework of employment relations has emerged now. It is marked by flexible deployment, customer focus, performance focus, project work, human spirit at work, commitment, L&D, and open information as the shared value of the principal actors (employer/employee/government).

[1] Thomas Davenport, Jeanne Harris, and Robert Morison, *Analytics at Work: Smarter Decisions Better Results* (Boston, MA: Harvard Business Press, 2010).

CHAPTER 14

Human Resource Information and Analytics

LEARNING OBJECTIVES

After completing this chapter, the student will be able to:

- Understand the contextual factors that caused the accelerated interest in HR analytics
- Define HR information system and HR analytics
- Explain the differences between metrics and analytics
- Illustrate the applications of HR analytics
- Cite the specific challenges and opportunities for predictive analytics in future

Opening Case Making Sense of Data to Solve People Issues

When Amit Sehgal took over as CHRO at Cognizant Petroleum Company in December 2002, he was not quite sure what he wanted or needed to do. Coming from a background in ERP technology project team, he was used to dealing with information about various aspects of the company's business: the sales, inventories, operations, and others on a 24/7 basis; yet, as he quickly learned, HR activities were not organized enough to provide daily data on operations and programs. He recognized the potential value of having even basic statistics about the HR department, its employees, and its operations—to highlight opportunities to leverage and how minute shifts in these values could signal gathering problems. However, since these data were not currently available or easily developed, he identified an employee in the HR team, with an IT background, who could mine data from the organization's current ERP systems and create a factsheet on HR relevant information.

Over a period of time, various important trends started coming to the surface. It was reported that instrumentation engineers (a key talent in the refinery) with a five-year work experience showed an attrition rate of 35%, which was 15% higher than engineers in other streams. Further analysis showed that instrumentation engineers, being recruited from premier engineering colleges, had 75% more probability of quitting within the first 10 years than instrumentation engineers from non-premier colleges. Further analysis of data of performance appraisals revealed that engineers recruited from premier institutes figured in the list of 'outstanding' rated employees in almost equal frequency as engineers from non-premier institutes. Further data revealed interesting trends in the compatibility between the boss and subordinate engineers based on the institute they had studied in. Eventually, it helped Mr Das in putting forward a proposal for changing the ratio of recruitments from premier and non-premier institutes, which eventually helped in reducing the attrition rate among trained instrumentation engineers by around 50%.

Discussion Questions

1. Evaluate the effectiveness of Amit Sehgal's approach to use information as the basis for the HR policy change.
2. What is your merit about the traditional HR approach of using qualitative assessment vis-à-vis the quantitative-based analytics?

14.1 INTRODUCTION

For many years, HR, as a function, abhorred data. Its strength lay in intuitive, emotionally intelligent 'touchy feely' approaches to dealing with people issues. Its sole contact with data was in collecting and maintaining employees' personal information. The rules of the game have, however, been changing drastically, especially over the last few decades, impacting the way HR managed its information. The explosion of digital information from innumerable sources has sent waves to HR shores also. Worldwide, as the economic uncertainties have persisted, businesses have been desperately searching for magic levers to achieve competitive advantage, and the use of information and analytics seem to have provided the answer. Sysco, a Fortune 500 company, has been using analytics around work climate, employee satisfaction, productivity and retention, and seven other dimensions. One of the gains has been substantial cost reduction in hiring and training costs of new associates.

14.2 HUMAN RESOURCE DATA

HR data is employee-related information. It can be qualitative or quantitative. Qualitative HR data is numerical and can be measured, for example, employee headcount, attrition rate, and absenteeism rate. Qualitative information are based on individual perception and assessment and cannot be measured.

14.3 HUMAN RESOURCE INFORMATION SYSTEM

14.3.1 Definition

The domain of HRM has been subjected to frequent and numerous innovations in technology. Some of the terms include the HR information system (HRIS), electronic HRM (e-HRM), and virtual HRM (VHRM). According to Tannenbaum, HRIS is '[O]ne which is used to acquire, store, manipulate, analyze, retrieve and distribute information about an organization's human resources.'[2] Later, HRIS was also defined as 'the composite of databases, computer applications, and hardware and software

2 S. I. Tannenbaum, 'Human Resource Information Systems: User Group Implications,' *Journal of Systems Management* 41, no. 1 (1990): 27–32.

necessary to collect/record, store, manage, deliver, present, and manipulate data of human resources.'[3] Hendrickson has defined HRIS 'as integrated systems used to gather, store and analyze information regarding an organization's human resources.'[4] According to Hendrickson, 'HRIS is not only about just technology, or bounded by the computer hardware and software applications that comprise the technical part of the system: it also includes the people, policies, procedures and data required to manage the HR function.'[5]

14.3.2 Objectives of HRIS

Following are the important objectives of HRIS:

- Reduce cost
- Improve administrative efficiency by deleting repetitive work
- Provide better client/customer service
- Align HR strategy to business
- Make innovation easier
- Integrate the various HR functions

14.3.3 History and Evolution

The growth and evolution of HRIS was connected with the increasing sophistication of the HR function, originally in the form of personnel function. During the early days of personnel management, HRIS did not exist. The only data management work that HR personnel did was maintaining employee record. From the 1960s onwards, the emergence of HR function and its escalating influence in business coincided with the slow evolution of HRIS. Several factors facilitated the process: the availability of low cost, generic, flexible, easy to install, and easily customizable window-based products helped smaller software houses to write affordable, easily customizable, modular HRIS with better sophisticated reporting capabilities. The new HR function, entrusted with the role of legislative compliance, had to collect, analyze, and report voluminous data to statutory authorities. HR departments felt the pressure to embrace computer technology for quick processing of employee data. The evolution of technology and related vendor activity brought in a comprehensive MIS for HRM. The mounting employee costs and the progressive affordability of computer technology necessitated the development of computer-based HRIS as a business decision.[6]

With the increasing development in technology in the recent years, opportunities have been created to provide real-time, information-based self-service, and to construct interactive work environment. Thus, employee data systems have matured from the automated employee record-keeping used in the 1960s into more complex reporting and decision systems. The first decade of the new millennium

---

3 R. Broderick and J. W. Boudreau, 'Human Resource Management, Information Technology, and the Competitive Edge,' *Academy of Management Executive* 6, no. 2 (1992): 7–17.

4 A. R. Hendrickson, 'Human Resource Information Systems: Backbone Technology of Contemporary Human Resources,' *Journal of Labor Research* 24, no. 3 (Summer 2003): 381–394.

5 Ibid., 381.

6 Faruk Bhuiyan, Mustafa Manir Chowdhury, and Farzana Ferdous, 'Historical Evolution of Human Resource Information System (HRIS): An Interface between HR and Computer Technology,' *Human Resource Management Research* 4, no. 4 (2014): 75–80.

witnessed a phenomenal proliferation in the number of organizations making use of HRIS for acquiring, storing and analyzing, and using human resource data. Over the years, the HR function has developed capability to manage change and transformation faster than at any time before by leveraging HRIS, given the authority and relevant accessible information for decision-making. In recent years, HRIS has become critical to the operations of HR departments of large companies. Information system in personnel has evolved from the automated employee record-keeping system of the 1960s into complex reporting and decision systems of today. Although these systems may rely on centralized hardware resources for their operations, they are increasingly being managed, supported, and maintained by a small group of information systems (IS) specialists, who reside within the personnel department and operate as a microcosmic MIS area.

The HRIS is designed to support the planning, administration, decision-making, and control activities of HRM. Applications such as employee selection and placement, payroll, pensions and employee benefits management, intake and training projections, career-pathing, equity monitoring, and productivity evaluations are supported by HRIS.

14.3.4 Users of HRIS

HR Professionals

- Reporting and compliance
- Payroll and compensation analysis
- Benefits administration
- Applicant tracking, skills inventory

Functional Managers

- Performance management and appraisal
- Recruitment and resume processing
- Team and project management
- Training and skills testing
- Management development

Individual Employees

- Self-service benefit options
- Career planning
- T&D

As organizations add self-service centers, employees use the HRIS for benefit selection and enrollment. Career planning and records of T&D can be maintained by the employees themselves thereby keeping the records up-to-date and saving labor and, therefore, cost, for the HR department.

14.3.5 Benefits of HRIS

Efficiency

According to Hendrickson,[7] increased efficiency is a benefit of an HRIS. Both time and cost efficiency can be addressed with the ability to do more transactions with fewer fixed resources. This can specifically be seen in areas such as payroll and benefits.

Effectiveness

In terms of accuracy, the HRIS helps in transactions. Additionally, the technology can be used to simplify processes.[8] Some information is only available through technology. Many types of computer-based training, Internet access to the recruitment world, and the use of certain programs to assess employees in the hiring process are only available for those with technology-rich environments. In short, timelessness in data application, removal of data duplication, and improvement and streamlining of HR functions helps in employee-service orientation. Besides, introduction of Web-based HRIS shifts HR activities to LMs and employees through self-service technology. Overall, time squandered on basic administrative tasks can be better spent on strategic issues and implementing progressive plans. It also allows HR professionals to help employees design their career plans, T&D, and so on.

14.3.6 Use of HRIS

According to Martinson, HRIS has dual usages. In the first place, its most common application lies in simple automation such as payroll and benefit administration, and employee record-keeping for the purpose of cost reduction and administrative efficiency. The second usage is strategic: for business analyses and analytics-based decision-making.

Reporting

Perhaps the biggest application area of an HRIS is its ability to create reports and presentations. An HRIS typically holds all information surrounding the firm's HR initiatives, including details regarding the group's hiring practices, such as a comprehensive listing of all job applicants, an up-to-date index of job openings, electronic copies of each employee's onboarding paperwork, and so on. It also holds data regarding the salary and incentive compensation of each staff member. Results of annual performance appraisals and any disciplinary actions that have been taken toward members of the team are included as well. Since these figures are held in one database, a business owner possesses the capability of running a variety of detailed reports that encompass some or all of this information. For example, when looking to hire additional staff, he can run a report of past candidates who possess a specific skill set. Alternatively, he can run a compensation report to obtain needed information when preparing the annual budget.

Recruitment

In support of a firm's staffing efforts, many HRISs provide a sophisticated interface allowing the use of the HRIS by both internal employees and external job applicants. An HRIS allows candidates for open positions to submit their resumes and contact information to a potential employer from a

[7] Hendrickson, 'Human Resource Information Systems.'

[8] Ibid.

remote computer. The system then collects the information and archives it, so it is easily accessible by the hiring manager. When seeking candidates, the manager is able to perform detailed searches of collected resumes, using a variety of queries, including location, level of education, years of professional experience, and technical skill set. In addition, the software also allows current employees to electronically apply for new positions.

Benefits of Administration

An HRIS allows a business to streamline the administration of employee benefits. In many cases, employees and new hires may electronically enroll in benefit plans. They may also have the capability of logging onto the system to monitor and update their current coverage throughout the year, changing status, dependent information, and contact data as required. A self-service system allows for benefits to be efficiently administered with as little manpower as possible, saving an organization's time and money.

Many studies have been carried out about various applications of HRIS. A study in Taiwan found that HRIS is most extensively used at the electronic data processing level, followed by MIS and digital satellite system levels.[9] A study in Indian companies found major applications in recruitment and selection (67.2% and 71.9%, respectively), payroll services (67.2%), compensation (67.2%), performance appraisal (62.5%), and job analysis and design (62.5%).[10] A later study, entitled 'Application of HRIS in HRM in India: A Study,' by Kundu and Kadian[11] had the following highlights:

- The most frequent application of HRIS was in 'employee record' followed by 'payroll' in organizations Indian and multinational, manufacturing, and service.
- Scope of HRIS applications has broadened in India. There is an increase in HRIS application in sophisticated activities and decision-making.
- In HRIS, use in technical and strategic HRM, performance and reward management, corporate communication areas, and service companies had an edge over manufacturing industries.

A subsequent study on employees in 71 different organizations operating in different sectors, such as IT, real estate, BPO, financial services, manpower consulting, and travel and tourism, on a sample size of 385 respondents,[12] had the following key conclusions:

- Major organizations in the IT, real estate, BPO, financial services, manpower consultancy, and travel and tourism have HRIS installed just between 3 and 5 years.
- Major organizations in the IT, real estate, BPO, financial services, and travel and tourism have HRIS installed, except for the manpower consultancy where the number of organizations that do not have HRIS installed are more than the ones that have it installed and are using it.

---

9 C. Y. Y. Lin, 'Human Resource Information Systems: Implementation in Taiwan,' *Research and Practice in Human Resource Management* 5, no. 1 (1997): 57–72.

10 T. Saharan and S. Jafri, 'Valuation of HRIS Status: An Insight of Indian Companies' Perspectives,' in *Business Management: Key Research Issues*, eds. S. C. Kundu, B. K. Punia, K. P. Narwal, and D. Singh (New Delhi: Excel Books, 2012): 113–127.

11 S. C. Kundu and Rajesh Kadian, 'Applications of HRIS in Human Resource Management in India: A Study,' *European Journal of Business and Management* 4, no. 21 (2012): 34–41.

12 Mohammed Owais Qureshi, Manjeet Kaushal Kaur, and Syed Rumaiya Sajjad, 'An Empirical Analysis of Organizations Using Human Resource Information System (HRIS) in India: An Employee Perspective,' *International Journal of Economics and Management Sciences* 2, no. 9 (2013): 54–63.

- It was further analyzed from what more than 10% of the respondents from the finance, manpower, and travel and tourism companies replied that the current HRIS has been installed just 1–6 months back.
- Although the services sector and real estate sector are growing by leaps and bounds, at the same time, the results indicate that companies in these sectors have to significantly improve their practices regarding the implementation and use of HRIS. The companies should focus on implementing a good HRIS and proper budget allocation should be done for the same.

14.3.7 Some HRIS Terminology

- **HRIS** Generic term referring to any information system used for obtaining relevant and timely information on which to base HR decisions.[13]
- **ERP** (Enterprise resource planning). Software system that integrates several data sources and processes into a unified system. An ERP system provides the functions of at least two separate systems, namely, accounting and inventory management.[14]
- **SAP** (System applications and products). World's largest business software company providing integrated software systems. In business since 1972.
- **ESS** Employee self-service is Web-based applications that provide employees with access to their personal records and payroll details. ESS features include allowing employees to change their own contact details, family members, and banking information and benefits. ESS also allows administrative tasks such as applying for a leave, reviewing of timesheet, inquiring about available loan programs, requesting for overtime payment, viewing of compensation history, and submitting of reimbursement slips. With the emergence of ESS, employees are able to transact with their HR office without physical appearance that is considered irrelevant in some transactions. ESS may be operated on an employer's intranet or via a Web service.

14.4 HUMAN RESOURCE METRICS

HR metrics are a vital way to quantify the cost and the impact of employee programs and HR processes and measure the success (or failure) of HR initiatives. They enable a company to track year-to-year trends and changes in these critical variables. It is how organizations measure the value of the time and money spent on HR activities in their organizations.

14.4.1 Categories of Human Resource Metrics

HR Efficiency Metrics

- **Cost per hire** It is the cost associated with a new hire. It is not only important to know how much it costs in hiring, but it is also important to see if the money spent is used to hire right people.
- **Time to fill up the open position** It is the total days to fill up a job opening per job. The shorter the time, the most efficiency required of the HR department in finding the replacement for the job.

[13] Mondy, R. Wayne, *Human Resource Management* (Upper Saddle River, NJ: Pearson Prentice Hall, 2008). Available at: www. bestpricecomputers.co.uk/glossary (accessed on January 7, 2008).

[14] Available at: https://www.shrm.org/.../teachingresources/ (accessed on December 16, 2017).

- **HR expense factor** It is the ratio between total company expense and HR expense. It shows if the expenses on HR practices are too much in terms of the whole company expense.

HR Effectiveness Metrics

- **Training ROI** It is the total financial gain an organization has from a particular training. It shows the effectiveness of the training program and how much benefit was brought to the company after the training.
- **Absent rate** It determines whether the company is having an absent problem from the employees. It also reflects the effectiveness of the HR policies as well as the company's own policies. It always goes along with employee satisfaction.

HR Capability-building Metrics

- **Revenue factor** It indicates the effectiveness of company operation with the use of the employees as its human capital.
- **Defects rate** It indicates the number of defective products in the operation. The lower the defect rate, the more effective the HR practices in developing company's core competency in terms of reducing cost.

HR Metrics According to Domains

Recruitment

Recruiting metrics measure activities involved in the stages of attracting and selecting top talent. Decision-makers frequently want to quantify variables, such as new hire performance, turnover rates of new hires, impact of a poor hire, and ROI in a new hire, in order to measure the success of the recruiting process.

Retention

Retention metrics often measure important aspects of turnover. Management often wishes to quantify such variables as turnover rate, average tenure, the rate of a veteran worker, or the financial impact of employee turnover. Results often indicate how much each separating employee is costing the company and help the company create proactive plans to prevent the loss of top talent.

Training and Development

T&D metrics quantify the learning processes of new employees and include activities such as orientation, training process time and costs, and the time and cost of on-the-job learning. Results often demonstrate the success of professional development processes and how much they help the organization achieve its business goals.

Staffing

Staffing metrics quantify the ROI in your employees. These measures include metrics such as cost per hire, recruiting efficiency ratio, and the cost to replace an employee.

Talent management

- Percentage of performance goals met or exceeded, showing if the organization is meeting the performance goal aligned with its mission

- Percentage of employees' rate at the top performance appraisal level who are paid above average salary
- Percentage of top performing employees who resign for compensation-related reasons
- Turnover percentages of low-performing managers
- Percentage of employees in performance management programs that show improvement within a year
- Percentage and rate of involuntary turnover in key positions

14.4.2 Human Capital and HR Metrics

Human capital is defined in the *Oxford English Dictionary* as 'the skills the labor force possesses and is regarded as a resource or asset.' It encompasses the notion that there are investments in people (e.g., education, training, health) and that these investments increase an individual's productivity. 'Based on corporate culture, organizational values and strategic business goals and objectives, human capital measures indicate the health of the organization.'[15]

One way to measure the human capital is through key performance indicators (KPIs). It helps measure human capital outcomes, such as talent management, employee engagement, and high performance; illustrates the firm's business, financial, and strategic goals; and promotes partnership with senior management for organizational performance and growth.[16] The best KPIs should be able to reflect the human capital performance, such as financial outcomes and performance drivers. At the same time, when determining strategic KPIs, it is essential to consider who designs human capital measures and how they are created.[17] A model way to design a good KPI is by consultation with the line/business managers who are accountable for the business performance. Lockwood prescribes the following steps that HR can use to create a better KPI:

- HR becoming aware of the overall business strategy
- Enlisting leaders outside of HR to help develop the KPIs
- Collaborating with business managers to ensure KPIs link to business unit strategic goals
- Focusing on links between people measures and intermediate performance drivers (e.g., customer satisfaction, engagement, and so on)
- Increasing manager acceptance through training programs and concrete action plans
- Working with HR to simplify metric and automate data collection[18]

HR or workforce analytics is different from the HR metrics in the sense that while metrics are concrete data containing some descriptions of certain processes or results (e.g., attrition rate of probationers), analytics indicate strategies to integrate data elements into metrics and for determining interrelationships or changes in metrics. The purpose of analytics is to provide usable information to the managers about the state of human capital to enable effective managerial decisions. Thus, the clear context of analytics is the problems or the opportunities facing the business and the managers.

---

15 N. Lockwood, 'Maximizing Human Capital: Demonstrating HR Value with Key Performance Indicator,' *HR Magazine* 51, no. 9 (2006): 1–10.

16 Ibid.

17 Ibid.

18 Ibid.

14.5 HUMAN RESOURCE ANALYTICS

14.5.1 Introduction

Analytics have breached the final frontier—the domain of people or human resource. In the Deloitte *Global Human Trends 2015* survey, people analytics presented the second largest overall 'capability gap' for organizations, trailing only the need to build better leadership. Analytics is on the agenda of almost every HR team that was surveyed, with three in four respondents rating it as 'important' or 'very important.' But despite this interest, the survey shows only a marginal rise in analytics capabilities. A total of 35% of the respondents reported that HR analytics was 'under active development' at their organizations—just slightly more than the proportion of respondents who said the same last year (33%). Only 8.44% of the respondents surveyed believe their organizations have a strong HR analytics team in place, a very slightly higher percentage than last year's figure. The conclusions drawn indicate that while new vendor tools have hit the market, teams are still not fully enabled, trained, or organized to succeed.

Analytics establish the cause and effect relations between sets of data on the basis of two factors: correlation or causation. Correlation connotes a mathematical relationship between two factors or events often using numerical of 0–1, indicating zero or a full predictive relationship. Causation is when one event, occurring or non-occurring, results in another event occurring or non-occurring.

Business Analytics

Analytics is the discovery and communication of meaningful patterns in data (Table 14.1). Done well, data analytics is built on a firm grasp of statistics and probability. These skills are used to discover useful information, suggest conclusions, and support decision-making.

Table 14.1 How companies use analytics to track different aspects of business?

Function	Description	Exemplars
Supply chain	Simulate and optimize supply chain flows; reduce inventory and stock-outs.	Dell, Wal-Mart, Amazon
Customer selection, loyalty, and service	Identify customers with the greatest profit potential; increase likelihood that they will want the product or service offering; retain their loyalty.	Harrah's, Capital One, Barclays
Pricing	Identify the price that will maximize yield, or profit.	Progressive, Marriott
Human capital	Select the best employees for particular tasks or jobs, at particular compensation levels.	New England Patriots, Oakland A's, Boston Red Sox
Product and service quality	Detect quality problems early and minimize them.	Honda, Intel
Financial performance	Better understand the drivers of financial performance and the effects of non-financial factors.	MCI, Verizon
Research and development	Improve quality, efficacy, and, where applicable, safety of products and services.	Novartis, Amazon, Yahoo

Source: Thomas H. Davenport, 'Competing on Analytics,' *Harvard Business Review* 84, no. 1 (January 2006): 6.

Business analytics describes the skills, technologies, and practices for relentless iterative inquiries into past business performance to develop new perspectives and to anchor business planning. It aims at surfacing new insights and understanding of business performance while relying on data and statistical methods. Traditionally, BI relied on a set of metrics, also based on data and statistical methods, to measure past performance and drive future business plans.

Business analytics use statistical analysis, including explanatory and predictive modeling, and fact-based management to enable effective decisions. In this way, it is connected with management science. Analytics may be used as input for human decisions or may drive fully automated decisions. BI is querying, reporting, online analytical processing (OLAP), and 'alerts.'

Thomas Davenport, Harris, and Morrison[19] identify these characteristics of an organization that are apt to compete on analytics:

- One or more senior executives who strongly advocate fact-based decision-making and, specifically, analytics
- Widespread use of not only descriptive statistics, but also predictive modeling and complex optimization techniques
- Substantial use of analytics across multiple business functions or processes
- Movement toward an enterprise level approach to managing analytical tools, data, and organizational skills and capabilities

In his book *Analytics at Work*, Davenport and others suggest that businesses can better compete in the current environment of rapid changes by finding answers to some fundamental questions about its business.

These questions are organized across two dimensions: time frame (past, present, or future) and innovation (known information or new insight). Querying, reporting, OLAP, and alert tools can answer questions such as what happened, how many, how often, where the problem is, and what actions are needed. Business analytics can answer questions such as why this is happening, what if these trends continue, what will happen next (i.e., predict), and what is the best that can happen (i.e., optimize).

It is now believed that if organizations are to make better decisions and take right actions, then they must use analytics. It is believed that for too long important calls have been based not on data, but on the experience and unaided judgment of the decision-maker. One research suggests that 40% of the major decisions are based not on facts, but on the manager's gut.[20]

Sometimes intuitive and experience-based decisions work well, but often they either go astray or end in disaster: executives pursue mergers and acquisitions to palliate their egos, neglecting the sober considerations that create real value; banks make credit and risk decisions based on unexamined assumptions about always–rising asset value. In other words, non-analytical decisions do not always lead to tragedy, but they do leave money on the table.

Reflection Point

Companies leveraging HR analytics for their business decisions experience an astounding 82% increase in their three-year average profits! This insight is based on a Deloitte study that highlights the incredible potential of HR analytics.

A study by McKinsey's research revealed that companies well-versed in HR analytics saw an 80% increase in recruiting efficiency, making their hiring processes highly effective. Additionally, their overall business productivity received a substantial 25% boost, resulting in increased output and efficiency across the board.

Conduct a mini research on the Internet to list out the various areas where the use of HR analytics is providing competitive advantage to businesses. Also discuss the areas in which the organizations should be cautious.

Source: http://www.peoplematters.in.Accessed 15.11.2023

[19] Davenport et al., Analytics at Work.

[20] Ibid.

14.5.2 HR Analytics–Definition

> HR analytics is the application of mathematical, statistical, and data mining techniques to HR and business data to explore concepts and ideas and solve HR-related business problems. HR analytics enables better decision making by providing an organization with insights about the workforce and the HR policies and practices that support them. Analytics may be used to look at the traits of the workforce, in particular its human capital: the value of individual knowledge, skills and experience of individuals and teams. This is also known as human capital analytics. When an organization reports on the insights gathered through HR analytics, it is often known as human capital reporting.[21]

Many of the HR metrics most frequently used in organizations can be traced to the pioneering work of Dr Jac Fitz-enz and the early benchmarking work he conducted through the Saratoga Institute. In 1984, Fitz-enz published *How to Measure Human Resources Management*, currently in its third edition,[22] which is still a highly valued overview of many HR metrics and the formulas used to calculate them. These metrics were developed through the joint efforts of the Saratoga Institute and the American Society for Personnel Administration, the forerunner of the current SHRM.

14.5.3 Activities in HR Analytics

Reporting

Reporting involves the following decisions:

1. What set of metrics would be appropriate in the context of specific challenges and opportunities for the business?
2. Are the content of the metrics clearly understood by the target stakeholder groups and the manner of transmitting (emails, presentation or posting in the Website) the metrics agreed upon?
3. What will be the frequency of the metric reports?
4. Who should receive the metric data (the top leaders, middle leaders, or the junior executives also)?

Dashboards

A dashboard is an easy to read, often single-page, real-time user interface, showing a graphical presentation of the current status (snapshot) and historical trends of an organization's or computer appliances KPIs to enable instantaneous and informed decisions to be made at a glance. It is an evolved element of reporting. It aligns real-time analysis of organizational and HR processes to total organizational data. It helps managers to further explore metrics on several levels within the organization and presents an up-to-date status of critical HR metrics.

Benchmarking

Saratoga Institute's pioneering work on building standard HR metrics as benchmarks can be used to gain important insights on what is possible. However, benchmarked HR metrics of one organization is rooted in the culture and typical problems and challenges that the organization may be faced with, and, therefore, not always comparable with another organization with different contexts, size, demographics, or so on.

---

[21] CIPD Factsheet on HR Analytics, July 2015.

[22] Jac Fitz-Enz, *How to Measure Human Resource Management* (New York, NY: McGraw-Hill Education, 2002).

Data Mining

Data mining analyzes data from different perspectives and summarizes it into information that can be used to increase revenue, cuts costs, or both. Data mining is one of a number of analytical tools for analyzing data in order to discern patterns or causal mechanisms between different sets of data. It uses statistical tools such as correlation and multiple regression methods to track patterns in complex datasets. For example, the correlation between the new performance incentive system and the employee morale. Data mining needs to be done with care, because it is possible to statistically establish absurd correlations also.

Predictive Analyses

In predictive analysis, models of organizational systems are developed that can help predict results of future actions/hypothesized changes in organizations. For instance, if the organization discovered a correlation between incentive system and change in employee morale, the data could be used to initiate suitable modification in the incentive or reward system. Leading indicators, in the balanced scorecard system, can serve as the basis for predictive analyses.

Thomas Davenport[23] gives an example of predictive analytics in the form of a customer lifetime value measure. It uses analytics to determine how much a customer will buy from the company over time. Similarly, a 'next best offer' or product recommendation capability is an analytical prediction of the product or service that the customer is most likely to buy next. Forecast of next quarter's sales, use of digital marketing models to determine what ad to place and on what publisher's site are forms of predictive analytics.

Workforce Modeling

Workforce modeling is the process by which the need for employees with specific competencies at a given point in time is matched with the availability and preference of employees having the skills. It can project how an organization's human capital needs would change in response to some expected changes in the organization's environment. The resulting mathematical models may be used to perform sensitivity analysis and generate data output in the form of reports and schedules.

Exhibit The Story of Project Oxygen

Google is one of several companies that are applying analytics in new ways. Until recently, organizations used data-driven decision-making mainly in product development, marketing, and pricing. However, these days, Google, Procter & Gamble, Harrah's, and others take that same approach in addressing human resource needs. In early 2009, Google People Analytics team set out to find answers to one question, which had come up again and again since the company's founding: Do managers matter? The team reviewed exit-interview data to see if employees cited management issues as a reason for leaving Google. Though they found some connections between turnover rates and low satisfaction with managers, those did not apply to the company more broadly, given the low turnover rates overall. Nor did the findings prove that managers caused attrition. As a next step, the team examined Googlegeist ratings and semiannual reviews, comparing

[23] Thomas H. Davenport, 'A Predictive Analytics Primer,' *Harvard Business Review* (September 2, 2014). Available at: https://hbr. org/2014/09/a-predictive-analytics-primer (accessed on January 25, 2018).

managers on both satisfaction and performance. For both dimensions, he looked at the highest and lowest scorers (the top and bottom quartiles). The solution came from applying sophisticated multivariate statistical techniques, which showed that even 'the smallest incremental increases in manager quality were quite powerful.' For example, in 2008, the high-scoring managers saw less turnover on their teams than the others did—and retention was related more strongly to manager quality than to seniority, performance, tenure, or promotions. The data also showed a tight connection between managers' quality and workers' happiness: Employees with high-scoring bosses consistently reported greater satisfaction in multiple areas, including innovation, work–life balance, and career development.

In light of this research, the Project Oxygen team concluded that managers indeed mattered. However, to act on that finding, Google first had to figure out what its best managers did. So the researchers followed up with double-blind qualitative interviews, asking the high- and low-scoring managers questions such as 'How often do you have career-development discussions with your direct reports?' and 'What do you do to develop a vision for your team?' Managers from Google's three major functions (engineering, global business, and general and administrative) participated; they came from all levels and geographies. The team also studied thousands of qualitative comments from Googlegeist surveys, performance reviews, and submissions for the company's Great Manager Award. (Each year, Google selects about 20 managers for this distinction, on the basis of employees' nominations.) It took several months to code and process all this information.

After much review, Oxygen identified the following eight behaviors shared by high-scoring managers:

1. Is a good coach
2. Empowers the team and does not micromanage
3. Expresses interest in and concern for team members' success and personal well-being
4. Is productive and results-oriented
5. Is a good communicator—listens and shares information
6. Helps with career development
7. Has a clear vision and strategy for the team
8. Has key technical skills that help him or her advise the team

Source: David A. Garvin, 'How Google Sold Its Engineers on Management'. Available at: https://hbr.org/2013/12/how-google-sold-its-engineers-on-management (accessed on January 25, 2018).

14.5.4 Benefits of HR Analytics

The value of HR analytics is in helping firms to effectively analyze their employee data and discover solutions to diverse, wide-ranging issues of problems such as improving effectiveness of the sales personnel to measure the quality of training programs. It helps LMs and teams to get a handle on the complexities of the individual and group dynamics in their organization—how people perform and create value for the organization. On qualitative areas, the application of HR analytics is helping firms to acquire concrete data on the time lag for a new employee to become productive. Organizations can now access the vast reservoir of employee data to make well-considered, high-quality decisions pertaining to employees and thus achieve better business outcomes. A study by the *Harvard Business Review* group established a link between improved profitability (by around 65%) and advanced usage of HR analytics.[24] HR analytic instruments are going a long way to synthesize employee metrics with business strategies by various HR processes including acquisition of strategic talent, making detailed HRP, gauging employee motivation, and so on. Significantly, HR analytics is proving to be useful in surfacing the real issues in employee engagement in an organization, exposing the limitations of unreliable surveys and instruments transplanted from organizations in another cultural context, often using sentiment analysis to gauge real-time engagement.

At a far more fundamental level, HR analytics is helping the HR professionals to perform a complete makeover of their own image as a number–shy, business-illiterate function to one that is comfortable with numbers and understands which sets of employee analytics have the most impact and leverage. Previously, before the era of analytics, HR, as the custodian of employee data, traditionally managed the role by collecting and maintaining the personal and professional data of employees such as payroll, employee benefits, and reports of performance appraisals. HR analytics has taken a quantum leap from the customary MIS, through the stage of dashboards to predictive reporting—metamorphosing from 'what' analytics to the 'why' analytics. Further, it has become possible to quantify the erstwhile nebulous link between HR initiatives and business goals. No longer is HR solely precedent-driven, nor does it make its people projections in the touchy feely, intuitive manner. Analytics and big data have empowered HR to make well-informed, well-considered decisions in a sure-footed manner, which is unprecedented. This newfound confidence is most dramatically captured in what Google asserts about employee-management decisions acquiring level of engineering decisions. In short, analytics has highlighted the power of number and thus enabled HR to use more influence in dealing with LMs with its perspectives on people issues.

The challenge of HR analytics is judicious selection of the useful and strategic information to ascertain what information should be mined and the effective way to sweat the data 'to model and predict capabilities so the organization gets an optimal ROI on its human capital.'[25]

14.5.5 The Scope for HR Analytics Capability

HR analytics uses workforce or HR data, either qualitative or quantitative, to investigate a certain concept with the help of computer programs and modeling techniques. There are three main levels of HR analytics capability. Most organizations are able to do level 1 only, very few are able to complete level 3 analytics:

- **Level 1 (basic analytics)** The use of descriptive data to illustrate a particular aspect of HR, for example, recording absence, annual leave, and attrition and recruitment rates. At level 1, no analysis is applied to the data beyond using it to describe a certain concept, or illustrate its change over time (sometimes called trend analysis).
- **Level 2 (using multi-dimensional data)** Combining different data sets or types of data, to investigate a specific idea can help to uncover interesting relationships between different HR activities and processes. Using two different types of data to create an analytics output is known as multi-dimensional analytics (e.g., combining leadership capability data with engagement scores to measure leadership effectiveness).

[24] L. Bassi and D. McMurrer, 'Maximizing Your Return on People,' *Harvard Business Review* 85, no. 3 (March 2007): 115–123, 144.

[25] Rajib Kumar, 'HR Analytics: Where Do We Stand,' October 2016. Available at: https://www.magzter.com/article/Business/ Human-Capital/HR-Analytics-Where-Do-We-Stand (accessed on November 16, 2017).

- **Level 3 (predictive analytics)** Some HR data can be analyzed and used to predict future trends in data. Using data this way can help HR departments to plan for future events and scenarios, and ensure they are able to deliver to the business. Predictive analytics for forecasting requires high-quality and robust data, and specialist technology and capability.

14.5.6 Application of HR Analytics

There are five different categories of human capital analytical applications.[26]

1. Identify and manage critical talent (e.g., high performers, high potentials, pivotal workers)
2. Manage critical workforce segments accordingly (e.g., underperforming units are identified and helped to improve)
3. Predict employee preferences and behaviors, and tailor HR practices to attract and retain talent
4. Forecast business requirements and staffing requirements (e.g., workforce skills needed in different business scenarios)
5. Adapt rapidly and scale recruiting-supply channels and targets (to make use of best talent sources available) to meet changing business conditions, objectives, and competitive threats

Narrated further are some more examples of analytical approaches, while keeping in mind the virtually infinite predictive possibilities, given the availability of good data such as candidate demographics and background data, psychometric data, structured interview data, assessment data, performance data, onboarding evaluation data, training data, and so on.

Predict Hiring Success

Predictive hiring algorithms will allow you to reevaluate your current hiring assumptions and raise the prospect of an upswing in profitability through data-based hiring. You will also be able to predict profiles of candidates with a higher risk of leaving your organization or who are (or will be) performing below standard.

Predict Recruitment Advertising or Channel Effectiveness

With predictive algorithms, you can now use your data from previous campaigns to avoid contacting candidates or using channels that do not provide a positive response and focus on those that do.

Predict High Potentials

Organizations using predictive algorithms will be able to predict which new hires, based on their profile, are likely to be high-potential employees. This allows you to move them in to your high-potential programs with much greater confidence of success.

Predict Employer Brand Strength

A predictive algorithm is able to predict when and why your employer brand strength will increase or decrease, compared to others. Combining external and internal employer-brand survey data can increase both the tenure and the productivity of your workforce.

[26] J. G. Harris, E. Craig, and D. A. Light, 'The New Generation of Human Capital Analytics' (Research Report, Accenture, 2010). Available at: http://www.accenture.co.uk/ Site Collection Documents/PDF/ (accessed on January 13, 2012).

Predict Contingent Workforce Effectiveness

A growing number of organizations are using contingent workforce strategies. Finding the balance between fixed or contingent labor force is complex and decision-making can be improved by using predictive algorithms, identifying hidden patterns and connections that may lead to productivity risks.

14.5.7 Some Practices by Global Firms Using HR Analytics

1. Harrah's Entertainment used insights derived from data to put the right employees in the right jobs and created models that calculate the optimal number of staff members to deal with customers at the front desk and other service points. Today, the company uses analytics to hold itself accountable for the things that matter most to its staff, knowing that happier and healthier employees create better satisfied guests.
2. Starbucks, Limited Brands, and Best Buy can precisely identify the value of a 0.1% increase in engagement among employees at a particular store. At Best Buy, for example, that value is more than US$100,000 in the store's annual operating income.
3. Sprint has identified the factors that best foretell which employees will leave after a relatively short time, which helps control employee attrition.
4. To protect its investments, soccer team AC Milan created its own biomedical research unit that draws on some 60,000 data points for each player. These units help the team gauge player's health and fitness and make contract decisions.

Exhibit Innovative HR Practices at Google Using HR Analytics

1. PiLabs is a subgroup that conducts experiments on effective approaches for managing people and support a productive environment. Its scope includes what rewards make the employees the happiest. The lab even improved employee health by reducing the calorie intake of its employees at their eating facilities by relying on scientific data and experiments (by simply reducing the size of the plates).
2. Google developed a mathematical algorithm to proactively and successfully predict which employees are most likely to become a retention problem. This approach allows management to act before it is too late and it further allows retention solutions to be personalized.
3. It developed predictive models with 'what if' analysis to continually improve their forecasts of upcoming people management problems and opportunities. Some other areas of application of analytics are: build effective workforce planning; improve diversity through more effective recruiting, retention, and promotions (especially among women engineers).
4. Developed an algorithm for predicting probability of success in new employees. Its research indicated the inefficacy of interviews beyond four, thus dramatically shortening the cycle time of recruitment. The hiring decisions at Google are made by a group in order to prevent possibilities for short-term hiring by individual hiring managers. 'Project Janus,' created an algorithm for each large job family, which analyzed rejected resumes to identify any top candidates, who they might have missed. They found that they had only a 1.5% miss rate, and as a result they hired some of the revisited candidates.
5. Calculated the performance differential between an exceptional technologist and an average one (as much as 300 times higher). Proving the value of top performers convinces executives to provide the resources necessary to hire, retain, and develop extraordinary talent.

6. Focused on increasing collaboration between employees from different functions. It has found that increased innovation comes from a combination of three factors: discovery (i.e., learning), collaboration, and fun. It consciously designs its workplaces to maximize learning, fun, and collaboration (it even tracks the time spent by employees in the café lines to maximize collaboration). Managing 'fun' may seem superfluous to some, but the data indicates that it is a major factor in attraction, retention, and collaboration.

Source: John Sullivan, 'How Google Became the #3 Most Valuable Firm by Using People Analytics to Reinvent HR,' February 25, 2013. Available at: https://www.ere.net/how-google-became-the-3-most-valuable-firm-by-using-people-analytics-to-reinvent-hr/ (accessed on November 2, 2017).

14.5.8 Importance Assigned to Various HR Analytics and Research Instruments

A study titled 'The HR Analytics Project Conducted by the Organizational Intelligence Institute and Drexel University' was conducted covering Fortune 1000 as well as select global firms (chosen on the basis of annual gross revenue) with the objective to gain insight into the extent to which these high-performing companies were conducting HR research and analytics practices. Of the 220 companies that participated, 195 were Fortune 1000 companies and 21 were global firms headquartered outside of the United States. Of significance, 39 participating companies were Fortune 100 firms.[27]

Some of the findings of the study were as follows:

1. 'Employee and organizational surveys' received higher priority from Fortune 100 and global firms than other participants. High-performing companies in terms of size and gross revenue tend to invest a significant amount of resources and time on employee and organizational survey initiatives. Over a third of all respondents reported employee and organizational surveys as the most expensive or costly to perform and the third most time-consuming HR research and analytics practice.
2. The larger companies, such as Bank of America, Dell, Eli Lilly, Ford, Google, Intel, Microsoft, Nike, IBM, Target, and SAP, benchmark and compare their survey results through employee-research membership consortiums, such as the Mayflower Group and Information Technology Survey Group. In doing so, member companies can make industry and cross-industry comparisons by job family, similar groups, business units, and/or functions.
3. Advanced organizational behavior (OB) research and modeling was rated as the most time-consuming and difficult to perform. Talent supply chain (e.g., analytics to make decisions in real time for optimizing immediate talent demands in terms of changing business conditions) was rated the second most difficult to perform, which is consistent with previous research and observations.[28]
4. Operations research and management science received the lowest rating (2.33) in terms of facilitating HR strategy and decision-making, although interest in optimization methods as well as the emerging application of AI (i.e., expert systems and machine learning) to

[27] Salvatore Falletta, 'In Search of HR Intelligence: Evidence-based HR Analytics Practices in High Performing Companies,' *People and Strategy* 36, no. 4 (2014): 28–37. Available at: https://issuu.com/guy2marsh9/docs/in_search_of_hr_intelligence_eviden (accessed on February 2, 2017).

[28] T. H. Davenport, J. Harris, and J. Shapiro, 'Competing on Talent Analytics,' *Harvard Business Review* 88, no. 10 (October 2010): 52–58.

HRM decisions are likely to increase as advancements in skills, capabilities, and technology continue.[29]

14.5.9 HR Analytics Process

The HR analytics process should follow nine steps from planning through to the evaluation of the process:

1. **Plan** Develop the goals and purpose for the analytics activity. Map the requirements of the customer and plan questions/queries, which will be answered by the analytics process.
2. **Define critical success factors** Define the measures that will show if the project has been a success. Examples of what these can be based on include delivery on time, impact of project, and feedback from users.
3. **Data audit** Map the data that is currently available and grade its quality. This will illustrate where any gaps in data may be, which should be filled before progressing.
4. **Design the process** Define roles and set objectives for team members. Define resource requirements and map stakeholders for the project.
5. **Design the data collection strategy** Design the collection and processing stages of the analytics activity.
6. **Data collection** Collect data from data sources. This can be from drawing on established data sets (e.g., absence records) or running new-data collection processes (e.g., engagement survey).
7. **Analyze data** Depending on the customer requirements, analyze the data and develop insights in the form of recommendations and guidance for the users of the data.
8. **Report data** Report in a clear and simple way illustrating a solution to their issue, or further areas of investigation if further data is required.
9. **Evaluate** Review the data-analytics-insights process and evaluate impact. Review and update process as required.

Source: CIPD Factsheet.

14.5.10 Challenges to Effective Use of HR Analytics

The challenges to the effective use of HR analytics are:

1. Identifying the right metrics to measure what is relevant and meaningful to the business by monitoring and analyzing the measures that improve decisions and actions, which contribute to better business results.
2. Developing a collaborative effort between HR, finance, and IT with significant input from LMs and executives.
3. Increasing the quantitative skills of HR professionals that are conventionally less.
4. Creating a culture that promotes use of analytics through strong communication and change management plan.

[29] James C. Cecil, *Applying Advanced Analytics to HR Management Decisions* (New York, NY: Pearson): 22.

14.5.11 Maturity Models for BI

Business Intelligence Maturity Models (BIMMs) help to 'describe, explain and evaluate growth life cycles.' The basic theme in all business models is the inevitability of changes in business, and the possibility of anticipating much of the changes in order to prepare for it and to control the effects over time. It has been observed from existing literature that there are multiple models coming up all the time and they evolve and get more and more perfected with time on the basis of experience.

The value of maturity model for BI lies in the fact that it charts a path for the business organization and assists in integrating analytics with its business strategy and performance. Organizations find ease at different levels of maturity, and make choices of appropriate levels to suit their business needs—some staying at lower levels, some using the upper levels. Some organizations make business analytics the fulcrum of their business strategy and for them the choice of analytics covers grounds beyond technology to cover people and business goals as well.

Essentially, the purpose of the maturity models is to help organizations in self-assessment and to decide action plans for getting better. The focus of this assessment is captured in the following questions:[30]

1. Where in the organization is most of the reporting and business analysis done today?
2. Who is using business reports, analysis, and success indicators?
3. What drives BI in the organization?
4. Which strategies for developing BI are in use today?
5. What business value does BI bring?

The models emphasize three indicators for effective business analytics—alignment and governance, leverage, and delivery—and seven key areas on assessment, namely, BI strategic position, partnership between business units and IT, BI portfolio management, information and analysis usage culture, process of improving business culture, process of establishing decision culture, and technical readiness of BI/data warehousing.[31]

Business analytics can operate at three basic levels: at the lowest level, where the information pertains to 'what' business users want to access and are usually in a form of data elements, which are passed from end users to the IT department; in the middle level, go beyond the sheer data to the reasons for requiring the information, graduating from the 'what' into the 'why,' and this information connects even the 'who,' 'when,' and 'where' with the internal processes that support business goals. At the third level, the information engages the entire organization where data is used. The focus lifts to how to manage business processes and organizational transformation. The existing decision processes, not found right, give way to modified decision processes, which optimize the usage of information throughout the whole organization.[32]

[30] Irena Hribar Rajterič, 'Overview of Business Intelligence Maturity Models,' *Management: Journal of Contemporary Management Issues* 15, no. 1 (June 2010): 47–67.

[31] Steve Williams and Nancy Williams, *The Profit Impact of Business Intelligence* (San Francisco, CA: Morgan Kaufmann Publishers, 2007).

[32] Nancy Williams and Jim Thomann, 'BI Maturity and ROI: How Does Your Organization Measure Up?' (2003). Available at: http://www.decisionpath.com:8180/docs_downloads/TDWI%20Flash%20-%20BI%20Maturity%20and%20ROI%20110703.pdf (accessed on April 19, 2009).

BI Maturity Models

Some examples

Gartner BI MM

Gartner's BIMM converges on three areas—people, processes, and metrics or technologies—and across five maturity levels, namely, unaware, tactical, focused, strategic, and pervasive. This model is useful for auditing the maturity levels of business and also of individual departments.

The Ladder of BI (LOBI)

The LOBI is a model used to create the IT plan and apply IT to business. This model applies three key process areas—technology, processes, and people—and across six levels, namely, facts, data, information, knowledge, understanding, and enabled intuition.

This model, though applicable to the knowledge management field and the author-constructed maturity levels from a technical point of view, it is not well documented and the criteria to evaluate the maturity level are not well defined. This model mainly provides IT perspective.

The HP BIMM

The HP BIMM consists of five stages based on the evolution of business enablement, information technology, and strategy/program management: operation (running the business); improvement (measuring and monitoring the business); alignment; empowerment; and transformation.

The business-enablement dimension describes types of business requirements and problems that are solved with BI solutions; the IT dimension describes information solutions a company adopts to serve differences of business needs, while the strategy and program management dimension describes management skills as a key enabler and catalyst for BI success. The HP BIMM depicts the maturity levels from a business/ technical aspect.

Source: Adapted from Kristen Gill, 'Roundup of Business Intelligence Maturity Models from Key Analysts and Experts in BI,' July 30, 2015. Available at: https://www.pyramidanalytics.com/blog/bi-maturity-models (accessed on November 16, 2017).

People Matters Workforce Analytics Study 2016 has used Gartner's Analytics Maturity Model and superimposed the HR analytics to report the following findings:

1. A majority of 38% of the surveyed companies are at their infancy when it comes to adoption of analytics. It means that they only use it for basic reporting, and in that 70% still use spreadsheets.
2. About 36% answer the 'what' and 'why' questions and are, therefore, in a stage of advanced reporting. These companies, however, do not seek to assess patterns and predict future behaviors.
3. About 26% of the companies have reached the stage of predictive and prescriptive workforce analytics.

14.5.12 HR Predictive Analytics

In 2007, with the sponsorship of companies such as Accenture, Blue Shield, Ceridian, Fidelity, Monster, Oracle, Success Factors, Target, and others, Dr Jac Fitz-enz built out the Predictive Management Model. The operating model is divided into four phases or steps:

1. **Comprehensive scanning** All functions contribute to a master list of external and internal forces that might affect the company's human capital, structural capital, or relational capital. In an experiment with top 40 managers of a 35,000-strong employee base, a multinational engineering company built a leadership development and succession plan in six months. It included high potential (HiPo) employees' career paths, their T&D and L&D needs, and identification of potential successors.
2. **Capability planning** Capabilities were divided into four categories regardless of departmental boundaries:
   (i) *Mission critical*—necessary for survival
   (ii) *Unique and differentiating*—provide competitive advantage
   (iii) *Operationally necessary*—keep the machine running
   (iv) *Movable*—can be retrained, transferred, eliminated, or outsourced

   It is found that (based on research of 714 companies in 2007) there is a connection between succession planning and top-line revenue if:
   (i) A senior executive is responsible and accountable for managing the succession plan
   (ii) HiPo employees are identified and development plans designed
   (iii) T&D plans are directly aligned with corporate strategy
   (iv) HiPo plans are reviewed, modified, and reinforced at least annually
   (v) Performance of the group is correlated with top-line revenue growth

   The research showed that when at least 75% of mission critical and differentiating positions have a fully qualified replacement, top-line revenue begins to increase.
3. **Process optimization** Processes are judged on their ability to 'return more money to the firm than they cost in terms of invested capital.' Processes are treated in two ways:
   (i) *Applied statistical analysis*—For example, the hiring process is divided into inputs (sources of job applicants), throughputs (selection and induction methods), and outcomes (new-hire performance, potential, turnover predictability, and the like). Predictive measurement identifies the most value-generating combination of inputs and throughputs to optimize outcomes.
   (ii) *Integrated delivery schedules*—Operations done in a silo are inward-looking and inefficient. They conflict with each other when they touch their customer, the manager or the employee.
4. **Predictive measurement** It consists of a 3-part system tying together strategic, operational, and leading metrics.
   (i) *Strategic*—Provides the big picture quickly. Some human capital metrics doing it are:
   - Revenue per FTE
   - Human capital value added (HCVA): Non-human expenses divided by number of employees. This is more precise than revenue per FTE, which ignores the effects of non-human investments.

- Human capital ROI: Same as HCVA except divide by cost of pay and benefits. This yields a ratio of 1:1.
- Human capital economic value added (HCEVA): HCEVA per employee, the ultimate human-productivity metric.
- Turnover of mission critical and differentiating personnel.

(ii) *Operational*—These contain the lagging indicators:

- Cost per unit of product or service: Hiring, training, paying, benefits processing, and such others.
- Timeliness: Time to fill jobs, deliver training and leadership development, respond, and solve problems.
- Quantity: Volume of output over input, numbers hired, trained, and so on, with a given commitment of resources.
- Reaction: Satisfaction of employees and managers with HR services.

(iii) *Leading*—These intangibles are directly related to strategic level metrics:

- Readiness: Percentage of mission critical and differentiating positions with at least one fully qualified replacement.
- Leadership: Employee survey results indicating degree of commitment to corporate leadership; these directly correlate with employee engagement and turnover.
- Employee engagement: Employee surveys indicate willingness to give more than the basic effort, correlates with revenue per FTE.
- Employer brand: Correlates with the cost to hire and retain top talent.
- Employee retention: Percentage of mission critical and differentiating positions not losing employees; reverse engineering retention uncovers the reasons for turnover.

14.5.13 The Current Status of HR Analytics

In 2010, the Center for Advanced Human Resource Studies (CAHRS) at Cornell University launched a series of working groups to gauge how partner companies are using HR analytics and what challenges remain. Over 50 participants from nearly 30 CAHRS partner companies participated in the working groups, which covered four key areas:

1. **Application** How are organizations applying HR analytics?
2. **Value** How much do organizations value using HR analytics, and how do they communicate this to the larger organization?
3. **Systems and structures** What resources support HR analytics initiatives? How does technology help or constrain these efforts?
4. **The future** How can organizations facilitate and enhance HR analytics? How will its practice evolve?

In response, all participants confirmed using HR data for basic reporting purposes; about 80% indicated having reports of key HR data in dashboard or scorecard; 73% had in-house expertise in quantitative analysis techniques; and 67% felt they had the support of senior leaders for HR analytics projects and initiatives. But the bad news is only 27% felt they had a strong team of analytical talent who could execute HR analytics projects; only 33% agreed with the statement 'Front line HR generalists understand the value of HR analytics'; just 13% felt they had the necessary technology/

systems to facilitate HR analytics; and only 1 in 5 respondents strongly agreed that they trusted the reliability and accuracy of their organizational data.

14.5.14 Enablers for HR Analytics

1. **Centralized data** While some had systems that linked data from different sources (finance, HR, marketing), others did not. The organizations with access to centralized data could conduct analyses to understand how factors such as leadership, operational efficiency, and customer/financial outcomes are interrelated. Those without such access lacked suitable data, or lacked in-house resources to analyze, interpret, and disseminate the information.
2. **Field training of HR users** Hands-on use in the field helps employees to understand what data is available, how to use it, and how to ask for help in assessing/analyzing it. Working with data in the field also allows users to hone their skills detecting patterns of relationships and communicating messages to LMs at different levels.
3. **Support from senior leaders** It brings credibility and resources to the endeavor.
4. **Enhanced technology** If the organization is already on the agenda of upgrading the existing technology, it can create a need for HR analytics.
5. **Supportive culture** An organizational culture that endorses HR analytics at the highest levels and communicates this widely; provides a supportive environment for employees to experiment and test hypotheses in real workforce situations.

14.5.15 Inhibitors for HR Analytics

1. Organizational barriers—Many managers and frontline HR generalists are not yet comfortable talking about HR in terms of testing and evidence, or lack the skills to know which data to use for the right analyses—that is, those that will help them identify process improvements, and strategic and financial outcomes. Top executives may also shy away from making big decisions using incomplete data.
2. Unresponsive culture—A culture wary of embracing HR analytics subtly ensures that its employees will be wary too.
3. Managing data from multiple countries.
4. Lack of incentives for others to share data across functions.
5. Lack of sophistication—fear of numbers, poor data analysis, and communications skills—among potential data users.
6. Inability to match data across sources.
7. Tailoring and communicating findings to different levels of the organization.
8. Data credibility concerns, perhaps caused by limited manpower resources, privacy and security issues, legal and financial constraints, old data, employee-driven entry for some of the data, and other factors.
9. Controlling access to data when slicing and combining.

A TJinsite[33] survey from TimesJob.com across industries corroborates some of the aforementioned findings:

---

[33] Available at: http://content.timesjobs.com/docs/TJNewsletterMarch2015.pdf (accessed on November 16, 2017).

1. 90% of the companies surveyed say predictive analytics is the future of talent hunting.
2. 7% employ it to find right hire.
3. 65% plan to employ predictive talent analytics in the next one year.
4. 12% think it will take them a year to move into predictive analytics.
5. 18% plan to climb the maturity curve in the next six months.
6. 5% of the organizations said that they had no plans on the card.

Some possible areas of applications of predictive modeling in HR are:

Training and Learning

Learning algorithms can be used to segment employees with particular training needs as well as detect trends in areas such as program enrollment, diversity, and so on. The segments could be based on demographics, skills, educational background, experience, and designation together with data on roles and responsibilities to create such segments. This can lead steps to improve employee-engagement scores. It can also indicate employee readiness to leverage learning opportunities or volunteer for new assignments.

Employee-risk Analysis

Based on data of employee turnover, organizations can develop risk quotient of individual employees. This can enable organizations to reduce the probability of loss of critical talent, ensure that there are no disruptions in business, and identify committed employees. The analyses can use various data related to employee demographics, performance, compensation and rewards, market data, training data, behavioral data, and employee survey scores. Managers can isolate the triggers for attrition and thereby prevent it.

HR Demand Forecast

HR managers can predict manpower inventory and future requirements, and thus draw up precise plans for recruitment, training, and infrastructure development. The pattern of attrition rates and business growth forecasts for each department or unit can help estimate the employees staying on and also future requirements.

Candidate Profile

By mining the current employees' data, including performance and productivity statistics, employee turnover details, and employee value indices, HR can profile potential employees. A correlation between employee value and profile variables such as education and experience can help identify the most suitable profiles. This helps increase quality, productivity, and customer-satisfaction scores, and reduce recruitment cost substantially, creating sustainable value for the organization.

Employee Morale Analysis

Data from multiple sources can help HR to design, develop, or modify their initiatives. Analyses of employee morale by monitoring, analyzing, and dissecting key topics that are most relevant to employee morale over a period can provide candid feedback, unavailable in traditional employee surveys. This could use internal data related to the respective HR initiative or change, as well as data from external social media such as Facebook, Twitter, and LinkedIn.

14.6 ARTIFICIAL INTELLIGENCE IN WORKPLACE

Businesses are viewing artificial intelligence for multiple ways to improve productivity. There are several benefits: one, it can perform repetitive work in every part of the organization so that employees can focus on creative solutions, complex problem-solving, and impactful work. One example of that being chatbots; two, it can help companies decipher their data and gain valuable insights from it without a data scientist. It's impossible to run a competitive business without data. And even if you obtain it, hiring someone to read all of that data and provide valuable insights is even harder. Good data scientists are almost impossible to find in today's market.[34]

There are, however, concerns too. One application of AI in workplace is the increasing adoption of what is known as Emotion AI, which is to 'sense, learn about, and interact with human emotional life' through statistical analysis, affective computing, and machine learning. Emotion AI promises organizations the knowhow to access, manage and track employees' interior states and personality attributes for the purposes in ways that support organizational goals, including productivity improvement, mitigated security and safety risks, increased customer loyalty and sales, and improved corporate wellness. Workplace surveillance is expanding to include automatic monitoring of worker emotion, mood, affect, and related constructs.[35]

Such wanton use of surveillance may not have a smooth sailing. A study on US adult workers have revealed concerns for deep privacy violation in matters of workers' sensitive emotional information, and the fear that workers may get harmed as a consequence. Findings reveal the need to recognize and define an individual right to *emotional privacy*, and how to protect and preserve emotional privacy within and beyond the workplace.

Case The ILmits of Analytics

It was a typical IR scenario in a large manufacturing MNC. The months' long wage negotiation was coming to a closure. Out of the two operating unions, one has agreed to the terms offered by the management after negotiations. The other, the challenger to the first, older union, of course, did not agree to the terms. They wanted some more, that will give them a handle to wean away some members from the first union.

The management was in a dilemma. It was necessary that the second union also signs. But the issue was what tactic to use. Should it go ahead and implement the agreed terms with the first union? Technically it could, as it had the blessing of the state labor ministry. In that event it would hope that the members of the second union will get restless and put pressure on its own union to sign. But it could go horribly wrong also. Supposing the members of the first union felt that the leadership was sold out and then decided to break ranks and join the second?

In this kind of stalemate situation with unions, the IR professionals would have a chance to show their mettle. A stalemate in wage negotiation always threatens a situation of industrial unrest. Business leader, LMs, sales executives all get concerned as to how and when things

34 Three surprising benefits of Artificial Intelligence in the workplace. Christian Crossman. July 2023. https://www.beekeeper.io/blog

35 Emotion AI at Work: Implications for Workplace Surveillance, Emotional Labor, and Emotional Privacy. Kat Roemmich. Proceedings of the 2023 CHI Conference on Human Factors in Computing Systems

will normalize. It depends on reading the minds of the trade union leaders, especially their top leader. The IR professionals hold rounds of formal and informal meetings with the trade union leaders to read their mind and keep the communication to the business leaders and all LMs on what is their 'hunch', or 'sensing' about what will break the impasse.

Discussion Question

1. Can technology and analytics help to get into the minds of the trade union leaders to anticipate their strategy, and then adopt a counter strategy?

14.6.1 Future of HR Technology

HR technology relates to the use of digital technology to identify and solve people-related challenges in the organization. The sweeping waves of digitalization are altering how people live, work, and conduct their business. This digital phase besets the HR professional with a dual challenge. First, HR should influence the business leaders and employees to adapt to a digital way of thinking, managing, and leading change. Second, HR can orchestrate an entire employee experience by redesigning its own processes, systems, and the HR function with the aid of digital platforms, apps, and ways of delivering HR services.

There is an estimated 7 billion mobile devices in the world, and more than 40% of all Internet traffic is driven by these devices. Yet less than one-fifth of companies conduct their HR and employee-productivity solutions on mobile apps. Digital HR, which brings together social, mobile, analytics, and cloud (SMAC) technologies, provides a new platform for employee and candidate experience.

With the emergence of Workday in 2005, the procurement of Success Factors by SAP in 2011, and the purchase of Taleo by Oracle in 2012, HR is at the cutting edge of the move to digital and the cloud in the workplace. The use of mobile devices has been melting the walls separating work from personal life. The employee preference for the mobile as a channel presents organizations a lever to embrace mobile HR technologies to an extent hitherto unimaginable with traditional HR platforms. HR is thus in the cusp of a probable metamorphosis of its mental models, by prioritizing connectivity, real-time operations, platforms, automation, and mobile-first.

SUMMARY

The HRIS was defined as 'the composite of databases, computer applications, and hardware and software necessary to collect/record, store, manage, deliver, present, and manipulate data of human resource.'[36] HRIS improves the efficiency and effectiveness of HR processes. It is useful in two ways. In the first place, its most common application lies in simple automation such as payroll and benefit administration, and employee record-keeping for the purpose of cost reduction and administrative efficiency. The second usage is strategic—for business analyses and analytics–based decision-making.

HR metrics is a vital way to quantify the cost and the impact of employee programs and HR processes, and measure the success (or failure) of HR initiatives. They enable a company to track year-to-year trends and changes in these critical variables. It is how organizations measure the value of the time and money spent on HR activities in their organizations. There are HR efficiency metrics

[36] R. Broderick and J.W. Boudreau, 'Human Resource Management, Information Technology, and the Competitive Edge.'

such as cost per hire, time to fill up the open position, among others. HR effectiveness metrics include training ROI and absent rate.

HR capability-building metrics include revenue factor and defects rate.

Analytics is the discovery and communication of meaningful patterns in data. Done well, data analytics is built on a firm grasp of statistics and probability. These skills are used to discover useful information, suggest conclusions, and support decision-making. Equipped with the powerful tool of HR analytics, the HR professional is able to project an image of business savvy, number crunching bunch of functionaries, in complete contrast to their traditional image of being number shy, and overtly reliant on qualitative and subjective assessments.

Some of the areas of application of analytics in HR processes are identifying and managing critical talent (e.g., high performers, high potentials, pivotal workers); managing critical workforce segments accordingly (e.g., underperforming units are identified and helped to improve); predicting employee preferences and behaviors, and tailoring HR practices to attract and retain talent; forecasting business requirements and staffing requirements (e.g., workforce skills needed in different business scenarios); and adapting rapidly and scaling recruiting-supply channels and targets (to make use of best talent sources available) to meet changing business conditions, objectives, and competitive threats.

With the emergence of Workday in 2005, the procurement of Success Factors by SAP in 2011, and the purchase of Taleo by Oracle in 2012, HR is at the cutting edge of the move to digital and the cloud in the workplace. The use of mobile devices has been melting the walls separating work from personal life. The employee preference for the mobile as a channel presents organizations a lever to embrace mobile HR technologies to an extent hitherto unimaginable with traditional HR platforms. HR is thus in the cusp of a probable metamorphosis of its mental models, by prioritizing connectivity, real-time operations, platforms, automation, and mobile-first.

Short-answer Questions

1. What are the objectives of the HRIS?
2. Describe HR efficiency metrics.
3. Define HR analytics.
4. What is data mining?
5. Explain workforce modeling.
6. Present some of the applications of HR analytics.
7. Describe three challenges for effective use of HR analytics.
8. What is comprehensive scanning?
9. Mention four enablers of HR analytics.
10. What is the purpose of Employee Morale Analysis?

Discussion Questions

1. Discuss the historical evolution of HRIS. What were the reasons for its limited application?
2. Distinguish between HRIS, HR metrics, and HR analytics.
3. Illustrate some of the HR analytics maturity models.
4. What makes predictive analytics a key aspect of the HR of the future? What are the challenges in using it?
5. What are the critical success factors for HR analytics in modern organizations?

CHAPTER 15

Employment Relations

LEARNING OBJECTIVES

After completing this chapter, the student will be able to:

- Distinguish between ER and IR
- Identify the drivers of change leading to the emergence of employment relations as a subject of study
- Discuss the roles of the employer, employee, and the government
- Present the frameworks of employment relations
- Discuss the challenges of employment relations in a transnational context
- Project the directions of employment relations in future

Opening Case Time Traveler

A time traveler traveling through the landscape or terrain of employment relations in India, post-Independence until the current times, would be astounded by the changes over time. Say, he chooses to visit the new joint venture of Maruti Suzuki in the 1980s. He would be stunned by the harmony, the unitary spirit of management and labor. He could notice a long queue of personnel professionals trying to understand the secret behind the hugely successful employee-participation processes particularly the suggestion schemes. He could also walk into the canteen where the workmen and executives are seated together in their same blue uniforms, eating the same meal by paying the same price. Imagine his shock and consternation when he passes through the times between 2000 and 2014 in the same organization, and observes labor management standoffs, often leading to locked gates, angry demonstrations, mayhem, and even imprisonment.

Many changes have been happening since the decade of the 1990s, which would have turned the architecture of employment relations on its head. The changes do not always follow a pattern; in fact, there are considerable divergences across units and across states. In some cases, organizations have created magic harmony in their workplaces (TVS Motors lauded for being a model employer), while in the same auto sector adversarial relations have often reached a nadir and resulted in loss of lives and considerable production and market share (incidents of unrest occurring in some of the automobile-manufacturing companies such as Honda Motors and Maruti Suzuki in the pre-2014 days).

Discussion Question

1. Identify some of the significant shifts in the domain of employment relations that have occurred during the last 30 years. What were the triggers of these changes?

15.1 THE DEFINITION

Employment relations is defined by *Cambridge Dictionary* as 'behaviour and interaction between an employee and their employer, especially relating to employees' rights and their happiness in their jobs.' According to Rasmussen and Lamm,[1] it is concerned with employment, unemployment, and self-employment; how individuals, groups, organizations, or the state have their interests represented; what these interests are; how individuals manage and promote their interests within an organization; and the way conflict is managed and regulated. According to ILO, the employment relationship is the legal link between employers and employees. It exists when a person performs work or services under certain conditions in return for remuneration.

It is through the employment relationship, however defined, that reciprocal rights and obligations are created between the employee and the employer. It has been, and continues to be, the main vehicle through which workers gain access to the rights and benefits associated with employment in the areas of labor law and social security. The existence of an employment relationship is the condition that determines the application of the labor and social security law provisions addressed to employees. It is the key point of reference for determining the nature and extent of employers' rights and obligations towards their workers.[2]

To put it simply, an employment relation occurs between an employer and an employee as and when the latter starts to work for the former in lieu of payment of wages. Such a relationship can be on the level of the two as individuals, or between one employer and multiple employees, or multiple employers dealing with multiple employees. The exchanges, arising out of these relationships, could happen at different levels in an organization—at individual or collective levels. The various actors or groups in employment relations have been categorized into three clusters—primary, secondary, and tertiary. The employer and the employees constitute the primary parties. A network of formal and informal rules, agreements, and procedures, and such factors as employment contracts, employee handbooks, and informal customs and practices connect these two parties. The secondary level comprises of the management and trade unions, who represent the primary parties.[3]

Interactions between primary and secondary parties result in employment relations practices. The tertiary parties are primary agents of state, who attempt to mediate between different sets of primary and

1 E. Rasmussen and F. Lamm, *An Introduction to Employment Relations in New Zealand*, 2nd ed. (Auckland: Pearson Education, 2002).

2 Available at: www.ilo.org/ifpdial/areas-of-work/labor-law (accessed on December 8, 2017).

3 D. Farnham, *The Changing Faces of Employment Relations: Global, Comparative and Theoretical Perspectives* (London: Palgrave MacMillan, 2015): 672.

secondary parties, provide stable employment relations and prescribe floors of employment standards.[4] State policies influence distribution of power between the primary and secondary parties, and hence their functions and decisions.[5] National unions, employers' associations, and political parties, which influence formulation and implementation of public policies, also act as tertiary parties. In addition, some institutions and factors outside national boundaries such as ILO Conventions and policies of MNCs also influence a firm's employment relations.

Interactions in organizations take complex forms. They include a series of interrelationships between different groups and individuals: employers and employees, managers and workers, unions and managers, and among different workers. The parties in employment relations interact at different levels and between levels. In order to explain these complex details of the real world of work, literature in employment relations often explicitly or implicitly uses a systems approach. In this approach, an employment system is seen as a collection of interrelated components that work together to accomplish the employment process. The employment relationship system concept is variable in scope and can characterize an immediate workplace, an immediate workplace, an enterprise, an industrial sector, or a country as a whole.[6] However, this approach, with assumed homogeneity within the national systems, failed to explain the continuing and persistent variations in employment systems across firms within countries.[7]

Parties in employment relations interact and produce rules, processes, and outcomes that characterize firms' employment systems. Attributes of the parties are inputs for employment systems, but they do not describe the system completely. A firm's employment system is described by such inputs as quality of employment, processes such as organizational practices, teamwork, and wage bargaining, and outcomes such as wages, benefits, and productivity. Employment systems are dynamic entities with inner consistencies between their parts. The systems continually interact with their environment, change, and adapt to develop congruence between people, process, structure, and external environment. A significant change in one of the elements displaces an old equilibrium and creates a new position.[8] Economic, technical, legal, social, political, and physical environment in which a firm operates influences its employment systems and sets context in which the firm functions.

It will be interesting to travel through the experiences of Bharat Petroleum Mumbai Refinery between the decades 1980 and 2010, to understand the shifts occurring in employment relations in India.

Case Evolution of Employment Relations at a Refinery

Bharat Petroleum Mumbai Refinery (BPMR) is located in Mumbai, Maharashtra, India. It was commissioned in 1955 with a design capacity to process 2.2 MMTPA of crude oil as Burmah Shell Refineries Ltd. It was nationalized in 1976 by Government of India and joined the public sector mainstream as BPCL Refinery. With progressive debottlenecking,

4 D. Farnham, *Employee Relations in Context* (London: Chartered Institute of Personnel & Development, 2000).

5 A. Fox and A. Flanders, 'The Reform of Collective Bargaining: From Donovan to Durkheim,' *British Journal of Industrial Relations* 8, no. 2 (July 1969): 11–41.

6 Dunlop John T., *Industrial Relations Systems* (New York, NY: Henry Holt and Company, 1958).

7 Harry C. Katz and Owen Darbishire, *Converging Divergences: Worldwide Changes in Employment Systems* (ILR Press | Cornell Studies in Industrial and Labor Relations).

8 Thomas G. Cummings, *Systems Theory for Organization Development* (New York, NY: Wiley, 1980): 76–77.

addition of critical facilities and introduction of state-of-the-art process-control system, the installed capacity of the refinery was gradually increased to the current level of 12 MMTPA of crude oil of both indigenous and imported varieties. The Refinery is spread over an area of approximately 454 acres.

To meet a significant part of the country's requirement of petroleum products, the Refinery manufactures LPG, naptha, motor spirit, aviation turbine fuel, kerosene, high speed diesel, low sulphur heavy stock, furnace oil, and bitumen. The Refinery also manufactures special products such as food grade hexane, benzene, and toluene.

The Refinery currently has about 3000 direct and indirect labors and 500 executives. It has three unions based on craft lines—Process Technicians Union (PTU), representing the process technicians; BPCL Refinery Union (BPCRU); representing the maintenance and general workmen; and Petroleum Employees Union (PEU), representing the clerical staff. The PTU, which has a membership of around 500 workmen, is considered to have more impact on the flow of operations in as much as the member workmen, either by sitting on the panel or being in the fieldwork, monitor and control the entire process of processing of crude oil by temperature control. The profitability of the Refinery depends on the operation of extracting the maximum yield from the crude oil. The process technicians are science graduates with due training in process-control work. Many of them were earlier engaged in supervisory, executive category in smaller chemical firms and had joined BPCL for better pay and working conditions.

Historically, the Indian petroleum industry was controlled by few Anglo-American companies. They maintained their dominance until the end of the 1950s. After independence (1947), the newly independent State wanted to play significant role in this vital industry. The industry policy resolution of 1948 and 1956 has clearly documented the government's aspiration and future plans for core industries such as petroleum. All future development of petroleum industry was reserved for PSUs. In the 1980s, the government decided to invite private companies in the refining sector. The private company Reliance Petroleum Ltd (RPL) has become the second largest player in oil refining sector with 27 MMTPA state-of-the-art refinery at Jamnagar, Gujarat. Apart from approving new refineries in the private and joint venture (involving Indian and foreign companies), there has not been any major policy change in the establishment of new refineries in the 1990s. However, from June 1998, the refining sector has been delicensed. Moreover, private and joint sector refineries have been permitted to import crude oil freely without import license for actual use in their own refineries. This will have adverse effect on the operating cost of public sector refineries should international crude oil price fall below the domestic price.

Today, there are 19 refineries in the country, 17 in the public sector, one in joint sector and one in private sector. The installed refining capacity was only 0.3 million tons in 1950–1951, which rose to 121.8 million metric tons in 2003–2004. Seventeen public sector refineries are located at Guwahati, Barauni, Koyali, Haldia, Mathura, Digboi, Panipat, Chennai, Narimanam, Bongaigaon, Mumbai (HPCL), Vishakhapatnam, Mumbai (BPCL), Kochi, Numaligarh, Tatipaka (ONGC), and Bina (Madhya Pradesh). Bina refinery was inaugurated in June 2003. Aggregate refining capacity of these plants is 75.95 million tons per annum. One refinery in joint sector is at Mangalore in Karnataka. It has a refining capacity of 9.69

million tons per annum. Private sector refinery of RPL was commissioned at Jamnagar in 2001. With an installed capacity of 27 million tons, it is the biggest refinery in the country.

IR—from 1976 until 2000

On January 24, 1980, a charter of demands was submitted by the unions for permanency, increase in age of retirement, and revision of pay scales. It was followed by various forms of unrest/industrial actions such as demonstrations, one-day strike to protest against the arrest of President of Union Dr Datta Samant, march by the employees to the refinery staff colony to press their demands, and so on. The trade union activities and agitations were on increase, culminating in a threat to serve a strike notice if the management did not accept their demands. This was recorded in a letter, dated November 7, 1981, addressed by the union to the management of the Corporation. The union served an ultimatum in its letter, dated December 28, 1981, that their major demands should be met within 10 days.

In a specific event on January 5, 1982, about 250 workmen assembled outside the administrative building inside the Refinery premises and demonstrated for two hours by remaining unauthorizedly absent from the work. The management wrote to the union expressing its keenness to have a long-term settlement on a condition that the employees' union should withdraw the pending cases filed by them. On January 13, 1982, the unions informed the management that 92% of the workmen had voted for going on an indefinite strike. It appeared that in a general meeting of the workmen, members of the union were convened to take secret ballot to find out the willingness or otherwise of the workmen to go on an indefinite strike. In the secret ballot held on January 12–13, 1982, according to the union itself, a large number of workmen favored such a strike.

On January 14, 1982, though the workmen had entered the premises of the factory, they did not do any work. The management made an interim offer to the workmen but the same was rejected. At 7:30 PM on January 14, 1982, in a gate meeting, a decision was taken to reject the offer of the management and to continue the strike until all the demands were accepted. On January 15, 1982, the workmen in LPG filling plant, bitumen filling, and maintenance entered the Refinery but did not do any work. Again, on the same day, members of the Process Technicians Associations Union, fire security utility, and others also abstained from work and none of the labor category workmen attended to work from 11:45 pm, and therefore the management was compelled to phase out catalytic plant and sought help of process technicians in the same. However, such help was refused. In the aforesaid circumstances, according to the management, it was compelled to phase out operating plant one by one and had informed the Government of Maharashtra about the whole situation that had arisen in the Refinery. The clerical staff, who had continued to work until January 15, 1982, also stopped working thereafter. Following this, the management declared a lockout that lasted until June 17 when the Refinery reopened.

The Bombay High Court held the unions' strike call to be totally unjustified on two counts. One, the unions' demand or dispute was pending before the Industrial Court. They should have waited for the result of the said litigation. Second, having submitted their charter of demands for rise in wages, DA, and so on, the union could not have resorted to a strike to achieve those demands. They ought to have approached the adjudication machinery provided under Sections 10 and 12 of the ID Act.

Post the lockout, the scars of a fragmented relation remained, leading to occasional ruptures. The trust deficit between the executives and the workmen deepened, leading to rigid demands on work procedures (e.g., manning complements, holiday work, and others), considerable muscle flexing, and occasional strike/work stoppage. The compulsion of not shutting the operations often made the supervisors acquiesce, thus further reinforcing the hardliners' stance in the unions. Eventually, in 1999, the unions were successful in securing a handsome compensation package through a long-drawn collective bargaining process. The looming prospects of disinvestment made the management reach out to the unions for support, collaboration, and a spirit of partnership.

IR in the New Millennium

The context of employment relations in BPCL Mumbai Refinery had started changing. The large number of refineries that came up since around the turn of the millennium and the additional refining capacity available (about 100 MMTPA) in public sector, the joint ventures and the private sector and also the product-sharing agreement changed the compulsion of the management to run operations at any cost.

The management took a two-pronged strategy of slowly weakening the iron hold of the unions, specially the Bharat Petroleum Technician's Union (BPTU), through some careful restructuring of the work process. As the first step, in the year 2008, the management changed the job specification of the process technicians, while replacing the retiring workmen. They revised the educational qualification threshold from graduates to diploma engineers with a minimum three years of supervisory experience in a comparable large chemical plant. Second, the management also adopted an assessment-center approach to ensure that candidates with personal ambition, drive for results, and learning orientation only came in.

As the second part of the strategy, the management tabled a proposal for converting the critical role of panelists into executive cadre with requirement for decision-making on the spot for operations control. The BPTU opposed the proposal tooth and nail, aware that it will sound the death knell for union activism and rob them of their power to hold up the Refinery operations. But the management team kept the agenda alive, bringing it up through formal and informal union–management discussions. Eventually, the time came for the renewal of the long-term settlement through fresh rounds of collective bargaining. In response to the union's charter of demand, the management made the proposal for upgradation of panelist role conditional for any discussion on wage revision. The impasse continued for more than three years, but slowly the pressures started building up on the BPTU (the other two unions had no stake) from its general members for settling wage revisions, and from the younger members for accepting the management proposals as they were aspiring for career growth. Eventually, the BPTU gave in and accepted the management proposal in return for a decent wage revision.

Following the last long-term agreement, the unions (mainly the activist BPTU) lost its sting. The new group of panelist executives had 50% of its complement drawn from the young process technicians who came in 2008. The operations in Refinery became smooth. The chronic niggles that characterized the post-1990 time had stopped. Unions were divided whenever there was talk of strike. The shop floor achieved rising productivity. The morale of the supervisors rose with more workplace flexibility and overall quality of interaction and camaraderie between workmen and supervisors improved considerably.

The company took drives to improve employee engagement specially by restructuring the suggestion scheme, which was lying dormant. There were focused inputs for employees, specially the new workmen-turned executives.

The old timers, however, cautioned against reading too much into the change. There is a view that unions will regroup themselves, whenever an opportunity comes in future.

The aforementioned case captures the shifting nature of the employment relations triggered by interplay of multiple contextual and internal forces. It would be worthwhile to analyze the evolution of employment relations, the changes and the factors responsible, and the road ahead.

Discussion Question

1. Does the evolution of employment relationship decimate the importance of the unions?

15.2 TRADITIONAL EMPLOYMENT RELATIONS

The traditional employment relationship has been in existence for over 200 years since the Industrial Revolution. A critical feature of the traditional employment relationship is the hierarchical power of employers over employees. This hierarchical power has three subsets: (a) directional power (the power to allocate work and to issue instructions/directives to employees); (b) control power (the power to check the performance of allotted work and fulfillment of the orders); and (c) the disciplinary power to take action, reward or punishment, on the basis of acceptable or unacceptable performance. It is the presence of hierarchical power in a working relationship that differentiates employment from self-employment, and provides the platform for a plethora of regulations intended to shield the employees in the different areas of employment.

Dr Tim Baker[9] uses the following model (as shown in Table 15.1) to demonstrate the different facets of the traditional employment.

15.2.1 Traditional Employment Relations in India

Employment practices that prevailed in the initial years of Independence in India are similar to the same in the West till the turn of the millennium. In this system, the hierarchical pattern of relationship was the central structure, with the supervisor wielding complete power to recruit, terminate, or compensate the employees. In some kind of internal labor market, the decisions are made by managers and implemented by the employees. The companies hire unskilled workers, train them, and move them around the organization depending on acquired skill sets. In the face of continuous and mounting pressures for improving productivity, principles of scientific management system were used to organize work, to compensate the employees, and to formulate employment rules. Trade unions joined the fray to protect the employees' interests and government took it upon itself to ensure industrial peace and harmony. The powerful role played by the government in determining the compensation and the employment terms can be traced back to the British period when, during the war years, the government

---

9 Timothy Bond Baker, 'Towards a New Employment Relationship Model: Aligning the Changing Needs of Individual and Organization,' *Leadership & Organization Development Journal* 30, no. 3 (2009):197–223.

Table 15.1 Traditional employment relationship

Shared value	Employee mindset	Employer mindset
Specialized employment	Work in a clearly defined employment area	Offer clearly defined and specialized employment opportunities
Internal focus	Follow organizational policies and practices	Reinforce the need to follow organizational policies and practices
Job focus	Fulfill job requirement	Link rewards and benefits to fulfilling job requirements
Function-based work	Focus on job functions	Structure work around functions
Human spirit at work	Value a stable and secure job	Offer secure jobs
Loyalty	Display loyalty to the employer	Reward employees who are loyal to the company
Training	Commit to gain technical qualification	Provide opportunities for employees to develop technical skills
Closed information	Comply with managerial instructions	Provide sufficient information for employees to do their job

Source: T. B. Baker, 'Towards a new employment relationship model: Aligning the changing needs of individual and organization,' Leadership & Organization Development Journal 30, no. 3 (2009): 197–223. Available at: https://doi.org/10.1108/01437730910949508 (accessed on February 15, 2018).

sought to ensure uninterrupted flow of production through several ways, one of them being the Defense of India Rules. The legacy was continued in the post-Independence period also.

The guiding principles in the industrial policy in India post-Independence were: setting up of heavy industry, public ownership, import substitution, and protection for both capital and labor. For commencement or expansion of business, one required a license and thus businesses were immunized from internal and external competition. Employment relation was characterized by state intervention to determine compensation and employment terms for workmen. The setting up of Wage Boards (jute, cement, coal, and the like) and the Bureau of Public Enterprise (for determining PSU payment rules) are some evidences. Two distinct phases are visible: the stage of state-driven industrialization in which the state took upon itself the role of custodian of workers' interests, followed by a stage of fragmented trade-union movement characterized by multiplicity of unions—national and local.[10]

The employment practices that developed and existed in the pre-liberalization period were diverse, though stable and consistent across large sections of society. There were traditions of collective bargaining between employer groups, trade union federations, and labor ministry; the legal framework enabled the government to create a state-driven IR system. There will be a movement towards stable and harmonious employment relations in the country conducive to the growth of business.

The Winds of Change

Since the mid-1980s through the 1990s, certain changes in national context and also in response to changes in global context tilted the balance in capital–labor power balance. There were rumblings of change as early as the 1970s. The failures of the over-restrictive and regulatory framework, the experiments with PSUs and the hamstrung private sector were evident. In 1988, the government enacted the Sick Industrial Companies Act for sick and unviable industries. Finally, in 1991, the proverbial last

[10] Subesh Das, *Managing People at Work* (New Delhi: SAGE Publications, 2010).

straw was added by the International Monetary Fund (IMF)–World Bank (WB) proposed structural adjustment unleashing a slew of reforms including removal of import restrictions, reduction of import duties, and abolition of 'license raj.' What followed were policy changes, started in the mid-1980s and accelerating in the 1990s, culminating in the State beating a retreat from the economic area. It is worthwhile to examine some of the contextual factors that have ushered in the shift.

15.2.2 Globalization

In the last three decades, governments of many countries have changed their development strategies and adopted policies that favor deregulation, privatization, and liberalization of trade and commerce. The programs, on the guidelines of WB/IMF, include a bunch of measures that include discontinuance of import licenses, reduction of import duties, attempts to attract foreign investment, and encouragement for private sector engagement. Indian firms have been enabled by the absence of tariff barriers and reduction of import duties to explore foreign markets to sell their wares. Another direct consequence of globalization has been the renewed activities of the MNCs, who are drawn to the developing countries by low wage rates and the withdrawal of restrictions on foreign investments. The local firms, driven by increased competition from national and foreign firms, are compelled to reduce cost of manufacturing and simultaneously upgrade their product quality to internationally acceptable standards.

15.2.3 Economic Reforms

The economic policies of the government have an indirect, but powerful bearing on the employment relations. A policy thrust on creation of job/employment opportunities boosts union power, and contrarily, if the policy aims at reducing inflationary rate, then it creates an upswing in the employer power.[11] The focus on heavy industries and public sector led to industrial behemoths with high costs and created a happy hunting ground for powerful trade unions, and a structured, rigid process of collective bargaining. The spate of nationalization of banks, coal mines, and insurance industries bolstered this trend.

The break from the aforementioned trend came in the form of Sick Industrial Companies Act in 1985. The private sector suddenly found a much larger role especially with the dilution of regulations and control. Then the unthinkable started happening. Sick industrial units in public sector were on offer for privatization. It broke the mental models that sick units can linger on and expect the healing touch of nationalization. As a matter of fact, many sick industries were forced to close their business.

15.2.4 Technology Adoption

There is an unresolved debate between the technological deterministic school and the skeptics whether global diffusion of technology removes the national boundaries in employment relations. It is, however, undeniable that technological changes do significantly influence the employment relations in a firm.[12] Rush for new technology has been a marked feature of the liberalized environment. The disappearance of import license and the foreign participation in Indian firms have facilitated the induction of global technology in many industries. While technology adaption often results in reorganization of work, the inevitable fallout on employment relations is the pressure for reskilling and redundancy management often leading to job cuts.

11 Farnham, *Employee Relations in Context.*

12 Das, *Managing People at Work.*

15.2.5 Social, Political, and Legal Factors

The important social factors influencing employment relations include population growth, poverty, literacy, and unemployment rate. With a population of 1.21 billion and growth rate of 1.41%, the population will only grow more enormous in size. However, when age structure of India is considered, 65% of India's population is of the age group 15–64, and 30% of the population being under the age of 15, it can be inferred that India's population is very young. When literacy rate of India is considered, it stands at 74.04% as per 2011 census. India's literacy rate at the time of Independence was mere 14%; over the years, literacy rate has been increasing but with varied rates in different states, with some states such as Kerala and Mizoram well above national average and Bihar with a dismal rate of 63.8%.[13]

The decades since the 1990s have been termed by critics as eras of jobless growth. The unemployment rate in India averaged 7.32% from 1983 until 2013, reaching an all-time high of 9.40% in 2009. Although, the rate has dipped in 2013 to 4.90, the demand for employment is still a major factor influencing employment relations. Another social factor influencing the employment relations has been the literacy level of the individual worker and his growth aspirations.

One of the most powerful political factors influencing employment relations in India is the extent of hold the political parties exercise through their associations with the affiliated unions. There are clear signs that the stranglehold of political parties over employees through trade unions has slackened considerably in the liberalized era. The younger, literate workers now show more awareness of their rights and have no difficulty in finding their own voice. This is one of the factors largely explaining the preference for non-unionized workplaces in services sectors and specially the IT/ITeS businesses.

Governments also play a deterministic role in employment relations through legislation or administrative actions. In India, the government created legal structures for interventions, as indicated in Table 15.2.

Table 15.2 Framework for government intervention in employment relations

Intervention	Provision in India	Act and rules
Protection of workers' rights	Workers can form unions. Unions can negotiate wages and conditions of work	Trade Union Act 1926; ID Act 1948
Protection of the vulnerable	Regulation and prohibition of child labor; equal wage and equal employment opportunity for women; maternity benefit	Child Labor Act 1986; Equal Remuneration Act 1976; Maternity Benefit Act 1961
Establishment of minimum compensation for work	Workers to be paid minimum wages, and minimum non-wage benefits such as medical, housing, and others	Minimum Wage Act 1948; Plantation Labor Act 1951
Assurances of decent working conditions	Minimum occupational and safety health standards, maximum hours of work	Factories Act 1948
Provisions for income security	Social security. Workers get payment during sickness, disability, or old age	Provident Fund Act 1952; ESI Act 1948; Payment of Gratuity Act 1972; Workmen Compensation Act 1923
Provisions for job security	Limited right not to be dismissed. Compensation when retrenched	ID Act 1948

Source: Das, *Managing People at Work*, 42–43.

[13] Navinchandra R. Shah, 'Literacy Rate in India,' *International Journal of Research in All Subjects in Multi Languages* 1, no. 7 (October 2013): 12–16.

There are other factors also leading to a shift in the employment relations. Shifts in the beliefs/values of professional managers caused by 'isomorphic pressures' exerted by consultants, business publications, and others, and the paradigm shift in the practices of HR professionals have molded the emergent employment relations. There have been growing managerial awareness for communication, empowerment, and collaboration. Finally, a shift in the labor–capital power equilibrium is clearly visible. It is reflected in the aggressive stance taken by employers in creating non-union workplaces.

15.3 ACTORS IN THE FRAY–ROLE-TAKING

In the context of the swirls of change unleashed by the different contextual factors, it will be interesting to examine the roles played by the three actors in employment relations.

15.3.1 The Management

Before independence, the managerial style, mostly of private owners, was authoritarian and employment relations issues were typically addressed in an ad hoc manner. After independence, the government's drive for industrialization saw the emergence of large industrial enterprises in the public sector. The sheer size of the enterprises ruled out the earlier ad hoc style and paved the way for a systematic management's function-based management structure, which included a personnel department.[14]

Gradually, the management system that evolved, shaped by a combination of social, economic, religious, and political factors, is a unique high-context culture where work relationships are personalized rather than contractual.[15] The managerial style mirrors manifold influences of authoritarian practices within the family, the educational system, society's hierarchical structure, and religious institutions to create a strong sense of dependence.[16] Other factors that are believed to have influenced the managerial style are the traditional values of renunciation, giving away, self-sacrifice, and self-denial.[17] The followership styles have the influence of the cultural traits of submissiveness, fatalism, power consciousness and possessiveness towards subordinates, fear of independent decision-making, and resistance to change.[18]

Currently, Indian managers are arming themselves with the global managerial techniques and toolkit. A significant thrust in the endeavor is the urge to create decent workplaces and manage harmonious employment relations particularly in such areas as career management, performance management process, total reward system, employee participation and engagement, managerial styles, and talent management. There are also serious thrusts to the development of human resource in Indian organizations. Such a realization is based on the understanding that without the development of human resource, Indian organizations will not be able to adopt successfully the new technology, improve the

[14] Pawan S. Budhwar, 'Employment Relations in India,' *Employee Relations* 25, no. 2 (2003): 132–148.

[15] Jai B. P. Sinha, *Patterns of Work Culture: Cases and Strategies for Culture Building* (New Delhi: SAGE Publications, 2000).

[16] I. Dayal, *Can Organizations Develop Leaders? A Study of Effective Leaders* (New Delhi: Mittal Publication, 1999).

[17] R. K. Gupta, 'Employees and Organizations in India: Need to Move Beyond American and Japanese Models,' *Economic & Political Weekly* 26, no. 2 (1991): 68–76.

[18] P. R. Sparrow and P. Budhwar, 'Competition and Change: Mapping the Indian HRM Recipe Against Worldwide Patterns,' *Journal of World Business* 32, no. 3 (1997): 224–242.

quality of their products, reduce costs of production, achieve optimum capacity-utilization of resources, and rationalize the workforce, and hence compete with overseas competitors.[19]

15.3.2 Trade Unions

The trade unions form the next group of actors of the employment relations system (ERS). Trade unionism in India can be traced back to the 19th century.[20] Mankidy[21] identifies four key cycles: the early years (1850–1900), the growth years (1900–1947), the militancy phase (1947–1970s), and the decline phase (the 1980s).

The mighty trade unions started collapsing in the early 1980s. The decline is attributed to several factors—the failure of a number of strikes as a result of which workers started losing faith and confidence in militant trade unionism.[22] The Bombay Textile Strike is considered to be a unique strike that was not resolved, even after 30 years, accounting for the indescribable suffering caused to thousands of workers and their families. Some researchers have also pointed out a downward spiral of growing alienation between trade unions and members.[23] Some other factors that have also accelerated the decline of trade unions in India are: emergence of the new, literate workers with vastly different aspirations, skill sets, individual attributes such as self-confidence and communication skills, the loosening grip of national federations over enterprise unions,[24] and multiplicity of unions. The waning influence of the trade unions is reflected in the plunging number of lockouts, duration of strikes, and ID.[25] It is, however, too early to write off the trade unions in India as spent forces.

The loss of membership is only one part of the setback being witnessed by trade unions, the other source of trouble is the enormous pressure the trade unions are facing to protect the workmen from loss of jobs. Introductions of new technology and work processes, pressure to reduce cost in the market are leading employers to decide on mass job cuts, reductions in manpower complements, retrenchment of labor, and so on. Such pressures are expected to reduce the tempo of union mobilization. Since the organized labor force is in a minority, barely 7% of the total workforce, with the changing nature of employment, the bargaining power of trade unions is expected to decline further. The experience of industrially advanced countries shows that the part-time workforce has less interest in unionization and active participation in trade union affairs.[26]

The unions are also unsettled by the pro-employer stance taken by some of the states, which is in marked contrast to the protectionism uniformly enjoyed by the trade unions from the government according to the stated policy. The trade unions have tried to regroup and collaborate across national

---

19 C. S. Venkata Ratnam, 'Economic Liberalization and the Transformation of Industrial Relations Policies in India,' in *Employment Relations in the Growing Asian Economies*, eds. A. Verma, T. A. Kochan, and R. D. Lansbury (London: Routledge, 1995): 248–314.

20 C. S. Venkata Ratnam, *Industrial Relations in Indian States* (New Delhi: Global Business Press, 1996): 12.

21 J. Mankidy, 'Changing Perspectives of Workers' Participation in India with Particular Reference to the Banking Industry,' *British Journal of Industrial Relations* 33, no. 3 (1995): 443–458.

22 H. Das, 'Trade Union Activism—Avoidable or Inevitable?' *Indian Journal of Industrial Relations* 35, no. 2 (1999): 224–236.

23 N. R. Seth, 'We, the Trade Unions,' *Indian Journal of Industrial Relations* 32, no. 1 (1996): 1–20.

24 E. Ramaswamy, 'Organised Labor and Economic Reform,' in *Indian Briefing: Staying the Course*, ed. P. Oldenburg (Armonk, NY: M. E. Sharpe, 1995).

25 Venkata Ratnam, *Industrial Relations in Indian States*.

26 S. Kuruvilla, 'Linkages Between Industrialization Strategies and Industrial Relations/Human Resource Policies: Singapore, Malaysia, the Philippines and India,' *Industrial and Labor Relations Review* 49, no. 4 (1996): 635–657.

trade unions, irrespective of the political color. The most visible evidence of the same was noticed in the united stance taken by all national trade unions on the issue of proposed labor reforms.

15.3.3 The State/Government

The State is the third and final actor in the employment relations arena. Over the years, certain common strands were noticed in the labor policy of the government. One classification detected four such elements:[27]

1. Encourage trade unions
2. Maintain industrial peace
3. Involve unions in the formulation of Five-year Plans
4. Exercise political control over the Union movement without jeopardizing the legal rights of unions (i.e., giving personal liberties to union leaders)

The State has used various mechanisms to achieve the aforementioned objectives. In the first place, suitable labor legislations were passed. A series of laws were enacted in 1948, and several others came at different points of time (e.g., Payment of Bonus Act came in 1965, Payment of Gratuity Act came in 1972). Efforts were made to find solution to a number of chronic issues affecting employment relations (e.g., recognition of trade unions and unfair labor/management practices) through commissions such as National Commission on Labor and commissions for workers participation in management. Tripartite fora such as National Labor Conference were created to anchor effective conversations between worker representatives and employer representatives. At present, there are over 200 state laws and 50 central laws related to labor.

Over a period of about 40 years, prior to liberalization, the government was very pro-labor and played the role of protector of the interests of labor, but slowly the winds had started blowing to another direction due to the opening up of the economy and the need to persuade global employers to invest in India. The long period of passive encouragement to trade unions and restrictions on any form of termination (including lay-off, retrenchment, and closures) had given rise to workplaces where the employers did not have flexibility to be globally competitive. In specific cases, the labor laws proved counter-productive (for instance, the inclusion of Section 11A in the ID Act); the judicial process was time-consuming and a multiplicity of unions sprang up and turned the workplace into a battlefield of adversarial, often political, unionism.

To wrap up, the employment relations scenario in India over the last five decades has been witness to fundamental shifts in which the nature and function of the three actors have also undergone certain clearly noticeable changes that have transformed the Indian employment relations (from often a combative, adversarial position of actors to a more collaborative stance). On the one hand, this is characterized by changing efforts initiated in state policies, ideology of trade unions, and the attitudes of management toward their employees and, on the other hand, by changes in the workplace practices at large. Significant changes are also noted in the nature of workplace practices such as breaking up of the lifelong employment system, initiation of performance-related compensation, and adoption of a more rationalized and structured approach to HRM.[28] The remainder of the chapter provides research evidence regarding the changing nature of the employment relations scenario in Indian organizations.

[27] C. K. Johri, 'Industrial Relations as Regulated by Law: Suggestions for Change,' *Indian Journal of Industrial Relations* 31, no. 4 (1996).

[28] P. Budhwar and N. Khatri, 'Comparative Human Resource Management in British and India: An Empirical Study,' *International Journal of Human Resource Management* 13, no. 5 (2001): 800–826.

15.4 THE NEW FRAMEWORKS FOR EMPLOYMENT RELATIONS

The future, as it can emerge, is nicely captured by Dr Tim Baker[29] where he talks about flexible deployment, customer focus, performance focus, project work, human spirit at work, commitment, and open information as the shared value of the principal actors (employer/employee). I would like to offer a detailed revised role of all the three actors.

The three actors in the employment relations need to take a hard look at pursuing a two-pronged strategy: accelerating the growth of the economy while catching the headwinds of economic reforms and globalization, and at the same time taking the initiative to build what ILO has categorized as 'decent workplaces.' The trade unions need to shun adversarial stance and shed political agendas from their trade union activities. They could develop commercial orientation (a la Singapore) and experiment with running businesses to get into the shoes of the employer. They need to undertake reskilling and literacy programs for their members. There should also be partnership with the employer to build the quality of their leadership by getting trained in advanced negotiation techniques and teamwork and collaboration.

The employer needs to make up his mind and champion industrial democracy. It is idiosyncratic that while the larger political system is democratic, often the managers play out an authoritarian, regimented style. The employer should have a clear, principle-based approach about dealing with collectives. It could be either in the form of Walmart's famous stand on 'no unions' or ITC's equally famous acceptance of the positive role played by trade unions in the growth of the firm. In case of a preference for non-union workplace, the employer needs to create an empowered workplace where the individual workplace is valued and treated with respect. While focusing on cost control, the employer also needs to draw a line on greed and equity in compensating his direct and indirect employees, specially the temporary labor (in line with recommendations by CII to pay more than minimum wages when the means are there). There should be an unqualified acceptance of 'equal pay, equal wages' irrespective of whether the government finally gets up to the task of enacting a law.

Finally, the role of the government. There is no denying that labor reforms are necessary and some of the archaic parts need to be jettisoned. The government, however, could take some fresh look at how the reforms would be brought about. First, let the government revisit the past. Several times, the Government of India had set up committees, many of which had thrown up ideas that are worthwhile. For example, the Second NCL, 2002, appointed to look into the broad framework of labor laws including the ID Act and suggest changes, had suggested a fine balance between business need and workers interest. It had suggested that prior permission may not be necessary in respect of lay-off and retrenchment, but it would serve the workers' interests better than currently if the retrenchment compensation is revised from the present 30 to 45 days. For closure of the enterprise too, the compensation (which is 30–60 days' salary), depending upon whether it is a sick and ongoing industry, should be increased. Second, there needs to be serious rethink on dilution of the inspection system (which needs to balance with self-certification to conform to ILO standards of decent workplaces). It calls for serious restructuring, induction of technically skilled personnel, empowerment of the inspectors, and design processes to prevent corruption. Third, government needs to pay attention and initiate action to extend the coverage of minimum threshold of protection laws to unorganized sector (constituting around 93% of the manufacturing sector). Finally, the government needs to initiate a broad-based dialog to create a shared vision of economic progress by engaging

[29] Timothy Bond Baker, 'Towards a New Employment Relationship Model.'

all the stakeholders, including employers and employee groups in the same manner, as carried out recently by Germany and followed by France.

15.4.1 Employment Relations in a Transnational Environment

Multinational corporations (MNCs) or transnational corporations (TNCs) have been spearheading the process of globalization by seamlessly moving capital, labor, technology, skills, and knowledge across borders and within international supply chains. The World Investment Report 2009, published by the United Nations Conference on Trade and Development, states there is a total of 889,416 MNCs around the world: 82,053 parent corporations and 807,363 affiliates. Even the recent global financial crisis has not halted the process, accelerated by the growth in information, communication, and transportation technologies.[30] There is a school of opinion that holds that the logic of technology and markets are overriding the divergences in national cultures towards globally valid 'best practice' managerial techniques, for example, the implementation of a range of specific employment practices identified with the so-called Malcolm Baldridge or European Foundation for Quality Management Models of Business Excellence. There are also contrary viewpoints that believe in the capacity of management practices to demonstrate the uniqueness of their national culture. It will, therefore, be relevant to take a stock of the trends of the MNC practices in India post-liberalization and their impact on employment practices.

One approach of the MNCs is to create mirror images of the employment relations technique that they developed at home in their foreign subsidiaries, virtually in the same form regardless of the local environment. This approach is largely visible in the manner in which the MNCs operate in the UK have gone about developing 'distinctive innovative and innovative approaches to managing employment relationships.'[31] The opposite also is known to have happened, whereby the traits of the local environment have deeply shaped the employment relations strategy in multinational subsidiaries.[32] For example, in their study of an American MNC ITCO, Almond et al.[33] reported on the relative ease in transplanting its chosen practice of non-union employment relations in the UK and Ireland as compared to the rest of Europe.

The MNCs, however, do not always act in a calculated manner, and sometimes are vulnerable to power dynamics or internal political cross currents like any typical organization. They could, therefore, be seriously constrained in its capacity to command the compliance of its foreign subsidiaries.[34] Even managers of subsidiaries can play crucial power games in blocking or modifying aspects of the policies made by corporate HQ that do not suit their interest.

---

30 Pauline Stanton, John Burgess, John Lewer, and Anthony McDonnell, 'Exploring Employment Relations Practices of MNCs in Australia,' paper presented at the 15th World Congress of International Industrial Relations Association, Sydney, August 24–28, 2009.

31 A. Ferner and J. Quintanilla, 'Multinationals, National Business Systems and HRM: The Enduring Influence of National Identity or a Process of 'Anglo-Saxonization',' *The International Journal of Human Resource Management* 9, no. 4 (1998): 710–731.

32 Tony Edwards, 'The Nature of International Integration and Human Resource Policies in Multinational Companies,' *Cambridge Journal of Economics* 35, no. 3 (May 1, 2011): 483–498.

33 P. Almond, T. Edwards, T. Colling, A. Ferner, P. Gunnigle, M. Müller-Camen, J. Quintanilla, and H. Wächter, 'Unravelling Home and Host Country Effects: An Investigation of the HR Policies of an American Multinational in Four European Countries,' *Industrial Relations* 44, no. 2 (April 2005): 276–307.

34 A. Ferner and T. Edwards, 'Power and the Diffusion of Organizational Change Within Multinational Enterprises,' *European Journal of Industrial Relations* 1, no. 2 (1995): 229–257.

In the final analysis, MNCs are often seen to use their considerable clout to subvert existing employment relations arrangements in the host countries to suit their interests. The subversion can be in avoidance of collective bargaining process or denial of the right of employees to participate in decisions affecting them. The host countries frequently offer MNCs incentives, such as exemption from employment regulations, or even changes in employment laws as a way of attracting investment or of preventing them from going elsewhere. The MNCs can shrewdly use the threat of withdrawal, of disinvestment, to secure government favor or control their employees' behavior. This also highlights the potential for MNCs to engage in 'regime competition,' a term used to indicate how decisions about investments or divestment are based on the comparative allure of a country's employment regime (its employment laws and regulation).

MNCs in India

Several similarities in trends have been reported in the MNC functioning in India, which, instead of setting benchmarks for global best practices, have often been associated with unsatisfactory employee relations. The trends are:

1. New centers of industrial strife (such as Gurgaon, Manesar, Pune, Jaipur, Chennai, and Bangalore) have replaced traditional centers of union militancy such as Bengal or Ahmedabad in the same way traditional industries have given way to new industries such as automobiles, auto ancillaries, telecom equipment as areas of strident unionism.
2. Managerial strategy for union avoidance and issues of union recognition emerged as a key issue for disrupting harmony in employment relations. Many of the mobile phone companies showed an antipathy for unions and a preference for leveraging disposable cheap labor consisting of very young workforce, mostly women, outstation workers hired for subsistence level wages.
3. The pressures of global competition and consequent quest for labor flexibility resulted in growing use of temporary workers. Das[35] refers to practices in Japan for having non-regular employees, part-time and temporary workers engaged directly by the company and contract workers who are registered with a third party.
4. Managerial style was another source of discord. It often manifested in summary suspensions and dismissals pay cuts, intolerance for any interference in their own production plans, insistence on written undertakings of good conduct. The HR practices reflected pseudo-participative systems where committees are formed but workers have little or no influence on decision-making. Several Indian companies use Japanese managerial and work practices such as teamwork, total employee involvement, Kaizen, 5-S, suggestion systems, and rewards, among which are Jaya Shree Textiles, Ingersoll Rand, Alstom Power, Infar India, and Hindustan Unilever. However, in all of these, unions are involved in the schemes and in their introduction.
5. Matched by managerial insensitivity, worker militancy formed another trend. The trade unions had affiliations to left-wing as also the right-wing political parties.

The other disturbing trends were rampant—use of contract and casual labor, low wages, the proneness of state governments to overlook many aspects of labor rights in the interests of investment. The collective bargaining processes were inadequate to resolve some chronic disputes and even wage settlements were challenged by dissident groups before the time ran out. Overall, there was a lack of

[35] S. Das, *Managing People at Work: Employment Relations in Globalizing India* (New Delhi: SAGE Publications, 2011): 153–165.

a sure-footed approach to resolve conflicts within the plants and the preferred approach was to use the goodwill of the state to arm-twist the nascent unions.

15.4.2 Employment Relations in SMEs

SMEs play a crucial role in national economies throughout the world and are, for this reason, described as the nurseries for entrepreneurship. SMEs generate a wide variety of products targeted at the local as also the global customers and the national and international value chains.[36] Apart from being a large employer, SME contribution to the GDP is also substantial. SMEs are expected to be in the forefront in employment generation, innovation, and new patterns of work.[37]

Researches on the status of employment relations practices in SMEs have indicated a general lack of formal processes and a prevalence of informal engagement in routine day-to-day tasks. Formal people practices are conspicuous by their absence, and the internal environment is relaxed and friendly with strong focus on relationships. Employees in SMEs have been described as 'the invisible workforce.'[38] Going further, Prof. Sisson has painted a bleak portrait of workplaces in the non-unionized, individualized workplaces in SMEs as 'bleak houses.'[39] According to Sisson, who based his observation on findings from the British Workplace Industrial Relations Survey 1990, non-union workplaces revealed poor process of consultation and employee involvement, high incidence of unorganized conflict such as absenteeism or high turnover; preference for temporary labor and compulsory redundancies, and absence of grievance procedures and consultative committees.

Research on SMEs in India, though limited, indicates incidences of employees in many SMEs being able to unionize themselves through tenacity and determination or political support, but with the general decline in the incidence of unionism at the global level, including in India, unionization is now becoming more and more difficult.[40] A more recent study of eight SME firms situated in the western industrial belt of India covering multi-sector organizations with investments ranging from ₹25 lakhs to ₹10 crore explored the state of HR practices in SMEs[41] has thrown up some key findings:

1. Employee relations were characterized by informality and close personal ties. Union representation was unusually low and workers voluntarily decided to lead a union-free workplace since most of their needs were taken care of beyond expectation by their employers. Most owner managers also felt that employees are better off without a trade union.
2. There was a strong sense of community within the firm, a context reminiscent of the Bolton[42] 'happy ship.' SME owners in the current study shared various initiatives they take to develop a familial work environment. One of the owners in the current study shared: 'I consider the employees as my own family. To make their working comfortable, as head of the family, I

---

[36] S. Marlow, D. Patton, and R. Ram (eds.), *Managing Labor in Small Firms* (London: Routledge, 2013).

[37] Carol Atkinson, 'Building High Performance Employment Relationships in Small Firms,' *Employee Relations* 29, no. 5 (2007): 506–519.

[38] James Curran, 'What Is Small Business Policy in the UK for? Evaluation and Assessing Small Business Policies,' *International Small Business Journal* 18, no. 3 (2000): 36–50.

[39] Keith Sisson and John Storey, *The Realities of Human Resource Management: Managing the Employment Relationship* (Buckingham and Philadelphia: Open University Press, 1993).

[40] D. S. Saini and P. S. Budhwar, 'Managing the Human Resource in Indian SMEs: The Role of Indigenous Realities,' *Journal of World Business* 43, no. 4 (2008): 417–434.

[41] U. A. Agarwal and S. Jha, 'Human Resource Practices in Indian SMEs: An Exploratory Study,' *Indian Journal of Industrial Relations* 50, no. 4 (2015).

[42] J. Bolton, 'Small Firms-Report of the Committee of Enquiry on Small Firms' (London: HMSO, 1971).

often go beyond what I can afford' and cited various welfare facilities that were offered to employees.

3. The SME owners were all aware of the statutory requirements that they were required to adhere.
4. Although emphasis was on developing good social relationships among employees and owners and the organizations were analogous to 'family,' the relationship between owners and employees was based on trust and respect
5. Most SMEs studied seemed to be under the assumption that, given the scale of operations, formal HR systems are not needed and day–to-day work can be easily carried out in a familial work environment.

15.5 THE FUTURE OF EMPLOYEE RELATIONS

As the millennium progresses, a clear consensus seems to be emerging among researchers regarding the slow liquidation of the traditional work arrangements in organizations. Constantly evolving technology, rapid globalization, and the arrival of new millennial employees—all are combining to unsettle the arrangements that have been regulating the modern workplace. 'Ten years ago, Facebook didn't exist. Ten years before that, we did not have the Web. So, who knows what jobs will be born a decade from now?'[43] The overwhelming concern is that

> [t]he work based society of the last century, which was built on the idea of people gaining security and sense of personal and social usefulness through productive employment has been seriously undermined by neoliberal economic policies, labor market flexibility, new management practices, consumerism, globalization and the like.[44]

While it is true that to prepare for the future of work, an organization must be mindful to adopt changes in the evaluation of skill sets, the employer value proposition, the available labor force, and the relevance of collective representation and action, whether through trade unions or not, is likely to endure. The advocacy for continued relevance of employee relations should have four key planks:[45]

1. Work dominates and is likely to dominate the lives of people and the vast multitude of them are employees, rather than employers. In work, of key importance for them is the terms and conditions of their work, that include both the market exchange that they enter into with their employer, and also the managerial relations to which they are subjected. Embedded in the former is the expectation of equitable return on their effort; in the latter, is the fear of abuse.
2. The management of employees, both collectively and individually, is the fulcrum of organizational life. Despite the competitive edge provided by such factors as product innovation, technology, and others, there is still truth in the oft repeated view by Alfred Marshall in his treatise *The Principles of Economics* about most valuable of all capital being human beings.
3. It is difficult to hoist a unitary mindset on the employees or compel the development of common interest between the manager and the managed. On the contrary, it is the view of

43 The New Work Order: The way we will work, *Time*, 2009. Available at: http://content.time.com/time/specials/packages (accessed on January 18, 2018).

44 Paul Blyton and Peter Turnbull, *The Dynamics of Employee Relations* (Basingstoke: Palgrave, 2004).

45 Ibid.

pluralists that certain divergences in the objective between management and employees are likely to remain as potential sources of conflict and tension.

4. Finally, the decline of trade union and the march of HRM notwithstanding, it is expected that as long as work continues to get done through cooperative endeavor, a balance will always be necessary between individualism and collectivism in an organization.

To crystalize the aforementioned view, while employment relationship comprises important individual aspects, it is only by recognizing the simultaneous existence of collective dimensions in this relationship that an adequate picture can be constructed of the employment relationships of the future. The focus of HRM on the individual and its general unwillingness to acknowledge the existence of distinct interests within workplace has created a blinkered and simplistic vision of common interest among managers and the managed.

Social scientists have long been arguing that individualization is a salient feature of the development of Western societies, while at the same time admitting that 'a substantial majority across Europe believes employees need the protection of strong trade unions.' This is also true of developing countries, especially India, where individualism is characteristic of large numbers of white-collar workers in emerging industries, such as IT. Yet studies show that white-collar workers in high-tech industries in India are not averse to unionization, or have already opted for some kind of collective organization. In a research conducted in 2013 among the employees of SMEs in manufacturing and IT, these workers expressed a pronounced need for union protection and collective organization, especially because many were deprived of the right to unionize.

There is, however, no denying that current state of employment relations is far from coherent. The colors in its landscape run into one another, showing huge diversity in both policies and practices. Many employee relations practices are deeply embedded in traditions and obsolescence, while some in new directions and clear discontinuity with the past manifest. If employment relations has to remain relevant, it needs to define a coherent set of values and priorities: greater equity, trust, and reciprocity; improved employment standards required by a decent workplace that will incorporate fair wages; greater employment security; flexibility in work to create a work–life balance demanded by the new employees; a slew of legislations to foster industrial democracy, and individual and collective employment rights; and a strategy for vocation-oriented curricula, learning, and skill enrichment.

Closing Case The Return of the Labor Unrest

Globalization and the allure of cheap labor have led many an MNC to set up their manufacturing units in India. These companies represent the best brands of the world, where landing a job means a jump in social status, hefty pay packages, and a promise of a better life. Yet, of late, the Indian workforce seems to be on the warpath against some of these very organizations.

While strikes and protests are common global phenomena, in India, these have been under the media glare over the last one year primarily because of the names involved—Hyundai, Honda, Nokia, Bosch, Pricol to name a few—most of which represent the best across industries. Although Indian companies are often the target of random strikes, it's the MNCs which get attention because of their profile—the strike at Hyundai's Tamil Nadu factory, earlier in June 2010, being a case in point.

The surge in trade activism in certain pockets comes at a time when strikes have actually been on the decline in the country with less number of workers getting affected. From a whopping 4.5 lakh workers affected due to strikes and lockouts in 2008, the number came down to a mere 90,000 in 2010 so far. While this can be seen as a reflection of increasing employee satisfaction, a section of employees, who feels short-changed, can still trigger a strike or create trouble for the employer.

That's not all. According to data available with the ministry of labor, so far 2010 has been a comparatively quieter year with 41 strikes and just 15 lockouts. In comparison, 2008 saw 109 strikes and 148 lockouts. In 2009, it had gone down to 62 strikes although the number of lockouts stood at 172.

Despite the fall in number of strikes, the bad blood between managements and unions is palpable. 'If an employee, who gets one of the best salaries in the country, is going out there, risking his job and huge pay to strike work, something must be definitely wrong. Isn't it?' asks A. Soundararanjan, Tamil Nadu's state general secretary of Marxist trade union CITU.

Patience no longer seems to be a virtue. A routine change of shift of an employee leads to protests, which gives the trigger-happy management an opportunity to 'discipline' workers and suspend them en masse. The result: Prolonged shutdown or lockout or if things get out of hand, bloody violence and even deaths.

Earlier in 2005, protesting workers of Honda Motorcycle plant at Manesar in Haryana were brutally beaten up by the police. They were demanding reinstatement of their colleagues dismissed for forming a trade union.

Later, in September 2008, a group of dismissed employees lynched L. K. Chaudhury, the chief executive of Oerlikon-Graziano Transmissions India, the Indian subsidiary of an Italy-based company in Udyog Vihar of Greater Noida. Exactly a year later, striking workers of Pricol, a Coimbatore-based automobile instruments maker, allegedly attacked and killed the HR vice-president Roy J. George.

In March this year, workers of another auto component maker, Bosch, physically intimidated and threat-ened their managers and officials, leading to a lockout.

In some cases, these issues have dragged on. For instance, take Hyundai Motor India. Employee relations at Hyundai—Tamil Nadu's biggest investor—have been under the weather for the last two years. The company saw four sit-in strikes in the last one year, and the state labor department had to intervene on all occasions. The bone of contention was the Hyundai bosses 'unbending stand' against trade unions. Instead, the company recognises 'works committee'. Though the 'works committee' is also an elected body, the 'rebel' union wants the committee disbanded, and recognition for the rebel union.

Similarly, Finnish cellphone maker Nokia has also faced the heat. Last year, the company suspended 60 workers for 'indiscipline,' leading to a strike and disruption of work for more than two days. A couple of weeks ago, employees once again went on a flash strike following a meeting of the employees' union and the management to fix long-term wages.

Trade union activists say the increasing number of contractual workers being drafted in by the managements and the issue of recognition of trade unions is a major reason for these protests.

'A union can stand up for the employees' rights with the management. Also, with companies now employing more people on contract, permanent employees are feeling the jitters who feel they will lose their livelihood. Their job security is under threat,' says a trade union leader.

According to the law, companies, apart from those in Maharashtra and West Bengal, are not legally bound to recognize workers' unions. The Tamil Nadu government is considering introducing a piece of legislation making it mandatory for companies to allow trade unions.

Discussion Questions

1. List the factors responsible for the return of labor unrest in India.
2. Recommend two actions each that the employers, the government, and the employees should take to create a decent workplace in the current globalized scenario.

Source: T. K. Rohit, 'The Return of Labor Unrest,' TNN, July 26, 2010, 12.09 EST.

SUMMARY

According to Rasmussen et al., the term 'employment relations' is concerned with employment, unemployment, and self-employment; how individuals, groups, organizations, or the state has their interests represented; what these interests are; how individuals manage and promote their interest within an organization; and the way conflict is managed and regulated. According to ILO, the employment relationship is the legal link between employers and employees. It exists when a person performs work or services under certain conditions in return for remuneration.

The guiding principles in the industrial policy in India post-independence were: setting up of heavy industry, public ownership, import substitution, and protection for both capital and labor. For commencement or expansion of business, one required a license and thus businesses were immunized from internal and external competition. Employment relations was characterized by state intervention to determine compensation and employment terms for workmen. The setting up of Wage Boards (jute, cement, coal, and the like) and the Bureau of Public Enterprise (for determining PSU payment rules) are some evidences. Two distinct phases are visible: the stage of State-driven industrialization in which the State took upon itself the role of custodian of workers' interests, followed by a stage of fragmented trade union movement characterized by multiplicity of unions—national and local.[46]

The employment practices that developed and existed in the pre-liberalization period were diverse, but stable and consistent across large sections of society. There were traditions of collective bargaining between employer groups, trade union federations, and labor ministry; the legal framework enabled the government to create a State-driven IR system.

Since the mid-1980s through the 1990s, certain changes in national contexts and also in response to changes in global context tilted the balance in capital-labor power balance. What followed were policy changes, started in the mid-1980s and accelerating in the 1990s, culminating in the State beating a retreat from the economic area. Some of the contextual factors that have ushered in the shift are globalization, technology adaption, sociopolitical and legal factors, and economic reforms.

A new framework of employment relations has emerged now. It is marked by flexible deployment, customer focus, performance focus, project work, human spirit at work, commitment, L&D, and open information as the shared value of the principal actors (employer/employee/government).

The MNCs have a significant role in shaping the employment relations. They are often seen to use their considerable clout to subvert existing employment relations arrangements in the host countries to

[46] Das, *Managing People at Work.*

suit their interests. The subversion can be in avoidance of collective bargaining process or denial of the right of employees to participate in decisions affecting them. The host countries frequently offer MNCs incentives, such as exemption from employment regulations, or even changes in employment laws as a way of attracting investment or of preventing them from going elsewhere. MNCs can shrewdly use the threat of withdrawal, of disinvestment, to secure government favor or control their employees' behavior. This also highlights the potential for MNCs to engage in 'regime competition,' a term used to indicate how decisions about investments or divestment are based on the comparative allure of a country's employment regime (i.e., its employment laws and regulation).

A special area of study of employment relations is the SMEs. Researches on the status of employment relations practices in SMEs have indicated a general lack of formal processes and a prevalence of informal engagement in routine day–to-day tasks. Formal people practices are conspicuous by their absence, and the internal environment is relaxed and friendly with strong focus on relationships. Employees in SMEs have been described as 'the invisible workforce.'[47]

In the new millennium, the traditional work arrangements in organizations are undergoing transformation. Constantly evolving technology, rapid globalization, and the arrival of new millennial employees—all are combining to unsettle the arrangements that have been regulate the modern workplace. The overwhelming concern is that

> The work based society of the last century, which was built on the idea of people gaining security and sense of personal and social usefulness through productive employment has been seriously undermined by neoliberal economic policies, labor market flexibility, new management practices, consumerism, globalization and the like.

If employment relations has to remain relevant, it needs to define a coherent set of values and priorities: greater equity, trust, and reciprocity; improved employment standards required by a decent workplace that will incorporate fair wages; greater employment security; flexibility in work to create a work–life balance demanded by the new employees; a slew of legislations to foster industrial democracy, and individual and collective employment rights; and a strategy for vocation-oriented curricula, learning, and skill enrichment.

Short-answer Questions

1. Define employment relations.
2. Mention five key features of traditional employment relations in India.
3. How has globalization affected employment relations?
4. In what ways do technology changes impact employment relations?
5. In what ways does the government intervene in employment relations?
6. Describe Dr. Tim Baker's new framework on employment relations.
7. How have MNCs influenced employment relations in India?
8. Mention some important features of employment relations in SMEs.
9. Mention some shifts that have occurred in Employment relations in India.
10. What are some of the concerns of the future of Employment Relations in India?

47 Curran, 'What Is Small Business Policy in the UK for?'

Discussion Questions

1. What role do you see trade unions playing in the emerging context of employment relations?
2. How will HR processes adapt to the new frameworks of employment relations?
3. What positive influence could the MNCs exert in bringing about a decent workplace?
4. It is said that the concept of work is going to undergo massive change due to advancement in digital technology. What, in your view, then will be the effect on employment relations?
5. What should the government do to ensure a balance in employment relations in the emerging workplaces?

CLUSTER 8

HUMAN RESOURCE BLUE OCEAN

Chapter 16

Human Resource Management in Small and Medium Enterprises

Chapter 17

Human Resource Management in the Services Sector

In the famous book *Blue Ocean Strategy*, the authors Kim and Mauborgne talk about opportunities to foray into 'blue oceans' of uncontested market space, as opposed to 'red oceans' where competitors fight for dominance, the analogy being that an ocean full of vicious competition turns red with blood. In the same way, HRM has the invitation to create value in two unexplored/little explored kinds of organizations where the ocean is not full of blood from the play of traditional HRM.

The new areas require a different starting block for HR. In service organizations, the business outcomes are determined by the customer preferences, and therefore the task for HR is to help create a service culture by aligning a bunch of high-performance work systems. There is a dilemma whether trade unions and service culture or quality culture can coexist. In a unionized environment, in a service organization, HR has to do tightrope walking and adopt effective influencing strategies to balance the power equation between the employer and the collective to support the desired culture. In union-free environment, HR processes should enable effective employee engagement and employee voice.

In SMEs, the challenge for HR is even more daunting. Most SMEs, which include start-ups, do not have HR function, and apparently can do without formal HR. There are several reasons, including budget constraint and smallness of the workforce. There are opportunities for HR to get in and contribute on talent acquisition and management, compensation, and alignment of employer values with those of the employees in an interactive way to build a value–based culture.

CHAPTER 16

Human Resource Management in Small and Medium Enterprises

LEARNING OBJECTIVES

After completing this chapter, the student will be able to:

- Connect the current business context with the relevance of HR in SMEs
- Distinguish between the focus in HR processes in the SMEs and large organizations
- Discuss the unique challenges faced by the SMEs
- Highlight the link between organizational performance and HRM in SMEs
- Present the evolution of HRM in Indian SMEs
- Discuss the factors influencing the adoption of HR processes in SMEs

Opening Case Sphinx India Ltd

Sphinx India Ltd (SIL) is a fully integrated construction organization that was established in 1983, in technical and financial collaboration with Bygging-Uddemann AB, with the main objective to introduce new and novel construction techniques in the field of construction of high-rise reinforced cement concrete (RCC) structure, silos, chimneys, and erection of storage tanks by hydraulic jacking system to the Asian construction industry. The collaboration ensures access to the long and rich Swedish experience and know-how. The company is jointly controlled by the Indian and Swedish promoters.

Furthermore, SIL has also developed another novel formwork system, the NBS cellular construction system, whereby steel formworks are deployed for the wall and slabs, which are cast simultaneously as a monolithic structure.

For the past 20 years, SIL has earned a reputation for having introduced hydraulic jacking technology in the field of erection of storage tanks and construction of high-rise civil structure by hydraulic slip forming and also for completing time-bound projects in record times without any cost overrun. The customers of SIL include the core industries such as power generation, petrochemicals, refineries, chemical, sugar, fertilizers, paper, cement, soy bean/food grains, and so on.

At present, it has approximately 20 project sites in various stages of execution across India and one project in Sudan. It employs around 400 employees, including around 100 at its head office at Andheri, Mumbai. SIL has set for itself ambitious targets in line with its growth strategy. Its current turnover is ₹200 crores. It envisages the existing businesses of chimneys and silos to increase by 30–40% in FY2011-12.

SIL further intends to widen its product offerings by including design and erection of RCC cooling towers, specialized building projects and infrastructure work in power plant projects, along with its core products—chimneys and silos.

In addition, SIL is also tapping new geographies and has already grabbed a project in Sudan. It intends to grow at a CAGR of 57% over the next 3 years (Table 16.1).

Table 16.1 Business plan for SIL

Business plan					
Verticals	**S. No.**	**Type of projects**	**2011–2012 (₹ crore)**	**2012–2013 (₹ crore)**	**2013–2014 (₹ crore)**
New	1	Cooling Towers	20.0	50.0	100.0
	2	Infra Work	20.0	60.0	125.0
	3	Specialized Building Projects	–	25.0	50.0
		Sub Total A	**40.0**	**135.0**	**275.0**
Existing	1	RCC Chimney	180.0	230.0	300.0
	2	RCC Silos	20.0	30.0	40.0
	3	International Works	50.0	75.0	100.0
		Sub Total B	**250.0**	**335.0**	**440.0**
		Total (A + B)	**290.0**	**470.0**	**715.0**

- Short-term strategy—To increase the annual turnover to ₹290 crore by 2011–2012.
- Medium-term strategy—To increase the annual turnover to 715 crore by 2013–2014.

The Challenges

The CEO realized that meeting all of the aforementioned parameters will require a technically proficient, energetic, and committed workforce. SIL would need to build a reputation so that it could attract and retain young talented workforce to achieve sustained excellence in its operations. Currently, its share of technical to non-technical employees is 40:60, and the attrition rate among technically qualified engineers is at 40%. The other problems faced by the CEO were:

Centralized Decision-making Authorities

Currently, the CEO and MD, Mr S. Modi oversees the day-to-day functioning of all the key functionaries, who are his direct reportees, including the project manager, the HR manager, the finance manager, and so on.

Mr Modi is a graduate in commerce. His business had a high growth trajectory during the last five years, when it grew from ₹100 crore to ₹200 crore by riding the business wave.

Now, he has high optimism about growing it several times. For technical guidance, he trusts the judgment of Mr P. Bansal, who is the CEO of the Delhi office. Mr Modi spends a lot of time on supervising the design and drawing of chimneys and silos, taking decisions on new recruitment, and so on. Most of the financial and administrative decisions are referred to him. He is the sole authority for signing checks. As per a recent analysis, he signs 30–40 checks per day. Evidently, he has stress-induced illnesses such as high BP and cardiac condition, and he finds it difficult to prioritize and focus on the strategic issues of the business. Decision-making process is slow because it has to move from the project sites to the MD for final approval.

Customer Acquisition and Retention

SIL keeps enquiries from potential clients for new business and from existing clients for additional business, but it often finds that it is unable to convert queries into business because of lack of focused business development. As a result, it already has a very poor order pipeline.

Usage of Outdated Technology

At present, SIL uses FoxPro that is a database management system and it does not support relational database management system, not an enterprise-wide solution. Resource allocation and planning is not done in a scientific manner using technology, which also leads to delay in project execution and completion. Therefore, SIL misses out on the opportunity for MIS and cutting-edge project management efficiency.

Data entry of attendance and leaves is done manually at head office, since there is no direct employee interface available for the employees at the site. This means that one employee at head office is required to punch in data for all the employees. The attendance records are couriered by all the site managers. In the absence of timely receipt of these records, the salary remittance gets delayed.

Even departments such as purchase, stores, HR, and accounts rely on MS Excel files and outdated software. In addition, some project sites have Internet facilities and some not. In spite of employees having company's ID, they prefer to communicate on their personal Gmail IDs.

Organization Structure

Leadership Team as shown in Figure 16.1.

SIL's organization structure has evolved as the business grew without any kind of scientific approach ever applied for organization design.

The existing organization structure does not define the clarity on basis of designation and the roles of employees, which leads to the unbalanced delegation of authority amongst the employees.

Technicians who, by and large, represent the field force on the ground look after arrangements of lighting and winch-machine connections, and maintenance of machinery. They report to the supervisors who are responsible to ensure that the utilities are in place for construction. The prime responsibilities of supervisors are checking for proper functioning of all the equipment at the site, ensuring proper implementation of rules and regulations, and supervising laborers and labor-requirements planning and management. The supervisors report to the site incharge.

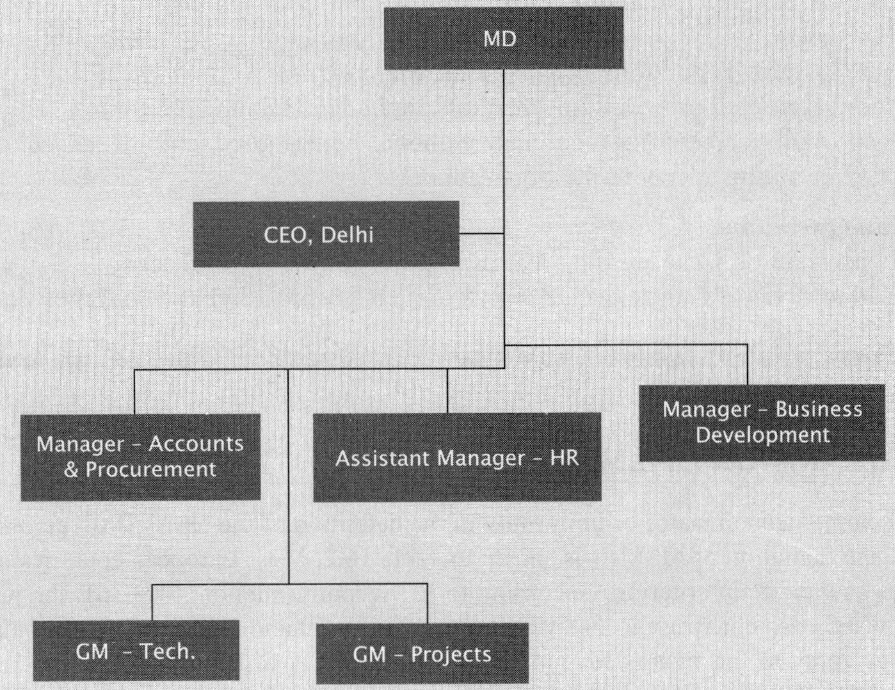

Fig. 16.1 The Organization Structure of SIL

The engineers are responsible for the construction activity and they too report to the site incharge or on-site project manager. The key responsibilities of the site incharge are project activity scheduling, resource management, coordination with the regional or head office, and client relationship management. The site incharge reports to senior managers, who typically manage multiple (approx. 3) project sites. These senior managers directly report to CEO or MD, appraise the progress of the project work, and are accountable for the timely execution of the projects. The CEO is accountable for business development, project execution, and financial control. The CEO reports to the MD.

Currently, however, the MD is also actively involved in minor issues of operational nature that have resulted in most of the employees reaching out to the MD for guidance and approvals. In addition to the minor operational issues, the MD also overlooks the filing of tenders, cost estimation, project planning, and managing finances. This is preventing the MD and CEO from focusing on the strategic issues that need their immediate attention.

Recently, Mr Modi had engaged an auditor to assess the business capability at SIL. His observations included the following:

1. Project management process not defined. Currently, project management is done in an ad hoc manner, resolving issues as and when they arise.
2. No one to lead the business development independently apart from Mr Modi. Also, SIL does not have anyone capable to lead and build its cooling tower business.
3. No proper documentation of policies and procedures for the departments such as HR, safety, and purchase.

4. SIL relies on FoxPro (outdated IT). Hence, the quality of management of information available is poor.
5. Resource planning is not done in a scientific manner.
6. No defined system of project-wise, activity-wise budgeting and cost control.
7. No mechanism for performance management, hence good employees do not find themselves wanting to stay in the organization.

Discussion Questions

1. Conduct an audit on what are the areas of improvement of HR processes.
2. If you had to advise on strategy to improve the HR practices, what would they be?

16.1 DEFINITION OF SMEs

There is no common denominator or uniformity in the definition of the term 'SME' across countries. The World Bank definition of MSMEs is shown in Table 16.2. Most European countries use number of employees as their main criterion. According to EU recommendation 2003/361, the main factors determining whether an enterprise is an SME are staff headcount and either turnover or balance sheet. These ceilings apply to the figures for individual firms only. A firm that is part of a larger group may need to include staff headcount/turnover/balance sheet data from that group too. According to Workplace Employment Relations Surveys, UK, small, medium, and large firms are those whose employees number 5–49, 50–249, and 250 and above, respectively. Some other countries use firm's assets and revenue as the additional criteria. SMEs in Malaysia are defined based on the twin criteria of annual sales turnover or number of full-time employees in the respective sectors. However, in India, the small-scale industries (SSIs) are defined in terms of investment limits in plant and machinery. The definition is derived from the original criterion used by Industries (Development and Regulation) Act, 1951 (IDRA). In India, the concept of medium enterprises (MEs) was unknown until recent times.

Table 16.2 World bank definition of micro, small, and medium enterprises (MSMEs)

Firm size	Employees	Assets US$	Annual sales US$
Micro	<10	<10,000	<100,000
Small	<50	<3 million	<3 million
Medium	<300	<50 million	<15 million

Source: World Bank. Available at: www.worldbank.org/en/.../msme-finance-expanding-opportunities-and-creating-jobs (accessed on December 12, 2017).

The term 'SSI' has been in circulation since a long time in India, which is different from the SME sector elsewhere. The investment parameter-based definition of the terms 'small' and 'medium' enterprise in India is a departure from the practice in rest of the world where the basis is a medley of standards such as terms of employment, assets, and sales, or a mixture of these factors. In the natural process of evolution through organizational life, SSI units graduate into MEs. The Ganguly Committee, constituted by the Reserve Bank of India (RBI) in 2003–2004, recommended the creation of a separate category on the basis of turnover.

In February, 2006, the Government of India introduced the Micro, Small and Medium Enterprises Development (MSMED) Act. As per the Act, the activities are classified into manufacturing and service category. RBI later provided the definition of the services sector and the activities that can be covered under MSMED (services) sector (Table 16.3).

Table 16.3 Difference between MSMEs

Nature of the enterprise	Micro enterprise	Small enterprise	Medium enterprise
Manufacturing sector	Investment in initial fixed asset (plant and machinery, which excludes land and building) does not exceed ₹2.5 million.	Investment in initial fixed assets (plant and machinery, which excludes land and building) more than ₹2.5 million, but does not exceed ₹50 million.	Investment in initial fixed assets (plant and machinery, which excludes land and building) more than ₹50 million, but does not exceed ₹100 million.
Services sector	Investment in equipment does not exceed ₹1 million.	Investment in equipment exceeds ₹1 million, but does not exceed ₹20 million.	Investment in equipment exceeds ₹20 million, but does not exceed ₹50 million.

Source: Pankaj M. Madhani, 'Matching Compensation Strategies,' SCMS Journal of Indian Management (January–March, 2012): 14–22.

In the light of the aforementioned definition, an SME in the Indian context would mean an enterprise in which the investment in plant and machinery is between 2.5 million and 100 million. The criterion of capital investment, adopted by the government for defining SMEs, creates a deterrent for the units to advance from micro- and SSI to medium-scale for fear of losing the facilities/incentives attached to them by the government. Recognizing the importance of SMEs in the industrial development of the country, the government has initiated a range of programs in diverse areas, namely, financing, technology, innovation, market information, technical training, and developmental assistance. These initiatives are important in facilitating the growth of the SMEs. But it will be the competitiveness of individual units and internal dynamics of industries that will give a thrust to the emergence of SMEs.[1]

16.1.1 Importance of SMEs

In the globalized and neoliberal economy of the 21st century, SMEs have become the new engines of growth-promoting vigorous business climate, economic efficiency, and power for economic development, particularly in developing countries. In developing economies, large-scale industries have given way to SMEs that are agile, adaptable, less capital-intensive, productive, and low cost. Despite some limitations, they are relatively more immune from economic volatility by virtue of their flexibility and adeptness to adjust to the changing business environment. SMEs are vital actors for enhancing innovation, competitiveness, entrepreneurship, and the establishment of an effective innovation system for developing countries.

Today globally, SME sector has become an important partner in achieving key socioeconomic objectives, such as employment growth, higher productivity, favorable balance of payments, and promotion of entrepreneurial culture (Table 16.4). According to current empirical studies, SMEs contribute to over 55% of GDP and over 65% of total employment in high-income countries. SMEs and informal enterprises account for over 60% of GDP and over 70% of total employment in low-income

[1] Pankaj M. Madhani, 'Matching Compensation Strategies,' *SCMS Journal of Indian Management* 9, no. 1 (January–March, 2012): 5–22.

Table 16.4 Share of SMEs in different countries

	USA	Germany	Japan	France	England	South Korea	India	Turkey
SMEs in total enterprises (%)	97.2	99.8	99.4	99.9	96	97.8	98.6	99.5
SMEs in total employment (%)	50.4	64	81.4	49.4	36	61.9	63.2	61.1
SMEs in total investment (%)	38	44	40	45	29.5	35.7	26.8	56.5
SMEs in total value added (%)	36.2	49	52	54	25.1	34.5	50	37.7
SMEs in total credits (%)	42.7	35	50	48	27.2	46.8	15.3	4
SMEs in total exports (%)	32	31.1	38	23	22.2	20.2	40	8

Source: Yılmaz, Kobi'lerin Finansman Sorunlarına Bir Çözüm Önerisi: —Risk Sermayesi Finansman Modeli, DıĞ Ticaret Dergisi, DTM Yayını, Yıl:9, Sayı: 33. Available at: http://eprints.ibu.edu.ba/151/1/ISSD2010_Economy_Management_p183-p192

countries, while they contribute over 95% of total employment and about 70% of GDP in middle-income countries. Important contribution is also on exports and on productivity growth.[2] SMEs also play a promoting function in innovations in organizations expanding the competitive edge of the countries/regions.[3]

It was as early as the decade of 1940 that governments started formulating targeted policies (grants, subsidized credits, special tax treatment, and so on), setting up support agencies (e.g., publicly funded SME agencies—1948 in Japan, 1953 in the USA, 1954 in India, 1966 in Tanzania, 1976 in Turkey)[4] to foster the growth of SMEs as a vehicle for economic progress. While the size and importance of the SME sector diverges across national economies, there is growing acknowledgement of the role it plays in industrial countries, especially for developing nations since the last few decades. SMEs are important to almost all economies in the world, but especially to those in developing countries.[5] The relevance of SMEs in a developing economy is on dual counts: first, its promise as a suitable vehicle for poverty-eradication programs; second, its potential for facilitating organizational innovation and sustainable growth. The two factors are interconnected: most of the international evidence says that growth and real poverty reduction go hand in hand. If SME development helps growth, more than likely, it helps reduce poverty as well.[6]

In India, SMEs are catalyzing economic progress by providing large-scale employment opportunities at comparative low cost capital, and increasing industrialization in the rural areas. Indian SME sector, which accounts for more than 98% of the enterprises in India, has shown impressive growth, with gross production rising from 11.5% in FY '03 to 15.8% in FY '06. As per the fourth All India Census of MSMEs, 2006, there are more than 36 million MSMEs in India contributing 45% of industrial output, 40% to India's exports, and approximately 8% to Indian's GDP.[7]

[2] OECD, 2004. Available at: http://www.oecd.org/cfe/smes/31919278 (accessed on January 12, 2016).

[3] Hidayet Keskin, Senturk, Sungur and Kiris, 'The Importance of SMEs in Developing Economies,' 2nd International Symposium on Sustainable Development, Sarajevo, June 8–9, 2010.

[4] OECD 2004.

[5] Berry, 'The Importance of SMEs in the Economy,' paper presented at the ITD Global Conference on Taxation of Small and Medium Enterprises, Buenos Aires, Argentina, October 17–19, 2007.

[6] Andrew Warner, 'Small and Medium Sized Enterprises and Economic Creativity,' in *Improving the Competitiveness of SMEs in Developing Countries: The Role of Finance to Enhance Enterprise Development* (New York and Geneva: UNCTAD, 2001).

[7] A. A. Ghatule and S. R. Dubey, 'Importance and Implications of SME Sector in Indian Economy,' *International Journal of Science, Technology and Management* 5, no. 3 (March 2016): 557–562.

16.2 HUMAN RESOURCE MANAGEMENT AND ORGANIZATION PERFORMANCE IN SMEs

Increasingly, strategic partnership is emerging as the central focus of HRM activities, much in the line of how Schermerhorn[8] described HRM as the 'process of attracting, developing and maintaining a talented and energetic workforce *to* support organizational mission, objectives, and strategies.' It is widely held, based on evidence from traditional large organizations, that HRM contributes to cost reduction. The key role that the SMEs are currently playing as the principal vehicle of economic progress, and the war for and concurrent draught of critical talent in the knowledge-driven organizations indicate the need for effective HRM practices in the small firm.[9] At present, firms are acknowledging the efficient HRM as a critical factor in their success or failure.[10]

According to the resource-based view of management,[11] irrespective of the firm size, employees are a strategically important, indispensable resource to achieving an organization's objective. Despite the critical role the HR practices play in enhancing organizational efficiency, mainstream management has focused on investing the role of HR practices in larger firm's research, ignoring them in SME sector.[12] This paucity of research persists even with the current surge of interest in the use of HR practices in SMEs during the last few years.[13]

While there has been very little research into the performance effects of HRM adoption on SMEs, a common thread in the arguments presented in prior studies on HRM in SMEs is that as SMEs grow, unsophisticated people management approaches become increasingly inadequate.[14,15] When this occurs, owners and managers of SMEs may come to realize the importance of formally adopting HRM systems and the associated benefits of nurturing people's creativity, and even the creation of competitive advantage and growth through people.[16]

Some empirical researches conducted with SMEs establish connection between HRM and improved organization performance:

1. Hayton[17] reported on the positive impact of discretionary HRM practices 'designed to promote the discretionary performance of employees by offering incentives and mechanisms

---

8 John R. Schermerhorn Jr., *Management*, 6th ed. (New York, NY: John Wiley and Sons, 2001).

9 D. B. Audretsch and A. R. Thurik, 'What's New About the New Economy? Sources of Growth in the Managed and Entrepreneurial Economies,' *Industrial and Corporate Change* 10, no. 1 (2001): 267–315.

10 J. Paauwe, *HRM and Performance: Achieving Long-term Viability* (Oxford: Oxford University Press, 2004).

11 J. B. Barney, 'Integrating Organizational Behavior and Strategy Formulation Research: A Resource Based Analysis,' in *Advances in Strategic Management*, Vol. 8, eds. P. Shrivastava, A. Huff, and J. Dutton (Greenwich, CT: JAI Press), 39–61.

12 J. Purcell and S. Hutchinson, 'Front-line Managers as Agents in the HRM Performance Causal Chain: Theory, Analysis and Evidence,' *Human Resource Management Journal* 17 (2007): 3–20.

13 Jan de Kok and Lorraine M. Uhlaner, 'Organization Context and Human Resource Management in the Small Firm,' *Small Business Economics* 17, no. 4 (2001): 273–291.

14 Kaman, V., McCarthy, A. M., Gulbro, R. D., and Tucker, M. L., 'Bureaucratic and High Commitment Human Resource Practices in Small Service Firms,' *Human Resource Planning* 24, no. 1 (2001): 33.

15 B. Kotey and P. Slade, 'Formal Human Resource Management Practices in Small Growing Firms', *Journal of Small Business Management* 43, no. 1 (2005): 16–40.

16 Kerr and McDougall, 'The Small Business of Developing People,' *International Small Business Journal* 17, no. 2 (January 1999): 65–74.

17 James C. Hayton, 'Strategic Human Capital Management in SMEs: An Empirical Study of Entrepreneurial Performance,' *Human Resource Management* 42, no. 4 (2003): 375–391.

for exchanging knowledge and encouraging organizational learning' on entrepreneurial performance in SMEs.

2. In another research finding, Welbourne and Cyr[18] informed of the improved firm's performance on two key result areas (long-term stock prices and earnings performance) as a direct consequence of induction of two HR executives in the top leadership level of an SME.
3. An initiative in employee counseling was reported to have considerably boosted sales, profit, productivity, product/service improvement, and cash flow in an SME.[19]
4. Another research finding presented evidence that education, T&D policies and practices in some medium-sized companies were positively linked to performance.[20]
5. A series of positive relationships between T&D plan and improved performance was reported by Wong et al. on three dimensions: (a) management (increased preference for employee development as against reliance on recruitment from outside, acceptance of development, and culture orientation in training); (b) organization of work (improved organization of business and HRP, management of team formation, formulating job descriptions and appraisals); and (c) external relations (new technology adoption, better production flow, financial control, customer care, and external image).[21]
6. HRM practices were also found to have affirmative causal link with improved strategy in SMEs. Chandler and McEvoy[22] established in a sample of 66 small- and medium-sized manufacturing organizations that use of training and group incentives scheme contributed to the effective roll out of a TQM strategy.

It is, however, clear that studies on HRM in SMEs have been few, and one dimensional, in that the bulk of them tended to merely investigate the existence of HRM practices in SMEs, and rarely went beyond that to explore the impact of the HR practices on firm's performance. Among the few studies to have done so (e.g., the impact of management training on SME performance), some have been criticized for having derived inconclusive findings or at best indicating only a weak relationship.

16.3 THE DIFFERENCE IN ADOPTION OF HUMAN RESOURCE MANAGEMENT—SMEs AND LARGE FIRMS

Most studies on HRM within SMEs are based on qualitative researches. This lack of information about HR in SMEs is considered 'problematic for theory, research and practice.'[23] The studies indicate relatively far lesser use of professional HR practices in SMEs than in larger firms. Some of the differences are discussed further.

---

[18] T. M. Welbourne and L. R. Cyr, 'The Human Resource Executive Effect in Initial Public Offering Firms,' *Academy of Management Journal* 42, no. 6 (1999): 616–629.

[19] J. Rocha and M. Khan, 'The Human Resource Factor in Small Business Decision Making,' *American Journal of Small Business* 10, no. 2 (Fall 1985): 53–62.

[20] D. Storey, 'Education, Training and Development Policies and Practices in Medium-sized Companies in the UK: Do They Really Influence Performance?' *Omega* 30, no. 4: 249–314.

[21] N. Marshall, N. Alderman, and A. Thwaites, 'Management Training in Small and Medium Sized Enterprises: Methodological and Conceptual Issues,' *International Journal of Human Resource Management* 8, no. 1: 44–65.

[22] G. N. Chandler and G. M. McEvoy, 'Human Resource Management, TQM, and Firm Performance in Small and Medium-Size Enterprises,' *Entrepreneurship: Theory and Practice* 25, no. 1 (2000): 43–57.

[23] R. L. Heneman, J. W. Tansky, and S. M. Camp, 'Human Resource Management Practices in Small and Medium-sized Enterprises: Unanswered Questions and Future Research Perspectives,' *Entrepreneurship: Theory and Practice* 25, no. 1 (2000): 11–26.

Adoption and deployment of HRM practices

1. Koch and McGrath[24] observed that generally larger firms had more incidences of HRM planning and formal training, and with higher level of overall HR sophistication in comparison with SMEs.
2. Westhead and Storey[25] found fewer probabilities for formal training for both managers and employees in a small firm.
3. In another study, based upon data obtained from 267 organizations, smaller companies were found to have less formalized performance appraisals, less likelihood of bonuses based on company productivity, and less training than do larger companies (with more than 1000 employees).[26]
4. Larger firms were found to have more structured recruitment practices than SMEs in another study.[27]
5. Another difference noted by Rainnie[28] is that small firms tend to provide more power to the managers, making the managerial prerogative largely unrestricted.[29]
6. A further area in HRM where SME practices vary from the larger firms is employment relations. Ram et al.[30] argue that employment relations in SMEs are characterized by 'unwritten customs and the tacit understandings that arise out of the interaction of the parties at work,' with the close working proximity and mutual dependence of employer and employee leading to informal accommodation and flexibility.[31]

Exhibit SMEs in Automobile Components in India–HR Issues

The Indian automotive component industry is small in size compared to the world market (₹740,000 crore). The industry has been experiencing a high growth rate of 27% over the period 2001–2006 and is expected to grow at a rate of 13% over the period 2006–2014. The quality of components made in India has improved significantly in the last decade and about 11 Indian auto component companies have won the Deming Prize so far. India is estimated to have the potential to become one of the top five auto component economies by 2025.

Major Characteristics

The Indian auto component industry is a thrust sector for India. The direct employment generated by the medium and large firms in the organized sector is 2.5 lakhs. In terms of location, over 70%

[24] M. J. Koch and R. G. McGrath, 'Improving Labor Productivity: Human Resource Management Policies Do Matter,' *Strategic Management Journal* 17, no. 5 (1996): 335–354.

[25] P. Westhead and D. J. Storey, 'Training Provision and the Development of Small and Medium-sized Enterprise: A Critical Review,' *Scottish Journal of Adult and Continuing Education* 5, no. 1 (1999): 35–41.

[26] S. E. Jackson, R. S. Schuler, and J. C. Rivero, 'Organizational Characteristics as Predictors of Personnel Practices,' *Personnel Psychology* 42, no. 4 (1989): 727–786.

[27] H. Aldrich and N. Langton, 'Human Resource Management Practices and Organizational Life Cycles,' in *Frontiers of Entrepreneurship Research*, eds. P. D. Reynolds, W. D. Bygrave, N. M. Carter, P. Davidsson, W. B. Gartner, C. M. Mason, and P. P. McDougall (Wellesley, MA: Babson College Center for Entrepreneurship, 1997).

[28] A. Rainnie, *Industrial Relations in Small Firms* (London: Routledge, 1989).

[29] Ibid.

[30] M. Ram, P. Edwards, M. Gilman, and J. Arrowsmith, 'The Dynamics of Informality: Employment Relations in Small Firms and the Effects of Regulatory Change,' *Work, Employment and Society* 15, no. 4 (2001): 845–861.

[31] Ibid.

of the automotive components companies are situated in either the northern or western regions. Delhi, Pune, and Chennai have traditionally been the most important clusters for the automotive components segment in India. The industry has 500 medium and large key participants in auto components in the organized sector, along with 6000 ancillary units. The unorganized sector predominantly caters to the aftermarket. Manufacturers in this sector operate independently with little investment and on a small scale. They generally produce components based on copied drawings and their quality is below average. Most components required by the Indian automobile industry are manufactured locally. Import dependence is estimated to the tune of 13.5% of the domestic demand.

Manpower/Human Resource-related Issues

Availability of trained manpower and productivity

1. A large chunk of available manpower from the automotive industry is going to either the service industry or to the new manufacturing units that have come in recent past. Retention of skilled manpower is proving to be a challenge. If companies do not plan ahead, there may be disruptions in production. The quality requirements from the industry are changing with the global requirements and achieving skill development for a new set of employees on a regular basis is a challenge. For improving productivity, need for skill development and attitudinal training of workforce is being increasingly felt by the industry. Production heads of auto component manufactures feel that job security has vitiated the work culture at the lower level. The workforce at lower level spends time less productively during working hours. Some experts have also echoed similar views.
2. Rising wage cost: Minimum wages in several states has gone up by over 30% in the last six months. This has severe implications on the profitability of the companies employing low wage earning workers. The implications are equally relevant for automated manufacturing systems because of the cascading effect of minimum wages among the middle level and senior level employees. Labor laws SMEs in auto-component sector feel that the current labor laws have resulted in poor productivity in India. These companies expect productivity friendly labor laws. The general feeling is that Chapter 5B of the industrial dispute act should be done away with. Under provisions of this act, companies cannot retrench more than 100 workers without prior permission from the Government even if the company does not have enough work for them. At few places, the Government is pressurizing companies to make the contract labor permanent, which the companies cannot afford. The Government of India is already working on a policy to mitigate the situation.

Source: Excerpted from 'Defining the Role of the Government in the Transnationalisation Efforts of the Indian SMEs in the Auto Components Sector,' paper prepared for Department of Scientific & Industrial Research (DSIR), Ministry of Science & Technology, New Delhi, August 2008.

16.4 INDIAN EXPERIENCE

16.4.1 The HR Challenges in SMEs

According to the estimates of the Ministry of SMEs, the sector contributes around 40% of the manufacturing output, accounts for over 8% of the national GDP, and creates more job opportunities both in rural and urban parts of the country. Being on a significant growth trajectory has made the sector vulnerable to a bunch of associated people challenges:

1. Acquiring talent to navigate the enterprises through double-digit growth rate is the key challenge facing many enterprises. Intense competition, lack of coherent acquisition capability including low salary, along with weak employer brand, create serious constraints for the enterprises.
2. Currently, big businesses are making investments to relentlessly upgrade the skill and competencies of their critical employees, by tie-ups with reputed foreign universities and engaging consultants. SMEs rely on in-house training due to tight budgets.
3. Most SMEs do not have processes to systemically track employee performance, or conduct performance counseling for generating developmental inputs and capture employee insights for performance improvements.
4. Retaining employees at the junior level is a challenge in Indian SMEs. The junior levels mostly comprise of employees with functional skills such as electricians, or field sales people. This class is highly mobile and change jobs frequently and may even quit without a prior notice. It becomes a big challenge for the HR to fill vacant positions at a short notice.[32]

Although there are currently more than 3200,000 SMEs in India, the extent of adoption of formalized HR practices is insignificant. According to a survey conducted by CII, 20% of medium- and 80% of small-sized businesses have no HR departments. This obviously restricts the SMEs' ability to deal with the various emergent people issues associated with a growing enterprise, the key one being talent acquisition in terms of building an effective employer brand that can attract talent. Several probable reasons have been ascribed to the lack of formal HR departments or processes in SMEs: budget constraints; focus more being on the growth and scale, rather than being people- and culture-related; perception of HR department being a cost center; and smallness of teams rendering it unnecessary to establish HR systems.

A study was undertaken covering 143 Indian SMEs (89 small enterprises and 54 medium enterprises) on the level of formalization of 12 HR functions. Formalization is defined as the extent to which regular and written-up procedures exist, a stated policy is in place, and a specialist designs and executes the HR systems. It was found that the level of formalization of HRM systems in SMEs was low and owner-managers played a central role in the HR functions of their enterprises. The direct involvement of the owner-manager led to ad hoc and informal HR practices. Compared to small enterprises, the level of formalization was found to be higher for medium enterprises. The level of formalization increased with increase in employee strength. An inverse relationship between the extent of involvement of the ownerimanager in HRM and the existence of a formal policy for HRM was evidenced.[33]

Another study conducted by Upasna Agarwal and Sumi Jha[34] on owners of eight small and medium enterprise firms covering different sectors (electronics component, textile and garment, auto ancillary,

[32] People Matters, 'Challenges for HR in SMEs,' February 14, 2017. Available at: https://www.peoplematters.in/article/ strategic-hr/challenges-for-hr-in-smes-14956?utm_source=peoplematters&utm_medium=interstitial&utm_campaign=learnings-of- the-day (accessed on November 17, 2017).

[33] Manjari Singh and Neharika Vohra, 'Level of Formalisation of Human Resource Management in Small and Medium Enterprises in India,' *The Journal of Entrepreneurship*, 18, no. 1 (March 1, 2009): 95–116.

[34] U. Agarwal and S. Jha, 'Human Resource Practices in Indian SMEs: An Exploratory Study,' *Indian Journal of Industrial Relations* 50, no. 4 (April 2015): 680–695.

IT, financial services, and renewable energy) sought to examine the HR practices in SMEs in India. The findings are as follows:

1. Recruitment
   (i) There was variance in practices of recruitment.
   (ii) Some showed reluctance to use formal approaches to recruitment (i.e., using the job centers or advertising in newspapers); discomfort in going to any technical institute or school for campus recruitment; preference for employee referrals or handpicking them from known acquaintances.
   (iii) Some of the respondents expressed a contrary view and supported the need for building professional team through a formal process; some confirmed conducting walk-in interview, online job postings for junior positions, and seeking references from reliable professionals for senior positions.
   (iv) There was an emphasis to get the 'right worker' and culture fit was important.
   (v) There was no strategy for retention.

   The aforementioned corroborated some of the empirical research findings:

   - In SMEs, managers tend to look for match of applicant competencies to general organization needs rather than to specific job requirements.[35] This involves 'aligning the applicant competencies with organizational values and culture rather than aligning basic knowledge, skills, and abilities.'
   - Recruitment practices in small enterprises rely on sources that are 'convenient, inexpensive, and directly controllable by the company, such as direct applicants, personal and employee referrals, and newspaper ads.'[36]
2. Compensation
   (i) Pay was more than the statutory minimum wages.
   (ii) Pay hikes were based on good business performance, not guaranteed.
   (iii) The enterprises followed an implicit norm of sharing revenue increase, if warranted by changes in the business cycle, through bonus payment.
3. Training
   (i) There was no policy for formal training. The sole focus of employee development was learning on the job.
   (ii) The high attrition rates in SMEs discouraged the enterprises from making investments in training to employees and to thus become kind of 'learning schools' for competitors.
   (iii) Primary concern was to get the product out of the door, not to improve the employability of the employees, in case of job loss.
4. Performance Appraisal
   (i) Performance Appraisal was the owner's prerogative and done on the basis of personal impression of the owner-manager.
   (ii) There were no formal job designs. Given the nature of work in SMEs, it was not possible (or feasible) to construct objective measures of employee performance.

---

[35] H. G. Heneman and R. A. Berkley, 'Applicant Attraction Practices and Outcomes among Small Businesses,' *Journal of Small Business Management* 37, no. 1 (1999): 53.

[36] Ibid.

5. Industrial Relations
   (i) Employee relations was marked by informality and close personal ties.
   (ii) There was low union density across the enterprises. Workers generally opted for union-free workplace, since most of their needs were taken care of beyond expectation by their employers.
   (iii) Owner-managers did not want unions.
   (iv) The respondents talked about a strong sense of community within the firm.
   (v) Owners practiced various employee-engagement initiatives.

16.5 IMPACT OF WEAK ADOPTION OF HUMAN RESOURCE MANAGEMENT IN SMEs

The lack of formal HR practices in SMEs has been associated with a number of adverse HR outcomes. A study conducted by McEvoy in 1984 in Midwest Metropolitan area covering 84 SMEs (with a 36-item questionnaire) established the key finding that the lack of emphasis on HRM in SMEs was one of the main reasons for business failures.[37] It was a confirmation of the several previous surveys (including a 1970 survey conducted by Dun and Broadstreet, which indicated that business problems cited by small-business managers were personnel-related). A Roper organization poll reported that the most difficult problem for small business was finding competent workers, and then motivating them to perform. A recent study by Puplampu[38] suggested that efficiency and performance of human resource were the most significant reasons of any SME to be unsuccessful.

In the UK, SMEs are the major principal source of unfair dismissal claims before UK employment tribunals.[39] In addition, surveys of SMEs indicate that a lack of skilled labor impedes small-firm growth. In another survey, almost one-third of SMEs identified training (32%) and employment topics (30%) among the top live issues facing the business in the coming year.[40]

In India, the problems of small enterprises related to HRM are failure to attract talent, motivate employees, and retain key employees, due to deficient recruitment, compensation, and training practices.[41] In Indian SMEs, HRM is perceived as 'unresponsive or not tailored to their needs,' and it is considered too costly an activity to carry for an SME.

16.5.1 Informality

SMEs are characterized by an informal environment. Owners prefer informal and unstructured processes in the hope that it would help in cost control and provide operational flexibility.[42] This

37 G. M. McEvoy, 'Small Business Personnel Practices,' *Journal of Small Business Management* 22, no. 4 (1984): 1–8.

38 Bill Buenar Puplampu, 'Skills, Structure and Leadership: Critical Variables for SME Internationalisation,' in *Internationalisation and Enterprise development in Ghana*, ed. John Kuada (London: Adonis and Abbey Publishers Ltd: Business and Economics): 129–194.

39 J. Earnshaw, M. Marchington and J. Goodman, 'Unfair to Whom? Discipline and Dismissal in Small Establishments,' *Industrial Relations Journal* 31 (2000): 62–73.

40 Small Business Service, 'Small Firms: Big Business. A Review of Small and Medium Sized Enterprises in the UK,' (London: HMSO).

41 Manjari Singh and Neharika Vohra, 'Strategic Human Resource Management in Small Enterprises,' *Journal of Entrepreneurship* 14, no. 1 (2005): 57–70.

42 M. Scott, I. Roberts, G. Holroyd, and D. Sawbridge, 'Management and Industrial Relations in Small Firms' (research paper no. 70, Department of Employment, London, 1989).

explains why the bulk of the SMEs favor informal and loose structures, maintain status quo, and remain where they are. In the opinion of some, an informal approach helps the SMEs to battle through the high degree of uncertainty in the business environment.

In a study covering 40 firms, Marlow and Patton[43] reported of a dilemma faced by the business owners whether to choose a formal or an informal management practice in general. On the positive side, informality generates employee motivation; however, on the contrary, it may also involve arbitrary treatment to an employee. The problem arises when issues of discipline have to be managed. In short, small firms thus face a struggle between building a positive and collaborative environment and maintaining discipline.[44]

Some critics attribute the choice of informality to the absence of foresight/resources endemic in SMEs. It reflects a failure to realize the strategic importance for key HR practices, for instance, L&D, which is sometimes considered to be a luxury, only affordable when the firm is making large profits.[45] And Golhar and Deshpande[46] argue that a lack of understanding of HRM issues by small-business owners may be one of the explanations for firm-size differences in HRM practices.

16.5.2 Degree of Specialization

The small firms are often less specialized than larger firms.[47] Larger firms demand the services of specialist employees, whereas in smaller firms' employees require to be multiskilled to perform multiple and a wide variety of tasks. Therefore, specialists are rarely found in smaller firms. This view is corroborated by a research finding, where in a random sample of 117 companies with less than 100 employees, Heneman and Berkley found that only 15 have an HR department.[48]

16.5.3 Legal Compliance

Compliance of all statutory requirements is an important condition for successful business conduct and it applies to SMEs also. For many SMEs, the failure to implement a structured compliance system is a significant risk and could lead to the enforced closure of the business.

It is, however, widely argued that SME owners are allergic to legal regulation. In Europe, administrative burdens related to law of employment affect the recruitment decisions of an estimated 31% of SMEs, with managers in these firms handling complex and obscure employment legislation (European Commission). The main concerns pertain to laws regarding minimum wage, health and safety, and working time.[49] Moreover, not only are SME owners and managers largely ignorant of the detail of legislation and resistant to increasing employment regulation, employees in SMEs have a low

---

43 S. Marlow and D. Patton, 'Minding the Gap Between Employer and the Employee: The Challenge for Owner-managers in Smaller Manufacturing Firms,' *Employee Relations* 24, no. 5 (2002): 523–539.

44 Ibid.

45 C. Hendry, A. Jones, M. Arthur, and A. Pettigrew, 'Human Resource Development in Small to Medium Sized Enterprises' (research paper no. 88, Department of Employment, London, 1991).

46 D. Y. Golhar and S. P. Deshpande, 'HRM Practices of Large and Small Canadian Manufacturing Firms,' *Journal of Small Business Management* 35 (1997): 30–38.

47 N. Bacon, P. Ackers, J. Storey, and D. Coates, 'It's a Small World: Managing Human Resources in Small Business,' *The International Journal of Human Resource Management* 7, no. 1 (1996): 82–101.

48 H. G. Heneman and R. A. Berkley, 'Applicant Attraction Practices and Outcomes Among Small Businesses,' *Journal of Small Business Management* 37, no. 1 (1999): 53–74.

49 *Small Business Service*. 2001. 56

level of awareness of legal entitlements and are reluctant to exercise their rights due to employment insecurity.[50] In India also, it is reported in the *Economic Times* that

> [m]ost SMEs have limited knowledge and awareness of compliances that impact them and often delegated this responsibility to junior management or outsourced it to consultants. Compliance has been synonymous with tax filing and SMEs are not really aware that there are 275-plus Acts that could impact them.[51]

16.5.4 Start-ups

Start-ups are known to evolve an informal work culture marked by distinctive dress code, communication style, and a flat organizational structure. But new challenges come up when they grow in size (in some cases, much quicker than planned), the principal one being the acquisition of a larger workforce. HR of a start-up or an innovative SME differs from that of a traditional firm as its growth is enmeshed in the aspirations of the young, the millennial, and the Net generation, who are averse to protocols and seek quick growth.

Like other SMEs, most start-ups do not have a full-fledged HR department, as HR function is considered an additional cost and never budgeted for. Initially, they are close knit and there is a certain bonhomie in the team, but as they gather momentum, it becomes necessary to scale up. Personal touch, which was possible earlier, disappears and internal communication becomes harder. Many of them still avoid setting up a HR function. Instead, they turn to outsourced or software-built services that fill the gaps. Trinet, Zenefits, and Justworks, for example, offer digital dashboards to onboard and keep track of employees similar to what a traditional HR person would do in the past. But, as one start-up founder wrote in a review of the Zenefits platform, '[It's] especially great for early stage companies, but once you reach about 50 employees, you'll need something more.'[52]

Exhibit The HR Challenges in Indian Start-ups

Manpower is inadequate, funding and resources are scarce and the route to growth is often an uncharted territory. Welcome to the startup environment. And it is in this environment that HR professionals need to deliver and do it right each time to ensure success. 'The role of the HR department in startups is to drive the workforce through effective action and not by means of their position,' Flipkart's Chief People Officer Mekin Maheshwari said.

New recruits need to have the right personality mix, skills and qualifications, and the ability to deliver beyond the expected job responsibilities. 'Start-up hires must have the skill and commitment to play multiple roles and don various hats as the company grows. There comes a time when one needs to go beyond the job description,' said Ganesh Shankar, MD of FluxGen Tech, a Bengaluru-based technology firm. Here are some of the key processes HR professionals in start-ups need to focus on: identifying and recruiting the right group of talent; creating appropriate job

---

50 Marlow 2002.

51 Thomas Abraham, 'View: Do You Know Your Law? 275 Acts Increase the Risk of Non-compliance in SMEs,' *The Economic Times*, January 7, 2017.

52 Cathy Weissman, 'The Future of HR and Why Startups Should Not Reject It,' *Fast Company*, October 2016. Available at: https:// www.fastcompany.com/3059673/the-future-of-hr-and-why-startups-shouldnt-reject-it (accessed on November 17, 2017).

descriptions to attract suitable talent; dividing job roles/responsibilities within the company as it grows; ensuring ongoing constructive communication among team members. Given further are some of the suggested actions.

Being Different

HR professionals in start-ups have to be able to create something important and big from almost nothing. Thus, the ability of constraints bringing out the best in them is a key requirement. Maheshwari of Flipkart said,

> HR folks in start-ups need to be a different blend of individuals who keep challenging themselves to do more. They need to be focused and have enhanced skills in their domain to identify the exact requirement or at least the ability to derive the precise skills needed by a team. Often, they must wear multiple hats and have to be more innovative to attract, retain and develop talent without adequate resources, especially during their foundation days.

Innovating as They Go Along

'The way HR managers manage people and teams in a start-up makes all the difference. In fact, in start-ups, management and innovation go hand in hand,' said Neetu Bansal of Vibrant Serve, a technology-skill services provider for top management. 'In contrast to large established companies, start-ups, especially today, need HR managers who come with a combination of passion and the ability to change the game as they go along.'

Ensuring Employee Engagement

Bansal said,

> In a start-up, we do things no one has done before. Thus, instead of specifying people with 5 yearsof experience in something, it is often smarter to look for people who can learn fast and have greaterexperience or have raw skill sets. Identifying people with these abilities is the effort the HR managerneeds to focus on to make it a success.

Source: Adapted from Kanchana Dwarakanath, 'HR Can Make or Break Your Start-up,' *The Economic Times*, May 13, 2015.

Despite the aforementioned studies, the picture is not as black and white as it would appear. There is some evidence, based on case/pilot studies, establishing sophisticated HRM practices in typical small firms.[53] Similarly, Hornsby and Kuratko[54] find that while firms of all sizes use primarily informal recruitment and selection techniques (mainly employee referrals and the interview), even among small firms, HR practices are often more sophisticated than they had expected. Using a small set of cases, Hill and Stewart[55] also demonstrate variation in level of sophistication of HRM practices among smaller organizations. It is possible that the importance of HR practices is not lost on the SMEs. Research

[53] S. P. Deshpande and D. Y. Golhar, 'HRM Practices in Large and Small Manufacturing Firms: A Comparative Study,' *Journal of Small Business Management* 32, no. 2 (1994): 49–56.

[54] Hornsby and Kuratko, 'Human Resource Management as Small Businesses Grow,' *American Journal of Business* 5, no. 1 (1990): 31–38.

[55] Hill and Stewart, 'Human Resource Development, Small to Medium-sized Enterprises, Investors in People,' (MCB UP Ltd, 1999).

in SMEs demonstrates that not only are high-performance work systems (HPWSs) utilized in some businesses,[56] but also the linkage between HRM and organizational outcomes does exist in SMEs.[57] In addition to these, the literature seems to suggest that the difference in HR practices between the large firms and the SMEs are of degree—a relative rather than an absolute absence of structure.[58]

Questions have also been raised whether HR practices in small- and medium-scale organizations are different. In a research done by Economic and Social Research Council (ESRC) Centre for Business Research in 2000, it was observed that the propensity for adopting HRM practices grew with the size in the sample organizations (Table 16.5).

Table 16.5 Propensity of adoption of HR practices by MSMEs

Size of firm	Quality management	Job rotation and multi-skilling	Performance-related pay	No. of firms
Micro	20	22.9	20.9	1023
Small	42.8	42	37.5	1075
Medium	58.9	54.6	52.7	275

Source: Frank Wilkinson, 'HRM and Business Objectives and Strategies in Small and Medium Sized Business,' (working paper no. 184, ESRC Centre for Business Research, University of Cambridge, Cambridge, September 2000).

In a study covering 170 entrepreneurs and owners, 16 HR practices were ranked by the respondents in order of importance. The ranking of the small enterprises group differed from that of the medium enterprises group in this manner for the first five items: open communication, pay for performance, training for new employees, collective responsibility, and competitive wages (small enterprises group); pay for performance, job security, open communication, collective responsibility, and fairness in promotion for the medium enterprises group.

16.6 FACTORS INFLUENCING THE ADOPTION OF HUMAN RESOURCE MANAGEMENT PRACTICES IN SMEs

Arguably, a number of factors, both internal and external to the firm, influence the extent and the manner in which HR practices are implemented within the SME sector. These factors include the SME's internal capabilities and also its access to external networks that have the potential to provide the knowledge necessary to innovate and grow.

16.6.1 Skill Requirements of Employees

The level of skill requirement of employees can influence the firm to decide on adopting formal HR practices. It is reasoned that where the business objectives of the firm depend on employees with high skills/competencies, choice of good practices in recruitment, development, and retention is imperative. Competent employees in high-technology sectors create competitive advantage and, for this reason, are scarce. Such candidates can be attracted and retained not only by attractive compensation package but also the existence of a proper career path, congenial management style, and employer brand. In

56 N. Bacon, P. Ackers, J. Storey, and D. Coates, 'It's a Small World: Managing Human Resources in Small Business.'

57 S. Snell, P. Pedigo and G. Krawiec, 'Managing the Impact of Information Technology on Human Resource Management,' in *Handbook of Human Resource Management*, edited by N. Ferris, S. Rosen and D. Barnum (Oxford: Blackwell): 159–174.

58 M. Cully, S. Woodland, A. O'Reilly, and G. Dix, *Britain at Work* (London: Routledge, 1999).

case of low skill requirement, the employees can be sweated and formal HR practices are considered unnecessary.

Small and medium enterprises who find it difficult to match the larger firms on the prospect of stable employment, given their unclear career paths, tend to source locally rather than nationally. This explains why in most SMEs the quality of human resources is indifferent in terms of skill, education, or commitment, except firms with predominantly professional employees, such as consultancy firms, where the evolution of a sophisticated work environment may be facilitated by the smallness of the firm. The SMEs are further constrained by scarcity of resources to adopt a systematic employee development program, who thus have low employability outside the organization. The scene is different though in Japan, where employee skill is built through elaborate on-the-job training.

16.6.2 Impact of National Policies

National policies or legislations also impact HRM in SMEs. In India, the need to build large industries led to industrial policies being heavily oriented to large enterprises to the neglect of SMEs. Laws related to employees had threshold, leading to exclusion of SMEs in case they managed to keep the number of employees less than the threshold. For example, important provisions of a key labor law—the ID Act—required minimum 50 workmen for qualifying for lay-off or retrenchment allowance. Factories Act, another principal law, has a threshold of 20 workmen without using power. In contrast, legislation in post-war West Germany was designed to protect independent Small and Medium Business Units (SMBUs) from 'inadvertent domination' by larger firms, while national standards insisted on high skill levels even in smaller firms. Similarly, in Japan, SMBUs were granted a clear place in a national strategy aimed at high innovation that in turn called for continuous learning among employees.[59] For both West Germany and Japan, national policy is credited with bringing about a more stable and more skilled workforce.

16.6.3 Customer Relations

Big customers can sometimes facilitate diffusion of HR practices through network of partnerships or by making it a condition for the SMEs to follow healthy HR practices to ensure delivery of quality of product and services. Similarly, Kinnie et al.[60] found that supply chain pressures and the demands of customers have a significant impact on SMEs' 'management structure, work organization and HR practices and policies.'[61,62] A partnership with a powerful, larger organization may save an SME's innovation costs and result in the adoption of sophisticated HR practices.[63] Such a partnership can work the other way around in the form of domination with 'dependent' SMEs being forced to adopt authoritarian management, tight supervision, and low wage levels.

[59] Clark, 'Education and Behaviour Modification,' *Journal of Philosophy of Education* (July 1979). Available at: http://onlinelibrary. wiley.com/doi/10.1111/j.1467-9752.1979.tb00522.x

[60] N. Kinnie, J. Purcell, S. Hutchinson, M. Terry, M. Collinson and H. Scarbrough, 'Employment Relations in SMEs: Market driven or Customer-shaped?' *Employee Relations* 21, no. 3 (1999): 218–238.

[61] Gales and Blackbum, 'An Analysis of the Impact of Supplier Strategies and Relationships on Small Retailer Actions, Perceptions, and Performance,' *Entrepreneurship Theory and Practiçe*. Available at: http://journals.sagepub.com/doi/abs

[62] 'HRM in the SME Sector. Valuable Employees and Coercive Networks'. Available at: https://www.researchgate.net/... HRM

[63] Goss, D., D. Adam-Smith and A. Gilbert, 'Small Firms and HRM: Exceptions that Prove the Rule?' *Journal of Small Business and Enterprise Development* 1, no. 2 (1994): 2–8.

16.6.4 Product Strategy

The product life cycles (introduction, growth, and maturity) require corresponding alignment of appropriate HRM focus, for example, supporting product strategy by shifting focus from innovation at introduction, to productivity at growth, and to efficiency at the maturity stage. But the SMEs are more vulnerable than the larger firms to neglect of this need to match the stage in product life cycle. The evidence of this neglect could be in developing HR policies post-hoc in the introduction stage;[64] fire-fighting in the recruitment and training of new employees at the growth stage;[65] and struggle to control employees in the matured stage.[66]

The strategy of multiplicity of products at different life-cycle stages causes high level of 'complexity for HR function,' which needs to balance organizational flexibility against possible local cultural/behavioral rigidities. These challenges are better met by SMEs as compared to larger firms. Indeed, the creation of SME activity through large-firm fragmentation and subcontracting has been directly attributed to this HRM advantage.[67]

16.6.5 Innovation

In line with Schumpeter's[68] classical view, SMEs are major actors in technological innovation.[69,70] 'Small-business owners, with their intimate knowledge of their customers, actually are incredibly well-positioned to innovate.'[71] Innovative SMEs have the edge over large enterprises by virtue of lack of bureaucracy and efficient communication channels despite limited resources,[72] qualities that associated HRM systems might be expected to support. Innovative firms invest more heavily in training[73] and high-growth new technology-based SMEs pursue HRM policies that nurture employee commitment and career development to compensate for higher large-firm salaries.[74]

16.6.6 Technology

Technology acts as the predictor of HR practices in two ways. First, by determining organization structure, recruitment, training, pay systems, and so on, appropriate for technology-driven processes.[75]

64 *Lawler*, J., Chen, S.-J., Wu, P.-C., Bae, J., Bai, B., 'The Role of *HRM* in Improving Labour Productivity: An Analysis of Manufacturing *SMEs* in Japan,' *Sri Lankan Journal of Human Resource Management* 44, no. 2 (2011): 165–169.

65 T. A. Kochan and J. Chalykott, 'Human Resource Management and Business Life Cycles: Some Preliminary Propositions,' Paper Presented at the Conference on Human Resources and Industrial Relations in High Technology Firms (Los Angeles, CA: March 1985).

66 Imrie and Richard, F., 'Work Decentralisation from Large to Small Firms: A Preliminary Analysis of Subcontracting,' *Environment and Planning* 18 (1986): 949–965.

67 Luis Suarez-Villa, 'Metropolitan Evolution, Sectoral Economic Change, and the City Size Distribution,' *Urban Studies* 25, no. 1 (1988): 1–20.

68 Ernst F. Schumacher, *Small Is Beautiful: Economics as if People Mattered* (New York, NY: Harper Perennial, 1939).

69 W. Adams, and J. W. Brock, *The Bigness Complex: Industry, Labor, and Government in the American Economy* (Stanford, CA: Stanford University Press, 1986).

70 R. Rothwell, 'Reindustrialisation, Innovation and Public Policy,' In *Technology, Innovation and Economic Policy*, edited by P. Hall, 65–83 (Oxford: Philip Allan, 1986).

71 Innovation lessons from small businesses. Callahan. March. 2009. Forbes

72 R. Rothwell, 'Reindustrialisation, Innovation and Public Policy.'

73 S. E. Jackson, R. S. Schuler and J. C. Rivero, 'Organizational Characteristics as Predictors of Personnel Practices,' Personnel Psychology 42, no. 4 (1989): 727–786.

74 M. Dodgson, 'Organisational Learning: A Review of Some Literatures,' *Organisation Studies* 14, no. 3 (1993): 375–394.

75 Jackson et al., 'Organizational Characteristics as Predictors of Personnel Practices.'

Second, firms, faced with frequently changing business environment, may respond with 'flexible specialization' made possible by linked technology and HRM systems. Firms thus achieve versatility in manufacturing with the help of a skilled, cohesive, and adaptable workforce.[76] SMEs are more suited to this arrangement than larger enterprises.

16.6.7 Services

Services sector has been the growing sector since the last few decades accounting for the bulk of new jobs. The work in the sector in areas such as hospitality, professional work, health care, IT, and ITeS has certain characteristic attributes.[77] The internal processes have a dominant customer-centricity (unlike in manufacturing) that HRM has to embed in its policies (particularly, selection and training), practices, and also in the organizational culture. HRM systems in service firms should value client perceptions of service delivery, and indeed are more likely to incorporate client input into performance appraisal.[78]

16.6.8 Proprietary Control and Governance

Divergence in ownership and governance is also a determinant of HRM. SMEs' degree of isolation from or connectedness with other organizations can determine the extent of adoption of HR practices.[79] Second, SMEs, being mostly single-location based, tend to get managed in an ad hoc, authoritarian, and informal manner. Firms that have multiple units require to develop centralized HR systems at corporate level to guide the units. Extending the same logic, it can be expected that SMEs with multiple units have a better probability to embrace formal HR practices. Similarly, affiliating with trade-name franchises may prove to be an accelerated learning curve to master HR expertise for the SMEs. On the contrary, family-owned and controlled SMEs get anchored in 'negotiated paternalism' as informal family loyalties create a spirit of mutual obligation eliminating the need for formal HR processes and systems. This condition prevents proper transfer of knowledge in family-owned businesses. Non-family-owned businesses, however, do not suffer from any such constraints.

In the final analysis, family-owned businesses have generally been marked by inadequate acceptance of modern HR systems. The vision and the values of the owner and his obligations to the family determine the selection of appropriate HRM systems. There is also a strong underlying drive to stay independent and remain in control of the firm. It is also established through past studies that owner-employers normally perceive formalized HR systems and processes with suspicion, and fear the loosening of their hold over the employees, and this amply explains why family ownership is related to introduction of formal HR practices.

16.6.9 Trade Unions

Trade unions can exert a positive influence in adoption of formal HR policies and best practices. For the USA, several studies have found relations between unionization and HR practices with medium-

76 M.J. Piore and C.F. Sabet, *The Second Industrial Divide: Possibilities for Prosperity* (New York, NY: Basic Books, 1984).

77 Hendry, Chris, Pettigrew, Andrew and Sparrow, Paul, 'Linking Strategic Change, Competitive Performance and Human Resource Management: Results of a UK Empirical Study,' In *Frontiers of Management*, edited by Mansfield, Roger (Abingdon: Routledge, 1989): 195–220.

78 Jackson et al., 'Organizational Characteristics as Predictors of Personnel Practices.'

79 Rainnie, *Industrial Relations in Small Firms*.

sized enterprises.[80] For example, Green[81] found that, where present, trade unions could exert a positive influence pressurizing firms with fewer than 25 employees to provide training opportunities. The labor government elected in 1997 recognized the role of unions in stimulating demand for training,[82] although this pressure may be weaker in the SME sector because overall levels of unionization and collective bargaining are lower.[83,84]

According to Kirton and Read,[85] unionization efforts face several hurdles in SMEs: employment relations are based on informality, and highly individualized interpersonal relations are characterized by proximity (between employer and employees, and among colleagues); employers abhor collective expression of grievances; and trade unions generally neglect SMEs. The 2004 Workplace Employment Relations Survey (WERS) in Britain[86] also corroborated part of this view and attributed the low unionization to the preference of SME managers for direct interaction with employees. Some researchers have also ascribed the general adversarial position of employers toward unions to the reluctance to share control and receive criticism.[87] The employers' attitude undoubtedly molds employees' union membership, perception, and experience. Nevertheless, it can be stated that the few SMEs who have union recognition experience more openness to formal HR processes than those without unions.

16.7 FUTURE OF HUMAN RESOURCE MANAGEMENT IN SMES

16.7.1 HR Outsourcing

Today, globalization is a major factor that has opened up opportunities for every business, including SME business. However, according a to a report of United Nations Industrial Development Organization (UNIDO),[88] most SMEs are ill equipped to compete effectively for reasons of internal resource gaps. 'SMEs in global value chain are even more vulnerable as they often bear the brunt of the difficulties of the large firms.'[89] Due to the impact of global crisis on SMEs constrained by resource limitations and the heat of competition, SMEs are seeking solutions in cost reduction and in leveraging external resources.[90]

Cost optimization is a major driver for HR outsourcing by a large number of SMEs. Setting up an HR department is considered expensive for the size of an SME organization. Small firms pursue outsourcing where the HR function is relatively undeveloped. In medium firms, finance and HR

80 D. J. Flanagan and S. P. Deshpande, 'Top Management's Perceptions of Changes in HRM Practices after Union Elections in Small Firms,' *Journal of Small Business Management* 34, no. 4 (1996): 23–34.

81 F. Green, 'The Impact of Trade Union Membership on Training in Britain,' *Applied Economics* 25 (1033–1043).

82 E. Keep and H. Rainbird, 'Training,' In *Industrial Relations*, edited by P. Edwards, 392–419 (Oxford: Blackwell, 2003).

83 J. Atkinson and N. Meager, 'Running to Stand Still: The Small Firm in the Labour Market,' In *Employment, the Small Firm and the Labour Market*, edited by Atkinson, J. and Storey. D. (London: Routledge, 1994).

84 D. J. Storey, *Understanding the Small Business Sector* (London: Routledge, 1994).

85 G. Kirton and Ian Read, 'Inequalities in Europe's SMEs: The Challenges for a Trade Union Agenda,' *Transfer: European Review of Labour and Research* 13, no. 1 (Spring 2007): 131–146.

86 J. Forth, H. Bewley, and A. Bryson, *Small and Medium-sized Enterprises: Findings from the 2004 Workplace Employment Relations Survey* (London: ESRC, ACAS, and PSI).

87 Ibid.

88 UNIDO, 2003. Available at: http://www.unido.org (accessed on November 17, 2017).

89 OECD, 'The Impact of Global Crisis on SME Constrained by Resource Limitations and the Heat of Competition, SMEs are Seeking Solutions in Cost Reduction and in Leveraging External Resources,' (2009). Available at: https://www.oecd.org/cfe/smes (accessed on February 15, 2018).

90 Available at: https://www.oecd.org/cfe/smes (accessed on November 17, 2017).

functions are largely occupied with routine transactions, and thus offer themselves easy targets of outsourcing. The HR functions being outsourced by SMEs include hiring, training, managing the PMS, and payroll processing. The in-house HR team consequently finds a strategic bandwidth and is able to tap the sophisticated HR systems and processes characteristic of large corporations at a relatively cheaper rate.

The outsourcing of time-consuming and expensive formal HR processes and functions improves the 'creditworthiness of a firm' by 'creating more bandwidth to focus on things that really matter.' The organization becomes more cost-efficient, better organized, and result-oriented.[91] Apart from cost consideration, there are other benefits of HR outsourcing for the SME owner. Talent acquisition is a major challenge for an SME in India, especially for family-run businesses, on account of deficient HR systems and practices, limited opportunity for growth in a flat organization, and unclear roles. Outsourcing improves the brand of the SME in the talent market, enables the SMEs access high quality professional expertise and experience of senior level consultants, without incurring any permanent cost burden. Outsourcing also frees the time of owners–managers to devote on the core business.

Ghodeswar and Vaidyanathan[92] have grouped reasons for outsourcing into four clusters: organizational drivers (focus on core business, flexibility, access to new technology, and so on); improvement drivers (improve productivity and quality, manage time better, acquire expertise, and so on); financial and cost drivers (reduce investment in assets, control operating costs, achieve economies of scale, and so on); and revenue drivers (growth objectives, leverage service providers' expertise, and so on).

SMEs path to HR outsourcing is not full of roses. The risks involved are also multiple: higher cost of coordination, emergence of quality and service problems, post-contractual revenue, costs of monitoring the contractual relationships, and loss of control over critical areas.[93] There are challenges of quality, security, and confidentiality involved in outsourcing, and the SMEs will have learn to resolve them as they grow more used to it. In the final analysis, HR outsourcing seems to be suited to the unique multiple needs of the SMEs, and the challenges of HR outsourcing seem to be far outweighed by the benefits in the form of cost-effective solutions that also leverage technology to provide a cutting edge to the SME in a competitive environment.

Closing Case Ziacom Inc

Ziacom 18 Media Pvt Ltd is a medium-sized 50/50 joint venture firm in India (between Ziacom Inc. and the Network18 Group), with interests in television, Internet, filmed entertainment, mobile content, and allied businesses, comprising brands such as CNBC TV18, CNBC Awaaz, Newswire18, moneycontrol.com, CNN-IBN, IBN 7, Homeshop18, and E18, among others. They have around 150 employees. Last year, the PBT was ₹8 crore.

Ziacom 18 Media Pvt. Ltd operates six general entertainment channels—MTV, Nickelodeon, Vh1, COLORS, SONIC, Comedy Central, and film business through Ziacom18

[91] Rajiv Shirali, 'Outsourcing will Improve the Creditworthiness of SMEs: Yogesh Dixit,' Interview with Director, CRISIL SME Ratings. Available at: http://www.business-standard.com/article/sme/outsourcing-will-improve-the-creditworthiness-of-smes-yogesh-dixit-113010100076_1.html (accessed on November 17, 2017).

[92] Bhimrao Ghodeswar and Janardan Vaidyanathan, 'Business Process Outsourcing: An Approach to Gain Access to World-class Capabilities,' *Business Process Management Journal* 14, no. 1 (2008): 23–38.

[93] Ajay K. Rajan and Suman Pahal, 'Human Resources Outsourcing in SMEs: An Exploration of Critical Areas,' *International Journal of Marketing, Financial Services and Management Research* 1, no. 6 (June 2016).

Motion Pictures that produces, acquires, and distributes Hindi films. This apart, Ziacom18 also runs Ziacom's consumer products division in India.

Ziacom 18 is faced with a situation where they have grown rapidly, without seriously looking at their people practices. They are poised for a 20% growth, but currently have worries about holding on to their creative personnel, and also attract more creative talents from the market. Another problem, which is slowly raising its head, is attrition rate (10%) among the creative personnel to some of their competitors. A year back, the company designated M.P. Joshi, an existing senior sales professional, as an HRBP, who now operates with a secretarial assistant, but no HR department. Most of the HR operations such as recruitment and pay roll are outsourced.

The new HR person has been proactive and enjoys the support of the CEO. He understands that since the mission of any entertainment company is to impress and delight customers, excellent service counts more than ever before. How will he ensure that Ziacom builds up a significant pool of employees who can consistently perform and deliver extraordinary service? On the basis of informal focus group discussions, he has felt that the company should formalize its PMS, along with KRAs and KPIs, for its employees and link them with a pay-for-performance scheme.

Discussion Questions

1. What are the challenges and opportunities for HRM in Ziacom?
2. What should be the strategy for Mr M.P. Joshi?

SUMMARY

SMEs are considered to be the principal anchor of both national and regional development in many countries. In India, which is poised to emerge as one of the leading economies of the world with the size of US$5 trillion by 2025, SMEs are considered as the 'backbone' of the national economy and major impetus is being given for their development.[94] According to the information provided by the Union Minister of MSME to Lok Sabha, the estimated contribution of MSME sector, including service segment, to the country's GDP during 2012–2013 was 37.54%; while the total employment in the sector is 805.24 lakh; and the share of MSMEs in India's total export for the year 2014–2015 was 44.70%.[95]

In recent years, human resources have gained acceptance as the vehicle of growth both at the microeconomic level as also at the micro level. At the macro level, the importance is associated with emergence of knowledge economies. At the micro level, it is considered a central pillar of sustained competitive advantage for businesses. HRM, however, receives a cold shoulder in bulk of the SMEs. Thus, there is a paradoxical situation where the ascendency of the knowledge-based economy is witnessing a concurrent decline of HR practice in organizations. Consequent to the lack of professional HR set-up and processes, there are typical problems faced by the SMEs related to

94 *The Economic Times*, 'Indian SME Trends: The Year Gone By and 2017,' December 30, 2016.

95 SMEStreet, 'MSMEs Contribute for More Than 37% of GDP and Employment for 805 Lakh Indians,' July 29, 2015. Available at: http://smestreet.in/msmes-contribute-for-more-than-37-of-gdp-and-employment-for-805-lakh-indians/ (accessed on November 17, 2017).

human resources—the major ones related to the talent-difficulty in acquiring, retaining, and engaging. The compensation structure is conservative, training opportunities are limited, and employees lack motivation. There are, however, reverse trends also, in isolated SMEs that match larger organizations in pursuing high-performance work practices. The factors influencing such variation in adoption and the implementation of HRM are manifold: skills requirement, product strategy, innovation, customer relations, trade unionism, and others.

SMEs, being aware of the need for sophisticated people processes, have mostly continued to shun formal HR set-ups. Instead, they found succor in HR outsourcing. Cost optimization has been the major driver for HR outsourcing by a large number of SMEs. Setting up an HR department is considered expensive for the size of an SME organization. Small firms pursue outsourcing where the HR function is relatively undeveloped. In medium firms, finance and HR functions are largely occupied with routine transactions, and thus offer themselves easy targets of outsourcing. The HR functions being outsourced by SMEs include hiring, training, managing the PMS, and payroll processing. The in-house HR team consequently finds a strategic bandwidth and is able to tap the sophisticated HR systems and processes characteristic of large corporations at a relatively cheaper rate. There are risks of quality and confidentiality, though the benefits seem to be greater than the costs.

Short-answer Questions

1. Define SMEs.
2. What is the importance of SMEs in India?
3. In what ways does firm size impact HRM adoption?
4. Mention some of the HR-related issues in automobile components manufacturing in India.
5. Mention three key HR challenges of SMEs in India related to talent acquisition.
6. What are some of the characteristics of IR in the SMEs?
7. 'SMEs are characterized by informality'. Explain.
8. How do skill requirements cause weak adoption of HRM in SMEs?
9. How does diversity in ownership and governance impact HR adoption in SMEs?
10. Write a short note on HR outsourcing in India.

Discussion Questions

1. What are the specific competencies that an HR professional need to possess to create value to the business?
2. What should be the specific talent strategy that SMEs should adopt to balance their concern for cost with cutting-edge capability?
3. Do you agree with the view that trade unionism would help the SMEs to improve their employee-engagement level?
4. In what ways can HR outsourcing improve competitiveness for an SME?

CHAPTER 17

Human Resource Management in the Services Sector

LEARNING OBJECTIVES

After completing this chapter, the student will be able to:

- Discuss the uniqueness of the services sector as different from the manufacturing sector
- Describe the impact of the special nature of services sector on the HR function
- Discuss the important normative approaches to the HR function in the services sector
- Discuss the nature, issues, and trends in specific services sector
- Discuss the role of trade unions

17.1 INTRODUCTION

HR function has often attracted criticism at the way it cocooned itself from the rest of the organization and pursued its own agenda. A particularly harsh joke on the traditional HR function ran like this:

Place 400 bricks in a closed room. Put your new employees in the room and close the door. Leave them alone and come back after 6 hours.

Analyze the situation you find:

(a) If they are counting the bricks, put them in the Accounting department.

(b) If they have messed up the whole place with the bricks, put them in Engineering.

(c) If they are arranging the bricks in some strange order, put them in Planning.

(d) If they are throwing the bricks at each other, put them in Operations.

(e) If they are sitting idle, put them in HR.

The good news is that the situation just discussed has gone through a significant transformation. In 2009, an article in the *Economist*[1] reports of a

> [m]assive restructuring of corporate HR departments that took place in the decade or so after 1995. Before that, the staff in HR departments had generally been seen as

[1] The Economist, 'Human Resources Transformation,' May 26, 2009.

> administrators, not as people to be involved in high-level strategic discussions. HR staff saw themselves as lifetime career specialists with little need for knowledge or experience of what the rest of the business was about.

The article goes on to elaborate how with the growing appreciation of the value of a company's human assets, and a need to ensure that the talent that an organization requires is not just onboard but also properly motivated, the role of HR has more and more come to be seen as strategic. 'The old-style HR that dealt with strikes, bonuses and gripes was rarely suited to this task.'

What triggered this transformation? The reason could perhaps be found in the emergence of the services sector as the dominant sector in the industry, which accounted for this tectonic change in the contours of the HR function.

17.2 THE EMERGENCE OF THE SERVICES SECTOR

In today's world, the third sector, labeled as the 'economy of services,' plays a dominant role with respect to contribution to GDP, job creation, and supporting the progress in standard of living and quality of life. Traditionally, economic activities are clustered into three sectors: agriculture, industry, and services. Services include banking, communications, wholesale and retail trade, all professional services such as engineering, computer software development, and medicine, non-profit economic activity, all consumer services, and all government services. Manufacturing has steadily been taking a back seat in developed countries and the proportion of the world economy devoted to services grew steadily during the 20th century. In the United States, for example, the services sector accounted for more than two-thirds of the economy in 1978 and more than three-quarters in 1993. In the early 21st century, service industries accounted for more than three-fifths of the global GDP and employed more than one-third of the labor force worldwide. The services sector now accounts for over 70% of employment in the industrialized economies of the world, with Norway and the United States upfront at over 75% of employment.[2]

Telecommunications, transportation, wholesale/retail, finance, insurance, and business services account for about 60% of all employment created in the industrialized economies over the past decade, while community, social and personal services, including health and education, account for the remaining 40%. Looking ahead, this growth is expected to continue, with nearly 20% employment growth expected in services in the next decade in the USA, with no change expected in manufacturing employment.[3]

The services sector is considered to be an engine of India's economic growth. According to a recent report published by the CII and KPMG, India has moved up to become the fastest growing service economy in the world. It contributed around 66.1%t of its gross value-added growth in 2015–2016, thereby emerging as an important net foreign exchange earner and the most attractive sector for FDI inflows.

---

[2] *OECD*, 'Growth in Services. Fostering Employment, Productivity and Innovation,' Meeting of the *OECD* Council at Ministerial Level (OECD, 2005).

[3] Geittel and Seidner, 'Human Resource Management in the Services Sector,' In *The SAGE Handbook of Human Resource Management*, edited by Adrian Wilkinson, Nicolas Bacon, Tom Redman and Scott Snell, 509 (SAGE Publications, 2006).

Exhibit Services Sectors Included in the National Industrial Classification 2008

• Wholesale and retail trade; repair of motor vehicles and motorcycles • Transportation and storage • Accommodation and food service activities • Information and communication • Financial and insurance activities • Real estate activities • Professional, scientific and technical activities • Administrative and support service activities • Public administration and defence; compulsory social security • Education • Human health and social work activities • Arts, entertainment and recreation • Other service activities • Activities of house-holds as employers; undifferentiated goods and services producing activities of households for own use • Activities of extraterritorial organizations and bodies.

Source: Extracted from 'National Industrial Classification,' Central Statistical Organisation, Ministry of Statistics and Programme Implementation (MOSPI), Government of India, 2008. Available at: http://mospi.nic.in/Mospi_New/upload/nic_2008_17apr09.pdf (accessed on May 2, 2012).

According to the Central Statistics Office (CSO) assessments, the growth in this sector is pegged at 8.8% in 2016–2017. According to a report by leading research firm Market Research Store, the Indian telecommunication services market is expected to grow by 10.3% year-on-year to reach US$103.9 billion by 2020.[4] India's services sector covers a wide variety of activities that have different features and dimensions. They include trade, hotel and restaurants, transport, storage and communication, financing, insurance, real estate, business services, community, social and personal services, and services associated with construction. Services in India are emerging as a prominent sector in terms of contribution to national and states' incomes, trade flows, FDI inflows, and employment.

The compound annual growth rate (CAGR) of services-sector GDP was 8.5% for the period 2000–2001 to 2013–2014. As per the survey, in India, the growth of services-sector GDP has been higher than that of overall GDP between the FY'01 and FY'14. Services constitute a major portion of India's GDP with a 57% share in GDP at factor cost (at current prices) in 2013–2014, an increase of 6% points over 2000–2001.

The growth in the services sector can be attributed mostly to the emergence of the Indian IT and ITeS sectors as well as e-commerce.

17.3 IMPLICATIONS FOR HUMAN RESOURCE MANAGEMENT FUNCTION

The uniqueness in services sector is intangible products mostly based on knowledge. Unlike the manufactured commodities, in service delivery, bulk of the employees is in direct contact with the customers/service users whose needs are more complex and varied. The typical customer-related work can include customer information, customer services, negotiation and contract of service, delivery of service, creation of customer value for retention, and collection of market information. The HRM in the services sector has the following issues: new methods of motivations; careful selection, based on rational and emotional intelligence skills; personnel T&D; orientation toward knowing the service and behavior in contact with the customers; and setting work procedures and performance standards.

4 Available at: https://www.ibef.org/in. (accessed in March 2017).

Traditionally, the HR function consisted of five sets of activities: planning, staffing, compensation, employee training and employee relations, and performance management. Given that these existing HR practices were developed in the context of manufacturing, the emergence of the services sector signaled a shift in the paradigm. The focus has shifted to address the need to pursue high quality services, via a set of sophisticated 'high cost and high skill employment strategies.'[5]

17.4 DIFFERENCES BETWEEN SERVICES SECTOR AND THE MANUFACTURING SECTOR

In layman's parlance, a 'manufacturing industry' is the one that is involved in the production of goods to be sold in the marketplace. These are further categorized as process industries (flow production or continuous process production industries) and discrete manufacturing industries. 'Service industry,' on the other hand, provides services of certain kinds. The uniqueness of service industry lies in the fact that usually the service is received and consumed while it is in the process of generation. Hospitality, advertising, banking, insurance, consultancy, and logistics are some of the examples of service industries.

There are five main points of difference between service and manufacturing organizations: the tangibility of their output; production on demand or for inventory; customer-specific production; labor-intensive or automated operations; and the need for a physical production location. However, in practice, service and manufacturing organizations share many characteristics. Many manufacturers offer their own service operations and both require skilled people to create a profitable business.

17.4.1 Tangibility

The key difference between service firms and manufacturers is the tangibility of their output. The output of a service firm, such as consultancy, training, or maintenance, for example, is intangible. Manufacturers produce physical goods that customers can see and touch.

17.4.2 Inventory

Manufacturers hold their produce in stocks, while services sector does not hold inventory; their product is service that is created when a client requires it. Manufacturers produce goods for stock, with inventory levels aligned to forecasts of market demand. Some manufacturers maintain minimum stock levels, relying on the accuracy of demand forecasts, and their production capacity to meet demand on a just-in-time basis. Inventory also represents a cost for a manufacturing organization.

17.4.3 Customers

Service firms do not produce a service unless a customer requires it, although they design and develop the scope and content of services in advance of any orders. Service firms generally produce a service tailored to customers' needs, such as 12 hours of consultancy, plus 14 hours of design and 10 hours of installation. Manufacturers can produce goods without a customer order or forecast of customer demand. However, producing goods that do not meet market needs is a poor strategy.

5 H. Francis and D'Annunzio-Green, 'HRM and the Pursuit of a Service Culture,' *Employee Relations* 27, no. 1 (2005): 71–85.

17.4.4 Employees

A service organization acquires employees with specific, right kind of competence in the disciplines that it offers. Service delivery relies on people to deliver and machines cannot replace them, although knowledge-management systems enable a degree of knowledge capture and sharing. In manufacturing, processes are continuously automated to reduce their labor requirements, although some manufacturing organizations are labor-intensive, particularly in countries where labor costs are low.

17.4.5 Location

Service firms do not require a physical production site. The people creating and delivering the service can be located anywhere. For example, global firms such as consultants Deloitte use communication networks to access the most appropriate service skills and knowledge from offices around the world. Manufacturers must have a physical location for their production and stock-holding operations. Production does not necessarily take place on the manufacturer's own site and can take place at any point in the supply chain.

17.5 DIFFERENCE IN HUMAN RESOURCE MANAGEMENT PRACTICES IN SERVICES AND MANUFACTURING SECTORS

Service organizations have been described as differing from manufacturing organizations in three ways: (a) their 'products' are intangible rather than tangible; (b) customers are actively involved in the production of services; and (c) the consumption of services occurs simultaneously with their production.[6–7]

The intangible nature of services means that performance is difficult for supervisors to monitor directly, so employees must be trusted to monitor their own performance.

The fact that customers are actively involved in the service production process means service providers must be sensitive to clients' needs; they must monitor these needs; and use the cues they receive from clients to guide their job behaviors. Because of these characteristics of service jobs, service organizations should be more likely than manufacturers to include both employee input and client input as sources of performance appraisal information.[10]

The simultaneity of the production and consumption processes also has implications for HRM practices.[11] For example, quality control cannot be achieved by the inspect-and-correct method commonly used in manufacturing plants. Instead, quality control occurs at the point of service

---

6 Daft 1986.

7 Mills and Margulies, 'Toward a Core Typology of Service Organizations,' *The Academy of Management Review* 5, no. 2 (April 1980): 255.

8 Mills and Moberg, 'Perspectives on the Technology of Service Operations,' *The Academy of Management Review* 7, no. 3 (July 1982): 467–478.

9 Larsson and Bowen, 'Organization and Customer: Managing Design and Coordination of Services,' *Academy of Management Review* 14, no. 2 (1989): 213–233.

10 Mills and Morris, 'Clients as 'Partial' Employees of Service Organizations: Role Development in Client Participation,' *Academy of Management Review* 11, no. 4 (1986): 726–735.

11 Schneider and Schecter, 'Development of a Personnel Selection System for Service Jobs,' In *Service Quality, Multidisciplinary and Multinational Perspectives*, Edited by Stephen W. Brown, Evert Gurmnesson, Bo Edvardsson, and BengtOve Gustavsson, 217–236 (Lexington, MA: Lexington Books, 1991).

delivery.[12,13] In order to maintain control over quality, service organizations are likely to seek ways of controlling the process of service production rather than the outputs. They may invest more resources to train new recruits, with the objective of socializing them to be effective monitors of their own service production behaviors.[14] They could also revise their personnel selection system.[15] Another way to gain more control over performance would be to use performance appraisal results in making compensation decisions. Job design practices could also be used to enhance service quality. Enriched jobs should encourage self-monitoring because employees then feel a greater sense of responsibility for their performance and they are more aware of their significance to the firm.[16] This line of reasoning implies that the following practices would be more prevalent in service-based firms:

- Job designs that are 'enriched,' in that they are characterized by autonomy, variety, and interdependence
- Employee input into performance appraisals
- Client input into performance appraisals
- Use of performance appraisal results to assess training needs
- Extensive training of new employees, with emphasis on performance on their current jobs
- Use of performance appraisal results in determining compensation

It should be noted here that in comparing service-based and manufacturing firms, these predicted differences would be found for both managerial employees and lower-level employees. However, the differences are likely to be greater for lower-level employees, although differences in the tasks performed by service-based employees and manufacturing employees are particularly pronounced.

17.6 HUMAN RESOURCE MANAGEMENT AND SERVICE QUALITY CORRELATION

17.6.1 Human Resources and Service Climate

In a service organization, the key stakeholder is the customer and the key activity is to deliver service of quality. The very nature of services, that is, their intangibility, poses difficulty in evaluation of quality. Service organization is thus 'in need of mechanism by which it can reduce this input of uncertainty and acquire the information necessary for effective service production and delivery.'[17] There are problems of consistency, as services tend to be different each time they are performed, because either the customer does not articulate his needs or the service provider is responsible for a variation.

[12] Christian Gronroos, 'Service Management and Marketing: Managing the Moments of Truth in Service Competition,' (Lexington, MA: Lexington Books, 1990).

[13] Heskett, Sasser and Hart, 'The Profitable Art of Service Recovery,' *Harvard Business Review* 68, no. 4 (1990): 148–156.

[14] D. E. Bowen and B. Schneider, 'Services Marketing and Management: Implications for Organizational Behavior,' *Research on Organizational Behavior* 10.

[15] Schneider and Schecter, 'Development of a Personnel Selection System for Service Jobs,' In *Service Quality, Multidisciplinary and Multinational Perspectives*, edited by Stephen W. Brown, Evert Gurmnesson, Bo Edvardsson, and BengtOve Gustavsson (Lexington, MA: Lexington Books, 1991): 217–236.

[16] G. R. Oldham and J. R. Hackman, 'Work Design in the Organization Context,' *Research in Organizational Behaviour* 2 (1980): 247–278.

[17] Siehl and Bowen, 'The Role of Rites of Integration in Service Delivery,' *International Journal of Service Industry Management* 2, no. 1 (1991): 15–34.

Sustained quality of service can only happen in a service climate. Service climate has been defined as employees' perception that (a) practices and procedures were in place to facilitate the delivery of excellent service, and (b) management rewarded, supported, and expected excellent service.[18] Kordupleski[19] presents a differentiation between 'true quality' that is customer-perceived quality and internal quality, which is business process quality. The customer assesses the true quality during and after his encounter with the service provider. Difference between the expected and perceived quality leads to a phenomenon called disconfirmation—either negative or positive.

In service industries, there are no frontiers separating the employee from the customer, unlike the manufacturing industry where the employee can remain incognito to the customer. The customer experience in service is often interwoven with the feel of the place, the style of delivery, and the way in which services are delivered, and that feel or tactile experience determines the overall customer satisfaction. It is because, when a customer is receiving a service, that service delivery is not an offer of consumption, but rather an individualized and emotional experience. It has thus been argued that to enable the customer to experience delight with services, it is essential to influence employee experience with positive work climate. There are two factors to emphasize in this regard: (a) due to close and frequent employee–customer interfaces in the physical environment through work, talk, and observation, the entire organization, and not merely specific customer-handling staff, should smell quality; (b) there is no margin for correcting the quality, unlike manufacturing, because the exchange occurs in real time.

A study conducted by Schneider and Bowen[20] on 28 branches of a bank sought to test the correlation between five aspects of HRM practices (work facilitation, supervision, organizational career facilitation, organizational status, and new employee socialization) and five aspects of service climate (managerial behavior, systems support, customer attention/retention, logistical support) with five facets of customer service-experience dimensions (courtesy, utility/security, adequate staff, employee morale, and branch administration). The results show that the employees' impressions regarding both service quality and HR practices in their own workplace get mirrored in the customers' experience of service quality. Based on the insights of this research, it becomes imperative that when managers try to improve the customer service quality, they need to turn their attention on both the climate of service and a climate for employee well-being.

17.6.2 TQM in Services and HR Processes

Although the master of TQM had expressed faith in the employees being naturally oriented to quality in their work, given a supportive environment and right tools, the softer processes received less attention in TQM approach, which could be the reason for the majority of TQM failures. In the same way that Purcell had suggested bundling of HR practices to support business strategy, there could also be an alignment of key HR process to create a quality climate.

---

18 B. Schneider and D. E. Bowen, 'The Service Organization: Human Resources Management is Crucial,' *Organizational Dynamics* 21, no. 4 (1993): 39–52.

19 A. J. Kordupleski, R. T. Rust and A. J. Zahorik, 'Why Improving Quality Doesn't Improve Quality (or whatever Happened to Marketing)?' *California Management Review* 35, no. 3 (Spring 1993): 82–95.

20 Ibid.

Recruitment and Selection

The alignment with quality process commences with acquisition of employees with certain orientation, attitude, and behavior that foster quality. A TQM environment requires more of flexibility and customer service-orientation, rather than skill or qualification levels. Even advertisement methods also can be carefully designed to source applicants with necessary orientation, for example, job advertisements based on life themes and key competencies can attract applicants with the desired attitudes. Similarly, selection methods can be designed to test for aptitudes in problem-solving and team-working. A selection process that assesses the compatibility between the candidate and the organization's culture will be more apt. A TQM selection system for a service organization should rely more on assessments of work ethic, personality, teamwork and cooperation, and problem-solving ability than a selection process of a manufacturing organization.

Employee Retention

The retention of key employees is particularly important. For example, experienced sales agent is a key talent in insurance business because of the complexity of the role where the customer needs to be informed that the insurance investment is different from normal investment. The loss of key players, therefore, hurts the business. Similarly, a spate of resignations at Infosys in mid-2017 led the market to speculate on the impact of the turnover on the future of technological innovation work. The key HR task here is to ring fence the strategic talent. The retention reputation builds the employer brand that leads to selection attractiveness, which in turn enhances the firm's ability to recruit employees who fit in with its culture.

High turnover rate can sometimes set in a repetitive process or a 'cycle of failure' where it leads to low productivity, poor service, angry customers, even more discontented workers, and thus leading to another process starting with high turnover.[21] According to Sellers, 'customer retention and employee retention feed one another' and result in quality improvement.[22] The value of the staying employee lies in the fact that his intimate knowledge of organizational 'routines' has deepened with the years spent in the organization, and in the process the customers have also built bonds of trust and expectations. When such an employee leaves, the bonds break as well. This affects the organization in another way. With each important exit, a vacancy chain is set in motion resulting in internal reshuffles that disrupt the normal flow of work in the organization, eventually telling on quality at the end of the chain with external customer.[23]

T&D

Success of implementing TQM program rests heavily on the supportive process of T&D. Studies across several industries have revealed the inadequacies in quality training in service industries, in comparison with other sectors. The deficiencies occur when the focus of training is only on the middle managers, to the neglect of the front-level employees, or the preference for hard tools and not on the soft processes. In successful development of TQM practice, it has been found teamwork processes

---

21 L. A. Schlesinger and J. L. Heskett, 'Breaking the Cycle of Failures in Services,' *Sloan Management Review* 32, no. 3 (1991): 17–28.

22 P. Sellers, 'What Customers Really Want,' *Fortune* (June 4, 1990): 62–70.

23 Tom Redman and Brian P. Mathews, 'Service Quality and Human Resource Management: A Review and Research Agenda,' *Personnel Review* 27, no. 1 (1998): 57–77.

and interpersonal skills are more relevant, especially in services, and the employees do not seem to really apply the knowledge of statistical tools and techniques that they got trained in.[24]

Performance Appraisal

The conventional wisdom in TQM literature is that TQM and performance appraisal are mutually exclusive. Much of Deming's arguments are against the traditional performance appraisal system, on account of failure to (a) desegregate performance failures from systems failure and (b) empower the employee as an essential condition of customer care. In response, the new PMSs that are being evolved with employee performance standards based on customer care indicators, which often combine 'hard' quantifiable measures such as 'delivery of a customer's first drink within two minutes' with soft qualitative standards such as 'a warm and friendly greeting,' as used at Forte Roadside Restaurants, are now used in performance appraisal systems.[25]

The data is gathered through a variety of channels: customer surveys, through electronic surveillance, through 'mystery shopping,' and through internal service-level agreements. The HR has to ensure that the measures of customer care are realistic, achievable, and measurable and to ensure that data gathering process is congenial for employees. For example, mystery shopping that often offends the employees could become more acceptable if used for rewards, and not for punishments and for training purposes.[26]

Rewards

The jury is still out on the usefulness of rewards to develop quality culture, with Deming having asserted that financial rewards undermine the spirit of cooperation necessary for continuous improvement, while the United States' Baldridge Award for quality excellence guidelines prescribing linking of performance reviews, compensation, and rewards to support quality improvement.[27] Several researches, including a survey by KPMG's Peat Marwick, reported a tendency for organizations that had been involved with TQM for a greater period of time to place more reliance on financial incentives to motivate employees to work toward quality improvement. In the final analysis, it does appear that strategies to incentivize quality-related behavior help in reviving waning interest for quality improvement after the first wave marked by managerial push declines.[28]

17.6.3 Normative Models of HRM Work in Services Sector

The Production Line Approach

In the past, before the phenomenal growth in services sector, one influential approach to services sector that held sway was offered by T. Levitt.[29] Levitt sought to correct what he considered the flawed thinking of manufacturing in 'technological terms' and service in 'humanistic terms.' Levitt

---

24 J. R. Hackman and R. Wageman, 'Total Quality Management: Empirical, Conceptual and Practical Issues,' *Administrative Science Quarterly* 40 (1995): 309–342.

25 Internal Revenue Service, 'The Customer is Boss: Matching Employee Performance to Customer Service Needs,' *Employment Trends* 585 (1995): 7–13.

26 S. Cook, *Customer Care: Implementing Total Quality in Today's Service-Driven Organization* (London: Kogan Page, 1992).

27 Hart and Schlesinger, 'Total Quality Management and the Human Resource Professional: Applying the Baldrige Framework to Human Resources,' *Human Resource Management* 30, no. 4 (Winter 1991): 433–454.

28 Redman and Mathews, 'Service Quality and Human Resource Management.'

29 Theodore Levitt, 'Production-Line Approach to Service,' *Harvard Business Review* (Sept–Oct 1972): 41–52.

felt that this was the reason why services sector lagged behind the manufacturing sector. The correct way of thinking, according to him, would be to adhere to certain clear technological principles to service work, namely, (a) simplification of tasks, (b) establishment of a clear division of labor, (c) the application of technology and systems as substitutes for service workers, (d) the development of tighter and more systematic control of service workers, and (e) the reduction of discretion in service jobs.

The aforementioned production line approach has been criticized for contributing to failure in services sector[30] on the ground that it resulted in poor service mentality and employee attrition due to boredom as the work became low skilled and technology-driven. In a chain reaction, it adversely affected customer perception and loyalty and thus the profit level dipped.

The New Service Management School—The Satisfaction Mirror

The New Service Management School, which came as a deviation from the production line approach, relied on what was known as the 'satisfaction mirror.'[31] It indicates a strong positive relationship between customer satisfaction and staff job satisfaction within the service organization. To elaborate the point, when the frontline employees are satisfied, they in turn will render high quality service to the customer. The mirror reflects relatedness between satisfaction of the two actors–the customer and the employee. A correlational analysis between customer satisfaction and overall job satisfaction has been reported in the range of 0.34–0.53. Heskett also suggests that 'the (in)ability to satisfy customers is the primary determinant of frontline workers job (dis)satisfaction.'

According to this formulation, the state of worker satisfaction, which is the source of customer satisfaction, can be achieved through a bouquet of new HR practices that would constitute a kind of 'cycle of capability.' This includes careful selection, high quality training, well-designed support systems, empowerment, teamwork, appropriate measurement, rewards and recognition, and the development of a service culture. The model for achieving 'cycle of success' in interactive service works is known as the high-involvement work systems (HIWS). HRM thus becomes a catalyst in what DuPuy[32] describes as the 'Customer's victory' over the production line approach of the past.

The Cycle of Capability of HRM

Careful selection

The emphasis is on selecting for attitudes or personality traits, 'nice persons,' not so much on technical skills and knowledge.

High quality training

Firms are advised to provide high-quality technical training, which could include 'working with accounting systems in hotels, cash machine procedures in a retail store, underwriting procedures in an insurance company.'[33] Another high valued skill is interactive skills to frontline employees to enhance customer satisfaction. Another powerful training is to foster learning by assigning newly hired workers with high-performing, service-oriented existing workers.

---

30 Schlesinger and Heskett, 'Breaking the Cycle.'

31 J. Heskett, W. E. Sasser, and L. Schlesinger, *The Service Profit Chain* (New York, NY: Free Press, 1997).

32 F. DuPuy, *The Customer's Victory: From Corporation to Co-operation* (London: McMillan, 1999).

33 V. Zeithaml and M. Bitner, *Services Marketing* (New York, NY: McGraw-Hill, 1996).

Well-designed support system

It is emphasized that customer centricity also requires provision for support systems such as IT and physical facilities of the organization. Adequate IT helps the service organizations to make the most in moments of truth situations when the customer comes in contact with the organization.

Empowerment

It is widely recognized that it is essential to dismantle some of the formal web of rules and procedures disabling the frontline employee and to enable him to have sufficient authority to decide on customer requirement and also to quickly recover when things suddenly go wrong in respect of the customer.

Teamwork

It is further imperative to break down functional boundaries between sets of people who impact the customer including the back-end and front-end groups and to create a seamless teamwork to create total customer experience.

Appropriate measurements, rewards, and recognition

In contrast to the company-based measurements that are integral part of production line approach, in this new service management approach, the emphasis is on customer-based measurements. There is an advocacy for both hard and soft customer based standards. There are proponents for rewarding performance with pay and also to intrinsic measures.

Development of service culture

Service connotes performance of work for another. Culture has been defined by *Merriam Webster* as 'a way of thinking, behaving, or working that exists in a place or organization (such as a business).' A service culture emerges when each employee in the organization automatically adapts a customer-centric approach in the performance of their regular work activities. The frontline staff (in sales and services) unfailingly keeps the customer requirements uppermost while offering solutions/support to customer issues. The backend or the support staffs also play their part in contributing to make customer satisfaction happen.

A service organization needs a service culture because it is otherwise impossible to direct the actions of all the employees, scattered over a large geographical spread, to a customer–centric direction otherwise than through building their commitment, which underlies such a culture. It has thus been defined as 'a culture, where an appreciation of good service exists, and where giving good service to internal as well as ultimate, external customers is considered a natural way of life and one of the most important norms by everyone.'[34]

A combination of well-designed support systems and aligned HRM practices unleash a virtuous cycle of capability whereby the resultant passion for service by the employees convince the customers of the service quality that in turn results in job satisfaction of the employees. Thus, a win-win-win scenario is created in the service triangle.[35]

The premises of the service management school have similarities with earlier approaches, a prominent example being the principles laid down by Peters and Waterman in *Search of Excellence* and also in the concepts of TQM and BPR. The customer-centricity is reminiscent of 'close to the customer

34 Gronroos, *Service Management and Marketing.*

35 Marek Korczynski, *Human Resource Management in Service Work* (UK: Palgrave MacMillan, 2001).

theme' of Peters and Waterman; the TQM approach of customer orientation, process orientation and continuous improvement, and 'value to the customer' implanted in BPR approach.

The criticism against the new service management line is its underpinnings of an essentially unitarist philosophy. Second, research on the subject does not provide any evidence of the efficacy of the approach.

George Ritzer's Concept of Macdonaldization

Another important perspective for looking at service work is provided by George Ritzer in his thesis on Macdonaldization of society. The key concept here is bureaucracy that has an underlying logic of formal rationality. Ritzer argues that Macdonald's is a clear model of this process of rationality in its extreme form. Macdonaldization has four components:

- **Efficiency** The optimal method for accomplishing a task. For a McDonald's customer, it is the fastest way to get from being hungry to being full. In the context of the organization, the implication of efficiency is the minimization of time.
- **Calculability** Objective should be quantifiable (e.g., sales) rather than subjective (e.g., taste). The equivalent of a high quality product in this context is the delivery of a large amount of product to the customer in a short amount of time. Customers are thus able to quantify how much they are getting versus how much they are paying. Organizations want consumers to believe that they are getting a large amount of product for not a lot of money. Workers in these organizations are judged by how fast they are instead of the quality of work they do.
- **Predictability** It implies guaranteed occurrence irrespective of time and place. As far as workers are concerned, they are required to perform highly repetitive, routine, and predictable work.
- **Control** The ability of one party to determine an entire process. It also implies substitution of people with technology.

Ritzer argues that 'the process of Macdonaldization is leading to the creation of more and more McJobs. The services sector, especially at the lower end is producing an enormous number of jobs, most of them requiring little or no skills.' He also opines that the worker is thus reduced to being a 'mechanical nut.' Ritzer describes a process of deskilling the service sectors worker to the extent that not only their actions but the script of what they will speak are also controlled. The unprecedented system of control dehumanizes the workers and turns them into robots so that they even lose their ability to resist.

du Gay–Enterprising Self

du Gay argues that the customer-centricity is embedded in the organizational structures, practices, and technologies in such a way that it seems to be relied upon to justify all management actions. He also offers the concept of 'enterprising self.' To elaborate, the worker in a service organization is required to be enterprising and the customer also does likewise. Instead of being determined by roles, the individual worker as also the customer are looking to create their identity and find meaning.

Feminist Analyses

The proponents of this approach argue that bureaucratic organizations have usually a hidden gender bias and women employees find themselves at a disadvantage as compared to their male counterparts.

The structures and processes are built on assumptions of men. There is, therefore, a need to deconstruct and analyze HR policies for concealed gender subtext.

In the end, all the aforementioned schools have their own implications on HR policies, as shown in Table 17.1.

Table 17.1 Implications for HRM on different perspectives on service work

Perspectives	Implications for content of HR policies	Implications for interpreting HR policies and their effect on service workforce
New Service Management School	Policies to achieve cycle of capability	HR practices develop win-win scenario. Highly satisfied and motivated workforce created.
Ritzer-Macdonaldization	Cost minimizing and bureaucratic policies	HRM as part of an overall process of dehumanization. Workers increasingly become robot-like.
du Gay	Imposition of market relations; development of enterprising culture	HRM as part of wider tantalizing discourse of the enterprising self. Workers increasingly conceive of themselves in enterprising terms.
Feminist analyses	HRM policies to achieve customers' (gendered) expectations of service quality	HRM policies as gendered. Workforce increasingly subject to gender-based servility.

Source: Korczynski, *Human Resources Management in Service Work*, 55.

To conclude the discussion on approaches, it is pertinent to refer to another classification of HRM approaches—the hard and the soft approaches. While the aforementioned perspectives fall in the classification of soft HRM approaches, other writers[36,37] tend to dispute the existence of the 'soft' side of HRM approaches in the service sector. Instead, contingent and well-calculating 'hard' HRM approaches are more often adopted by services firms in their utilization of human resource.[38] The hard approach is seen to be an instrumental and economically rational approach to HRM. In this view, people management practices are driven by strategic considerations to gain competitive advantage, maximizing control, while achieving the lowest possible labor cost. This approach is quantitative and calculative, and labor is considered to be a commodity and resource.

17.7 SOME SPECIFIC INDUSTRIES IN SERVICES SECTOR

17.7.1 Hospitality Industry

HRM Approaches

1. On a conceptual level, a number of studies have highlighted an essential paradox in the hospitality industry—between standardization and customization. From one particular research conducted on a large American hotel chain covering the USA and several European countries,

[36] Hoque, 'New Approaches to HRM in the UK Hotel Industry,' *Human Resources Management Journal* 9, no. 2 (1999): 64–76. Francis and D'Annunzio-Green 2005.

[37] P. Worsfold, 'HRM, Performance, Commitment and Service Quality in the Hotel Industry,' *International Journal of Contemporary Hospitality Management* 11, no. 7 (1999): 340–348.

[38] R. Lucas, 'Fragments of HRM in Hospitality? Evidence from the 1998 Workplace Employee Relations Survey,' *International Journal of Contemporary Hospitality Management* 14, no. 5 (2002): 207–212.

it was found that while empowerment was high, and both hiring and training focused on customer service skills, the hotel employees were still subject to pervasive performance measurement.[39] Another study by Shamir[40] on UK hotels reported the duality between a demand for flexibility and a demand for high degree of control and coordination. These studies capture an almost universal struggle experienced in hotels for a balance between customer orientation and rationalization for cost control.

A large number of hotels, in particular, have historically been dominated by images of poor working conditions and underdeveloped HR practices, which largely focus on cost control, instead of employee commitment. It may appear reasonable that an organization choosing to compete in a labor-intensive, high-volume, low-cost industry is likely to adopt HRM policies that treat employees as a variable input or a cost to minimize.

Indian Hotels

The Indian Hotels Company Limited (IHCL) and its subsidiaries are collectively known as Taj Hotels Resorts and Palaces, and is recognized as one of Asia's largest and finest hotel companies. Incorporated by the founder of the Tata Group, Mr Jamsetji N. Tata, the company opened its first property, Taj Mahal Palace hotel, Bombay, in 1903. The Taj, a symbol of Indian hospitality, completed its centenary year in 2003.

Taj Hotels Resorts and Palaces comprises 93 hotels in 55 locations across India with an additional 16 international hotels in the Maldives, Malaysia, Australia, the UK, the USA, Bhutan, Sri Lanka, Africa, and the Middle East.

Taj Hotel is well known for its innovative HR practices. One of the oft quoted philosophies behind their hiring and training practices is 'The employees can be trained to be better chefs or waiters, but they cannot be taught to be good individuals.'

- Build Leaders—Each employee is given an authority to take the decisions pertaining to his work and this empowers them and helps in building a leader in all.
- Some of their HR initiatives include Employee Satisfaction Tracking System (ESTS) and Special Thanks and Recognition System (STAR). In 2002, they were awarded Hermes Award for their HR practices.

The Taj Group of Hotels, however, would appear to be a tiny minority in the Indian hotel industry who are committed to proactive HRM. The Federation of Hotel & Restaurant Associations of India (FHARI) Annual Report (2009–2010) revealed the average staff turnover in five-star deluxe hotels in India is 24.14%. The Indian hospitality industry is characterized by a weak internal labor market. There is a stream of 10,000 hospitality students graduating every year (Ministry of HRD, Government of India) from various public and private institutions. However, the management trainee positions are merely restricted to about 100–150. Most graduates join as operations trainees and then wait for another few years to become management trainees. The working condition in most hotels in India apart from top luxury brands leaves a lot to be desired. The attrition rates are high.

---

[39] C. Jones, G. Taylor, and D. Nickson, 'Whatever It Takes? Managing 'Empowered' Employees and the Service Encounter in an International Hotel Chain,' *Work, Employment and Society* 11, no. 3 (1997): 541–554.

[40] B. Shamir, 'Between Bureaucracy and Hospitality: Some Organizational Characteristics of Hotels,' *Journal of Management Studies* 15, no. 3 (1978): 285–307.

Long work hours with low compensation motivates employee to look for greener pastures. Many of the multinational brands act as a training ground for interns who later take up more lucrative assignments elsewhere. The reason for shifting jobs are slight increments in salary, lack of openness in the work environment, and almost no norm for sharing of concerns by employees. The employee-to-room ratio is extremely high. Hotels deploy more people rather than investing in a multi-skilled task force.

Kusluvan[41] in his study 'Managing Employee Attitudes and Behaviours in the Tourism and Hospitality Industry' observed that normative HR practices have largely not been implemented in industry, although some improvements have begun to be noted, once again in larger organizations. For example, recruitment and selection is generally conducted intuitively and unprofessionally, orientation and training has largely been neglected for both management and the employees, although this is starting to improve somewhat in larger organizations where service quality and consumer satisfaction have been recognized as important; there continues to be lack of opportunity for promotion and career development, although evidence of the use of internal labor markets has begun to be found, the industry continues to be notorious for its low wages and lack of benefits, particularly at lower organizational levels; results of empowerment and employee participation are mixed, with some studies finding increasing relates and others suggesting managers are becoming increasingly hierarchical and autocratic, and the industry can be characterized by a poor leadership style with managers largely being described as poorly equipped to manage professionally and as exhibiting unbridled individualism, although a more consultative approach has begun to be observed in some chain hotels.

17.7.2 Health Care

Like many other sectors, winds of change have been blowing in health care sector also for over two decades now. The emphasis has been on structural change, cost containment, and introduction of market mechanisms while the importance of HRM has often been overlooked.[42] The shift has been from the rule of professionals to that of the customer. The shift to 'customer'-oriented policies has also seen systematic pressures to rationalize health care production, increase efficiency, and cut costs.

The motto for the hospitals is to keep the manpower levels to a minimum without undermining their concern for quality health care. Health care employees expect their employers to provide infrastructure, HR practices, and support, which they can link to improved performance, especially in relation to patient care and service innovations. At the same time, effort is maintained toward immediate patient care even when employee expectations remain unmet.[43] The duality may create a blur in the focus of the health care. If the customer is the king instead of the consultant, there is the risk of the nursing domain seeing the intrusion of non-medical managers with the aid of performance appraisals and the 'targets.'

---

41 S. Kusluvan. (Ed.), 'Characteristics of Employment and Human Resource Management in the Tourism and Hospitality Industry,' In *Managing Employee Attitudes and Behaviors in the Tourism and Hospitality Industry* (New York, NY: Nova Science, 2003).

42 Keith Townsend and Adrian Wilkinson, 'Managing Under Pressure: HRM in Hospitals,' *Human Resource Management Journal* 20 (2010): 332–338.

43 P. Hyde, C. Harris, R. Boaden, and P. Cortvriend, 'Human Relations Management, Expectations and Healthcare: A Qualitative Study,' *Human Relations* 62, no. 5 (2009): 701–725.

Indian Context—Report of a Study

There are some studies that address the health care sector in the Indian context but most of these features either the rural or the public sector hospitals and health care facilities. The existing studies are mostly on health care facilities of rural India[44–46] and education about health in urban India.[47] There are very few studies in the Indian public health care context that focus on influence of HR practices on doctors' work attitudes, including professional and organizational commitment.[48]

A seminal study conducted by Avantika Tomar and Amit Dhiman[49] covered a hospital that was established in 1999 and, within a time span of nine years, the group had 26 running hospitals (including 11 satellite/heart command centers) with several more in the pipeline. The findings show that the emphasis is more on supreme hospitality and patient amenities than medical treatment. The health care industry is witnessing a significant change. A consultant is no longer the 'king'; this position has now been taken by the patients. Of late, the emphasis is on patient satisfaction in terms of the facilities provided rather than the nature of medical treatment given. This is primarily so for organizations, such as this hospital, which aim at providing world-class care and for which 'patient-centricity' is the hallmark. HR specific issues such as standardization of nursing activities, appraisal systems, effective communication channels, and compensation structure, all affect the quality of service provided in a hospital.

17.7.3 Call Centers

The need for call center arose out of BPR initiatives and organizations found it attractive for two key reasons: first, the logic of efficiency, a potential for a dramatic reduction in costs per customer transaction, as compared to face-to-face interactions; second, the opportunity to reconfigure the processes to align to the customer preferences (e.g., transactions outside normal duty hours and one-stop shop for their problems). However, as it turned out, there were unforeseen negative consequences. The work pressures of uninterrupted and endless sequence of repetitive conversations with customers the employee never meets created enormous pressures as did the long hours of work. Thus, the work experience, in the words of Arzbächer,[50] fell in between 'neo-Taylorism and customer orientation' and the workplace appeared similarly hanging between 'modern sweatshops and positive modern workplace.'

---

44 M. Pathak, V. A. Ketkar, R. D. Majumdar, 'Perceived Morbidity, Utilization of Health Services and Factor Affecting it in a Rural Area,' *Health and Population Perspective and Issues* 4, no. 1 (1981):79–85.

45 L. Bhandari and S. Dutta, 'Health Infrastructure in Rural India,' In *India Infrastructure Report 2007: Rural Infrastructure*, edited by P. Kalra and A. Rastogi, 265–285 (New Delhi: Oxford University Press, 2007).

46 J. Sharma and R. Narang, 'Quality of Healthcare Services in Rural India: The User Perspective,' *Vikalpa* 36 (2011): 51–60.

47 L. Bhandari, 'Social Infrastructure: *U*rban Health and *E*ducation,' India Infrastructure Report (2006): 232–257.

48 Maheshwari, Sunil Kumar, Bhat Ramesh and Dhiman Amit, 'Implications of Human Resource Practices and Other Structural Factors on Commitment of Public Medical Professionals in India,' IIMA Working Papers WP2007-08-04 (Ahmedabad: Indian Institute of Management Ahmedabad, Research and Publication Department, 2007).

49 Avantika Tomar and Amit Dhiman, 'Exploring the Role of HRM in Service Delivery in Healthcare Organizations: A Study of an Indian Hospital,' *Vikalpa* 38, no. 2 (2013): 21–38.

50 Sandra Arzbächer, Ursula Holtgrewe, and Christian Kerst, 'Call Centers: Constructing Flexibility,' Paper presented at the Workshop 'Are Regimented Forms of Work Organisation Inevitable? Call Centres and the Chances for an Innovative Organisation of Service Work in Europe,' December 2–3, 2000, Gerhard Mercator University of Duisburg, Duisburg. Available at: https://www. researchgate.net/publication/48667053_Call_centres_constructing_flexibility (accessed on November 17, 2017).

The implications for HRM are similarly dual. Both hard and soft HR approaches became necessary. The HRM practices included training, development of interpersonal and problem-solving skills, and provision of resources to support employees. From the limited group of studies conducted so far, it appears that the success of service businesses is reliant on the delivery of quality customer service, which in turn depends on employee commitment and satisfaction. The focus of HRM on recruitment, training and skill development, as well as on resource support is the key to enhance employee commitment and satisfaction, which in turn increase the service capacity and ultimately better overall firm performance.[51,52]

Call Centers in India

There are three delivery methods for contact centers: on-premise, hosted, or cloud-based. In case of on-premise system, the hardware and software is set up deployed and maintained in the premises of the contact center. An outside service provider is relied upon for a hosted system. Cloud computing uses physical resources like processors and storage as Internet resources. (Available at: http://www.callcentertimes. com/Articles/tabid/59/ctl/NewsArticle)

The Indian Contact Center (Call Center) Market is one of the fastest growing and competitive markets in the world with a CAGR of 45% over the past five years. An Overview Report on Contact Center Outsourcing Industry in India has considered the hosted contact center approach with its utility-based pricing model, on demand capacity, and virtualization/integration capabilities as the best solution for success.[53]

Major drivers low investments

1. **Investment required is modest** Be it inbound call center or telemarketing, lead generation profile of outbound call center, cost of operations or overheads get reduced to half.
2. **Geographic advantage** India has the time zone advantage. The 12-hour time difference enables global organizations to provide their customers with 24 × 7 × 365 days services. By taking this advantage of time difference, companies have been able to ensure that their customers receive round-the-clock customer support.
3. **Latest technology** Contact centers in India employ latest technology, software, and high-end infrastructure to provide high-quality customer support services.
4. With privatization and reduction in the tariff of Internet services and cellular services, India has an advantage over other locations in terms of infrastructure.
5. **Quality of service delivery** Contact centers are synonyms of quality. The agents are overseen for the call waiting time, average time to answer, number of calls taken to monitor the quality of service given to the clients.

---

[51] Little, M. M., and Dean, A. M., 'Links Between Service Climate, Employee Commitment and Employees' Service Quality Capability,' *Managing Service Quality* 16, no. 5 (2006): 460–476.

[52] Tsaur, S.H. and Lin, Y.C., 'Promoting Service Quality in Tourist Hotels: The Role of HRM Practices and Service Behavior,' *Tourism Management* 25, no. 4 (2004): 471–481.

[53] Lahiri and Pangrikar, 'An Overview Report on Contact Center Outsourcing Industry in India,' *Global Journal of Management and Business Studies* 3, no. 3 (2013): 295–302.

17.8 TRADE UNIONS IN SERVICES SECTOR

Case Trade Unions Fight to Find a Foothold in Retail Industry

Twenty-four-year-old Amit wades through sacks of rice and wheat in the air-conditioned aisles of Big Bazaar, a supermarket in central Mumbai that belongs to the country's large listed retailer, Pantaloon Retail India Ltd. In his hot pink T-shirt and shiny black shoes, sales assistant Amit, who did not give his second name, looks like one of the many young shoppers that the store attracts.

With its blaring music, buzzing nightclubs, bowling alleys and television screens, the mall complex where the store is located is a world away from the nearby textile mill where Amit's father worked for 30 years. 'If the workers came inside, they would never recognize where they worked,' Amit says. Yet, the reinvented mall is seeing the rise of one of the ubiquitous symbols of Mumbai's mills—trade unions.

Amit, whose father was a unionized textile worker, is part of a group of 200 Pantaloon employees that claims to have formed a union under the banner of the Bharatiya Kamgar Sena (BKS), an arm of local right-wing party, the Shiv Sena. In March, the union shut down four of Mumbai's Big Bazaar stores, protesting against the sacking of 12 workers hired to work at a store whose opening was delayed.

Mumbai's textile mills bred one of country's strongest union movements, where migrants from across the state and the country fought for benefits and eight-hour work days, among other things.

The retail unions are nowhere close to being as powerful. The newly formed unions at Big Bazaar and Metro AG, a German retailer with two stores, are still finding their feet. They are fighting for better pay, shorter hours, faster promotions, staff rooms, educational and medical facilities, and other benefits. The union at Big Bazaar hopes for higher increments this year. Starting salaries for employees have gone up to ₹3,800 a month from ₹2,800 when Amit started three-and-a-half years ago.

The first trade union in an organized retail chain in India is in the process of being registered at Metro. It is fighting the company over the sacking of its members in labor court. Pantaloon and Metro have not recognized the unions.

'Wherever we tried to form unions in Mumbai and Bangalore, the staff members were fired. We are now trying to form a general union including mall workers,' says M.K. Pandhe, general secretary of the Communist Party of India (Marxist)'s Centre of Indian Trade Unions.

Most jobs in retail are not permanent; instead, employees are hired on contract and can be more easily fired than permanent employees. That makes it difficult for the workers to form unions.

'It is hard for mall workers to be unionized. Their jobs are largely unorganized,' says L.K. Deshpande, a labor economist at Mumbai University.

The Shiv Sena has been more successful than the CPM in making inroads in this sector. 'We start by giving written petitions to managements. Then we send reminders. But if they don't respond, we storm their offices and they are forced to recognize us,' says Suryajant Mahadik of BKS, whose union operates in city hotels, airports, banks, ports and auto firms across the city.

The unions at Big Bazaar and Metro say they have been around for more than a year without the companies recognizing them.

Sanjay Jog, who heads HR at Pantaloon, says the company does not have a union. However, he admits that Pantaloon downed shutters in four stores because of an employee protest.

Jog says the company has a grievance redressal mechanism through which it regularly talks to all employees. He adds that the company tries to hire staff who belong to the area adjoining its stores as far as possible. Jog claims a majority of staff at the company's Parel store are children of textile mill workers.

A spokesperson for Metro, too, says the company does not have a union. 'Metro Cash & Carry is an equal opportunity employer and has ... HR procedures which are practised globally,' he adds in a written statement.

Internationally, too, employees have not found it easy to form unions in retail chains. Wal-Mart Stores, Inc. has always been opposed to them, for instance. Although retail is India's second largest employer, after agriculture, only 4% of the more than $300 billion (₹12.2 trillion) retail market is organized, according to some estimates. With organized retail growing at around 40% a year, the sector could add up to 2 million jobs, according to the Retailers Association of India, an industry body.

The retail unions claim that even as they fight for recognition, they are beginning to make a difference. Big Bazaar union member Mayur Vankar says workers now put in nine-hour shifts compared with 12-hour days earlier. At Metro, union member Kartik Shekhar says, the company now makes provident fund payments for all employees.

Both unions say they have represented cashiers who may have been asked to personally make up for shortfalls in cash collection. They need to do more, says Deshpande. Given the demand for jobs, unions need to under-score the need for them to be there, he says. 'Not everyone in this sector wants to be in a union because there are no comparable jobs that are better,' he adds.

Amit knows that being part of a union can cut both ways. His father stayed jobless for four years after his textile mill shut down in 1999. Mumbai's textile mill owners preferred to relocate or down shutters rather than deal with unions. Amit dropped out of college and took the Big Bazaar job in desperation after his father waited for years for his dues. Amit's father now works as a security guard in a mill-turned-mall and refuses to talk to *Mint* because he is scared that he could lose this job, too.

Amit's peers are either jobless or have harder jobs without the medical and continuing education opportunities he now has. Amit himself hopes to graduate this year and stay on in the retail business. Pantaloon offers a retail MBA program for graduates in association with a few B-schools. Smiling shyly, Amit says he is aware that there is a buzz around the retail business these days.

Discussion Questions

1. Many employers do not want unions in their industry.
2. What is your view about unionization in the services sector?
3. What constructive role can the unions play to balance the employees' interests with those of the business?

Source: Saumya Roy, *Live Mint*, August 6, 2007.

17.8.1 Decline of Trade Unions in Service Industry

Globally, trade unions are often seen as symbolic of the dyeing historical legacy from the time of manufacturing sovereignty. In the USA and the UK, the numbers have dwindled (14% in the USA, 30% in the UK). In India, the trade union density is cited as 9% only. The decline has been largely attributed to the emergence of the services sector. There are several barriers to the functioning of trade unions in a services sector.

On the basis of research, it is observed that union membership tends to grow with the size of the organization. In services sector, because of the simultaneity of production and consumption, the locations get decentralized and the size smaller (one study conducted in US industries put the size of a services sector location at one-fourth of the manufacturing location).

The rise in services sector has also coincided with a shift in the composition of the workforce. Globally, it is observed that more women and part-timers have been joining the workforce, and the unions find it less easy to mobilize such groups. The high rate of attrition in the services sector also discourages unionization.

17.9 MODELS OF UNION STRATEGIES

Essentially trade unions choose out of two alternate strategies depending on the nature of workplace relations between the employer and the union. If the perception is that there is a great potential for cooperation in the service work, then unions have an option to adapt what is known as the social partnership approach. Conversely, if service work is increasingly mired in conflict, then an organizing model is deemed appropriate where union would encroach on no-union areas and assert themselves.

Indian Scene

In India, services sector is partly unionized. Traditional services such as hospitals, hotels, government enterprises and offices have had unions, and employers such as the house of Tatas and ITC have been public in their tolerant view about employees organizing unions. However, the new service industries such as IT and ITeS have successfully remained union-free. There are also examples of deunionization of industries.

Unionization at BPOT

To counter the general democratic deficit within Indian BPO, union for ITeS employees (UNITES) was formed in September 2005 following an initiative by global union federation Union Network International (UNI) through its Indian Liaison Committee, preparatory organizing efforts under the provisionally named Centre for Business Process Outsourcing Professionals (CBPOP) and an organizational break from the Information Technology Professionals Forum (ITPF) which orientates on software/IT professionals.[54] UNITES was therefore the first explicit attempt to give BPO employees an independent voice.

17.9.1 Trade Unionism in BPOs

The BPO-ITeS industry in India came about in the late 1990s, and as of 2012, employed around 2.8 million. Annual revenues are around US$11 billion, around 1% of GDP. There has been controversies

---

54 Hirschfeld, 'IT Professional's Forum in India: Organization at a Crossroads' (Nyon: Unted Network International).

about the status of BPO-ITeS employees who according to a recent report by a government-sponsored labor institute (V. V. Giri National Institute of Labor, India) are compared to galley of slaves in the Roman ships. Some Indian writers—such as Praful Bidwai and Chetan Bhagat—have criticized BPO-ITeS industries for exploiting workers and making them work as cyber coolies.[55]

Commenting on the work environment in Indian BPOs, some researchers have talked about a 'democratic deficit,' stating that there is evidence that customary Indian hierarchical work cultures have been transposed to BPO, and not merely to its third-party and domestic segments.[56] There are reports on high-handedness by manager/supervisory staff, arbitrariness, harsh punishments including dismissals on flimsy or no reasons. Employee communications are always top-down[57] and employee-engagement initiatives aim solely at raising productivity and quality, and not at employee participation in management.[58] Finally, under-scoring this deficit, although many UK offshoring companies recognize trade unions, they do not extend this right to their Indian operations. In fact, industry analysts and ITeS trade body of India (NASSCOM) have called the idea of a union preposterous, because workers do not desire union in this sector. According to industry analysts, unionization of BPO-ITeS industry may drive away customers and cause a threat to the 'India Advantage' factor.

The first effort to form association among BPO employees was made in 2000, and the second ongoing effort since 2004. Eventually, UNITES was formed in September 2005, arising out of a move by global union federation UNI (Union Network International) through its Indian Liaison Committee, preparatory organizing efforts under the provisionally named Center for Business Outsourcing Professionals (CBOP) and an organizational break from the ITPF that orientates on software/IT professionals.[59] UNITES was therefore the first explicit endeavor to give BPO employees an independent voice.

The UNITES' founders, conscious of employer hostility to trade unionism and of employees' powerful sense of professional identity, promoted UNITES as 'a community of professionals,' sharing data, advice, and training facilities for its members to help them with their careers. Surmounting bureaucratic barriers, UNITES obtained legal status through the Labor Commission in Karnataka and gained 'Provisional Affiliation' to Indian National Trade Union Congress (INTUC). It had organizing centers/'chapters' in Bangalore, Hyderabad, New Delhi, Chennai, Mumbai, and Kochi.[60] The distinction between fully paid-up members (600 rupees per annum)[61] and those paying an initial registration (100 rupees) is important. Officers report a willingness to pay the initial fee but some difficulty in translating 'sign-ups' into full membership. Thus, it is helpful to think of UNITES membership as stratified, with a committed core and a looser periphery, surrounded again by non-members who comprise a broader, interested constituency.

---

55 A. Sandhu, 'Why Unions Fail in Organizing India's BPO-ITES Industry,' *Economic and Political Weekly* 14 (October 2006): 4319–4322.

56 P. Taylor and P. Bain, 'Work Organisation and Employee Relations in Indian Call Centres,' in *Developments in the Call Centre Industry*, eds. J. Burgess and J. Connell (Abingdon: Routledge, 2006).

57 Nasscom, 'Strategy Review 2003: The IT Industry in India,' (New Delhi: Nasscom, 2003).

58 R. Batt, V. Doellgast, H. Kwon, M. Nopany, P. Nopany, and A. da Costa, 'The Indian Call Centre Industry: National Benchmarking Report Strategy, HR Practices, & Performance,' CAHRS Working Paper 05–07 (Ithaca, NY: School of Industrial and Labor Relations, Center for Advanced Human Resource Studies, Cornell University, 2005).

59 Hirschfeld, 'IT Professional's Forum in India: Organization at a Crossroads.'

60 UNITES, 'Review of UNITES @ One,' (Bangalore: UNITES, 2006).

61 Ibid.

According to findings of a research conducted on trade union mobilization in Indian call centers, although 7000 recruits were claimed by late 2006, the general secretary estimated full membership at 700–1,000 (interview November 19, 2006).[62]

The reasons explored in the aforementioned research as to why employees join UNITES, the reasons were found to be several, the most common being the instrumental basis (individualist/ collectivist) to improve compensation and working conditions and to obtain information/advice about rights. Interview evidence in the research reveals several instances where UNITES had intervened externally and internally on behalf of employees over pay-related grievances (the withholding of pay/bonuses, unpaid overtime, under-paying). Others expressed the view that while UNITES could not impact pay rates in the short term, its future ability to do so influenced decisions to join. Clearly for members in domestics who benefit from the collective agreements, their responses reflect a more immediate, explicitly collectivist reality.

News Item 1—Nurses of Private Hospitals Continue Strike

Hundreds of nurses from three corporate hospitals boycotted work on Saturday, as a result of which hospitals deployed their nursing students and tutors to attend to the patients. While the nurses of Madras Medical Mission, Mogappair, continued their strike on Saturday, those in Fortis Malar Hospital, Adyar, and Apollo Hospitals, Greams Road, also struck work.

According to Jinu Varghese, secretary of All India Private Nurses' Association, around 60 nurses in Malar Hospital had been issued suspension orders and male nurses had been asked to vacate the hostel in Thiruvanmiyur. In both hospitals, the nurses plan to continue their strike, Mr Varghese said. A representative of the 800 nurses on strike at Apollo Hospitals said that they would continue their strike on Sunday and stick to their demand for a monthly salary of ₹15,000.

In a press release, Brig. Joe Curian, CEO, Madras Medical Mission, said that at the end of an eight-hour discussion with the representatives of the striking nurses and the Additional Commissioner of Labor C. Somburajan on Friday, the management had agreed to discuss the nurses' demand of ₹15,000 as salary and that a decision would be announced on March 19. It would return nurses' certificates after verification; provide double payment for overtime instead of extra weekly offs and issue experience certificate after one year of service.

The management would not insist on executing bonds and has sought a notice of 14 days from nurses for going on strike. It has also stated that participants of the strike would not be penalised but salary would not be paid to those participating. According to Mr Curian, the nurses were continuing their strike despite agreeing to rejoin duty on Saturday. Global Hospitals, MIOT Hospitals and Billroth Hospitals issued a joint statement along with the three affected hospitals stating that indirect benefits such as accommodation, transportation and meals provided to the nurses formed part of the overall remuneration package. 'Beyond these costs incurred by the hospital organization, as mentioned, an enormous amount is spent on training the nurses and skill building for which the nurses are not charged,' the statement said.

[62] Ibid.

Salaries for nurses are commensurate with their qualification, said A. K. Ravi Kumar, secretary, Tamil Nadu Private Nursing Homes Board. According to him, the demand for paramedical staff is high across the world, and hence the high attrition. Corporate hospitals are only slightly better off as they can fall back on nursing students until they finish their education.

'Since qualified nurses move for better salary, most of the small and medium hospitals contend with poorly trained nurses. To prevent this, we have proposed that the smaller institutions which send their students to us for six months training should register with the Board,' he said.

Discussion Questions

1. Should employees working in services industry resort to strike? What is the impact of the strike onthe customers?
2. What specific HRM interventions are required to prevent the possibility of disruption of servicesby way of work stoppage by employees in services industry?

Source: R. Sujatha, *The Hindu*, March 4, 2012.

News Item 2—Apollo Hospitals Management Too Gives in

The management of Apollo Hospitals reached an agreement with the striking nurses on Thursday evening, bringing to close the week-long agitation by nurses from various private hospitals in the city.

'The impasse has been resolved,' said V. Satyanarayana Reddy, CEO, Apollo Hospitals, in a brief statement. Monthly emoluments for nurses had been fixed at ₹12,000. They will get 'a speciality/JCI weightage in addition,' he said. He expressed confidence that the nurses would return to work for the first shift on Friday morning.

Thursday began with nurses in Apollo Specialty Hospital, Teynampet, and Apollo First Med Hospital, Poonamallee High Road, joining the strike. According to them, even as they kept out of the hospital, representatives of the Apollo Welfare Association for Registered Nurse held discussions with the management. The stalemate continued throughout the day and hundreds of nurses, most of them in their twenties, marched from Rajaratnam Stadium in Egmore to Langs Garden Road, carrying placards and raising slogans.

Earlier in the day, Mr Reddy had issued a statement terming the strike illegal and requesting the nurses to 'please allow us to provide high standards of patient care.'

He clarified that he had already placed his offer with the unions, and that it was the best in industry package effective April 2012. He further said that the hospital outcomes depend on 'coordinated effort of the entire hospital team and not only the nursing community.'

He noted that 'the number of occupied beds had been slightly scaled down' as it was the hospital's policy never to compromise on patient safety and care.

Also, student/trainee nurses provided bedside support and not clinical care to patients who had come from various locations in the country and did not want to go elsewhere.

Even as the nurses' demonstration on Langs Garden Road concluded and their representatives held discussions with the hospital's management, the Greams Road Apollo

Hospitals was a picture of quiet on Thursday night. A family from Oman waiting outside the hospital said they had admitted a patient on Wednesday.

Discussion Questions

1. If you had to do an HR audit at Apollo Hospital after the resumption of duties by the nurses, what questions would you ask and from whom?
2. What did the situation reflect on the state of HRM function at the hospital? What went wrong?
3. What would be the strengths of the organization in the case that you would use?

Source: R. Sujatha, 'Nurses' Strike Pays Off,' *The Hindu,* March 9, 2012.

SUMMARY

The services sector is considered to be engine of India's economic growth. According to a recent report published by the CII and KPMG, India has moved up to become the fastest-growing service economy in the world. It contributed around 66.1% of its gross value-added growth in 2015–2016, thereby emerging as an important net foreign exchange earner and the most attractive sector for FDI inflows. According to the CSO assessments, the growth in this sector is pegged at 8.8% in 2016–2017. According to a report by leading research firm Market Research Store, the Indian telecommunication services market is expected to grow by 10.3% year-on-year to reach US$103.9 billion by 2020.

There are five main differences between service and manufacturing organizations: the tangibility of their output; production on demand or for inventory; customer-specific production; labor-intensive or automated operations; and the need for a physical production location. However, in practice, service and manufacturing organizations share many characteristics. Many manufacturers offer their own service operations and both require skilled people to create a profitable business.

Traditionally, the HR function consisted of five sets of activities: planning, staffing, compensation, employee training and employee relations, and performance management. Given that these existing HRM practices were developed in the context of manufacturing, the emergence of the services sector signaled a shift in the paradigm. The focus has shifted to address the need to pursue high quality services, via a set of sophisticated 'high cost and high skill employment strategies' (Francis and D'Annunzio-Green 2005, 71).

Unlike the traditional manufacturing industry, a service organization needs a service culture because it is otherwise impossible to direct the actions of all the employees scattered over large geographical spread, to a customer–centric direction otherwise than through building their commitment, which underlies such a culture. It has thus been defined as 'a culture, where an appreciation of good service exists, and where giving good service to internal as well as ultimate, external customers is considered a natural way of life and one of the most important norms by everyone.'[63]

One of the controversial aspects of the service culture having implications on HRM is the way work is organized. One of the methods has been described as the process of 'Macdonaldization,' which is breaking the work into atomic units. According to Ritzer, the services sector especially at the lower end is producing an enormous number of jobs, most of them requiring little or no skills. He

[63] Gronroos, Service *Management and Marketing.*

also opines that the worker is thus reduced to being a 'mechanical nut.' Ritzer describes a process of deskilling the services sector workers to the extent that not only their actions but the scripts of what they will speak are also controlled. The unprecedented system of control dehumanizes the workers and turns them into robots so that they even lose their ability to resist.

The new services sector is known to prefer union-free workplace, and thus intent on creating a workplace culture of employee engagement and decent HR practices. In the traditional industries in services sector, there is partial unionization. Traditional services such as hospitals, hotels, government enterprises and offices have had unions, and employers such as the house of Tatas and ITC have been public in their tolerant view about employees organizing unions. However, the new service industries such as IT and ITeS have successfully remained union-free. There are also examples of deunionization of industries.

Short-answer Questions

1. Why is services sector important in India?
2. What is the role played by HRM in the services sector?
3. Explain tangibility.
4. What are the five main points of difference between the services sector and manufacturing sector?
5. How does simultaneity of production and consumption process affect HRM in the services sector?
6. Describe service climate.
7. What is production line approach?
8. How does reward system impact service culture?
9. Explain satisfaction mirror.
10. What are the four components of George Ritzer's concept of Macdonaldization?

Discussion Questions

1. Explain the factors that differentiate services sector from manufacturing sector.
2. How does the 'soft' approach to HRM vary from the 'hard' approach of HRM?
3. What are some challenges faced by different industries in India? How are they being currently met?
4. Are trade unions an anachronism in the services sector?
5. What is satisfaction mirror? How does it impact the HR role in an organization?
6. What are the important activities that constitute the cycle of capability of HRM?
7. What would be the relevance of the new approaches of HRM for the manufacturing sector?

CLUSTER 9

INNOVATE AND TRANSFORM

Chapter 18

Organization Transformation and the Human Resource Leadership

Chapter 19

Human Resource Management Innovations

In the pathbreaking book *The Innovator's Dilemma*, Clayton Christensen presents the dilemma for successful, outstanding companies, who may do everything 'right' and yet still lose their market leadership, or even fail, as new, unexpected competitors rise and take over the market. The key is to abandon traditional business practices, and disrupt to innovate, but the dilemma for the manager is to choose the time.

Caught in the maelstrom of vicious and unexpected changes in market, organizations that thrive on stability are compelled to get out of their comfort zones to continuously change and innovate. There are two ways in which HR can support innovativeness of organization: first, by helping to create a culture of innovation through bunching of certain relevant HR processes to create a capability and motivation for innovation; second, by adopting innovative practices. Design thinking and use of social media for recruitment are some examples of HRMI.

Organizations seem to have progressed from episodic changes, to continuous change, or to a state of 'punctured equilibrium.' HR has the task of building the change capability of organizations, where resistance to change is met and resolved quickly. HR also can play the role of change leadership and become 'change enablers,' 'change drivers,' 'change accelerators,' 'catalysts,' or 'change levers.'

CHAPTER 18

Organization Transformation and the Human Resource Leadership

LEARNING OBJECTIVES

After completing this chapter, the student will be able to:

- Discuss the triggers for organizational transformation and change
- Evaluate the factors the leaders should use to decide on initiating a change process
- Describe the process and stages of organizational transformation
- Identify the role of HR professionals in helming transformation
- Identify the reasons for resistance to change and ways to overcome such resistance

Opening Case BPCL—The Story of Organizational Transformation 1996-1997

Background

Bharat Petroleum Corporation Ltd was a downstream oil company, engaged in refining of crude petroleum oil and marketing of petroleum products all over India. Its products included petrol, diesel, kerosene, LPG, industrial fuels (such as naphtha, furnace oil, and lubricants), aviation turbine fuel, and industrial feedstocks (such as benzene and toluene). It was a public sector company with a sales turnover of ₹55,000 crore; profit after tax (PAT) ₹1694 crore; sales volume 19.2 million tons; market share 21.4%; 12,500 employees. It had two subsidiaries—Kochi Refineries Ltd and Numaligarh Refineries Ltd.

In the year 1996, BPCL embarked on a major initiative for organization transformation. There were three key drivers for the change decision: (a) impending deregulation of the hydrocarbon industry, (b) changing needs of multiple stakeholders, and (c) potential benefits from performance improvements. The compulsions in the prevailing situation were caused by the dual factors of predicted growth in the demand for hydrocarbon products with the entry of the multiple players in the market, including private enterprises such as Reliance and Essar, which provided a sharp edge to the competitive business environment.

On behalf on the nodal ministry, the Ministry of Petroleum and Natural Gas, Government of India, Dr Kelkar, the petroleum secretary, initiated deregulation process in the Industry and advised BPCL to commence the restructuring process. M/s Arthur D. Little (ADL) was appointed to assist BPCL in the transformation program. A steering committee was constituted with the top leadership of the company to provide the scope and guidance for the restructuring process, and a project group was created consisting of 22 full-time resources drawn from various functions in the middle management cadre. The project was christened Customer Service and Customer Satisfaction (CUSECS), a unit of water released from a dam, a metaphor for transformation and fertility.

The Change Process–The Change Plan

The change process design had two stages. The purpose of Phase I was to prepare a blueprint for change for subsequent implementation in Phase II. The first phase had three segments: envision the future, assess current reality, and develop the change plan. The second phase consisted of two segments: develop implementation plan and implement.

The assessment of current reality stage started with identification of the stakeholders, which included not only the shareholders but also employees, customers, suppliers and contractors, and the government. The project team then branched out to different parts of the company for collection of both hard as also soft data. Teams/consultants visited a large number of locations engaging large parts of the organization in candidly talking about their experience of the organization, conducting interviews with cross section of each set of stakeholders, but also with all trade unions and management staff associations. The assessment of the current reality was presented to the management council (MC) in January 1997 in which enablers of change were identified for each of the functional areas. Subsequently, the enabler group conducted several workshops for each of the functions to validate the current reality assessment and identify improvement opportunities. During the current-reality assessment stage, the enabler group realized that each employee had his/her own perception of the current reality. The current-reality assessment process thus helped in creating common collective understanding of current reality.

In the next stage, in early December 1996, the functional directors met for a two-day intensive workshop to explore their aspirations—individual as well as for the organization. Later, in the same month, members of the MC and the CUSECS project team went through a similar exercise and created a vision for BPCL. Participants could appreciate the benefits—cohesion and alignment. These two exercises were helmed by the consultant. The steering committee members then were trained to conduct similar visioning exercise. Thereafter, the steering committee cascaded the visioning exercise to the rest of the organization. Eventualities, in March 1997, at the end of the exercise, a majority of employees at all locations were covered for the visioning exercise. The exercise yielded a set of 12 corporate visions:

1. Make BPCL a great place to work
2. Develop effective boundary management
3. Fulfill social responsibilities
4. Apply the best technology
5. Be an ethical company

6. Adopt strong and dynamic systems
7. Focus on sound business performance and operational efficiency
8. Evolve good corporate strategy
9. Establish first-class brand and corporate image
10. Have excellent customer caring and customer service
11. Strive to be the best
12. Make people a source of our improvement

The underlying theoretical construct for the current reality and visioning exercise was based on Peter Senge's *The Fifth Discipline.*[1] The assumption was that transformation process becomes effective when the stakeholders are allowed to tell the truth about the current reality and then build a shared vision for the future. The gap between the two went to establish a creative tension that provided the ideas and energy for change. It was learned during the visioning exercise that each person had his/her own vision and the shared visioning process really helped to align the visions of individuals with that of the organization.

In the next stage, the change plan was prepared documenting in great detail the corporate vision, the corporate strategic questions to be addressed, and the broad outline of the organization structure with the outline of the SBUs/support functions. It also included the vision, the assessed current reality, the key improvement opportunities and the planned steps to foster new behaviors. Regarding the organization design, several alternatives were considered and evaluated on the basis of various enabling factors for competitive edge. Table 18.1 summarizes the evaluation.

Table 18.1 Organization design evaluation matrix

Factors	Option 1 existing with some enhancements	Option 2 regional with dedicated sales force	Option 3 business units with support services
Customer focus	Low	Moderate	High
Responsiveness to market conditions (e.g., speed of decision-making)	Moderate	Moderate	High
Cost benefit approach to decisions	Moderate	Moderate	High
Consistency with best practices	Low	High	High
Ease of implementation	Low	Low	High

It was decided to adopt the design of SBUs with support services. The process of organization redesign had four elements: the vertical structures, the lateral linkages, the integrated organization, and the experimentation and adjustment.

Along with visions, a new set of core values were also evolved. They were trust, collaboration, involvement, flexibility, candor, willingness to take risks, and discipline. Performance measures were equally carefully chosen for all SBUs. For example, retail SBU chose the measures of return on capital employed (ROCE), customer loyalty index, cycle time of retail engineering projects, security of sites, and morale of staff.

1 Peter Senge, *The Fifth Discipline: The Art & Practice of the Learning Organization* (New York, NY: Doubleday/Currency, 1990).

Once the change plan was ready, it was widely disseminated throughout the organization at all levels. A series of workshops were conducted by the CUSECS team to communicate the essence covering a large majority of BPCL staff. Complete sets of the plan were provided to all management/non-management associations/unions. It was loaded in the PCs at all locations.

The Change Process: The Implementation of Plan

The implementation phase started with selection of the new SBU leaders by the directors. The design of the strategy, structure, and roles of the SBUs was done by the designate SBU leaders with the help of teams from the CUSECS group. A unique democratic process was adopted for redistributing staff form the old structure to the new structure. Union leaders were sent in batches for workshops organized by Institute of Management and Development, New Delhi to inform them of emerging trends in the trade union movement in India and abroad.

At this stage of the project people in the organization realized that the restructuring was for real. Apprehensions mounted. Communication was the key to dealing with the situation. We communicated in various ways. The CUSECS team held monthly communication meetings with MC to apprise them of the work done by the team. Regular communication workshops were conducted by each MC member with his respective staff using standard presentation packs made by the CUSECS team.

At every BPCL location in the country, a person in job group F or above went to attend the Independence Day function that year. Opportunity was taken to talk about the changes in the offing and address questions of staff at all levels—from the cleaner to the location-in-charge. Town meetings were held in all major BPCL locations by a two-person team comprising of one MC member and one CUSECS member to communicate the new organization design as well as to address the apprehensions of employees.

At the heart of the new organization design are six SBUs that will focus on different customer segments/key asset. Each SBU has embedded in it all critical functions. Financial powers were delegated very substantially to the lowest possible level in the SBUs.

BPCL was mindful to continuously build the skills and knowledge of the employees through training programs, seminars, engaging specialists in the field in which we are taking on new initiatives.

The harder part is to change behaviors. To truly gear up for competition, we need to adopt new behaviors. What are these behaviors?

To spread the 'learning' culture, BPCL created a community of internal coaches, selected from all across the functions based on passion and threshold communication expertise. The community of coaches was specially trained by Innovation Associates—a company promoted by Peter Senge. The coaches disseminated the five disciplines through a training program called 'Foundations of Organization Learning' (FOL). Another program called 'Visionary Leadership and Planning' (VLP) program was conducted with intact teams. This was in the nature of an 'action learning' program. This was a huge exposure of the internal coaches to large group internal facilitation skills.

The Positive Impact on Organization Performance

BPC's growth rate of 3.59% has been higher than the industry growth rate of 0.13%. A comparison of the various business results is given in Figure 18.1.

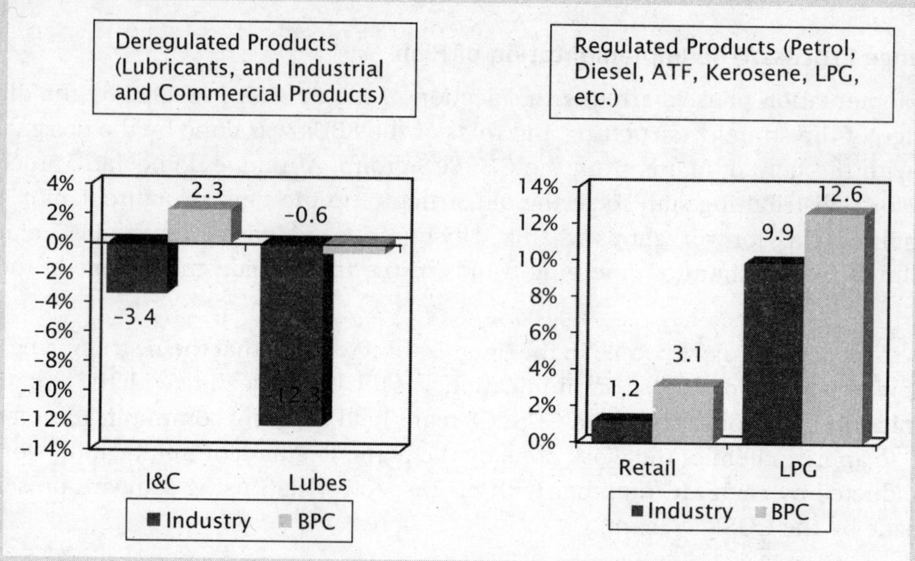

Fig. 18.1 BPCL performance *vis-à-vis* Industry

In organizations, most change programs fail to achieve the desired results because the people within the organization do not feel committed to change. A key reason for the success of BPCL organization transformation is the adherence to the wisdom captured in the old Chinese proverb that states that 'Tell me and I will forget. Show me and I may remember. Involve me and I will care.'

The Insights

1. For a large-scale change project to succeed, it has to be led from within. This is because only internal role holders have the credibility to convince employees of the need for major changes and enroll them in the process with the aid of their in-depth knowledge of the business (a lot of which is often tacit). Involvement is the key to overcoming resistance to change. Different levels of people have differing levels of involvement.
2. The selection of the consultant is crucial. The consultant has a major role to play though largely as a facilitator. Some of the key ways in which the consultant helped were: building the skills of the project CUSECS team for effective presentation, holding effective meeting, and facilitating/anchoring productive conversation. The consultant also shared relevant conceptual frameworks and best practices in global organizations. Some of the best practices shared included overall change management frameworks, dynamic brand management frameworks, VLP framework, creating a safe place to talk candidly about uncomfortable issues/undiscussables, and providing reassurance to/keeping up the spirits and morale of the management when things looked really grim

(Figure 18.1). The consultants, a global expert on organization transformation, carried a reputation and credibility. Finally, the consultants also showcased cutting-edge program management for large-scale projects encompassing a large organization.

3. The role of the top management, throughout the transformation endeavors, was to 'shepherd' the entire process. The top management provided overall direction, but carefully took only a very few top-down decisions. Some of these rare but critical decisions taken by the C&MD and the functional directors were on:
   (i) Appointment of the consultants
   (ii) Selection of the CUSECS team
   (iii) The broad overall design of the new organization structure
   (iv) Who will be the leaders of the newly created SBUs

The top management, however, made themselves continuously available and remained in touch with the project CUSECS team to remain updated on developments in the project, to encourage the team, to trouble-shoot and debottleneck when necessary, and manage the external environment, especially the government in BPCL's context.

Discussion Questions

1. What are the broad learnings on effective change management?
2. What are the factors that helped the transformation efforts in BPCL?

18.1 INTRODUCTION

Tumultuous waves of change have been rocking the shores of business organizations since the first waves of globalization in the last decades of the last millennium. This creates a contradiction as by nature organizations are wired to pursue stability.[2] To organize is to systematize, to make behavior predictable. All organizations are based on systems of internal and external expectations. The external expectation can be informal, in the form of a customer want, or formal in the form of regulations by the government. Similarly, internal expectations also can be formal or informal. As a consequence, organizations evolve a pattern of learned, predictable behavior. When the expectations suddenly change, organizations suffering from inertia die the death of dinosaurs. It has been reported that the average lifespan of a company listed in the S&P 500 index of leading US companies has decreased by more than 50 years in the last century, from 67 years in the 1920s to just 15 years today, according to Professor Richard Foster from Yale University. Today's rate of change 'is at a faster pace than ever,' he says. Professor Foster estimates that by 2020 more than three-quarters of the S&P 500 will be companies that we have not heard of yet.[3]

Organizations that have the chance of beating the pace of corporate funerals are those who can change and adapt. Nokia was a pulp manufacturer before it got into electricity and then mobile phones; at some point, its brand name was even used on galoshes. Or, take Berkshire Hathaway, which began

[2] Robert E. Quinn, *Deep Change: Discovering the Leader Within* (San Francisco, CA: Jossey-Bass, 1996).

[3] Kim Gittleson, 'Can a Company Live Forever?,' BBC News, New York, January 19, 2012. Available at: http://www.bbc.com/news/business (accessed on November 15, 2017).

as a textile mill in Rhode Island. In India, ITC, a cigarette-manufacturing company, makes profits from its food business.

The original meaning of the French term 'changer' was bend or turn like a tree or a vine searching for the sun. The idea that the only constant in change has been a truism since the time of Heraclitus, circa 500 BC. According to *Cambridge Dictionary*, change is 'to make or become different.'

According to Graetz et al.,[4] change itself is undergoing change. The incremental change of the 1970s has given way to revolutionary change, which is driven by deregulation, information age, globalization, and technology. All industries are challenged by it, while some industries are challenged almost continuously. As a consequence, the traditional static organizations are giving way to dynamic organizations. Graetz et al. have reported a central tension within organizations between continuity and change, and the need to reconcile this tension with a pluralistic approach by managing five key dualities: simultaneity, relational, minimal threshold, dynamism, and improvisation.

18.2 TERMINOLOGIES

18.2.1 Change

Change Management

Change is considered as something that can make or break an organization. It follows, therefore, that there should be a conscious process to control it by providing leadership and direction in a manner that the outcomes are those desired. Change management is the process by which change is brought about. It is, however, a non-linear, iterative, cumulative, and reformulation–in-use process, because of the differing interests of individuals within organizations and unpredictability the future holds.[5]

18.2.2 Types of Change

The changes that an organization requires to make at any given point of time may vary in nature and intensity. It is, therefore, necessary to understand the nature of change required so that appropriate strategy can be deployed, as otherwise it will amount to searching for an unknown destination without a road map. Change can be classified in multiple ways, such as push or pull, top-down or bottom-up, and so on.

According to Linda Ackerman,[6] there are three types of change:

1. **Developmental** It can be planned, evolved, or incremental. It is aimed at adding to or altering existing aspects of an organization, often targeting skill or process improvement.
2. **Transitional** It describes a quest for an envisioned state that is different from the current state. It is episodic, planned, or radical. This is the conventional topic of change in organizations.
3. **Transformational** It is fundamental in nature. It demands a shift in the mental models of the organization and employees. Transformation can lead to the evolution of a different

---

[4] Fiona Graetz, Malcolm Rimmer, Aaron Smith, and Ann Lawrence, *Managing Organizational Change* (Sydney: John Wiley & Sons, 2005).

[5] Michael Armstrong, *Armstrong's Handbook of Human Resource Management Practice* (London: Kogan Page, 2009).

[6] L. Ackerman, 'Development, Transition or Transformation: The Question of Change in Organizations,' in *Organization Development Classics*, eds. Donald F. Van Eynde, Judith C. Hoy, and Dixie Cody Van Eynde (San Francisco, CA: Jossey Bass, 1997).

organization that varies vastly in structure, processes, culture, and strategy. It may, therefore, see the emergence of a learning organization.

4. Planned versus emergent change.

The traditional approach in responding to change is by planning in anticipation. It consists of sequential steps for modifying institutional or individual behavior. It normally follows an identified need to change, on the basis of a forced field analysis of enablers/disablers in the environment.[7]

Kurt Lewin offered a three-stage model about change in organizations. The model, considered for long a classic of change literature, was influential for about four decades until the recent economic recession. The model brings together elements from field theory, group dynamics, and action research. Lewin suggested the present state as a dynamic social equilibrium, or a condition of balance maintained by active driving and resisting social forces. His model describes change as planned, collective, goal-oriented moves. In his model, Lewin indicates a succession through three transitional phases to balance the enablers/ disablers in the contextual factors that demand the change. In the first stage, termed 'unfreezing,' undesirable behavior is surfaced and 'disconfirmed,' and the needs for specific change are identified and articulated. 'Disconfirmation' is feedback that one's present behavior is ineffective, or less than effective. In the next stage termed 'moving,' the change gradually slowly gets effected through a process of trial and error. It involves conceptualizing a problem, obtaining data about concerned forces, identifying or formulating alternative solutions, and deciding on an action plan. In the final 'refreezing' stage, the change gets embedded to enable learning and assimilation for sustainability in the future. This stage relies on confirmation, psychological support, and heightened confidence. Confirmation comes in the shape of feedback on the effectiveness of performance on the basis of task measurements, responses of others that validate a new level of effectiveness, social comparison with another social unit, or a self-assessment. Confirmation may be reflected in financial or non-financial rewards.

Lewin's model of planned change initiatives, with its time-consuming, step-by-step process, and involvement of groups, has come to be criticized for being slow, stationary, and unsuitable for complex, rapidly evolving conditions like the current times. Burns has gone to the extent of asserting that planned change can be an unethical, fear-producing 'vehicle for domination'[8] reinforcing the top-down approach of change management. It is also pointed out by some critics that Lewin's model does factor in the corporate business environment, which is increasingly complex, interconnected, and globalized. It is also true that planned change initiatives often fail, up to 70%.[9]

The proneness for failure of most change initiatives has been attributed by various authors to various factors. In his book *Leading Change*, Kotter[10] mentions eight factors: failure to establish adequate urgency to change; an insufficiently powerful guiding coalition; a missing, blocked, or under-communicated vision; failure to create short-term wins; declaring victory too soon; and not anchoring changes in the corporation's culture. Some other factors believed to be adversely impacting planned change initiatives include difficulty in negotiating conflicting group identities, leadership issues, inertia deriving from a company resource position, and indifference to organization–environment

7 B. Burns, 'Complexity Theories & Organizational Change,' *International Journal of Management Reviews* 7, no. 2 (2005): 73–90.

8 B. Burns, 'Kurt Lewin and the Planned Change Approach to Change: A Reappraisal,' in *Organizational Development*, ed. J. Gallos (San Francisco, CA: Jossey-Bass, 2006), 133–157.

9 S. Sackman, P. Eggenhofer-Rehart, and M. Friesl, 'Sustainable Change: Long-term Efforts Towards Developing a Learning Organization,' *Journal of Applied Behavioral Science* 45, no. 4 (2009): 521–549.

10 J. P. Kotter, *Leading Change* (Boston, MA: Harvard Business School Press, 1995).

interdependencies and connectivity.[11] In the final analysis, planned change has been found to be most suitable when there is an anticipated need for structural changes that, nonetheless, has limited impact on organizational learning or the sustainability of change efforts.

In contrast, the unfurling of change in a seemingly natural and unprescheduled way is known as emergent change. This change cannot be foretold or planned. It can occur anywhere, and can be self-organizing in a limited way. Most organizations these days find themselves at the 'edge of chaos and far-from-equilibrium,' swinging between stability and variability. As Stacey has pointed out, organizations have to get used to running in these conditions, as excessive security and control may insulate them from their environment, thus precipitating their demise.

There can be two typical situations for emergent change:

1. Environmental factors (such as the national economy, sudden shift in consumer behavior, a new strategy from the competitors requiring immediate action, or the changes in political power dynamics) can create an emergent change situation. Even internal factors such as readjustment of power structures between groups, the emergence of new centers of expertise, and so on can cause emergent changes, not pre-meditated by the managers. Sometimes, the implementation of planned change initiatives can throw up surprises requiring emergent course changes.
2. Sometimes managers make some decisions based on unspoken assumptions, which, however underlying, are interconnected in an invisible way. These implicit beliefs then govern the direction and course of the decisions, thereby shaping the change process by 'drift' rather than by design.[12]

Since emergent change takes place in real time, it helps organizations to continuously adapt to the changing environment, thereby learning and formulating more effective strategies. They also result in

> [s]ensitivity to local contingencies; suitability for on-line real-time experimentation, learning and sense-making, comprehensibility and manageability; likelihood of satisfying needs of autonomy, control, and expression; proneness to swift implementation, resistance to unraveling; ability to exploit existing tacit knowledge; and tightened and shortened feedback loops from results to action.[13]

Episodic Versus Continuous Change

Episodic change connotes changes that are occasional, discontinuous, and deliberate. This kind of change is tagged 'episodic' because takes place in indefinite time periods, warranted by external events such as technology change or a change in key leadership. Sometimes described as 'radical' or 'second order' change, episodic change often involves replacement of one strategy or program

[11] M. Liebhart and L. Garcia-Lorenzo. 'Between Planned and Emergent Change: Decision Maker's Perceptions of Managing Change in Organizations,' *International Journal of Knowledge, Culture and Change Management* 10, no. 5 (2010): 214–225.

[12] 'Change Management.' Available at: https://www.jisc.ac.uk/guides/change-management (accessed on November 18, 2017).

[13] K. E. Weick, 'Emergent Change as Universal in Organizations,' in *Breaking the Code of Change*, 223–241, eds. M. Beer and N. Nohria (Boston, MA: Harvard Business School Press, 2000).

with another.[14] Such change occurs during periods of divergence when an organization has decided to move out of its comfort zones.

This situation arises when there is a disconnect between the internal structure of the organization and assessed needs of the business environment.

Continuous change indicates ongoing, evolving, and cumulative changes. The distinctive quality of continuous change is the idea that small continuous adjustments, created simultaneously across units, can cumulate and create substantial change. That scenario presumes tightly coupled interdependencies. When interdependencies loosen, these same continuous adjustments, now confined to smaller units, remain important as pockets of innovation that may prove appropriate in future environments. Also referred to as 'first order' or 'incremental' change, continuous change is characterized by people constantly adapting and editing ideas they acquire from different sources. At a collective level, these continuous adjustments made simultaneously across units can create substantial change.

First Order and Second Order Change

Watzlawick et al.[15] differentiated between two levels of change. It implied a distinction between qualitative changes to the system itself and adjustments within it. Bartunek and Moch[16] explained that first-order change indicated gradual modifications that make sense within an established framework, while second-order change warranted modifications to the framework itself. Levy[17] defined first order as incremental adjustments that do not alter the system's core, while second order implies differences in the basic governing rules. For Ford and Backoff,[18] second-order change meant a step toward a different plane of understanding or a shift in deep structures.

Radical and Incremental Change

Pennington[19] makes a distinction between radical and incremental change to illustrate the degree of difficulty in implementing any change. Radical changes to an organization's core business are likely to result in higher level of disturbances and involve higher degree of risk than incremental changes. Incremental changes describe the peripheral changes, considered to be low disturbance and low risk, and can be accommodated if the concerned people have had a successful past record of continuous change (Figure 18.2).

18.2.3 Forces Driving Change

A variety of forces are driving change in the world. Globalization has become relentless, with outsourcing and offshoring becoming the clear choice of the large enterprises. In developing economies, service industries hold the sway, with intellectual capital providing greater competitive advantage than

14 Karl E. Weick and Robert E. Quinn, 'Organizational Change and Development.' Available at: http://www.AnnualReviews.org (accessed on November 18, 2017).

15 J. H. Weakland and R. Fisch, *Change: Principles of Problem Formation and Problem Resolution* (New York, NY: Norton, 1974).

16 J. M. Bartunek and M. K. Moch, 'First-Order, Second-Order, Third-Order Change and Organization Change Interventions: A Cognitive Approach,' *Journal of Applied Behavioral Science* 23, no. 4 (1987): 483–500.

17 A. Levy, 'Second order Planned Change: Definition and Conceptualization,' *Organizational Dynamics* 15, no. 1 (1986): 5, 19–17, 23.

18 J. D. Ford and R. W. Backoff, *Organization Change In and Out of Dualities Paradox* (Ballinger: Cambridge, 1988).

19 G. Pennington, 'Guidelines for Promoting and Facilitating Change,' LTSN Generic Centre, 2003. Available at: https://www.heacademy.ac.uk/system/files/id296_promoting_and_facilit‑‑ting_change.pdf (accessed on February 15, 2018).

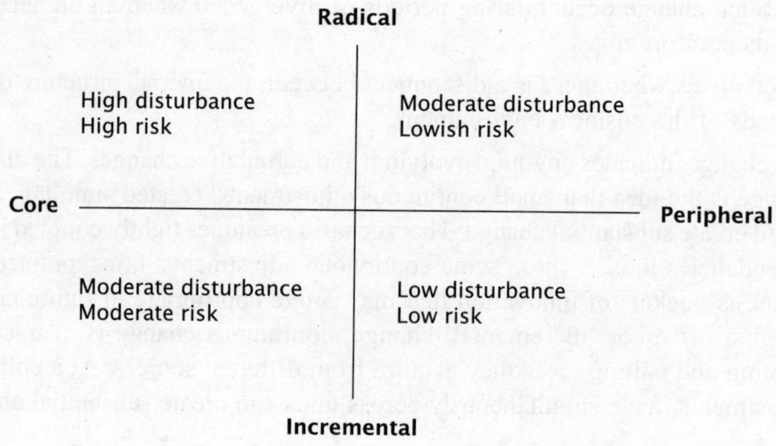

Source: Pennington, 'Guidelines for Promoting and Facilitating Change.'

Fig. 18.2 Radical–incremental and core–peripheral

physical and financial capital. Security has become a primary objective crossing virtually every sector of the economy and society. At the same time, according to Thomas Friedman,[20] the world has become flatter. Developing countries have leveraged digital capabilities to swiftly ascend the growth path to catch up with the First World. For example, China and India graduate one million engineers per year while the US graduates 65,000. There are a good number of theories on the drivers of the necessity for a change, which is whatever gave birth to the desire or need for change in the organization. Such drivers of the need for change include, for example, increasing globalization, emerging new Internet capabilities, and changes in consumer behavior.[21] Besides, new leadership, laws, regulations, and competitors can also drive the need for change.

Noel Tichy[22] articulated a three-dimensional structure to explain the various forces that exert pressures for change on organizations:

1. **Technical** Relates to pressures for change exerted by changes in technology and economic conditions (e.g., advanced high-tech equipment, changing interest rates, and increased competition).
2. **Political** Indicates compulsions for change created by issues concerning the play of power, influence, and the allocation of resources (e.g., who has authority, who is rewarded, and who decides how rewards and resources are allocated).
3. **Cultural** Implies the need for change triggered by values and beliefs of people (e.g., demographic composition and cultural diversity of the labor pool and societal values).

According to Dick,[23] a key force pushing for change is the desire to gain competitive advantage. The culture shifts in the 1980s and the 1990s in Xerox and GE were to reclaim falling market. Xerox's

[20] Thomas Friedman, *The World is Flat*, 1st edition (New York, NY: Farrar, Straus and Giroux, 2005).

[21] J. Thompson and R. Sanders, *Reinventing Public Agencies: Bottom-up Versus Top-down Strategies* (San Francisco, CA: Jossey-Bass, 1998).

[22] Tichy, Noel M., *The Leadership Engine* (New York: Harper Collins, 1997).

[23] Todd D. Dick, 'Accelerating Change for Competitive Advantage,' *Organizational Dynamics*. 24, no. 1 (Summer 1995): 77–82. Available at: http://www.sciencedirect.com/science/article/pii/0090261695900373 (accessed on November 19, 2017).

experience, called 'Leadership Through Quality,' not only pulled back their falling market but also became a benchmark for companies trying to introduce major quality management programs. The GE experience, called 'Workout,' transformed a bureaucratic, command-and-control culture into one of speed, simplicity, and self-confidence. Simon Collyer[24] opines that technology explosion is considered as an important force to induce change.

Since the mid-1980s itself, the world has been witnessing a technological explosion with 90% of our technical knowledge having been generated in the last 55 years, and the technological knowledge is expected to grow exponentially. Technology growth requires accelerated change by breaking down traditional barriers to entry, such as start-up costs and the need for economics of scale. Furthermore, globalization rapidly spreads from one part of the world to another through social network, mass marketing, international trade, and global travel. Frohman brought in a completely different perspective on the basis of researches conducted in over two dozen organizations in the USA, ranging in size from a US$5-million contract research and development (R&D) organization to several of the top ten Fortune 500 industrial companies—service companies as well as manufacturers. The changes in these organizations were brought about based on personal initiatives. The initiators were known in the organizations (by the CEOs, senior VPs, and their colleagues and peers). They were differentiated both by their very active, energetic, and focused behavior, and by their attitudes. Their attitudes were independent yet loyal to the organization, respectful yet questioning of the status quo and authority, determined to make a constructive impact yet not driven by personal ambition. They were not the 'organization men' of the 1950s and 1960s.[25]

Morrison[26] indicated three very powerful driving forces coming together simultaneously to drive proactive change initiatives by good organizations—new technologies such as the Internet and other networked communications; new consumers, who are more discerning, better informed, more individualistic; and new geographical markets in the developing countries such as in China with its 1.3 billion population. These forces are collectively creating considerable insecurity and unease in the boardrooms of large corporations, demanding change.

To summarize, the various perspectives on what drives change in an organization, it is noted that there are a number of factors responsible for creating compulsions for change in an organization. These factors are both internal and external. The external factors are those affecting the organizations both directly and indirectly. As regards external factors, since the organizations lack control over the variables in such an environment, they need to change themselves to align with the environment. These factors include technology (e.g., manual supervision becoming redundant with computerization and robotics), market conditions (e.g., the option of digital advertising reducing the impact of print media), social changes (e.g., the trend for diversity in the workplace and demand for equal remuneration for equal work), and political dynamics (e.g., the reforms of regulatory frameworks). The internal factors, which are far more enigmatic, include the demographic profile (e.g., the need of the millennials for their engagement have brought in experiments in creating workplace flexibility), the emergence of new managers (e.g., the propensity of out-of-the-box and global thinking abilities), and so on.

---

24 Simon Collyer, *Managing Among Rapid Change* (Newtown Square, PA: Project Management Institute, 2015).

25 A. Frohman, 'Igniting Organizational Change from Below: The Power of Personal Initiative,' *Organizational Dynamics* (Winter 1997): 39–53.

26 J. Ian Morrison, 'The Second Curve: Managing the Velocity of Change,' *Strategy & Leadership* 26, no. 1 (1998): 7–11.

18.2.4 Factors that Enable Change

Changes in organization occur over a period of time. There are certain factors that help the change process. They are variously named 'change enablers,' 'change drivers,' 'change accelerators,' 'catalysts,' or 'change levers.' The prevalence of these factors increases the probability of the success of the change efforts. These factors are of diverse nature, including 'events, activities, or behaviors that facilitate the implementation of change.'[27]

Shared Vision of Change

Organizational change efforts gather momentum when the important stakeholders of the organization, including the employees, start thinking positively about the vision of the change and show acceptance through their conduct. This is well supported by a number of researches on change implementation. A key finding in a research conducted at a Midwestern financial company by Gradwell[28] indicated the importance of the leaders standing in front of a crowd and

> Champion the change efforts by articulating a clear vision, communicating that vision, involving employees in implementing the vision, and reinforcing the vision. On the other hand, when leaders do not articulate a clear vision or involve employees in a change effort, or if employees do not buy into the change, the change will go unnoticed and employees will be more apprehensive about the nature of the change, the reason for the change, and the direction of the change.

It is also reported that even only setting a clear, compelling change vision may not work; it is necessary to get the enrolment of such stakeholders.

Clarifying on what would constitute a compelling vision, Kotter[29] clarified that the vision should be in the form of a picture of the future easy to communicate; appealing to customers, shareholders, and employees; and contain something that helps to clarify the direction in which the organization needs to move. Such vision should be more than the numbers. In aborted change efforts, even in cases where the leaders had a vision, they are not specific enough or compelling enough to employees, and thus are not accepted and employees do not change. Henings et al. conducted a study on a major organizational change effort in a corporate audit department of a US bank to explore the components of comprehensive change processes as initiatives move from the organizational level to the group and individual levels of implementation. He reported, as a finding, that an accepted change vision is connected generally to the initial steps of the change process, specifically progressing the vision to the group level and, sometimes, with individual adoption of change initiatives.[30]

---

27 K. S. Whelan-Berry, J. R. Gordon, and C. R. Hinings, 'The Relative Effect of Change Drivers in Large-scale Organizational Change: An Empirical Study,' in *Research in Organizational Change and Development*, eds. W. A. Pasmore and R. W. Woodman, vol. 14 (Greenwich, CT: JAI, 2003), 99–146.

28 S. S. Gradwell, 'Communicating Planned Change: A Case Study of Leadership Credibility,' Available at: https://idea.library. drexel.edu/islandora/object/idea%3A324/datastream/OBJ/download/Communicating_planned_change__a_case_study_of_ leadership_credibility.pdf (accessed on February 15, 2018).

29 Kotter, 'Leading Change,' *Harvard Business Review* (1995).

30 C. R. Hinings, J. L. Brown, and R. Greenwood, 'Change in Autonomous Professional Service Organizations,' *Journal of Management Studies* 28, no. 4 (1991): 375–393.

Leadership

Leaders' change-related behavior is widely considered as a key change driver. What is critical for success of change implementation is not only the top leadership support, but a wider involvement of the entire leadership and endorsement of change throughout the organization, permeating teams, departments, and locations. Leadership works as a change driver when leaders actively support the change vision or, in other words, leaders 'walk the talk' of the change initiative throughout the change implementation process, as opposed to providing the vision and walking away to other priorities. It also requires that the leaders demonstrate the actions that they want others to and manage resistance to change. It could be said that all change drivers result from leaders' change-related actions due to the formal power and authority that leaders have in the organization.

In the context of change, the primary expectation of employees is that the formal leader will provide explanations, legitimacy, and logic for change in work activities. In practice, however, employees look for more than the symbolic activities of their leaders. They judge the leaders' competence and experience, evaluate the leaders' willingness to implement change and measure their credibility to lead change. Employees seek answers to their questions on how the leaders are trying to bring about change, do they 'energize and enthuse others,' do they explain reasons for decisions? A study by Sally Woodward and Chris Hendry (to identify and describe variability in change in financial service institutions in the city of London as led by top managers and as experienced by employees, which highlights the clear judgmental aspect of the relationship between leaders and led) reported among other findings that when change is being initiated or executed, employee adaptation is influenced by assessments of management support, credibility, and competence. Employees, instead of being passive receptacles, act like imaginative consumers of leaders' visions and of manipulated cultural artifacts.[31]

Research has also confirmed that visible leadership commitment to change and the animated engagement of leaders act as change catalysts. The interaction of leaders with employees significantly impacts the overall change process in a positive manner. When the senior leaders take actions to fix accountability for realizing the change goals at the group and individual levels, the change process gets anchored in the organization. Employee adoption of the change initiative also can be enabled when leaders enroll the employees to get personally engaged. Leaders assist in sustaining momentum and institutionalizing the change initiative in numerous ways, such as paying attention to the progress of the change initiative and removing obstacles encountered, developing appropriate structures and establishing necessary monitoring mechanisms, and communicating the relationship between the change efforts and organizational success.[32]

Communication

A study conducted in a national insurance company who were in the process of change in working conditions showed that employees who felt they had received high-quality information about the proposed changes were more inclined to be in high levels of readiness for the change.[33] Failure to communicate effectively during change efforts is cited as a major reason for its failure. Larry

[31] S. Woodward and C. Hendry, 'Leading and Coping with Change,' *Journal of Change Management* 4, no. 2 (June 2004): 155–183.

[32] K. S. Whelan-Berry and K. A. Somerville, 'Linking Change Drivers and the Organizational Change Process: A Review and Synthesis,' *Journal of Change Management* 10, no. 2 (June 2010): 175–193.

[33] V. D. Miller, J.R. Johnson, and J. Grau, 'Antecedents to Willingness to Participate in a Planned Organizational Change,' *Journal of Applied Communication Research* 22, no. 1 (1994): 59–80.

Smeltzer[34] under-scored the value of communication and collaboration in his study of change in 43 organizations. In situations where management fails to provide proper update, inaccurate and negative rumors abound, thus hurting the change efforts. Smeltzer provides some evidence of communication failure by the management such as being more concerned with communicating with the public and stockholders than with employees; using 'lean' channels of communications such as memos, in preference for face-to-face methods and others.

It is emphasized by change specialists that effective communication serves as the building block for deepening employees' understanding of the need for the change initiative. It can also, for example, provide the status of the change implementation and address points of resistance.[35] The specific kind of communication, having maximum impact on change implementation, is the one that is providing information and seeking opinions both ways. Employee briefing about the status of implementation of change plan indicates that the change process is being monitored, and is on track. It showcases the plucking of the low-hanging fruits and the decongestion of bottlenecks. The stories of early successes build morale of the employees.

Based on research on successful change programs, Peter Richardson and D. Keith Denton[36] have suggested some actions for effective communication. Some examples are:

- Top leadership to demonstrate wholehearted and visible support.
- Inform employees early and in detail.
- Persist with communication all along, even after the change.
- Conduct face-to-face communications as much as possible. Next in order of priority should be satellite hook-ups, teleconferences, or other interactive ways of employee contact.
- Communicate through supervisors and managers. Encourage, train, and hold them accountable for keeping employees informed and providing a lot of interpersonal communication regarding the changes.
- Accept that there will be emotional and rational ones and handle them with sensitivity. Use group meetings, toll-free telephone lines, and frequent newsletters.
- Involve employees in the change process and in decisions about change as much as possible.

Training

Training is considered a powerful factor facilitating change by equipping employees with new knowledge, skills, or behaviors. Employees learn new technology, processes, work processes or routines, and behaviors that embody the change vision. Further, training often provides meaning for the change vision, that is, what the organizational change vision means at the group level. A survey of 565 trained and 365 untrained municipal employees by Bennett, Lehman, and Forst[37] established that employees who felt blocked from applying training reported significantly less customer orientation than employees who were untrained.

[34] L. R. Smeltzer, 'An Analysis of Strategies for Announcing Organization-Wide Change,' *Group and Organization Studies* 16, no. 1 (1991): 5–24.

[35] Edgar H. Schein, *Organizational Culture and Leadership: A Dynamic View* (San Francisco, CA: Jossey-Bass, 1985).

[36] P. Richardson and D. K. Denton, 'Communicating Change,' *Human Resource Management* 35, no. 2 (Summer 1996): 203–216.

[37] Joel B. Bennett, Wayne E. K. Lehman, and Jamie K. Forst, 'Change, Transfer Climate, and Customer Orientation: A Contextual Model and Analysis of Change-Driven Training,' *Group & Organization Management* 24, no. 2 (1999): 188–216.

Employee Involvement

Involving employees in the change process is generally regarded as essential for the success of transformational programs. The involvement could be tried out at various levels—face-to-face meetings and discussions, modeling vital behaviors, or formally designed platforms, such as implementation planning or pilots and so on.[38] The employees feel empowered when they are invited to provide recommendations, or they see visible actions being taken in response to their concerns. As individual employees engage in change-related work, they revert back to their team with better comprehension of the change initiative and clarity about change vision, its issues and gains for their group, and become de facto change champions in that group. These participation strategies have acted as determinants of employee opinions of change. As a specific example, Whelan-Berry[39] found that participation in pilots and in shaping change initiatives altered individual frameworks, increasing understanding and commitment to change initiatives, and increasing employee enthusiasm.

Convergence of Practices, Structures, Processes, and Systems

In order to sustain the positive effects of change, it is essential to primarily integrate the relevant HR practices (training, recruitment and selection, performance management, compensation, and so on) that are regarded as change drivers with the broad themes and visions of change. For example, if the organization has decided to change for better customer-centricity, then the selection process should be geared to identify candidates with customer-oriented competencies. The same logic will apply to onboarding process, and so on. Prior researches have confirmed that performance appraisal and related reward systems, aligned to reflect the behavior, skills, or work demanded by the change initiative, work as strategic enablers of change adoption by individual employees.[40] Convergence of recruitment, selection and socialization of new employees, and the behavioral systems and processes support the momentum of the change implementation and institutionalize the change. Until the time new behaviors get anchored in organization culture, ‘they are subject to degradation as soon as the pressure for change is removed.’[41]

Other than HR practices, the structure and certain organizational processes such as planning, budgeting and reporting, operations, and customer and technology systems also need to converge with the change themes to yield maximum impact of change endeavors. Researchers have emphasized the criticality of certain systems and processes, which can help track and evaluate the change efforts, and thus enable the organization to take appropriate and timely remedial measures.[42] The employees get a clear message that the change initiative is valuable enough to be monitored, measured, and managed.

18.2.5 The Change Process

There is a virtual unanimity among both scholars and practitioners, given the blistering pace of change, that change processes are both complex and challenging for organizations embarking on such

[38] S. K. Piderit, ‘Rethinking Resistance and Recognizing Ambivalence: A Multidimensional View of Attitudes Toward an Organizational Change,’ *Academy of Management Review* 25, no. 4 (2000): 783–794.

[39] K. Whelan-Berry, ‘Change Catalysts: Source of Individual Change in the Context of Organizational Change,’ 1997, Dissertation Abstracts International, UMI No. 9725149.

[40] A. Armenakis, S. Harris, and H. Field, ‘Making Change Permanent: A Model for Institutionalizing Change Interventions,’ in *Research in Organizational Change and Development*, eds. W. Pasmore and R. Woodman, 97–128.

[41] Kotter, ‘Leading Change,’ *Harvard Business Review* (1995).

[42] T. Vollman, *The Transformation Imperative: Achieving Market Dominance Through Radical Change* (Boston, MA: Harvard Business Press, 1996).

a path. Simultaneously, the know-how about how to plan and implement plans for organizational transformation and change, is also limited. According to earlier researches, abortive change initiatives range from one-third to four-fifths of change endeavors.[43] In a 2013 Strategy&/The Katzenbach Center survey of global senior leaders on culture and change management, the success of major change initiatives was found to be only 54%. The consequences of such failures are significant—destroyed morale, wasted resources, increased turnover, and plunging bottom line.[44] Yet, organizational change considered as a constant and essential part of the competency set of millennial leaders and managers. It is therefore imperative to develop a clear understanding of organizational change process, its multiple contexts, levels, and choices about or during change.

Two models of change process are being shared further.

Kotter's Eight-stage Process of Creating a Major Change

The eight-stage process has been described by some as a vision for the change process. It describes a sequence of steps to be taken to arrive at the organizational change vision. Some of the distinctive features of Kotter's change process are: its clear accent on leadership role in change and regarding change as topdriven; focus on organizational culture; and orientation to the private sector. Critics have labeled it as bestfit for emergent, rather than planned change management. Kotter's eight-stage process can be summarized as follows:

1. Establishing a sense of urgency
   (i) Examine the market and competitive realities
   (ii) Identify and discuss crises, potential crises, and opportunities
2. Creating the guiding coalition
   (i) Put together a group with enough power to lead the change
   (ii) Get the group to work together like a team
3. Develop a vision and strategy
   (i) Create a vision to help direct the change effort
   (ii) Develop strategies for achieving the vision
4. Communicating the change vision
   (i) Use every vehicle possible to constantly communicate new vision and strategies
   (ii) Have the guiding coalition role-model the behavior expected of employees
5. Empowering broad-based change
   (i) Get rid of obstacles
   (ii) Change systems and structures that undermine the change vision
   (iii) Encourage risk-taking and non-traditional ideas, activities, and actions
6. Generating short-term wins
   (i) Plan for visible improvements in performance and wins
   ii) Create those wins
   (iii) Visibly recognize and reward the people who made those wins possible

[43] Whelan-Berry and Somerville, 'Linking Change Drivers and Organizational Change Process.'

[44] Brent Gleeson, 'Leading Change: 6 Reasons Change Management Strategies Fail,' *Forbes*, December 7, 2016. Available at: https://www.forbes.com/sites/brentgleeson/2016/12/07/leading-change-6-reasons-change-management-strategies-fail/#34e36f025d9e (accessed on November 19, 2017).

7. Consolidating gains and producing more change
   (i) Use increased credibility to change all systems
   (ii) Hire promote and develop people who can implement the change vision
   (iii) Reinvigorate the process with new projects, themes, and change agents
8. Anchoring new approaches in the culture
   (i) Create better performance through customer-oriented behavior
   (ii) Articulate the connect between the new behavior and organizational process
   (iii) Develop means to ensure leadership development and succession planning

Source: Adapted from J. P. Kotter, 'Leading Change: Why Transformation Efforts Fail,' *Harvard Business Review* (March–April 1995).

Kotter's process has been well received as effective and is popular and highly influential in change management literature. The critics of the model state that (a) Kotter essentially prescribes the what of the change process, but not the how; (b) it is not sufficiently detailed to guide change management in all situations; (c) not being general enough for some kinds of change; (d) being overly planned, and not tuned to the practicalities of organizational life. It needs to be kept in mind that there can be no panacea to the challenges of organizational change.

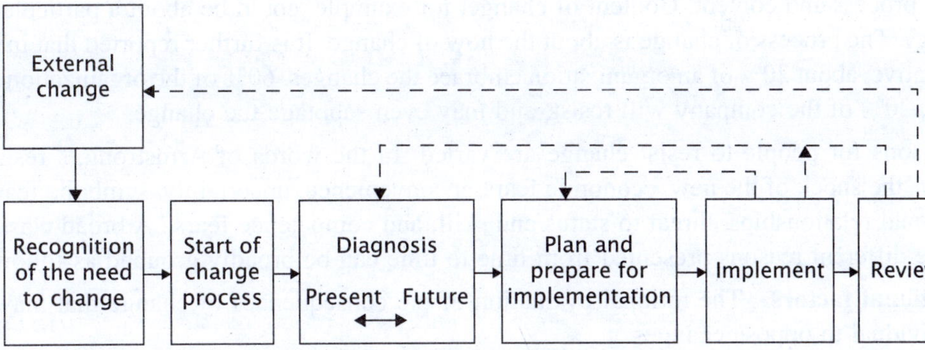

Source: J. Hayes and P. Hyde. 'Process Model of Change', in *the Theory and Practice of Change Management*, ed. J. Hayes, 3rd ed, 47–54 (London: Palgrave McMillan, 1998).

Fig. 18.3 Process model of change

The second model to be presented is formulated by Hayes and Hyde (Figure 18.3):[45]

1. Recognize that external events or internal circumstances require a change to take place.
2. Start of the change process. Decide
   (i) Who to involve?
   (ii) What to make public?
   (iii) Who should have management responsibility?

[45] J. Hayes and P. Hyde, 'Process Model of Change,' In *The Theory and Practice of Change Management*, edited J. Hayes, 3rd edition, 47–54 (London: Palgrave McMillan, 1998).

3. Diagnosis—Corresponds to what Kurt Lewin called unfreezing.
   (i) Identify the current scenario
   (ii) Develop the preferred scenario
4. Prepare and plan for implementation—Corresponds to the stage of moving in Lewin's model.
5. Implement change.
6. Review and consolidate—Similar to the stage of refreezing in Kurt Lewin's model.

18.2.6 Managing Resistance to Change

Resistance to change is widely considered as an important determinant of successful or failed change initiatives. A study undertaken by Maurier[46] revealed that resistance was a 'little recognized, but critically important contributor' for abortive change initiatives. CIPD[47] defines resistance to change as 'an individual or group engaging in acts to block or disrupt an attempt to introduce change.' In the opinion of Hughes,[48] most traditional change management texts avoid the topic of resistance to change and there is a tendency for it to be depicted as 'something to overcome.' For example, Armstrong says, 'resistance to change can be difficult to overcome even when it is not detrimental to those concerned, but an attempt must be made.'[49] However, CIPD[50] identifies that resistance to change is not necessarily negative, as it may be an indication that the change initiative needs rethinking.

Change literature abound in different types of resistance. CIPD[51] classifies resistance to change on the basis of process and content. Content of change, for example, could be about a particular change in technology. The process of change is about the how of change. It is further reported that in a typical change initiative, about 20% of an organization embrace the changes, 60% of the organization tolerates it; however, 20% of the company will resist, and may even sabotage the change.

The reasons for people to resist change are varied. In the words of Armstrong,[52] resistance is triggered by 'the shock of the new, economic fears, inconvenience, uncertainty, symbolic fears, threat to interpersonal relationships, threat to status and skill, and competence fears.' A broad classification covering the different reasons presented from time to time can be broadly grouped as follows:

(a) **Rational factors** The rational evaluation of the consequences of change that may lead an individual to oppose changes.

(b) **Non-rational factors** An individual's preferences and biases that guide his choice of a position on change. Can include emotional factors!

(c) **Political factors** Colored with political dynamics and may include factors such as favoritism or scoring a point.

(d) **Management factors** Inappropriate management style.

---

[46] R. Maurer, 'Using Resistance to Build Support for Change,' *Journal for Quality and Participation* 19, no. 3 (1996): 56–63.

[47] CIPD, 2014. Available at: http://www.cipd.co.uk (accessed on November 19, 2017).

[48] M. Hughes, *Managing Change: A Critical Perspective* (CIPD, 2010).

[49] Armstrong (2009, 431).

[50] CIPD (2014). Available at: https://www.cipd.co.uk/Images/ (accessed on January 20, 2017).

[51] Ibid.

[52] Armstrong, *Armstrong's Handbook of Human Resource Management Practice.*

Resistance to Change Methods for Reducing Resistance to Change

Line manager's role

It has been found from experience that resistance triggered by anxiety and uncertainty can be addressed effectively, if LMs take a proactive role in imparting information.[53] It calls for simultaneous flow of communication from change leadership to the LMs and from them to the employees. The reason the LMs often prefer to withhold information until the last minute is the apprehension of backlash in the form of negative emotions from employees. But the unintended consequence of this secretiveness is the inability to make complete communications and to resolve issues arising out of change on time. Therefore, an open communication on the pros and cons of change can help reduce change-associated ambiguity and create clarity about the compelling reason for change.[54]

Dealing with individual issues

There is a view that employee resistance, far from being inherent, is caused by anticipated negative consequences of change. It would help to embed a process in the change management strategy to address upfront and change employee's perceptions, and in some cases carry out a course correction in change strategy itself, based on interactions and feedbacks. This reinforces the necessity to implement suggestions by the employees to demonstrate the value of employees.

Care in implementing technological change

The resistance associated with technological change are commonly of two types: functional or dysfunctional. In case of functional resistance, it probably signals the prevalence of issues with the technology or its impact and the appropriate response should be to take corrective steps. Dysfunctional resistance, however, creates organizational disruptions,[55] and the way to deal with it would be to explore the root causes of resistance and then to determine ways of solving the issues.

Encouraging employee participation

Several researches conducted, including that by Lewin in 1991, revealed that employee participation in the learning, planning, and implementation stages of a change process substantially improves change adoption and reduces resistance. This strand of thought eventually led to the evolution of new management schools of thought, including OD and HRD.[56] The reverse is also true. An 'attitude that gets staff people into trouble is the expectation that all the people involved will resist the change. It is curious but true that the staff person who goes into a job with the conviction that people are going to resist any new idea with blind stubbornness is likely to find them responding just the way the staff specialist thinks they will.' The process is clear: Whenever the people who are supposed to buy new ideas are treated as if they were bullheaded, the way they are used to being treated changes; and they will be bullheaded in resisting that change.[57]

---

53 Ibid.

54 W. Bridges, *Managing Transitions: Making the Most of Change* (London: Nicholas Brealey Publishing, 1995).

55 Rivard, Suzanne and Lapointe, Liette, 'Information Technology Implementers' Responses to User Resistance: Nature and Effects,' *MIS Quarterly* 36, no. 3 (2012): 897–920.

56 C. R. Milton, Lanny Entrekin and B. W. Stening, *Organizational Behaviour in Australia* (Sydney: Prentice–Hall of Australia, 1984).

57 Paul R. Lawrence, 'How to Deal with Resistance to Change,' *Harvard Business Review* (May–June 1954): 49.

Finally, a question needs to be asked 'Is resistance to change bad?' Not always is the opinion of many change writers. According to Haltman,[58] 'There are times when resistance is the most effective response available.' The trend to resist all resistance and to consider all change as good may be fallacious, because the only measure of an effective change is the impact that it makes, and that may only play out in time, not immediately. In organizations, there is always a dilemma of what to change and what to keep, to maintain a balance between stability and disruption. Employee resistance may provide the handle to keep the equilibrium, when change is toxic and dysfunctional. As Maurer stated, 'Resistance is what keeps us from attaching ourselves to every boneheaded idea that comes along.'[59]

18.2.7 Strategy for Change through Adoption of Technology

Changes in technology always present opportunities for organizations to leverage the same for improving their competitive ability. Unfortunately, often the technologies are either grossly under-utilized or discarded. Such failed investments in technology may have negative consequences: financial loss and demoralized employees. Studies in the past have focused on answering the question: what determines the success in implementing technology use. Two models have been presented: Technology adoption model (TAM) and Technology readiness Index (TRI).

According to the first model, TAM, the answers lie in two areas: perceived usefulness and perceived ease of use, which was presented through a model. *Perceived usefulness* refers to 'the degree to which a person believes that using a particular system would enhance his or her job performance'; and *perceived ease of use* refers to 'the degree to which a person believes that using a particular system would be free of effort'.[60]

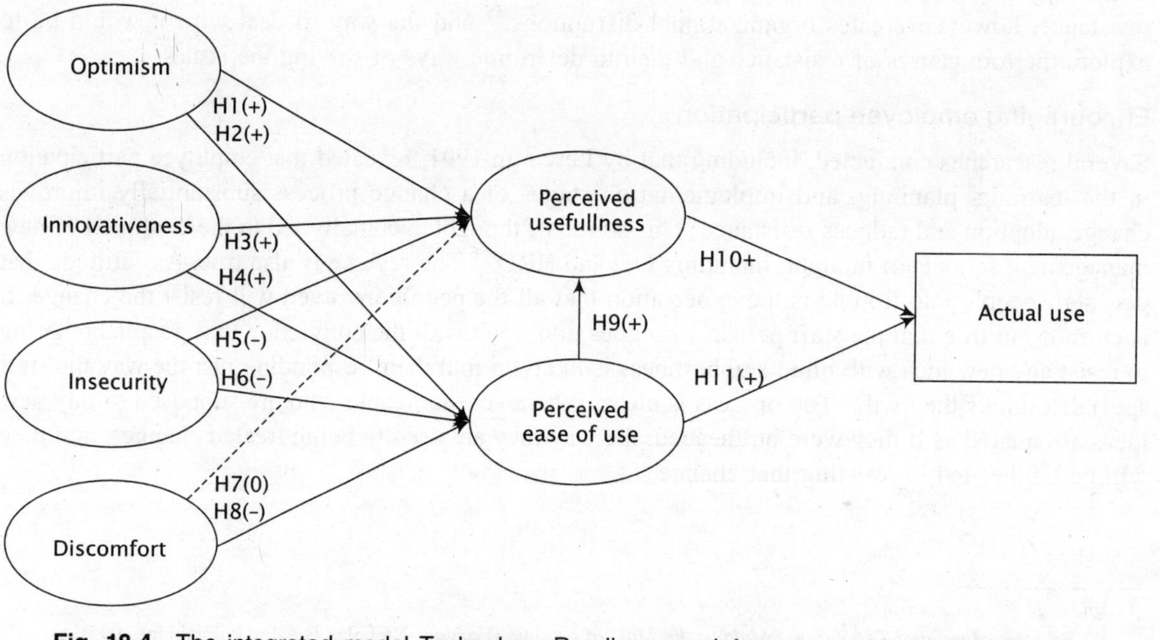

Fig. 18.4 The integrated model Technology Readiness and Acceptance Model (TRAM) with hypothesized relations among study variables

---

[58] K. Hultman, *The Path of Least Resistance* (Denton, TX: Learning Concepts, 1979).

[59] R. Maurer, 'Using Resistance to Build Support for Change.'

[60] Davis, Fred D. 'Perceived usefulness, perceived ease of use, and user acceptance of information technology.' *MIS quarterly* (1989): 319-340.

The second model-TRI[61] refers to 'people's propensity to embrace and use new technologies to accomplish goals in home life and at work'. It combines certain positive and negative beliefs related to technology. The beliefs vary among individuals and determine a person's inclination to deal with new technology. These beliefs were categorized into four dimensions: optimism, innovativeness, discomfort, and insecurity.

The above two models were integrated into a third model by Lin and others[62].

Case Developing Strategy for Leading Change through Technology Adaption

In Premier Cements Company (PCL) contract labor was the lifeline of manufacturing, constituting about 75% of the workforce. The traditional process required low technology, skill, and literacy, and to an essentially entrepreneurial management, contract labor provided just the right choice in terms of easy availability and low cost. The plant management also preferred the freedom to engage labor 24/7 to meet sudden, sporadic requirements for additional production, or long shift hours. Employment of such high numbers of contract labor led to issues (of compliance of legal requirement, unsafe work and conditions, lack of discipline in manpower utilization) inviting adverse internal audit comments.

Efforts were made by the HR department to improve by adopting a framework for a Contract Labor Management system, and to create enthusiasm for the system a trendy logo (called the Pyramid0 was created, which mapped the key action areas at two levels—compliance related and internal process related, with accountabilities for several interfacing functions (like HR, legal, procurement, and manufacturing) to develop a healthy contract labor manufacturing system. Over a period of time, however, due to lack of co-ordination between different functions, and fuzzy accountabilities, the system was reduced to only Access control system registering. It was not what she envisioned. She felt that the issue needs to be looked at from fresh perspectives, with a clear solution-oriented approach. She thought of assigning the task to Rahul, the new General Manager-ER, who recently joined from Procter & Gamble.

Rajeev, the newly appointed General Manager (HR), PCL, was tasked with the responsibility to ensure a well-functioning, clean, compliant contract labor system. Rajeev knew the challenges, which were as follows:

(a) Inaccurate reporting on headcount

There was no accurate data of how many contract labors were engaged in a day. From the beginning manpower engagement was ad hoc, without any systematic approved plan. Some of its plants were set up by the company, while some other plants were acquired from other companies. There was no centralized HR Planning, and each plant followed its own unique systems. This issue was endemic in the cement industry because of the over reliance on cheap, easily available labor.

There was an Access Control system, used by the contract labor for card punching, but the data did not flow into the system. So, if HQ required data on contract labor, it would be manually compiled, leading to inaccuracies.

61 Parasuraman, Ananthanarayanan. 'Technology Readiness Index (TRI) a multiple-item scale to measure readiness to embrace new technologies.' *Journal of service research* 2.4 (2000): 307-320.

62 Lin, Chien-Hsin, Peter J. Sher, and Hsin-Yu Shih. 'Past progress and future directions in conceptualizing customer perceived value.' *International Journal of Service Industry Management* 16.4 (2005): 318-336.

(b) Low skill and literacy, low potential for up-skilling

The cement manufacturing process was labor oriented, with a workforce having low level of skill and literacy. The company tried to bring in world-class technology, but for that the workforce had to be up skilled. The plant management, who were happy with the existing process and work of the employees, were reluctant to let go of the workmen. Besides, management feared resistance from the unions as well as the local community whose cooperation was crucial for managing cement manufacturing operations.

(c) Concerns on safety and legal compliance

The incessant pressure for produce at any cost, and absence of modern systems and processes, led to abysmal safety record for the plant. There were work related fatalities every year. Things never went out of control because of the goodwill of the local community leaders.

The unplanned, highly localized way of inducting workforce posed a peculiar problem for the corporate leadership: at any given point of time it was impossible to obtain accurate data on the workforce-numbers as well as skill levels. The problem could not be resolved more because of the resistance of the local management to revealing data, for fear of being pulled up by the corporate leadership. But senior corporate leadership was seriously concerned about the adverse comments from internal audits, rising cases of litigations arising out of deficient recruitment process, and the violations of safety. Rahul listed the key issues requiring attention, as under:

(a) Unregulated entry and exit of the contract labor.
(b) Proxy entries for absent employees.
(c) No record of the number of contract labor working on a given day, nor the exact duration of such work.
(d) No comprehensive database of contract labor.
(e) No documentation of training imparted, especially the mandatory safety training.
(f) Unavailability of data for corporate reporting.

The failure to rationalize the process and introduce systems in the past was mainly due to resistance from the Unit Heads, LMs, the contractors, and the contract labor. Besides, the Line viewed it as an HR initiative and that led to inadequate enrolment of the key actors. Gradually, the corporate leadership also gave up on the matter.

Two-faced solutions

Rahul realized the solutions to the above issues will have two aspects: the system with a SOP and the change management process to implement.

(d) The change management process choices

(i) Top-down approach: Contact providers of Access Control. Get the senior leadership to approve the proposal. Instruct the plants to implement the system from a given date.
(ii) Bottom-up approach: Check out from the first LMs the issues in introducing the system.
(iii) Mixed approach: Get the senior leadership on board, and then create a process to check and work on the concerns/suggestions of the LMs.

What would Rahul do?

18.2.8 Strategies for Effecting Change

Thurley and Wirdenius[63] have posited five different models of change.

Directive

The foundation of this approach is the belief that it is the manager who is responsible for managing change. Therefore, the manager can use his authority to direct the implementation of change plan, with or without consultation or participation of employees. The approach can ensure speed in execution, but by ignoring views of the stakeholder it fails to use all relevant inputs to make change effective.

Expert

This approach, suitable for implementing technological change, relies on expertise of few to lead change. It seeks no input from the multitude of stakeholders, affected by change. The advantage is that it is solution-focused, and experts can swiftly implement the solutions also. It suffers from the possibility of resentment of those who not being a party to the solution search have to accept them.

Negotiation

In this strategy, the change managers are flexible to bargain and concede on issues. It results in a higher probability of change adoption, since it accepts the stakeholders' say on changes that affect them. Conversely, it can consume time, and the eventual outcome may not be on planned lines.

Education

It aims at moving the employees to a set of shared values and employs a combination of methods to win their hearts (usually with the help of external or internal consultants)—education, training, persuasion, consultation, and so on. It builds employee enrolment in change, but entails a time-consuming process.

Participative

It engages people to the maximum extent possible, and although driven by senior managers, it is largely led by teams and individuals. It considers the views of the people affected by change in a comprehensive manner. It is a costly and time-consuming approach, but it has the potential for being most effective among all strategies by virtue of its focus on building stakeholder commitment.

Closing Case Pidilite Story of Organizational Transformation: What to Change and What to Keep

Pidilite Industries Limited, founded in 1959, is an India-based adhesives-manufacturing company, with corporate headquarters in Mumbai. Its products range also includes art material, construction chemicals, and industrial chemicals. It markets the Fevicol range of adhesives: Fevikwik, Dr. Fixit, Roff, Cyclo, Ranipal, Hobby Ideas, M-seal, and Acron. The company has manufacturing facilities in India, including Mahad (Maharashtra), Vapi (Gujarat), Baddi (Himachal Pradesh), and Kala Amb (Himachal Pradesh). In 2016, its gross

63 K. Thurley and H. Wirdenius, *Supervision: A Reappraisal* (London: Heinemann, 1973).

sales was ₹5066.53 crore, an increase of about 8% over 2015, and PAT at ₹700 crore, an increase of about 40% over 2015.

A wholly owned subsidiary in Singapore, under the banner 'Pidilite International Pte Ltd' was incorporated by the company in 2005 for its international operations, covering the acquisition of overseas companies and joint ventures. Currently, it has a number of overseas businesses, including those in the USA, Brazil, Thailand, UAE, and Singapore. The company has been experiencing exponential growth, especially since the 1990s.

Despite being a traditional family-run enterprise, Pidilite has navigated through several phases of transformation in its growth trajectory over the years. Madhukar Parekh, the chairman, has led his company through major changes. In the late 1980s and the early 1990s, Pidilite transitioned from a production-oriented industrial products company to a marketing-oriented consumer company—a major change indeed. The chairman's brother and company director Ajay Parekh, 57, remembers the time well and says, 'That transition was entrepreneurial, led by the family.'

The challenge of change in the new millennium is different. The owners realized that to sustain growth and manage operations and markets across continents the family had to stop micromanaging and let people learn for themselves. It was a difficult decision, but the family decided to take it and learn. One of the dilemmas was around what to change and what not to change. Would Pidilite jump into the bandwagon and imitate what every other enterprise was doing in search of cost optimization, through reduction of head-counts? Manish Modi, Pidilite's President, Business Resource Group, found out the answer when he went to the C&MD with a proposal to lay off some employees at the height of the downturn. Formerly, the CEO of Datamatics Technologies, Modi, who was recruited to head the HR function, had conducted a thorough review of Pidilite's organizational structure and made a list of positions deemed redundant. The C&MD would have none of it. 'He said we could re-skill, re-deploy, but there's no question of laying people off, even in loss-making time.' Modi remembered.

The reason for avoiding the beaten path for the C&MD can be traced to the deeply held cultural ethos at Pidilite. Every other year, Pidilite Industries throws a big party for retired employees and their spouses at its campus in Andheri, Mumbai. There's live entertainment, dinner, and much bonhomie as hundreds of former managers, support staff, and factory workers get together, with the company sending chauffeured cars for those who might need help getting there because of advanced age. It is a remarkable do, as corporate events go, but as C&MD Madhukar Parekh says, 'People who work with us today need to realize the contribution of those who came before.'

Modi overcame his disappointment over time when he realized that, being new, he was unaware of the cultural nuances in the organization. He modified his HR plan, and in subsequent years went ahead to recruit over 80 top executives for Pidilite, as part of a process to transform the company from a family-run enterprise to a professionally run company. Aiding the process were headhunting firm Egon Zehnder and Pidilite's board of directors, who helped in identifying possible candidates and in the selection interviews. A list was made of 20 admired target organizations for recruitment of professionals with minimum 12 years' experience and having grown up the ranks. The powerful brand image of Pidilite products helped to attract the talent.

Interestingly, the top leadership knew what role to play in this change. They were aware that Pidilite's employer branding was undermined by its reputation as a family-run company, with one or the other family member heading every business line and function. 'We were recruiting very senior people, so it was a challenge,' says Parekh. 'There were long conversations where I had to articulate the company's values and convince them that family members were preparing to disengage from day-to-day management.' Pidilite eventually acquired a core group of new professionals, drawn from some of India Inc.'s most respected companies, such as ITC, Cadbury India, ICI (to name a few), with very strong cultures of their own. In order to ensure they assimilated in Pidilite's milieu, the first few recruits were attached to the chairman's office in staff roles before being given operational responsibilities. Significantly, one of the first to come over was Sandeep Batra, former CFO of ICI, who is now Pidilite's director for finance, a function that was previously a forbidden territory for outsiders and was with the chairman's cousin, Apurva Parekh. 'When we first met, the chairman told me he was hiring a full management team. It was going to add to costs, but he said the promoters were committed to it because their involvement in operational decision-making could only take the company so far. He wanted to free them for strategy,' says Batra.

With an annual turnover of ₹4000 crore, Pidilite has grown to a size that the Parekhs no longer have the bandwidth required to manage operations efficiently. The change has paid off for Pidilite. One of Batra's noteworthy achievements is improved investor relations, something the promoters had been neglecting. From zero in 2008, the number of brokerages covering Pidilite has now increased to 14, thanks to a system of quarterly earnings calls. Pidilite has five members of the Parekh family in the management, with the chairman's uncle N. K. Parekh representing the first generation and the others forming the second generation. The third generation of the family to come of age so far is all daughters, who have not entered the business. In the earlier scheme of things, when Pidilite was a much smaller company, functional roles would go to the family member most interested in handling them. Now Pidilite has senior people in the CFO and CIO roles and Apurva Parekh, who was handling both, has disengaged from both functions. 'The big challenge was not recruitment but integrating the new people so that they succeed. We have tried to ensure that Pidilite's core values are not diluted even as we absorb the best of outside culture,' he says.

At the heart of the aforementioned transformation was a shift in the talent acquisition strategy. In the late 1990s, the company targeted the entry levels through a management trainee program, where it recruited from top engineering and business school campuses. The program was abandoned when the company found it could not retain the recruits. The next strategy was to recruit at middle management level, but even here the Pidilite's leadership development efforts left much to be desired, which is why it eventually had to recruit top executives from outside.

Now that the second rung of leadership takes figurative, if not literal, ownership of Pidilite, the campus recruitment program has been revived, and it seems to be working. Currently, 50 management trainees are deployed in various divisions of the company, and leadership development has been taken up as priority by the new CEOs. 'We've spent the last five years inducting talent from outside, now we have to build from within. We have to develop people, give them cross-divisional exposure, and define career paths. These practices were absent before,' says Kavinder Singh, designated CEO, consumer products, Pidilite, who joined from ITC Foods, and was initially designated president, strategic initiatives.

The owners are now set to move on to the next phase. 'We now have a leadership team, which is integrated with our way of doing things,' Madhukar Parekh says. 'In the first phase, we held their hands, worked together with them. Now we can let go, spend less time with them. I sit with them only once in a quarter, for the quarterly review.' Certain things, however, do not change in Pidilite. Every Thursday, the family has lunch with employees whose birthdays fall in that week. On any given Thursday, there are usually20 employees and at least three family members present at the lunch party. Are the new CEOs invited? 'Only if it's their birthday,' says Ajaybhai, with a chuckle. 'This gives the family a chance to connect with employees, stay in touch with older ones who we have known for very long.' Does the older set complainabout the new professionals? 'Much less now,' says Ajaybhai. 'They usually come to us only if they feel they are not being heard by the managers and that is becoming much less.'

Discussion Questions

1. What are the factors that helped the change process in Pidilite?
2. Why did the earlier strategy of inducting talent at the bottom and at the middle did not work?
3. Evaluate the factors the promoters should consider while deciding on transformation.

Source: Adapted from Dibyendu Ganguly, 'Move over Family, Pidilite Makes Way for Outsiders at the Top,' *The Economic Times*, August 1, 2014. Available at: https://economictimes.indiatimes.com/magazines/corporate-dossier/move-over-family-pidilite-makes-way-for-outsiders-at-the-top-rung/articleshow/39356823.cms (accessed on November 19, 2017).

SUMMARY

Organizations have been constantly coping with tumultuous waves of change, ever since the last decades of the last century. Change has become the mantra for organizational survival. It has been reported the average lifespan of a company listed in the S&P 500 index of leading US companies has decreased by more than 50 years in the last century, from 67 years in the 1920s to just 15 years today, according to Professor Richard Foster from Yale University. Today's rate of change 'is at a faster pace than ever,' he says. Professor Foster estimates that by 2020, more than three-quarters of the S&P 500 will be companies that we have not heard of yet. Change has been categorized in different ways by researchers. It includes planned change and emergent change; transactional change and transformational change; episodic and continuous change; first-order and second-order change; and radical and incremental change. There are several change models.

Technical change relates to pressures for change exerted by changes in technology and economic conditions (e.g., advanced high-tech equipment, changing interest rates, and increased competition). Political change indicates compulsions for change created by issues concerning the play of power, influence, and the allocation of resources (e.g., who has authority, who is rewarded, and who decides how rewards and resources are allocated). Cultural change implies the need for change triggered by values and beliefs of people, (e.g., demographic composition and cultural diversity of the labor pool and societal values). Change can be introduced following different strategies. Some of the strategies are directive, expert, negotiation, education, and participative.

There are certain factors that help the change process. They are variously named 'change enablers,' 'change drivers,' 'change accelerators,' 'catalysts,' or 'change levers.' The prevalence of these factors increases the probability of the success of the change efforts. These factors are of diverse nature including 'events, activities, or behaviors that facilitate the implementation of change.' Some of the change enablers are shared vision, communication, alignment of systems and processes, employee involvement, and training.

Many change initiatives flounder due to resistance. The reasons for people to resist change are varied. In the words of Michael Armstrong, resistance is triggered by 'the shock of the new, economic fears, inconvenience, uncertainty, symbolic fears, threat to interpersonal relationships, threat to status and skill, and competence fears.' The factors that cause resistance can be classified as rational factors, non-rational factors, political factors, and management factors.

Short-answer Questions

1. Define change management.
2. What are the types of changes?
3. What is the difference between episodic and continuous change?
4. How is the first order change different from second order change?
5. Why is shared vision important for creating change?
6. Differentiate between radical and incremental change.
7. Discuss the role of training for creating conditions for change.
8. What role is expected from leadership to bring about change?

Discussions Questions

1. What are the forces that cause organizations to change and transform? What impact do internal and external forces have in organizational change?
2. What are the different models of organizational change?
3. Why do employees resist change? What should be done to reduce resistance?
4. Describe the change process. What are the critical steps in the change process?

CHAPTER 19

Human Resource Management Innovations

LEARNING OBJECTIVES

After completing this chapter, the student will be able to:

- Describe the context of organizational innovation
- Define innovation
- Learn the conditions/factors congenial for organization innovation
- Know the characteristics of HRM innovation
- Learn the building blocks for creating a culture of innovations

Opening Case Zodiac Ltd—HRMIS

In June 2013, Lata Bhosle reflected on her 52-week long journey at Zodiac Ltd. She fondly remembered her first day in office, the highlight being the discussion with her boss who explained that her position as the general manager of OD and the change facilitator had been created to smoothly progress the company from a functionally organized, traditional business to an athletic organization, ready to race with the competition and win through best HR practices in the pharmaceutical industry. Her boss was warm in his welcome and full of confidence in her for managing transformation as she had a back- ground of change implementation in the automobile industry. Her progress at Zodiac Ltd had been tracked by many of her professional colleagues and by headhunters. Consequently, she had received two job offers with promising job profiles, but her own sense of failure in the tasks given to her at Zodiac Ltd had prohibited her from accepting these offers and influenced her to increase her efforts with the existing job. Now, she wondered what she could do differently to successfully manage change.

In 2012, Lata had thoroughly researched Zodiac Ltd before accepting the offer. Zodiac Ltd was considered a top-10 pharmaceutical company in India. From 2000 onwards, the Indian pharmaceutical industry was rapidly globalizing and faced challenges similar to those faced by the automobile industry.

The industry was growing exponentially and went from a few companies to many, with new entrants making a foray into the segment and growing. Both sectors had strong statutory and regulatory bodies. However, a major difference was that the pharmaceutical industry was largely family-owned and many firms were managed like family businesses. Lata discovered that Zodiac Ltd too had been founded by the father of the current chief managing director, Sekhar Dubey, in 1962. Empowered by the Indian Patents Act of 1970, the firm had diligently worked to carve out a niche, both in Indian and global markets. Based on expertise in reverse engineering, a new process for manufacturing drugs at low costs, the firm had built competitive advantage over other firms of a similar size and stature. The firm was becoming more progressively professional under the guidance of leading consultants. Managing an HR excellence campaign and developing state-of-the-art people processes in an industry that Lata had never worked in appeared challeng- ing, but the financial reward was good. When Lata began working with Zodiac Ltd, she felt that this could be an opportunity to advance her career.

Since 2007, Zodiac Ltd had been led by Sekhar Dubey, who was a second-generation entrepreneur known for his aggressive, hands-on leadership style. Sekhar Dubey introduced a policy of organic and inorganic growth. Organic growth steadily increased the customer base through new geographic locations and the addition of new formulations; inorganic growth was based on mergers and acquisitions where many strategically aligned businesses were acquired and integrated with the main business. In early 2012, Zodiac Ltd hired Pharmacon, a United Kingdom-based consulting agency, to improve the quality of the company's technical knowledge. In 2012, Zodiac Ltd had a consolidated revenue of ₹2500 crore, with an earning before interest, tax, depreciation, and amortization margin of 23% (which was above the industry average) and a PAT of ₹200 crore. The company had a presence in more than 15 countries and employed more than 8500 employees. Interviews with Sekhar Dubey revealed that the company prioritized research-led growth with the goal of making Zodiac Ltd a globally recognized pharmaceutical company.

To align the organization with this growth strategy, Lata's role was to aid Sekhar Dubey by aligning talent management. Accordingly, her mandate was to work with the HR department to (a) conduct an organizational excellence audit, (b) identify areas of improvement in HR processes related to team alignment and performance, and (c) execute a holistic change strategy in consultation with the VP of HR. Initially, Lata decided to create certain amount of goodwill among employees in the organization, and target the low-hanging fruits. Since the young employees (up to 35 years of age) constituted the critical mass in the employees, she introduced the following initiatives, targeted at millennials:

1. 'Keep Smiling,' was a process for affecting an instant recognition for great performance by an employee. The mnemonic 'Smiling' beautifully captures the spirit behind the initiative: **S**—Shoulders Additional Responsibility; **M**—Multi-tasking Ability, Meticulous Planning; **I**—Initiative, Innovative; **L**—Leading ability; **E**—Empathizing, Effective Communication; **I**—Innovation; **N**—Novel; and **G**—Grand (SMILING). The intention of this initiative is to recognize efforts by employees going beyond pre-determined roles, domains, and work arenas, where one has willingly taken on challenges and assignments in a display of 'high levels of commitment, perseverance, ability to stretch the body, and mind and love for work.'

2. 'Shaktiman' is another new initiative for reward and recognition, but conducted once a year, based on a rigorous process of layered selection. Shaktiman was intended to be a platform for recognizing outstanding contributions at workplaces in creating value for the company beyond the realms of normal duty. Either the LM or the employees themselves could do the nomination, which would subsequently be scrutinized by a panel and the best 10 were selected to go into the Hall of Fame.
   This event was scheduled once in a year and the award presentation (citation and cash prize of ₹5000 each is presented) in a glittering ceremony in the presence of a Director.
3. Face-to-face: Twice a year open houses were organized and attended by all the staff. The initiative was based on informal conversations with some of the young employees who spoke about their experiences of excessive control by the senior leaders in the work organization. Face-to-face had been an initiative to provide a platform for young workforce with few years of experience to bind with the senior leadership team wherein the employees were encouraged to express their challenges and concerns on a wide variety of areas. The senior leadership team also utilized the opportunity to convey the young workforce the path of the organization with the challenges and opportunities ahead for them.
4. Gurukul: All new entrants (management trainees) to the organization were groomed through a structured mentoring process conducted by an outside consultant. The mentoring workshop was a three-day workshop wherein the specified mentors and mentees were matched and an agreement was reached about the roles, boundaries, and the process. The seniors who volunteer to mentor were familiarized with the best practices in mentoring process and skills. Subsequently, the mentors were required to help the mentees as buddies (familiarizing them with the work environment and helping in problem-solving) and teachers.

After the first 6 months, on an informal review with the boss, Lata noted that in the first two initiatives the employees engaged enthusiastically. Even the senior leaders backed the said initiatives. Face-to-face received lip service from the seniors and the enthusiasm started petering out. Mentoring improved the performance and the cycle time for familiarization of the new entrants, but the older employees, barring a few, started backing out of the activity that required them to spend their own time. On the suggestion of the VP HR, Lata prepared a roadmap for an HR audit and consulted the VP HR to discuss its development. Once her plans were in place, she began collecting the data required to assess the organization by conducting in-depth interviews with senior executives and surveys at all levels of the employee hierarchy, and by reviewing HR documentation. After six weeks, she had gathered the required data for analysis that confirmed her plans for improvement.

1. Data suggested that the employees had great expectations from the HR, which was perceived to focus generally on time-keeping and policing jobs to ensure statutory compliance.
2. Interdepartmental collaboration was low. The relationship between the VP of HR and the VP of finance was strained because both VPs spent more time attempting to prove who contributed more toward organizational performance than undertaking valuable work. Interdepartmental liaising was weak, and all functional heads competed internally for their share of attention and recognition from the founding members of the company.

3. Lata also diagnosed role-related issues in the production department. Mulayam Singh, the VP of production, was an old-guard employee who had been with the organization for 25 years, but he delegated minimal work to his juniors. His instructions were ambiguous, and employees did duplicate jobs and wasted time completing redundant documentation processes. His leadership style lacked clarity and an understanding of reporting structures or job role systems, leading to overlapping roles and conflicts within the production team.

Lata understood that the important thing to do was to help create an organizational vision and engage employees in the process. The next steps would be to initiate organizational transformation by creating clear roles, compensation system based on job evaluation, PMS, and other HR processes. HR needed to change gear and balance transactional role with transformational and strategic role. She had a frank discussion with the VPs of HR and production to prepare and deliver a plan of action with a committed timeline and detailed activity schedule for these interventions. The VP of HR had worked for the firm for more than five years and advised her to go slowly by first aligning with the group norms, gaining confidence, and then changing the dysfunctional aspects of roles or task performance. He told her that she was new to the system and that her ideas, though relevant and of organizational interest, would meet resistance because they would challenge the contributions of existing employees. He recommended aligning with departmental heads to create an urgency for change and to identify supporters and opponents. He also informed her that the company employed an old, family-owned structure with several informal but powerful channels of communication and influence. The relationships between the owners and some employees were deep. He warned her to be careful during the implementation of any changes because, although her reports identified the need for change, which people would acknowledge and to which pay lip service publicly, there were undercurrents of resistance, largely from old members of the firm who were also part of the cohort of the owners.

The reality of introducing innovation stunned her soon. When she organized a meeting with all departmental heads and HR managers to brief them about the findings and enroll them for change, she experienced cold vibrations, with support from only a few employees. The subsequent meetings were worse, with low attendance, lukewarm support, and some clear resistance. Her own team of colleagues did not back her. Mr Singh was openly cynical and his team members put up dogged resistance. Now, as she was taking stock of her first 365 days into an extremely thrilling assignment, the shine had worn off from the role. She wondered what she needed to do differently.

Discussion Question

1. What are some of the key lessons learnt about implementation of HRM Innovations?

19.1 INTRODUCTION

In the current, globalized business environment, characterized by keen domestic and global competition, rapid technological change, and bounded resources, business organizations are keenly trying to achieve a capability to innovate. Innovation is the key idea that is shaping corporate life, helping leaders conceive previously unimagined strategic options. Being innovative can help organizations discover opportunities, anticipate on (future) trends, and increase effectiveness, productivity, and profitability. Besides, different types of innovations (incremental, radical, or a combination of both) help achieve not only major business changes, but also greater focus on existing business processes and practices, reduce/eliminate waste, and attract/retain talent. In their book *The Game-Changer*, the authors A. G. Lafley and Ram Charan[1] gave several examples on how P&G used innovations to leverage its acquisition of Gillette to accelerate profitable topline revenue growth and enhance capabilities. We learn about how Nokia became number one in India by using innovation to create 200 million customers. Nokia first observed the unique needs of Indian customers, particularly in rural villages where most of the population resides; it segmented them in new ways; and put new features on handsets relevant to their unique needs. In the process, it created an entirely new value chain at price points that give the company its desired gross margin. Innovation here lay in creating customers by attracting new users and building stronger loyalty among current ones. According to the authors, the real value for a business organization lies in putting innovation at the center of the business, from top to bottom, the effect being that not only the organization achieves improvement in top/bottom line, it also leads to the discovery of a superior way of doing things—'more productive, more responsive, more inclusive, even more fun. People want to be part of growth, not endless cost cutting.'

Innovations, however, can yield desired results for the business organization only when it is viewed not as a stand-alone, exclusive activity by an elite group, but rather as something that is routine and process-driven, while riding on the capabilities of normal employees, particularly the knowledge workers. But innovations do not guarantee business success, unless it is embedded in the culture of the organization. There is an entire process of managing the transition from formulation of a new solution or a new product to the market through making the right connections in a repeated manner. And this process can only happen when people do that simple, but critical activity—connect to share problems, opportunities, and learning. The leaders need to map, systematize, manage, measure, and improve this process to generate a consistent flow of innovations, and occasionally the real big one. Innovations, in this demystified avatar, become a journey that can be plotted, replicated, and can demand changing everything from budget and strategy to capital allocation and promotions.

The term 'innovation' has had many definitions over the years, each bringing in a new facet. According to Joseph Schumpeter,[2] innovation covers a wide field including introducing a new product or modifications brought to an existing product; a new process of innovation in an industry; the discovery of a new market; developing new sources of supply with raw materials; and other changes in the organization. Business Council Australia[3] has a crisp definition: Innovation is adoption of new or significantly improved elements to create added value to the organization directly or indirectly for its customers. On the basis of various readings on innovation literature, the term 'innovation' is generally held to have two different connotations. First, to indicate the process of bringing new products, equipment, programs, or systems into use;[4] second, to imply the object of the innovation

[1] A. G. Lafley and Ram Charan, *The Game-Changer: How You Can Drive Revenue and Profit Growth With Innovation* (New York: Crown Business, 2008).

[2] Joseph Schumpeter (1930). Available at: https://www.investopedia.com/terms/j/joseph-schumpeter.asp (accessed on February 15, 2018).

[3] Joan Lala Popa, Gheorghe Preda and Monica Boldea, 'A Theoretical Approach of the Concept of Innovation,' Business Council Australia (1993). Available at: ftp://ftp.repec.org/opt/ReDIF/RePEc/bbu/wpape

[4] F. Damanpour, 'Organizational Innovation: A Meta-Analysis of Effects of Determinants and Moderators,' *Academy of Management Journal* 34, no. 3 (1991): 555–590.

process, that is, the new product, equipment, program, or system.[5] While using this term some have also raised questions whether 'objective newness' is considered an important criterion of innovation. According to Daft,[6] objective newness is an important parameter of innovation, others regard it as 'a product, program, or system which is new to the adopting organization.'[7]

19.2 HUMAN RESOURCE MANAGEMENT AND INNOVATIONS

HRM innovations (HRMIs) have been defined as *any intentional introduction or change of HR program policy, practice or system, to influence or adapt the skills, behaviors*, and interactions of employees and have the potential to provide, both, the foundations for strategy formulation and the means for strategy implementation that is perceived to be new and creates current capabilities and competencies.[8]

There are several theories on the synergy between HRM and innovation. Zhou et al.[9] reason, on the basis of AMO model (ability, motivation, and opportunities), that HRM develops abilities, motivation, and opportunities, thereby improving employee performance, apart from boosting financial performance. One way in which HRM can directly improve capability to innovate is by building a strategic focus of employee development strategy in that direction. The resource-based view states that organizations achieve sustainable competitive advantage by creating resources that are unique, inimitable, valuable, and non-substitutable. Human resource also represent a valuable resource that should, according to Beugelsdijk,[10] be managed toward being unique so that it is superior to the human resource of other organizations. Besides, since innovation is development of new ideas and also the process of actually putting the new ideas into practice, the development of ideas mainly occurs through creative employees, individually or in teams.

Jiang et al.[11] also take this argument further and define the people within an organization as 'the foundation of innovation' and declare, if an organization views its employees as the most important asset and invests in it by creating a supportive work environment, employees will feel committed to the organization. The feeling of being valued leads to an increased inputs-to-return creativity. Beugelsdijk[12] has identified individual HR practices that have different effects on two types of organizational innovation: incremental innovations and radical innovations. Incremental innovation, which is concerned with the enhancement and upgrading of existing products, services, and processes within a company, can be organized by incentive systems and training programs. The relevant HR practices that aid incremental innovation are: training and schooling, job autonomy, and performance-

[5] P. Attewell, 'Technology Diffusion and Organizational Learning: The. Case of Business Computing,' *Organization Science* 3, no. 1 (1992): 1–19.

[6] R. L. Daft, 'A Dual-Core Model of Organizational Innovation,' *Academy of Management Journal* 21, no. 2 (1978): 193–210.

[7] (Damanpour 1991)

[8] A. Som, 'Bracing MNC Competition Through Innovative HRM Practices: The Way Forward for Indian Firms,' *Thunderbird International Business Review* 48, no. 2 (2006): 207–237. Available at: https://www.researchgate.net/.../228666900_Innovative_human_ resource_management (accessed on January 20, 2018).

[9] Y. Zhou, Y. Hong, and J. Liu, 'International Commitment or External Collaboration? The Impact of Human Resource Management Systems on Firm Innovation and Performance,' *Human Resource Management* 52, no. 2 (2013): 263–288.

[10] S. Beugelsdijk, 'Strategic Human Resource Practices and Product Innovation,' *Organization Studies* 29, no. 6 (2008): 821–847.

[11] J. Jiang, S. Wang, and S. Zhao, 'Does HRM Facilitate Employee Creativity and Organizational Innovation? A Study of Chinese Firms,' *International Journal of Human Resource Management* 23, no. 19 (2012): 4025–4047.

[12] Beugelsdijk (2008).

based pay. Radical innovation, on the other hand, poses far more challenges and intricacies, warrants employees' empowerment at work and flexible working hours. It is further argued by the author that firms with a decentralized organizational structure and an employee-empowerment orientation are able to achieve higher levels of product innovation. Jiang et al.[13] also hold that by enhancing the competencies and motivation of employees to be creative, more innovative ideas can be generated. Creativity at employee level may lead to the development of innovative products at organizational level. The following HR practices facilitate creativity: hiring and selection, reward, job design, and teamwork.

On the basis of various views on the linkages between HRM and organizational innovation, it can be summarized that HRM contributes to innovation by playing two different roles: (a) facilitation of an innovative organization culture and (b) adoption and implementation of innovation activities through its own processes or HRMIs.

Exhibit Innovations in HR

Technological advancement in organizations has led to the rise of chatbots and AI in simplifying HR functions. When it comes to workplaces professionals worldwide concur to the need to have technology ease processes. One such area is the HR function in a number of organizations that has actually gone ahead and digitized its work with great efficiency with the help of chatbots. Chatbots are computer programs that are designed to simulate conversations with human users over the Internet through computers or mobile devices.

Companies like InMobi, Bank Bazaar and Yes Bank are a few of the first ones to have integrated chatbots into their HR functions. These automated virtual assistants are designed to take over many of the critical as well as time-consuming HR tasks, leaving HR heads and managers with more time to take up more strategic work within their function. A case in point being HR SaaS solution company, PeopleStrong, which launched India's first HR chatbot called 'Jinie'. Jinie plays the role of an employee's personal work assistant, and also helps solve HR-related queries such as applying for leaves, collating and completing employee data, answering company policy-related FAQs—Jinie can help an employee with all of that and more.

Performance management, one of the biggest and most time-consuming HR activities, is also set to see a bot revolution. Instead of waiting for six months or a whole year to receive feedback from employees on their work, bots help facilitate feedback in real-time, in a transparent manner without back and forth human intervention. Lengthy and tedious appraisal forms are getting replaced by feedback sharing through an automated chat mechanism.

As per PeopleStrong Co-founder and CEO, Pankaj Bansal's estimate, at least 30 million of the 100 million people in HR functions will be actively using chatbots to ease their work by 2020. With easy access to a range of employee and performance related information, bots are all set to making life simpler and change the way we work.

Source: Excerpted from 'Chatbots: The Latest Technology Fad in HR.' April 12, 2017. Available at: https:// www.peoplematters.in/article/hr-shared-service/chatbots-the-latest-technology-fad-in-hr-15293?utm_source=peoplematters&utm_medium=interstitial&utm_campaign=learnings-of-the-day (accessed on November 8, 2017).

13 Jiang et al. (2012).

An HRMI is an 'idea, program, practice, or system which is related to the HRM function and is new to the adopting organization.'[14] It is an innovation which contributes to any of the standard HRM functions such as recruiting and selection; appraisal; T&D; and rewards and benefits. For example, Reebok set up a CrossFit Workout Center wherein employees were motivated to sweat it out. It was found that the center not only helped employees shed their extra pounds but also made them see the importance of Reebok's vision that in turn helped the employees engage in their duties more passionately. In another instance of an HRMI, Zappos, an online shoe store, has a novel hiring system that includes telephone interviews, lengthy personal interviews, and other detailed processes. Once selected, the candidates present themselves in informal events such as happy hours or lunch events to show how they socialize with the company staff and enroll in the culture. The successful candidates then receive an onboard training. At the conclusion of the training process, the candidates get a strange offer—US$3000 to leave. Around 3% does take up the offer but those who choose to stay are the ones that actually understand the company's vision and culture, and they do have a long-term association with the company.

19.3 FACTORS AFFECTING THE INNOVATION PROCESS IN ORGANIZATIONS

The innovation process has four sequential steps: conception of an idea, proposal, decision to adopt, and finally the implementation. What are some of the determinants of organizations? Why is it that some organizations become like dinosaurs and some change their orientation and focus and survive? Researchers on organization innovation have been at work for a long time on what specific conditions help organization innovation.[15–18] The different factors surfaced by various studies include structural features specific to big organizations, strategic orientation, learning and flexibility, and internal and external factors (internal factors—market orientation, learning and technology policy, designed to enhance a firm's innovative behavior—and external factors—industry concentration and barriers to entry) that directly affect the organization's attitude toward innovation or by inhibiting or stimulating related work.[19]

1. It is widely accepted that leadership plays a decisive role in innovation process. Some of the factors that have been held as facilitators of innovation are elite values toward change, the status and sociometric centrality of the organization's top administrators, and the cosmopolitan orientation of top administrators and administrator motivation to innovate.[20] There are several reasons for the critical role of leaders in organizational innovation: The leaders serve as a bridge connecting the organization with the technological environment. Their exposure, status, and rank enable them to initiate change into the organization. They get ideas, their

[14] Richard A. Wolfe, 'Human Resource Management Innovations: Determinants of Their Adoption and Implementation,' *Human Resource Management* 34, no. 2 (1995): 313–327.

[15] Capon, Lehmann, Farley and Hulbert, 'Profiles of Product Innovators Among Large U.S. Manufacturers', *Management Science* 38, no. 2 (1992): 157–169.

[16] Fritz, 'The Path of Least Resistance,' (Oxford: Butterworth Heinemann, 1989).

[17] Kraft, 'Market Structure, Firm Characteristics and Innovative Activities,' *Journal of Industrial Economics* 37 (1989): 329–336.

[18] R. A. Wolfe, '*Organizational Innovation*: Review, Critique and Suggested Research Directions,' *Journal of Management Studies* 31, no. 3 (1994): 405–431.

[19] H. Salavou, G. Baltas, and S. Lioukas, 'Organisational Innovation in SMEs: The Importance of Strategic Orientation and Competitive Structure,' *European Journal of Marketing* 38, no. 9/10 (2004): 1091–1112.

[20] Richard L. Daft, 'A Dual-Core Model of Organizational Innovation,' *Academy of Management Journal* 21, no. 2 (1978): 193–210.

ideas matter, and the sanction of funds requires their approval. They can also exert critical influence in change.

2. An influential stream of research has held that organizational innovations occur in two distinct zones. William Evans,[21] the originator of this approach, has argued that innovations can be started at both leadership level and bottom levels, depending upon the nature of innovation to be proposed and a good way to maximize adoptions is to encourage the generation of innovative ideas at both the ends of the organizational hierarchy. Organizational innovations follow different routes from conception to implementation: while administrative innovations occur near the top of the hierarchy and trickle down, the technical innovations start some place at the bottom of the hierarchy and trickle up.
3. Richard A. Daft has taken the aforementioned proposition to present the theory of the dual-core model of organizational innovations. The model describes dual cores of organizations—a technical core and an administrative core—each having a part to play. Innovations in technical core directly cover basic work activities and can concern product, process, or technology. Innovations in administrative core cover areas of organization management and can involve organizational structure and administrative processes; their link to the basic work activities is indirect. There are populations in each core having goals, problems, activities, technology, and an ecology. Each core can play host to innovations. The administrative core is above the technical core in the hierarchy, and the domain of the administrative core includes the organization itself. If the degree of professionalism is high, the coupling of the two cores is loose and the technical core has a fair amount of independence, but if the professionalism is low then the technical core acts subservient and the administrative core plays the big brother role.

   According to the research findings by Daft, the innovation strategy depends on the needs of the organization: when innovation is desired in technical core, the organization requires to focus on acquisition of highly professional employees for the technical core, empowerment of such employees to manage innovation (on the premise that they are well versed in the state-of-the-art technology), and making approval process routine and simple. Where the acquisition of highly professional employees becomes difficult due to financial constraints, then the administrators may need to assert.
4. According to Coral,[22] the most crucial influencers of innovative behavior of organizations are (a) institutional arrangements, (b) technological and organizational capabilities, (c) organizational learning, and (d) entrepreneurial or risk-taking behavior. Furthermore, he refers to individual factors that also influence the overall innovative behavior of organizations. Especially, the (e) individuals' intention to take on certain behavior is essential for predicting innovative behavior of an entire organization.

19.4 CHARACTERISTICS OF HUMAN RESOURCE MANAGEMENT INNOVATIONS

The HRMIs have several broad characteristics:

---

[21] W.M. Evan, 'Organizational Lag,' *Human Organization* 25 (1966): 51–53.

[22] C. Montalvo, 'What Triggers Change and Innovation?' *Technovation* 26, no. 3 (2006): 312–323.

1. **Uncertainty** Since innovations in the area of HRM are intangible, it poses serious challenges for predicted outcome or in business terms 'return on investments.' The ambiguity or lack of knowledge about the nexus between the inputs, processes, and outcomes is inbuilt in most HRMIs. Therefore, the conventional computational methods are less applicable to HRMI outcomes as compared to the organizational innovations in other fields such as, marketing or operations (e.g., cost–benefit, ROI, payback analyses). The lack of concreteness of HRMI measures, along with the complexity in assessing their impacts, creates uncertainty that typifies HRMI.[23]
2. **The perceived threat to vested interests** Resistance to innovation efforts is unconnected with the inherent features of the innovation subject. According to Kimberly, the potential benefits of an innovation notwithstanding, its adoption and implementation will militate against some interests and imperil some coalitions. In case the innovation is radical in nature demanding change in behavior, the degree of both uncertainty and resistance is likely to be higher than in normal cases of innovation.[24]
3. **Two other attributes associated with HRMI are**
   (a) *Magnitude* The extent of change to existing structure, personnel, and financial resources implied by an innovation; and
   (b) *Pervasiveness* The number of organizational members who are expected to change their behaviors due to an innovation.[25]

HRMIs with little magnitude and pervasiveness would tend to engender minimum resistance. Examples of such HRMIs include innovative job posting and peer recognition approaches. On the other hand, HRMIs such as flextime, new bonus programs,[26] flexible work arrangements, and parental leaves[27] can imply considerable displacement of existing organizational procedures and/or substantial change in the behaviors of organizational members. Such HRMIs, therefore, result in considerable perceived threat to the status quo and, thus, in resistance. A summary of innovation attributes most relevant to HRM is given in Table 19.1.

19.5 CONDITIONS NECESSARY FOR SUCCESSFUL HRMI IMPLEMENTATION

Based on experiences of organizations the successful implementation of HRMIs requires the following conditions:

1. **Innovation champions** It has been found that very often there are many factors present in organizations that act as disablers for a new initiative. As has been mentioned, HRMIs are often associated with uncertainty and, therefore, the innovation efforts need to be tangible and personified in innovation champions. In successful HRMI implementation, innovation champions bring vigor and positive spirit to create momentum for the innovation implementation.

---

23 Frost, P. and C. Egri, 'Political Process of Innovation, Research in Organizational Behaviour' (1991): 229–296.

24 Nord, W. R., and S. Tucker, 'Diffusion, Uncertainty, and Firm Size,' International Journal of Research in Marketing 6 (1987): 109–128.

25 J. M. Beyer and H. M. Trice, *Implementing* Change (New York, NY: Free Press, 1978).

26 E. E. Kosseck, *The Acceptance of Human Resource Innovations* (Quorum Books, 1989).

27 E. Galinsky, Dana E. *Friedman*, and Carol A. Hernandez, *The Corporate Reference Guide to Work-Family Programs* (New York: Families and Work Institute, 1991): 212–213.

Table 19.1 Coverage of HRMIs in a hospital

Category	Human resource management processes	Coverage
Employment innovations	1. Talent management 2. Reward management 3. e-HRM	Blended learning/e-learning, talent management pool, labor market communication program, employer branding, education and performance program, employee development plans, generic job descriptions, sickness absence management, introduction to recruitment department, flexible labor office, monitoring employee satisfaction, workability plans.
Work innovations	1. Employee engagement and empowerment 2. Management responsiveness 3. Job design 4. Working conditions	Introduction of nurse practitioner, introduction of physician assistant, introduction of lower-level nurses, dual management, manager participation in nursing work, changing teams, job rotation, job crafting, internal mobility paths.
Organizational innovations	1. Culture 2. Strategic HRM 3. Communication 4. Digitalization	Organizational restructuring, HR department restructuring, cultural change programs, family centered care, process improvement techniques: theory of constraints, business process redesign, lean management for healthcare, capacity management care, centralized scheduling, digitalization, operating room checklist, safety rounds, network with other healthcare providers, network with other business organizations.
Miscellaneous	1. Barriers 2. Causes 3. Cooperation vs Competition	

Source: 'Taking Care of Innovations: An Exploratory Research on Dutch General Hospitals,' Master Thesis, University of Twente, August 2016.

2. **Power dynamics** Due to the aura of uncertainty and the threat to vested interests, HRMI unlash political dynamics inside the organizational environment. If the innovation champions wield more power than the opponents, then it creates favorable headwind for the HRMI implementation. The innovation champions are able to effectively challenge the detractors and provide necessary resources to the threatened groups.
3. **Organizational context** There are internal and external factors that also determine the success of HRMIs. Internal factors include size, complexity, extent of unionization, strength of the culture, commitment to HR function and a desire to improve the quality of organizational life. External factors include increased foreign competition, government regulations, labor market conditions, and institutional pressures to imitate other organizations. If the innovation is in sync with the organization context, then the innovation champions do not have to use influence to implement innovation. On the contrary, if there is dissonance between the innovation and the organization context, then it becomes imperative for the innovation champions to use power and pressure to make innovation happen.[28]

[28] Wolfe, *Research Handbook on Comparative Employment Relations* (1995).

19.6 CURRENT TRENDS IN HUMAN RESOURCE MANAGEMENT INNOVATIONS

19.6.1 Design Thinking in HR

The origin of design as a way of thinking is attributed to Herbert A. Simon's 1969 book *The Sciences of the Artificial.* In the 1990s, David M. Kelley of Stanford University, the founder of the design consultancy IDEO, started using design thinking for business purposes. In 1992, an article 'Wicked Problems in Design Thinking' by Richard Buchanan broadened the scope of design thinking to cover complex human issues and concerns with application of design. It makes use of the creative strategies designers employ during the process of designing. Design thinking also evolved as a problem-solving approach. It capitalizes on the designer's sensibility and methods to harmonize people's needs with technological feasibility, and convert business strategy, customer experience, and market opportunity. It follows a path very dissimilar to analytical thinking. Instead of the convergent approach of breaking issues into pieces, it relies on building up ideas, virtually without boundaries, through a process of brainstorming, thereby eliminating anxiety and unlocking spontaneous energy.

There are different practice approaches for design thinking, and the oft-used approach consists of seven stages: define, research, ideate, prototype, choose, implement, and learn. The various stages provide opportunities for framing of problems, asking questions, generation of ideas, eventually leading to choice of the right solutions. The process is not circular; it can move sequentially, at random, at the same time, or even repetitive. According to Plattner et al., 'While the stages are simple enough, the adaptive expertise required to choose the right inflection points and appropriate next stage is a high order intellectual activity that requires practice and is learnable.'[29]

Design thinking is receiving increasing attention in HRM, especially in the context of the emergent strategic partner role of HR. Design thinking, with its inherent people-centricity, has clear application in HRM, particularly in managing the people aspects of organization transformation that implies a transition from an actual state to a desired state. A classic change management program consists of communication, training, workforce transition, and so on. In each of these areas, design thinking can make a difference in improving the quality and overall effectiveness of the activity. L&D programs, as we know, are a key enabler to reskill groups of affected employees and an important lead indicator for managing change. In a typical condition, training programs operate at a very low ROI. The participants of such sessions generally get into a mode of passive learning with the onus of skill transfer resting primarily upon the transformation team. With the aid of design thinking, the T&D strategy could be two-tiered: socialization and actualization. In the socialization stage, all problems could be identified in an exhaustive manner, covering select stakeholders, engaging them in design discussions, and arriving at the solution design based on their views. The design thinking tool thus would create value through fostering better engagement of the stakeholders, deriving certain key themes and archetypes from the data, and weaving them into the design fabrics. In the actualization phase, a product/service prototype is developed on the basis of the design elements, followed by iterations and validations, leading to a final design that, while being aligned to business needs, enrolls the affected stakeholders.[30] The same effect can be achieved in formulating high-quality communication program, which is also

[29] Hasso Christoph Meinel, and Larry J. Leifer, eds., *Design Thinking: Understand — Improve — Apply. Understanding Innovation (Berlin; Heidelberg:* Springer-Verlag).

[30] Anudyuti Das, 'Design Thinking to Aid Transformation,' *Human Capital* 20, no. 4 (September 2016).

a key measure for organization transformation. Very often transformation efforts flounder on two counts: first, lack of understanding of the divergent communication needs of different stakeholders for change; and second, the failure to craft the communication style to the unique cultural shades of the employees at work.

There are other areas of HRM that can be improved with the help of design thinking. One such area is talent engagement. The multiplied complexity of work and the scarcity of talent make it imperative for the HR professional to play a dual role of facilitating employee engagement and to arm the LM with the tool kit of mentoring and training. To effectively balance this role, the challenge for HR is to get fully conversant with the work content and context of both the employee and the LM. For example, to understand employee issues, HR must be aware of the drivers of employee engagement from the employees' perspective. For the employee, both the rational and emotional aspects would need to be paid due attention, considering their constraints in clearly articulating his problems. The HR personnel should familiarize him with the job context and then be able to hold informal conversations with employees in their workplace. Empathy maps, a design thinking instrument, could be handy in developing a deep understanding. An empathy map captures information under four components—think: the user's opinions on the subject of interest; feel: the user's emotional reactions on the issue of interest; do: the user's actual actions related to the subject; and say: verbatim quotations. The relevance of the instrument in this context is that it yields data based on the user's perspective, and by creating scope to capture data from multiple channels—emotional as well as rational—comes up with an authentic employee-centric view of a situation. A leader may not feel threatened or offended that his team members call him 'busy,' but an empathy map could reveal that, for some team members, busy could imply 'difficult to approach.'[31]

19.6.2 Gamification

One of the ways organizations are differentiating from each other is user-creating stakeholder experience—be it customer, candidate, or audience. In HR processes, recruitment and selection activity provides a natural platform for crafting an experience for a job seeker in the reality of the work environment. In experiential recruiting, an emergent field, the innovations being currently tried out include coding marathons, hacking events, complex problem-solving exercises, and solving cryptic puzzles.[32]

Gamification indicates use of game thinking and mechanics in business processes. In HRM, it is considered applicable to the areas of recruitment, T&D, and employee engagement. In the recruiting process, gamification brings out applicants' natural propensities for competitiveness, self-expression, closure, and even altruism—all the while allowing them to navigate situations that replicate the tasks necessary to be successful on the job. For employers, talent acquisition software that incorporates gamification can generate hard data on a candidate and gain insight into a candidate's specific personality traits as well as his or her ability to multi-task and handle stress on the job. It integrates features such as fun, play, design, competition, and addiction into the need for achievement, status, rewards, and self-expression and makes it attractive to the millennials. Game mechanics can be applied for screening or selecting the candidates. It includes visual cues, response objects, badges, levels, leaderboards, challenges, and progress bars; it can even create candidate experience where

[31] Available at: https://www.peoplematters.in/article/technology (accessed on November 20, 2017).

[32] Ruchika Kinger, 'Augmenting Experiential Recruiting Through Gamification.' Available at: https://www.peoplematters.in/article/strategic-hr/augmenting-experiential-recruiting-through-gamification-15658 (accessed on November 20, 2017).

candidates can compete with each other and check their application stage vis-à-vis the other candidates. The current application areas of games include campus recruitment, shortlisting, employee referrals, sourcing, and onboarding or employer branding. For example, gamification of employee referral program could happen through developing a scorecard and adding to scores per referral.

Exhibit Gamification in Recruitment

Some Current Experiments

Google's Code Jam

A multi-service Internet phenomenon, Google launched an annual software-writing competition to find fresh, exceptional talent. The Google Code Jam provides the participating developers and engineers not only a shot at displaying their skills as potential hires for the company, but also a chance to win up to US$50,000 in monetary prizes.

Formaposte French Postal Service—A Day in the Life

A French postal service that was constantly faced with the challenge of maintaining loyal employees once they were hired, launched Jeu Facteur Academy. This talent-assessment software enabled potential new hires to experience virtually what a week in the life of a postal carrier is like. From waking up before dawn to under-standing the intricacies involved in postal work, the candidate game presented applicants with realistic expectations of the job prior to accepting a position with the postal service. As a result of utilizing gamification in recruitment, employees who quit their job at the postal service dropped from 25% to just 8%.

UK Government Communications Headquarters—Cracking the Code

Government Communications Headquarters (GCHQ), the British intelligence and security agency, created an intriguing encrypted message on a Website CanYouCrackIt.co.uk. It was part of an application process for new hires. Candidates had to literally crack the code on the Website and then succinctly decipher the hidden message in order to be able to advance in the application process. As a result, the GCHQ was able to easily screen the applicants without having to rely strictly on a candidate's resume as the weeding-out process before the interview.

Domino's Pizza—Designing Pizzas for Cash

Affirming that Domino's is an innovative and fun place to work, Domino's created the Pizza Mogul game. While at first glance it may seem like a creative way for customers to earn money by coming up with off-the-wall ideas for new pizzas, the mindset behind embracing the concept of gamification in recruitment was to attract and inspire young job seekers to their brand by presenting it as a truly hip place to be employed. Users who log on to play the game get to pick and choose the toppings they think would make an appealing pizza. Then they can name their creation, and for every version of their pizza that is sold, they earn cash.

Source: Excerpted from http://www.furstperson.com/blog/gamification (accessed on January 11, 2017).

Gamification can help in observing human behavior too. The data, which traditionally were collected through cumbersome questionnaires or interviews, can now be generated quite simply and accurately through observation of an individual's game behavior. Gamification can serve as an assessment tool by providing information to analyze non-linear relationships and predicting outcomes. Gamification can also enrich the performance management process through transparent leaderboards with badges that can be attached to each level enabling the employees to keep tab on the status of their on-the-job performance. It has become common for organizations to provide an internal social media platform where employees can update posts and chat with each other internally. HR department can improve employee engagement by creating clear, mission-based career paths so that employees know where they can head in the organization and work out an L&D plan as appropriate.

An Indian company cracked the gamification code for time and attendance (T&A). The employees resist compliance. Non-adherence to T&A and leave management processes are a big headache to HR managers. It is not just a process issue but people issue. We often see the HR and employees breaking their heads over a petty attendance regularization. Every correct action on the attendance platform earns points for an employee. Weekly and monthly winners are announced. Here comes the bigger surprise—all the points earned can be redeemed into gifts, coupons, buying stuffs, and offers to choose from a large collection.[33]

19.7 INNOVATIVE HUMAN RESOURCE MANAGEMENT PRACTICES IN INDIA

In a study conducted on 194 Indian organizations in 2008, Som reported the following key findings:

1. HRM function has become more proactive, fair, helpful, respected, and acts as a coach and tries to benchmark with global excellent practices. Indian firms are focusing on innovative recruitment and compensation practices to improve their performance.
2. Among the five key HR practices that were tested (role of HRD, recruitment practices, retraining–redeployment practices, performance appraisal practices, compensation and reward practices), not all were targets of innovation. With liberalization, which created a deregulated hypercompetitive environment, retaining key talent has been one of the important resources for competitive advantages for firms. Indian firms are using flexible hours, competency-based payment schemes, and clear remuneration policies to attract and retain talent. In the study, it came out that innovative recruitment and compensation practices were preferred for improving firm's performance.[34]

19.7.1 Workforce Downsizing and HRMI in India

Manpower downsizing is the most preferred response for organizations seeking to improve their organizational efficiency, cost and performance. Research on the impact of downsizing, however, is inconclusive and a large number of companies rather than becoming 'lean and mean, often end up lean and lame' as a result.[35] In another study on the innovative practices in Indian firms, Som reported on two companies (State Bank of India and Mehta Group of Industries) who dealt with the issue of redundancy in different ways. State Bank of India (SBI), India's largest public sector bank, under severe competitive pressures post-liberalization for cost optimization (from both the Indian private as well as foreign banks), decided to restructure and implement the right HR practices in order to retain its talented workers. Mehta Group is a leading conglomerate with two cement companies (Gujarat

33 Pankaj Shah and Dhwani Mehta, 'An Indian Company Cracked the Gamification Code for Time & Attendance.' Available at: https://www.peoplematters.in/article/technology/an-indian-company-cracked-the-gamification-code-for-time-attendance-15294 (accessed on November 20, 2017)

34 Ashok Som, 'Innovative Human Resources Management and Corporate Performance in the Context of Economic Liberalization in India,' *The International Journal of Human Resource Management* 19, no. 7 (2008): 1278–1297.

35 R. Henkoff, 'Getting Beyond Downsizing,' *Fortune* 129 (1994): 58–64.

Sidhee Cement and Saurashtra Cement in Western India) was faced with the task of revitalizing a sick unit and a loss-making firm. A strategy of 'synergy' between the two companies (to reduce competition and the declining market share) was devised with focus on introduction of innovative HRM practices. In the wake of this decision, there was organization restructuring, recast of roles and job descriptions, creation of new positions, and adoption of competency modeling measures. Rather than embracing a retrenchment and recruitment philosophy, the group chose a redeployment policy. Employees were classified into clusters of technical experts, industry experts, and market research personnel. By enhancing HRD within the company, Mehta Group was able to record significant improvement in performances and was able to optimally utilize its resources.[36]

19.8 HOW HUMAN RESOURCE PRACTICES CONTRIBUTE TO ORGANIZATIONAL INNOVATION

Employees are regarded as the key resources for an innovative organization. It is also widely acknowledged that innovations occur regularly when they are managed, motivated, and rewarded in the right manner. There are some HR processes that have touch points with organizational innovation. The linkage between HRM practices and organizational innovation has been the subject of considerable interest in recent times and there is a body of researches done on the subject. In a study, based on a sample of 178 organizations operating in the Greek manufacturing sector,[37] a mediation model was tested to assess the connection between HRM and organizational performance. The findings of the study confirmed the hypothesis that the relationship between the HRM practices of resource development and reward relations, and organizational performance is catalyzed through the HR outcomes of skills and attitudes. In another research, covering 173 Spanish firms, Jiménez-Jiménez and Sanz-Valle[38] applied structural equations modeling on the data to report the findings that innovation contributes positively to business performance and that HRM enhances innovation. These and several other researches on the same theme have supported the hypotheses that an innovation-driven business strategy needs to be backed by robust and bundled HR practices. The assortment of HRM practices is characterized by extensive T&D, extensive employee involvement and empowerment, high levels of autonomy and flexibility, and performance related rewards and recognition.[39] It has been reasoned that the resultant improvement in psychological outcomes such as commitment and engagement would translate into productivity and creativity.[40]

Some of the innovative HR practices fostering innovations in well-known MNCs are indicated further.[41]

---

36 Som, 'Bracing MNC Competition Through Innovative HRM Practices.'

37 A. Katou and P. Budhwar, 'Human Resource Management Systems and Organizational Performance: A Test of Mediating Model in the Greek Manufacturing Context,' *International Journal of Human Resource Management* 17, no. 7 (2006): 1223–1253.

38 D. Jiménez-Jiménez and R. Sanz-Valle, 'Could HRM Support Organizational Innovations?,' *International Journal of Human Resource Management* 19, no. 7 (2008): 1208–1221.

39 D. Guest, N. Conway, and P. Dewe, 'Using Sequential Tree Analysis to Search for 'Bundles' of HR Practice,' *Human Resource Management Journal* 14, no. 1 (2004): 79–96.

40 F.L. Cooke, 'The Important Role of Maintenance Workforce in Technological Change: A Much Neglected Aspect,' *Human Relations* 55, no. 8 (2002): 963–988.

41 Ashok K. Gupta and Arvind Singhal, 'Managing Human Resources for Innovation and Creativity,' *Research-Technology Management* 36, no. 3 (1993): 41–48.

19.8.1 Human Resource Planning

Venture Teams: One of the ways in which innovations occur in organizations is through venture teams (VTs). A VT comprises individuals with varied experience and expertise, who are assigned a project on the premise that the output of the team will be greater than individual output taken together. To encourage innovation, HR planners should get people with divergent qualities and skill mix. Some of the skill sets identified by some organizations that are reputed for innovations are: 'openness to new ideas, a tolerance of ambiguity, and an eagerness for new experience' (Motorola); 'technically excellent, but broad enough to understand what others have to say, share goals, and exercise people skills' (Apple Computers); 'an artist as a scientist or business man' (DuPont); 'genuinely want to serve the customer, create superior product, willing to stick their necks out to do new things.'[42] The next step in HRP is to formulate appropriate selection process, for example, adopting 10 in-depth interviews to select a technologist,[43] building consensus by a committee of union members and management, and looking for technical skills as well as interpersonal skills (GMs Saturn Plant).

19.8.2 Performance Appraisal

Performance management process is a critical determinant of employee motivation. The performance measures drive the desired behavior. For example, in a technology-based company, where the cycle time between the research initiation and successful launch in the market is long, speaking of things such as number of patents, publications, or research grants may fail to enthuse innovators. In such situations, risk-taking can be encouraged and failure should not be responded with punishment. Organizations stress on creation of new ideas, and have gone to the extent of awarding adoption of ideas from elsewhere (Not Invented Here Award in Raychem). There is also a practice of linking percentage of sale to a new product (3M allots 25% of sale from products introduced during last five years). For performance evaluations, organizations have deviated from the 90-degree appraisal to set up system of self-policing for new product innovations and technical audit (3M).

19.8.3 Reward Systems

Employee reward systems that drive innovative behavior include freedom for creativity, free time to engage in own research, hefty research budgets, and in-house grants. The approach of the organization toward failure in innovation initiative is also an important determinant of innovation. In the company 3M, in case of a failed project, there is no punishment; instead, the employees are told to continue with the next project. The Golden Step Award is given to the employee who develops a new product. In Merck, pay-raise policies vary between innovators and non-innovators. Besides basic pay, the creative performers get other financial or non-financial rewards.

19.8.4 Career Management

There are Catch-22 situations when a scientist/technical professional becomes due for promotion to the next level, which often involve additional administrative/managerial work. Organizations have circumvented this quandary by inventing a dual-track system. In such a system, an employee can choose an administrative track or a technical track. Both tracks have proportionate and comparable pay,

42 A.K. Gupta and A. Singhal, 'Managing Human Resources for Innovations and Creativity,' *Research Technology Management* (May-June 1993): 41–48.

43 Ibid.

status, and influence. A 'third-ladder' system, which is an improvement on the dual-track system, gives opportunity to a scientist/ technical person to engage in a challenging research project (Table 19.2).

Table 19.2 HRMIs in Indian owned Indian-invested companies

Types of HR practices	No. of responses (N = 54)
L&D	
T&D	48
Career development planning	3
Management/leadership development	5
Learning organization	15
Knowledge management	10
Employee involvement and quality initiatives	
Suggestion schemes	45
Quality initiatives	32
Performance management	
Performance appraisal	28
Performance-related pay	24
Profit-sharing	4
Performance/merit-based promotion	20
Employee recognition awards	33
Employee welfare and engagement	
Employee welfare schemes	7
Employee-engagement initiatives	11
Other HR initiatives reported	
Recruiting creative employees	3
Empowerment	7
Autonomy	2

Source: Fang Lee Cooke and Debi S. Saini, '(How) Does the HR Strategy Support an Innovation Oriented Business Strategy? An Investigation of Institutional Context and Organizational Practices in Indian Firms,' *Human Resource Management* 49 (May–June 2010): 377–400.

19.8.5 Indian Context

The liberalization of the Indian economy in the 1990s has contributed to a spectacular growth in the number of privately owned Indian firms that have been growing into globally competitive MNCs. Meanwhile, intensified competition and market volatility has caused PSUs restructuring their organization and reconfiguring their business strategy. These changes require a new way to manage human resources. A study covering 54 managers from Indian-owned, Indian-invested companies, each working in a different company spread across a range of business areas (e.g., banking, telecommunications, IT, consulting, commercial, aerospace, pharmaceutical production research and development, railway engineering, automotive production, energy, oil, minerals, and shipping) explored the types of innovations and level of innovativeness, types of HR practices adopted, their effectiveness, and areas for improvement. The respondents listed a range of HR initiatives as having been adopted by firms to support their innovation-oriented business strategy. In particular, L&D, employee involvement and quality initiatives, performance management schemes, and employee welfare and engagement schemes were the most commonly reported HR practices.

> It is interesting to note that what Indian managers see as effective HR practices that will support innovation and organizational performance appear to be in line with those prescribed in Western HRM literature and what has been found being practiced by firms. This suggests either the universality of the strategic HRM principles as Kim and Bae[44] suggest or that these EMBA graduate managers have been heavily influenced by Western business and management education materials and actually believe that these are the 'best practices.' Given the eagerness of Indian firms to catch up with the global firms as latecomers and the growing number of Western MNCs operating in the country, we cannot rule out the normative isomorphic effect facilitated by Western MNCs, HR consultants, and HRM/HRD professional networks and associations.[45]

19.9 HOW TO MAKE HUMAN RESOURCE MANAGEMENT INNOVATIONS SUSTAINABLE

A good number of HRMIs have a short shelf-life. The reason can be explored in the way innovations are conceptualized in HRM. Unlike an R&D facility or an academic zone, HRM does not command resources of social science researchers or data scientists. Instead, its ideas for innovation spring from professional networks, seminars, or articles. Listening to a talk, one can suddenly make a connection between a new idea and workplace challenge. It is reported in neuroleadership researches that people, when compared with others, experience a 'threat response' in their brains, and the resultant rising high cortisol levels make it difficult for them to consider other data for analysis. So, people end up grabbing 'that bright, shiny object and take it home, in the form of pages of excitedly scrawled notes and an intense resolve to get the team working on it.'[46] Mindless adoption of trendy ideas, in an indiscriminate manner, and implementing them superficially, can lead to certain failure of the innovation.

So HRMIs, in order to be sustainable, will have to factor in the hidden structure and the informal networks that are more influential than hierarchies and the formal structures. John Boudreau and Steven Rice suggest, based on their experience of Juniper Networks (a Silicon Valley–based innovator of high-performance networking technology), a four-step approach for responsibly bringing new ideas to the organization. Juniper's method—getting the big picture, seizing on insights, applying them

[44] Kim and Bae (2005).

[45] Fang Lee Cooke and Debi S. Saini, '(How) Does HR Strategy Support an Innovation Oriented Business Strategy? An Investigation of Institutional Context and Organizational Practices in Indian Firms,' *Human Resource Management* 49, no. 3 (May–June 2010): 377–400.

[46] John Boudreau and Steven Rice, 'Bright, Shiny Objects and the Future of HR,' *Harvard Business Review* 93, no. 7/8 (July/August 2015). Available at: https://hbr.org/2015/07/bright-shiny-objects (accessed on January 20, 2018).

wisely, and ensuring their impact—may be useful to you. It has enabled this company to move from one-off programs and unconnected experiments to a system that is always evolving in exciting and consistently business-aligned ways.

19.9.1 Problem Orientation

There is a need to avoid the easy temptation to run after every new practice, but instead spend more time and effort in developing deeper understanding of the problem itself. When the challenge has been studied in sufficient depth from different perspectives, it helps achieve best-fit solutions. The appreciation of the problem widens the field of options leading to better solutions.

19.9.2 Adopting a Macro View

One requires developing a perspective for the big picture—the business context that cries for the intervention. Sometimes innovations become imperative when the business has hit a plateau and the business strategy needs to be reinvented. It may imply restructuring the HR function itself to be able to align to the changing business conditions.

19.9.3 Business Literacy

Close familiarity with business processes can enable HR to keep track of innovative management concepts and couple them to what is pivotal in the organization. From the experience, tying together values, performance assessment, and neuroscience is one example in Juniper's experience. Another is improving customer service by analyzing an organizational network—and this effort put HR directly into the operations of the business.

19.9.4 Care in Application

The next step is to carefully blend the learning with ongoing other projects. The HRMIs, in order to have a lasting impact, must be purpose-built. It may mean shunning the path of 'best practice,' and instead breaking it down to reveal insight useful for the organization and then working it out into work plans, customized for the company's unique climate, brand, and business objectives. Prototyping the application of an idea in some fertile area of the organization is a valuable way of working out the necessary synergies. It also offers proof of concept through experience. You cannot just tell people about a great idea and expect them to pick it up and run with it; they need to see and experience its value. HR plays a big part in creating such experiences. One example of how Juniper put its own stamp on a research idea lies in the area of boundary-spanning leadership.

19.9.5 Metric for Business Impact

It is well known that what gets measured gets done. HR needs to apply its mind in developing suitable metric for the business impact of the innovations. A new HR approach would also entail a new tool to measure progress and impact. The intent of the measurement devices should be to keep people's focus on the key business imperatives. It should have future orientation and emphasize lead measures, rather than historical accomplishment and lag measures. Metrics should yield deep learning on what to keep and what to change with the initiatives. HR should be prepared to accept lapses on the chin and revise. On the contrary, successful innovations may also surface fresh new metrics.

Closing Case Challenges for HRMIS at TPL Plant

Established in 1924, Texaco Pharmaceuticals Limited (TPL) is a global research-focused health care and pharmaceuticals company providing prescription medicines and vaccines. The company is the market leader in most of the therapeutic categories in which it operates. TPL also offers a range of vaccines for the prevention of hepatitis A and hepatitis B. TPL has two manufacturing facilities in India, at Nashik and Thane. The plant at Nashik was set up in the year 1983. The state-of-the-art plant at Nashik makes formulations.

The senior leadership team seeks performance improvement of the plant particularly in quality standards. In recent times, the plant has received adverse internal audit report on account of violations of the quality specifications and, more alarmingly, dispatched goods have, on some occasions, been returned with customer complaints. A key challenge impacting employee performance is the effectiveness of the frontline managers to manage employee performance. A summer intern, who was recently engaged on a two-month project, has given a report, highlighting the following:

1. The organization had a certain approach to working that has not kept pace with the changing times. The regulatory requirements are becoming stringent but the organization is too busy trying to deliver to make any fundamental changes.
2. Capacity expansion—Due to pressures of more delivery, operations have increased multi-folds. However, facilities, manpower numbers and capabilities, and equipment have not kept pace with these changes.
3. Drastic reduction in manpower (both operatives and supervisor) while simultaneously demanding more output. This has happened during a two-year period between 2008 and 2010. Supervisor's workload have resultantly increased manifolds.
4. Attrition of experienced managerial staff—Continuous movement of people out of the organization has led to a lack of continuity among people.
5. New senior leadership team—Credentials of the new team are still viewed with suspicion by the HODs and other team members. There is also an absence of visibility or authority of leadership. There is no vision or energy in the organization to unite people.
6. Organizational culture—It is viewed as too lenient and numbers-oriented but lacking a quality focus. Quality becomes a concern only in cases of failures or audits otherwise it is kept on a backburner by people across all levels.
7. Unclear accountability and responsibility—People are unsure about their powers. Supervisors are not sure if they can take independent actions or not.
8. Role of supervisor—There is lack of role clarity and assertiveness. Supervisors are reluctant to confront non-performers and table important issues for resolution.
9. Exercises of authority—Supervisors are afraid to exercise their authority. There is a fear of being singled out or victimized if they take any action and/or flag issues. There is an unwillingness to take action and the approach is to let things be. There is also a fear that if they report deviations, they will be held accountable for them. What follows is a scapegoating exercise rather than a root-cause analysis exercise. Deviations are not looked at as opportunities for improvement. People get into defensive behaviors.
10. SOPs—There appear to be multiple concerns related to SOPs, people may not know SOPs, they are too complex and cannot be followed in practice, they take too much of

time and, therefore, managers feel justified in bypassing them and so on and so forth. Efforts need to be made to increase awareness regarding the what and why aspects of SOPs.

11. Acceptance of authority—People who moved up from the ranks are not being accepted in the supervisor's position by the lower ranks.
12. Transparency—Should become more transparent in terms of the activities that happen, if they notice something wrong, they should inform instead of withholding information.
13. Handling discipline issues—There is a feeling of leniency and absence of fear if people do not follow SOPs or organizational norms. Supervisors do not feel empowered to take action against people.
14. Career progression—While some people are frustrated because of lack of opportunity to move up, others do not want to move up and want to remain where they are.

Assignment

You have joined the TPL plant as a senior operations executive. You have been asked by the plant manager to observe the plant condition over a period of time, and prepare an innovative plan for HR intervention. You have had experience of working in several very good plants before coming here and you think what needs to be done.

SUMMARY

A critical success factor for business in a time of unprecedented change is the ability to come up with new ideas to keep operations, products, and services fresh. According to a study by Accenture, more than 90% of executives believe long-term success of their organization's strategy depends on their ability to develop new ideas. Being innovative can help organizations discover opportunities; anticipate on (future) trends; and increase effectiveness, productivity, and profitability. Besides, different types of innovations (incremental, radical or a combination of both) help achieve not only major business changes but also greater focus on existing business processes and practices, reduce/eliminate waste, and attract/retain talent. In their book *The Game-Changer*, the authors A.G. Lafley and Ram Charan[47] gave several examples on how P&G used innovations to leverage its acquisition of Gillette to accelerate profitable top-line revenue growth and enhance capabilities. We learn about how Nokia became number one in India by using innovation to create 200 million customers. Nokia first observed the unique needs of Indian customers, particularly in rural villages, where most of the population resides; it segmented them in new ways, and then put new features on handsets relevant to their unique needs.

Organizational innovation process has four sequential steps: conception of an idea, proposal, decision to adopt, and finally, the implementation. The different factors determining the level of innovation include structural features specific to big organizations; strategic orientation, learning and flexibility, and internal and external factors (internal factors—market orientation, learning and technology policy, designed to enhance a firm's innovative behavior—and external factors—industry concentration and barriers to entry) that directly affect the organization's attitude toward innovation or

[47] *Game Changer* (Innosight President Scott D. Anthony interviewed Procter & Gamble Chairman and CEO A.G. Lafley as part of a keynote session at the May 2008 PDMA and IIR Front End of Innovation conference in Boston). Available at: https://www.forbes. com/2008/08/28/pg (accessed on January 20, 2018).

by inhibiting or stimulating related work. Dual-core model is an influential model, suggested by Richard A. Daft. The model describes dual cores of organizations—a technical core and an administrative core—each having a part to play. Innovations in technical core directly cover basic work activities and can concern product, process, and/or technology. Innovations in administrative core cover areas of organization management and can involve organizational structure and administrative processes; their link to the basic work activities is indirect.

HMRIs have been defined as any intentional introduction or change of HR program, policy, practice, or system, designed to influence or adapt employee the skills, behaviours, and interactions of employees and have the potential to provide both the foundations for strategy formulations and the means of strategy implementation that is perceived to be new and creates current capabilities and competencies.[48]

One way in which HRM can directly improve capability to innovate is by building a strategic focus of employee development strategy in that direction. The resource based view states that organizations achieve sustainable competitive advantage by creating resources that are unique, inimitable, valuable, and non-substitutable. Human resource also represents a valuable resource that should, according to Beugelsdijk, be managed toward being unique so that it is superior to the human resource of other organizations. Besides, since innovation is development of new ideas and also the process of actually putting the new ideas into practice, the development of ideas mainly occurs through creative employees, individually or in teams. Based on experiences of organizations, the successful implementation of HRMIs requires the following conditions: innovation champions, power dynamics, and organizational context—internal and external.

Most major HR processes (selection, T&D, performance management, and compensation management) can have a bearing on fostering innovations. Currently, the innovative practices adapted for improving HRM effectiveness include different employee-engagement initiatives, application of design thinking for L&D, and gamification for making talent acquisition more fun and attractive to the millennials. There are, however, challenges for overdoing the innovation. The factors that will ensure that HRMIs are sustainable are: problem orientations, adopting a macro view, business literacy, care in application, and selection of proper metric for business impact.

Short-answer Questions

1. Define HRMI.
2. Explain Coral's concept of crucial influencers of innovations in organizations.
3. Mention the attributes of HRMI.
4. Mention three conditions for successful implementation of HRMI.
5. Write a brief note of the connection between Gamification and HRM.
6. Narrate Som's research findings of innovations in Indian organizations.
7. How does workforce downsizing affect innovations in India?
8. How do venture teams impact HRP?
9. Suggest two steps to make innovations sustainable in India.
10. In what ways do HR practices determine the level of innovations in an organization?

---

[48] Som, 'Bracing MNC Competition Through Innovative HRM Practices.'

Discussion Questions

1. Which HR process, in your opinion, has the maximum impact on fostering innovation in organizations?
2. What are some of the innovations in Indian organizations?
3. Can innovations be suitable for hard areas in HRM such as using a bell curve for performance appraisal? Work out details of the plan.
4. What competencies will an HR professional require to foster innovations in organizations?

CLUSTER 10

REIMAGINING HUMAN RESOURCES MANAGEMENT

Chapter 20
Diversity, Equality, and Inclusion

Chapter 21
Workplace Wellness

During the cataclysmic time of the global pandemic, certain new realities dawned. Essential workers at risk. Entire companies suddenly working from home. Office buildings abandoned. Suddenly HR, the function, which in many organizations perched awkwardly between its legacy as a transactional function and its future as a strategic partner, emerged as the knight in the shining armour.

Employee-centricity defines the new HR. From a holistic approach to employee well-being and an improved hybrid workplace to working in the metaverse to a diverse community at work. It would not be far-fetched to say that the future of HR will surprise employees pleasantly as the decade progresses.

Organizations are coming to the conclusion that a diverse, inclusive and equitable culture positively affects the business transformation and profitable growth for a company. Chapter 20 discusses at length the multiple facets of DEI- the benefits, the challenges, the benchmarked practices and the future.

Chapter 21 deals with Wellness at workplace. A recent study by the McKinsey Health Institute found a 22% gap between employer and employee perceptions of well-being at work and identified a strong correlation between toxic work cultures and employee burnout. So HR needs to lead the design of 'The Healthy Organization' — a holistic and more inclusive enterprise-wide approach to well-being'.

CHAPTER 20

Diversity, Equality, and Inclusion

LEARNING OBJECTIVES

After completing this chapter, the student will be able to:

- Understand what is Diversity/Inclusion
- Describe the benefits of Diversity and Inclusion
- Explain barriers for DEI
- Understand the conditions necessary for DEI
- Explain the challenges in a Multicultural Workforce
- Describe the future of DEI

Opening Case A Moment of Truth for DEI Champions

On the phone the Sales Head sounded distraught. 'Listen, we need to take a call on Vandana. Today she made a big scene with one of our old customers when she had gone to negotiate a new contract. A small issue of discount went into a big fight. Fortunately, the team leader acted cool and controlled the damage. Vyom, the HR Manager, assured him that he will look into the issue.

Vandana Nair came through their trusted search firm about five years back with two years of post-MBA experience and a good profile. She was initially well received, and she worked well on her assignments, showing a grasp of customer wants and a sharp mind for analytics. But things started changing since last two months, reportedly after a break up with a long standing partner. Incidents started occurring of uncontrolled emotional outbursts, frenzied behavior, especially if there were discussions about a particular political party and its leader, who she worshipped. She started getting irregular at work.

Vyom works in a lubricant manufacturing and selling company. It is a self-declared champion of Diversity and Equality at workplace. DEI is also part of its brand proposition. The company is quite tolerant about little lapses in orderly behavior on behalf of their employees. After all, with long hours and demanding customers, nerves can get frayed sometimes. But now he needs to talk to her gently and counsel her on observing some ground rules, especially in dealing with outsiders.

Vyom talked to some of her colleagues, who complained about her behavior. He spoke to Dr. Joshi, the part-time employee counsellor, who reported that Vandana has been seeing him recently, and showing symptoms of mild depression. She was advised to see a psychiatrist.

Vyom was in a dilemma. He did not know how the bosses would look at this issue. From his understanding, diversity here largely consisted of periodic awareness workshops and following a quota for recruitment/promotions of women employees.

Discussion Questions

Vyom has the following options:

1. Call Vandana to the conference room and ask her to look for a job in another organizations. Promise her a special leave. He can suggest Accenture and Cognizant for example as prospective employers.
2. Ask her to go for a comprehensive check up with a psychiatrist to ascertain whether she could manage to keep her illness under control with appropriate medication.
3. Take time to look for a manager who is experienced to deal with people with mental illness. He knew of a few.
4. Talk to the senior leadership about the company's broad approach on PWDs, before initiating any step.

Discuss the pros and cons of each of the above options in a group.

Source: Adopted from The Tapestry of a Diverse Workforce. Oct. 2018. https://www.linkedin.com/pulse/tapestry-diverse-workforce-amitabha-sengupta

20.1 INTRODUCTION

Diversity, equality, and inclusion (DEI or EDI) seems to be the zeitgeist of our times. In 2021, *New York* magazine stated 'The business became astronomically larger than ever'. As per a report of '*The Economist*', research on MNCs indicates that the number of people hired for jobs with 'diversity' or 'inclusion' in the title has grown more than four times during the last decade or so.

The key features of the workforce of the 21st century may be presented as larger number of women, minorities, ethnic backgrounds, multi-generational employees, and different lifestyles. Besides, organizations have understood that a necessary condition of succeeding in the globally competitive marketplace would be how effectively these demographic workforce variations are managed. This may explain why over three-fourths of Fortune 1000 companies have embraced diversity initiatives. However, the adoption of diversity by organizations widely varies in scope: at the basic level, it covers limited recruitment initiatives, education and training, career development, and mentoring programs to increase and retain workforce heterogeneity in organizations. At the other end of the spectrum, many organizations also widened the coverage to include employee participation and communication strategies, and emphasized on *inclusion* in the management of diversity and community relations, thus indicating that it is essential to remove the hurdles that hold back the employees from utilizing the full range of their skills and competencies in organizations.

20.2 WHAT IS DIVERSITY?

In India, where the 1.4 billion-strong population speaks more than 450 languages, diversity not only means having more female workers, but also hiring employees from different cultural, linguistic, and socioeconomic backgrounds; of different sexual orientations; and with different physical abilities

Coming to the organizational context, diversity now is not merely about gender, ethnicity, and culture, but has infinite range of differences such as relations-oriented diversity (gender, age, and religion); task-oriented diversity (education level, experience, and cognitive abilities); readily detected diversity (differences of age, nationality, etc.); and underlying diversity (differences in personality or attitudes).[1]

20.2.1 Diversity—Definitions

Some of the definitions of diversity can be made note of:

Diversity is

1. 'about all the ways in which people differ from each other.'[2]
2. 'the fact of many different types of things or people being included in something; a range of different things or people.'[3]
3. 'the degree to which there are objective or subjective differences between people in the group.'
4. 'the similarities and differences in such characteristics as age, gender, ethnic heritage, physical abilities and disabilities, race and sexual orientation among the employees of organizations.'
5. 'employing people who may be different from each other and who do not all come from the same background. The differences may be those of national origin, physical appearance, religion, education, age, gender, or sexual orientation.'[4]
6. 'similarities and differences in characteristics such as age, gender, ethnic heritage, physical abilities, and disabilities, race and sexual orientation among the employees of organizations.'[5]

20.3 WHAT IS EQUALITY?

In essence, equality is about fairness, about not discriminating in treating individuals, or groups because of their protected characteristics. Equality is based on the intention that all individual should have the same chance and opportunity.[6] Straw categorized equality as:

1. **Equal chance** Having the same chance or opportunity in the workplace, for example, in training, selection or promotion.
2. **Equal access** Having the same opportunity to enter an organization.

---

1 Jackson and Joshi (2011). Work team diversity, In Zedeck, S. *APA handbook of industrial and organizational psychology,* 1, 651–686.

2 Joplin, J. R. W., & Daus, C. S. (1997). *Challenges of leading a diverse workforce.* Academy of Management Executive, 11(3), 32–47

3 https://dictionary.cambridge.org/dictionary

4 https://www.encyclopedia.com/finance/finance-and-accounting-magazines/diversity-workplace

5 Griffin, R.W. and Moorhead, G. (2006) Fundamentals of Organizational Behavior: Managing People and Organizations. Houghton Mifflin Company, Boston.

6 Straw. 1989. Equal opportunities: the way ahead. Institute of Personnel Development.

3. **Equal share** Having proportionate representation within all groups and all levels within the organization

The right to equality is considered a fundamental aspect of our constitution, and a part of the fundamental rights of every citizen:

1. Art 14 No Indian citizen should be denied equality before the law or equal protection of the laws.
2. Art 15 The state shall not discriminate prohibition of discrimination on grounds of religion, race, caste, sex or place of birth
3. Art 16 Equality of opportunity for all citizens in matters of public employment or appointment to any office under the State
4. Art 17 Abolition of untouchability and prohibition of its practice
5. Art 18 Abolition of titles except military and academic.

20.4 WHAT IS INCLUSION?

It can be said that diversity prepares the soil, and inclusion sows the seeds for new workplace culture. A diverse workforce needs to be carefully blended into the social fabric of the workplace. Organizations can truly thrive when they adopt an inclusive approach to create a spirit of multi-culturism. Researchers claim that organizations, which ignore differences, and try an assimilation approach to diversity, rather than an approach of integration and inclusion, fail to reap the full rewards of diversity. On the other hand, a culture of inclusion accelerates the emergence of a kind of unity and harmony amongst employees. In such a culture, difference are not driven under the carpet, but rather acknowledged, valued, and engaged. Divergences are considered as not only normal, but as creating new opportunities to explore better organizational processes like decision-making and problem-solving, and promoting creativity.

Reflection Point

Air India v. Nargesh Meerza case of 1981

Air India, a state-owned company, required female flight attendants to retire under three circumstances: (1) upon reaching 35 years of age, (2) upon getting married, or (3) upon first pregnancy. In the instant case the employee got married after four years and later became pregnant. The company terminated the services on grounds of pregnancy. The court struck the rules down, holding that these requirements constituted official arbitrariness and hostile discrimination.

Discussion Question

1. There are two approaches to Equality—relying on legal sanctions for non-compliance, or tackling underlying cultures within the organization. Discuss the pros and cons of both approaches.

In respect of diversity theme, there are two prevailing approaches in the usage of the terms Equality, Diversity, and Inclusion (EDI) and DEI. While equality assumes that all people should be treated the same, equity takes into consideration a person's unique circumstances, adjusting treatment accordingly so that the end result is equal. Bill Schaninger, a McKenzie Senior Partner explains the difference 'There's a real difference between equal and equitable. Suppose we say, 'All interns are created equal. We pay them nothing.' The people who can afford an entire summer without getting paid are likely already coming from a position of privilege.[7]

20.4.1 Benefits of Diversity

1. Cost Savings

A continuous flow of employees having diverse capabilities help build a learning environment in the organizations to stay ahead of the curve. Diversity positively impacts the organizations' bottom line through leveraging its talent pool. On a more micro level, cost savings also occurs through lowering absenteeism rates. Absenteeism can occur when individuals do not feel secure about their status, as insecurity prevents employees from fully engaging at work.

Monks suggest that the introduction of diversity initiatives has a positive influence on absenteeism rates, tending to result in a reduction of both labor turnover and absenteeism levels. The final aspect of the cost savings argument focuses on lawsuits on sex, age, and race discrimination, or, perhaps more specifically, a strategic organizational effort to avoid their occurrence.[8]

2. Talent Imperatives

A systematically gathered diverse workforce can provide a unique competitive advantage to business through opening a wider and richer pool of talent which can be leveraged to stay ahead in a fiercely competitive market. It has been found, based on research, that organizations that are able to recruit, develop, retain, and promote diverse employees, reap the benefits of diversity in multiple ways: (1) talented employees will be attracted to organizations that value their capabilities; (2) they will also be motivated to engage in productive activity if they think they are being treated fairly, and career opportunities are available to them; (3) besides a diverse workforce allows diverse employees to identify with the company, making the company attractive to other diverse potential employees.

3. Broadening Community Engagement

In a time when business recognizes the virtue of multiple stakeholders, diversity can open the door for potential source of competitiveness beyond the considerations of the current supply chain. Diversity can help widen the network of businesses to get in touch with different combinations of people and open opportunities for future business opportunities. Business could connect with diverse ensemble of prospective stakeholders—business associates, vendors, employees, volunteers, investors, customers, etc. Diversity thus has the potential of augmenting the reach, visibility, and support base of the organization to significant proportions.[9]

4. Legal compliance

Diversity programs should help improve compliance with laws (Prevention of sexual harassment at the workplace, Presidential Directive for SC, ST, and backward classes, etc.) in respect of discrimination/harassment, and make sure that policies and processes are in place in organizations to discourage litigation. Organizations that embrace diversity in their approach to different HR processes like recruitment and selection and training and leadership development are more likely to take timely appropriate measures to foresee problems, thus obviating the probability of lawsuits.

---

[7] *What is Diversity, equity, and inclusion*? https://www.mckinsey.com

[8] Monks, K. (2007). *The business impact of equality and diversity: The international evidence.* Dublin: *The Equality Authority and National Centre for Partnership & Performance.*

[9] *Diverse reasons to embrace diversity.* Rajib Kumar.www.humancapitalonline.com.

5. *Brand Enhancement*

Organizations can focus on improving the company's public image or enhancing its image by using diversity management. It can specifically work as an employer branding initiative and create the organizational reputation and image as an inclusive employer leading to improvements in the recruitment and retention of high-calibre employees.

Reflection Point

It is opined that current concepts of career management are based on masculinity and are suitable for males; women face different obstacles in their lives and the career ladders are not aligned to their needs

Discussion Question

1. Do you agree? Give reasons.

6. *Higher Stock Prices*

It has been observed that stock markets is also responsive to the level of diversity in an organization. As the market buzz of a company, doing a great job of using a diverse workforce, grows, it can positively affect the stock prices of the company. There are indications that commitment to diversity also can be used by investors as a criterion for assessing how well a company is being managed.

20.5 THEORIES/APPROACHES TO DIVERSITY MANAGEMENT

20.5.1 Institutional Theory of Diversity Management

The underlying premise of this theory is that an organization structure cannot be designed ignoring the social environment prevailing in the organization. The social environment includes the laws, rules, regulations, and social and professional norms. Therefore, organizations adapt administrative structures in sync with those norms and regulations. This in a way provides legitimacy for their operations, and through that organizations try to indicate their priorities, and thereby start to mobilize material resources from others. In short, as laws demand that organizations embrace diversity, it becomes imperative for them to showcase their compliance to both their employees and to the external stakeholders. Default in conforming to the laws and norms shall make the organizations liable to be questioned and punished.

20.5.2 Resource-Based Theory of Diversity Management

Organizations possess four kinds of resources/capital: physical, financial, human, and corporate. The success of organizations is determined by the dexterity in managing these resources. From a purely commercial viewpoint, an organization with diversity in human capital acquires an edge over traditional organization which is built on homogeneity. Research have indicated a correlation between racial diversity and growth/innovation leading to financial performance.[10] Another study done in 1999 by Richard and Johnson attributed a low turnover rate, better innovation, market performance, and improved productivity to diversity practices.

---

[10] Richard, 2000; Richard, Barnett, Dwyer, & Chadwick, 2004; Richard et al., 2003 as cited in Yang & Konrad, 2011.

The Practitioner/Consultant Approach

The core theme of this approach is that diversity enables economic success and benefits business. Dietz and Peterson (2006) gave reasons that diversity provides a business solution when organizations seek scarce critical talent by widening the net to cover minorities and other potential employees who could be easier/ready for hiring. This approach also points out that a diverse set of employees is better positioned to understand the needs of a diverse set of consumers. In short, the benefits cited by this approach are:

1. Competency utilization
2. Reinforcing commitment
3. Brand building for the organization
4. Greater adaptability of employees
5. Talent acquisition and retention of talent
6. Cost reduction due to turnover, absenteeism
7. ROI from various initiatives, policies, and practices

The Mainstream Approach

In this approach, there are two perspectives: the macro and the micro.

Macro view

At the organizational level, diversity management is to moderate and to keep a watch on the impact of diversity on performance. Thomas and Ely suggest three perspectives: discrimination-and-fairness, access-and-legitimacy, and integration-and-learning. The one way found most congenial for work groups, according to Thomas and Ely, is the integration-and-learning perspective. The key features of this perspectives are creating positive inter-group relations, feelings of being valued and respected by other group members, and the individual's comfort with their racial identity at work.[11]

Micro view

The focus here, at the individual employee level, is understanding and managing stereotypes, prejudices, and discrimination, which, act as the antecedents of discrimination in the workplace.[12] According to Dietz and Peterson (2006) also present several other causal factors of discrimination:

1. Emergence of social identities and social categorizations
2. Realistic group conflict
3. Interaction with demographically different persons

Dietz and Peterson (2006) reported that relationships with demographically diverse employees are still adversely impacted by rising levels of prejudices, the elimination of which should be the key strategy for diversity management at the micro level. Discrimination is often legitimized by issues of employee pay or productivity. This calls for management interventions to control or eliminate: stereotypes or prejudices, and discrimination.

[11] Thomas & Ely 1996.

[12] Dietz and Petersen 2006. The way to remove / limit discrimination by controlling prejudices and stereotypes.

Critical Approaches

According to Prasad et al. (2006), excessive focus on managing diversity and the value of holding training/workshops sidesteps the core issues caused by inequality and discrimination and their impact on organizational outcomes. In examining the role of managers/policymakers on the theme of diversity, Lorbiecki and Jack's (2000) reported that managers view diversity as an area to be managed, and their perception of groups as having distinct and different identity helps to rub out the differences found between diverse individuals.

Experts have also opined that the traditional approach of assigning diversity to individuals as diverse inside an organization, compels the co-workers also to look at them in a certain light, thereby making it hard to enable movement within or between diverse groups. Prasad et al. (2006) have suggested that in traditionally multi-cultural, the Anglo-Saxon method of viewing diversity could be questioned, and there should be endeavors to explore fresh ways to manage diversity.

20.6 CHALLENGES FOR DIVERSITY

20.6.1 Similarity–Attraction Phenomenon

A common human tendency is to be attracted to similar individuals. People experience difficulty in communicating with those who are dissimilar whether on account of race, age, gender, profession, and so on. On situations when people report being discriminated against, the root cause could be the similarity–attraction phenomenon. It can happen with recruitment when the selection has been influenced by the recruiter belonging to the same community as the selected candidate and speaks the same language.

It has also come up through many studies that, in organizations where there is no formal mentoring program, young employees seek out influencers/informal mentors, based on certain similarities in demographic traits. Thus, employees, who cannot identify such mentors, lose out on the fruits of such mentoring, and such a loss can limit their grooming process. The informal mentors, thus chosen, prefer to have more daily interface with their informal protégés, driven by the latent similarity–attraction factor. In a conventional male majority workplace, the choice for the 'similar like me' phenomenon fall on male protégés, who thus get a leg up in the career building phase, as they get more exposed by their male mentors to important decisions.

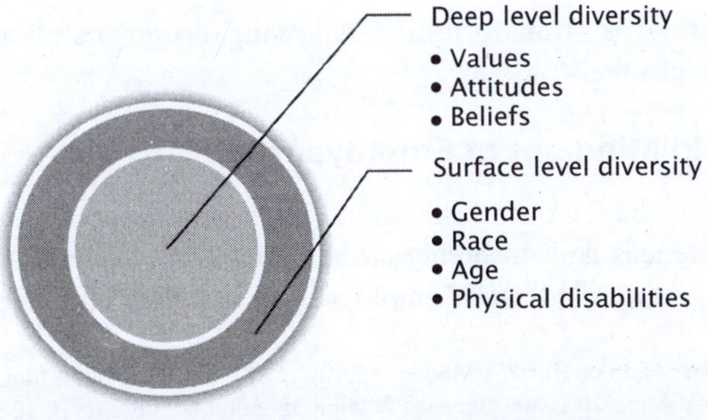

Fig. 20.1 Individuals often initially judge others based on surface-level diversity. Over time, this effect tends to fade and is replaced by deep-level traits such as similarity in values and attitudes.

An effective way to disable the similarity attraction phenomenon is to carefully monitor the development of the new employees early on by adopting formal mentoring programs and by providing appropriate training programs to all of them.

As you may see, while similarity-attraction may put some employees at a disadvantage, it is a tendency that can be managed by organizations.

20.6.2 Faultline

A faultline happens when a fracture in the ground that causes great shifts, even earthquakes, causing great destruction. When it is applied to teams, it has the potential to be disruptive in much the same way. When applied to groups a faultline implies an attribute along which a group is broken into subgroups. Bezrukova et al. explained that faultlines 'occur when multiple attributes (e.g., race, age) of group members come into alignment and divide a group into relatively homogeneous subgroups.'[13] For example, consider a Project Team consisting of four people from the Production Department and three people representing Quality Control Department, functional loyalty may act as the faultline, as the Production employees see themselves as separate from Quality control employees. Now, if in both teams some are pass-outs from reputed engineering colleges and some are ordinary technicians who got promoted based on work experience, profession and level of education can further split the groups into sub groups. Faultline crevices destroys team cohesion.

In an increasingly globalized workplace, leaders face deep faultlines: 'residual bitterness between historical enemies, culture clashes, turf battles and generation gaps.' Yet, an overwhelming number of the leaders in the study did not know how to build strong, diverse teams across these differences.

Developing faultlines is a possibility in a diverse team, but not a certainty. Researchers, Ernst and Chrobot–Mason offer six strategies for leaders to bridge these intense, emotional boundaries.[14]

1. Create a sense of psychological safety for their team by shielding members from threats such as ridicule, judgment, etc., and maintaining entity of a team.
2. Foster open discussion between group members.
3. Encourage one-on-one interactions by team members preferably at neutral zones like a cafeteria.
4. Build a shared purpose including by rallying against a competitor team.
5. Do 'weaving,' i.e., integrating different groups with unique skill sets to work together towards a common goal.
6. The last strategy is 'transforming.' Allowing group members time and space to 'open themselves to change.'

20.6.3 Change in Mind-set of Employees

Just because diversity is the flavour of the times, employees do not discard their deeply held cultural values, lifestyle preferences and differences when they come to work. The challenge is to manage a real transformation in the mind-set of employees so that they embrace an accommodative attitude

[13] Do Workgroup Faultlines Help or Hurt? A Moderated Model of Faultlines, Team Identification, and Group Performance. Organization Science. Volume 20 Issue 1January 2009pp 35–50https://doi.org/10.1287/orsc.1080.0379).

[14] *The challenge of leading on unstable ground*: *Triggers that activate social identity* faultlines. Chrobot-Mason, D., Ruderman, M. N., Weber, T. J., & Ernst, C. (2009). *The challenge of leading on unstable ground: Triggers that activate social identity faultlines. Human Relations,* 62(11), 17631794. https://doi.org.

towards people from different background by addressing their diverse lifestyles, needs, aspirations, interests, capabilities, and work styles. There is also an additional issue of the impact of diversity on HR practices, which have to accommodate all demographic and social factors. The issue of cross-cultural communication is important too while dealing with diversity.[15]

Exhibit How to Bake Multiple Generations Together at Workplace

1. **Build a regular platform for sharing** A platform, where employees can share their wisdom, or perspectives and their stories of success and failure, can go a long way in creating inclusiveness. It may take the shape of a morning team huddle for exchanging the plan for the day or making a space in a normal team meeting for one person sharing their significant learning from the past few weeks?
2. **Look for and use 'wisdom workers'** Every organization has wise seniors who are sage souls, enabling quiet, invisible productivity, and providing informal counseling to juniors. Such people can be identified through informal grapevines or employee satisfaction surveys. They can be given roles of internal counselors or informal role models. One of the ways to leverage such workers will be to allow them to spend a percentage of time acting as internal coaches in the company. Procter and Gamble developed with their 'Masters' program, an honor bestowed on those in the global company with decades of internal wisdom who can serve as wise beacons for those newer to the organization.
3. **Adopt a mixed mentoring culture** Mixing regular mentoring with reverse mentoring can seamlessly integrate multiple generations at work. In July 2023 PepsiCo India launched YCom, a forum of millennials elected by their own members—as a parallel board to the executive committee. It has various plans, including reverse mentoring the Executive Committee on Digital Technologies. Companies such as PepsiCo, GSK Consumer Healthcare India, Jubilant FoodWorks, Microsoft, Vodafone, and Mindtree are championing reverse mentoring.
4. **Encourage Employee Resource Groups (ERGs)** About 90% of Fortune 500 companies have ERGs, but very few groups dedicated for older demographic groups. Bringing your 'Modern Elders' together can help leverage their institutional wisdom and insight.

Discussion Questions

1. Do you think it is necessary to take a targeted strategy for creating inclusion for multi-generational workforce?
2. Do a mini research on the Internet on what are the various ways companies integrating the multi-generational workforce.

Sources

1. Professional Transitions-4 Ways to Help Different Generations Share Wisdom at Work. Chip Conley. May, 2018. Harvard Business Review.
2. To tap into Gen Y ideas, leaders become mentees. Sreeradha D Basu and Prachi Verma. ET Bureau. May 9 2017. https://economictimes.indiatimes.com

20.6.4 Enrolment of Managers

One reason why diversity efforts fail is the lack of enthusiasm on the part of managers. In case, due care has not been taken by the organization to equip the managers and enthuse them for the gains of

[15] *Diversity Management Practices in Select Firms in India: A Critical Analysis:* Author(s): Sanghamitra Buddhapriya Source: *Indian Journal of Industrial Relations*, April 2013, Vol. 48, No. 4).

the organization, the task of building and nurturing a diverse workforce may appear as a burdensome, new work for them. The job may appear truly rigorous when the managers are also required to deliver diversity strategies, without the backup of specific support system in the organization. As a result, managers may think of diversity as a low priority, fringe activity, choosing to spend as little effort as possible, for the barest compliance, rather than being proactive, focusing on probable positive outcomes.

The senior leadership needs to believe in the value of diversity and demonstrate its genuine support and commitment. The commitment gets communicated not only through words but through the manner in which this gets translated in the form of allocation of resources like human, financial, and technical. It is for this reason that the commitment from the organization's leadership is widely regarded as an important element in a best practice approach to diversity management. However, while crucial, the top management support alone is not sufficient. The use of champions for diversity at lower levels in the organization, and employee involvement in driving diversity, is also of great importance.[16]

Reflection Point

Atul is an HRBP in a Refinery. One day he receives a request from the Head, Inspection department, for recruitment of an Instrumentation Engineer. While going through the manpower inventory, he found at least four women engineers and two male experienced diploma holders suitable for the role. When he questioned the HOD, he stated that he does not want to take responsibility to put women in the shifts and would prefer a male role holder. While checking others, he found that women engineers are considered to be suitable for only office jobs. There is also a mind-set that diploma engineers are less competent than graduate engineers. He found that both the presumptions are not based on facts.

Atul had women co-students in his engineering class and felt that there is no ground to take such a discretionary view about women at workplace. When he raised this issue with the HR Head, he surprisingly appeared to share the same view as of the HOD, Instrumentation.

Discussion Question

1. What are the consequences of informal stereotyping of employees?
2. What are the effective ways to eliminate such biases?

20.6.5 Reverse Discrimination

In certain kinds of workforce composition, diversity initiatives may also trigger apprehensions of reverse discrimination. If the existing workforce community perceives the diversity focus as a smokescreen for side-lining them, then there may be probability of a strong resistance to such initiatives. Such perception may manifest in the Resistance Paradigm for managing diversity, whereby the majority may be afraid of being disrupted by newcomers. This paradigm paints all the push for diversity as threats. To obviate such misperceptions, it is necessary to include the prevalent communities in the process of building future vision for diversity, and their role in realizing such vision. Indeed, according to some research, issues like work from home and work-life balance and organizations embracing them

16 Miller, S. K., & Tucker, J. J. (2013). *Diversity trends, practices, and challenges in the financial services industry. Journal of Financial Service Professionals,* 46–57.

in redesigning their policies is viewed by large number of men as policies for women's problems, even though such policies are gender neutral.[17]

20.6.6 Stereotypes

Stereotypes are general assumptions held by individuals in respect of other individuals based on differences in socio-economic or other characteristics. This poses a major peril for managing a diverse workforce by leading to unfair decision-making. For example, 'Men are from the Mars, women are from Venus. For example, a recruitment manager holding the stereotype that women engineers are unsuitable for working in shifts, may prefer to recruit a lower-ranked male engineer in campus recruitment. An effective way to eliminate the adverse effects of stereotypes on decisions is to become conscious of it.

20.6.7 Age Diversity in the Workplace

In India, 62.5% of the population is in the age group of 15–59 years; around 66% of the total population (more than 808 million) is below the age of 35 years. There is a multi-generational workforce at work, and it poses certain challenges.

Table 20.1 The attributes of multi-generational workforce

S.No	Values	Veterans	Baby boomers	Gen X	Millennials
1.	Level of trust	Respect authority	Self-confident, not reliant to authority	Less toward authority	High toward authority
2.	Loyalty to institutions	Commitment and scarify	Cynical attitude	Considered adolescent	Committed to work
3.	Most admire	Comfortable with managing style	Acceptance of delightful charge	Creativity based operations	Follow a hero of reliability
4.	Career goals	Duty is prime	Stellar career	Portable career	Many careers
5.	Rewards	Quality of work	High recognition	Lack of restriction	Significant job
6.	Parent–child involvement	No involvement	Moving back	Isolated	Obtrusive
7.	Having children	Controlled	Parental guidance	Separated	Confined
8.	Family life	Traditional	Pamper as children	Hesitant	Explicit
9.	Education	As per requirement	Freedom of expression	Pragmatic	Structure of accountability
10.	Retention	Lifetime	Security	Growth	Oppose it
11.	Evaluation	Not	Once a year	Fear	Instant

Source: Managing multi-generational workforce: challenge for millennium managers. Dr. Namita Rajput and others. IJMRA.

20.6.8 Religious Diversity in the Workplace

Article 25 of Indian Constitution guarantees the freedom of conscience, the freedom to profess, practice, and propagate religion to all citizens. Employees are expected to make reasonable accommodations to ensure that employees can practice their beliefs without causing hardship for the employer.

[17] P. & O'Donovan, D. (2016). What is the impact of flexible working on the worker and the workplace? Paper presented at the Irish Academy of Management Conference Proceedings, University College Dublin, August 31st to September 2nd.

Accommodating someone's religious preferences may also require companies to relax their dress code to take into account religious practices such as wearing a turban for Sikhs or covering one's hair with a scarf for Muslim women.

20.6.9 PwD at Workplace

About 2.2% of India's population lives with some kind of physical or mental disability, as per the National Statistics Office report on disability released in 2022. Article 15(1) enjoins on the Government not to discriminate against any citizen of India (including disabled) on the ground of religion, race, caste, sex, or place of birth.

The challenges are: employer reluctance, peer acceptance and inclusion, the absence of special conditions necessary for the afflicted people like leave for long absences mood variations, etc., the bias against differently-abled people, lack of growth and developmental opportunities, the psychological safety needed for them, the lack of sensitization of the managers, etc.

Exhibit Statutory Provisions in Respect of PWD

In compliance with UN Convention on the Rights of Persons with Disabilities, 2008. India enacted the Rights of Persons with Disabilities Act, 2016 (the 'New Act') and the rules there under (the 'Rules') in 2017. It defines a 'person with disability' as someone with long-term physical, mental, intellectual, or sensory impairment which, in interaction with barriers, hinders his/her full and effective participation in society equally with others.

Under the New Act, persons with at least 40% of a disability (referred to as 'persons with benchmark disability') are entitled to certain benefits. One such benefit is that at least 4% of the total number of vacancies in Indian Government establishments in specified categories (and 1% in certain others) are required to be reserved for their employment.

The New Act requires establishments to prepare and publish an Equal Opportunity Policy (the 'EOP') for persons with disabilities with (a) details regarding amenities and facilities put in place for persons with disabilities; (b) lists of posts identified for such persons; and (c) details of training, promotion, allotment of accommodation and provision of assistive devices and barrier-free accessibility for such persons.

Source: Rights of Persons with Disabilities in India and Other Jurisdictions Ius Laboris, https://www.lexology.com/library/detail.asp)

20.6.10 Diversity of Sexual Orientation

A key challenge here is the dilemma of coming out with disclosure of sexual identity in the workplace, leading to non-disclosure by a large percentage of lesbian, gay, and bisexual employees at work. People with different sexual orientation are apprehensive about possible reactions of peers and superiors, preferring secrecy and as a result suffer from some negative effects such as lower job satisfaction and organizational commitment, and the decision to quit. The answer lies in building an inclusive and positive work environment which make employees comfortable regardless of their sexual orientation.

20.6.11 Cultural Diversity

Culture refers to values, beliefs, and customs that exist in a society. Globally, the workforce is becoming multicultural. In addition, the world of work is becoming increasingly international. In the churn that occurred post-globalization, the BRICS countries have emerged as key players in world economics.

International business has opened possibilities of tapping resources, source raw materials and access a much larger customer base. Apple Inc gets its iPhone manufactured at cheap cost at locations in Korea, China, and India, while Lenovo rose to third largest maker of PCs after it acquired IBM PCs.

20.6.12 Glass Ceiling

In traditional organizations women may be represented in lower-level positions, but rarely in top echelons of leadership. In fact, while women constitute close to one-half of the workforce, men are four times more likely to reach the highest levels of organizations. An ILO Report compiled in 2011 reported:

1. Women are more likely to live in poverty
2. Overall, women's pay is about 70-90% of that of men
3. Progress in many areas, but still some challenges.

According to a 2022 ILO report, only 22.5% of women participated in senior managerial role in Asia-Pacific.[18]

LinkedIn Opportunity Index 2021 reported the prevalence of considerable gender discrimination at work. As a result, four out of five working women had their gender to blame for missing out on a promotion or a raise at the workplace. The study pointed out that India's working women faced the strongest gender bias among all Asia-Pacific countries. Whether it is managing a career along with a family or facing discrimination vis-à-vis household duties, women felt their career growth being stifled because of reasons beyond their control. More than 50% of women seek recognition, equal treatment, and inclusivity at their workplace. However, it is easier said than done. As a result of this, businesses are producing a lesser number of women leaders than it can or should.[19]

20.7 DIMENSIONS OF DIVERSITY

There are two dimensions of diversity: surface-level diversity and deep-level diversity.

1. Surface-Level diversity It is about character traits that are visible, such as race, gender, age, ethnicity, visible disabilities, body shape, and size.
2. Deep-level diversity It includes values, beliefs, and attitudes. We want to interact with those who share our values and attitudes, but when we meet people for the first time, we have no way of knowing whether they share similar values or not. As a result, we tend to use surface-level diversity to make judgments about deep-level diversity.

Research shows that surface-level traits affect our interactions with other people early in our acquaintance with them, but as we get to know people, the influence of surface-level traits is replaced by deep-level traits such as similarity in values and attitudes. Age, race, and gender dissimilarity are also stronger predictors of employee turnover during the first few weeks or months within a company. It seems that people who are different from others may feel isolated during their early tenure when they are dissimilar to the rest of the team, but these effects tend to disappear as people stay longer and get to know other employees.[20]

---

18 The business case for change. https://www.ilo.org

19 Glass ceiling and beyond: Status of women in leadership. April 29, 2023. Aarti Sharma in Voices, Business, TOI. https://timesofindia.indiatimes.com.

20 Managing a Diverse Workforce. Social Science Libre texts. https: //socialsci.libretexts.org)

Exhibit Diversity Practices in Select Indian Companies

Tata Group of Companies[21]

1. Tata LEAD: the diversity and inclusion program that engages the talent and the group companies on initiatives to strengthen D&I and foster an inclusive culture.
2. Tata SCIP: specific on boarding process for women returning back to work after a break.
3. TATA Gear-up: specific developmental program for the women mid-managers.
4. MOSAIC Wings: ERG for the LGBTQ+ community.
5. Pathways to Success: targeted at women with 5-8 years of work experience to enable them to help confront and address the unique challenges that women face in their careers.
6. The Reach Out program: meant for senior women leaders to connect build effective network with leaders and peers across a group of likeminded organizations.
7. CXO Workshops: to sensitize senior leadership teams on DEI and build business case. and deal with unconscious biases.
8. Power of Inclusive Management Workshops (POIM): to sensitize the middle management across the group about diversity and inclusion.
9. Mentoring Program at Tata Mentors.
10. Women of Mettle: engineering college-level competition especially women students for scholarship and possible employment.
11. Paternity leave for ten days: to enable male employees to share the parental responsibility.

Mahindra Group[22]

1. Women Leaders Program (WLP): 18-month developmental training program for women in middle management
2. Unconscious Bias training to mid-level managers
3. Project Surya Shakti: to break gender stereotypes in an unconventional sector, an initiative to train women for solar power installation.

Godrej Group[23]

1. Godrej Women's Leadership Network: Specific platform to help women employees with mentoring, leadership development, and regular networking opportunities.
2. Godrej Alliance for Parents: platform for employees, often with their spouses and partners, share experiences on childcare, children's education, and tips to maintain a healthy work-life balance.
3. Unlabel Workshop: to sensitize on how unconscious biases affects their decisions regarding employees.
4. Partnership with UNHRC: to learn on global standards for tackling bias against LGBTI.
5. Godrej Cultural Lab to foster inclusion and diversity of all spectrum.

XYZ Group[24]

1. Pragya Initiative: to build a culture of diversity and inclusion through conclaves, summits.
2. VOICE: platform to voice unresolved workplace concerns and seek resolution.
3. Springboard: an accelerated development program for high potential women managers.
4. ONUS: to support senior women leaders in sustaining career aspirations.

---

[21] http://www.tatasecondcareer.com/tata-lead.asp

[22] special/mahindra-group-to-turn-employees-into-leaders-with-women-leaders-program/44245

[23] https://economictimes.indiatimes.com/news/politics-and-nation/how-the-godrej-group-is-creating-an-inclusive-culture.

[24] Author

20.8 INCLUSION

Indian Labor Organization defines Inclusion in the following words: 'Employees need to feel that they are valued, respected, fairly treated and empowered through inclusive business practices, inclusive organizational culture and inclusive leadership. It is this transformational approach to diversity and inclusion that makes significant contributions to overall business performance.' The new ILO report further explains inclusion' as the experience people have in the workplace and the extent to which they feel valued for who they are, the skills and experience they bring and the extent to which they have a strong sense of belonging with others at work.[25]

20.8.1 The Benefits of Inclusion

In the new global marketplace, inclusion presents a competitive edge. It is well known that the profile of the new customer and her tastes and preferences are vastly different from those of the traditional customer. She needs to be represented in the firm, because, locking oneself off from such emergent customers, who will be integral to the new global consumer universe, will otherwise become the USP of their competitors.

There is another case for inclusion. After the passing out of the Gen X, Gen Y and Gen Z will be the cohorts who will move into the vacated space, to create success for organizations. The new generations are programed differently. The old command and control management approach will not drive efficiency for them. Such people will respond favourably to Inclusive work environment, resulting in higher productivity, retention, engagement, morale, and innovation. It is claimed that for most industries,' innovation is not an option; it's a business imperative'. Forbes quotes a study by sociologist Martin Ruef–who, in a study covering 766 graduates of the Stanford Business School, reported that those entrepreneurs, with the most diverse friendships scored three times higher on metric of innovation, thus proving that pooling diverse ideas together drives innovation.[26]

Inclusion can also lead to several other benefits:

1. Enhanced morale, feelings of support and job satisfaction; employees will respond to the trust of the employers by developing enhanced loyalty and commitment to the organization.
2. Diversity and inclusion policies can be embedded in specific recruitment and retention policies which will widen the reservoir from which they can source future recruitment and thus create an employee brand and value proposition in the form of a fully inclusive culture.
3. When the workforce becomes a mirror image of the organization's customer base, and the organization is able to leverage the similarity to design better product or service offerings, the organization's outputs can be closely aligned with the customer preferences. This can considerably boost customer satisfaction.[27]
4. A report examining global diversity and inclusion published by Forbes, in 2011, 85% of executive respondents concurred with the view that a diverse, inclusive workforce is essential for stirring varied ideas and perspectives that enable innovation.

[25] Deborah France Massin, Director, ILO Bureau for Employers' Activities. *Greater progress on diversity and inclusion essential to rebuild productive and resilient workplaces.* https://www.ilo.org/global/about-the-ilo/newsroom/news.

[26] How Companies Can Benefit From Inclusion. Dan Schawbel. https://www.forbes.com/sites/danschawbel/2012/05/13.

[27] Ferdman, B. M. (2003). *Accounts of inclusion (and exclusion). The Industrial- Organizational Psychologist*, 40(4), 81–86.

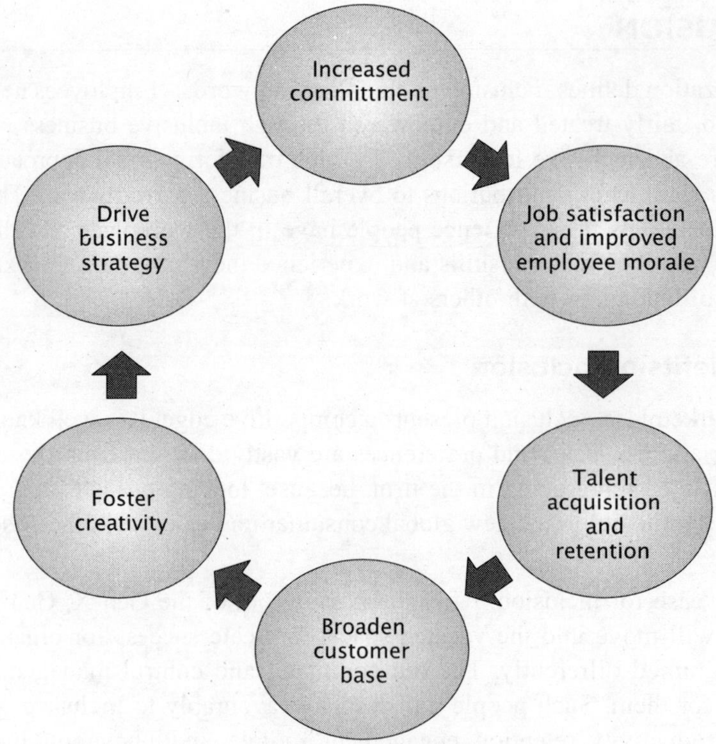

Fig. 20.2 The benefits of inclusion

Diversity and Inclusion–A Reality Check

International Labor Organization brought out a report (Transforming Enterprises through Diversity and Inclusion. April. 2022) on enterprises of all sizes in lower-middle-income and upper-middle-income economies covering a diverse mix of staff, managers, and senior executives. Some of the highlights were:

1. Only 50% of respondents reported said that proper identification and resourcing in their workplaces' culture and strategy. Inclusion was measured in only 1/3rd of enterprises.
2. The respondents felt that workplace inclusion was more likely to be associated with seniority than personal background or characteristics such as age, gender, or ethnicity/race/religion. 92% of senior staff reported feeling included, as against 76% of lower-level respondents. The workforce in medium-sized, large, and multinational enterprises were also more likely to feel positive than those in small and national enterprises.
3. Only 1/4th respondents reported about that women being a 'critical mass (40-60%) of top management'; 1/3rd reported zero representation of PwD (PwDs) at senior level of management. Minority groups were similarly clustered at junior levels.
4. Two-thirds of respondents reported observing greater emphasis on diversity and inclusion in the workplace since the start of the pandemic and that the pandemic had increased their expectations on employers to promote diversity and inclusion.

Discussion Questions

1. How critical is it to increase diversity at the leadership?
2. Discuss in your group and suggest three measures which organizations could take to improve diversity at senior levels.

Source: Greater progress on diversity and inclusion essential to rebuild productive and resilient workplaces. ILO Report.https://www.ilo.org/global

20.8.2 Strategies to Create a diverse, Equitable and Inclusive Workplace

An ILO report outlines four key principles for achieving transformational and sustainable change which are applicable globally and to all workforce groups and levels:[28]

1. Diversity and inclusion should be a priority and part of strategy and culture.
2. There must be diversity in top management.
3. Senior leaders, managers and staff must be accountable as role models. a
4. Actions must apply throughout employment–covering recruitment, retention, and development.

Reflection Point

The term 'dog-whistle diversity' appeared first in TIME in 2017 coined by Author Christine Michel Carter. The origin of the phrase lay in dog-whistle politics. Dog whistle diversity is defined as the hiring of groups who have historically been under-represented or subject to discrimination by organizations for the social aspect of environmental, social, and corporate governance (ESG). To investors and stakeholders, hiring these groups sends a coded message that the organization is more open to a diverse workforce, but to the groups hired it suggests the organization lacks effective diversity management or inclusion.

Discussion Question

1. Do you agree with the view that efforts to use as a brand can damage the development of genuine DEI efforts?

Source: We Need to Talk About Dog-Whistle Diversity'. Time. 2017-11-29. Retrieved June 21 2023

20.9 DIVERSITY SHOULD BE PART OF CULTURE

At United Parcel Service of America Inc. (UPS), the international shipping company, which operates in 200 countries, 58% of all senior officers are women or minorities. UPS has never created a role of a Diversity Officer, because they believe that it cannot remain as an accountability of a single role holder. In the most successful companies, diversity management is the job of every employee, beginning with senior most levels leadership to the bottom-most levels of employees. In such a culture, respect for others is part of the DNA. A strong culture—where people have a sense of shared values.

[28] *Greater progress on diversity and inclusion essential to rebuild productive and resilient workplaces.* ILO Report.https://www.ilo.org/global

Loyalty to the organization is rewarded, and team performance is celebrated. It enable employees with vastly different demographics and backgrounds to feel a sense of belonging.

Google in India identifies 200 women engineers from economically backward sections, who are trained for two years in technology. They are also imparted soft skills training to make them ready to join the workforce. In the words of Anurag Bansal, chief sales officer at TalentSprint, a technology training firm, who are partners with Google, 'they are fully equipped to be part of the organization, and they don't feel that they are a separate group or they have been taken into the organization as a special initiative. That is the bottoms-up approach to inclusion.'[29]

Exhibit ERGs as Instruments to Build Inclusive Culture

The ERGs are voluntary, employee-led groups whose aim is to foster a diverse, inclusive workplace aligned with the organizations they serve. They are usually led and participated in by employees who share a characteristic, whether it's gender, ethnicity, religious affiliation, lifestyle, or interest. ERGs started more than sixty years back at Xerox as a forum of black workers to discuss race-based tension in the workplace. ERGs, apart from creating a safe space for employees sharing their difficulties experience, help with individual/career development.

Godrej and Adobe are two of the prominent companies in India who have used ERGs to embed inclusion as part of their culture. In Godrej, the three pillars that shape the ERG and its strategies are: Represent, be better together, and make a difference. The network for women meets to brainstorm ways by which the company can better support women monthly. At Adobe four prominent ERGs are Access at Adobe, Pride at Adobe, Women at Adobe, and Veterans at Adobe.

Discussion Questions

1. Do a quick Internet research to find out the best practices in ERGs in Indian Companies.
2. What are the challenges in making ERGs as effective instruments of DEI?

Source: What are Employee Resources Groups. https://www.greatplacetowork.com/resources/blog/what-are-employee-resource-groups-ergs

20.9.1 Diversity in Senior Management

When there is diversity in top leadership, it has greater depth of experience and multiple perspectives than a non-diverse team and can nurture creativity and acquire a certain depth of understanding of employees and clients. Diversity in top leadership team positively impacts the bottom line, with companies showing more diversity at the executive level and are being more likely to generate higher profits. According to a McKinsey survey, companies in the top quartile for gender diversity at the executive level are 21% more likely to generate higher profits and 27% more likely to have superior value creation. Those in the top quartile for ethnic/cultural diversity on executive teams are 1/3 more likely to have industry-leading profitability.[30]

[29] *The Next Level of Diversity for Companies in India.* Shefali Anand January 12, 2022. https://www.shrm.org/resourcesandtools.

[30] Diversity in leadership: why it matters and what you can do. https://resources.workable.com/stories-and-insights.

20.9.2 Accountability of Managers as Role Models

It is said that whatever is measured gets done. One way to ensure that DEI programs are implemented is to develop a dashboard, a set of diversity metrics, monitor, and track. For example, in PepsiCo, during the tenure of former CEO Steve Reinemund, half of all new hires had to be either women or minorities. Bonuses of managers partly depended on whether they had met their diversity-related goals. When managers are evaluated and rewarded based on how effective they are in diversity management, they are more likely to show commitment to diversity that in turn affects the diversity climate in the rest of the organization.

In an interview with Sodexo Inc, Rohini Anand, CDRO, while emphasizing the commitment and engagement of management at all levels for the right behavioral outcomes, refers to the value of robust metrics for incentivizing the implementation of diversity 'You can have good initiatives and programs, but the idea is to really make sure you are changing behaviors and cultures within the organization.'

20.9.3 HR Role in D&I Process

HR needs to make conscious efforts to align all the people processes to D&I strategy. In order to avoid the trap of tokenism, organizations need to closely look at systems, not at gestures. It is, therefore necessary to audit all aspects of HR that impact diversity. The HR processes include recruitment, on boarding, compensation and rewards, training, performance management, career management and leadership development. Addressing the core system, would enable creating a DEI mind-set of the employees over time and help the DEI processes to become sustainable.

20.10 TRAINING

Many companies have made it a practice to provide training programs for different levels of employees to sensitize them about issues and opportunities in DEI. The critical success factor for such programs is the integrity with the organizational culture. A study of over 700 companies identified the enablers of the efficacy of such programs as: the commitment of top management, rewards for contribution to DEI, and the training programs being made mandatory for managers.

20.11 RECRUITMENT

Companies may want to increase diversity by targeting a pool that is more diverse. Many companies, including Ernst & Young Global Ltd, uses mentoring for undergraduate students. Companies may also benefit from reviewing their employment advertising to ensure that diversity is important at all levels of the company.

Similarly, there are multiple ways to include synthesize diversity and inclusion in the design of on boarding programs. The practices adopted by different companies include keeping a module on the basics of DEI and the importance for their organization, sensitization workshop for new managers and mentorship programs.

20.12 COMPENSATION

There are several ways in which compensation and rewards system can positively impact diversity and inclusion. One, the principle of equity should underlie the compensation system. Additionally, analytics can be built around fair and equitable pay, so that when the compensation data is mined it can tell the story of the company's commitment to D&I, specially about discrimination based on gender or supervisory biases. One can also do benchmark surveys to compare with the industry trends. It can also help in talent retention and enhance employer brand.

A second effective way to link compensation and reward system would be to incentivize employee behaviors that goes in tandem with the corporate strategy. For example, executive compensation can be tied to balanced scorecard measures that reflect DEI goals. Managers can have performance measures related to diversity and employees at all levels can participate in appropriate training and activities.[31]

20.13 PERFORMANCE MANAGEMENT

As the old wisdom goes what gets measured gets performed, DEI objectives can get embedded in the system of employee performance management through appropriate dashboards and a mix of qualitative and quantitative measures.

At the beginning, the employees need to have standards what behavior will foster inclusivity as an organizational norm. The leaders need to role model such behavior standards.

Leadership/Employee behavior that enable diversity and inclusion[32]

• Visible commitment–articulate genuine commitment to diversity	• Humility–be modest about capabilities and admit mistakes
• Awareness of bias–show awareness of personal blind spots	• Curiosity about others–be open and listen without judgment
• Cultural intelligence–be attentive to others' cultures and adapt if needed	• Effective collaboration–empower others and embrace diverse thinking

Source: Six Signature Traits of Inclusive Leadership by Deloitte. How performance management can foster diversity and inclusion.

There are two kinds of dashboards which are currently in use: Diversity Score card and Diversity Reports.

1. Diversity scorecards are visual snapshots of an organization's progress with its DEI goals, tracking their representation using data. It helps evaluate the effectiveness of DEI initiatives and to decide on modification or retention of the existing performance metrics. This scorecard can be integrated to the balanced scorecard on L&D dimensions.

---

31 *Compensation Trends in 2022: Diversity, Equity, and Inclusion*. June 2022. https://www.beqom.com).

32 https://www.small-improvements.com

2. Diversity report is compiled to present trends over a specific period of time. Currently there is a practice of Organizations publishing Annual DEI report as a method of transparently tracking their year-over-year progress toward their DEI goals.[33]

20.14 DIVERSITY ANALYTICS AND MEASURE

Imagine in a company, when the CEO asks the Chief Diversity Officer (CDRO) anticipates such questions and knows the answers because the DEI vision and goals had been set at the beginning and revisited from time to time. Some of the goals which were set were: increase the representation of women at the top management levels, critical talent retention, improvement in the creativity and innovation for problem solving, among others. The metrics for measurements were in tune with the goals. They included: diversity data, employee surveys, performance reviews, 36-degree feedback, and the business results.[34]

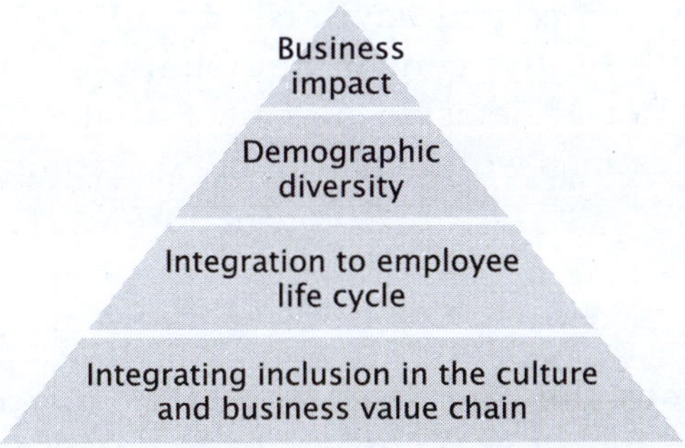

Fig. 20.3 Four-level model for measuring DEI

Level 1: **Business impact** Different sets of metrics for different DEI goals. For example, for affirmative action objectives, the metrics could be: percentage of women/PwDs, LGBTIQ+ in the workforce; in case of goals to mirror customer demography with employee demography, the metrics could be rate/cost of new customer acquisition, Engagement rate with new customers, etc.

Level 2: **Demographic diversity** Simplest set of metrics to use. For example: percentage of diversity employees across various diversity groups in the organization.

Level 3: **Integration to employee life cycle** Different set of metrics for different stages. Attraction-percentage of diverse pool created for core roles; Selection-percentage hiring of diversity candidates; on boarding-time for productivity of new hires; Reward and Recognition-percentage of diversity role models in the organization.

Level 4: **Integration of inclusion** Inclusion, being fundamentally an experience, measures should be qualitative, and can include face to face interviews and employee surveys.

[33] *Source:* 25+ Examples of DEI Scorecards and DEI Reports. Senior Media Editors. May 2023.https://seniorexecutive.com/diversity-scorecards

[34] *Source:* Why blend in when you can stand out? Rao & Joshi. Page 209. Invincible Publishers.

Closing Case Story of Gayathri, a Variable Worker

Gayathri's Special Day

Today is a special day for Gayathri. She will be starting to work, a part of the variable workforce of XYZ as a Field Sales Agent and will experience the happiness in sharing the position of a breadwinner in her family with her father. This will change her life from being patriarchy driven to a role of shared responsibility.

Variable Workforce

Businesses have dramatically increased their use of variable workforce over the past decade as they struggle with rising labor costs and the need for a workforce that can quickly adapt to market conditions. Variable workers are people who are not on the company payroll but provide services to an organization, such as contractors, consultants, temps and advisers. According to a report by McKinsey & Company, racially, ethnically, gender, and ability diverse companies perform 35% better, are 87% better at decision making and are 40% more likely to have higher revenue. Organizations worldwide spend $1.7 trillion on the non-employee workforce annually.

Benefits

By adopting a variablised workforce model, organizations can reap numerous benefits. Firstly, it allows for increased flexibility in workforce management, enabling businesses to quickly scale up or down based on demand fluctuations. This agility is particularly advantageous in industries with seasonal variations or rapidly changing market dynamics like XYZ Capital. Moreover, this model promotes innovation and diversity within organizations. By bringing in individuals with diverse backgrounds and experiences, organizations can foster creativity and generate fresh perspectives, leading to improved problem-solving and decision-making processes. Workforce diversity is of growing importance to all organizations. This is not just because it's the right thing to do. It's also because diverse companies perform better.

Challenges

However, implementing a variablized workforce model is not without challenges. Organizations must carefully navigate legal and ethical considerations, such as ensuring compliance with labor regulations and protecting the rights of the part-time workers. Managing a diverse workforce with varying employment arrangements requires robust talent acquisition and management strategies, including effective communication, collaboration, and performance evaluation mechanisms.

The Company

XYZ Capital is a prominent entity within the XYZ Group, a leading conglomerate based in India. While XYZ Capital serves as the financial services arm of the group, XYZ Money Limited operates as a subsidiary focusing specifically on wealth management and financial advisory services.

With a strong presence in the Indian market, XYZ Capital aims to cater to the diverse financial needs of its customers, providing them with comprehensive and tailored solutions. XYZ Money Limited, a subsidiary of XYZ Capital, specializes in wealth management and financial advisory services. The company offers a range of products and services, including stock broking, portfolio management, mutual funds, insurance, and wealth planning. With a focus on delivering personalized investment strategies and expert advice, XYZ Money Limited aims to assist individuals and businesses in managing their wealth and achieving their financial goals.

Under XYZ Money Limited, the Financial Product Distribution (FPD) channel was launched in September 2022 to cater to the dynamic financial needs of the market. This channel offers a range of financial products to meet the diverse requirements of customers. One of the unique selling points (USPs) of the FPD channel is the opportunity it provides to earn passive income. Through the distribution of financial products, individuals can earn commissions or incentives based on the sales they generate. This passive income stream can be a significant motivation for individuals looking to supplement their earnings or build a rewarding career in the financial services industry.

The Variablized Workforce Model

At XYZ Money Limited, the variablized workforce model is embraced and complemented by the Financial Product Distribution (FPD) channel. This combination allows for a dynamic and agile approach to talent management while effectively catering to the financial needs of the market. The variablized workforce model at XYZ Money Limited entails the utilization of various employment arrangements beyond traditional full-time employees. This includes engaging contingent workers, freelancers, and part-time employees who possess specialized skills and expertise. By adopting this flexible workforce approach, the company can quickly scale its workforce based on demand fluctuations, enhance operational efficiency, and access a broader talent pool. The FPD channel, launched in September 2022, aligns with the variablized workforce model by offering individuals the opportunity to participate in financial product distribution as a source of income. Through this channel, individuals can become financial advisors or distributors, allowing them to leverage their expertise and market knowledge to sell a range of financial products. This aligns with the concept of a variablized workforce, as individuals have the flexibility to work independently, sell multiple products, and earn passive income based on their sales performance. The combination of the variablized workforce model and the FPD channel at XYZ Money Limited brings numerous advantages. It enables the company to tap into a diverse pool of talent, including individuals with specialized financial expertise who may prefer non-traditional employment arrangements. This enhances the overall capabilities and expertise of the workforce, benefiting both the organization and its clients.

Gayathri's joy and anxieties

Gayathri, a resident of Palakkad, and the eldest of three daughters of a lower income family, had joined Kudumbashree three years back to explore ways to become financially independent. She had heard from a neighbour that Kudumbashree provides support for livelihood development in the form of loans, infrastructure development and trainings. She received training for the existing MEs and second for the new ones which includes general orientation training.

Today she has been asked to see the HR Manager at the office of Kudumbashree for orientation. She is full of joy and anxiety. How will her life be shaped now?

Discussion Questions

1. What are the challenges and opportunities in a variable workforce?
2. What is the role of HR in integrating the diverse elements to create a harmonious unit?

SUMMARY

The workforce of the 21st century is a mosaic of larger numbers of women, minorities, and ethnic backgrounds, multi-generational employees with different cultures, practices and lifestyles. Organizations have accepted that a necessary condition of succeeding in the globally competitive marketplace would be how effectively these demographic workforce variations are managed. This may explain why over three-fourths of Fortune 1000 companies have embraced diversity initiatives. However, the adoption of diversity by organizations widely varies in scope: at the basic level it covers a limited recruitment initiatives, education and training, career development and mentoring programs to increase and retain workforce heterogeneity in organizations.

The universe of diversity has three facets—diversity, equality/equity, and inclusion, making it a composite whole. Diversity implies employing people who may be different from each other and who do not all come from the same background. The differences may be those of national origin, physical appearance, religion, education, age, gender, or sexual orientation. Equality is about fairness, about not discriminating in treating individuals, or groups because of their protected characteristics. Equality is based on the intention that all individuals should have the same chance and opportunity. Inclusion means the process of true assimilation of diverse people into the fabric of the organization. In an inclusive culture, differences are not driven under the carpet, but rather acknowledged, valued, and engaged. Divergences are considered as not only normal, but as creating new opportunities to explore better organizational processes like decision making and problem solving, and promoting creativity.

An EDI environment yields many benefits. Better business performance, talent availability, creativity and innovation, synergy with customers in a global market. It has challenges too: stereo types, glass ceiling for women, faultlines, reverse discrimination, differences of multi-generational workforce, etc. Therefore, organizations have to adopt robust strategy to build an EDI work environment with the following steps:

1. Diversity and inclusion should be a priority and part of strategy and culture.
2. There must be diversity in top management.
3. Senior leaders, managers and staff must be accountable as role models.
4. Actions must apply throughout employment–covering recruitment, retention, and development.

EDI also requires appropriate metric for reviewing the effectiveness of the diversity initiatives. Such measures need to be embedded in the HR process.

Short-answer Questions

1. Describe two major challenges for implementing diversity and inclusion.
2. What is the most effective step in ensuring that employees adopt an inclusive approach?
3. What is dog-whistle approach?
4. Explain the four model approach to diversity management.
5. Explain the purpose for ERG.
6. What legal right is available to PWDs in India?
7. What is cultural diversity?

Discussion Questions

1. What are the ways in which an organization manage diversity effectively?
2. What outcomes need to be monitored to indicate managing diversity effectively?
3. Describe some of the important benefits of effective diversity management.
4. What is 'similarity–attraction' phenomenon? If uncontrolled, what are the problems this tendency can cause?
5. What is the pay gap? What are the reasons behind the earnings gap?
6. What, in your opinion, are the limitations of laws and regulations in eliminating discrimination in the workplace? Why or why not?
7. Reflect on a time when you experienced a different culture or interacted with someone from a different culture. How did the cultural differences influence your interaction?

CHAPTER 21

Workplace Wellness

LEARNING OBJECTIVES

After completing this chapter, the student will be able to:

- Understand what is wellness
- Know benefits of wellness
- Learn types of wellness
- Explain issues of wellness
- Understand roles in wellness
- Learn barriers to wellness at workplace
- Grasp strategies for creating wellness at workplace

Opening Case Strategizing Wellness at Workplace

Purnima Chibber, a marketing professional, took over the reins of HR department of a large FMCG MNC in Kolkata, just when employees were returning to their workplaces after the pandemic was easing. She was a high-energy, optimistic person with a strong bias for action. She did not like the fear and worry on the faces of the employees and was set about doing something immediately. She started a two-pronged wellness program: one, called Sanjivani, based on physical workouts with trendy measures like pedometers. She also made it competitive among groups by organizing annual event for the winners in September every year. And other a spirituality-based initiative called Prashanti, which included talks by specialists like Brahmakumaris, and also organized occasional workshops for yoga and meditation.

Purnima, was also a health enthusiast herself, having been a national-level badminton player at one time but a freak knee injury prompted her to retire from active sports. She genuinely wanted employees to be healthy and fit, and always motivate others to participate in different physical activities. She believed that the engagement of employees in physical exercises made the workplaces more vibrant and positive, so that they could look forward to come for work. A good number of employees responded enthusiastically to Purnima's sincere messages. Even the trade unions welcomed the initiatives and encouraged their members to cooperate.

Later, buoyed by the success of the first few initiatives, Purnima invited employees to use the existing Suggestion Scheme to give their suggestions on how to improve the health and wellness of the employees. Based on their suggestions, some more initiatives were added:

1. Chirag An innovative Employee Assistance Program for 24/7 face-to-face or online counseling provided by empanelled professionals for employees and their families.
2. Chaitanya A Webinar series, conducted periodically to educate and spread awareness among employees on holistic wellness. The topics covered were mental health, stress management, mindfulness, and work–life balance.
3. Dostana Employees tend to develop a circle of close friends at the workplace, whom they can confide in. Some of them can be trained and made available to play the role of a confidant when a co-employee faces an emotional crisis in personal or professional life. This acts as a vent for sharing the pressures with a trusted friend and for eventually finding a way out of the situation.

The above measures went a long way in improving the work ambience in the company, as confirmed by a dipstick survey conducted by the HR department at the end of the year. Purnima won an award for her presentation at National Workplace Wellness Seminar conducted by an Employer Federation. However, there were some more challenges coming up in her way in the next three months, which includes shifting the existing office from the current leased premises to a new premise owned by the company about ten kilometres away, which could create some inconvenience to employees and could lead to some resistance by the trade unions.

Discussion Questions

1. Evaluate the strategy adapted in improving wellness at work. What were the advantages and what were the disadvantages?
2. What steps should now be taken to align HR processes to sustain the interest of the employees in wellness at workplace?

21.1 INTRODUCTION

Industrial Revolution, which ushered in an era of growth and material progress, brought in a new workplace, which, for all its positives, also exposed workers to serious health hazards. 'Every morning just at five, gotta get up dead or alive' is the song refrain that novelist Charles Dickens used to describe the state of weariness or hardship that men, women, and children felt about their lives, which were due to the industrial revolution. Long hours of work, child labor, cramped work areas with poor ventilation, trauma from machinery, and toxic exposures to heavy metals, dust, fumes, and solvents made the workplace unhealthy and dangerous.

As public unrest mounted, governments formulated norms to make the workplace safer and healthier. The first set of laws on working conditions in factories came about in the late 19th century in England, and India, followed by other industrialized countries, that results in improved working conditions leading to better health. The significant measures for impacting health are: limiting working hours, abolishing child labor, provisions for rest hours, weekly off, leave, accident benefits, and several major welfare facilities.

The outbreak of Coronavirus brought in a fresh set of health problems. Apart from the dangers posed by the illness itself, the actual work also became more challenging and mentally taxing. The remote work culture created longer working hours to accommodate teleconferences from other time zones. People could not escape the work environment fully with off-hours emails needed to be monitored. Employees miss their office camaraderie and professional growth. In a nutshell, modern workplaces are becoming increasingly stressful as triggers being longer, ever-increasing working hours, smaller, stretched workforces, higher workloads and uncertain business environments, absenteeism, presenteeism (the act of attending work while sick), and staff turnover.

In the context of the above, there is a growing awareness of the need to focus on the wellness of the employees. The more progressive organizations from quite some time have been vocal about the critical value of their human resource, and other organizations are also joining the bandwagon on employee wellness issues. It is evident that many of the workplace problems originate from a lack of commitment to the needs of their workers. The key to unlock the desired employee contributions is by fostering wellness at work. It is also appreciated that even beyond playing an influential role, they also have an onus to help employees embrace certain healthy behaviors leading to sound physical and mental health. It can be said that wellness now transitioned from being a topic of opinion to an agenda for action.

Currently, numerous workplaces and workplace practices embed employee wellness to design work schedules and other routines. This is an evidence of openness on the part of the employers such as providing more flexibility, increasing insurance coverages, budgetary provisions for wellness focus, and many more. During the pandemonium, organizations provided vaccination for self and family, sanctioned special leaves, declared 'no meeting days', limited the meeting time and calls beyond office hours, etc. Some organizations have gone further ahead to formulate comprehensive health and wellness solutions, keeping in mind the employee's unique requirements. Besides, wellness programs have also become a part of talent acquisition strategy.

21.1.1 Definitions

'Wellness is not a 'medical fix' but a way of living – a lifestyle sensitive and responsive to all the dimensions of body, mind, and spirit, an approach to life, we each design to achieve our highest potential for wellness now and forever.'[1]

Workplace wellness is a comprehensive term covering all areas of work life, from the quality and safety of the physical environment to the perceived meaningfulness of their work, their working environment, the climate at work, and work organization. Workplace wellness aims to create conditions to enable workers feel safe, healthy, satisfied, and engaged at work. From an organizational viewpoint, workers' wellness is considered necessary for an organization's long-term effectiveness, correlated to productivity.

According to McKinsey's Future of Wellness survey, 'Wellness consists of six dimensions: better health, better fitness, better nutrition, better appearance, better sleep, and better mindfulness'. Although

1 Greg Anderson, Author of 22 Non-negotiable Laws of Wellness

of the six dimensions, the key one is better health. The relative importance varies between countries as consumers in Japan prefer appearance, while in Germany fitness is priortized.[2]

Exhibit Trends in Workplace Wellness in 2023

1. Creating Flexibility personalizing the work experience, from remote work policies to offering time away from the job.
2. Preventing burnout by providing leave, sabbatical, or other methods of time off to enable recharging.
3. Supporting caregiving through paternity leave, elder care, etc.
4. Help with financial planning as apprehension on lay-offs and rising prices create stress and anxiety.
5. Emphasizing mental health.
6. Foster a spirit of ownership and camaraderie.
7. Leverage technology.
8. Build a culture of deep listening

Source: Eight top workplace wellness to watch in 2023. Ted Kitterman. *Great Place to work*. March 2023. https://www.greatplacetowork.com

21.2 TYPES OF WELLNESS

Many traditional corporate wellness programs only recognize the physical component of health. Employers that only emphasize physical health are missing out on a significant opportunity to positively impact their organization. That is because this type of approach does not account for all of the different elements of employee wellness. And it certainly does not recognize all the things that affect a person's life and happiness.

The trick to a successful employee wellness program and healthier employees is to learn how to connect all of the components of employee wellness. These components include physical, financial, emotional, and social wellness. It is essential for employers and employees alike to understand how these different components of wellness influence one another. For example, if an employee is having difficulties with their financial wellness, they are most likely feeling the emotional and physical impacts of that as well. When one aspect of wellness is lacking, it's difficult for employees to feel and perform their best at work.

This is why it's a good idea for employers to re-think their traditional approach to employee wellness. Before we can dive in on how to connect these elements, it's crucial to fully understand each component of employee wellness. Let's break it down:

21.2.1 Physical Wellness

When we talk about wellness or wellness, we normally have in mind the physical health. It is about how we feel and what we see. This is an important facet of wellness pointing to the general health of the body. It covers goal-driven activities or exercises, nutrition, development of certain regular habits

2 Feeling good: the future of the $1.5 trillion wellness market. https://www.mckinsey.com.

to be in good health, and preventative healthcare. Physical wellness implies fitness, the capability to lead a healthy life. When an organization seeks to promote the physical wellness of its employees, it means it actively seeks to help them become immune to the risk of chronic illness, chronic fatigue, or headaches, maintain healthy weight, and prevent other health-related issues. An agenda for workplace physical wellness can go a long way in improving the lifespan of employees. Such an agenda can cover:

- Ergonomic furniture and standing desks to create ease of work.
- Breaks to enable a short walk or a quick snack/coffee break in their cabin/workstation
- Annual biometric screenings
- Annual corporate flu shot clinics
- A workplace gym and lounge area for employees
- Health, safety, and nutrition education
- Healthy office snacks
- Healthy lifestyle education

21.2.2 Financial Wellness

According to Gallops research experts, financial wellness is about effectively managing one's economic life. In basic terms it includes the four domains:

1. Thrift-keeping or spending within one's means
2. Preparedness for financial emergencies
3. Easy access of data to make good financial decisions
4. Keeping a plan for the future

Financial wellness often impacts other areas of wellness, especially mental and physical wellness, and, therefore, need to be given due attention. According to one study by Green Path Financial Wellness, 58% of employers reported that financial 'illness' plays a role in employee absenteeism while 71% of employees say their top source of stress is personal finances.[3]

Making financial wellness program as an integral part of a workplace wellness program makes the employees more informed on their personal finances. It helps eliminating a powerful stressor at work, thus helping employees to fully focus on their work, with little to worry about managing personal finances. Financial wellness can help companies reduce unnecessary expenditures due to absenteeism, lost productivity, and benefit cost overruns.

Employers can incorporate the financial component of wellness into their employee wellness program by:

1. Providing financial resources to employees.
2. Organizing tuition assistance programs that enhance money management skills and help employees create and build assets.
3. Providing newsletters and other periodic publications.
4. Organizing investment, retirement, college, emergency and health-care planning seminars.
5. Organizing debit and credit-related programs.

---

3 *Is It Time to Rethink Your Employee Wellness Strategy?* Alan Kohl. 2018. https://www.forbes.com

21.2.3 Emotional Wellness

Emotional wellness implies 'an awareness, understanding, and acceptance of one's emotions and an ability to manage effectively with adversity, challenges and change' according to the National Centre for Emotional Wellness. Being tuned into one's emotions, one becomes aware of one's physical sensations. Acting on one's feelings and emotions, can help one to become stable and reliable. Those, who develop a habit of staying in the present and experience mindfulness, without spending their time excessively in the past or the future, can achieve a higher level of emotional wellness than others.[4]

Emotional wellness (or emotional wellness) implies an ability to overcome stressful situations in life, and adjust in trying times, and acheive progress in life. It lies in the extreme end of the scale of emotional experience opposite to emotional ill-being at the other end. So, there is no marked threshold beyond which one achieves emotionally wellness. Rather, the endeavor of the most people is to move along the scale towards emotional wellness.

Exhibit Psychological Safety at Workplace

Psychological safety is a term that is in circulation since the Pandemonium. It is experienced when the team believes that it is ok to take risks, express ideas and concerns, speak up with questions, and admit mistakes without worrying about adverse consequences.

According to a study (GI Group Holdings), quoted by Times of India, in-office workers experience the least degree of psychological safety when compared to hybrid or remote workers.

How work modes fares in terms of psychological safety. (Ratings on a scale of 1-5):

In-Office 3.1

Remote 3.7

Hybrid 3.9

Discussion Question

1. Project Aristotle, a study of hundreds of teams initiated by Google, listed psychological safety as the no. 1 predictor of team performance. List the leader behavior essential to improve psychological safety at workplace.

Source: Workers feel at home in office with hybrid. Namrata Singh. 5/6/23. https://timesofindia.indiatimes.com

The key to improve emotional wellness is to build some emotional skills such as to learn and to understand one's emotions so as to be able to work with them, control them, and overcome dysfunctional emotions faster. In a workplace setting, it helps the managers to become aware of the impact the emotional state of their team members will have on performance.

According to the APA, poor emotional wellness and high stress levels can lead to health problems, like high blood pressure, weakened immune systems, and poor sleep, which in turn can manifest in poor performance and deviant behavior at workplace. Employees with poor levels of emotional wellness may experience more sick days and higher rates of absenteeism. Absence of emotional wellness can affect team work, employees' confidence and identity at work, competency for productive work, absenteeism, and the comfort with which to keep or gain work. Positive emotional wellness contributes to a healthy mental state and optimism. It helps in better stress management, and collaboration. Without positive emotional wellness, the potential of employees to work hard or feel their best at work get severely restricted.

[4] *What is emotional wellness.* Diana Raab. 2019. *Psychology Today.* https://www.psychologytoday.com/us.

The various measures taken by many employers to embed emotional element of wellness into their employees' wellness program are:

- Workplace meditation programs before or after the regular work schedules
- Pranayama or breath control exercises
- Mental health days
- Stress management programs
- Emotional/mental health education and resources
- Mindfulness programs
- Employee counseling programs
- Values and vision workshops
- Employee assistance programs
- ERGs or affinity groups

21.2.4 Social Wellness

During the days of isolation of the pandemonium period, many employees became aware of a sense of isolation, and the shattering impact of such isolation on wellness. Lonely employees are liable to suffer from alienation from their jobs, which adversely affect their performance. Employers and employees both became aware of how powerful relationships at work and prospects for social connection in the workplace are fundamental conditions for employee job satisfaction, happiness, and overall wellness.

Social wellness indicates a robust support system based on connectedness and a sense of belonging. People look for assurance and help from their close relationships when they get stuck with hard times. As employees get on with their careers, they also simultaneously pay attention to balance their social life with their professional life. Having a helpful social network enables them to build assertiveness, become confident and comfortable in their own skin in social situations. A positive social network also instils self-respect. Social wellness also helps to define boundaries that boosts communication, trust and dealing with disagreements. Furthermore, social wellness also serves as a bedrock of emotional resilience.

In a nutshell, social wellness covers the following:

- Relationships with colleagues, managers and having wider social network
- Company values and CSR
- Social inclusion and a sense of belonging
- Feeling valued as a person, colleague and employee.[5]

Steps to improve social wellness

- Review the existing benefit policies connected with social wellness: Hybrid working creates opportunities for social activities. Paternity leave and leave for elder care indicate an employer's appreciation.

---

5 What is social wellness and why should employers care? Employee Benefits. https://employeebenefits.co.uk/what-is-social-wellness

- Review the work culture especially the scheduling. Break times and opportunities to pursue community activities, e.g., club membership which help employees to relax and pursue hobbies/ extra-curricular activities.
- Create an ambience where employees can express themselves in creative ways through their attires and the artefacts.
- Encourage employees to embrace diversity.
- Pursue a set of CSR activities where employees can participate and experience service to the community.
- The social ceremonies (like Foundation Day, Annual Picnic, Annual Sports, etc.) should be arranged in such a manner as to cater to the needs of the employees and their families.
- Some of the other ways of contributing to social wellness of employees are: team outings, book clubs, employee of the month event, creating a space for community assemblies and activities, and so on.

21.2.5 Environmental Wellness

- David Suzuki, the world leader in sustainable ecology, emphasizing the value of environment in our lives had said 'The environment is so fundamental to our continued existence that it must transcend politics and become a central value of all members of society.'
- Environmental wellness connotes one's sense of safety, comfort, and connection with one's physical surroundings. It involves considering the interactions between one's environment, one's community, and oneself. The way to expand it is to feel a deeper sense of harmony with the earth and the community. It begins with the immediate surroundings. One's personal space is connected with one's state of mind, emotional wellness, and productivity. Environmental wellness also stretches beyond the personal space to larger communities, geographic areas, and earth.[6]

21.3 BENEFITS OF WELLNESS AT WORKPLACE

The rationale behind why organizations spend on employee wellness lies in myriad factors – including ethical, legal and economic. Employee health issues can cause rise in costs and fall in revenues for any organization. This constitutes the basic commercial logic for employers to embrace wellness.[7] A survey by Assocham across multiple sectors was carried on with the basic premise that 'On an average for every rupee being spent on employee wellness program, employers get ₹132.33 as a saving on absenteeism cost and ₹6.62 back as reduced health care costs'.[8]

Research supports the belief that worksite fitness programs bring down employees' absenteeism and job turnovers,[9] Studies in commercial banks in Kenya have also established strong relationship

6 *Six ways to enhance your environmental wellness.* Ben Mumme. April. 2021. https://medium.com/change-becomes-you

7 Wright and Marsden 2005. A response to the CCA report 'making companies safe: what works?'. Research Report 332. HSE Books, Sudbury) Wright and Marsden surveyed and collected data from 500 organizations and found that 73% of employers believe health and safety requirements benefit their business as a whole, and 64% say that they save money in the long term.

8 https://indianexpress.com/article/lifestyle/health/over-52-employees-say-no-wellness-prog-by-firms-survey.

9 Miller, Pamela, and Cheryl Haslam. 'Why employers spend money on employee health: Interviews with occupational health and safety professionals from British Industry.' *Safety Science* 47.2 (2009): 163-169.

between physical wellness and employee's performance.[10] Other benefits of wellness programs include: better time management by employees, meeting performance goals and deadlines, improved job satisfaction, harmony in the family and resultant qualitative improvement in productivity.

A survey of senior HR Directors indicated that organizations offering better combination of wellness programs scored higher on performance such as ability to attract essential employees' quality of relations between management and employee and product quality. Such practices help reduce work life conflict and increase positive appraisals of one's organization. These effects are often associated with employee attitudes such as increased job satisfaction and enhanced control over their work schedule.[11]

Wellness programs have great rub off effect on employers' brand. Employers who improve wellness programs for workers are likely to have a competitive advantage in the market. Being perceived as champion of wellness at workplace the employers make a differentiation to the potential employee who look forward to a buzzing workplace where wellness is a top priority. Employees who get support in wellness programs become brand ambassadors of the company spreading messages of goodwill for the organization.

During the tumultuous days of pandemic, companies who demonstrated exemplary concern for wellness over all other interests gained a positive, indelible image in the minds of their employees. 'Organizations that are committed to stand by their people during such turbulent moments have a far better employee experience and work culture. Considering that group health insurance tackles both physical and mental wellness as well as positively impacts financial wellness, this is a holistic approach that can become a game-changer'.[12]

Exhibit State of Wellness Globally

Global Status of Wellness

Out of the 3.4 billion workers, 74% are inadequately paid, even less than $13/day; 45% are in low-skill/manual jobs; 77% are in part-time or unstable jobs;. 18% of the workforce will be over 55 by 2030; 52% are overweight/obese, and 76% report that they are struggling with their wellness.

Reach of Wellness Programs

Only 9% of the global workforce has access to some form of wellness program at work. The breakdown in penetration: North America 52%, Europe 23%, Middle East/North Africa 7%, Latin America/Caribbean 5%, Asia 5% and Sub-Saharan Africa 1% of employees.

The Cost

Worldwide, the cost of unwell workers represents 10-15% of global economic output.

---

10 Kamau, S., Tuwai, B., & Kuria, S. 2015. Effect of corporate wellness practices of employee's performance among commercial banks in Kenya. *International Journal of Scientific & Research Publications.*

11 Ioan, L., Codruta, O., & Patricia, R. (2010*). The Role of W.L.B. Practices in order to improve organizational performance, European Research Studies,* 8(1))

12 '*How employees wellness can be a game changer for the organization's growth*'. Raghuveer Malik. https://www.peoplematters.in/article

Future of Wellness

In future, the information age will be succeeded by a 'Wisdom' or 'Human' age: as robots and AI co-opt many work tasks, Qualities (collaboration, creativity, empathy, constant learning, etc.) not replicable by machines will be in high demand and will need the highest level of mental and physical wellness

Source: The Future of Wellness at work. Global Wellness Institute. https://globalwellnessinstitute.org. January. 2016.

21.4 CHALLENGES FOR WELLNESS AT WORKPLACE

According to a survey conducted by Assocham across sectors such as FMCG, Media, IT/ITES and Real Estate, over 50% of employees in India reported the absence of wellness programs in their company, and 62% of the balance respondents opined the existing programs inadequate. It further said that 83% of sample population were ready to contribute part of their salary in company-sponsored wellness program, but 17% do not intend to participate.[13]

It is observed that there is still a mixed bag on wellness at workplace in India. While the many benefits of these programs have been researched and established, there are bottlenecks in achieving wellness visions. Some of the challenges are:

21.4.1 Not Enough Time

Because of the traditional mind-set, many employers think activities away from work will be time lost to business. They are averse to provide time to their employees away from their work duties to take part in wellness programs. In the same way, employees who hold an instrumentalist view of 9-to-5 work schedule, do not want to 'waste' time at the office either during lunch hours or after having punched out. The employers' tactic of circumventing this problem by scheduling wellness events during recess hours or mandatory break times, also often gives an impression that the employer is merely using such events for winning some brownie points in employer branding, and really not committed to create employee experience of wellness.

21.4.2 No Enthusiasm

Mobilizing interest in a workplace wellness program can be daunting. Employees, who get on board to improve their health, experience a decline in interest when facing the normal rigours involved in initiatives to improve their health. The challenges are typical of implementing a change for oneself, especially the adjustment to the lifestyle, and the need to let go of some toxic habits.

21.4.3 What is all this for?

Sometimes workplace wellness programs are taken up without crafting a broad vision, and building a shared purpose. For example, if an external survey has faulted the employer or there have been reports of resignation on account of burnout, the company may introduce an Employee Assistance Program, without caring to explain to the employees the need for the same. It does not enthuse the employees, who may think of the same as just another fad which will pass.

---

13 https://indianexpress.com/article/lifestyle/health/over-52-employees-say-no-wellness-prog-by-firms-survey

21.4.4 At What Cost?

There are multiples ways to create a wellness program. Some of it may require budget provision and prove expensive, i.e., setting up a gym or hiring of experts to conduct health awareness workshops, etc,. There are also enough low-cost options like group walks, morning meditation/yoga sessions by in-house experts, or disincentivizing smoking.

For the employee, the deterrent factors are rising health care costs, increased prevalence of chronic illnesses, proliferation of healthcare providers, increased prescription drug costs, etc.

21.4.5 Who/how/what should be Communicated?

Wellness programs, like most other well intended change initiatives can flounder, if they short-change the critical step of communicating the long- and short-term benefits of such programs. In a survey reported by Colonial Life & Accident Insurance Co. in a white paper '*Well on the Way: Engaging Employees in Workplace Wellness*. July', 2012, more than half employees, whose employers offer wellness programs say they are only somewhat or not at all knowledgeable about them. Lack of knowledge is higher among young workers, less educated workers and lower-paid workers.[14]

21.4.6 How to Leverage the Technology?

In this digital age, technology holds endless possibilities to aid wellness. Wearable instruments for tracking healthcare and nutrition and Web and mobile-based lifestyle behavior coaching programs are two examples of how technology can be the building block for a right employee wellness initiative. Organizations lagging behind in proper technology solutions, get hamstrung either to collect or to analyse the employee health data, and consequently unable to build strategies for preventive, predictive and highly personalized healthcare service for employees. The failure to leverage technology and make use of tools suitable for the organization, pull the organization back in its endeavor to create conditions for an effective employee wellness program.

21.4.7 How to Deal with Mental Illness?

A McKinsey survey reports predicts poor mental health taking a heavy toll, affecting a high percentage of people of middle/high-income countries, and causing declining mental health for 42% of employees globally. The decline is most prominently manifest in depression, anxiety disorder, substance abuse and burnout leading to absenteeism, presenteeisms, and low productivity. The loss of productivity globally, as per a World Health Organization estimate, is to the tune of $1 trillion annually.[15]

The deeper problem of mental health lies in the stigma attached to it and the reluctance of the persons to admit how it impacts their performance at workplace. The stiffest hurdle for creating wellness at workplace lies here, whereas the first step in seeking solutions will require that the employers design a workplace ambience of psychological safety where mental health issues are discussed at the same level of comfort as physical illness. Employees are more likely to use solutions when they are positively framed—for example, as a way to boost wellness and performance.

---

[14] *Communication is the key to wellness success.* Stephen Miller. 2012. https://www.shrm.org.

[15] *Using digital tech to support employee mental health and resilience.* July. 2021. https://www.mckinsey.com/industries.

Case Does being Abusive Get Results?

In a video, which went viral, the cluster head in a Kolkata branch of the private bank, was seen engaging in misconduct and screaming at his employees in Bengali.

The video gained significant traction on social media and was widely shared on multiple platforms. Users expressed concerns about the senior executive's behavior and demanded immediate action against him. In response to the incident, the bank released a statement indicating that it had suspended the employee in question and initiated an investigation based on a preliminary inquiry.

For those familiar with banking and financial services industry (BFSI) and or been at the receiving end of their so-called relationship banking pitch, knows the reality. That such behavior is common and across the industry. The incident serves as a wake-up call for both the financial industry and society at large.

It is not surprising that there has been such peer pressure of high target setting. It starts from the top. Financial services entities use as much as target setting as any other consumer business. These targets are steered with regulations in mind, and not much of consumers' financial interests at the core. A mere candid conversation with mid-level executives and Direct Selling Agent from BFSI would give horror stories. Here is why financial regulators should take note, if they mean consumer protection.

Toxic sales cultures are characterised by intense competition, unrealistic targets, and a focus on maximising profits at any cost. The pressure to meet these targets can lead to unethical practices, such as mis-selling products, pressuring customers to purchase unnecessary services, and withholding important information.

Performance-driven workplace and abusive leadership style, has an impact on wellness.

Numerous studies have established that leaders' adverse attitude have damaging properties on subordinates' physical and psychological wellness. In supervision it has been declared significant for the healthiness as well as wellness of subordinates. Supervisors can affect the healthiness of their employees either in a direct manner by showing uncooperative behavior, and through an indirect manner by affecting subordinate responsibilities.

Another study provides insights to managers about the link between abusive supervision and employee performance. In addition, it recommends that leaders at all levels adopt abusive supervision when they can properly consider a specific employee's perception of the reasons for their behavior. They must consider the previous inclusion in the manager's circle of members, as well as the link between the challenging pressures they face and innovative work behavior to deal with such management behaviors.

A different study covering 500 employees and their supervisors in a field study conducted by Shannon Taylor, Professor from the University of Central Florida examined the differences in attitude and behavior of supervisors who had been abused by their superiors and those who had not and, in turn, how each group treated their employees. The findings, published in the *Journal of Applied Psychology*, showed that abused supervisors who purposefully distanced themselves from their manager expressed respect and kindness towards their own employees, despite the poor treatment they received from their own boss.

Discussion Questions

1. It has been said that the Bank's action of suspending the officer is merely to distance itself from the incident. What other actions would the bank need to do to ensure that such incidents are merely one off?
2. Is it true that abusive style of leadership works in a target driven, high growth sector? What steps could be taken to ensure psychological safety in such workplaces?

Sources:

1. 'Senior HDFC-bank exec abuses colleagues during online meeting suspended-after video goes viral' https://www.cnbctv18.com.
2. Coach Soch Toxic Behaviour in Banking - its Not a Shocker, its Pervasive Industry Culture. https://www.cnbctv18.com/views
3. Schyns, B., & Schilling, J. (2013). *How bad are the effects of bad leaders? A meta-analysis of destructive leadership and its outcomes. The Leadership Quarterly*, 24(1), 138-158.
4. *When Does Abusive Supervision Affect Job Performance Positively?* Fuda Li and others. November 2022.
5. *Benefits of an abusive boss.* https://www.tribuneindia.com.

21.5 ISSUES IN WELLNESS

21.5.1 Stigma on Mental Illness

One of the reasons that employees often struggle in silence is the stigma attached to need of the help on mental illness. The best way employers can begin to support the mental wellness of their employees is to simply...talk about it. In a recent article in *Harvard Business Review*, executives at Mind Share Partners, a non-profit organization, changed the culture of workplace mental health, discussed how managers support employees' by modeling healthy behaviors and sharing their own mental health challenges. When we normalize seeking support and remind employees to take stock of how they are feeling, we can have a profound impact on how employees view and treat their own emotional wellness. Our biggest challenge to create employee wellness is not the retirement gap. It's likely mental wellness. And it is time to talk about it.[16]

21.5.2 Limited Coverage

According to a survey done by Redseer Management Consulting Co. only 15% of the eligible employees are covered under any wellness program. The beneficiaries are largely restricted to MNCs and knowledge-intensive industries (e.g., finance, investment, consulting, information technology, high-tech, higher education, and creative industries). The contract workers, the platform workers or those comprising the band called precariat are excluded from these programs.

21.5.3 Siloed and Reactive Programs

Most employers offer a cross-section of separate programs, services, and benefits that address different aspects of employee wellness. It includes workplace wellness programs, Employees Assistant Programs (EAPs), occupational safety and health programs, and workers' compensation and accident insurance.

---

16 *Kelly Odonnell,* Chief Client Officer at Edelman Financial Engine. April. 2021. https://www.linkedin.com)

These programs usually operate in silos; they are not coordinated with each other and are disconnected from other employer-sponsored benefits and policies, such as compensation, health/medical benefits, paid time off, retirement, and child care benefits.[17]

21.5.4 Unsustainable Solutions to Systematic Problems

Workplace wellness programs are largely a makeshift structure, quite inadequate on preventing strategies. In a time of heated competitiveness, where cost considerations are driving companies to outsource all activities except the core, the employer can hardly be expected to take long-term approach to employee wellness issues.

21.5.5 Lopsided Focus

The drift of most wellness programs seems to be in problems which are carry over from outside the workplace. But objectively looking, the focus needs to be primarily on work related wellness, as health issues generated in workplaces also have an enormous, and often negative impact on the employees' wellness. Workplaces often pose serious occupational hazard and besides work poor pay, long workdays, lack of work-life balance, toxic relationship with managers and peers can also cause mental and emotional distress.

21.5.6 Ineffective or Counter-productive Programs

Based on a cultural and historical analysis on wellness ideas, André Spicer, a professor at Cass Business School at City University London, claimed that wellness programs yielded low returns on investment. In some cases it, produced opposite results by turning happy employees into anxiety–ridden unhappy ones, as they worried that not being perceived healthy, and not looking attractive would make them vulnerable for job loss.[18]

21.5.7 More of a Brand Proposition than Good of the Employees

Spicer also opined that corporate wellness is a huge industry, with power to push its agenda on companies. Secondly, large part of the public has got enrolled to the idea of wellness. Besides, the business logic for wellness is the belief that healthy people are productive people.

21.6 ROLES IN MANAGING WELLNESS AT WORK

21.6.1 Employee's Role

The employee is primarily responsible for two things: his personal wellness by taking charge of own physical, emotional, and mental health and safeguarding his health at work and to decide his role as a part of the workplace community. Unsafe, whimsical actions can pose a threat to the work environment and jeopardize others' lives. For example, if guards are put on the moving parts of the machine at workplace for safety, and an employee removes the guards for his convenience, then he

---

17 *Improving workplace wellness in Asia: a business case, approaches and successful practices.* Yeung and Johnston. A whitepaper of Global Wellness Institute. Asian development Bank. December. 2019

18 Corporate wellness programs make us unwell. An interview with Andre Spicer by Scott Berinato.

not only creates risk for self, but also for co-workers. Employee is thus fully responsible for adherence to norms and communication.

21.6.2 Managers Role

Since, work gets done through interaction between the manager and the employee, the role of the manager is of utmost value for the success of the wellness programs, and their commitment is crucial. However, when the managers only focused on business results and target achievements, they may feel tentative of the role of promoting employee wellness. The ambiguity about their role as champions of employee well–being can seriously impede employee wellness agenda.

According to Gallup, managers play four concrete roles.[19]

1. Invite Instead of driving the employees, managers should adapt advocacy and empowerment to improve their wellness.
2. Provide Offer information and opportunities-serving as a conduit to wellness. Provide a safe, comfortable work environment, encouraging participation in wellness activities
3. Model Role model appropriate behavior/practices and exemplify wellness practices authentically enthuse and enrol employees in wellness programs.
4. Care Demonstrate interest and genuine concern for each employees' wellness by uplifting their lives—their purpose, social, financial, community and physical wellness.

21.6.3 Role of Top Leadership

An APA report recently found that '81% of workers agree that how their employers support mental health will be an important consideration for them when they look for future work.' However, as we emerge from the pandemic and employers face new macroeconomic and geo-political challenges, there is an obvious danger that wellness slips as a priority for leaders.

Jeffrey Pfeiffer, Professor at Stanford Graduate School of Business, in his book 'Dying for a Pay Cheque', discusses the damaging effect of the professions on the physical and emotional health of employees. According to him, as organizations are stepping up their demands for more hours of work, the workplaces are becoming more and more toxic.

Pfeiffer mentions two pillars of workplace wellness—job control and social support. A reference is drawn to Whitehall studies which established the correlation between chronic stress at work with higher probability of metabolic syndrome (risk of cardio-vascular disease) compared with those who have no work stress. In a condition of low job control, their lack of responsibility and discretion can make the employees feel incompetent and starved of a sense of accomplishment, they may experience stress, anxiety, and depression. Secondly, social support is another determinant of employee wellness. Numerous studies have regularly shown link between social support and wellness and that close relationships shields from the impact of different kinds of psychosocial stresses which can undermine health. It has been claimed by some experts that those with low levels of social support have higher mortality rates.

The need of the hour is to create a model workplace, that should be fostering and stimulating, which is only possible with leaders who are kind and caring and value holistic wellness of their employees. They are well-positioned to champion wellness and overall health of employees. The

[19] Managers role in employee wellness. Wood and Bailey. Nov. 2017. https://www.gallup.com/workplace/236249.

role of the leader in such situations is to design caring cultures. They need to be compassionate and take preventing measures, instead of resorting to conventional remedial measures. True wellness need psychologically safe workplaces, where employees have flexibility in how and where they work.[20]

Exhibit Some Model Wellness Programs

1. Mandatory Mental Illness Certification by at least one member of HR department
2. Flexible time away from work
3. Emotional Wellness Programs such as a quiet room in the campus to meditate or reflect, walking trails, outdoor sitting areas, keeping plants inside office area.
4. Wellness Ambassadors assigned to meet and talk about aspects of wellness
5. Mindful Pauses—Guided mindfulness breaks, break of 15 minutes between meetings
6. Walking Meetings
7. In-house Yoga—Getting in a Yoga instructor at least once a week
8. Massage Therapy/Ergonomical furniture
9. Health Exchange Program
10. Financial Wellness—To help employees with budgeting, planning, investing and goal-setting, to create better financial security, thus reducing stress
11. Themed Wellness Days—To promote healthy eating habits or encourage employees to compete to get the highest number of steps during the workday or reach some other fitness goal
12. Wellness Challenges, as a fun way to gamify wellness by which employees can earn points and badges for any or all activities that they complete and can have a choice in what those activities are–physical wellness, mental wellness, etc. They can form teams and compete as individuals or groups

Source: Twelve Wellness programs that actually help. Forbes Human Resources Council. May. 2020.https://www.forbes.com/sites

21.7 WELLNESS PROGRAMS BEST PRACTICES[21]

1. Leaders must play an active role in envisioning, exemplifying the right habits, allocating budget, deploying the resources, reviewing and advocating.
2. There should be an employee health assessment. The wellness programs should be carefully curated to suit the unique needs of the employees as reflected in the basic health data.
3. Partnership of employees, employer, organizations, and local community.
4. It should be holistic and should be aimed at the key dimensions of wellness, particularly physical, mental, financial, spiritual and environmental.
5. The programs need to be operationalized in a systematic, step by step process, with tangible and clear targets, milestones measure and standards, accountability and time specific review process.
6. Employees should be motivated and enrolled in the process at all levels.

[20] *The overlooked essentials of employee wellness.* Jeffrey Pfeffer. McKinsey Quarterly. 2018.

[21] Based on Hoffman, L. and Kennedy-Armbruster, C (2015). Case Study Using Best Practice Design Principles for Worksite Wellness Program, *ACSM Health and Fitness Journal,* April/May 30-35

7. A comprehensive multi media two-way communication plan with formal and informal exchanges should be drawn up.
8. The entire wellness program should make use of proper analytics and metrics for evaluating the effectiveness.

21.8 WELLNESS METRICS

Peter Drucker's famous words 'If you can't measure it, you can't improve it' applies to wellness endeavor at workplace too.

Using metrics helps to check whether wellness programs are working or not. Employers should assess not only the degree of employee participation but also the return, tangible /intangible, on the money spent. The kind of return that one can seek could include: reduction in sick leave, claims for medical re-imbursement, number of smokers, number of workplace injuries, attrition rate; improvement in health index, fitness levels, engagement levels and productivity.

A Deloitte *Global Human Capital Trends* study (2020) reported that 61% of respondents reported absence of any metrics for the impact of wellness initiatives on organizational performance in their organization. Ironically, in another *Global Human Capital Trends* survey (2021), wellness was ranked as the third-highest priority by the workers for work transformation efforts in the previous one to three years, but the executives ranked it at second-to-last priority.

Wellness metrics include:

1. Financial outcomes – savings on illness expenses
2. Health impact – Improvement over last assessed health survey
3. Organizational support – based on anonymous survey
4. Productivity and performance – differential
5. Value on investment (VOI)
6. Utilization and program uptake – no. of employees accessing the program
7. Communication and awareness – based on an employee survey
8. Employee satisfaction – employee survey, mystery audits
9. Employee turnover – exit rate, exit interview qualitative data
10. Changes in absenteeism and annual healthcare costs per employee – Cost saved on account of differential absenteeism rate
11. Demographics – program participation by different demographic groups based on age, language, sex, orientation, etc
12. System Severity – based on anonymous surveys
13. Time to service – cycle time between request for and receipt of help

Apart from the above, it must be kept in mind that a variety of modifiable health risk factors, such as excess weight, poor diet, smoking and lack of daily exercise, affect both medical costs and work performance. A system of metrics which will be useful should be related to a comprehensive health risk assessment.[22]

[22] Based on Metrics Beyond ROI Can Capture Wellness Outcomes. Stephen Miller. March. 2015. https://www.shrm.org and Employee wellness metrics to track now. *Academy of Innovative HR.* https://www.aihr.com

21.9 WELLNESS PRACTICES IN GLOBAL COMPANIES[23]

Name of the company	Programs
Asana Collaborating software company	1. 'Nap rooms' for employees to take some time out, recharge, and de-stress. 2. Unlimited paid time-off to employees. 3. In-house culinary team responsible for whipping up delicious meals. 4. Free executive coaching sessions.
Google	1. On-site healthcare services. 2. Physical therapy sessions. 3. Massage services. 4. Fitness classes. 5. Learning opportunities including: a. Guitar lessons. b. Coding classes. c. Cooking sessions. 6. Micro-kitchens and cafes stocked with nutritious meals for employees.
Microsoft	1. Free education and resources on how to manage weight, get fitter, or quit smoking. 2. Gym memberships and other fitness purchases for their employees. 3. 'Know your numbers' screening event each year, with information about cholesterol levels, blood pressure, and more. 4. Family and personal counseling 5. Stress management sessions.
Rodale, Publishing company	1. Energy Centre', an on-site gym offering free fitness classes. 2. Meditation room. 3. Opportunities to boost health and fitness with training sessions and athletic opportunities in the office. 4. Organic cafeteria providing locally-sourced, healthy food.

21.10 HOW TO DESIGN AN EFFECTIVE WELLNESS STRATEGY

An effective workplace wellness framework must be holistic and focus first on wellness challenges that arise within the workplace.

21.10.1 Safe and Healthy Working Conditions

Employers have a responsibility to comply with legal standards/norms at workplace and implement the basic requirements such as securing the moving parts of the machine, taking fire prevention measures, specify means of entry and exit, arrange proper ventilation and temperature control, report dangerous occurrences, etc. Thirty years ago, WHO (World Health Organization) coined the term 'sick building syndrome' to raise awareness of indoor air quality which was identified as major concerns, advising the employers to be mindful of the need to create healthy interiors.

In short, the baseline should be to comply with the occupational health and safety laws and with the standards and regulations. The good employer needs to go beyond mandatory requirements

23 Time for a brand check-up: how corporate wellness strategies benefit your brand. Steve Harvey. https://fabrikbrands.com/corporate-wellness-strategies

and proactively embed health and wellness-enhancing elements into the work environment so that employees feel cared for and motivated to be productive.

21.10.2 Promote Healthy Behaviors at Work

Experts talk about five major determinants of people's health (genetics, behavior, social circumstances, environmental and physical influences, and medical care). The conditions in which we are born, grow, work, age impacts and the way we behave.

Employers can design the work environment in ways which may exert powerful impact on employees' behavior at work. Many employers are leveraging technology to bring in small changes in designing amenities. These include ergonomic workstations and tools, standing and treadmill desks, private spaces (e.g., nap/meditation rooms, lactation rooms, canteens with options for healthy food, on-site fitness facilities, etc). to foster healthy habits at work.

It is also important to foster camaraderie and 'best friends at work', as Gallup's work emphasizes. Progress in neurosciences and related domains have unearthed the link between human interactions, emotions, motor and cognitive abilities, and our physical health and mental resilience.

21.10.3 Cultivate a Healthy Work Culture

As defined by WHO, wellness is a state in which 'every individual realizes his or her own potential, can cope with the normal stresses of life, can work productively and fruitfully, and is able to make a contribution to her or his community' (WHO, 2004). The culture at the workplace which includes basic hygiene factors (Herzberg, 2004), the quality of communication, information flow, social support, and having regard for individual abilities shape employees' experience of wellness.[24] Both research and anecdotal evidence suggest that the most effective employee wellness initiatives are implemented within the context of a broader organizational culture of wellness.

Leaders have an enormous responsibility in moulding the workplace culture, which in turn influences social interactions at work. If the employees perceive the leader focused on bottom line only, wellness of employees will then be kept at the back burner. If a leader not only talks about caring for people, but consistently mirrors it in his/her actions and decisions, the employees will feel reassured and trust his words.

21.10.4 Support Healthy Habits Outside Work

Many wellness programs fall into a set pattern: going off the block with a health risk assessment, or a biometric tool, followed by a virtual awareness /education session to deal with individual health risks and sometimes following them up with lifestyle-related services or benefits to incentivize healthy behaviors, e.g., gym memberships, free health screenings, or yoga classes.

Such initiatives are exemplary, if it takes in consideration the varieties across demographics, locations and socio-economic environments. The need of a Gen. Z workers will be different from those of the Baby boomers. Similarly the need of a worker engaged in coal mines will be different from those working in an IT office. In one case it may be basic clean air and proper safety gear; in other case it could be wearable. Companies are increasingly relying on technology solutions and local

[24] *The Effect of Organizational Culture on Employee Wellness: Work-Related Stress, Employee Identification, Turnover Intention*. Klajko and others. Research Gate November 2019.

wellness traditions (e.g., Ayurveda and traditional Chinese medicine), to support customization and to increase program flexibility.

Closing Case Wellness Programs at Deutsche Bank

At Deutsche Bank, in operation since 1870, wellness initiatives gained momentum in 2013 with first Employee Assistance Program and Health Screening Vendors. Employees were sensitized between 2014 and 2016. Wellness initiatives like Zumba, nutrition classes or Step Athlon with over 1000 employees participating in the global race, Deutsche Bank adopted a wellness first approach across all levels and locations.

Below is a snapshot of the wellness architecture that Deutsche Bank follows:

1. Purpose statement
   Enable our employees to take ownership of own wellness by providing a framework environment and giving them the support to be mentally and physically healthy, financially secure and productive.
2. Definition of wellness
   Foster a resilient environment which allows to take responsibility for their health and wellness enabling them to be the best they can do at home and at work

Physical	Mental	Social	Financial
Improve health and lifestyle behavior, take steps to avoid preventable diseases, manage existing conditions	Foster mental health by providing preventing support of mental health issues (i.e. stress, depression and anxiety)	Allowing time and valuing involvement with family, friends, co-workers and wider members of community/society	Have knowledge and control over finances, protect against the unexpected and save for the future

At Deutsche Bank, wellness goes beyond physical and mental health and being a financial firm, the concept of financial wellness is naturally ingrained into the culture. Core values of client centricity and integrity are thus not only applied to external clients but also to internal clients-employees. Keeping the value of partnership in mind inspired the genesis of social wellness at Deutsche Bank.

This year, the bank plans to roll out an elaborate wellness framework globally which will serve as the platform for strengthening and structuring the focus on wellness.

Discussion Questions

1. Evaluate the wellness Strategy of Deutsche Bank in terms of sustainability.
2. In another news report it transpired that Deutsche Bank planned to lay off 800 employees as part of a new cost saving initiative. This is despite higher than anticipated profit in the first quarter. (2023 Lay-offs: A timeline of job cuts in top companies. https://www.peoplematters.in/news/strategic) Given that businesses operate in a VUCA environment, what are the ways businesses can balance their concern for employees with concern for the bottom line?

Source: Based on and excerpted from 'Banking on wellness: Deutsche Bank's take on wellness at work https://www.peoplematters.in

SUMMARY

Following the trauma of COVID-19, there is a growing awareness of the need to focus on the wellness of the employees. The more progressive organizations from quite some time have been vocal about the critical value of their human resource, and other organizations are joining the bandwagon on employee wellness issues. It is becoming evident that much of the workplace problems originate from a lack of commitment to the needs of their workers and the key to unlock the desired employee contributions is by fostering wellness at work. It is also appreciated that even beyond playing an influential role, they also have an onus for helping employees embrace certain healthy behaviors leading to sound physical and mental health. It can be said that wellness now transitioned from being a topic of opinion to an agenda for action.

Companies have discovered that embedding wellness in their policies and practices brings in multiple benefits. It saves cost and improves employee morale. It enhances their brand. A survey of senior HR Directors indicated that organizations offering better combination of wellness programs scored higher on performance such as ability to attract essential employees' quality of relations between management and employee and product quality. Such practices help reduce work life conflict and increase positive appraisals of one's organization. These effects are often associated with employee attitudes such as increased job satisfaction and enhanced control over their work schedule.

There are important roles to be played by the employee, the manager and the senior leadership. The role of the senior leadership is crucial: to create a model workplace, that should be fostering and stimulating, which can be possible with leaders who are kind and caring and value holistic wellness of their employees. The leadership is well-positioned to champion wellness and overall health of employees.

It is essential to review the effectiveness of wellness programs to check whether they are working. Using metrics helps to check whether wellness programs are working or not. Employers should assess not only the degree of employee participation but also the return, tangible/intangible, on the money spent. The kind of return that one can seek could include: reduction in sick leave, claims for medical re-imbursement, number of smokers, number of workplace injuries, attrition rate; improvement in health index, fitness levels, engagement levels, and productivity.

Short-answer Questions

1. Define wellness.
2. Explain 'psychological safety at workplace'.
3. What, according to Gallops, are the four concrete roles in the wellness of a manager?
4. Please mention the highlight of the survey conducted by Assocham on wellness.
5. Describe any two key issues in wellness programs at workplace.
6. Explain environmental wellness.
7. What are the keys to emotional wellness?
8. How are the organizations designing wellness to suit the different needs of multi-generational workforce?
9. What does the McKenzie report of July 2021 reveal about mental wellness?
10. Mention two financial metric for wellness.

Discussion Questions

1. What is wellness?
2. What are the benefits of wellness? Is there a co-relation between business success and wellness?
3. Is well-being about fitness alone? What are the different types of wellness?
4. What are some of the issues of wellness? What needs to be done to resolve them?
5. What is the role of senior leadership in ensuring wellness? What does he need to do to ensure sustenance of well-being?
6. What are strategies for creating wellness at workplace?